THE
NEW INTERNATIONAL
LESSON ANNUAL
1996–97

September–August

THE
NEW INTERNATIONAL
LESSON ANNUAL
1996–97

September–August

ABINGDON PRESS
Nashville

The New International Lesson Annual

Copyright © 1996 by Abingdon Press

All rights reserved.

This book is printed on recycled, acid-free paper.

Scripture quotations, unless otherwise labeled, are from the New Revised Standard Version Bible, Copyright ©
1989, by the Division of Christian Education of the National Council of the Churches of Christ in the USA.
Used by permission.

Scripture quotations noted KJV are taken from the King James Version of the Bible.

Scripture quotations noted NIV are taken from the *Holy Bible: New International Version.* Copyright © 1973,
1978, 1984 by the International Bible Society. Used by permission of Zondervan Bible Publishers.

Scripture quotations noted JB are from *The Jerusalem Bible,* copyright © 1966 by Darton, Longman, & Todd, Ltd.
and Doubleday & Company, Inc. Used by permission of the publishers.

Scripture quotations noted NASB are from the *New American Standard Bible,* © The Lockman Foundation 1960,
1962, 1968, 1971, 1972, 1973, 1975, 1977. Used by permission.

Scripture quotations noted NAB are from *The New American Bible,* © 1987 by Thomas Nelson, Inc.

Scripture quotations noted NJB are from *The New Jerusalem Bible,* copyright © 1985 by Darton, Longman &
Todd, and Doubleday & Company, Inc. Reprinted by permission of the publishers.

Scripture quotations noted NKJV are from The New King James Version. Copyright © 1979, 1980, 1982,
Thomas Nelson, Inc., Publishers.

Scripture quotations noted REB are from *The Revised English Bible.* Copyright © 1989 by The Delegates of the
Oxford University Press and the Syndics of the Cambridge University Press. Reprinted by permission.

Scripture quotations noted NEB are from *The New English Bible.* © The Delegates of the Oxford University Press
and The Syndics of the Cambridge University Press 1961, 1970. Reprinted by permission.

Scripture quotations noted GNB are from the Good News Bible—Old Testament: Copyright © American Bible
Society 1976; New Testament: Copyright © American Bible Society 1966, 1971, 1976. Used by permission.

ISBN 0-687-002796
ISSN 1084-872X

96 97 98 99 00 01 02 03 04 05 —10 9 8 7 6 5 4 3 2 1

PREFACE

We're glad you're back, or joining us for the first time, as we prepare to launch into another year of exciting study. Our mission at Abingdon Press is to provide you with the best resource available for delving deeply into the Scriptures so as to understand them in their original context, interpret them for contemporary Christian disciples, and share them with all who will hear the story of God's creating, sustaining, and redeeming love.

To accomplish our mission, we have selected writers who are known in the church for their work as scholars, pastors, and/or teachers of adults. These leaders can provide you with the information you need to open the Word and mine its meaning. Our focus, as symbolized by the lighthouse on the cover, is God's Word as a lamp that lights our way (Psalm 119:105). That's where we start, with the Word. However, we don't end there. We cannot stop with information alone because, as James reminds us, we are called to be doers of the Word, not merely hearers (James 1:22). The risen Christ calls us to active discipleship. We are disciples, witnesses, stewards, evangelists, prophets, and teachers. Therefore, we must let God's Word not only inform us but transform us. Paul tells us that this transformation is brought about by the renewing of our minds (Romans 12:2). A Bible study class provides an ideal setting for this renewal. Through the work of the Holy Spirit in our lives, we can step out in faith, boldly proclaiming the Word to a troubled world that desperately needs to hear good news.

The lessons in *The New International Lesson Annual* have session plans that help you study and live out the meaning of the Scriptures. These plans, found under the heading Sharing the Scripture, will provide those of you who are class leaders with ideas for presenting the lesson. Teaching methods include class discussion, small group sharing, occasional activities based on art or music, silent reflection, brief lecture ideas, and a variety of ways of studying the Bible. The point here is to invite the learner—which is the meaning of the word "disciple"—into active engagement, rather than passive listening to, God's Word. To this end, we also suggest ways to help participants act on what they have learned once they leave the class each week.

As we work to create this volume that is used among churches in denominations across the theological spectrum, we recognize that people of strong Christian faith and practice do differ in their understanding and application of the Scriptures. Consequently, it is unlikely that every reader will agree with all points that are made here. Other readings of the same passage are indeed possible. However, you may be assured that the contents of this book are rooted in the belief that God has spoken through the biblical writers and that we as God's people are in dialogue with them, seeking to learn what God expects of us in the time and place in which we are privileged to live out our high calling as Christian disciples.

In closing, we are always aware that this book is for you. Your feedback is extremely important, so we hope that you will complete the evaluation form at the end of this book and return it to us. If you have any further comments or questions, please write to me, Dr. Nan Duerling, at Abingdon Press, 201 Eighth Avenue South, P. O. Box 801, Nashville, TN 37202.

Dr. Nan Duerling, *General Editor*

CONTENTS

FIRST QUARTER

God's People Face Judgment

UNIT 1: RESPONSES TO WRONG
(September 1–29)

UNIT 2: JUDAH'S INTERNAL DECAY
(October 6–27)

UNIT 3: THE FALL OF JERUSALEM
(November 3–24)

SECOND QUARTER

New Testament Personalities

UNIT 1: PERSONS IN JESUS' NATIVITY AND EARLY LIFE
(December 1–29)

UNIT 2: PERSONS IN JESUS' MINISTRY
(January 5–26)

UNIT 3: PERSONS OF THE NEW TESTAMENT CHURCH
(February 2–23)

THIRD QUARTER

Hope for the Future

UNIT 1: STAND FAST IN THE LORD
(March 2–30)

UNIT 2: LETTERS TO CHURCHES
(April 6–27)

UNIT 3: A MESSAGE OF HOPE
(May 4–25)

FOURTH QUARTER

Guidance for Ministry
(June 1–29)

A Call to Faithfulness

UNIT 1: THE GREATNESS OF CHRIST
(July 6–27)

UNIT 2: BE FAITHFUL FOLLOWERS OF CHRIST
(August 3–31)

FIRST QUARTER

SEPTEMBER 1, 1996—NOVEMBER 24, 1996

Our Sunday school year opens with a study of Israelite history from the fall of Samaria in 722 B.C.E. (Before the Common Era) to the fall of Jerusalem in 587 B.C.E. In Unit 1, "Responses to Wrong," we learn about the efforts of Hezekiah, Josiah, Jeremiah, and Habakkuk to be faithful to God in the midst of the sin and apostasy of Judah. Unit 2 clearly shows how far Judah, also known as the Southern Kingdom, has strayed from God. The fall of Jerusalem is detailed in our final unit.

In Unit 1, the first response to wrong that we encounter is King Hezekiah's attempt to remain steadfast in the faith, as recorded in 2 Kings 18:1-8 and 20:16-21. His reforms are short-lived, however, for his successor again leads the people away from God. As we see in the second lesson from 2 Kings 23:1-8a, another king, Josiah, prompted by the discovery of scrolls of the covenant during Temple renovations, encourages the people to renew their covenant with God. In Lesson 3, Jeremiah is called to be God's prophet. Jeremiah 1:4-10, 14-17 records God's call and the young prophet's response. Jeremiah 7:1-15, the basis for our study on September 22, demonstrates that Jeremiah faithfully proclaims God's word and confronts the hypocrisy of the people. As this unit closes, we read in Habakkuk 2:1-4 and 3:17-19 of the prophet's continuing trust in God during the difficult days leading up to the destruction of Jerusalem.

Unit 2, "Judah's Internal Decay," opens with a study of Jeremiah 5:1-6 in which the prophet searches in vain for truth and justice among God's people. As we read in Jeremiah 28:5-14, Jeremiah challenges the well received false prophecy of peace proclaimed by Hananiah. On October 20, we hear in Ezekiel 2:3-7 and 3:4-11 the prophet calling the rebellious people of Israel to listen and obey. He also teaches in Ezekiel 18:1-5, 7-13, 19-20 that they must accept personal responsibility for what is happening, rather than blame their ancestors.

As Unit 3 begins on November 3, we again listen to the prophetic words of Ezekiel, who symbolically demonstrates the doom of Judah in Ezekiel 4:1-13. The following week, we see the horrendous picture of Jerusalem under siege by King Nebuchadnezzar, as recorded in 2 Kings 24:20b–25:12. Now that the unbelievable has occurred—the Holy City of David has been torched and most of the remaining residents were deported to Babylon—we hear the cries of people longing for restoration in Lamentations 5:1-10, 19-22. The unit concludes with a word of hope from Ezekiel 37:1-12, 14. This passage assures the exiles, and us, that God can make dry bones live again.

As you prepare to teach this quarter, we would recommend that you use *The Devotional Companion to The International Lessons 1996–97* (available from Cokesbury, ISBN 0-687-002796) as a guide for class worship. In keeping with our emphasis on God's Word as the light for our way, you may also want to use the refrain from the song "Thy Word Is a Lamp" (*The United Methodist Hymnal*, page 601) as a regular part of your weekly devotions.

Since this quarter's lessons include historical and geographical references, we would also recommend that you have on hand a copy of *Bible Teacher Kit* (available from Cokesbury, ISBN 0-687-77786-0). This teaching resource will provide you with maps, timelines, and a glossary that you will find very helpful. Specific suggestions for use are made under the Sharing the Scripture portion in various lessons.

MEET OUR WRITER

DR. NAN DUERLING

Currently the general editor of *The New International Lesson Annual*, Dr. Duerling has written church curriculum for youth and adults since 1984. She has served as a voting member of the Curriculum Resources Committee of The United Methodist Church, as well as the Curriculum Consultant in the Mid-Atlantic region for The United Methodist Publishing House. A former secondary and university level English teacher, Nan teaches in the Course of Study School at Wesley Theological Seminary in Washington, D.C. She also enjoys teaching adult classes at Linthicum Heights UMC where she and her husband, Craig, are both active laypersons. The Duerlings live in Crownsville, Maryland.

STEADFAST FAITH

FOCUSING ON THE MAIN QUESTION

Wars, political alliances forged to defeat enemies, intrigue, and religious conflicts. These issues are often at the root of breaking news stories in our own day. They are also found in the history of the Israelite people as told by the Deuteronomic historian(s) in Deuteronomy through 2 Kings.

Our unit this quarter begins about 721 B.C.E. (before the common era) with the fall of Samaria. The Northern Kingdom (also called Israel) and the Southern Kingdom (known as Judah) had split apart after the death of King Solomon in 928 B.C.E. For almost two hundred years both kingdoms were ruled mainly by corrupt kings whose craving for power was insatiable. They plotted against or assassinated whomever threatened their rule. Most of these kings turned aside from God, preferring instead to take authority into their own hands. Prophets warned against the sin and rebellion of these rulers and their subjects, but to no avail. Ultimately, Israel fell to the Assyrians. Their defeat was explained neither as a military loss to a superior power nor as God's inability to protect them, but as the stubborn refusal of the people to listen to God and turn from their evil ways (see 2 Kings 17).

Now Judah faces the same danger. The Southern Kingdom's future looks bleak, for King Ahaz is just as corrupt and idolatrous as most of his predecessors. Ahaz dies and his twenty-five-year-old son, Hezekiah, ascends to the throne. Hezekiah "did what was right in the sight of the LORD" (2 Kings 18:3) and, therefore, Judah does not suffer immediate devastation.

We too are often confronted by pressure to adhere to standards that are contrary to God's call upon our lives. Like the Judeans, we have our own pantheon of idols. Many of us value status, material goods, influence, and power. We set aside God as we pursue the goals of our professional or personal lives. Yet, not everyone succumbs to such pressures and temptations. Some persons hold fast to God, just as Hezekiah did. The willingness to remain steadfast has important consequences not only for the faithful themselves but also for generations to come. As we study today's lesson, we will focus on this question: *How can steadfast faith become a transforming response to sinful situations?*

READING THE SCRIPTURE

NRSV
2 Kings 18:1-8

1 In the third year of King Hoshea son of Elah of Israel, Hezekiah son of King Ahaz of Judah began to reign. 2He was twenty-five years old when he began to reign; he reigned twenty-nine years in Jerusalem. His mother's name was Abi daughter of Zechariah. 3He did what was right in the sight of the LORD just as his ancestor David had done. 4He removed the high places, broke down the pillars, and cut down the sacred pole. He broke in pieces the bronze serpent that Moses had made, for until those days the people of Israel had made offerings to it; it was called Nehushtan. 5He trusted in the LORD the God of Israel; so that there was no one like him among all the kings of Judah after him, or among those who were before him. **6For he held fast to the Lord; he did not depart from following him but kept the commandments that the Lord commanded Moses.** 7The LORD was with him; wherever he went, he prospered. He rebelled against the king of Assyria and would not serve him. 8He attacked the Philistines as far as Gaza and its territory, from watchtower to fortified city.

Key Verse

NIV
2 Kings 18:1-8

1 In the third year of Hoshea son of Elah king of Israel, Hezekiah son of Ahaz king of Judah began to reign. 2He was twenty-five years old when he became king, and he reigned in Jerusalem twenty-nine years. His mother's name was Abijah daughter of Zechariah. 3He did what was right in the eyes of the LORD, just as his father David had done. 4He removed the high places, smashed the sacred stones and cut down the Asherah poles. He broke into pieces the bronze snake Moses had made, for up to that time the Israelites had been burning incense to it. (It was called Nehushtan.)

5Hezekiah trusted in the LORD, the God of Israel. There was no one like him among all the kings of Judah, either before him or after him. **6He held fast to the LORD and did not cease to follow him; he kept the commands the Lord had given Moses.** 7And the LORD was with him; he was successful in whatever he undertook. He rebelled against the king of Assyria and did not serve him. 8From watchtower to fortified city, he defeated the Philistines, as far as Gaza and its territory.

Key Verse

2 Kings 20:16-21

16 Then Isaiah said to Hezekiah, "Hear the word of the LORD: ¹⁷Days are coming when all that is in your house, and that which your ancestors have stored up until this day, shall be carried to Babylon; nothing shall be left, says the LORD. ¹⁸Some of your own sons who are born to you shall be taken away; they shall be eunuchs in the palace of the king of Babylon." ¹⁹Then Hezekiah said to Isaiah, "The word of the LORD that you have spoken is good." For he thought, "Why not, if there will be peace and security in my days?"

20 The rest of the deeds of Hezekiah, all his power, how he made the pool and the conduit and brought water into the city, are they not written in the Book of the Annals of the Kings of Judah? ²¹Hezekiah slept with his ancestors; and his son Manasseh succeeded him.

2 Kings 20:16-21

¹⁶Then Isaiah said to Hezekiah, "Hear the word of the LORD: ¹⁷The time will surely come when everything in your palace, and all that your fathers have stored up until this day, will be carried off to Babylon. Nothing will be left, says the LORD. ¹⁸And some of your descendants, your own flesh and blood, that will be born to you, will be taken away, and they will become eunuchs in the palace of the king of Babylon."

¹⁹"The word of the LORD you have spoken is good," Hezekiah replied. For he thought, "Will there not be peace and security in my lifetime?"

²⁰As for the other events of Hezekiah's reign, all his achievements and how he made the pool and the tunnel by which he brought water into the city, are they not written in the book of the annals of the kings of Judah? ²¹Hezekiah rested with his fathers. And Manasseh his son succeeded him as king.

UNDERSTANDING THE SCRIPTURE

2 Kings 18:1-8. The Deuteronomic historian(s), who writes Israel's history as it appears in the books of Deuteronomy through 2 Kings, devotes three chapters of 2 Kings (18–20) to Hezekiah. The son of King Ahaz, Hezekiah instituted reforms during his twenty-nine-year reign (715–687 B.C.E., according to many scholars, though the dates are in dispute). He reversed his father's support of pagan cults in Judah by destroying shrines and other objects of worship. Hezekiah faithfully adhered to the commandments given by Moses. During the years of the divided monarchy (922–721 B.C.E., when Israel fell to the Assyrians), when kings in both the Northern (Israel) and Southern Kingdom (Judah) were often corrupt, Hezekiah stands out in the opinion of the historian for his faithfulness to God.

2 Kings 18:9-12. This brief story of the fall of Samaria, the capital of Israel, repeats the account found in 2 Kings 17:5-6. King Shalmaneser of Assyria (727–722 B.C.E.) attacked the Northern Kingdom and, after a three-year war, seized Samaria. At that time, Hoshea ruled the Northern Kingdom. According to the historian, Hoshea "did what was evil in the sight of the LORD" (2 Kings 17:2). The defeat, which ended the Northern Kingdom forever, is attributed by the historian to the unfaithfulness of the people and Hoshea, for they had sinned by disobeying God and ignoring the covenant. Most scholars date the fall of Samaria to 721 B.C.E., which would have been during the reign of Ahaz in Judah, but the Deuteronomic historian claims this catastrophic event occurred during the reign of Hezekiah.

2 Kings 18:13-37. Sennacherib, King of Assyria from 704–681 B.C.E., invaded Judah in 701 B.C.E., capturing forty-six towns. Hezekiah sent a message of submission and a huge sum of silver and gold to Sennacherib who was at Lachish, a walled city located about thirty miles southwest of Jerusalem. Not satisfied with these terms, Sennacherib demanded that Jerusalem surrender. He sent Assyrian officials, along with a large army, to persuade the people in Judah not to listen to Hezekiah but to make peace with Assyria. Instead of using Aramaic, the diplomatic language of the day, the envoys spoke in Hebrew so that the residents could understand them. The envoys mocked God and made promises, but Judah did not surrender. Another account of Sennacherib's attack is found in Isaiah 36.

2 Kings 19:1-37. Hezekiah's spokespersons returned to tell him what had happened. The king tore his clothing, put on sackcloth, and went into the house of the Lord, as signs of repentance and mourning. He dispatched several officials and priests to consult with Isaiah. The prophet assures the inquirers that they need not fear Sennacherib, for God will deal with him. Having heard a report from Rabshakeh ("chief butler"), Sennacherib sent messengers to Hezekiah. The message, found in 19:10-13, seems to be a condensed version of 18:29-35. Hezekiah not only reads the letter but also takes it to the house of the Lord and spreads it out for God to see (19:14). Hezekiah then prays to God (19:15-19). Acknowledging that the Assyrians have been able to win over the gods of other nations, Hezekiah implores God to act so as to make God's unmatched power and sovereignty clear. God responds to this prayer through Isaiah, who sends a lengthy word of prophetic judgment against Assyria to Hezekiah. The prophet states that God will prevent Sennacherib from entering Jerusalem (19:32) and that the city will not fall because God will defend it. No battle ensues. Instead, the Assyrian warriors were struck down in the night. How they died is not known for certain. Sennacherib himself lived, but was assassinated at home by his own sons (19:37) in 681 B.C.E.

2 Kings 20:1-11. Hezekiah's illness and recovery is also recorded in Isaiah 38. This incident occurred during the Assyrian crisis (20:6), so it is out of order in the narrative. In response to Isaiah's announcement of Hezekiah's impending death, the king prays to God, not for the nation but for his own recovery. He reminds God of his own faithfulness. In response to the king's prayer, God orders Isaiah to go back to Hezekiah and promise him healing and an additional fifteen years of life. God also announces intervention so that Jerusalem will be delivered from Assyria. Acting as a doctor, Isaiah calls for a lump of figs, a commonly used poultice, to bring about healing. Hezekiah asked for and received a supernatural sign (the retreat of a shadow) to show that he would be healed.

2 Kings 20:12-19. Merodach-baladan, known also as Marduk-apaliddina, ruled Babylon from 720–709 B.C.E. and briefly in 703 B.C.E. Merodach-baladan sent envoys to Hezekiah as part of a Babylonian plot against Assyria. Apparently flattered that the Babylonians wanted him as an ally, Hezekiah showed the emissaries everything Judah had to offer. Isaiah rebuked Hezekiah for this action and warned of the danger of invasion by the Babylonians. Hezekiah heard the prophet's word as "good," for the events Isaiah prophesied would not take place during the king's life. Such an invasion did take place much later, resulting in the destruction of Jerusalem in 587 B.C.E. and captivity of the Judeans in Babylon.

2 Kings 20:20-21. The Deuteronomic historian closes this lengthy account of Hezekiah's rule with a reference to Hezekiah's tunnel. This conduit system, which runs through 1700 feet of solid rock, was constructed to ensure a water supply in the event of attack. It still exists today. Hezekiah was succeeded by his son, Manesseh, an evil monarch who reversed his father's reforms.

INTERPRETING THE SCRIPTURE

Hezekiah Did What Was Right

Although today's lesson includes three chapters from 2 Kings as background reading, the lesson itself focuses on several verses, 2 Kings 18:1-8 and 20:16-21, that describe King Hezekiah himself. His steadfast faithfulness gives us an example of how God expects us to respond to the sin and evil around us.

The Deuteronomic historian begins 2 Kings 18 by telling us that Hezekiah was twenty-five years old when he ascended to the throne. While many scholars believe his reign began in 715 B.C.E., the exact year of his ascension is in dispute. If he became king in "the third year of King Hoshea" Hezekiah would have been ruling when the Northern Kingdom fell to the Assyrians in 721 B.C.E. Most scholars, however, believe that Hezekiah's father, Ahaz, was king of Judah when Israel fell. The defeat at the hand of the Assyrian King Shalmaneser is recorded briefly in 2 Kings 18:9-12. A more thorough account is found in 2 Kings 17. Recall that the Deuteronomic historian recounts the story in Kings by going back and forth between the events in the Northern and Southern Kingdoms. This method, though repetitious and sometimes confusing to the reader, tells the story of both kingdoms as if they are operating on parallel tracks.

At the outset of the account of Hezekiah's reign in Judah, the historian tells us how highly this king is esteemed: "He did what was right in the sight of the LORD just as his ancestor David had done" (2 Kings 18:3). David, who ruled between 1005 and 961 B.C.E., is the standard by which all of the kings of Israel and Judah are judged. Although David initially became king of Judah (2 Samuel 2:1-11), the tribes of Israel came to him and asked that he be their king as well (2 Samuel 5:1-16). David found favor in God's sight and, despite his adultery with Bathsheba and his plot against her husband, Uriah, is considered righteous before God. For the historian to compare Hezekiah to David is high praise. Only Josiah, (whose story we will read next week) is more greatly revered.

Not only does the historian compare Hezekiah to David but he also contrasts him with his father, Ahaz. In 2 Kings 16:2b we read that Ahaz "did not do what was right in the sight of the LORD his God." According to the historian, Ahaz "walked in the ways of the kings of Israel" (2 Kings 16:3a). He "made his son pass through fire" (16:3b), a reference to the practice of child sacrifice. Moreover, as verse 4 shows, he actually worshiped pagan gods. Ahaz is the first of the Judean kings after Solomon to be personally charged with participation in pagan rituals. His even had an Assyrian altar that he had seen in Damascus copied and placed in the Temple at Jerusalem (2 Kings 16:10-16).

Instead of worshiping other gods as his father had done, Hezekiah disassembled their shrines. He removed the "high places," as required by Deuteronomy 12:2-3, where people had worshiped gods. The law according to Deuteronomy called for the centralization of worship in Jerusalem. The people of God were to come to Jerusalem to worship and sacrifice there and there alone. Hezekiah "broke down the pillars." Connected with Baal worship, these stone pillars represented the male god, while the sacred wooden pole represented the female consort, Asherah. These Canaanite cultic objects, associated with fertility rites, were commonly found in places of Israelite worship. Hezekiah even broke the bronze serpent of Moses (see Numbers 21:6-9). Called Nehushtan, this serpent had originally been made by Moses at God's direction so that persons who were bitten by poisonous snakes could look at it and live. By Hezekiah's time, people were apparently worshiping it, for the serpent was an important symbol in Baal worship.

Hezekiah Trusted God

Signs and objects of other religions could be found in places where the Israelites worshiped because they wanted to "hedge their bets." They worshiped God but also blended other religious practices and gods with their own. It was as if the people counted on God for some things but looked to other gods to meet additional needs. In contrast, Hezekiah trusted God completely. Instead of following other gods, Hezekiah held steadfast to God. His trust and obedience is demonstrated by his adherence to the commandments given by Moses. Again, such behavior stands in sharp relief against the disobedience of his father and the idolatrous ways of the people.

God's Word to Hezekiah

According to 2 Kings 20:12-15, the Babylonian king Merodach-baladan had sent emissaries to Hezekiah to enlist Judah as an ally against the Assyrians. Eager to show them how much he had to offer to a coalition, Hezekiah gave the envoys a complete tour. Opposed to such an alliance, Isaiah came to Hezekiah with a word from God. He prophesied against both Judah and Hezekiah's lineage, saying that the nation would be invaded, despoiled, and the residents carted off to Babylon. Furthermore, Hezekiah's offspring would be taken to Babylon to serve there as eunuchs in the palace.

In response to the prophet's word, Hezekiah acknowledges the appropriateness of God's decree. Unlike prior situations, Hezekiah does not pray or try to change God's mind. Hezekiah, however, is grateful that this fate will not befall Judah during his own reign.

Although the Deuteronomic historian has judged Hezekiah to be a good king, this word of the Lord comes to him because he is looking to military alliances, rather than God alone, for national security. The historian may have added the reference to the Babylonian captivity (beginning in 597 B.C.E., with the first deportation from Judah, through 538 B.C.E., when Cyrus of Persia issued an edict allowing the captives to return home) to help explain and prepare the reader for the exile to come. God's people are to worship God alone and put their complete trust in God's ability to guide and sustain them.

Hezekiah's Story as Our Story

As we read the story of Hezekiah's reign in 2 Kings 18–20 and examine his response to the evil he saw around him, we can see ways that Hezekiah's steadfast faith can inform our own response to evil. Hezekiah was judged a good king because, as our key verse states, "he held fast to the LORD . . . [and] kept the commandments." Disobedience to God and idolatry had already brought the Northern Kingdom down and would eventually bring the Southern Kingdom down as well. In both cases their defeats were military ones wrought by the Assyrians and Babylonians, respectively, but the Bible explains these actions as the will of God. Such catastrophic consequences could have been avoided had the people been steadfast and obedient unto God.

Although Hezekiah ascended the throne as a young adult, he did not hesitate to act on what he believed, even though he likely knew his actions would be unpopular. Similarly, in our own day we may be reluctant to speak out against evil and injustice. We may succumb to the pressures of society to conform to unjust behaviors, such as racism or sexism. We may shun the neighbors Jesus calls us to love simply because they are poor or immigrants or somehow "not like us." We may blithely assume that there are no consequences for our actions. Clearly, the experience of the divided kingdoms shows that there can be dire consequences if we continue to refuse to confront wrong. The lesson that Hezekiah teaches us is that even in the midst of decay within the community of faith and pressure from without

to knuckle under to political or military powers, we can be victorious if we do what is right and hold fast to the Lord. When we fail to be obedient and loyal to God, we do so knowing that we risk judgment that will surely come.

SHARING THE SCRIPTURE

PREPARING TO TEACH

Preparing Our Hearts

As you read the scripture, consider ways in which external military pressures and internal idolatry affected God's people in Hezekiah's day. What similar events are occurring today? How does God call us as Christians to speak out against the wrongs we see around us?

Preparing Our Minds

If you choose to do further background reading for today's lesson, remember that the chronology of the events recorded in 2 Kings 18–20 is debated by scholars. The Deuteronomic historian claims that Hezekiah was on the throne in Judah when Israel fell, while other biblical and extra-biblical sources date that fall at about 721 B.C.E. Only one attack against Judah by the Assyrian king Sennacherib can be documented, but the historian's narrative would indicate that two were mounted. The mention of King Tirhakah of Ethiopia (2 Kings 19:9) suggests that a second attack did occur because he did not ascend to the throne until 690 or 688 B.C.E. Some students may ask why Sennacherib's troops left Judah without attacking then (2 Kings 18). While you will want to be prepared to respond to questions, do not get bogged down in unclear details. The spotlight in this lesson is on Hezekiah himself

and the steadfast faith that enabled him to respond to the idolatry and disobedience to God that had infiltrated Judah.

Preparing Our Learning Space

If possible, post or duplicate maps of Israel, Judah, and the Assyrian Empire (available in Bible Teacher Kit by Abingdon, ISBN 0-687-77786-0) to help orient students to the land.

Write today's main question on newsprint or a chalkboard.

Since this is the first Sunday of a new church school year, you may want to spruce up your learning space with different posters, pictures, or flowers.

Have on hand:
- ✔ several Bibles for students
- ✔ newsprint and marker or chalkboard and chalk
- ✔ optional materials for a collage, including magazines that can be cut, scissors, glue, paper

LEADING THE CLASS

(1) Introduction

After welcoming the class and introducing any new members, ask:
- If God were to speak audibly this morning, what problems or issues within our society would God want the church to confront? Why?

• What kind of witness should the church be making in order to call people to living accountably before God?

Use information from Focusing on the Main Question to help class members understand the similarities between today's problems and the ones Hezekiah faced because the people were not living according to God's commandments.

If you have a large map of Israel and Judah, or if you have duplicated the map on page 143 of Bible Teacher Kit, briefly point out the two kingdoms as a means of helping the class to become oriented to where Hezekiah and the people of Judah were in relation to their neighbors. Show the map of the Assyrian Empire and note that Israel had already fallen to the Assyrians in 721 B.C.E. as the result of apostasy. Also point out Philistia and the city of Gaza, mentioned in 2 Kings 18:8, and Babylon, mentioned in 2 Kings 20:12, 17.

Highlight today's main question (written on newsprint or chalkboard) as the context for our study of Hezekiah's steadfast faith: *How can steadfast faith become a transforming response to sinful situations?*

(2) Hezekiah Did What Was Right

Choose a volunteer to read aloud 2 Kings 18:1-4.

Use information under this heading in the Interpreting the Scripture portion to help class members understand what Hezekiah did to purge Judah of idolatry. His steadfast faith motivated him to remove shrines erected to other gods.

Ask the class to put themselves in Hezekiah's place and answer these questions. As an alternative to a whole class discussion, break into groups or pairs.

• How did you think people would respond to your tearing down of shrines that your father Ahaz had constructed?

• Why you were motivated to fulfill God's commandments when other kings and the people had ignored them?

(1) What kind of spiritual legacy had you hoped to leave for the people?

(3) Hezekiah Trusted God

Choose someone to read aloud 2 Kings 18:5-8.

Point out, as noted under Interpreting the Scripture, that Hezekiah trusted God while others were "hedging their bets" by depending on the gods of their neighbors.

Ask these questions:

(1) In what ways do Christians today "hedge their bets"? In other words, we say that we trust in God, or that Jesus is all we need, but our actions may belie our statements. Where do we really put our trust?

(2) What changes need to be made if we are to exhibit the kind of steadfast faith that Hezekiah showed?

If your class enjoys hands-on activities, provide materials for collages (pictures cut out and mounted in overlapping fashion on paper). Instruct the group to create collages of the kinds of things Christians put their trust in. They can talk as they work about why people put their trust in things other than God.

(4) God's Word to Hezekiah

Read 2 Kings 20:16-21. You may want to choose someone to be a narrator, a second person to read Isaiah's message to Hezekiah, and a third to read Hezekiah's response.

Either before or after the scripture reading, give background, as found under Understanding the Scripture (2 Kings 20:12-19) and Interpreting the Scripture, concerning the events with the Babylonian envoys that preceded Isaiah's message. Point out that even Hezekiah, who had been faithful to God, had failed the people because he was so willing to try to make a good impression on the Babylonians. His decision to court political allies, rather than trust God alone, led to Isaiah's message.

Ask the class to respond to Hezekiah's response to God's message from Isaiah.

- What consequences did Hezekiah's behavior toward the Babylonians have for the Judeans?
- Why do you think God stated that catastrophe would not take place during Hezekiah's reign?
- How do you feel about Hezekiah's attitude toward this pronouncement?

(5) Hezekiah's Story as Our Story

As an option for a class that prefers lectures, read or retell this portion found under Interpreting the Scripture.

Encourage discussion of these questions either as a whole class or in small groups:

(1) **We do not have idols set up in our churches, but our society does have many idols, such as status, power, and money, that many Christians worship. How can we as people of God live a life that is in contrast to the idol worshiping of our society?**

(2) **If God were suddenly to judge the church, what sins of commission (things we do) and omission (things we fail to do) would God name?**

(3) **What positive steps can the church make to present a credible, positive witness to a world that desperately needs to know what God expects and how we can meet those expectations?**

(4) **How might our actions, rooted in steadfast faith, open the way for God to transform evil situations?**

HELPING CLASS MEMBERS ACT

Hezekiah ascended to the throne when he was twenty-five years old. Think of one young adult you know whose life exemplifies the kind of steadfast faith that enables this person to be a Christian role model for others. Contact this person and let him or her know how much this witness means to you.

Consider a situation in your own family, church, community, or workplace that God would judge as being unfaithful. Think of at least one concrete action you can take to name this situation and suggest a remedy for it. For example, a family may be so focused on amassing wealth that it is not giving time or money to God. That family could begin by naming their greed and inappropriate priorities and then set aside a percentage of their income and a specific amount of time to worship, learn about, and serve God.

Think about current social problems that will have an impact on children and grandchildren. Choose one of these problems to address by writing to a legislator and letting that person know how concerned you are that future generations will suffer the consequences of misspent money or special privilege or whatever your concern is.

PLANNING FOR NEXT SUNDAY

Invite the class members to prepare for next Sunday's lesson by reading 2 Kings 22:1–23:20, focusing especially on 2 Kings 23:1-8a (ending with Beersheba). This lesson, entitled "Beginning Again," concerns obedience to God's commandments. Ask the class to consider how, when we have been disobedient to God, we can begin anew to be obedient.

BEGINNING AGAIN

PREVIEWING THE LESSON

Lesson Scripture: 2 Kings 23:1-8*a*
Background Scripture: 2 Kings 22:1–23:20
Key Verse: 2 Kings 23:3

Focus of the Lesson:
the commitment King Josiah made to obey God by instituting reforms according to the forgotten covenant recently rediscovered during temple renovations

Main Question of the Lesson:
How can we begin anew to obey God's commands more faithfully?

This lesson will enable adult learners to:
(1) recognize Josiah's commitment to obey God's commandments.
(2) encounter God's call for obedience in their own lives.
(3) respond by making a commitment to obey God, beginning anew to do so if necessary.

Today's lesson may be outlined as follows:
(1) Introduction
(2) Josiah Responds to God's Commands
(3) Josiah Calls Others to Change Their Ways
(4) Josiah Institutes Reforms
(5) Josiah's Story Calls Us to Begin Anew

FOCUSING ON THE MAIN QUESTION

Last week we studied King Hezekiah, whom the Deuteronomic historian judged to be a good king. We skip over the story of two evil kings, Manasseh (687–642 B.C.E.) and Amon (642–640 B.C.E.), and move this week to the reign of King Josiah (640–609 B.C.E.). Josiah is highly esteemed by the historian because he institutes temple reforms that call the people to greater faithfulness to God's covenant.

Why were these reforms even needed? Hezekiah, as we recall, had already dis-

mantled shrines to other gods. Those efforts were short-lived, however, for his son Manasseh rebuilt them (see 2 Kings 21:1-9). As Judah moves closer to its destruction by the Babylonians, we again find a host of foreign cults being practiced among God's people. During temple renovations a scroll was discovered that probably contained at least a portion of Deuteronomy. The contents of this scroll clearly indicted the people for their apostasy. King Josiah, Hezekiah's great-grandson, took drastic action to rid the land of foreign gods. His reforms enabled the people to begin again to obey God.

Perhaps we too have been like the people of Judah. We make resolutions, promising to turn aside from behaviors and attitudes that we know do not conform to God's expectations of us. Maybe we succeed—at least for a while. But then we find ourselves drawn back to our former ways. Possibly we rebuild "shrines" that we had at one time rejected. We find it so easy to justify our behavior on the grounds that everyone else is acting the same way. Like the Judeans, we see nothing wrong with our behavior because it is so commonly accepted.

The kingdom of God, however, does not operate by majority rule. It functions according to the commands of God which we, like the Judeans, violate at our own risk and peril. At times, only a small minority—perhaps a minority of one—recognizes the wrong we are doing and calls us to return to faithful obedience to God. Josiah was one of those rare individuals who not only could perceive what God commanded but also could take decisive action to bring about the needed changes so that others could live obediently as well. As we consider today's lesson, we will ask: *How can we begin anew to obey God's commands more faithfully?*

READING THE SCRIPTURE

NRSV
2 Kings 23:1-8*a*

1 Then the king directed that all the elders of Judah and Jerusalem should be gathered to him. ²The king went up to the house of the LORD, and with him went all the people of Judah, all the inhabitants of Jerusalem, the priests, the prophets, and all the people, both small and great; he read in their hearing all the words of the book of the covenant that had been found in the house of the LORD. ³The king stood by the pillar and made a covenant before the LORD, to follow the LORD, keeping his commandments, his decrees, and his statutes, with all his heart and all his soul, to perform the words of this covenant that were written in this book. All the people joined in the covenant.

4 The king commanded the high priest Hilkiah, the priests of the second order, and the guardians of the threshold, to bring out of the temple of the LORD all the vessels made for Baal, for Asherah, and for all the host of heaven; he burned them outside Jerusalem in the fields of the Kidron, and carried their ashes to Bethel.

NIV
2 Kings 23:1-8*a*

1 Then the king called together all the elders of Judah and Jerusalem. ²He went up to the temple of the LORD with the men of Judah, the people of Jerusalem, the priests and the prophets—all the people from the least to the greatest. He read in their hearing all the words of the Book of the Covenant, which had been found in the temple of the LORD. ³The king stood by the pillar and renewed the covenant in the presence of the LORD—to follow the Lord and keep his commands, regulations and decrees with all his heart and all his soul, thus confirming the words of the covenant written in this book. Then all the people pledged themselves to the covenant.

⁴The king ordered Hilkiah the high priest, the priests next in rank and the doorkeepers to remove from the temple of the LORD all the articles made for Baal and Asherah and all the starry hosts. He burned them outside Jerusalem in the fields of the Kidron Valley and took the ashes to Bethel. ⁵He did away with the

Key
Verse

Key
Verse

⁵He deposed the idolatrous priests whom the kings of Judah had ordained to make offerings in the high places at the cities of Judah and around Jerusalem; those also who made offerings to Baal, to the sun, the moon, the constellations, and all the host of the heavens. ⁶He brought out the image of Asherah from the house of the LORD, outside Jerusalem, to the Wadi Kidron, burned it at the Wadi Kidron, beat it to dust and threw the dust of it upon the graves of the common people. ⁷He broke down the houses of the male temple prostitutes that were in the house of the LORD, where the women did weaving for Asherah. ⁸He brought all the priests out of the towns of Judah, and defiled the high places where the priests had made offerings, from Geba to Beer-sheba.

pagan priests appointed by the kings of Judah to burn incense on the high places of the towns of Judah and on those around Jerusalem—those who burned incense to Baal, to the sun and moon, to the constellations and to all the starry hosts. ⁶He took the Asherah pole from the temple of the LORD to the Kidron Valley outside Jerusalem and burned it there. He ground it to powder and scattered the dust over the graves of the common people. ⁷He also tore down the quarters of the male shrine prostitutes, which were in the temple of the LORD and where women did weaving for Asherah.

⁸Josiah brought all the priests from the towns of Judah and desecrated the high places, from Geba to Beersheba.

UNDERSTANDING THE SCRIPTURE

2 Kings 22:1-2. Eight-year-old Josiah (an age questioned by some scholars) succeeded his father, Amon, an evil king who had reigned only two years before being assassinated. People revolted against the conspirators and had Josiah installed as king. Like his great-grandfather, Hezekiah (see 2 Kings 18:3), Josiah "did what was right in the sight of the LORD, and walked in all the way of his father David." David is the highest standard by which the Deuteronomic historian judges all kings. Josiah is second only to David in the historian's opinion.

2 Kings 22:3-7. In 621 B.C.E. (Before the Common Era) Josiah sent his secretary, Shaphan, to the high priest Hilkiah (not the same person as in last week's lesson) to count money collected from the people for temple repair. Second Kings 12:9-16 explains the collection method. The funds were to be disbursed to the construction workers, whom Josiah trusted to deal honestly with the money.

2 Kings 22:8-10. The high priest Hilkiah

handed over to Shaphan a scroll that had been found in the temple or, as some scholars believe, had been known by Hilkiah but not brought forth until this time. No details are given, but possibly the scroll was found in the box (see 2 Kings 12:9) that Hilkiah had been instructed to open and count. This scroll contained a book of the law, likely portions of Deuteronomy. Shaphan read the book himself, but the historian makes no comment about his personal response. He returned and read it aloud to Josiah.

2 Kings 22:11-13. In contrast to Hilkiah and Shaphan, who make no overt response to the scroll, twenty-six-year-old Josiah tears his clothing as a sign of repentance and mourning. Deeply concerned that God is angry with the people, Josiah sends his advisors to inquire of a prophetess. Perhaps the scroll contained words such as Deuteronomy 6:13-15 or 28:15-24 that speak of God's anger being kindled against those who do not faithfully serve God and God alone. Josiah is aware of the numerous shrines and high places in Judah where gods of other cultures are worshiped. The historian writes in 2 Kings 21:1-9 of the cultic practices instituted by Josiah's own grandfather, Manasseh.

2 Kings 22:14-20. The prophetess Huldah, whose name means "weasel," gives a prophecy of doom on Judah. The reason Judah will be destroyed is that the people have practiced—and continue to practice—idolatry. God sends a word of comfort to the penitent Josiah, promising that he will die without seeing the destruction of Judah. The promise is fulfilled, though Josiah does not literally die "in peace." He is murdered in Megiddo by King Neco of Egypt, an ally of the Assyrians against whom Josiah had revolted (see 2 Kings 23:29).

2 Kings 23:1-3. Josiah took action upon hearing God's word from the prophetess. He gathered the people together and read from the scroll. The king was standing before two pillars of bronze at the entrance of the temple, which according to 1 Kings 7:21 are called Jachin ("God establishes") and Boaz ("He comes with power"), perhaps because they were words from an inscription. These pillars, which were about twenty-seven feet high and six feet in diameter, apparently had ceremonial significance (see 2 Kings 11:14), but their exact meaning has been lost. Josiah made a covenant to be faithful and obedient unto God, and the people agreed to follow. A covenant signifies a relationship based on commitment that generally includes both promises and obligations. Covenant is one of the most important theological concepts in the Bible.

2 Kings 23:4-8. Josiah set about destroying images and shrines to other gods associated with Assyrian, Canaanite, and Phoenician worship. He "deposed the idolatrous priests," meaning that he had them killed. He not only closed pagan shrines but also closed shrines to God located in the Judean countryside in an attempt to centralize the worship of God in Jerusalem.

2 Kings 23:9-20. Israelite priests could come to share the food of temple priests, but they could not serve at "the altar of the LORD." Josiah tried to end child sacrifice practiced at Topheth ("firepit") on behalf of the Ammonite god Molech. He also got rid of the horses and chariots that rode in processions to honor the sun as a god, as well as shrines and altars particularly associated with fertility rites. The king torched such shrines because places destroyed by fire could never be used again for worship, nor could places on which human bones had been burned, for they are unclean and, therefore, make the places they touch unclean.

INTERPRETING THE SCRIPTURE

Josiah Responds to God's Commands

At age twenty-six, King Josiah oversaw an extensive project of temple renovations. He was evidently an honest, trusting young adult, for he asked the high priest Hilkiah to count the money collected for the work and pay the builders without requiring them to give account of their expenditures. What began as an effort to repair the temple structure was soon transformed into a program of religious reform. Not only was the temple to be renewed but God's people were to be spiritually revitalized, turning from their wicked ways and beginning anew to serve God.

In the course of the temple renovations, the high priest Hilkiah found—or decided to bring forth—a book of the law, which was likely a scroll of a portion of Deuteronomy. While neither Hilkiah nor Josiah's secretary Shaphan, to whom the book was given, seemed particularly moved by the contents of this scroll, Josiah was cut to the quick. Shaphan's reading may have included these words from Deuteronomy 6:13-15: "The LORD your God you shall fear; him you shall serve, and by his name alone you shall swear. Do not follow other gods, any of the gods of the peoples who are around you, because the LORD your God, who is present with you, is a jealous God. The anger of the LORD your God would be kindled against you and he would destroy you from the face of the earth."

Josiah first made an individual response by tearing his clothes, as was the custom of those who repented. He then sent counselors to inquire of Huldah the prophetess and learned of the fate that would befall Judah for its sinful turning away from God. Josiah heard that God would indeed punish Judah for its stubborn refusal to worship God alone, though this catastrophic punishment would not occur in Josiah's lifetime.

Josiah Calls Others to Change Their Ways

Having made a personal response to the word of the Lord as it was written in the book and spoken by the prophet, Josiah called together the leaders and people of Judah. He was not about to keep what he knew to himself. Everyone, from the greatest to the least, was included in this important gathering.

Josiah met with the people at the house of the Lord. Standing in front of temple pillars that had symbolic significance, which is now lost to us, Josiah read the scroll for the people to hear. Josiah not only spoke to them but also challenged them to react by entering into a covenant with God. Covenant is a major theological theme in the Bible. The covenant was not a legalistic contract but the formulation of a relationship between God and human beings.

Covenant carried with it the idea of responsibilities and obligations, as well as rewards and punishments. In this covenant, Josiah promised to be obedient to God's laws and to perform what God had commanded. The historian writes that "all the people joined in the covenant" (2 Kings 23:3).

Josiah Institutes Reforms

Having secured the people's affirmation of the covenant, Josiah began major religious reforms. He started at home, ordering the high priest and other priests to remove from the Jerusalem Temple cultic objects used to worship Baal and his consort, Asherah. Second Kings 21:7 records the installation of Asherah in the temple during the reign of Manasseh. Josiah had objects carted out of the city and burned to ashes. Throwing ashes on bones or graves further defiled an idol and the site so that it could not be used again for worship. On Josiah's orders, priests who had offered sacrifices to idols were "deposed," that is, killed. Prostitution, commonly associated with the fertility rites of Canaanite worship, was ended.

Josiah was not content to confine his reforms to Jerusalem. He went into the towns of the Northern Kingdom and continued to destroy idols and their shrines. By trying to bring the worship into the central location of the Temple at Jerusalem, Josiah had hoped to curb apostasy. Clearly, the Judeans had been unfaithful to God. Their God had become one among many—a situation that God would not tolerate. Worshiping God along with other gods was not acceptable. The people had to choose to worship God alone or face catastrophic consequences for their unfaithful disobedience.

Josiah's Story Calls Us to Begin Anew

The people of Josiah's time had forgotten who they were and whose they were. While we know little about how the scroll that was found during the temple renovations had been lost (some scholars believe Deuteronomy was written in the period preceding and at the beginning of Josiah's reign), we know for certain that the people were not living as God had called them to live. They had gone their own way, choosing gods made of wood and stone instead of the living God who had created them and entered into human history.

Apparently, even the priests were unconcerned about this double-minded behavior. Hilkiah handed over the scroll to Josiah's secretary, but certainly no record of his anguish about the people's apostasy is mentioned. One person—Josiah—immediately recognized how far short they had fallen and acted to restore the covenantal relationship between the people and God. He attempted to purge the land of the symbols of the Judeans' disobedience and unfaithfulness. At the direction of their national leader, the people apparently accepted the changes he brought about, though we imagine that the historian chose not to record resistance that surely must have existed in some quarters.

We, too, find it hard to admit that we were wrong, that our loyalties were misplaced, that we have strayed from the God we claim to love and obey. Yet, life with God seems to be a series of new beginnings. Covenant is followed by disobedience, repentance, God's gracious forgiveness, and a new awareness of our relationship with God through Jesus. While some Christians certainly have been involved in other religious practices or cults, many have slipped into the idolatry of materialism or power. Our idols are not made of wood or stone but of green paper or shiny metal with horses under the hood or media stars whose decadent lifestyles we long to imitate.

When we are confronted with the terrible truth that we are not worshiping God alone, or as Jesus said in the Sermon on the Mount, seeking first the kingdom of God (Matthew 6:33), we ask how we can begin anew to obey God's commands

more faithfully. Josiah's reaffirmation of the covenant is surely a model for us, for we are part of the "new covenant in [Jesus'] blood" (Luke 22:20). Participation in the sacrament of Holy Communion is a tangible way in which we can renew the covenant and begin again to be the persons God calls us to be. We may need to reexamine our understanding of Communion and begin to recognize its power to heal us and bind us to God.

Yet, we must go beyond ritual, as important as that is, and take action that indicates we have indeed turned around, which is the meaning of the word "repent." Just as Josiah could not have the people simply reaffirm their covenant with God but called upon them to actively rid the land of foreign gods, so we cannot simply perform a ritual act, no matter how meaningful, and then let the matter rest.

Like the people in Josiah's day, we may find ourselves called to an entirely different lifestyle than the one our society touts. We cannot worship God and the idols of our society. We have to identify the idols in our own lives that prevent us from giving our wholehearted allegiance to God. We may even find, as the Judeans did, that our religious institutions need to be purged. Of course we do not have literal idols in our churches. But we may try to worship God on Sunday while making programmatic and financial decisions within the congregation as if God were not present. We may shut out the needy who desperately want to come into God's presence. We may be spending most of the money given to God through the church on ourselves, rather than heavily supporting missions and outreach programs. We may be relying on ourselves to meet a challenge or solve a problem rather than taking that situation to God in prayer and seeking the guidance of the Holy Spirit.

Perhaps one of our greatest obstacles to beginning anew to obey God's commands is that deep inside we think of ourselves as self-made individuals. We have difficulty thinking of ourselves as accountable—much less obedient—to someone else, even if that someone is God. Rugged individualism that claims to do it "my way" is incompatible with obedience to the God of the universe. To begin anew we must be willing to recognize, as Josiah did, who we are and whose we are. Once we can see ourselves at the foot of the cross, rather than enthroned on our own little shrine, we can become the faithful people that God calls—and enables—each of us to be.

SHARING THE SCRIPTURE

PREPARING TO TEACH

Preparing Our Hearts

As you read the scripture and lesson for this week's study, consider how God is calling you, your congregation, your denomination, and your country to be obedient. What role can you play in helping to bring about a new understanding and commitment to faithfulness to God? What changes do you need to make in your own life? If you keep a spiritual journal, record your thoughts.

Preparing Our Minds

If you have access to *The Interpreter's Dictionary of the Bible* or another Bible dictionary, you may want to look up King Josiah. You may also want to do some reading concerning Baal, Asherah, and other gods mentioned in today's reading.

As an optional activity, you or someone you enlist during the week may be willing to speak briefly about a religious cult that is active in your area. Be sure to present this information in a light that, on one hand, will help class members understand why such worship is not an alternative for Christians, while on the other hand, will not belittle others for holding beliefs we do not accept. Prepare to use this activity only if you have both available class time and sufficient knowledge of the cult.

Preparing Our Learning Space

If you have access to any artist's rendering of Solomon's Temple, that picture may help class members to envision themselves in the crowd as Josiah speaks to the people. If you have pictures of any cultic objects mentioned, you may also want to post them in the room. If your children's department keeps a picture file, this would be a good place to look for such pictures. Bible dictionaries are also good sources.

Have on hand:
- several Bibles for students
- newsprint and marker or chalkboard and chalk
- optional paper and pencil for each student
- optional pictures illustrating other gods, cultic objects, and Solomon's Temple

LEADING THE CLASS

(1) Introduction

Begin by asking the group:
(1) **How many of you make New Year's resolutions?**
(2) **How many of you keep New Year's resolutions?**
(3) **Why does it seem so difficult to turn away from a bad habit or begin a new one?**

Point out that we find it hard to remain faithful to our resolution to lose weight or spend more time with the family or whatever we have deemed important. Similarly, many of us have as much trouble beginning anew to live obediently before God after we have stumbled as we do keeping our New Year's resolutions.

As an alternative for classes that prefer a lecture format, read or retell the Focusing on the Main Question portion.

Close the introduction by telling the group that we will be focusing today on the commitment King Josiah made to obey God by instituting reforms according to the forgotten covenant that had just been located as the temple was being renovated. Note that this Bible study prompts us to ask today's main question: *How can we begin anew to obey God's commands more faithfully?*

(2) Josiah Responds to God's Commands

To set the stage for Josiah's challenge to the people to change their ways, provide background information from this portion under Interpreting the Scripture and from the entries for 2 Kings 22 under the heading Understanding the Scripture.

For emphasis, you may want to write the following information on newsprint or a board.

Josiah does not call the people to change their ways until he:

• is confronted by the Word of God (specifically the law according to Deuteronomy) and recognizes their sin.

• hears the words of the prophet regarding disaster because of the people's apostasy.

• shows by his actions that he is heartsick and repentant about the failure of the people.

(3) Josiah Calls Others to Change Their Ways

Prior to reading the scripture, show the class any pictures you have collected illustrating the kinds of cultic objects that the Judeans were worshiping. Also display any artists' renderings of Solomon's Temple you have found. Ask the adults to picture themselves in front of the temple, among the crowd who had gathered to hear King Josiah, as you read 2 Kings 23:1-3. Remind them that they have been wor-

shiping both the living God and the gods of other cultures.

When you have finished the reading, ask these questions:

(1) Had you heard Josiah, would you be convicted of the error of your ways? Why or why not?

(2) What changes would you be willing to make to become more obedient unto God?

(3) What difficulties would you expect to encounter as you sought to begin anew to be obedient?

(4) What do you perceive to be the significance of entering into a covenant with God?

(4) Josiah Institutes Reforms

Ask the group to close their eyes and picture the scene as you read aloud 2 Kings 23:4-8a (ending with Beer-sheba). If the students enjoy hands-on activities, give each one paper and a pencil and have them try to draw the scene. Stick figures are fine. What they mainly want to capture is the total fiery desecration of these gods and the priests who served them.

Whether the adults just listened or drew what they heard, talk for a few minutes about these questions:

(1) How does the act of destroying symbols of apostasy open the door for people to begin anew to be obedient to God?

(2) What does the fact that Josiah burned the idols to ash say to you about the importance God attaches to the single-minded worship of God?

(3) Suppose you had been present as idols you had previously worshiped were being destroyed. How would you feel about the leader who ordered this action? Would you, for example, be angry that such change was being foisted upon you?

(4) How would you feel about your own life before God as you watched symbols you had revered being turned to ashes?

? (5) What changes would you want to make?

(5) Josiah's Story Calls Us to Begin Anew

If your class prefers a lecture format, you may want to begin this segment by retelling "Josiah's Story Calls Us to Begin Anew" found under Interpreting the Scripture.

Have the class brainstorm answers to the following question. Record their answers on newsprint or a chalkboard.

• If we were to listen to the Word of God and faithfully obey its teachings, what behaviors or attitudes would we be forced to change? (This question is intentionally broad, but you may want to limit it, perhaps to the great commandment about loving God [Deuteronomy 6:5] and neighbor [Leviticus 19:18] as found in Matthew 22:37-39, Mark 12:29-31, and Luke 10:27.)

If the class is large enough, divide into pairs or teams and assign each one a behavior or attitude that the total group brainstormed. Have one person in each group act as a recorder/reporter. Ask the teams to consider (1) why this behavior or attitude is not in keeping with God's command, and (2) how Christians who practice this behavior or attitude can begin again so as to be obedient to God. Allow a few moments for the teams to work and then have them report back to the class.

Summarize this activity by pointing out that, like Josiah, we must be able to recognize our disobedience, repent of it, and call others to change their ways as well. We must make such changes with great discernment, lest a dominant figure (even a cult leader) draw us into a situation where we follow orders without question. In the case of Josiah and the Judeans, the witness of the Word of God, the message of the prophetess, and their own hearts were one: they had been disobedient and needed to make a total break with their past in order to live as God's faithful, obedient people.

As an additional, optional activity, you or someone you enlisted may want to give a short report on a cult that is active in your community. Class members can discuss why this particular group is not an appropriate alternative for Christians. They may also want to consider why this group is attracting persons that the church has obviously failed to attract.

HELPING CLASS MEMBERS ACT

Challenge class members to ask God during their own devotional time this week to show them ways in which they are living unfaithfully. They may want to meditate on these failures or write about them in their spiritual journals. For each one they consider, have them also ask God to show them how they can repent and begin anew to be the faithful people they are called to be as disciples of Jesus.

Have the class members use the same format above to consider ways in which their congregation is living unfaithfully and needs to repent and begin anew.

Encourage each class member to read the newspaper or a religious publication through the eyes of God. In what situations do persons who claim to be Christian seem to be acting disobediently? Ask the students to offer a prayer so that the persons whose stories they have read may experience the kind of transformation to which Josiah called the people of Judah.

PLANNING FOR NEXT SUNDAY

Encourage adults to prepare for next week's lesson, entitled "Responding to God's Call" by reading Jeremiah 1. We will focus on Jeremiah 1:4-10 and 14-17.

Ask them to think about how they hear God's call in their own lives and the ways in which they respond to this call.

RESPONDING TO GOD'S CALL

PREVIEWING THE LESSON

Lesson Scripture: Jeremiah 1:4-10, 14-17
Background Scripture: Jeremiah 1
Key Verses: Jeremiah 1:4-5

Focus of the Lesson:
the prophet Jeremiah's response to God's call upon his life

Main Question of the Lesson:
What does it mean to be called by God?

This lesson will enable adult learners to:
(1) become familiar with the process and purpose of God's call on Jeremiah's life.
(2) explore God's call on their own lives.
(3) respond by living out their own call.

Today's lesson may be outlined as follows:
(1) Introduction
(2) Hearing God's Call
(3) Receiving God's Touch
(4) Strengthened to Speak God's Word
(5) Jeremiah's Story Prompts Us to Respond

FOCUSING ON THE MAIN QUESTION

What does it mean to be called by God? This question will guide our study this week as we consider God's call on the life of Jeremiah, as well as God's call on our own lives. We may prefer to choose for ourselves what we will do with our lives without any direction from God. Perhaps Jeremiah would have selected another path, for his work as a prophet certainly did not allow him to win any popularity contests! Yet, God calls each of us to some task. Our willingness to accept this responsibility and challenge enables God's work to be done through us.

We often refer to ordained clergy or others who are professionally involved in the work of the church as having been *called*. And so they were—and continue to be—called and equipped to undertake leadership in the community of faith. A Christian vocation, however, need not be lived out professionally within the church. Some of us are called to make an impact in the classroom or operating room or dining room. Calls come at different points in life. A few persons, like Jeremiah, seem to know what they are to do from childhood, while others discover their calling as life unfolds and doors of opportunity are opened and closed.

Even when we recognize that we are to use particular talents or undertake a specific task or play a certain role, we still are not sure this is what we want to do. Like Jeremiah, we may find the odds stacked against us. We may question God, especially when others clearly let us know that they think we're headed in the wrong direction. God's call upon our lives does have consequences, whether we heard this call as a young person, like Jeremiah, or are hearing it as a middle-aged or older adult. God calls and we choose to obey, despite the difficulties and disappointments. Or, we choose to ignore that call and then experience the inner turmoil that does not let us rest until we heed God's will. When we step out in faith and respond positively to God's call, God will direct our steps, no matter how dark the path or difficult the walk.

READING THE SCRIPTURE

NRSV

Jeremiah 1:4-10

4 Now the word of the LORD came to me saying,

5"Before I formed you in the
     womb I knew you,
   and before you were born I
     consecrated you;
I appointed you a prophet to the
     nations."

Key Verses

6Then I said, "Ah, Lord GOD! Truly I do not know how to speak, for I am only a boy." 7But the LORD said to me,

   "Do not say, 'I am only a boy';
   for you shall go to all to whom I
     send you,
   and you shall speak whatever I
     command you,
8 Do not be afraid of them,
   for I am with you to deliver you,
            says the LORD."

9Then the LORD put out his hand and touched my mouth; and the LORD said to me,

   "Now I have put my words in
     your mouth.
10See, today I appoint you over
     nations and over
     kingdoms,
   to pluck up and to pull down,
   to destroy and to overthrow,
   to build and to plant."

NIV

Jeremiah 1:4-10

4 The word of the LORD came to me, saying,

5"Before I formed you in the womb I knew
     you,
   before you were born I set you apart;
   I appointed you as a prophet to the
     nations."

Key Verses

6"Ah, Sovereign LORD," I said, "I do not know how to speak; I am only a child."

7But the LORD said to me, "Do not say, 'I am only a child.' You must go to everyone I send you to and say whatever I command you. 8Do not be afraid of them, for I am with you and will rescue you," declares the LORD.

9Then the LORD reached out his hand and touched my mouth and said to me, "Now, I have put my words in your mouth. 10 See, today I appoint you over nations and kingdoms to uproot and tear down, to destroy and overthrow, to build and to plant."

NRSV

Jeremiah 1:14-17

14 Then the LORD said to me: Out of the north disaster shall break out on all the inhabitants of the land. ¹⁵For now I am calling all the tribes of the kingdoms of the north, says the LORD; and they shall come and all of them shall set their thrones at the entrance of the gates of Jerusalem, against all its surrounding walls and against all the cities of Judah. ¹⁶And I will utter my judgments against them, for all their wickedness in forsaking me; they have made offerings to other gods, and worshiped the works of their own hands. ¹⁷But you, gird up your loins; stand up and tell them everything that I command you. Do not break down before them, or I will break you before them.

NIV

Jeremiah 1:14-17

¹⁴The LORD said to me, "From the north disaster will be poured out on all who live in the land. ¹⁵ I am about to summon all the peoples of the northern kingdoms,"
   declares the LORD.

"Their kings will come and set up
   their thrones in the entrance of the
     gates of Jerusalem;
they will come against all her
   surrounding walls and against all
     the towns of Judah.
¹⁶I will pronounce my judgments on
   my people because of their
     wickedness in forsaking me,
in burning incense to other gods
   and in worshiping what their
     hands have made.
¹⁷"Get yourself ready! Stand up and say to them whatever I command you. Do not be terrified by them, or I will terrify you before them.

UNDERSTANDING THE SCRIPTURE

Jeremiah 1:1-3. Known as the superscription, these verses introduce us to the "words" or "history" of Jeremiah. His father, Hilkiah (not the same person as in either of the previous lessons), was a priest in Anathoth, a town about three miles north of Jerusalem. Likely he was a descendant of Abiathar, a priest who was banished to Anathoth by King Solomon (see 1 Kings 2:26-27). Depending upon how these verses are interpreted, Jeremiah began his prophetic ministry in 627 B.C.E. or he was born then. However, no oracles can be dated with certainty to this period. Consequently, some scholars question that Jeremiah was prophesying at that time, whereas others believe that chapters 2–6 retain the themes of his preaching prior to reforms made during Josiah's reign. The list of kings omits two who reigned for

three months each: Jehoahaz (609 B.C.E.) and Jehoiachin (598–597 B.C.E.). The events mentioned in the verses date the end of Jeremiah's ministry to August 587 B.C.E. Chapters 40–44 continue with prophecies that date to 580 B.C.E., after Jeremiah is exiled in Egypt. This apparent discrepancy may be explained if these initial verses introduced a shorter version (chapters 1–39) that was later expanded.

Jeremiah 1:4-10. These verses record a dialogue in which God calls Jeremiah to his prophetic ministry. Several active verbs in verse 5 demonstrate God's relationship to Jeremiah: formed, knew, consecrated, and appointed. God formed Jeremiah in the womb much as a potter forms and molds clay. God intimately knew this unborn child. God dedicated or consecrated him to a divine mission that would serve "all nations." As was true with other prophets, Jeremiah's message to the Israelites would also have a bearing on its neighbors, especially Assyria, Babylon, and Egypt, for God is the God of all peoples and history. Like Moses, Jeremiah protests. Whereas Moses claimed he had a speech problem, Jeremiah believed that his youth prevented him from speaking on God's behalf. God assures him that God will be responsible for the words he is to speak. God's presence will guide and sustain the prophet. The symbolic act of touching Jeremiah's mouth indicates that God is the one who will provide the words. Jeremiah is appointed to dislocate the familiar (pluck up, pull down, destroy, and overthrow) as well as bring about newness (build and plant) through the force of his prophetic words.

Jeremiah 1:11-13. These verses contain a play on words: the Hebrew word for almond (or waker tree) sounds like the word for watching. God watches over Jeremiah, who in turn is to act as a watchman (see Jeremiah 6:17) or sentinel to warn the Israelites of danger. In a second vision, Jeremiah sees a boiling pot, which may have been a wide-mouthed pot used for cooking, "tilted away from the north." The draft of the fire likely came from the north, just as troops that invaded Palestine generally came from the north. Perhaps we are to understand that God will tip the hot contents of this pot onto Jerusalem.

Jeremiah 1:14-17. In these verses, God explains the vision. Jerusalem will be struck by a disastrous invasion from the north. Although the enemy is not named, Babylonian troops did in fact invade from the north, having come through Syria and northern Israel into Judah in 605 and 597 B.C.E. The reason for this judgment and subsequent punishment, as seen in verse 16, is that God's people have engaged in idolatry. They have created idols, thereby forsaking both God and their own identity. God calls upon Jeremiah to "gird up [his] loins," that is, prepare for battle. Jeremiah is to tell the people everything that God commands him. The prophet is not to "break down" in the face of opposition, for if he does, God will break him down.

Jeremiah 1:18-19. Opposition will surely come from political and religious leaders, as well as from the people themselves. War imagery is used here to show how strong this opposition will be. Yet, God will make Jeremiah strong, like a fortified city, a city prepared to withstand the assault of enemies. Jeremiah will be like an iron pillar and bronze wall. Such promise of strength is also seen in the call of the prophet Ezekiel (3:8-9). Despite the overwhelming odds against him, Jeremiah will prevail because God promises to be present with him. Thus, Jeremiah is warned about the difficulty of the prophetic task facing him, but he is also assured of God's abiding presence, guidance, and salvation.

INTERPRETING THE SCRIPTURE

Hearing God's Call

The book of Jeremiah opens with a little background as to who Jeremiah was and when he lived. However, we have no clear-cut indication of the circumstances surrounding his call to be God's "prophet to the nations." Although Jeremiah argues that he is young and therefore unable to serve, the reader has no clue as to where Jeremiah was or what he was doing when the Lord spoke to him. Perhaps, like Moses, he was involved in the daily business of life and unexpectedly met God in the ordinariness of the day. Or maybe he, like Isaiah, was in the temple when the Lord came to him. He was, after all, the son of a priest. Whatever he was doing, we do know for sure is that Jeremiah was unquestionably chosen by God.

Jeremiah must have been overwhelmed. God created Jeremiah, knew him, consecrated him, and appointed him. The weight of God's words must have been awesome. By including these words, Jeremiah was reminding the people of his credentials as a prophet. He did not choose this vocation; God chose him. This reminder may be necessary because Jeremiah reaches a point in his ministry where he must send his scribe Baruch into the temple to read the scrolls because he is not allowed to enter (see Jeremiah 36:5-6). In this written record of the words he has received from God, Jeremiah feels the need to give the details of his original call to ministry.

The prophet continues the dialogue God initiated by responding that his youth prevents him from speaking properly on God's behalf. Age, however, is not the yardstick by which God measures those who are called to serve. In fact, by whatever criteria we imagine, none of us is capable of serving. Yet, God provides not only commandments and directions but words of comfort as well. Jeremiah is to speak out boldly, not the words he chooses but the words God gives him. Such words will be difficult both to speak and hear, but Jeremiah need not fear for God will be present and provide whatever the prophet needs to do the task.

Receiving God's Touch

Just as clergy have historically been ordained by the laying on of hands, prophets have been commissioned by recording that God or someone acting on God's behalf has somehow touched their mouths and given them words to say (see for example Exodus 4:12, 15-16; Deuteronomy 18:18; Isaiah 6:7; Ezekiel 3:2-3). Prophets have at their disposal the power and creativity of the word of God. That word created the universe according to Genesis 1. When it goes out, God's word fulfills its purpose and does not return empty (see Isaiah 55:11).

Although Jeremiah has been appointed "over nations and over kingdoms," he does not need to leave Jerusalem to accomplish his work. While he will proclaim both destruction and peace, he will not have to do anything to bring about activity. Jeremiah will not lead armies into battle but will simply speak God's word. And it will be so. Language is a powerful force that can shape the future.

Strengthened to Speak the Word

The prophet was called to speak the words of God but advised that many would not want to hear these words. Persons with political power and influence—the kings and princes of Judah—would surely not want to hear Jeremiah's words of warning and doom. Likewise, the priests do not want to hear Jeremiah's words, for as verse 16 reveals, God's judgment is coming because the people have not worshiped God alone. Surely the leaders of the religious community must bear at least some responsibility for allowing the people to turn aside from faithful worship and obedience. Similarly, the people themselves will not want to hear from Jeremiah because his words will indict them. They have fallen away from God, preferring instead the idols of their own making and the gods of their neighbors.

God lets Jeremiah know that everyone—the politicians, religious leaders, and public—will be against him. Such forewarning would be enough to cause the bravest, most experienced spokesperson to cower. God promises to be with this chosen, teenage prophet as he announces God's judgment on the people. Jeremiah will be strengthened in the face of the opposition that will definitely arise as a result of the message he is to proclaim. The prophet is warned, however, in verse 17 that he must not break down, for if he does, God will break him down.

What is the message he must declare? Disaster is irrevocably coming! This action will be military in nature: tribes and kingdoms will invade from the north. God is not meekly having Jeremiah announce this news as if God is powerless to stop the attack. Instead, according to verse 15, God is the one who is calling upon Judah's enemies to defeat God's own people! That defeat will be a total one, sparing none of the cities of Judah. By worshiping other gods, the people not only have been unfaithful to God but they have lost sight of their identity as well. They have forgotten who they are and whose they are. It is Jeremiah's privilege and burden to answer God's call to prophesy so that the people may not only understand the reasons for their impending destruction but also look ahead with hope to a time of restoration when, chastened for their unfaithfulness, they will return from the captivity in Babylon and begin to rebuild their temple and plant their vineyards.

Jeremiah's Story Prompts Us to Respond

Most of us are not like Jeremiah. We have no sense of having been imbued with special purpose even before our birth. Neither have we had the kind of face-to-face conversation with God that Jeremiah records. Nor have we likely been expected to proclaim such doomsday messages that people are ready to throw us in a pit and leave us to die (see Jeremiah 18:18-23).

Despite these apparent dissimilarities, we are in fact very much like Jeremiah. God has called us to a lifestyle of discipleship and perhaps to a specific task, and God expects us to respond to that call. That call is our vocation, not necessarily in the sense of a career but, in the words of Walter Brueggemann as quoted by James Fowler in *Becoming Adult, Becoming Christian*, "a purpose for being in the world that is related to the purposes of God." To discern this purpose, we need to recognize, as the people of Jeremiah's day apparently did not fully acknowledge, that we are God's people and within that identity lies our purpose. We cannot worship other gods, whether we call them Baal or mammon or by some other name.

Instead, we are called to give our full allegiance to God and to live in such a way that what we do reflects God's will and word in the world. Our lives must, in some tangible way, show forth the purposes of God. We will likely find our purpose as other persons help us to discern the abilities, hone the skills, and develop the personality that makes each one of us unique. However, no matter what our talents may be and no matter which path we are drawn to follow, God's creative word is working through us to witness to others.

Like Jeremiah, we probably find the idea of witnessing scary because we feel inadequate for the task. What will I say? Will anyone listen to me? Suppose they ridicule me or, as is true in some societies, physically harm me? What then? We want to back away from sharing the word of God, preferring a witness in which our actions substitute for our words, but neither words nor actions alone are sufficient. Jesus taught us by both his words and his actions. We too must learn to announce, even in difficult situations where we seem to be the only dissenting voice, what we understand to be the word of God. The future of a friend or family member, or possibly a nation, may hang in the balance.

Jeremiah certainly had not thought of himself as anyone special; presumably, we share his thought about ourselves. God's dialogue with Jeremiah underscores the fact that he was indeed someone with a specific task to do, a task so important that God had called even before birth and strengthened him to remain faithful to this task throughout his life. Most likely, your call and mine will not have the far-reaching impact that Jeremiah's did. Although we may not be able to change the world literally, we may be able to change the world for one person or a few people. If we are faithful in discerning and saying yes to God's call, we indeed will be able to find the purpose for our lives that is related to God's purpose for us. Whatever challenges, disappointments, or victories the fulfillment of that purpose may bring, it is indeed good news to know that we are in tune with the One whose kingdom is in the process of coming and that we in some very small measure are both witnesses and workers for that kingdom.

SHARING THE SCRIPTURE

PREPARING TO TEACH

Preparing Our Hearts

Early in the week, meditate on what you believe to be God's call on your life. Why do you teach a Sunday school class or give other leadership in the church? How does your paid or volunteer work reflect who you are and whose you are? If you keep a spiritual journal, reflect on your purpose and identity as a child of God.

Preparing Our Minds

As you read the scripture and lesson, try putting yourself in Jeremiah's place. How would you feel if God came to you and called you for such an apparently difficult task? What words would you have wanted to hear from God?

You may want to do additional reading about Jeremiah in a Bible dictionary. Volume 2 of *The Interpreter's Dictionary of the Bible* (Abingdon Press), includes a thorough discussion of the prophet's life and times.

Preparing Our Learning Space

Prepare questions on newsprint or chalkboard, as shown under "Jeremiah's Story Prompts Us to Respond." Cover them for use later in the class.

If possible, you may want to post several news or magazine articles regarding situations that modern-day prophets may be called to address. Articles showing the church speaking out against social problems (e.g., gambling, drug addiction) may be especially helpful.

Have on hand:
- several Bibles for students
- newsprint and marker or chalkboard and chalk
- optional news or magazine articles (see above)
- optional paper and pencils

LEADING THE CLASS

(1) Introduction

To help class members experience the kind of reaction Jeremiah may have had when he learned of God's call upon his life, try this guided imagery exercise. Read the words, pausing for ten to fifteen seconds as indicated by the word "pause." The class is to remain silent and in an attitude of meditation as you read.

Sit in a comfortable position. Relax. Breathe deeply. (pause) Now ask God to help you remember a time when you felt overwhelmed or inadequate to meet a challenge facing you. Perhaps you or a family member was seriously ill, suddenly unemployed, or faced with a difficult situation with a child or other loved one. Think about how you felt at that time. (pause)

Now recall or imagine God telling you that you were the one who was called to act in this situation. God told you that

R

R although the task would not be easy, you were not to worry. Listen and hear God promise to strengthen you and provide you with the resources you need to do the job. Think about how God's words make you feel. (pause)

Give thanks for God's call upon your life and God's ability to equip you for the task. As you are ready, open your eyes.

Now ask these questions either to the total class or in pairs or small groups:

? (1) **How does it feel to know that God has called you to do a job, even if you would prefer not to have to undertake it?**

(2) **What are the risks and rewards of responding to God's call with a resounding, "Yes, here am I"?**

Conclude this portion by noting that as we study Jeremiah's call today, we will be asking ourselves this main question: *What does it mean to be called by God?*

(2) Hearing God's Call

Use the information from Jeremiah 1:1-3 in the Understanding the Scripture portion to set the stage for the prophet's call. Keep this background information brief.

Choose a volunteer to read aloud Jeremiah 1:4-10. The scripture will come more alive if you select three persons, one to read a narrator's part, one to read Jeremiah's words, and one to read God's words.

Point out the four verbs in verse 5: *formed*, *knew*, *consecrated*, and *appointed*. Talk with the class about the meaning of these words in terms of how God actively shapes our lives. Information to help you is found under Understanding the Scripture (Jeremiah 1:4-10) and "Hearing God's Call" under Interpreting the Scripture. Ask these questions:

? (1) **What did God want Jeremiah to do?**

(2) **What was Jeremiah's response to God's call?**

(3) Receiving God's Touch

Note in verse 9 that God touches Jeremiah's mouth and puts words in his mouth.

Talk with the class about their understanding of what it means to be a prophet. Unlike the popular definition that conveys the notion of one who predicts the future, the prophet is one who is called to speak God's words to the people. The symbolic purification of the prophet's mouth and assurance that he had been appointed by God are both important points.

Ask:

(1) **Can you think of any modern-day prophets, that is, persons who continue to remind their church or nation or other group what God expects of God's people? If so, who are they?** ?

(2) **How do you sense that these persons have been truly touched to speak for God?**

(4) Strengthened to Speak the Word

Read Jeremiah 1:14-17 aloud.

Use information from the lesson to help the class understand that God has appointed Jeremiah to the difficult task of announcing disaster to the people because of their idolatry and turning aside from God. No one will want to hear Jeremiah's words, and persons of all stripes will oppose him.

Ask:

(1) **Suppose God sent a Jeremiah into our midst today. What would be the issues that God would expect that person to speak with us about? In other words, what would he be called to "pluck up" or "plant"?** ?

If the group enjoys hands-on learning, provide some news or magazine articles depicting injustices or other concerns that God may call modern prophets to speak about. Invite class members to work in teams or pairs, reading the article and imagining what God would want to have said. The teachings of Jesus, particularly the parables and Sermon on the Mount, offer modern Christians words and attitudes to apply to challenging situations.

(5) Jeremiah's Story Prompts Us to Respond

If available, distribute paper and pencil. Show the following questions that you wrote on newsprint or a chalkboard prior to class. Ask each person to think silently about the questions, writing responses if possible.

(1) The people in Jeremiah's day had little hope because they faced judgment for their apostasy. What situations within the church or society at large give you little reason for hope?

(2) How do you think God can use you to bring a word and deed of witness and hope to others, even on a very limited scale?

(3) How will you respond to that call?

(4) What price are you willing to pay to act as God's spokesperson?

Close this section by offering a prayer that everyone present will hear and act on God's word, knowing that God will strengthen them for the task ahead.

HELPING CLASS MEMBERS ACT

Challenge class members to consider their own call and take one step during the coming week to act on that call.

Encourage class members to speak out this week on one or more issues they feel are important to God. Perhaps they could write a letter to a newspaper editor or elected official. Maybe they need to challenge the church itself to take action on an issue about which the church has been complacent.

Suggest that class members affirm the calling of a child or teen in their own family or congregation. Many youth want to be actively involved in the life of the church, but they need adults who will help them find and express their gifts.

PLANNING FOR NEXT SUNDAY

Ask class members to read Jeremiah 7, particularly verses 1-15. Next week we will consider the word that Jeremiah is called to proclaim and how that word confronts the hypocrisy of the people.

CONFRONTING HYPOCRISY

PREVIEWING THE LESSON

Lesson Scripture: Jeremiah 7:1-15
Background Scripture: Jeremiah 7
Key Verse: Jeremiah 7:3

Focus of the Lesson:
God's challenge to the people, through the prophet Jeremiah, to change their sinful, hypocritical ways

Main Question of the Lesson:
What attitudes and actions are God's people called to change in order to be in a more faithful, obedient relationship with God and neighbor?

This lesson will enable adult learners to:
(1) analyze the hypocritical behavior Jeremiah identified in the people of Judah.
(2) identify hypocrisy in their own lives.
(3) respond by taking action to root out at least one hypocritical behavior or attitude.

Today's lesson may be outlined as follows:
(1) Introduction
(2) Misplaced Trust
(3) Amending Our Ways
(4) Actions Have Consequences
(5) Confronting Our Own Hypocrisy

FOCUSING ON THE MAIN QUESTION

Hy-poc-ri-sy: pretending to be what one is not, or assuming the appearance of religion. In more common terms, a hypocrite is one who talks the talk but doesn't walk the walk. One's words and actions belie the real attitudes of the heart.

God called Jeremiah to preach a sermon to confront the people of Judah with their hypocrisy. Signs of impending invasion notwithstanding, the people felt smug and secure because they lived in the shadow of the temple, the home of God. They reasoned that since God dwelled among them, they need not fear. Jeremiah warned the people that their trust was misplaced if they believed that God would offer automatic protection no matter how they acted. While professing to believe in God, the Judeans were also worshiping other gods. They baked cakes for a fertility goddess, built shrines, and sacrificed their children to a god of their neighbors. Despite these flagrant violations of God's moral and ethical commandments, the people flocked to the temple to offer their sacrifices to God. They envisioned themselves as a worshiping people. In reality, they mocked God, for they were unable to recognize that God sought not sacrifice but faithful obedience. Their outward actions belied their inward, ruptured relationship with God.

Like the Judeans, we too must confront our own hypocrisy. We may need to recognize that attending worship on Sunday is not enough to put us in a right relationship with God. Nor is belonging to a particular group or memorizing a certain

amount of Scripture or doing a certain amount of work for the church. Our relationship with the living God is rooted in our relationship with Jesus, whose life and teaching affirm the prophet's point: our relationship to God is integrally linked to our just relationship with other persons, particularly the most vulnerable members of our society. If we treat others unjustly, oppress the immigrant or the poor, or worship other gods no matter what their names may be, we are as guilty of hypocrisy as the people whom Jeremiah addressed. *What attitudes and actions are God's people called to change in order to be in a more faithful, obedient relationship with God and neighbor?* This is our main question for today's study.

READING THE SCRIPTURE

NRSV
Jeremiah 7:1-15

1 The word that came to Jeremiah from the LORD: ²Stand in the gate of the LORD's house, and proclaim there this word, and say, Hear the word of the LORD, all you people of Judah, you that enter these gates to worship the LORD. ³Thus says the LORD of hosts, the God of Israel: Amend your ways and your doings, and let me dwell with you in this place. ⁴Do not trust in these deceptive words: "This is the temple of the LORD, the temple of the LORD, the temple of the LORD."

⁵For if you truly amend your ways and your doings, if you truly act justly one with another, ⁶if you do not oppress the alien, the orphan, and the widow, or shed innocent blood in this place, and if you do not go after other gods to your own hurt, ⁷then I will dwell with you in this place, in the land that I gave of old to your ancestors forever and ever.

8 Here you are, trusting in deceptive words to no avail. ⁹Will you steal, murder, commit adultery, swear falsely, make

NIV
Jeremiah 7:1-15

1 This is the word that came to Jeremiah from the LORD: ²"Stand at the gate of the LORD's house and there proclaim this message:

" 'Hear the word of the LORD, all you people of Judah who come through these gates to worship the LORD. ³This is what the LORD Almighty, the God of Israel, says: Reform your ways and your actions, and I will let you live in this place. ⁴Do not trust in deceptive words and say, "This is the temple of the LORD, the temple of the LORD, the temple of the LORD!" ⁵If you really change your ways and your actions and deal with each other justly, ⁶if you do not oppress the alien, the fatherless or the widow and do not shed innocent blood in this place, and if you do not follow other gods to your own harm, ⁷then I will let you live in this place, in the land I gave your forefathers for ever and ever. ⁸But look, you are trusting in deceptive words that are worthless.

⁹" 'Will you steal and murder, commit

Key Verse

Key Verse

41

offerings to Baal, and go after other gods that you have not known, ¹⁰and then come and stand before me in this house, which is called by my name, and say, "We are safe!"—only to go on doing all these abominations? ¹¹Has this house, which is called by my name, become a den of robbers in your sight? You know, I too am watching, says the LORD. ¹²Go now to my place that was in Shiloh, where I made my name dwell at first, and see what I did to it for the wickedness of my people Israel. ¹³And now, because you have done all these things, says the LORD, and when I spoke to you persistently, you did not listen, and when I called you, you did not answer, ¹⁴therefore I will do to the house that is called by my name, in which you trust, and to the place that I gave to you and to your ancestors, just what I did to Shiloh. ¹⁵And I will cast you out of my sight, just as I cast out all your kinsfolk, all the offspring of Ephraim.

adultery and perjury, burn incense to Baal and follow other gods you have not known, ¹⁰and then come and stand before me in this house, which bears my Name, and say, "We are safe"—safe to do all these detestable things? ¹¹Has this house, which bears my Name, become a den of robbers to you? But I have been watching! declares the LORD.

¹²" 'Go now to the place in Shiloh where I first made a dwelling for my Name, and see what I did to it because of the wickedness of my people Israel. ¹³While you were doing all these things, declares the LORD, I spoke to you again and again, but you did not listen; I called you, but you did not answer. ¹⁴Therefore, what I did to Shiloh I will now do to the house that bears my Name, the temple you trust in, the place I gave to you and your fathers. ¹⁵I will thrust you from my presence, just as I did all your brothers, the people of Ephraim.'

UNDERSTANDING THE SCRIPTURE

Jeremiah 7:1-2. God calls Jeremiah to proclaim a sermon in the Temple at Jerusalem. Although the date is questioned by some scholars, according to Jeremiah 26:1 this event occurred early in the reign of King Jehoiakim (609–598 B.C.E.), a son of Josiah installed by the Egyptians. The Egyptians had killed King Josiah in battle and deposed the son who succeeded him, Jehoahaz, within three months of his ascension to the throne. Judah was deeply concerned about its security and future as Egypt and Babylon jockeyed for position to control Palestine. The prophet's message created such a stir, as attested to in a parallel account in Jeremiah 26 written from a more personal point of view, that the temple prophets and priests took legal steps to have Jeremiah executed. He was apparently accused of not speaking on

behalf of God because he prophesied the destruction of the temple. Since the people thought that God would always be present in the temple, they assumed that Jeremiah was a false prophet, an offense that was legally punishable by death (see Deuteronomy 18:20-22).

Jeremiah 7:3-4. Jeremiah's message calls the people to change their ways. The repetition of the words "the temple of the LORD" underscores the people's belief that the temple could not be violated. They assumed that God would alway be there, dwelling among them. Consequently, they believed that God would protect them, no matter what.

Jeremiah 7:5-7. The crux of the matter is that the people must change if God is to continue to dwell in the temple. The conditions they need to fulfill are specifically outlined. They must act justly. They must not oppress the helpless, shed innocent blood, or worship other gods.

Jeremiah 7:8-10. According to the covenant with Moses, the people are to adhere to certain moral and ethical behaviors. Yet, they have consistently violated the Ten Commandments and then gone into the temple mistakenly believing that they were safe despite their actions.

Jeremiah 7:11-12. The temple has become a place for the wicked to hide, but God knows what is going on.

Jeremiah 7:13-15. In about 1050 B.C.E., the shrine in Shiloh was destroyed by the Philistines. This central shrine, which pre-dated the Temple in Jerusalem, was located about eighteen miles north of Jerusalem. Since Jeremiah was descended from the priests at Shiloh who had been exiled to Anathoth, he would have known about the destruction there. Jeremiah prophesies that God will cast out all the people, just as happened at Shiloh. The temple sermon itself ends with verse 15.

Jeremiah 7:16-20. God tells Jeremiah that it will be useless to intercede for Judah because it is in a state of such grievous apostasy. The people are unabashedly worshiping other gods, including the queen of heaven, Ishtar, a Babylonian-Assyrian goddess. Families work together to worship these gods: children, men, and women each had a role to play. Prior religious reforms were obviously short-lived. God announces to Jeremiah that the people are hurting only themselves, for God will destroy them, their livestock, and the vegetation on which they depend.

Jeremiah 7:21-28. God's requirement of the people is faithful obedience, not sacrifice. When the people are in a right relationship with God, their sacrifices are acceptable. However, when they have disobeyed or ignored God and the prophets sent by God, no amount of sacrificial offerings can overcome that breach in their relationship with God. The people have chosen to follow their own ways, rather than God's way. They will pay a huge price for their "stiffened necks," a phrase Jeremiah uses to mean "hardness of heart." External actions are without value unless they are undertaken with a heartfelt sincerity.

Jeremiah 7:29-34. These verses, extending into Jeremiah 8:3, detail the fate that awaits Judah. The cutting off of one's hair is a ritual of mourning. Judah shall indeed mourn because God "has rejected and forsaken the generation that provoked his wrath." The people have defiled God's temple. They practice child sacrifice, a rite recognized by many of Israel's neighbors but forbidden by God (see Leviticus 18:21). God tells Jeremiah that this place will eventually be called the valley of Slaughter; child sacrifice will come to be understood as murder. Verse 33 paints a gruesome image of the bodies of the idolaters being picked clean by birds and other predators. The chapter closes on a very somber note using an image that appears again in 16:9. A major reversal will occur: the festivities of revelers will cease, for Judah will become a desolate waste.

INTERPRETING THE SCRIPTURE

Misplaced Trust

God called Jeremiah to stand at the temple and preach a sermon of warning to the people. Despite their appearances of religiosity and worship, they were guilty in God's sight of unfaithfulness and disobedience. They took for granted that God's presence in the temple provided the protection from enemies that they needed.

Such security was especially comforting in light of the military threat from the north. The people assumed that everything would work out for them. But they were wrong. Without question, God was capable of offering the protection they needed. However, the people mistakenly perceived that God could be toyed with. They wanted God to be available for them when they needed God, but they were unwilling to remain in the committed, faithful relationship that God expected of them.

Jeremiah's message to the people of Judah is one that must be heard and understood in our day as well. Trust is misplaced when we depend upon the outward trappings of our religion—or in the case of the Judeans, the temple of God—to take the place of a right relationship with God. How many times have we heard the term "Sunday Christians," referring to persons who regularly attend worship but who live by the expectations or ethics of other gods the rest of the week. Such persons erroneously believe that they can feud with a neighbor, engage in shady business practices, physically or emotionally abuse family members, and then return to church on Sunday morning as if all is well between them and God. All is not well. The prophet is not speaking to us about the errors and sins that even the most devoted Christians fall prey to. Instead, he is talking about a mind-set in which we assume that our only responsibility is to do the right outward actions or perform the proper rituals, no matter what is truly in our hearts. Jeremiah's call, as seen in our key verse, to "amend your ways and your doings" (7:3) was an apt word for both those who trusted that God would never desert the temple and those who believed that appearances, not the heart, are all that matters to God.

Amending Our Ways

Jeremiah's original sermon challenged the people to amend their ways in about 609 B.C.E. More than two millennia later, we recognize that we need to change the same things as the Judeans. Jeremiah 7:5-7 speaks conditionally. In other words, if the people act in certain specified ways, then God will respond by dwelling in the temple. The unstated corollary is, of course, that if the people act to the contrary, God will depart from them. What are these behaviors that can cause God to abandon the people?

First, Jeremiah tells the people that they are to act with justice. This is a bedrock biblical theme that has two facets. The notion of justice includes standards for penalties to be meted out to those who break social compacts. Justice also includes standards by which the advantages of life in community are distributed, so as to ensure opportunities for participation, material goods, and freedom for all.

In the Bible, benefits are distributed according to the standard of need. Persons who lack what they need to participate in the life of the community are entitled to receive justice. Needy persons are often identified not as named individuals but as groups: the orphan, the widow, the stranger, the sick, the prisoner, the poor. Powers that block needy persons so that they cannot get what they need are described as oppressive. Note that Jeremiah 7:5 calls the people to act with justice, while 7:6 admonishes them not to oppress others. The sin of injustice occurs either when other persons are intentionally barred from meeting their basic needs or when those who could help to bring about justice fail to act. Needs are met and justice is served when people have access to food, clothing, shelter, due process, and freedom. Not only are immediate needs met but also the persons are no longer oppressed; they have the means to be productive, participating members of the community. Jesus' ministry, as well as the law and the prophets of the Hebrew Scriptures, reflects the critical role that justice plays in the kingdom of God. God's people are called to act with justice, and a mark of their obedience and faithfulness is their willingness to act justly.

Notice in Jeremiah 7:6-7 that God will dwell with the people if and only if they both act justly and avoid oppressing others. But the people have not lived obediently. Instead, they have broken the Ten Commandments. As indicated in verse 9, they have committed theft, murder, and adultery, as well as borne false witness and worshiped other gods. Yet, they have had the audacity to go into the temple and act as if they are acceptable in God's sight. Instead of commending their worship, God asks if the temple has "become a den of robbers," the same description that Jesus used in Matthew 21:13 when he drove out the money changers.

Actions Have Consequences

God is watching what is happening, and God will not be fooled. In fact, if the people think they are safe, they only need to remember the destruction of the house of worship at Shiloh in the days of Samuel. Although the people do not want to hear the prophet's words (he was arrested after this sermon, according to Jeremiah 26:8), God proclaims that the Temple in Jerusalem will be destroyed as surely as the one in Shiloh was.

The reason for this intended destruction is that God has provided the people with what they need to know, but they have not wanted to listen. They have chosen to act hypocritically, ostensibly showing their love for God by their worship in the temple while at the same time breaking their covenant relationship with God by their idolatrous, immoral, and unethical actions. Despite their feelings of smugness, they will be cast aside in the coming military victory of Babylon and their exile in that country, just as the people of the Northern Kingdom (Israel, the "offspring of Ephraim") were overrun by the Assyrians. While they assumed they were safe, God's words show just how God will go in holding people to standards of obedience and justice.

Confronting Our Own Hypocrisy

If Jeremiah were alive today, what words would God have the prophet proclaim? Which of our actions have consequences that we either cannot or will not recognize? We still claim to be God's people, but many Christians are reluctant to speak up when decisions by elected leaders threaten to create or add to the injustices and oppression wrought on the most vulnerable members of society. Christians cannot sit idly by when the poor, the children, the widow, and others in our society who desperately need necessities are denied access to these basics. How are we acting justly, not only as citizens in a secular society but within our own congregations and denominations? Is our church providing food and volunteers for a soup kitchen? Do we support projects that help the homeless or people who live in substandard housing? How do we treat the prisoner or the immigrant (alien, in biblical terms)? In what ways do we tend the sick, such as those who have AIDS? If we are not reaching out to these vulnerable persons who are in need not only of a message about God's love but also of a living demonstration of that love, what words of judgment does God have for us?

As we think about what we as Christians are doing—and failing to do—perhaps Jeremiah's words will take on new meaning and greater urgency. While we may be faithful in attending church (and worship surely is important!), are we like the Judeans who felt that as long as they were observing their religious rituals other behaviors did not count? To be in a covenant relationship with God, either through the covenant with Moses or the new covenant in Christ, means that we are to make our relationship with God the top priority in our lives, to seek first the kingdom of God. In doing so, we discover that to be in a right relationship with God necessitates that we be in a right relationship with our neighbor. That, of course, does not mean that we must worship the gods our neighbor worships. It does, however, mean that we act with justice for all, oppress no one, and worship God alone. If we are not acting in ways that mirror a close, personal relationship with God, then we need to confront our own hypocrisy and seek God's forgiveness and guidance so that we may become the people God intends us to be.

SHARING THE SCRIPTURE

PREPARING TO TEACH

Preparing Our Hearts

Spend some time this week meditating on what hypocrisy is and how it may manifest itself in your own life and in the life of your congregation. You may want to record your thoughts in a spiritual journal.

Pray that God will enable you to proclaim God's word in such a winsome way this week that the class members who need to confront hypocrisy in their own lives will be open to doing so.

Preparing Our Minds

Read Jeremiah 7 several times, focusing especially on verses 1-15. Also read Jeremiah 26:1-6, which is another account of the same sermon written from a more biographical point of view.

You may want to review the Ten Commandments found in Exodus 20:1-17. Note that several of the commandments are mentioned in Jeremiah 7:9. Disobedience to these commandments prompted God to have Jeremiah confront the people with their hypocritical behavior.

Preparing Our Learning Space

If you have a list of the Ten Commandments, you may want to post it in your room. You may also want to post a map showing the location of Shiloh, mentioned in Jeremiah 7:12.

You may want to write the questions in the "Confronting Our Own Hypocrisy" portion on newsprint prior to class.

Have on hand:
- several Bibles
- newsprint and marker or chalkboard and chalk
- paper and pencils

LEADING THE CLASS

(1) Introduction

Begin today's lesson by asking class members to define the word "hypocrite." Then encourage them to give examples of the kinds of behavior that they consider hypocritical. Focus on general examples, such as cheating on income tax or fighting with a neighbor. Do not entertain specific cases that may hurt or embarrass individuals. In the course of the discussion, have class members say why they believe the examples they have given are hypocritical. In other words, what law or teaching does this behavior seem to violate? You may want to record this information on newsprint or a chalkboard.

Emphasize that one's relationship with other persons reflects one's relationship with God. If we engage in the outward rituals of our religion but are not in a right relationship with God, we are acting hypocritically. In today's lesson, Jeremiah preaches a sermon at the temple that calls the people of Judah to face their own hypocrisy.

As we study today's lesson, we will consider this main question: **What attitudes** *and actions are God's people called to change in order to be in a more faithful, obedient relationship with God and neighbor?*

(2) Misplaced Trust

Choose a volunteer to read aloud Jeremiah 7:1-4. Use information from Understanding the Scripture to set the scene.

Focus attention on verse 4. Invite class members with various translations to read the word that describes "words" in the first part of the verse. Answers include: "deceptive" (NRSV and NIV), "lying" (NKJV), and "delusive" (NJB). Help the class delve beyond the literal meaning of "This is the temple of Lord" (which in fact it was) to understand that the Judeans were putting their trust in their belief that God would neither destroy nor forsake the divine dwelling place, regardless of how they acted. Jeremiah's point is that such a belief is false or deceptive. The people are coming into the gates of the temple to perform their religious rituals, but their hearts are not right with God. They are not as safe as they think they are because their trust is misplaced.

Ask the class to consider these questions either as a whole group or with a partner:

[?] **(1) What actions, or group memberships, or other external "security blankets" do we rely on to vouchsafe our connection with God?**

(2) Is our trust misplaced? Why or why not?

(3) Would God say our trust is misplaced? Why or why not?

(3) Amending Our Ways

To help the class members hear the conditional nature of God's promise to be with the people if they amend their ways, select one person to read verses 5-6 (the "if" portion) and a second volunteer to read verse 7 (the "then" portion). Help the group understand that God promises to dwell with them if and only if they change their behaviors.

On newsprint or a chalkboard list the actions found in verses 5-6:
- Must act with justice
- Must not oppress the alien, the orphan, and the widow
- Must not shed innocent blood
- Must not worship other gods

Then brainstorm answers to these questions, recording the group's answers on newsprint:

(1) What are some ways in which we act [?] **with justice?**

(2) What are some ways in which we (as individuals or a church or a society) oppress the alien (stranger/immigrant), fatherless (NKJV), and the widow (or other persons who are alone)?

(3) How do we tacitly allow innocent blood to be shed?

(4) Who are some of the other gods we worship? (for example, mammon, status)

(4) Actions Have Consequences

Select a volunteer to conclude the reading of today's scripture lesson, Jeremiah 7:8-15. Fill in background concerning Shiloh as found in verses 13-15 in the Understanding the Scripture portion.

Distribute paper and pencils. Ask the class to work in small teams to write in a sentence or two the gist of what God is saying to the people through Jeremiah. Invite volunteers to share their responses. (Example: You are trusting in your belief that I the Lord your God will neither desert nor destroy the temple. You are wrong. You have broken my commandments and worshiped other gods. You paid no attention to the warnings I gave you. Just as I destroyed my dwelling in Shiloh, so will I destroy the Temple in Jerusalem and cast you out of my sight.)

(5) Confronting Our Own Hypocrisy

Refer back to the ideas brainstormed during the "Introduction." Invite the class to think about other hypocritical behaviors. You may wish to add ideas found in the first paragraph of the "Confronting Our Own Hypocrisy" segment of the Interpreting the Scripture portion.

Distribute paper and pencils to each person. Ask class members to meditate on the questions below that you have written on newsprint or a chalkboard. Some persons may want to write their thoughts. Assure the group that they will not be asked to share their responses with the class.
- If Jeremiah were alive today, what hypocritical behaviors would he be called to confront in me?
- If Jeremiah were alive today, what hypocritical behaviors would he be called to confront in our church?

Close by reading this litany. The class members' response is adapted from today's key verse, Jeremiah 7:3. You may want to write the response on newsprint or a chalkboard.

[R] **Leader:** We confess, O God, that we have at times acted unjustly. We have blamed the poor for their own plight, ignored the needs of the fatherless and widow, and worshiped gods of our own choosing.

Group: Help us to amend our ways, so that you will dwell with us, O God.

Leader: We confess, O God, that we have at times deliberately disobeyed your moral and ethical teachings. Forgive us for failing to live up to the high standards of conduct to which you call us.

Group: Help us to amend our ways, so that you will dwell with us, O God. **[R]**

Leader: We ask, gracious God, that we might live in such an intimate relationship with you that your words, will, and actions are reflected in all that we say, think, and do.

Group: Help us to amend our ways, so that you will dwell with us, O God.

HELPING CLASS MEMBERS ACT

Challenge class members to ask God to reveal hypocrisy in their lives and seek direction in overcoming this hypocrisy.

Suggest that class members note a current social problem as discussed on television or seen in a newspaper or magazine article. Ask them to consider these questions: (1) What is the problem? (2) How is our community (state, nation) handling the problem? (3) How would God call us to handle the problem, based on our understanding of justice? Encourage each member to take at least one action that is in keeping with a just response.

Invite class members to examine the actions of the congregation to see how the church may need to "amend its ways" so as to act with greater justice. Perhaps they could undertake a project to enable the church to reach out and act on behalf of the oppressed or others who are being treated unjustly. For example, the class could suggest that the church sponsor the building of a Habitat for Humanity home, or open an after-school tutoring center, or provide staff for a soup kitchen on a regular basis.

PLANNING FOR NEXT SUNDAY

Next week's lesson, "Continuing to Trust," will focus on Habakkuk, especially 2:1-4 and 3:17-19. Encourage class members to read all of the work of this minor prophet. Prompt them to think about their own level of trust in God, especially during difficult times.

CONTINUING TO TRUST

PREVIEWING THE LESSON

Lesson Scripture: Habakkuk 2:1-4; 3:17-19
Background Scripture: Habakkuk
Key Verses: Habakkuk 3:17-18

Focus of the Lesson:
the prophet Habakkuk's joy and absolute trust in God even under difficult circumstances

Main Question of the Lesson:
Can we trust God to care for us?

This lesson will enable adult learners to:
(1) examine the prophet's resolve to trust in God despite uncertainties.
(2) consider questions that arise in their own lives in difficult times.
(3) respond by trusting God in a difficult situation.

Today's lesson may be outlined as follows:
(1) Introduction
(2) Waiting for an Answer
(3) The Righteous and the Wicked
(4) Trusting in God
(5) Putting Our Own Trust in God

FOCUSING ON THE MAIN QUESTION

How many times have we questioned God about situations we just cannot figure out? We have worked hard and practiced high standards of ethics only to be the one caught in a layoff, while a co-worker who will trample anyone to get ahead is promoted during the company's reorganization. Why, God? we ask. We miscarry a child who is very much wanted only to read of yet another infant found stashed in a dumpster. Why, God? we ask. Sometimes life seems so unfair. The wicked appear to prosper and enjoy life, but we are beset by problems and setbacks. Where is God in the midst of our pain? *Can we trust God to care for us?*

The prophet Habakkuk would answer today's main question with a resounding yes. God is not only present but faithful. We can definitely rely upon God. Even when trouble surrounds us, we can know that God is our strength. Habakkuk lived in a time when Judah was threatened by the Babylonians. He could not understand where God was or whose cause God was championing. From the prophet's point of view, God seemed to be tolerating evil—an untenable position for the God whose "eyes are too pure to behold evil (Habakkuk 1:13)."

By means of a vision, the prophet is assured that God not only sees but also directs what is happening. In this case, God is using the Babylonians (also known as Chaldeans) to chasten Judah. For God to use the enemies of God's own people seems incomprehensible. In the end, however, God promises the prophet that justice will prevail. In God's own time the Babylonians will be punished for their

wickedness. They will ultimately drink the cup of humiliation that they have poured upon others as a result of their merciless, oppressive behavior. God's divine order–the kingdom–will come about in the time and way God chooses.

In the meantime, the prophet will continue to trust God. The historical realities of the prophet's life stand in sharp contrast to the vision of future vindication that God gives him. But the prophet believes that God is indeed trustworthy. Therefore, "though the fig tree does not blossom," Habakkuk will continue to rely upon and rejoice "in the God of [his] salvation." His prophetic word encourages us to do the same.

READING THE SCRIPTURE

NRSV
Habakkuk 2:1-4
1 I will stand at my watchpost,
   and station myself on the
      rampart;
 I will keep watch to see what he
    will say to me,
    and what he will answer
      concerning my complaint.
²Then the LORD answered me and
    said:
 Write the vision;
   make it plain on tablets,
   so that a runner may read it.
³For there is still a vision for the
     appointed time;
   it speaks of the end, and does
    not lie.
 If it seems to tarry, wait for it;
   it will surely come, it will not
    delay.
⁴Look at the proud!
   Their spirit is not right in
    them,
   but the righteous live by their
    faith.

NIV
Habakkuk 2:1-4
1 I will stand at my watch
   and station myself on the ramparts;
   I will look to see what he will say to me,
    and what answer I am to give to this
     complaint.

The LORD's Answer
²Then the LORD replied:
   "Write down the revelation
   and make it plain on tablets
   so that a herald may run with it.
³For the revelation awaits an appointed time;
   it speaks of the end
   and will not prove false.
 Though it linger, wait for it;
   it will certainly come and will not delay.

⁴"See, he is puffed up;
   his desires are not upright—
   but the righteous will live by his faith—

NRSV
Habakkuk 3:17-19

¹⁷Though the fig tree does not
blossom,
and no fruit is on the vines;
though the produce of the olive
fails
and the fields yield no food;
though the flock is cut off from
the fold
and there is no herd in the
stalls,
¹⁸yet I will rejoice in the LORD;
I will exult in the God of my
salvation.

¹⁹GOD, the Lord, is my strength;
he makes my feet like the feet
of a deer,
and makes me tread upon the
heights.

To the choirmaster: with
stringed instruments.

NIV
Habakkuk 3:17-19

¹⁷Though the fig tree does not bud
and there are no grapes on the vines,
though the olive crop fails
and the fields produce no food,
though there are no sheep in the pen
and no cattle in the stalls,
¹⁸yet I will rejoice in the LORD,
I will be joyful in God my Savior.

¹⁹The Sovereign LORD is my strength;
he makes my feet like the feet of a deer,
he enables me to go on the heights.

For the director of music. On my
stringed instruments.

Key Verses

UNDERSTANDING THE SCRIPTURE

Habakkuk 1:1. The superscription identifies Habakkuk as the prophet who gives this oracle, though nothing is really known about him. The word "oracle," which means "burden," is often used to describe a prophetic word. Habakkuk likely wrote this book during the years 608–598 B.C.E. The book can be divided into three identifiable literary sections that may have been separate units originally: 1:2–2:5 (a dialogue between the prophet and God); 2:6-20 (five woes proclaimed against a wicked nation); and 3:1-19 (a poem that bears similarity to the Psalms and in its current form was intended for use in worship).

Habakkuk 1:2-4. This portion begins a dialogue between the prophet and God. The prophet speaks to God in the form of a complaint. He wants to know how long the violence and injustice perpetrated by

the wicked will continue in Judah. "Violence" (see also 1:3, 1:9, 2:8, 2:17) refers to confusion and disorder.

Habakkuk 1:5-11. Someone (apparently God, though the speaker is not clearly identified) responds. God will use enemies of the people to bring about judgment (see other references to God using enemies: Isaiah 5:25-30, Jeremiah 32:4-5). Specifically, the Chaldeans, who are also called neo-Babylonians, will be the agents of God's punishment. They ruled the Near East from 612–539 B.C.E. The Babylonians sacked Jerusalem in 587 B.C.E. and took the people into captivity.

Habakkuk 1:12-17. The prophet raises a second complaint to God. This time he wants to know why God, whose "eyes are too pure to behold evil," looks on while the wicked persecute God's people. The prophet compares the Judeans to fish: they are leaderless and easily captured by God's enemies. Habakkuk cannot understand why a just God allows such action to take place at the hands of evildoers.

Habakkuk 2:1-4. Now that the prophet has voiced his complaints, he will take his watchpost (see also Isaiah 21:8) to await God's reply. The prophet clearly assumes that God will reply, and God does indeed give an answer through a vision. God assures him that although the prophet may not see the final vindication, divine justice is at work and divine order will come about at the appropriate time. The righteous live by faith, but the proud have a wrong spirit within them.

Habakkuk 2:5-6a. Verses 5-6 serve as a preface to a series of five woes directed against the oppressor, the Chaldeans (or Babylonians).

Habakkuk 2:6b-20. In the first woe (verses 7-8), God speaks against a nation guilty of plundering. Those who had been conquered by this nation will rise up and claim what was taken from them as spoils. The second woe (verses 9-11) is directed against the dynasties (houses) that have oppressed others. The building blocks of their own houses will cry out against them. Verses 12-14 call down disaster upon a government that tries to glorify itself by constructing impressive buildings at the expense of oppressing people. The fourth woe, recorded in verses 15-17, indicates that God will cause the merciless military power that has humiliated others to drink the cup of humiliation itself. The final woe, found in verses 18-20, is directed against worshipers of false gods. In contrast to lifeless idols, the holy God is living in the temple.

Habakkuk 3:1-16. The prophet combines prayer to God with a hymn that was obviously used for liturgical purposes. (Note the words "Shigionoth" [verse 1], "Selah" [verse 3], and "choirmaster" [verse 19]. These technical terms are found in the Psalms, Israel's book of worship.) In verses 3-7, the prophet describes a theophany or appearance of God. This vision of God is dominated by light and brightness. The prophet goes on to describe a vision of God in battle, a scene reminiscent of God's victory against the Egyptians in the days of Moses. The purpose of God's action is articulated in verse 13: God came to save God's people and anointed one (that is, the king of Judah) from the wicked. This vision grants the prophet foresight of the accomplishment of God's purpose. Despite current appearances to the contrary, God's justice will prevail and the faithful will inherit the kingdom.

Habakkuk 3:17-19. Although the actual situation of the people has not changed—the Babylonian threat is still very real—the prophet responds to the vision with words of trust. Habakkuk is living in the space of time between God's judgment and fulfillment. The prophet has seen a vision of what is to come and knows that he can trust God to save the people. In the end, Habakkuk can affirm that "GOD, the Lord, is [his] strength."

INTERPRETING THE SCRIPTURE

Waiting for an Answer

The prophet Habakkuk complained to God that violence and disorder reigned. Everywhere he looked there was trouble. The wicked seemed to be in charge. Where, he wanted to know, was God's justice? God gave the prophet an amazing answer: God was allowing evildoers—specifically the Chaldeans, known also as the Babylonians—to appear to be in control. In fact, they would punish God's own people, not because God could not contain them but because God chose them for this task. God would later punish the Chaldeans, but for now they were free to live according to their own immoral and unethical standards.

Habakkuk could not imagine that the holy God he worshiped would even look on such evildoers, much less allow them to chasten Judah. He asks how long God is going to stand by while these wicked persons persecute God's own people. In essence, Habakkuk wants something bad to happen to the people who have acted in ways so contrary to God's justice and holiness. After he sets forth his question, Habakkuk takes his place at a figurative watchpost to await the Lord's reply. The prophet's willingness to wait as a sentinel on duty indicates that he does, in fact, believe that God will speak to him. Surely he is convinced that God hears and will answer him. And he is not disappointed. God does respond with a vision "for the appointed time" (2:3). This vision is plain, as legible as a highway sign. It does not refer to the present but to a future, unspecified time. At that time the kingdom of God will come, though the prophet himself may not be alive to experience the final vindication of God's justice. Nonetheless, such a day will come. In the meantime, the prophet is to live in the space between the promise and the fulfillment.

The Righteous and the Wicked

By means of a vision, God reminds the prophet that the proud will not endure. They may seem to be in charge. Life may be going well for them. Such persons, however, are sowing the seeds of their own destruction. In the end, they will perish. A look at the pronouncement of five woes (2:6b-20) will help us to understand the behaviors that will cause disaster to come upon the wicked. The proud believe that they can walk over anyone. The Chaldeans, for example, have plundered the peoples they conquered. Their greed impels them to "heap up what is not [their] own" (2:6b). Such behavior will lead to a revolt by the ones whom they have oppressed. The tables will be turned so that the oppressors will owe money to the oppressed. In addition, the proud also think that their houses (or dynasties) are untouchable. Instead of offering security, the very stones of their homes will cry out against them. Moreover, the arrogant believe that they can expand their empires and build new cities by means of bloodshed and violence. However, such actions will come to nothing. The proud believe that they can act without mercy and justice toward others and continue to thrive. Yet, in God's own time, the Chaldeans will drink the cup of humiliation they have passed to other people. Finally, the evil worship lifeless idols. Such worship is useless because these mute gods have been created by the very people who worship them.

In contrast, the righteous choose to worship the holy, living God. They are called to live according to their faith in God. Their upright faith is what allows them to live, whereas the proud, unrighteous ones will surely succumb because "their spirit is not right in them" (2:4).

Trusting in God

Unlike the wicked, who live according to their own standards and worship idols they have crafted with their own hands, the prophet acknowledges God's holiness and seeks to live according to God's standard of justice. Habakkuk praises God for salvation. Despite his questions and uncertainties, the appearance of evildoers prospering, and the difficult circumstances among his own people, the prophet proclaims his trust in God.

Why, though, when everything the prophet could perceive with his own senses suggested that God was not in charge, that the forces of evil had taken over, would the prophet continue to trust God? He continued to do so because he knew what God had done in the past. Habakkuk stood in awe of God's saving work (3:2) and called upon God to do such work again. The glorious God who appeared as bright as the sun (3:4) had been able to save the people from their enemies. Habakkuk believed that God would save them again, despite appearances to the contrary. The prophet could look ahead to a future time when God would bring about justice and vindication. God would allow the Babylonians to chasten Judah, but in God's own time—a time Habakkuk did not expect to live to see—God would ultimately save the people of Judah. Salvation, justice, and the divine order of the kingdom of God would come about according to God's will and purpose.

As he looked ahead, Habakkuk joyfully proclaimed his trust in the God of his salvation (3:18), the God who gave him strength (3:19). He affirms that no matter how bleak the circumstances are, he can indeed continue to trust God.

Putting Our Own Trust in God

What about us? Are we willing to affirm God as our strength and our salvation? Are we willing to trust God in all situations? Are we willing to stand before God, ask our questions, and wait for an answer, believing that God will indeed respond?

Trusting may be hard for us, especially if our prayers seem to go unanswered. An injustice or difficult situation drags on for weeks, months, even years without a resolution in sight. Yet, we expect instant "customer service." Since our humanity limits us to space and time, we can only know for certain what is happening here and now. The future is a matter of faith. When we do not receive an immediate response from God, we may react in one of several ways. One option is to begin wondering if God is really listening. Another is to assume that God is able to act but no longer cares what happens to us. A third option is to assume that God is powerless to do anything about our situation. Or, like the prophet, we can trust that God will hear and respond in God's own time and way. This option may be difficult for us, but it is the most faithful way. We patiently wait for God to act on our behalf, trusting that God will do so.

Trusting God may also seem like a ludicrous idea when we see our enemies prospering. We want God to zap these people, but in God's infinite grace and mercy they continue to prosper. Sooner or later, however, the seeds sown by their own greed or unethical behavior sprout up and cause them to stumble. Whether we see their downfall or not is not at issue here. God promises that the righteous—the ones who live by faith—will live. Apparent victories, even those wrought by oppressors who think they are invincible, will only last for so long, for "the arrogant do not endure" (2:5).

Trusting God also seems difficult in the midst of adversity. Some persons only recognize God's existence when they are in trouble. They seek God and perhaps try to bargain, hoping that God will work everything out for them. Others want tangible evidence of God's presence before they will trust. They are like the man who has fallen from a cliff and is clinging to a branch. He continues yelling, but no one responds until God promises to rescue him. All the man has to do is let go of the branch. After thinking for a few moments, the man yells back: "Is anyone else up there?"

Some persons turn away from God when tragedy strikes. They forget that sin and death are part of the human condition. God does not necessarily intervene as a drunk driver kills a beloved family member. God does not necessarily change a weather pattern so that a devastating storm bypasses a heavily populated area. God does not necessarily prompt warring nations to hold their fire, despite the death and destruction that result from their animosity. In short, God does not guarantee us lives that are pain-free. God does, however, promise to be with us in our suffering. Sometimes that suffering can awaken us to greater trust in God. Jesus' trust in the garden and on the cross demonstrate to us the immeasurable trustworthiness of our loving God. The issue, then, is not whether God can be trusted, but whether we are willing to put our confidence in the One whose vision is not limited to the here and now but who holds the future— including our lives and the lives of those we love—securely within loving arms.

SHARING THE SCRIPTURE

PREPARING TO TEACH

Preparing Our Hearts

As you begin to prepare yourself spiritually to lead this week's lesson, think about at least one time in your life when you weren't too sure if you could trust God. Perhaps you or a family member was seriously ill, or you were experiencing serious financial problems, or someone's behavior had deeply hurt or disappointed you. You could not imagine that God could somehow work out this situation. Try telling God, either in an imaginary dialogue or by recording your thoughts in a spiritual journal, how you felt at the time and what convinced you that God did indeed care for you and could be trusted to resolve the situation.

Preparing Our Minds

Read all three chapters of Habakkuk several times, preferably in different translations. Try putting yourself in the prophet's place. Imagine yourself engaged in a dialogue with God about God's apparent unwillingness to listen or inability to act in the face of violence and injustice. Note that unlike most prophetic literature, where the prophet speaks messages of God to the people, Habakkuk is in dialogue with God.

In addition to reading the lesson, you may want to consult a commentary on Habakkuk.

Preparing Our Learning Space

Prepare sheets of newsprint with a sentence stem and questions, depending upon the activities you choose to use.

Have on hand:
- ✔ several Bibles for students
- ✔ newsprint and marker or chalkboard and chalk
- ✔ paper and pencils
- ✔ optional copies of *The United Methodist Hymnal* or other Psalter

LEADING THE CLASS

(1) Introduction

If possible in your learning area, have markers available and post a sheet of newsprint with the words, "I find it hard to trust God when . . ." If the class members do not know one another well, you may want to use the stem, "It seems hard to trust God when . . ." so as not to be so personal. As class members enter, invite them to finish the sentence stem by writing all around the paper, just as graffiti would be painted on a wall. As an alternative, hand out slips of paper and pencils to class members and ask them to complete the sentence. When you are ready to begin, collect the slips and read them aloud without identifying the writers.

Either way, discuss with the group reasons that people find it difficult to trust God completely. Close the introduction by pointing out today's main question: *Can we trust God to care for us?*

If the class prefers not to participate in a discussion, use the Focusing on the Main Question portion as your introduction. Be sure to lift up the main question.

(2) Waiting for an Answer

Provide background information on Habakkuk 1:1-17 from the Understanding the Scripture portion. Then choose a volunteer to read Habakkuk 2:1.

Invite class members to put themselves in the prophet's place and ask:

(1) You have complained that God seems neither willing to listen nor to act, despite the fact that the wicked are perverting justice. You have also complained that God just looks on while these evil persons trample the righteous. Why, then, do you think God will answer you?

(2) What kind of response do you hope to receive?

Now read God's response in Habakkuk 2:2-3 and ask:

(1) How does God answer the prophet?

(2) When can the prophet expect the vision to be fulfilled? (Be sure to note that though the vision is not yet fulfilled, it is in process and moving toward fulfillment.)

As an alternative, use information in this section of Interpreting the Scripture as the basis for a lecture.

(3) The Righteous and the Wicked

Ask several persons who have different translations of the Bible to read Habakkuk 2:4.

Divide a sheet of newsprint in half. On one side write, "Characteristics of the Righteous," and on the other, "Character-istics of the Proud." Encourage class members to suggest characteristics.

As appropriate, fill in background information about the proud as found in the Understanding the Scripture portion for Habakkuk 2:5-20 and the Interpreting the Scripture portion.

Summarize the answers, being sure to draw this distinction: the proud (or arrogant) will not endure (2:5), but the righteous live by their faith.

(4) Trusting in God

Provide background for Habakkuk 3, as found in Understanding the Scripture. Choose someone to read Habakkuk 3:17-19. Point out that verses 17-18 are today's key verses.

Distribute paper and pencils. Ask class members to work with a partner or small team to write a modern version of verse 17. In other words, have the students think of difficult situations in their own context. Here are some examples: even if the factory closes; even if my child experiments with drugs; even if my friend is killed in a car accident. Instruct them to add verses 18-19a either as they appear or rewritten in modern terms.

Invite a volunteer from each group to read what he or she has written. Affirm each group's work.

Point out that although the situations we face may be different from those the prophet encountered, they are no less serious. Like the prophet, we are called to respond to God with trust and praise.

(5) Putting Our Own Trust in God

Post the following questions and provide time for silent reflection. Some class members may want to write their responses, so be prepared with paper and pencils. Announce that answers are private and will not be shared with the group.

- Which of your prayers seem to be unanswered right now? How do you feel about that?
- Recall two or three very difficult times in your life. Did you begin to doubt that God would care for you? What happened? How was your faith renewed?
- Suppose a difficult situation should arise this afternoon. Would you be willing to trust God completely? On what ground do you base your answer?

Close this section of the lesson by dividing the class in half and reading responsively Psalm 27:1-6. If you have *The United Methodist Hymnal* (number 758-59) or other Psalter available, students may read from that. If not, they may need to share Bibles to be reading from the same translation. Point out that Habakkuk 3 is in the tradition of the Psalms and that Psalm 27, like Habakkuk 3:17-19, extols God's saving goodness.

HELPING CLASS MEMBERS ACT

Encourage class members to think of a current situation in their own lives that is testing their willingness to trust God completely. Urge them to (1) pray about this situation, believing that God will answer, (2) recall a difficult prior situation that God resolved, and (3) read Habakkuk 3:17-19 at least once each day as an affirmation of God's saving strength in even the most dire circumstances.

Challenge class members to become caregivers for someone who is experiencing a life crisis. Through their words and actions, students should share and demonstrate their trust that God is in charge of the situation and will bring it to a resolution in God's own time and way.

Tell class members to think about a national or world situation that involves violence or oppression. Invite the adults to take whatever action they can, including prayer, to speak out and act against this injustice.

PLANNING FOR NEXT SUNDAY

Next week we will begin Unit 2, entitled "Judah's Internal Decay," in order to understand the nature of Judah's apostasy. Ask class members to read Jeremiah 5, paying particular attention to verses 1-6.

SEARCHING FOR JUSTICE AND TRUTH

PREVIEWING THE LESSON

Lesson Scripture: Jeremiah 5:1-6
Background Scripture: Jeremiah 5
Key Verse: Jeremiah 5:1

Focus of the Lesson:
the prophet Jeremiah's pronouncements of impending punishment against Jerusalem for its lack of faithfulness, truth, and justice

Main Questions of the Lesson:
What pronouncements did God make against Judah?
What pronouncements would God make against us?

This lesson will enable adult learners to:
(1) examine reasons for Judah's impending punishment.
(2) relate Judah's behavior to the context of their own lives.
(3) respond by identifying and repenting of unjust and disobedient behavior.

Today's lesson may be outlined as follows:
(1) Introduction
(2) In Search of One Just Person
(3) None to Be Found
(4) Judgment Is Coming
(5) The Lesson of Judah for Us

FOCUSING ON THE MAIN QUESTION

Superman reportedly stands as a defender of truth, justice, and the American way. His Herculean accomplishments are all predicated upon the belief that the strong defend the weak, that good overcomes evil, and that truth will eventually win out over lies. Superman always manages to right the wrong.

We expect such behavior of Superman, but do we expect it of ourselves? Do we as Christians seek God's justice for all persons? Do we repent of our sin and walk in the way of the Lord? Do we declare our loyalty to God through Jesus and remain steadfast in our faith?

Or are we more like the people of Judah

whom God called Jeremiah to confront? God really wanted to forgive the people and was willing to save Jerusalem for the sake of "one person who acts justly and seeks truth" (Jeremiah 5:1). No one meeting that description—neither the rich nor the poor, neither the religious leaders nor the common people—could be found. Although people professed allegiance to God, their behavior proved that their profession was insincere. Judah was rotten to its very core.

God had sent prophets to warn the people to turn from their sinful ways, but they continued to live according to their own light, which was dark indeed. They could not imagine that God would judge them. After all, God's Temple was in Jerusalem, and God had promised that a descendant of David would always be on the throne.

They thought they could continue to pay lip service to God while behaving immorally and disobediently. But they were wrong. As much as God wanted the people to turn from their wicked ways, God knew they had reached the point of no return. God would not completely destroy these unfaithful people, but they had to be severely chastised for their unjust, immoral behavior.

Suppose God were to send a Jeremiah into our town—even into our church. Would the prophet find at least one just person? Or do we, like the Judeans, have much to repent of? Are we even aware of our unfaithfulness? As we study today's lesson, we will continue to ask: *What pronouncements did God make against Judah? What pronouncements would God make against us?*

READING THE SCRIPTURE

NRSV
Jeremiah 5:1-6
1 Run to and fro through the
       streets of Jerusalem,
    look around and take
       note!
  Search its squares and see
    if you can find one
       person
  who acts justly
    and seeks truth—
  so that I may pardon
       Jerusalem.
²Although they say, "As the
       LORD lives,"
    yet they swear falsely.

³O LORD, do your eyes not look
       for truth?
  You have struck them,
    but they felt no anguish;
  you have consumed them,
    but they refused to take
       correction.
  They have made their faces

NIV
Jeremiah 5:1-6
1 "GO UP and down the streets of Jerusalem,
  look around and consider,
       search through her squares.
    If you can find but one person
       who deals honestly and seeks the truth,
       I will forgive this city.
²Although they say, 'As surely as the LORD
       lives,'
    still they are swearing falsely."

³O LORD, do not your eyes look for truth?
       You struck them, but they felt no pain;
       you crushed them, but they refused
          correction.
    They made their faces harder than stone
       and refused to repent.
⁴I thought, "These are only the poor;
       they are foolish,

Key
Verse

Key
Verse

harder than rock;
they have refused to turn
back.
⁴Then I said, "These are only the
poor,
they have no sense;
for they do not know the way of
the LORD,
the law of their God.
⁵Let me go to the rich
and speak to them;
surely they know the way of the
LORD,
the law of their God."
But they all alike had broken the
yoke,
they had burst the bonds.

⁶Therefore a lion from the forest
shall kill them,
a wolf from the desert shall
destroy them.
A leopard is watching against
their cities;
everyone who goes out of
them shall be torn in
pieces—
because their transgressions are
many,
their apostasies are great.

for they do not know the way of the LORD,
the requirements of their God.
⁵So I will go to the leaders
and speak to them;
surely they know the way of the LORD,
the requirements of their God."
But with one accord they too had broken
off the yoke
and torn off the bonds.
⁶Therefore a lion from the forest will attack
them,
a wolf from the desert will ravage them,
a leopard will lie in wait near their towns
to tear to pieces any who venture out,
for their rebellion is great
and their backslidings many.

UNDERSTANDING THE SCRIPTURE

Jeremiah 5:1. Jeremiah 5 includes several oracles of judgment. God's people continue in their sinfulness, despite certainty of siege by the "evil from the north" (4:6). The Babylonians invaded and deported people from Judah in 598–597 B.C.E., though they did not destroy Jerusalem then. Although the exact date of this passage is unknown, the time for warnings has passed. All Jeremiah can do now is explain why the people are besieged. He focuses on their moral failings as the reason for attack. In verse 1, God instructs the prophet to scour the city in search of one just person. If such an individual can be found, God is willing to pardon all of Jerusalem. This verse is reminiscent of Abraham's attempt to find ten righteous people so as to save Sodom and Gomorrah (see Genesis 18:22-33).

Jeremiah 5:2. Although the people have covenanted to be faithful to God, they have sworn falsely and are guilty.

Jeremiah 5:3. The prophet responds to God, noting the people's obstinacy in the face of God's punishment.

Jeremiah 5:4-5. Everyone in the city has forsaken God's law. Perhaps the poor (the lowly) do not know any better, but the rich, those in power and leadership positions, are not morally better off than the poor. No one is living according to the covenant.

Jeremiah 5:6. The animals mentioned—beasts of prey—are the invaders who will destroy Judah (see Jeremiah 2:15; 4:7; Hosea 13:7-8; Habakkuk and 1:8; Zephaniah 3:3). The reason for this destructive action is the people's own apostasy.

Jeremiah 5:7-9. God's people are guilty of idolatry, adultery, and prostitution. In light of such behavior, what option does God have but to punish them?

Jeremiah 5:10-11. God instructs the prophet to partially destroy a vineyard. The vineyard is a symbol for God's own people. God had lovingly planted this vineyard from good seed (see Jeremiah 2:21 and Isaiah 5:1-7), but the vine has grown wild and must be destroyed. Israel (the Northern Kingdom, which has already been destroyed) and Judah have both been faithless.

Jeremiah 5:12-17. Jeremiah now speaks words of judgment. He says that the people have spoken falsely, not expecting God to take any action against them. They believed that God's presence in the temple and God's promise that a descendant of David would be on the throne shielded them from any drastic action against them. Since the people could not believe that war or famine would come upon them, the words of the prophets were ignored. The use of "wind" is a play on the Hebrew word that means "spirit," "wind," or "breath." Prophetic inspiration can come as the "spirit" or "breath" of God. In essence, Jeremiah is calling the other prophets "windbags." God will make the words in the prophet's mouth searing; they will devour the people. A merciless invader will come upon the people.

Jeremiah 5:18-19. These two verses of prose interrupt the poetry. Some scholars believe these verses are a later addition to the text that weakens the threats. The destruction will not be total, but it will be a judgment from God because the people have committed apostasy. Their punishment will be to serve others in a foreign land, which is exactly what happened during the Babylonian captivity.

Jeremiah 5:20-29. God has Jeremiah declare judgment against the people. The prophet reminds them of God's creative power to tame and limit the destructive forces of chaos. Such power should cause the people to revere and obey God. But they do not. Instead, they have shut their eyes and ears to God. They have rebelled and turned away from God. A drought during the growing season is to be seen, according to the prophet, as a punishment from God. Jeremiah goes on to discuss the sins of injustice and oppression that thrive in the midst of God's people. Just as the fowler snares unsuspecting birds in a trap, some of God's people have grown richer by defrauding the needy. Instead of calling for justice and defending the rights of the vulnerable, God's people have allowed wickedness to continue. Such faithless behavior deserves retribution from God.

Jeremiah 5:30-31. Wickedness abounds in the land, including among the religious leaders. The prophets—the ones who supposedly speak for God—are prophesying falsely. The NRSV says that "the priests rule as the prophets direct," whereas the NIV reads "the priests rule by their own authority." In either case, neither the prophets nor the priests are directed by God. No one seems to care, however, for God's people love and support the corruption of the prophets and priests. Chapter 5 closes by raising a terrifying question: "What will you do when the end comes?"

INTERPRETING THE SCRIPTURE

In Search of One Just Person

The LORD passed before him, and proclaimed,
    "The LORD, the LORD,
    a God merciful and gracious,
    slow to anger,
    and abounding in steadfast love
        and faithfulness,
    keeping steadfast love for the
        thousandth generation,
    forgiving iniquity and
        transgression and sin,
    yet by no means clearing the
        guilty,
    but visiting the iniquity of the
        parents
    upon the children
    and the children's children,
    to the third and the fourth
        generation."

These words spoken by God to Moses in Exodus 34:6-7 are echoed elsewhere (see Numbers 14:18; Nehemiah 9:17, 31; Psalm 103:8; Jeremiah 32:18; Jonah 4:2). This gracious, loving, forgiving nature is what prompted God to send Jeremiah into the streets of Jerusalem. God will punish the guilty, but God preferred to pardon the people. If, as our key verse states, the prophet could find one person—only one—who acted justly and sought truth, then God would have spared the city. God has shown such compassion before. God promised Abraham that Sodom and Gomorrah would be saved if the patriarch could find ten righteous people (see Genesis 18:22-33).

God sent the prophet into Jerusalem— the city of David and the site of God's temple. Surely in this holy place inhabited by people who were chosen by God and shepherded by a multitude of religious leaders, Jeremiah would have no difficulty finding a single individual who lived faithfully in covenant relationship with God. The prophet should be able to locate someone whose behavior testified to a love of God and love of neighbor. There must be one person willing to defend the oppressed and take the risk of speaking the truth on God's behalf.

None to Be Found

Like his predecessor Abraham, Jeremiah's search was in vain. While Jerusalem was home to many people who professed to be faithful to God, their oaths were false. They claimed loyalty to God, but their actions belied their profession of faith. In contrast to Jeremiah 2, in which Judah's sin is portrayed as strictly religious in nature, chapter 5 finds fault with the social and personal morals of the people. There was not one righteous person; not even (see Romans 3:10). Everyone had sinned.

Instead of righteousness, justice, and truth, Jeremiah found falsehoods, stubbornness, disobedience, ignorance of the ways of God, and violations of God's law. But there was no excuse for such behavior. God had clearly set forth expectations in the Ten Commandments and other laws given to Moses. Although Jeremiah made allowances for poor persons, who perhaps had not been educated about the covenant, even those persons with wealth or standing in the community, who should have known what God required, chose not to act on what they knew. Moreover, the people had been chastened and called to repentance, but to no avail. They defiantly continued in their wicked ways.

Judgment Is Coming

God's loving, merciful nature is slow to anger, but judgment will come. The Northern Kingdom (Israel) had been warned about its disobedience and apostasy, but the people would not turn from their wicked ways. God allowed the Assyrians to be the instrument of judgment against them in 722–721 B.C.E. Similarly, Judah had been warned repeatedly about its apostasy and failure to live in a right, covenant relationship with God.

Surely the people in the Southern Kingdom (Judah) would learn from the bitter example of the North. But they did not. God held off judgment because of faithfulness on the part of a few persons, including King Hezekiah and King Josiah, whom we have already studied. In mercy, God sent prophets to Judah to warn the people, but God never forces people to make the righteous choice. The people of Judah opted to continue hurtling headlong toward destruction.

God is slow to anger, but a time will come when the guilty will be punished. God had even told Judah, by means of prophesy, that invaders from the north would carry out God's purposes, though they were enemies of God's people. In Jeremiah 5:6, the ones who will execute the judgment against Judah are described as ferocious animals. Lions are mentioned as destroyers in Jeremiah 2:15; 4:7; Hosea 13:7-8; and Zephaniah 3:3. Wolves are cited in Habakkuk 1:8 and Zephaniah 3:3, and a leopard in Hosea 13:7.

The people of Judah have had their chance. God has patiently worked through prophets and two faithful kings, but the people refuse to repent. They have sealed their own destruction. Now, it will only be a matter of time before Jerusalem is again invaded by the Babylonians and torn to pieces as a wild animal decimates its prey.

The Lesson of Judah for Us

Suppose God sent a modern-day prophet to our community or church. Would this person find at least "one person who acts justly and seeks truth" (Jeremiah 5:1)? Or would this seeker have to go before God, as Jeremiah did, and report that the search was futile? Not one righteous person could be found. Although Jeremiah made allowances for poor people who may not have had access to knowledge, God had indeed provided the people with clear-cut expectations. God had entered into a covenant relationship, given the law, and sent prophets to let the Judeans know what they were to do.

How much more has God done for us? We have the benefit of easily accessible written Scriptures, the lessons of the history of God's people prior to the founding of the church, two thousand years of church history, and—most importantly—Jesus Christ. We too have the resources to be obedient, faithful people. The question remains: Are we? Are we truly different from the people of Judah? Or are we practicing the same old sins and disobedience in modern garb?

The Judeans professed to live unto God but, as the prophet discovered, "they swear falsely" (Jeremiah 5:2). In other words, they said one thing but acted in ways that were contrary to their profession. Not only that, they also refused to turn from their wicked ways. Don't we modern Christians do the same thing, at least at times? We claim to love God but we do not love our neighbor. Some Christians erect walls of hostility between themselves and persons of other nations, ethnic groups, religions, socioeconomic classes, ages, or other superficial categories, which deny that God's image exists in all persons. We may treat even our loved ones and closest friends rudely or contemptuously. We have our own "tests" to determine if a person is worthy to receive our help, whereas God's own standard is justice meted out according to need. We may know how to live in community, to care for our neighbor (whoever and wherever that person may be), but we do not necessarily choose to act on what we know to be God's expectations for us.

Like our Judean ancestors, modern Christians also commit sins of personal immorality. To our shame, adultery seems almost as common in the church—sometimes even in the parsonage!—as it is in the world. We also commit sins of greed when we have more than enough money and resources but refuse to share them with needy brothers and sisters. We wait apathetically for someone else to demand justice for all persons. We selfishly waste the resources of God's creation by consuming goods we do not really need. The list of our sins goes on and on.

Perhaps our problem, like that of the Judeans, is that we really do not believe God will act (Jeremiah 5:12). We mistake God's long-suffering graciousness for God's winking at our behavior. We continue to do whatever we choose, assuming that we will never be held accountable, that a day of reckoning will never come. God's response to the Judeans shows us otherwise. While we may not be able to legislate our own religious and moral beliefs in a pluralistic society, we can at least peacefully make our views known and live according to the beliefs we profess. If, for example, we recognize our proper role as stewards of God's creation, we can recycle, buy products from socially responsible companies, and cut back on the use of nonrenewable energy resources, whether these actions are mandated by law or not. We can put our faith into action.

In Jeremiah 5:3, the prophet commented that God had punished the people of Judah. Instead of repenting, they had hardened themselves, refusing to be corrected by God. We see this attitude in our day as well. We know what God calls us to do, but we have some excuse as to why we cannot—or will not—take the appropriate action. Repentance—turning from our sinful ways—is predicated on an understanding that we are accountable to God for our behaviors and attitudes. We can repent, knowing that God will forgive us. Or we can, like the Judeans, continue to deny that God will ever take decisive action in the face of our unfaithfulness and disobedience. If we choose the latter option, we do so knowing that judgment will come to us as surely as it did to Judah.

SHARING THE SCRIPTURE

PREPARING TO TEACH

Preparing Our Hearts

As you study Jeremiah's message of judgment to the people of Judah, ask God to show you shortcomings in your own life. How have you turned away from God? What do you need to do or change in order to become a faithful follower of Jesus?

Think, too, about your church. Would a prophet find one just person within your congregation (or your class)? If not, what changes need to be made? How can you as a church leader help to bring about these changes?

Preparing Our Minds

Read Jeremiah 5 from several Bible translations. If you have time, you may want to read Jeremiah 4:5–10:25. These passages form a series of oracles of judgment against Judah. God's judgment will be carried out by an enemy from the north. Note that we have alrady studied Jeremiah 7.

Preparing Our Learning Space

If you choose to do the debate described below, you may want to write the statement on newsprint prior to class.

Have on hand:
- ✔ several Bibles
- ✔ newsprint and marker or chalkboard and chalk
- ✔ optional paper and pencils

LEADING THE CLASS

(1) Introduction

Begin the class by asking the following question. You may want to record answers on newsprint or a chalkboard.

(1) What words or phrases would you use to describe the actions and attitudes God expects of Christians?

(This question can be answered in a variety of ways, but be sure the list includes traits noted in Jeremiah 5, such as: act justly, seek truth, obey God, are willing to repent and turn away from sins, and are familiar with what God expects of them.)

Then ask:

(2) If God were to send a prophet today to search for persons who practiced these actions and held these attitudes, what kind of report would the prophet have to give?

(Be careful not to let the discussion focus on particular individuals or certain groups within the church. Remind the class to speak in generalities, such as "Some of us seem unwilling to forgive others.")

Note that God has searched for faithful persons before. Today we will examine the results of one search conducted by Jeremiah. Conclude the introduction by announcing today's main questions. You may also want to write them so that the class can keep these ideas before them during the session. *What pronouncements did God make against Judah? What pronouncements would God make against us?*

If your class will not engage in a discussion, use ideas from Focusing on the Main Question to introduce the lesson.

(2) In Search of One Just Person

Read Jeremiah 5:1 aloud. Discuss the following theological question, either with the whole class or in small teams or pairs:

(1) What does this verse tell me about God?

(Answers may include: God is unwilling to give up on people; God wants to forgive us; God urgently seeks us; God sends persons to find us when we have sinned; God expects us to act justly and seek truth; God chastises us in order to bring us back.)

If you subdivide the class, allow time for teams or pairs to share their ideas. Then have students turn in their Bibles to Exodus 34:6-7. Invite them to add any characteristics concerning the nature of God that this passage prompts them to consider.

Check the "In Search of One Just Person" portion under Interpreting the Scripture for other ideas. Or, use this information as the basis of a lecture.

(3) None to Be Found

Choose a volunteer to read aloud Jeremiah 5:2-5 and ask the following questions:

(1) What does this passage tell me about the people of Judah?

(Answers may include: The people mouth pious words but do not speak truthfully; they have responded to God's correction by digging in their heels and refusing to budge; all are guilty of breaking God's laws.)

(2) What does this passage tell me about the relationship of the people of Judah to God?

(Answers may include: God will continue to seek the people and offer forgiveness, but God will ultimately punish them if they do not repent and turn away from their wickedness; God holds the people accountable because they are in a covenant relationship.)

(4) Judgment Is Coming

Now read Jeremiah 5:6. Ask:

[?] **(1) Does this verse in any way change your understanding of who God is or how God relates to people? If so, how?**

See Understanding the Scripture and this portion under Interpreting the Scripture for references.

You may want to bring up the story of Sodom and Gomorrah (Genesis 18:22-33 and 19:12-29). Here God responded to Abraham's plea with the same willingness to pardon the city if just ten righteous people could be found. This story reinforces both God's mercy and desire to pardon, as well as God's justice in taking decisive action when unrepented sin is rampant.

At the end of Jeremiah 5:6, God says that the people must be punished because "their transgressions are many, their apostasies are great." With the whole class, or with several persons serving as debaters, or within small groups, conduct a debate based on this statement:

[R] God did not really punish the people; they punished themselves as a result of their unwillingness to obey God.

(5) The Lesson of Judah for Us

Address the following questions by discussion, reading, or retelling this portion as it appears under Interpreting the Scripture.

[?] **(1) What can we as Christians learn about ourselves as we study these events concerning Judah?**
(2) What inferences can we draw about God's relationship to us from this passage?

If the class likes hands-on activities, distribute paper and pencils. Encourage class members, working either individually or with a partner, to write editorials regarding behaviors of Christians that indicate that we too have "sworn falsely" and have not lived in faithful obedience to the high calling of discipleship in Jesus Christ that is ours. The editorials may include statistics or particular kinds of behaviors, so long as they do not target a particular individual or identifiable group for censure. Provide an opportunity for volunteers to share what they have written so that the class may respond.

HELPING CLASS MEMBERS ACT

Encourage everyone to spend time in prayer and meditation this week focused on these two questions: (1) How do my actions reflect justice and truth? (2) What changes does God call me to make so as to be a more just and truthful person? Challenge each person to take at least one step toward enacting a change God has revealed needs to be made.

PLANNING FOR NEXT SUNDAY

In preparation for next Sunday's lesson, "Rejecting False Promises," ask class members to read Jeremiah 28:5-14. Those who have time will want to read the entire background scripture, Jeremiah 28–29. Suggest that the students consider contrasting ways we react to truth we do not want to hear as opposed to false promises that raise our hopes.

Suggest that class members be alert for opportunities to act in ways that promote justice and truth. These opportunities may arise at home or church, in the workplace or community, or during a fellowship time with friends. They may want to record their response to at least one of these incidents in a spiritual journal.

REJECTING FALSE PROMISES

PREVIEWING THE LESSON

Lesson Scripture: Jeremiah 28:5-14
Background Scripture: Jeremiah 28–29
Key Verses: Jeremiah 29:12-13

Focus of the Lesson:
Jeremiah's rejection of Hananiah's false promises of peace

Main Question of the Lesson:
How can we discern words from God, especially when we hear a more appealing message that raises false hope and offers false promises?

This lesson will enable adult learners to:
(1) discern the truth of Jeremiah's message.
(2) recognize the consequences of messages that supposedly speak God's word but in fact do not.
(3) respond by discerning the word of God in their own lives.

Today's lesson may be outlined as follows:
(1) Introduction
(2) Hearing What You Want to Hear
(3) Resisting the Will of God
(4) Recognizing False Promises Today
(5) Discerning the Word of God

FOCUSING ON THE MAIN QUESTION

God speaks to us in many ways. Sometimes we hear God's word through a sermon or hymn. We may hear it as we read the Scripture, pray, or meditate. Perhaps God comes to us as we hike along a trail or quietly paddle a canoe. The divine voice may call us through the words of a friend or the circumstances of our lives. Or possibly, we just hear a still small voice within us.

We hear so many communications that supposedly come from God. The question is: Do they? Are we responding to words from God, or do we simply say "amen" to words we really want to hear? Some persons claim to speak in God's name, calling others to support a cause or join a group that purports to be of God but actually holds beliefs and engages in practices that do not reflect the Way that Jesus taught. Such leaders may entice followers with their smooth words and soothing message. They may say exactly what their adherents want to hear. But they are not words from God.

What do we do when we know that some self-proclaimed prophet is leading people along a path strewn with false hopes and promises? How do we confront this person? Jeremiah had to face such a situation. No one wanted to hear his words of impending destruction. Instead people rallied around Hananiah, who confidently prophesied that God would "break the yoke of King Nebuchadnezzar" (Jeremiah 28:11). Hananiah assured his listeners that within two years the people exiled in the first deportation to Babylon would return home. Jeremiah knew otherwise, but no one wanted to listen to his gloomy message. No one wanted to hear that God was allowing Nebuchadnezzar to punish Israel for its apostasy and disobedience. Such a message, though true, was unthinkable.

Jeremiah's words from God were rejected in favor of Hananiah's false hopes for peace. Today's lesson from Jeremiah prompts us to ask: *How can we discern words from God, especially when we hear a more appealing message that raises false hope and offers false promises?* We will also consider ways in which we can confront false prophets in our own day.

READING THE SCRIPTURE

NRSV
Jeremiah 28:5-14

5 Then the prophet Jeremiah spoke to the prophet Hananiah in the presence of the priests and all the people who were standing in the house of the LORD; 6and the prophet Jeremiah said, "Amen! May the LORD do so; may the LORD fulfill the words that you have prophesied, and bring back to this place from Babylon the vessels of the house of the LORD, and all the exiles. 7But listen now to this word that I speak in your hearing and in the hearing of all the people. 8The prophets who preceded you and me from ancient times prophesied war, famine, and pestilence against many countries and great kingdoms. 9As for the prophet who prophesies peace, when the word of that prophet comes true, then it will be known that the LORD has truly sent the prophet."

10 Then the prophet Hananiah took the yoke from the neck of the prophet Jeremiah, and broke it. 11And Hananiah spoke in the presence of all the people, saying, "Thus says the LORD: This is how I will break the yoke of King Nebuchadnezzar of Babylon from the neck of all the nations

NIV
Jeremiah 28:5-14

5Then the prophet Jeremiah replied to the prophet Hananiah before the priests and all the people who were standing in the house of the LORD. 6He said, "Amen! May the LORD do so! May the LORD fulfill the words you have prophesied by bringing the articles of the LORD's house and all the exiles back to this place from Babylon. 7Nevertheless, listen to what I have to say in your hearing and in the hearing of all the people: 8From early times the prophets who preceded you and me have prophesied war, disaster and plague against many countries and great kingdoms. 9But the prophet who prophesies peace will be recognized as one truly sent by the LORD only if his prediction comes true."

10Then the prophet Hananiah took the yoke off the neck of the prophet Jeremiah and broke it, 11and he said before all the people, "This is what the LORD says: 'In the same way will I break the yoke of Nebuchadnezzar king of Babylon off the neck of all the nations within two years.' " At this, the prophet Jeremiah went on his way.

within two years." At this, the prophet Jeremiah went his way.

12 Sometime after the prophet Hananiah had broken the yoke from the neck of the prophet Jeremiah, the word of the LORD came to Jeremiah: ¹³Go, tell Hananiah, Thus says the LORD: You have broken wooden bars only to forge iron bars in place of them! ¹⁴For thus says the LORD of hosts, the God of Israel: I have put an iron yoke on the neck of all these nations so that they may serve King Nebuchadnezzar of Babylon, and they shall indeed serve him; I have even given him the wild animals.

¹²Shortly after the prophet Hananiah had broken the yoke off the neck of the prophet Jeremiah, the word of the LORD came to Jeremiah: ¹³"Go and tell Hananiah, 'This is what the LORD says: You have broken a wooden yoke, but in its place you will get a yoke of iron. ¹⁴This is what the LORD Almighty, the God of Israel, says: I will put an iron yoke on the necks of all these nations to make them serve Nebuchadnezzar king of Babylon, and they will serve him. I will even give him control over the wild animals.' "

NRSV
Jeremiah 29:12-13

¹²Then when you call upon me and come and pray to me, I will hear you. ¹³When you search for me, you will find me.

NIV
Jeremiah 29:12-13

¹²Then you will call upon me and come and pray to me, and I will listen to you. ¹³You will seek me and find me when you seek me with all your heart.

UNDERSTANDING THE SCRIPTURE

Jeremiah 28:1-4. During the fourth year of the reign of King Zedekiah the prophet Hananiah clashes with Jeremiah over the question of what God's will is for the people of Judah. Hananiah, whose name means "Yahweh has been gracious," insists that the yoke of Nebuchadnezzar, the king of Babylon, has been broken. Hananiah prophesies that within two years God will return to Jerusalem the vessels plundered from the temple (see 2 Kings 24:13), King Jeconiah (a variant spelling of Jehoiachin), and the exiles carted off to Babylon in 597 B.C.E. when Nebuchadnezzar and his troops attacked the holy city will also be returned. Hananiah's message was one of coming peace.

Jeremiah 28:5-11. Standing in the temple, Jeremiah publicly responds to Hananiah's prophecy. As he speaks, he is wearing a yoke, similar to one worn by oxen, that

God had commanded him to make (see Jeremiah 27:2). The yoke is a symbol of Judah's submission to Babylon. Jeremiah's reply indicates that the tradition of the true prophets is one of warnings and punishments. In contrast, false prophets have often promised peace and good fortune. Verse 9 alludes to the test of true prophesy, as found in Deuteronomy 18:20-22. If a prophet is truly speaking on behalf of God, the prophet's words will come true. While Jeremiah would like to see Hananiah's prophecy come to pass, he knows those words of peace do not proclaim God's truth. Hananiah responds by removing and breaking the yoke Jeremiah is wearing, thereby symbolizing his belief in the coming freedom from Babylon. Jeremiah does not argue with Hananiah; he simply leaves.

Jeremiah 28:12-14. Soon after the confrontation in the temple, Jeremiah received a message from God confirming Jeremiah's position. God is the one who has determined the role Nebuchadnezzar and Babylon will play.

Jeremiah 28:15-17. Jeremiah again confronts the false prophet and states that God did not send Hananiah to speak to the people. The important point here is that while Hananiah's words of peace may have brought comfort to the people of Judah and inspired them to patriotism, his words were false; they contradicted the will of God. Moreover, the people trusted these false words rather than the true, but devastating, message of Jeremiah. Through the prophet, God tells Hananiah that he will be dead within one year. This prophecy is swiftly fulfilled in the seventh month; Jeremiah 28:1 dates this conflict to the fifth month.

Jeremiah 29:1-3. In the same year (594-593 B.C.E.) Jeremiah writes a letter to those persons who were already in exile in Babylon. They had been exiled when Nebuchadnezzar captured Jerusalem in March 597 B.C.E. According to 2 Kings 24:14-16, the exiles were mostly leaders, warriors, and skilled craftspersons, numbering either ten thousand (verse 14) or eight thousand (verse 16). The letter is to be carried to Nebuchadnezzar by Gemariah and Elasah, who may have been the brother of Ahikim who saved Jeremiah from death (see Jeremiah 26:24). These two men were going to Babylon at the request of King Hezekiah of Judah.

Jeremiah 29:4-9. The letter opens with a clear word that God is responsible for the people being in exile. They are in Babylon not because of weakness on God's part, but in fulfillment of God's will. Jeremiah's basic message to the exiles is to settle in the land. Contrary to the message of the false prophets (29:8-9), the people will be in exile a long time. (In fact, the exile does not end until King Cyrus of Persia, who defeated the Babylonians, issues a decree in 538 B.C.E. allowing the exiles to return home and rebuild the temple left in ruins by the Babylonians.) Jeremiah tells them to build houses, plant gardens, marry, have children and grandchildren. In other words, they are to multiply and thrive in the land. They are not to rebel but to seek peace, for if Babylon prospers, so will they.

Jeremiah 29:10-14. The letter continues with a promise from God that the people will return home. God plans prosperity and hope for the future for them. As stated in today's key verses (12-13), God will be found by those who seek the Lord with all their hearts.

Jeremiah 29:15-23. In the letter, the prophet announces that King Zedekiah and others now in Jerusalem will be struck down because they did not heed God's words. Two false prophets who are with the exiles in Babylon, Ahab and Zedekiah son of Maaseiah, will be turned over to Nebuchadrezzar (a variant spelling in verse 21; the Babylonian form of the name is Nabu-kudurru-usur) to be executed by fire for their false prophecies and worship of other gods.

Jeremiah 29:24-32. Shemaiah, a prophet in exile in Babylon, responded to Jeremiah's letter by sending his own letter to Zephaniah, the priest charged with the responsibility of overseeing the Temple in Jerusalem. Shemaiah is outraged that Jeremiah was not arrested for the letter he sent to Babylon. Shemaiah denounces the letter for it contained reference to a lengthy stay in that country. Zephaniah read Shemaiah's letter aloud so that Jeremiah could hear it. Jeremiah responded with a word from God condemning Shemaiah: Neither he nor his descendants would live to see the restoration of the exiles to Jerusalem.

INTERPRETING THE SCRIPTURE

Hearing What You Want to Hear

Judah was in turmoil. In 597 B.C.E., Babylonian forces had invaded Jerusalem. As spoils of their conquest, they had carted off sacred temple objects and deported thousands of Jewish leaders and skilled craftspersons. The prophet Hananiah begins to proclaim that God will soon come to the rescue, and the nightmare will be over. Hananiah was so certain that God would break King Nebuchadnezzar's hold on Judah that in 593 B.C.E. he announced that the exiles would be returned within two years (Jeremiah 28:11).

Suppose you had been among the people who gathered in the temple and heard Hananiah's upbeat message. His words would have comforted you and all the others who remained in Judah in the midst of despair and defeat. Perhaps you could have begun to think positively about the future. Two years really is not a long time. You wonder what God has in store for Nebuchadnezzar. Whatever it is, you revel in the thought that God will show that evil king and his country a thing or two.

Just as you are breathing a sigh of relief and feeling a surge of patriotism, along comes that naysayer Jeremiah. He insists that Hananiah has it all wrong, that his words are false. Jeremiah reminds you that the prophets truly sent from God brought words of war, famine, and other harsh realities. You would like to throttle Jeremiah, but Hananiah steps up and breaks that ridiculous wooden ox yoke Jeremiah is wearing. Jeremiah seems so stunned that he just walks away. You don't want to hear any more of his message. In fact, you don't really believe that God is so angry with Judah that this current conflict with Babylon is anything more than a temporary state. Hananiah's words seem so positive, so hopeful. You want Jeremiah to lower the volume and sit down.

Resisting the Will of God

Hananiah's words sounded so much better than Jeremiah's. The problem was, however, that Hananiah lived in a fantasy world. His "feel good" message was not the word of God; it was false prophecy. On the other hand, Jeremiah's message, though painful to hear, was true. Jeremiah followed up his proclamation with a letter to the exiles in Babylon (Jeremiah 29:1-32). He told them to plan to settle in and do their best to help Babylon prosper. According to Jeremiah, the captives would be in Babylon for decades. This notion that the exiles would remain in the land of their captors long enough to have grandchildren enraged another false prophet, Shemaiah. He was so angry that he wrote to the temple overseer, Zephaniah, faulting him for his failure to punish Jeremiah. The possibility that Judeans would be in Babylon for several generations was too unbelievable to contemplate.

What was going on here? Surely anyone would be anxious to see the yoke of the oppressor Babylon removed. He could not announce an imminent end to exile, however, because he perceived Nebuchadnezzar's rule over Judah to be the will of God. This foreign king assuredly was no worshiper of God. He was, however, the instrument God was using to punish God's own people. To fight against Nebuchadnezzar, amounted to resisting the will of God.

Recognizing False Promises

Jeremiah recognized false prophecy and its consequences. He had tried to persuade King Zedekiah that his advisors were false prophets (see Jeremiah 27:12-15). Jeremiah also tried to convince the temple leaders that the prophets were speaking falsely (see Jeremiah 27:16-22). No one, however, wanted to listen to him. His message, though true, was just too painful to hear. Surely there was some mistake. This prophet, who was in a minority of one, must be wrong. According to the false prophets, God's will would be fulfilled in the near future. The yoke of Babylon would be thrown off. In retrospect, we can recognize that Hananiah's promises of coming peace were false.

We can easily discern false prophecy from a historical perspective because we can determine which words were true and which were false. But what happens when we are bombarded in the present by false prophecy, when we do not have the benefit of knowing how things turned out? Like Hananiah, self-proclaimed prophets are still uttering words that many people want to hear. Some preachers promise healing and blame the victim for lack of faith if recovery is not immediate or complete. Others promise an abundance of material goods to the faithful, leaving the poor (whom Jesus loved and served) to wonder what they had done to deserve their misfortune. Some false prophets arrogantly announce that they alone have the true word from God and that people must follow them if they expect to be saved. Another brand of false prophets insists that their political beliefs or the candidates they support truly represent God. Certain false prophets even try to predict the Second Coming of Christ—a date that Jesus himself did not know. Some of these extremists gather their adherents together in isolated compounds that are armed and prepared for the end of the world.

Discerning the Word of God

By whatever name we moderns call them, false prophets do exist and have a following of believers. However, just as Jeremiah knew that Hananiah's words were false, many Christians perceive that prophets such as those described above did not come from God. We have to ask: How then can we discern the word of God? How can we tell the difference between a true and a false prophet? Our problem in discerning the difference between a true and a false prophet is that the false prophet's words often are rooted in partial truth. Hananiah, for example, knew that God dwelled in the temple that had been pillaged by the Babylonians. Surely God would want the stolen equipment returned to the temple as soon as possible. Similarly, Hananiah knew that the Babylonians were enemies of God's people. How could people like that be God's chosen instruments? And why would God want to defeat God's own people? The victory by the Babylonians, according to Hananiah, would only be temporary. In a short time, God would liberate the Judeans. Hananiah's words seemed so reasonable. They seemed to be in keeping with what the people knew and expected of God. Yet, Hananiah was completely wrong. He had totally missed God's word. On the other hand, Jeremiah's words seemed too incredible to believe. He, however, was the one who spoke for God. In retrospect, the people knew that he was God's spokesperson because his words came true. Events confirmed his prophecies.

In trying to assess the truth of a speaker's words, Christians have the benefit of two complete testaments of written Scriptures. We can test the words of modern spokespersons for God against the Bible. Sometimes we can easily tell that a person was not sent by God because of that individual's hateful or destructive actions. For example, those who assassinate abortion doctors hardly can claim to believe in the sanctity of life. Their actions contradict both their testimony and the word of God. The skinhead who torments persons because of their race or ethnic origin certainly does not speak for the God who created all humanity in the divine image. Some of these false spokespersons may know better but, for whatever reason, choose to use the Scriptures for their own ends.

Followers of false prophets, however, are taken in by words and promises that offer exactly what they want to hear. They may accept violent means to achieve their ends, though Jesus himself acted peaceably. Jesus did not use the word of God to buttress his own position, as some false prophets do. Instead, he allowed the word of God to speak the truth. Jesus acted on these words, even though they cost him his life. He demonstrated to us the importance of allowing God's will to be done through us, rather than determining what we want God's will to be and then finding ways to support our claim.

Jeremiah, like Jesus, put God's word ahead of his own desires and physical safety. He confronted not only Hananiah but other false prophets and the people who followed them as well. We too are called to listen carefully to the words of persons who claim to speak for God. We can acknowledge that there are honest differences in interpreting the word of God. Often, though, we can recognize that the false prophet seeks personal advantage in proclaiming a certain message. We are called, just as Jeremiah was, to confront that false prophet and bear witness to the truth. When people who claim to be speaking for God are actually resisting the will of God we must announce the truth, as difficult as it may be to tell and hear. In faith, we can trust God to take care of the outcome.

SHARING THE SCRIPTURE

PREPARING TO TEACH

Preparing Our Hearts

Think about a time when someone gave you bad news. How did you respond to such news? Did you believe it, or did you want to think there had been some mistake, that the news you heard was false? How did your unwillingness to accept such news affect you and your attitude toward God?

Preparing Our Minds

Our background scripture includes Jeremiah 28 and 29. If you have time, also read chapter 27 to gain a greater understanding that God willed for Judah to be under the yoke of Babylon. To rebel against Babylon or predict that its yoke would soon be broken, as Hananiah did, was to resist the will of God. You may also want to read about the first fall of Jerusalem and deportation to Babylon as found in 2 Kings 24:1-17.

As an option, you may want to check news articles dating to the spring of 1993 to learn more about David Koresh and the Branch Davidians or other persons that most Christians would agree were false prophets. You can find such information in your local library.

Preparing Our Learning Space

Have on hand:
- ✔ several Bibles for students
- ✔ newsprint and marker or chalkboard and chalk
- ✔ optional magazines or newspapers that you have located detailing the activities of a person or group that may be identified as false prophets

LEADING THE CLASS

(1) Introduction

Open the session by asking:
(1) **How does God speak to you?**
(2) **What guidelines do you use to determine whether the words you are hearing are from God or from some**

other source that only seems to be speaking for God?

After discussing these questions for a few moments, ask:

(3) **Can you think of any modern-day false prophets? (Perhaps Jim Jones of Jonestown or David Koresh of the Branch Davidians in Waco, Texas, will come to mind.)**

(4) **What kind of messages do they proclaim?**

(5) **Why do you think these false prophets gain adherents?**

(6) **How do you decide that their message is false, even though they support their claims with the Bible?**

Connect this discussion to today's scripture lesson by pointing out, as seen in the Focusing on the Main Question portion, that Jeremiah was forced to confront the false prophet Hananiah, whose claims were not the word of God. Highlight our main question for today's lesson: *How can we discern words from God, especially when we hear a more appealing message that raises false hope and offers false promises?*

(2) Hearing What You Want to Hear

Provide background for today's scripture lesson from Jeremiah 28:5-14 by reading or retelling Hananiah's message in Jeremiah 28:1-4. Be sure class members understand that although Jerusalem has not yet been destroyed, the Babylonians have invaded. These enemies have made off with plunder from the temple and deported numerous leaders and skilled craftspersons.

Then choose a volunteer to read aloud Jeremiah's response to Hananiah as found in Jeremiah 28:5-11.

Invite class members to consider this story from the perspective of the crowd at the temple.

(1) **Suppose you had been in the crowd at the temple. Would you have preferred to have heard Jeremiah's message or that of Hananiah? Why?**

(2) **In your "heart of hearts," which prophet would you decide had really been speaking on behalf of God? Why?**

If your class prefers a lecture, use ideas found under this heading in the Interpreting the Scripture portion.

(3) Resisting the Will of God

Continue examining the story from the perspective of different characters.

(1) **Now suppose you had been Hananiah. Do you honestly believe that the oppressive yoke of Nebuchadnezzar and the Babylonians will be broken in two years? If so, what beliefs do you hold about God and God's relationship with people that make you so certain of your position?**

(2) **Now assume that you are Jeremiah. What is your message to the people? What makes you believe that Hananiah is a false prophet? (Note: You may want to refer to Deuteronomy 18:20-22 in relation to Jeremiah 28:9.)**

Hananiah's message is one of coming peace. He cannot believe that God will allow the Babylonians to oppress the Judeans for long. Read Jeremiah 28:12-14 and ask:

(3) **How does God deal with false prophets?**

(4) **What consequences do Hananiah's false words have for the people?**

(4) Recognizing False Promises Today

If the class enjoys hands-on activities, provide a news article on someone whom mainstream Christians would identify as a false prophet (such as David Koresh of the Branch Davidians). Have groups or individuals read the article, then ask:

(1) **What is this person's message?**
(2) **How does it deviate from God's word?**
(3) **Why do you believe the message is not from God?**

? **(4) How did this person's message harm his followers?**

As an alternative, use this portion under the Interpreting the Scripture heading to create a lecture.

(5) Discerning the Word of God

Read today's key verses, Jeremiah 29:12-13, in unison if possible.

Briefly discuss ways in which we discern the word of God even when we hear soothing words that lead us away from God's will. Use the "Discerning the Word of God" portion under Interpreting the Scripture to help you.

Lead the following guided imagery exercise. Be sure to pause for at least ten seconds at each break.

R Sit quietly and comfortably in your chair. Close your eyes and relax. (pause)

Picture yourself alone in prayer in the sanctuary. Feel the wood of the pew or altar rail. Imagine Jesus sitting or kneeling beside you. Hear him say these words of comfort from Jeremiah 29: "Then you will call upon me and come and pray to me, and I will listen to you. You will seek me and find me when you seek me with all your heart." (pause)

Ask Jesus whatever you will, believing that he will hear and respond. (pause)

Now listen as he speaks to you. (pause)

As you are ready, open your eyes.

Conclude the guided imagery exercise by asking:

? **(1) If you felt a response to your prayer (or will later receive such a response), what guidelines will you use to know if it is truly from God or simply words that you want to hear?** (Note that this discussion should focus on guidelines for discerning the difference between true and false words, rather than the content or message of an individual's prayer.)

HELPING CLASS MEMBERS ACT

Challenge class members to examine their own lives. When have they heard words of warning that they chose to ignore? (These may be words about their spiritual direction or health or safety or relationships. For example, someone may have warned them about smoking, but rather than heed the warnings, they chose to cite cases of Aunt Minnie and an elderly neighbor who both smoked and lived well into their nineties.) How did they respond to these words? Ask adults to think about how they knew whether or not these words were in keeping with God's will for their lives.

Ask the group to think about how false prophets may be working within the church today. (Recall that Hananiah was a prophet within the religious establishment.) Tell them to identify messages that seem to be out of step with God's will. Challenge them to take at least one action to confront this false prophet and lovingly point out why the message he or she proclaims is not of God. In doing so, individual class members must be ready to listen to the person they have identified as a false prophet because that person may, like Jeremiah, be the one who truly speaks for God.

PLANNING FOR NEXT SUNDAY

Invite the class to read next week's background scripture from Ezekiel 2:1–3:21, paying particular attention to 2:3-7 and 3:4-11. This lesson will focus on God's commission of the prophet Ezekiel to proclaim God's message to the people in exile, even if they rebelliously refuse to hear him.

LISTENING AND OBEYING

PREVIEWING THE LESSON

Lesson Scripture: Ezekiel 2:3-7; 3:4-11
Background Scripture: Ezekiel 2:1–3:21
Key Verse: Ezekiel 2:7

Focus of the Lesson:
the commissioning of Ezekiel to proclaim God's message fearlessly to the Israelites in exile, even if they rebelliously refuse to hear him

Main Question of the Lesson:
What is required of one who is commissioned to proclaim God's message to persons who refuse to listen and obey God's commands?

This lesson will enable adult learners to:
(1) study God's commission to Ezekiel.
(2) think about rebellion against God.
(3) respond by examining their own lives for areas of rebellion.

Today's lesson may be outlined as follows:
(1) Introduction
(2) Commissioned by God
(3) Living Rebelliously
(4) Speaking to Rebels
(5) Listening and Obeying in Our Day

FOCUSING ON THE MAIN QUESTION

Like a two-year-old who stamps his foot and yells "no" in response to a simple request, the Judeans living as exiles in Babylon still rebelled against God. Despite the apparent hopelessness of their situation, they would not change. They refused to listen and obey God, preferring to continue in the sinful ways that caused their punishment in the first place. An objective assessment of the situation would cer-tainly indicate that it was too late for prophecy to have any effect.

All was not lost, however. Just as parents do not give up on their two-year-olds, neither did God give up on the exiles. Instead, God raised up a prophet from within their ranks. God chose the priest Ezekiel, about whom we know very little, to undertake this difficult task. God prepared the prophet for discouragement by reminding him that since the people had not heeded God they would likely not listen to Ezekiel. Furthermore, his message, would not win him any popularity. Nonetheless, Ezekiel was to persevere and continue to speak the word of God, no matter what kind of reception he received.

We can envision ourselves as both the exiles and the prophet in today's scripture lesson. Sometimes we are like the rebellious exiles. We choose to clap our hands over our ears like the two-year-old who assumes that she will not have to obey if she cannot hear her parents. Or we may know what God expects of us, but we prefer to do things our own way. At other times, we are like the long-suffering prophet who tries to speak God's truth to others. Their lack of appreciation for what we are trying to do is disheartening. We decide that it is easier to give up than to forge ahead. But God calls us to be faithful to the task. So, in the face of what seems to be an exercise in futility, we continue to act on God's behalf. As we study Ezekiel 2:1–3:21 we are challenged by this question: *What is required of one who is commissioned to proclaim God's message to persons who refuse to listen and obey God's commands?*

READING THE SCRIPTURE

NRSV
Ezekiel 2:3-7

3He said to me, Mortal, I am sending you to the people of Israel, to a nation of rebels who have rebelled against me; they and their ancestors have transgressed against me to this very day. 4The descendants are impudent and stubborn. I am sending you to them, and you shall say to them, "Thus says the Lord GOD." 5Whether they hear or refuse to hear (for they are a rebellious house), they shall know that there has been a prophet among them. 6And you, O mortal, do not be afraid of them, and do not be afraid of their words, though briers and thorns surround you and you live among scorpions; do not be afraid of their words, and do not be dismayed at their looks, for they are a rebellious house. 7You shall speak my words to them, whether they hear or refuse to hear; for they are a rebellious house.

Key Verse

NRSV
Ezekiel 3:4-11

4 He said to me: Mortal, go to the house of Israel and speak my very words to them. 5For you are not sent to a people of obscure speech and difficult language, but

NIV
Ezekiel 2:3-7

3He said: "Son of man, I am sending you to the Israelites, to a rebellious nation that has rebelled against me; they and their fathers have been in revolt against me to this very day. 4The people to whom I am sending you are obstinate and stubborn. Say to them, 'This is what the Sovereign LORD says.' 5And whether they listen or fail to listen—for they are a rebellious house—they will know that a prophet has been among them. 6And you, son of man, do not be afraid of them or their words. Do not be afraid, though briers and thorns are all around you and you live among scorpions. Do not be afraid of what they say or terrified by them, though they are a rebellious house. 7You must speak my words to them, whether they listen or fail to listen, for they are rebellious.

Key Verse

NIV
Ezekiel 3:4-11

4He then said to me: "Son of man, go now to the house of Israel and speak my words to them. 5You are not being sent to a people of obscure speech and difficult language, but to the house of Israel— 6not to to the house of Israel— ⁶not to many peoples of obscure speech and difficult language, whose words you cannot understand. Surely, if I sent you to them, they would listen to you. ⁷But the house of Israel will not listen to you, for they are not willing to listen to me; because all the house of Israel have a hard forehead and a stubborn heart. ⁸See, I have made your face hard against their faces, and your forehead hard against their foreheads. ⁹Like the hardest stone, harder than flint, I have made your forehead; do not fear them or be dismayed at their looks, for they are a rebellious house. ¹⁰He said to me: Mortal, all my words that I shall speak to you receive in your heart and hear with your ears; ¹¹then go to the exiles, to your people, and speak to them. Say to them, "Thus says the Lord GOD"; whether they hear or refuse to hear.

many peoples of obscure speech and difficult language, whose words you cannot understand. Surely if I had sent you to them, they would have listened to you. ⁷But the house of Israel is not willing to listen to you because they are not willing to listen to me, for the whole house of Israel is hardened and obstinate. ⁸But I will make you as unyielding and hardened as they are. ⁹I will make your forehead like the hardest stone, harder than flint. Do not be afraid of them or terrified by them, though they are a rebellious house."

¹⁰And he said to me, "Son of man, listen carefully and take to heart all the words I speak to you. ¹¹Go now to your countrymen in exile and speak to them. Say to them, 'This is what the Sovereign LORD says,' whether they listen or fail to listen."

UNDERSTANDING THE SCRIPTURE

Ezekiel 2:1-2. Ezekiel, a priest exiled to Babylon in 597 B.C.E. when Jerusalem was invaded, is called by God to be a prophet in June/July 593 B.C.E. (1:2) according to a vision beginning in Ezekiel 1:1. What follows in chapters 2:1–3:15 is an account of the prophet's call and commissioning by God. The vision of God enthroned caused the prophet to fall on his face (1:28). Hence, in 2:1, a voice (which we assume to be that of God) calls Ezekiel to stand up. Whereas Ezekiel's experience in chapter 1 was basically visual, in chapter 2 he hears the word. A spirit that is not further identified energizes the prophet to stand. This upright position likely means that he is not experiencing this vision of commission in a sleeplike state but is awake. The term "mortal," which occurs over ninety times in Ezekiel (NRSV), is from the Hebrew and means "son of man." Ezekiel is addressed by this generic term that emphasizes his humanity, rather than by name. Since Ezekiel is the only human in this scene,

the term "mortal" clearly identifies him.

Ezekiel 2:3-7. God commissions the prophet to go to the people of Israel. They are described as having been rebellious and sinful for generations. Note that since Ezekiel's call occurs after many people have been deported to Babylon, God is still trying to deal with this faithless people prior to the total devastation of Jerusalem in 587 B.C.E. In mercy, God will send a prophet, though God warns Ezekiel that the people may not listen to him. Moreover, they may not just ignore him either. These rebellious people are like plants (briers and thorns) and insects (scorpions). Despite their ability to inflict pain, Ezekiel is not to be afraid of them. He is to speak, regardless of how the people respond. The phrase "thus says the Lord" is often used with words of prophecy.

Ezekiel 2:8-10. God tells Ezekiel himself not to be rebellious. Thus, Ezekiel does as God commands. As in verse 8, images of the mouth are often associated with the commissioning of a prophet (see Jeremiah 1:9 and Isaiah 6:6-7). Ezekiel is called to eat a scroll on which God's words were written. The prophet is not to speak his own words, only those that have been given to him by God. These words are not good news but, as in the case of funeral rites, words of lamentation and woe. Such words describe how the people will respond to events.

Ezekiel 3:1-3. Ezekiel does not rebel but takes and eats the unrolled scroll given to him by an outstretched hand. These words of sorrow taste "as sweet as honey" to him.

Ezekiel 3:4-11. Ezekiel is being sent to the people of the house of Israel, meaning the people of Judah who are living in exile in Babylon, as the prophet is. The "obscure speech and difficult language" (3:5) may be a reference to Akkadian, the language of the Babylonians. The people in exile surely heard languages other than their own. The point, however, is that the people will not listen to Ezekiel, not because they cannot understand the language, but because they refuse to hear the word of God. God again tells Ezekiel that the people will not listen to him because they will not listen to God. However, God will make Ezekiel, whose name means "God strengthens," even more determined to prophesy. He is to persevere, regardless of the reception he receives.

Ezekiel 3:12-15. The vision concludes with the spirit (or wind) lifting the prophet up and carrying him to Tel-abib, a name taken from the Akkadian "til abubi," which means "mound of the deluge." He finds himself at the river Chebar with other exiles from Judah. While Ezekiel 1:1, 3 would lead us to believe that Ezekiel was in Babylon when God commissioned him, some scholars argue that these verses from chapter 3 indicate that the prophet was sent from Judah to those living in exile. In either case, the prophet was physically moved from one location to another. Other examples of the prophet being lifted up and carried by a spirit are found in Ezekiel 8:3; 11:1, 24; and 43:5. The prophet went "in bitterness in the heat of [his] spirit" (NRSV, NKJV). The Revised English Bible reads that he went "full of exaltation, the power of the Lord strong upon [him]." This ecstatic state of the REB seems to mesh better with the idea that the prophet was stunned for seven days by the experience.

Ezekiel 3:16-21. After seven days, God again speaks to the prophet, telling him that he is to act as a watchman for God's people. He is to hear the word of the Lord and speak it to the people. Ezekiel is only responsible for telling the people what God commands him. As long as he raises the warning, as a sentinel is called to do, Ezekiel will not be held accountable for whatever choices the people make. However, if the prophet does not warn them, God will hold him accountable. Four different situations are described in verses 18, 19, 20, and 21.

INTERPRETING THE SCRIPTURE

Commissioned by God

Ezekiel had been exiled to Babylon during the first deportation in 598/597 B.C.E. along with other religious leaders. Since he had no sacred place in Babylon in which to offer sacrifices, he may have experienced what we call an identity crisis. How could he be who he was—a priest of the most high God—when the ritually significant temple and tools of his profession were no longer available? Even it he had a place to make a sacrificial offering, would the God he had worshiped prior to this catastrophe be present in this foreign land? If God was in Babylon, was God at all concerned about Ezekiel?

Suddenly, after about four years in captivity and with no apparent warning, God appeared to Ezekiel in a magnificent vision. The prophet saw the throne of God, the chariot with a wheel in a wheel. Words could not describe what Ezekiel alone beheld as he stood with other exiles at the river Chebar. He could only say that it had "the appearance of the likeness of the glory of the LORD" (Ezekiel 1:28). The visual impact of this scene was so overwhelming that Ezekiel fell on his face.

We can only imagine what Ezekiel must have thought about himself, about God, and about the other residents from Judah. God calls his chosen one to stand up so that God can speak with him. In this conversation, God commissions this dislocated priest to be a prophet. He is commissioned to speak the word of God. Moreover, he is empowered and energized by a spirit, though in Ezekiel's day this presence would not have been understood in the way Christians perceive the Holy Spirit. Ezekiel also is given a very specific task: He is to go to the people who are in exile because of their disobedience to God. He is to speak on God's behalf regardless of whether the people listen to him or not. They probably will refuse because, according to Ezekiel, they are "rebellious," "impudent and stubborn."

Living Rebelliously

Some people never learn. They continue doing whatever they choose whether their pattern of behavior helps or harms them. Like teens who believe that parents are too strict, certain individuals assume that rules are for everyone but them. They are unable to recognize that rules are designed to protect them and others; rules provide boundaries within which they will be safe. Breaking rules usually creates problems, even if no one else witnessed the disobedience. No other driver may be on the dark narrow road when we lose control of our speeding car and crash. Acting in any way that is against deeply held moral or ethical values gnaws away at us internally, even if we are certain nobody knows what we have done.

Breaking rules or moral laws may also cause someone else pain. A spouse decides to have an affair, which results in the disintegration of two families. The drunk driver walks away from an accident without a scratch, but innocent passengers in another car are killed or permanently injured. The con artist bilks vulnerable widows out of their savings.

We can cite numerous examples of the kinds of rebellion in which people freely engage. Usually people know when they are doing wrong, but they assume that either they won't get caught or, if they do, there will be no consequences for their actions. Sometimes, of course, they do "get away with it." But sooner or later their disobedience catches up with them and in some way they suffer for their rebellion.

Such was the case with the exiles in Babylon. Despite all the warnings God had sent to the people about their behavior—particularly their idolatry—the people assumed that nothing would happen to them. Even after the invasion of Jerusalem and their deportation to Babylon, they had not turned aside from their sinful ways. Most humans would have given up on these stubborn people but God, though hurt and angered by their continuing rebellion, loved them enough to raise up a prophet from within their midst. God provided someone to speak to the rebels.

Speaking to Rebels

Proclaiming the word of God to rebellious, hard-hearted people would be no easy task. Even as God commissioned Ezekiel to undertake this important mission, God warned him that these people likely would not listen and obey any more than their ancestors had. Whether the people heeded his words or not, Ezekiel was to forge ahead on his mission. Even if the people hurt him, as briers and thorns cut the flesh or as a scorpion's sting poisons the body, he was to remain faithful to his task.

God's instructions to the prophet seem so difficult to follow. We do become discouraged when others ignore us or dismiss our ideas. We do become fearful when people begin to threaten us for the stand we are taking. As someone once replied to a critic of the status quo, "People shot Abraham Lincoln and crucified Jesus. What do you think they will do to you?" What, indeed? Most of us do not want to hear that we are wrong or off track, especially if we are satisfied with the way things are going. Why listen to words that challenge our comfortable situation? Why presuppose that any change is needed?

God knew that the people would not listen to Ezekiel because they had a long history of refusing to listen to God. Prior prophets were rebuffed, unappreciated, and in some cases physically abused. Yet, God would provide the stamina the prophet needed to withstand the taunts of the rebels. The words that Ezekiel was to speak to them were not his own words but words that God had given him. All the people had to do was listen and obey, but as we know, they did not.

Listening and Obeying in Our Day

We like to think that we have come a long way since the days of the exile. We pride ourselves on being such an advanced civilization. Unfortunately, for many persons in our society "advancement" means flowing toward certain areas, such as science and technology, while ebbing away from God. Science and technology offer us many good and worthwhile things, but they cannot

replace God, though they may become a god. Like the Judeans who were captivated by other gods, many of our contemporaries neither listen to nor obey God. To them, God is an antiquated, irrelevant concept that rational people simply set aside, like putting toys we have outgrown in a box. To say that we believe in God is, in some quarters, an unpopular assertion that causes certain people to wonder about us. Even among the Christian community, the idea of listening for God's voice and obeying God's commands seems suspect, often with good reason. Some persons who claim to speak for God are truly mentally ill. Others are leaders of a cult that ensnares vulnerable persons who cannot or will not think for themselves about who God is or what God expects them to do.

While we must be ready to discern the Spirit of God, we cannot assume God is no longer speaking. We need to listen attentively for the word of God as it is proclaimed to us. We need to identify modern prophets, such as Martin Luther King, Jr., and Desmond Tutu, who taught us about the sins of racism and apartheid, or Mother Teresa, who demonstrates God's love for the poor and sick, or Dietrich Bonhoeffer, who was initially charged and imprisoned for aiding Jews in their flight from Hitler's regime. Tutu, King, and Bonhoeffer were ordained clergy whose prophetic words and actions cost them their lives.

If God were to commission us, would we have the courage to undertake such prophetic ministry? Would we keep talking and acting even if it seemed that no one was hearing us or offering support for our message? Could we trust God to keep our enthusiasm high even when objective circumstances indicated that we had every right to feel discouraged?

Although we may be called to prophetic ministry, we more likely will be the people in the crowd. Perhaps we act like the rebellious Judeans who suffered the consequences of refusing to hear and respond to

God's word. Maybe we are busy, modern Christians whose rebellion against God can more aptly be described as benign neglect. God is shoved to a corner of our lives, rather than treasured in the core of our being. The kingdom of God is not our first priority, as Jesus taught that it must be. Listening to God speak through the Scriptures, sermons, hymns, meditation, friends, or other ways is just not impor-tant. When we do not listen, we cannot obey because we have no idea what is expected of us. Often, however, we make the same mistake as the Judeans did. We do not what God expects of us, but we decide to do things our way. Ultimately, our rebellion has life-changing conse-quences that can never be undone, only regretted.

SHARING THE SCRIPTURE

PREPARING TO TEACH

Preparing Our Hearts

As you begin to spiritually prepare yourself to lead this lesson, examine your own life in relationship to that of the exiles. If God were to speak to someone else about you, would you be described as "rebellious," or "stubborn," or "impu-dent" as the Judeans were? If so, what changes do you need to make in your life to be obedient unto God?

Think also of yourself in relation to the prophet Ezekiel. Do you feel that God has commissioned you to teach this class? If so, how does God support you in this effort even when you feel discouraged?

Preparing Our Minds

Read Ezekiel 2:1–3:21, as well as the information in this lesson. Try to imagine yourself in Ezekiel's position. What would your response be if, seemingly out of the blue, God commissioned you to undertake a thankless task that appeared doomed to failure from the start?

You may also want to read the account of the prophet's vision in Ezekiel 1.

Preparing Our Learning Space

If you choose to use the "faith in action" activity under "Listening and Obeying in Our Day," you may want to do some research on a topic in advance and/or bring appropriate references for classroom use.

Have on hand:
- ✔ several Bibles for students
- ✔ newsprint and marker or chalkboard and chalk
- ✔ optional paper and pencils
- ✔ optional Bible references, such as con-cordances

LEADING THE CLASS

(1) Introduction

If the class enjoys hands-on activities, introduce today's lesson by having them work with a partner or team to write a "help wanted" ad for a prophet. Provide paper and pencils. The ad is to include traits the prophet should possess, as well as an indication of the kind of rebellious, stubborn people whom the prophet is called to address. Invite several teams to share their ad. If possible, draw parallels between their description and the task for which the prophet Ezekiel was commis-sioned. Here is an example:

Help Wanted: Strong person who is will-ing to listen to God and not be swayed by public opinion needed to take unpopular prophetic message to people with a long history of rebellion. Prophet must be able to overcome discouragement, disappointment, and possible physical abuse. The right candidate should be willing to persevere, despite repeated setbacks and apparent failure of people to listen and obey.

If the class members enjoy a high level of trust with one another, you may want to introduce the lesson by having them talk, perhaps with a partner or team, about moments of discouragement in their own lives. Have them describe the situation and why it caused them to feel so discouraged. Rather than sharing the entire story with the whole class, ask persons to give words or phrases to describe the situation and their response to it. You may want to record their ideas on newsprint or a chalkboard. Examples include: hopeless; no way out; felt like I was talking to a wall; people caved in to pressure rather than fight for what they knew was right.

If you prefer to open the lesson another way, read or retell the Focusing on the Main Question portion.

Whatever method you choose, be sure to introduce today's main question: *What is required of one who is commissioned to proclaim God's message to persons who refuse to listen and obey God's commands?*

(2) Commissioned by God

Ask class members to discuss what it means to be "commissioned." Some may have firsthand experience with commissions in the armed forces or as a notary public.

Move to a discussion of Ezekiel's commissioning by selecting a volunteer to read aloud Ezekiel 2:3-7. Ask the following questions, using information from the Understanding the Scripture or Interpreting the Scripture portions to fill in gaps as needed:

(1) **How did God describe the people that the prophet was being commissioned to address?**

(2) **What role was Ezekiel to play in deal-**

ing with the exiles? (Remember that he, too, was an exile.)

(3) **How would you have felt had God commissioned you to do what Ezekiel was to do?**

Point out that most of us are not commissioned to undertake the awesome task that God expected of Ezekiel. However, we each have at least one task to do to make God's presence known here on earth. Ask class members to think about the tasks to which God has called them. Provide a few moments of silent meditation for this activity. If it seems appropriate, you may want to close this quiet time with a prayer, such as: "We give you thanks, O God, for the tasks to which we have been called. We ask you to empower us that we might be able to do our work more faithfully. Undergird us with the strength and courage we need to act and speak as your people. In Jesus' name we pray. Amen."

(3) Living Rebelliously

Brainstorm answers to the following questions. You may want to record answers on newsprint or a chalkboard.

(1) **What biblical examples can you give of people living rebelliously?**

(2) **Why would God define each of the behaviors you have listed as rebellious?**

(3) **Has the nature of rebellion against God changed over the years? If so, how? If not, why do you think the kinds of rebellion that we engage in have remained the same?**

(4) Speaking to Rebels

Choose someone to read aloud Ezekiel 3:4-11. Then ask:

(1) **What kind of reception did God believe Ezekiel would receive? On what do you base your answer?**

(2) **Since God seemed to be so pessimistic about the people's response, why do you think God chose to send**

? a prophet anyway? What does this decision tell you about the nature of God?

(3) How did God prepare Ezekiel for the task he was being commissioned to undertake?

(5) Listening and Obeying in Our Day

Move the discussion to the present by asking:

? (1) **If God were to commission a prophet today, how do you think God would describe the state of the Christian church in general? How would God describe the state of your denomination? How would God describe your local church?**

(2) **What kind of message would a modern prophet be called to proclaim in your community?**

(3) **What kind of response do you think the community in general would make?**

(4) **What kind of response do you think Christians would make?**

If the class is willing to put faith into action, ask them to identify a problem (such as hunger or homelessness) that modern prophets are called to address. Provide some Bible references (especially concordances) so that students can look up related passages. If time is short and the class is large, you may want to do some of this research yourself and develop a list of appropriate Bible passages prior to class. Talk with the class about how they can lis-

ten to the word of God and respond to the problem. If, for example, they focus on hunger, they might choose to set up a work day in a soup kitchen, write to elected officials concerning the need for food programs for poor persons, design a fund-raiser for a hunger project, or covenant to pray for those who are hungry.

HELPING CLASS MEMBERS ACT

Challenge class members to examine their own lives this week to identify areas of rebellion. Specifically, ask them to look for behaviors or attitudes they hold that they know are contrary to God's will, but that they refuse to turn away from. Suggest that they determine one step they can take this week to overcome this rebellious behavior.

Invite class members to think of one person they know (perhaps a family member) who refuses to listen to God. Challenge them to speak a word of witness to that individual this week. Remind them that such a task needs to be undertaken with great tact and humility.

Encourage members to speak out at least once this week on behalf of God, even if the issue they address is one that may be considered unpopular or controversial by their neighbors or business associates. To undertake such a task effectively, they may need to study related scripture texts.

PLANNING FOR NEXT SUNDAY

Announce that next week's lesson, entitled "Accepting Personal Responsibility," will examine selected verses from Ezekiel 18. Class members may want to review Exodus 20:5 and Deuteronomy 5:9 (both part of the Ten Commandments) and Exodus 34:6-7, all of which make reference to the sins of one generation being visited upon other generations. Ezekiel proclaims a different message: All persons are responsible for their own actions.

ACCEPTING PERSONAL RESPONSIBILITY

PREVIEWING THE LESSON

Lesson Scripture: Ezekiel 18:1-5, 7-13, 19-20
Background Scripture: Ezekiel 18
Key Verse: Ezekiel 18:20

Focus of the Lesson:
God's message through Ezekiel that each individual is personally responsible for his or her own actions

Main Question of the Lesson:
How can I accept responsibility for myself, rather than shift blame to someone else, or hold myself accountable for another person's actions?

This lesson will enable adult learners to:
(1) examine Ezekiel's case studies of the behaviors of a grandfather, father, and son.
(2) understand biblical teaching concerning individual responsibility.
(3) respond by considering their own level of personal accountability.

Today's lesson may be outlined as follows:
(1) Introduction
(2) A Lack of Accountability
(3) Case Studies 1 and 2: A Righteous Man and His Violent Son
(4) Case Study 3: The Righteousness of the Third Generation
(5) Assuming Responsibility for Ourselves

FOCUSING ON THE MAIN QUESTION

"It's not my fault. I didn't do it. So and so is to blame." Many people simply refuse to be held accountable for their actions. If we are passed over for a promotion, for example, we assume the boss does not like us rather than examining ourselves to see how we have fallen short, or why the other candidate may be better qualified. If we are caught speeding, we tell the officer about the car that zoomed past us and plead that we didn't know we were driving too fast. If we improperly install or use a product, we are ready to sue the manufacturer for defective or falsely advertised merchandise.

Not only do many persons refuse to take blame for their own actions or circumstances, but they teach their children how to shirk responsibility, too. If our child does poorly in school, we reassure the young genius that it must be the teacher's fault. If our teenager becomes involved in substance abuse, we blame that on a zealous drug dealer or the wrong kind of friends. If our college-age adolescents cannot hang on to two nickels, we continue to send more money rather than insist that they develop a budget and live within it.

Absolving ourselves of responsibility almost seems to be a national pastime. But we are not alone, and we are hardly the first ones to play this game. In the days of the prophet Ezekiel, people did not hold themselves accountable either. Instead of blaming an employer, manufacturer, or teacher for their plight, the exiles believed that they were suffering for the sins of other generations. Their understanding was not groundless, for Exodus 20:5; 34:6-7; and Deuteronomy 5:9 indicate that God will punish the guilty to the third and fourth generation.

Ezekiel, however, proclaimed a radically different message: "It is only the person who sins that shall die" (18:4). The one who is guilty will be held responsible. This teaching would have forced the exiles to confront the extent of their own accountability. Their ancestors surely had sinned. So, too, had they. Ezekiel's teaching prompts us to ask today's main question: *How can I accept responsibility for myself, rather than shift blame to someone else or hold myself accountable for another person's actions?*

READING THE SCRIPTURE

NRSV
Ezekiel 18:1-4

1 The word of the LORD came to me: 2What do you mean by repeating this proverb concerning the land of Israel, "The parents have eaten sour grapes, and the children's teeth are set on edge"? 3 As I live, says the Lord GOD, this proverb shall no more be used by you in Israel. 4Know that all lives are mine; the life of the parent as well as the life of the child is mine: it is only the person who sins that shall die.

NRSV
Ezekiel 18:5, 7-13

5 If a man is righteous and does what is lawful and right— . . . 7does not oppress anyone, but restores to the debtor his pledge, commits no robbery, gives his bread to the hungry and covers the naked with a garment, 8does not take advance or accrued interest, withholds his hand from iniquity, executes true justice between con-

NIV
Ezekiel 18:1-4

1 The word of the LORD came to me: 2"What do you people mean by quoting this proverb about the land of Israel:
" 'The fathers eat sour grapes,
    and the children's teeth are set on edge'?
3"As surely as I live, declares the Sovereign LORD, you will no longer quote this proverb in Israel. 4For every living soul belongs to me, the father as well as the son—both alike belong to me. The soul who sins is the one who will die.

NIV
Ezekiel 18:5, 7-13

5"Suppose there is a righteous man
    who does what is just and right.
. . . .
7 He does not oppress anyone,
    but returns what he took in pledge
    for a loan.
He does not commit robbery

tending parties, ⁹follows my statutes, and is careful to observe my ordinances, acting faithfully—such a one is righteous; he shall surely live, says the Lord GOD.

10 If he has a son who is violent, a shedder of blood, ¹¹who does any of these things (though his father does none of them), who eats upon the mountains, defiles his neighbor's wife, ¹²oppresses the poor and needy, commits robbery, does not restore the pledge, lifts up his eyes to the idols, commits abomination, ¹³takes advance or accrued interest; shall he then live? He shall not. He has done all these abominable things; he shall surely die; his blood shall be upon himself.

but gives his food to the hungry
    and provides clothing for the
    naked.
⁸He does not lend at usury
    or take excessive interest.
He withholds his hand from doing
    wrong and judges fairly between
    man and man.
⁹He follows my decrees
    and faithfully keeps my laws.
That man is righteous;
    he will surely live,
        declares the Sovereign LORD.
¹⁰"Suppose he has a violent son, who sheds blood or does any of these other things ¹¹(though the father has done none of them):

"He eats at the mountain shrines.
He defiles his neighbor's wife.
¹²He oppresses the poor and needy.
He commits robbery.
He does not return what he took in
    pledge.
He looks to the idols.
He does detestable things.
¹³He lends at usury and takes excessive
    interest.

Will such a man live? He will not! Because he has done all these detestable things, he will surely be put to death and his blood will be on his own head.

NRSV
Ezekiel 18:19-20

19 Yet you say, "Why should not the son suffer for the iniquity of the father?" When the son has done what is lawful and right, and has been careful to observe all my statutes, he shall surely live. ²⁰The person who sins shall die. A child shall not suffer for the iniquity of a parent, nor a parent suffer for the iniquity of a child; the righteousness of the righteous shall be his own, and the wickedness of the wicked shall be his own.

NIV
Ezekiel 18:19-20

¹⁹"Yet you ask, 'Why does the son not share the guilt of his father?' Since the son has done what is just and right and has been careful to keep all my decrees, he will surely live. ²⁰The soul who sins is the one who will die. The son will not share the guilt of the father, nor will the father share the guilt of the son. The righteousness of the righteous man will be credited to him, and the wickedness of the wicked will be charged against him.

Key
Verse

Key
Verse

UNDERSTANDING THE SCRIPTURE

Ezekiel 18:1-4. As expressed in Exodus 20:5 and Deuteronomy 5:9 (both from the Ten Commandments), Exodus 34:6-7, and a popular proverb quoted in Ezekiel 18:2, children suffered for the sins of their parents. The prophet refutes this idea, insisting instead that each individual is personally accountable for his or her faithfulness to God and will be judged accordingly. Jeremiah also quotes this proverb and comes to the same conclusion in Jeremiah 31:29-30. All lives are in God's hands; one person will not suffer as a result of the actions of another. Each person is morally accountable for his or her own actions.

Ezekiel 18:5-9. In these verses, Ezekiel draws a picture of a righteous person, listing virtues from both a positive and a negative perspective. Actions related to religious observance and moral and ethical behaviors are lifted up. Some points on the list are clearly related to the Ten Commandments. The righteous person is faithful unto God, refusing to "eat upon the mountains," that is, refusing to eat meat sacrificed to idols. This person does not commit adultery or violate the laws of ritual purity associated with sexual intercourse. The righteous one is ethical, neither oppressing anyone nor stealing, acting charitably toward the poor, and handling money according to the economics of God, that is, without taking interest. Righteous persons act justly and walk in God's ways. Therefore, they live. This portrait of the righteous one is the first of three case studies.

Ezekiel 18:10-13. The second case study depicts the son of the righteous man described in 18:5-9. The son, however, is the exact opposite of the father. The father's righteous example apparently was rejected by the son, who chose to live according to his own ways. God says that the son shall die. His blood is "upon himself." In other words, he is accountable for his own behavior and will reap the consequences of his choices.

Ezekiel 18:14-18. A third portrait is included in this series of case studies. This one describes the son of the second man and grandson of the first. This man has seen the sins of his father but has chosen not to walk in his footsteps. Instead, he lives righteously. As verse 17 states, "he shall not die for his father's iniquity." The father is held accountable for his sins and will die, but the judgment against him will not cast a shadow of judgment on his righteous son.

Ezekiel 18:19-20. The prophet raises a question that the people have been asking: "Why should not the son suffer for the iniquity of the father?" The suffering of one generation for the sins of a former generation surely must have been a concern of the exiles. Were they in Babylon because their ancestors had sinned against God? Unquestionably, their ancestors had sinned. However, in the final case study it became clear that the son did not suffer for the sins of his wicked father. Similarly, the father/grandfather—the first person in the case studies—did not suffer because of the wickedness of his son. God held each one accountable. Similarly, the people of Judah were not in Babylon because of the sins committed by others. They were in exile because of their own sins.

Ezekiel 18:21-24. Repentance, or "turning" away from sin, does bring about life. Those who turn lead an upright life; their sins are blotted out. God's hope and intention is that the wicked should turn and receive new life. God takes no pleasure in unholy behavior. The opposite scenario is also possible: The person who has lived righteously can choose to "commit iniquity." If this should happen, that person will be judged accordingly and die.

Ezekiel 18:25-29. The saying "The way of the Lord is unfair" (NRSV) or "The way of the Lord is not just" (NIV) is found in verses 25, 29 and 33:17. This saying is false, however. God is just and fair because God treats the people on the basis of their own behavior. The people, not God, are unfair.

Ezekiel 18:30-32. In the closing verses of this chapter, the prophet announces God's judgment. He also calls the people to "repent and turn from all [their] transgressions." If the people elect not to repent, they will be judged and found wanting. If, however, they choose to turn, God will give them "a new heart and a new spirit." In other words, those who choose to turn to God will experience new life, a new relationship with God.

INTERPRETING THE SCRIPTURE

A Lack of Accountability

Life certainly seems easier when we can blame others for our sins, failures, and difficult circumstances. We can step aside from our own responsibility and whine about the actions or attitudes of another. Like a child, we insist that we did not trip over the shoelaces we forgot to tie; someone else stuck his foot in our path and caused us to fall.

Similarly, the exiles in Babylon avoided personal responsibility for their captivity by blaming prior generations. A proverb— "The parents have eaten sour grapes, and the children's teeth are set on edge" (Ezekiel 18:2)—deftly explains their predicament. They are the children who are suffering the ill effects of their ancestors' sinfulness. The idea of one generation suffering the consequences of the action of another is found within the Mosaic Covenant as recorded in Exodus 20:5 and Deuteronomy 5:9. Through the prophet Ezekiel, God tells the people that this proverb is no longer to be used. Instead of some kind of collective or generational guilt, wherein all suffer for the sins of others, God is now holding each person responsible. Only the guilty party will be accountable. Therefore, when people sin they can expect to be punished. Furthermore, those who suffer punishment cannot explain away their penalty as a burden to be borne as a result of someone else's action; they must accept personal responsibility.

Such a message must have created shock waves among the exiles. It is one thing to assuage suffering with the notion that you did not really cause the problem, that you are a victim of someone else's behavior. It is quite another thing, though, to confront the fact that you are suffering for your own sins, that your own unfaithfulness has put you in this devastating position.

Case Studies 1 and 2: A Righteous Man and His Violent Son

In Ezekiel 18:5-9, the prophet describes a righteous man. This person is faithful to God, following the moral and ethical laws of the covenant. He treats others with justice and generosity. This man practices biblical economics, which require that no interest be paid on a loan to the poor (see Exodus 22:25; Leviticus 25:36-37). He is also able to bring about reconciliation to conflict. In short, the prophet describes one who epitomizes righteousness.

Since this man was so clearly righteous, we would expect his son to follow in his footsteps. The father surely would have taught the boy his religious beliefs, not just by mouthing the words but by living a model life. The father likely would have surrounded his family with other persons who were good influences. One would certainly expect this child to grow up to be a pillar of the community.

Unfortunately, he did not. For whatever reason, the boy sets aside all he has been taught. Ezekiel 18:10-13 describes him as a violent murderer who consistently breaks the law of the covenant by living immorally and unethically. In verse 18, he is portrayed as an extortionist who even robbed his own brother. He practices idolatry and other abominations before God. According to the prophet, God holds the son accountable, and he will be required to pay for his own sins.

The text is silent about the righteous father's reaction to his son's behavior. We can fairly assume that the father was deeply pained by the son's rejection of all he had been taught and his embracing of such sinful, immoral actions. However, God does not hold the father accountable for his son's behavior. This rebel has chosen his own course and he must take responsibility for himself. God likely understands the father's predicament well because God has so clearly instructed the people how to live but time and time again they have gone their own way. God loves the people, even in exile, but God also holds them accountable.

Case Study 3: The Righteousness of the Third Generation

The prophet's lesson does not end with the second generation, however. He goes on to describe the son of the murderer. This young man has had a terrible role model for a father. We do not know whether he had a relationship with his grandfather that could explain where he got his understanding of righteousness. How he came to find God's way is not really important to Ezekiel, though. The prophet's emphasis is on the young man's free choice. He has the power to decide for himself how he will act. Ezekiel notes that he considers what his father has done "and does not do likewise" (18:14).

After describing the three generations, Ezekiel makes his point in 18:19-20: The son will not suffer for the sins of his father. Why should he? He has been faithful to

God's covenant and has lived a righteous life. Therefore, neither he nor his grandfather (the father of the murderer) will be held accountable for the sins of the second generation. In Ezekiel's words, "the righteousness of the righteous shall be his own, and the wickedness of the wicked shall be his own" (18:20).

Ezekiel's words may be comforting to us, especially if we have been trying to carry the burden of a family member who has an unlimited reservoir of excuses for ungodly behavior. We need to pray for that person and be supportive, of course, but we can let go of any guilt we may have about not being able to "fix" that person's problems. Likewise, Ezekiel's case studies help us to recognize that if we have been blaming others for our situation, we must begin to take responsibility for ourselves.

Assuming Responsibility for Ourselves

We can begin to take responsibility by recognizing who owns a particular problem. If we are holding ourselves accountable for actions over which we have no control (such as those of a grown child), we need to let go of that problem. On the other hand, if we have tried to rationalize our behavior, we need to stop blaming others and assume responsibility for our own circumstances. We in fact may be in a difficult position, but instead of blaming everyone around us, we need to pray that God will enable us to turn this situation around so that good will come out of it.

Ezekiel's example regarding parents and their children is particularly relevant in our own day. Like the father in the prophet's first case study, many parents adhere to high moral, ethical, and religious standards. They teach their offspring, by word and deed, what it means to be a child of God and disciple of Jesus. Despite their best efforts, the child rebels against the values of the parents. Although Ezekiel does not report on the father's feelings about his son's behavior, any parents who have seen a child veer so far off the narrow path are heartbroken in many ways. The parents feel anguish for the grown child whose life is in such a terrible state. They also engage in self-recrimination, wondering how they failed and what they could have done differently. People who are aware of the situation may also blame the parents for the way in which this child has turned out. So-called child-rearing experts have numerous theories to explain how parenting errors caused the child to develop into such a problem-riddled adult.

Ezekiel's reply to such theories and criticism would be "hogwash." God has created and endowed each human being with free will. We are able to make our own choices. That freedom is a God-given gift. However, with freedom comes the obligation to accept responsibility for our actions. No one is exempt. The father in the first generation of Ezekiel's case studies is not blamed for his son's immoral, unethical, antisocial behavior. Nor is the son of the evil man punished for his father's sinful ways. While we may argue that finding the right path in life is more difficult if one lacks appropriate teaching and role models, the third generation was able to choose the way of God in spite of his father's behavior. He is not punished for his father's sins but is judged by God on the basis of his own choices.

The prophet's teaching offers an effective antidote both to those who feel they are to blame for the failure of others and to those who refuse to accept responsibility for their own behavior. God deals with each one of us individually, but God is gracious and compassionate, for we have all fallen short. If we feel that we have caused someone else to stumble, we can ask forgiveness from God and that person, but then we must forgive ourselves. Similarly, if we have found it convenient to shift blame from ourselves to others, we must begin to be accountable. Even if someone else's behavior or attitude has caused us to be in difficult circumstances, we need to figure out how we, with God's help, can move beyond this situation.

SHARING THE SCRIPTURE

PREPARING TO TEACH

Preparing Our Hearts

As you spiritually prepare yourself to lead this week's lesson, ask God to help you be more accountable for your own actions and attitudes. Do you blame others for whatever goes wrong in your life, for whatever sins and errors you commit? Or do you take responsibility for yourself? If you find that you do not accept responsibility, ask God to enable you to change your ways.

Also ask God to show you situations in which you are assuming responsibility for someone else. Pray that God will give you wisdom to let go and allow this person to be accountable for himself or herself.

Preparing Our Minds

Read Ezekiel 18 and this lesson. You may also want to review Exodus 20:5; 34:6-7; and Deuteronomy 5:9, which teach that several generations are punished for sin.

Preparing Our Learning Space

If you plan to use the ranking activity for your introduction, prepare the statements ahead of time by writing them on newsprint, a chalkboard, or paper that can be photocopied.

If you plan to use the meditation time suggested under "Assuming Responsibility for Ourselves," write the questions on newsprint or a chalkboard prior to class.

Have on hand:
- ✔ several Bibles for students
- ✔ newsprint and marker or chalkboard and chalk
- ✔ paper and pencils

LEADING THE CLASS

(1) Introduction

Write the following information on newsprint, a chalkboard, or paper that can be photocopied:

Directions: Read each of the following statements and either circle the number of your choice or write it on paper. Number 1 shows least agreement; number 5 shows greatest agreement with the statement.

(1) If I make a mistake I am quick to admit it.　　　　1　　2　　3　　4　　5
(2) My problems that are often caused by other persons.　1　　2　　3　　4　　5
(3) I sometimes blame myself for my adult son or daughter's shortcomings.　　　　1　　2　　3　　4　　5
(4) I feel as if I have very little control over my life.　　1　　2　　3　　4　　5
(5) I have to help others make decisions.　　　　1　　2　　3　　4　　5

You may want class members to discuss their answers with a partner or team for a few moments. If so, ask them to explain why they marked their answers the way they did.

Conclude the introduction by noting that today's lesson concerns God's teaching through the prophet Ezekiel that we are all individually accountable unto God. We need not accept responsibility for another person's failure, nor are we to blame others for our own sins and shortcomings.

Make reference to today's main question: *How can I accept responsibility for myself, rather than shift blame to someone else or hold myself accountable for another person's actions?*

(2) A Lack of Accountability

Choose a volunteer to read aloud Ezekiel 18:1-4.

Look especially at the proverb in verse 2. Invite class members to explain what this proverb means. Or ask them to write a modern proverb that expresses the same idea, namely, that the children suffer ill effects from their parents' actions.

You may want to discuss ways in which this notion of one generation suffering for the sins of another is still present today. Some examples may include: children being born with AIDS or a substance abuse problem; parents who have been abused as children abusing their own offspring.

Then ask the class to discuss these questions as a whole or in teams:
(1) **What new concept is Ezekiel teaching the people?**
(2) **How do you think the concept of individual accountability affected the exiles?**
(3) **Does this teaching regarding individual accountability change the way you view your own life or circumstances? If so, how?**

(3) Case Studies 1 and 2: A Righteous Man and His Violent Son

Point out that Ezekiel does not talk in generalities about accountability but uses cases studies of a hypothetical man, his son, and grandson. Ask someone to read aloud Ezekiel 18:5-9. Then ask:
(1) **How would you describe this man in your own words?**
(2) **Given this information, what would you expect his child to be like?**

Now read Ezekiel 18:10-13. Ask:
(1) **How would you describe the son?**
(2) **How is he different than what you may have expected, given what you know about the father?**
(3) **How would you have described the father if all you knew about him was what you knew about the son?**

(4) Case Study 3: The Righteousness of the Third Generation

Read or retell the description of the third generation, found in Ezekiel 18:14-

18, which is not part of the scripture lesson. Ask:

[?] **(1) Is this young man what you would expect, given that you know his father was a violent man who murdered and extorted money from others?**

Now read aloud verses 19-20, noting that verse 20 is our key verse for today's lesson. Ask the class to summarize Ezekiel's teaching in one sentence.

(5) Assuming Responsibility for Ourselves

If the group enjoys hands-on activities, divide them into teams. Challenge each team to create a modern scenario or case study that reflects Ezekiel's teaching. Refer to the Focusing on the Main Question or Interpreting the Scripture portions if you want some suggestions for situations that modern families face. At a designated time, ask each team to report what they have developed, or to demonstrate their story by means of role-play.

Provide some time near the end of the session for individuals to reflect silently on the questions below. Prior to class, if possible, write them on newsprint or a chalkboard. If some students prefer to write their answers, distribute paper and pencils. Assure the group that their answers will not be discussed.

- What current problem or situation in my life am I blaming on someone else?
- What do you expect me to do, O God, to take responsibility for this problem?
- How am I taking responsibility for someone else's shortcomings?
- What damage am I doing to that person by acting as a crutch for him or her?
- How can I change my behavior, O God, to be supportive of another but not accept responsibility for that person's defeats?

You may want to conclude this time of meditation and/or spiritual journaling with a prayer, such as:

Gracious God, in your love and mercy [R] **you have given each of us the freedom to choose to walk the narrow path of righteousness or the broad path of sin. Help us to recognize that with this gift of freedom comes accountability. Forgive us for the times that we have blamed others for our own shortcomings. As we face difficult circumstances now, show us how to accept responsibility. Forgive us also, Lord, for shouldering responsibility that properly belongs to someone else. Enable us to let go and allow that person to begin to be accountable for his or her own actions. We pray for your guidance, O God, in the name of Jesus. Amen.**

HELPING CLASS MEMBERS ACT

This week ask class members to sit with a pad and a timer set for ten minutes. Have them list as many situations as possible in which they have blamed others for their own sins, failures, and inadequacies. Tell them to select one of these situations and analyze their own responsibility for the shortcoming. Have them follow up this exercise by taking whatever steps are necessary to begin to assume responsibility for their own actions.

Suggest that students who are members of official bodies in the church listen carefully at the next meeting for instances in which someone tries to blame another committee, the pastor, or a larger body for problems within the church. Encourage class members to take action when such situations arise so as to help the appropriate group take responsibility for its action.

PLANNING FOR NEXT SUNDAY

Next Sunday we will begin a new unit entitled, "The Fall of Jerusalem." Ask class members to study Ezekiel 4:1-13, in which Ezekiel prophesies against Jerusalem. To gain a fuller understanding of the background, suggest that students read Ezekiel 3:22–5:17. Ask them to begin thinking about how Jerusalem came to terms with its own impending defeat.

FACING DEFEAT

PREVIEWING THE LESSON

Lesson Scripture: Ezekiel 4:1-13
Background Scripture: Ezekiel 3:22–5:17
Key Verse: Ezekiel 4:7

Focus of the Lesson:
the punishment and coming defeat of Jerusalem as symbolized by the actions of Ezekiel

Main Questions of the Lesson:
How did Ezekiel prepare the people for defeat?
How do we acknowledge and face defeat in our own lives?

This lesson will enable adult learners to:
(1) study Ezekiel's actions symbolizing the imminent defeat of Jerusalem.
(2) examine situations that may lead to defeat in their own lives.
(3) respond by aiding those who have been defeated.

Today's lesson may be outlined as follows:
(1) Introduction
(2) Defeat Is Coming
(3) A Glimpse of Wartime Conditions
(4) Ezekiel Protests
(5) Facing Defeat in Our Own Lives

FOCUSING ON THE MAIN QUESTION

Endings are often difficult to face. Our baby, now a young adult, packs to move across the country and we know that our relationship can never again be the same as when he lived at home. During the final months before retirement, we look forward to a new phase in our lives but also mourn the loss of the familiar routine and personalities that are so much a part of our lives. A loved one is terminally ill and we struggle to make the remaining days as meaningful as possible, wondering how we will cope with this loss.

Sometimes, of course, endings are a natural part of the rhythm of life. We expect them, even if they are not always welcome. In other situations, though, an ending is not simply a transition to another phase of life but a gut-wrenching defeat. We sadly hang a "going out of business" sign on the window of a shop we tried so hard to make profitable. Or we decide to divorce a spouse we once deeply loved, feeling overwhelmed by feelings of failure as a mate. Or we are forced to sell a home that we cannot afford to keep. In any of these circumstances, we are sobered by the realization that defeat is at hand.

Although Judah was on the brink of defeat, the people still did not recognize that their beloved city of Jerusalem would soon be overrun by invaders from Babylon. They could not yet believe that God would punish them for their apostasy and continuing disobedience. To help them understand what was in store for them, God told Ezekiel to perform symbolic actions that would portray the coming military defeat and accompanying shortages of food and water. Without uttering a word, the prophet was to illustrate how Jerusalem would be defeated and how this defeat would affect the people.

We, too, may be facing defeat. While we may not experience the destruction, famine, and death caused by war, we may find ourselves on the brink of defeat. As we study today's scripture, let us consider these questions: *How did Ezekiel prepare the people for defeat? How do we acknowledge and face defeat in our own lives?*

READING THE SCRIPTURE

NRSV
Ezekiel 4:1-13

1 And you, O mortal, take a brick and set it before you. On it portray a city, Jerusalem; 2and put siegeworks against it, and build a siege-wall against it, and cast up a ramp against it; set camps also against it, and plant battering rams against it all around. 3Then take an iron plate and place it as an iron wall between you and the city; set your face toward it, and let it be in a state of siege, and press the siege against it. This is a sign for the house of Israel.

4 Then lie on your left side, and place the punishment of the house of Israel upon it; you shall bear their punishment for the number of the days that you lie there. 5For I assign to you a number of days, three hundred ninety days, equal to the number of the years of their punishment; and so you shall bear the punishment of the house of Israel. 6When you have completed these, you shall lie down a second time, but on your right side, and bear the punishment of the house of Judah; forty days I assign you, one day for each year. 7You shall set your face toward the siege of Jerusalem, and with your arm bared you shall prophesy against it. 8See, I am putting cords on you so that you can-

NIV
Ezekiel 4:1-13

1 "NOW, SON of man, take a clay tablet, put it in front of you and draw the city of Jerusalem on it. 2Then lay siege to it: Erect siege works against it, build a ramp up to it, set up camps against it and put battering rams around it. 3Then take an iron pan, place it as an iron wall between you and the city and turn your face toward it. It will be under siege, and you shall besiege it. This will be a sign to the house of Israel.

4"Then lie on your left side and put the sin of the house of Israel upon yourself. You are to bear their sin for the number of days you lie on your side. 5I have assigned you the same number of days as the years of their sin. So for 390 days you will bear the sin of the house of Israel.

6"After you have finished this, lie down again, this time on your right side, and bear the sin of the house of Judah. I have assigned you 40 days, a day for each year. 7Turn your face toward the siege of Jerusalem and with bared arm prophesy against her. 8I will tie you up with ropes so that you cannot turn from one side to the other until you have finished the days of your siege.

Key Verse

Key Verse

not turn from one side to the other until you have completed the days of your siege.

9 And you, take wheat and barley, beans and lentils, millet and spelt; put them into one vessel, and make bread for yourself. During the number of days that you lie on your side, three hundred ninety days, you shall eat it. ¹⁰The food that you eat shall be twenty shekels a day by weight; at fixed times you shall eat it. ¹¹And you shall drink water by measure, one-sixth of a hin; at fixed times you shall drink. ¹²You shall eat it as a barley-cake, baking it in their sight on human dung. ¹³The LORD said, "Thus shall the people of Israel eat their bread, unclean, among the nations to which I will drive them."

9 "Take wheat and barley, beans and lentils, millet and spelt; put them in a storage jar and use them to make bread for yourself. You are to eat it during the 390 days you lie on your side. ¹⁰Weigh out twenty shekels of food to eat each day and eat it at set times. ¹¹Also measure out a sixth of a hin of water and drink it at set times. ¹²Eat the food as you would a barley cake; bake it in the sight of the people, using human excrement for fuel." ¹³The LORD said, "In this way the people of Israel will eat defiled food among the nations where I will drive them."

UNDERSTANDING THE SCRIPTURE

Ezekiel 3:22-27. Just as he did in the first vision, Ezekiel experienced the glory of God, fell on his face, and was lifted up by the spirit. From the description of the place, the reader is to conclude that the prophet is in Babylon. This time, instead of calling him to speak, God tells Ezekiel to isolate himself within his house. He will be immobilized by cords so that he cannot go among the people and prophesy. God will also make him speechless. Recall that in 3:16-21 God would hold the prophet accountable for not speaking the words he was given. Here, however, God chooses to have Ezekiel remain silent rather than prophesy to the rebellious people. God will unloose his tongue when Jerusalem is destroyed (see Ezekiel 24:27). Then Ezekiel will be able to prophesy again. Some commentators understand this speechlessness to be rooted in a physical problem endured by Ezekiel.

Ezekiel 4:1-3. Although Ezekiel cannot speak, he is still able to communicate by means of signs and symbols. Such actions were understood in ancient societies not only as illustrative of an event but also as somehow causing it to be set in motion. First, the prophet is to take a mud brick and either etch or sculpt a picture of Jerusalem under siege on the brick before setting it in the sun to dry. The picture is to include the encampments and equipment of the attacking army. The iron plate or griddle is set up as a wall to symbolize God's part in the siege against Jerusalem. Through miming actions, the prophet shows the people what is going to happen, though he gives no verbal interpretation.

Ezekiel 4:4-8. By lying on his side as God commands, Ezekiel tells the people how long this punishment will last. One day is supposedly equivalent to a full year of exile, though how these numbers are calculated is unclear. Punishment for Israel (here, the Northern Kingdom, though Ezekiel often uses house of Israel to refer to Judah) was interpreted as three hundred ninety years, whereas Judah's period of exile was said to be forty years. God's command that Ezekiel "bear the punishment" (NRSV) or "iniquity" (NKJ) or "guilt" (NJB) suggests that Ezekiel, who is a priest as well as a prophet, is to serve as a scapegoat for the people (see Leviticus 16:20-22). The prophet both identifies with and suffers on behalf of the people.

Ezekiel 4:9-17. Symbolic action continues as God commands the prophet to bake bread from six ingredients, signifying the scarcity of any one type of food. He is to ration food and water, consuming about eight ounces of bread and two-thirds of a quart of water per day. Since Ezekiel is in Babylon and this food shortage will occur during the invasion of Jerusalem, the prophet is again identifying with the people in their suffering. How he is supposed to bake and eat this bread while lying on his side bound by cords is not explained (4:9). In addition to the concern about scarcity, Ezekiel raises the problem of ritual purity. If he baked his bread over human feces as God commanded, he would defile himself—a condition that he as a priest has never allowed to happen. God does allow the prophet to bake his bread over cow's dung, a commonly used fuel, though the people of Israel will eat defiled bread.

Ezekiel 5:1-4. In the final symbolic act of this series, Ezekiel is to cut his own hair and beard, a sign of mourning, with a sharp sword, signifying the enemy. Then he is to weigh, divide, burn, strike with the sword, scatter, and bind it to represent God's punishment. The three portions of hair may symbolize the burning of Jerusalem, death by the sword, and exile, respectively. Some of the people in Jerusalem may survive, as represented by the binding of a few hairs in the hem, but even many of these will later meet a violent end.

Ezekiel 5:5-17. The miming actions are followed by a prophetic word. God begins by noting the divine election of Jerusalem. The people have rebelled against God, adopting the ways of their neighbors. They have desecrated the temple. Therefore, God will come against them. Horrendous consequences of this judgment—including cannibalism and famine—are listed. Note in this section the use of phrases commonly associated with prophesy: "Thus says the Lord GOD" (5:5, 7, 8, 11) and "I, the LORD, have spoken" (5:13, 15, 17).

INTERPRETING THE SCRIPTURE

Defeat Is Coming

Again and again and again God had sent prophets to warn the people of Judah. Their message was simple: Turn from your sinful ways or face judgment. The people have heard but refused to believe that God would allow any harm to befall royal David's city. Surely God will protect Jerusalem and its residents. Although God earnestly desired to pardon the people, their continuing resistance to correction and increasing hardness of heart prompted God to take decisive action. In keeping with God's will that the people be punished for their apostasy, the Babyloni-ans were coming to defeat and destroy the city.

The clock was relentlessly ticking off the countdown to destruction. Prophetic warnings were of no avail at this point, but God did have a role for the prophet to play. Ezekiel, who had been sent to Babylon with the first group of captives in 598-597 B.C.E., was commanded to illustrate the fate of Jerusalem in pictures and symbolic actions. God commanded Ezekiel to etch (or perhaps sculpt) on a damp mud brick a picture of Jerusalem under siege. This artistic rendering of the city surrounded by battering rams poised for action and encamped enemy troops would have been a terrifying sight. The prophet is instructed to set his face toward an iron cooking griddle pressed against the siege as a sign of God's part in the coming military action.

The prophet is also told to lie first on his left side and then on his right. God will bind him with cords for three hundred ninety days and forty days, respectively, as an indication of the length of punishment first for Israel and then Judah. He is to prophesy against God's people. Moreover, God calls him to "bear their punishment" (4:5). This phrase can also mean "bear their sin" or "bear their guilt." The prophet becomes the figure of the scapegoat introduced in Leviticus 16:20-22. Ezekiel is called to assume both his prophetic role by prophesying against the city and his priestly role by bearing the guilt of the people before God.

A Glimpse of Wartime Conditions

Defeat was coming, but before it was final the people would experience severe hardship and deprivation. Using small quantities of wheat, barley, beans, lentils, millet, and spelt, the prophet demonstrated how difficult it would be to find enough of any one ingredient to mix a loaf of bread. Food would be so scarce that the people under siege would have less than eight ounces of bread and two-thirds of a quart of water to subsist on each day. Famine and thirst will lead to starvation, a condition that most persons would find more difficult to endure than the swift death caused by an invader's weapon.

In addition to the lack of food, the people would also suffer the indignity of eating food prepared under ritually impure conditions. God tells the prophet that he is to eat a barley cake baked over "human dung" (4:12). Although cow dung was a commonly used fuel for fire in ancient civilizations, human feces were not. In fact, Deuteronomy 23:12-14, which speaks of ritual purity within Israel's military camps, requires that an area be designated outside the camp for use as a latrine. The presence of human excrement within the camp would render it unholy. Whatever was cooked over human fecal matter was therefore impure.

Ezekiel Protests

Thus far, Ezekiel has been willing to do all that God has commanded. Yet, when God instructs him to cook and eat food that is ritually unclean, the prophet protests. Ezekiel had been called by God to the prophetic office; however, he had been born into the priestly office. He had been taught since birth what was required of him as a priest, and he had been faithful to the expectations of his office. He reminds God that he has "never eaten what died of itself or was torn by animals" (Ezekiel 4:14). Ezekiel's comments refer to stipulations found in Leviticus 22:8 that forbid the consumption of improperly slaughtered animals. Ezekiel also reports that he has never eaten meat ("carrion flesh") that has sat beyond the limited time set forth in Leviticus 7:18. His scrupulous conscience in these matters is repulsed by the suggestion that he engage in impure practices.

God hears the prophet's concerns. For Ezekiel to have eaten of bread cooked over an impure fire meant that he would have been ritually defiled—a state he has never experienced. Therefore, God relents and allows the prophet to cook his barley cake over cow dung. However, the people will "eat their bread, unclean, among the nations to which [God] will drive them" (Ezekiel 4:13).

Facing Defeat in Our Own Lives

Through the prophet Ezekiel, God made clear to the exiles in Babylon the terror of the coming siege. The people in Jerusalem would suffer hunger and thirst before they were defeated and Jerusalem was destroyed by enemies. In the process, the people would act in ways that were abominable before God. The prophet's actions pointed to a situation too horrible to imagine.

Many modern adults have experienced the ravages of war firsthand. Some may have been called upon to fight for their nation. Others may have lived in countries in which an enemy invaded and left a trail of bombed out buildings, decimated landscape, wounded victims, and families mourning their dead loved ones. Some may never forget the sound of air raid sirens piercing the blacked-out sky. Coupons to obtain rationed items were likely as closely guarded as today's plastic credit cards. Even as you read this lesson, there are probably persons somewhere in the world experiencing the kind of scarcity and degradation recorded in Ezekiel.

War, of course, is an example of catastrophic defeat not just of an individual or family but of a nation, perhaps a way of life or even an entire civilization. The history of the world is often recorded as stories of the victories and defeat of war. Yet, we face other defeats on a smaller, more personal scale. Throughout the world, persons experience grinding poverty that causes them to worry constantly about having enough food for themselves and their children. Each day requires a struggle just to obtain the basic necessities for survival. To tell a child or elderly adult that no food is available today represents a significant defeat for a family, especially its breadwinner.

The nation we live in may not be under siege by outside military forces, but many individuals feel threatened as they walk or drive through unsafe areas. Human life is particularly endangered by drugs, alcohol, and guns. The drug dealer, drunk driver, and gun-toter not only have the power to destroy themselves but others as well.

Where people once left their windows opened and doors unlocked, windows are barred and doors are secured with several locks, perhaps even a security alarm. People try to protect themselves, their loved ones, and their possessions, but disregard for human life and wanton destruction of private property have created a sense of futility in some quarters. Senseless killings on a street corner—even bombs that snuff out the lives of civilian workers and their children in an office building—engender feelings of fear and defeat.

Other persons are defeated not by external circumstances but by decisions they have made. Like the citizens of Judah, some individuals have set themselves on a doomsday course. A thief chooses to commit a crime and is punished with a jail sentence. A student caught cheating fails a course. A taxpayer who opts to underreport earnings is slapped with a fine. A drug addict finds it difficult to obtain and keep a job. A professing Christian engages in immoral or unethical actions that create inner turmoil and alienate him or her from God.

No matter what potentially difficult circumstances we find ourselves in, most of us are unwilling to admit defeat. We are hopeful about the future. Our optimism can be a very stabilizing force, but it can also be a Pollyannish attitude if we, like the Judeans, are responsible for the defeat we face. When our own behaviors are leading us toward destruction, we need to recognize how our failure to be faithful to God is stirring up trouble for us. Then we need to listen and respond, as the Judeans did not, to God's word as it comes to us through the Scriptures, a friend, a sermon, or in some other way. God does want to change our lives, but if we continue to stubbornly refuse to heed God's warnings, we will find ourselves facing defeat.

SHARING THE SCRIPTURE

PREPARING TO TEACH

Preparing Our Hearts

Spend some time this week thinking about defeats in your own life, particularly those over which you feel (at least in retrospect) that you had some control. You may want to record answers to the following questions in a spiritual journal: In one sentence, how would I describe the cause and effect of the situation? How might different actions on my part have eased or averted defeat? What steps have I taken to avoid similar circumstances?

Ask God to help you identify behaviors that have the potential to defeat you in the future. Pray for guidance in changing your ways.

Preparing Our Minds

Read Ezekiel 3:22–5:17. Look especially at chapter 4, verses 1-13. Try to visualize the picture of the siege that the prophet drew on the mud brick. Also, put yourself in Ezekiel's place and imagine lying bound for an extended period of time. Consider the level of obedience unto God and the love for God's people that would enable you to withstand such hardship. Keep that commitment in mind as you prepare and teach this week's lesson.

Preparing Our Learning Space

Class members may find it helpful if you (or an artistic student) draw your own rendering of Ezekiel's mud brick, illustrating Jerusalem with a wall erected by the enemy, battering rams, a ramp, and camps for the soldiers. For added realism, use chalk on a brick to make the drawing. The drawing may be done before class or as directed below. Also bring a heavy object to press against the completed drawing.

Have on hand:
- several Bibles for students
- newsprint and marker or chalkboard and chalk
- optional Play-Doh or other clay in several colors
- optional half loaf of bread
- optional quart container, preferably made of glass or clear plastic, about two-thirds filled with water

LEADING THE CLASS

(1) Introduction

Begin the session by asking class members to recall an incident of defeat, preferably one that is public knowledge rather than a private tragedy. If students are reluctant to comment, you may use an example from a local sports team or a political election.

After hearing a few examples, focus on one or two and ask the group these questions:

(1) What do you think caused this defeat?
(2) Was the defeat unavoidable? If not, how could it have been averted?
(3) How did the people involved in the loss respond? How might you have responded?
(4) What lessons might be learned from this defeat?

Move the discussion to today's Bible lesson by reminding the class that:
- Jerusalem was on the brink of defeat.
- the Babylonians would besiege and defeat Jerusalem.
- the defeat could have been averted had the people repented of their apostasy and changed their ways.
- God would no longer tolerate such sinfulness and, therefore, was allowing the Babylonians to strike Jerusalem.

Conclude this portion of the lesson by

raising today's main questions: *How did Ezekiel prepare the people for defeat? How do we acknowledge and face defeat in our own lives?*

(2) Defeat Is Coming

Because today's scripture lesson shows Ezekiel prophesying in pictures rather than words, you (or an artistic student with whom you have made prior arrangements) may want to draw an illustration of Ezekiel 4:1-2 on newsprint or a brick. The drawing could be done at this point in the lesson or prior to class. After showing the drawing, press a heavy object (preferably metal) against the paper or brick (as described in verse 3) and ask:

(1) What does this picture depict? (Talk about the details rather than simply saying "preparations for war.")
(2) Had you been one of the exiles in Babylon who had seen Ezekiel's picture, what might your reaction have been?

If you cannot use a drawing, read Ezekiel 4:1-3 and ask the questions above.

Continue to portray the siege of Jerusalem by asking a volunteer to read aloud Ezekiel 4:4-8. Use information under these verses in Understanding the Scripture and Interpreting the Scripture to help the group understand what Ezekiel is doing. Be sure to include a brief discussion of the term "scapegoat" and its reference in Leviticus 16:20-22.

(3) A Glimpse of Wartime Conditions

If you have access to Play-Doh or other multicolored clay, use it to continue your visual presentation of today's lesson. As you read Ezekiel 4:9, take several pieces of different colored clay and form a loaf. The variety of colors will help class members see how scarce each type of grain or other foodstuff will be when war comes.

Read verses 10-11, holding up a half loaf of bread and container of water, if you have brought them.

Invite class members to pause for a few moments to meditate silently on (1) what it must be like to subsist on such a small amount of food, and (2) the irony of people who disobeyed God by worshiping gods, including those who supposedly provided water and abundant crops, being reduced to starvation rations.

(4) Ezekiel Protests

Read Ezekiel 4:12-15 and discuss the issue of ritual impurity that Ezekiel raises. See Understanding the Scripture and Interpreting the Scripture for information, including references to the Law that prohibit certain methods of food preparation or consumption. Be certain to point out that these matters would be especially critical to Ezekiel, who was a priest. You may want to note that verses 14-15 are not part of today's scripture lesson, though they are included as background reading.

(5) Facing Defeat in Our Own Lives

Help the class members apply the lesson of Ezekiel to their own lives in one of two ways.

(1) If class members know and trust each other, ask them to work with a partner or small team. Stress that this activity must be entered into with respect for privacy and that comments made will be kept confidential. Ask each person to share a situation in which he or she experienced defeat. The sharing may include the following points, which you may want to list on newsprint or a chalkboard:

• A brief description of the circumstances
• The student's understanding of why the defeat occurred
• The student's comments on how the defeat could have been avoided
• How this defeat enabled the student to grow spiritually

(2) If class members are not well acquainted, divide into teams and assign

one of the following case studies to each team. You may either read aloud or write the cases where everyone can see them. The team is to consider these two points, which you may want to write on newsprint or a chalkboard: (1) how this imminent defeat could have been avoided if the individual had been more faithful to God, and (2) what the likely outcome of this case will be. One case may be assigned to more than one team.

CASE 1: A Christian business owner was becoming deeply mired in debt. He had been buying high-priced goods to make himself and his family appear prosperous. To pay for these items, he dipped into his business's capital to the point where the business was on the verge of bankruptcy. His creditors were demanding payment.

CASE 2: A teen raised by devoted Christian parents has fallen in with the wrong crowd. Against her parents' orders, she attends parties where alcohol is served, drugs are used, and couples sneak off to engage in sex. This high school junior had repeatedly told her parents that she was old enough to make her own decisions and that she did not need to discuss her business with them. She has come to realize that her life is out of control and fears that she may be an alcoholic. She wants to try to talk with her parents about her problems.

HELPING CLASS MEMBERS ACT

Challenge class members to examine their own lives to discern behaviors or attitudes that are leading them to defeat. Encourage them, with God's help, to change their course if possible. If defeat is unavoidable at this point, suggest that they take stock of what has happened and ask God to show them how to avert a similar outcome in the future.

Suggest that students consider taking an offering for persons living in war torn countries who need food or medical supplies. Money can be channeled through missions agencies such as UMCOR (United Methodist Committee on Relief) to assist victims.

Encourage adults to be on the lookout for news articles that focus on a message of impending doom or defeat. Examples may include: imminent invasion of one country by another, collapse of a government, an incurable epidemic. Have them consider the ways in which they react to this news; what, if anything, they feel can be done to reverse the situation; and how they may see God acting in this situation.

PLANNING FOR NEXT SUNDAY

Next week's lesson, entitled "Experiencing the Unbelievable," looks at the fall of Jerusalem as recorded in 2 Kings 24–25. Our lesson will focus especially on 2 Kings 24:20b–25:12. Ask the class members to read all of the scripture in preparation for the class. Tell them to imagine themselves in the midst of this destruction and reflect on how they would relate to God under these circumstances.

EXPERIENCING THE UNBELIEVABLE

PREVIEWING THE LESSON

Lesson Scripture: 2 Kings 24:20*b*–25:12
Background Scripture: 2 Kings 24–25
Key Verse: Jeremiah 13:17

Focus of the Lesson:
the Babylonian King Nebuchadnezzar's defeat of King Zedekiah and the destruction of Jerusalem

Main Questions of the Lesson:
How did the Babylonians experience the unbelievable event of the destruction of Jerusalem?
How do we cope with crises in our own lives?

This lesson will enable adult learners to:
(1) understand the account of the destruction of Jerusalem and deportation of its citizens.
(2) recall crises that had an impact on them.
(3) respond by empathizing with and assisting others who are experiencing crisis in their lives.

Today's lesson may be outlined as follows:
(1) Introduction
(2) Prophecy Becomes History
(3) Jerusalem Is Destroyed
(4) The People Are Exiled
(5) Crisis in Our Own Lives

FOCUSING ON THE MAIN QUESTION

We often chuckle at Chicken Little's doomsday warning that the sky is falling. Usually, it isn't. More likely, some gloomy reporter simply exaggerates the meaning of a particular event. However, rare moments do exist when Chicken Little seems to be absolutely right. Disaster is upon us. A country is stunned by the assassination of a popular president. The bullet strikes not only this father and world leader but the heart of the nation as well. One of the great scientific triumphs of all time explodes just seconds after liftoff as a horrified crowd of spectators watches the fragments plummet to earth. The image is replayed over and over again on television screens as viewers struggle to comprehend what has happened. An ordinary looking van parks in the business district of a city. Moments later, the crude, homemade bomb it contains explodes, ripping off the front of an office building and killing scores of innocent workers and their children. The nation that had seemed so invincible is rocked by terrorism in its own heartland.

Such events, catastrophic as they were, pale in comparison to the eighteen-month siege and total destruction of Jerusalem. The sky had truly fallen for the Judeans. Those who had not died from hunger or been killed by the invading Babylonians were carted off into exile. The liberation of the slaves in Egypt during the days of Moses—the defining event of Jewish history—had been reversed by Nebuchadnezzar and his troops. Yet, the Babylonians were not the ones who were truly in charge of God's people. The Creator of the universe had entered human history and, even now, was orchestrating events. The Babylonians were not victorious because God could not stop them but because God had allowed them to mete out punishment to the people of Judah, who had repeatedly sinned. For years, God had warned them about the consequences of their disobedience and unfaithfulness. In mercy, God had protected them, but now God was permitting the sky to fall upon their heads.

As we study today's lesson, we will want to ask these questions: *How did the Babylonians experience the unbelievable event of the destruction of Jerusalem? How do we cope with crises in our own lives?*

READING THE SCRIPTURE

NRSV

2 Kings 24:20b–25:12

20b Zedekiah rebelled against the king of Babylon. **25** ¹And in the ninth year of his reign, in the tenth month, on the tenth day of the month, King Nebuchadnezzar of Babylon came with all his army against Jerusalem, and laid siege to it; they built siegeworks against it all around. ²So the city was besieged until the eleventh year of King Zedekiah. ³On the ninth day of the fourth month the famine became so severe in the city that there was no food for the people of the land. ⁴Then a breach was made in the city wall; the king with all the soldiers fled by night by the way of the gate between the two walls, by the king's garden, though the Chaldeans were all around the city. They went in the direction of the Arabah. ⁵But the army of the Chaldeans pursued the king, and overtook

NIV

2 Kings 24:20b–25:12

20b Now Zedekiah rebelled against the king of Babylon.

25:1 So in the ninth year of Zedekiah's reign, on the tenth day of the tenth month, Nebuchadnezzar king of Babylon marched against Jerusalem with his whole army. He encamped outside the city and built siege works all around it. ²The city was kept under siege until the eleventh year of King Zedekiah. ³By the ninth day of the fourth month the famine in the city had become so severe that there was no food for the people to eat. ⁴Then the city wall was broken through, and the whole army fled at night through the gate between the two walls near the king's garden, though the Babylonians were surrounding the city. They fled toward the Arabah, ⁵but the Babylonian army pursued the king and him in the plains of Jericho; all his army was scattered, deserting him. ⁶Then they captured the king and brought him up to the king of Babylon at Riblah, who passed sentence on him. ⁷They slaughtered the sons of Zedekiah before his eyes, then put out the eyes of Zedekiah; they bound him in fetters and took him to Babylon.

⁸In the fifth month, on the seventh day of the month—which was the nineteenth year of King Nebuchadnezzar, king of Babylon—Nebuzaradan, the captain of the bodyguard, a servant of the king of Babylon, came to Jerusalem. ⁹He burned the house of the LORD, the king's house, and all the houses of Jerusalem; every great house he burned down. ¹⁰All the army of the Chaldeans who were with the captain of the guard broke down the walls around Jerusalem. ¹¹Nebuzaradan the captain of the guard carried into exile the rest of the people who were left in the city and the deserters who had defected to the king of Babylon—all the rest of the population. ¹²But the captain of the guard left some of the poorest people of the land to be vine-dressers and tillers of the soil.

overtook him in the plains of Jericho. All his soldiers were separated from him and scattered, ⁶and he was captured. He was taken to the king of Babylon at Riblah, where sentence was pronounced on him. ⁷They killed the sons of Zedekiah before his eyes. Then they put out his eyes, bound him with bronze shackles and took him to Babylon.

⁸On the seventh day of the fifth month, in the nineteenth year of Nebuchadnezzar king of Babylon, Nebuzaradan comman-der of the imperial guard, an official of the king of Babylon, came to Jerusalem. ⁹He set fire to the temple of the LORD, the royal palace and all the houses of Jerusalem. Every important building he burned down. ¹⁰The whole Babylonian army, under the commander of the imperial guard, broke down the walls around Jerusalem. ¹¹Nebuzaradan the commander of the guard carried into exile the people who remained in the city, along with the rest of the populace and those who had gone over to the king of Babylon. ¹²But the commander left behind some of the poor-est people of the land to work the vine-yards and fields.

NRSV
Jeremiah 13:17
¹⁷But if you will not listen,
    my soul will weep in secret for
        your pride;
my eyes will weep bitterly and
    run down with tears,
    because the LORD's flock has
        been taken captive.

NIV
Jeremiah 13:17
¹⁷But if you do not listen,
    I will weep in secret
        because of your pride;
my eyes will weep bitterly,
    overflowing with tears,
    because the LORD's flock will be taken
        captive.

Key
Verse

UNDERSTANDING THE SCRIPTURE

2 Kings 24:1-7. Nebuchadnezzar, who reigned in Babylon from 605–562 B.C.E., decisively defeated the Egyptians at the battle of Carchemish in 605 B.C.E. (24:1, 7). Jehoiakim, who had paid tribute to the

Pharaoh (23:35), decided to ally Judah with Babylon now that Egypt had suffered defeat. From 604–602 B.C.E., Judah was a vassal of Babylon, but when the Egyptians drove back Babylon in 601/600 B.C.E.,

Jehoiakim seized the opportunity to rebel. Nebuchadnezzar resupplied his Babylonian army (also called the Chaldeans) and then moved in to punish the rebels. The Arameans (Syrians), Moabites, and Ammonites had from time to time been at war with neighboring Judah. The Deuteronomic historian interpreted this military action against Judah as the punishment from God that the prophets had foretold. Manasseh's sins are detailed in 2 Kings 21:1-16. Jehoiakim died in 598 B.C.E. and his son Jehoiachin (also known as Jeconiah) ascended to the throne.

2 Kings 24:8-17. These verses describe the siege of Jerusalem by the Babylonians, who captured the city in March, 597 B.C.E. and deported many of the city's most able persons. Isaiah had prophesied this deportation to Babylon (see 2 Kings 20:12-19 and Lesson 1). The young King Jehoiachin ruled briefly in 598/7 B.C.E. before he, his family, and other palace officials were exiled. Verse 14 records that ten thousand persons were deported, whereas verse 16 says that eight thousand were taken. Valuable sacred treasures of the temple were plundered. Mattaniah (a son of Josiah), was installed as king. His name was changed to Zedekiah as a sign of vassalage. (See Ezekiel 17:11-21 for more information about Zedekiah.)

2 Kings 24:18-20. Zedekiah ruled between 597 and 587/6 B.C.E. As noted above (24:1), the Egyptians had been defeated by the Babylonians in 605 B.C.E. However, when Pharaoh Psammetichus II of Egypt began to exert influence in Palestine in 592 B.C.E., Zedekiah wavered between continuing the current Babylonian vassalage and forging a new alliance with Egypt. He decided to rebel against Babylon, a decision that had disastrous consequences.

2 Kings 25:1-7. As a result of Zedekiah's rebellion, Nebuchadnezzar and his troops stormed into Jerusalem for an eighteen-month siege that began in January, 587 B.C.E. As was customary (and depicted on the brick etched by Ezekiel, see Lesson 10), the Babylonians built siegeworks to isolate the city. The food supply was completely depleted, as Ezekiel also had foretold by means of symbolic action (see Lesson 10). When the city wall was breached in July, 586 B.C.E., Zedekiah and his troops tried to flee through a gate in the southeast wall. They were headed toward Arabah in the Jordan Valley between the Dead Sea and the Sea of Galilee when the Babylonians overtook them. Zedekiah's army deserted, and the Babylonians captured the king and brought him to their own king, who sentenced Zedekiah to witness the execution of his owns sons before he himself was blinded and carted off to Babylon.

2 Kings 25:8-12. The Babylonians burned the temple in August, 586 B.C.E., along with the rest of Jerusalem. They deported a second group of persons, leaving the poorest ones in Jerusalem.

2 Kings 25:13-21. The Deuteronomic historian gives a detailed description of the temple furnishings that the Babylonians destroyed and plundered. First Kings 7:13-50 records the making of these furnishings. The Babylonians rounded up the temple priests and other leaders and had them executed.

2 Kings 25:22-26. Nebuchadnezzar installed Gedaliah, a member of an important family in Judah, as the governor. Gedaliah apparently could have brought stability, though not freedom from Babylonian rule, to Judah. He counseled the people who remained in Judah to serve Nebuchadnezzar. If they did so, all would be well. However, a group of assassins led by Ishmael killed Gedaliah. (See Jeremiah 40:7–41:18 for another account of Gedaliah's reign and assassination.) They also killed those who were with him at Mizpah. Located about eight miles north of Jerusalem, this city may have been one of the few that remained after the Babylonian conquest. Survivors fled to Egypt.

2 Kings 25:27-30. The Deuteronomic historian's account closes on a hopeful note in terms of the future of David's monarchy. After thirty-seven years in prison, King Jehoiachin of Judah was released by King Evil-merodach, who ruled Babylon from 562 to 560 B.C.E. Evil-merodach treated Jehoiachin with kindness and respect, even giving the exile an allowance and inviting him to dine. Another account of this story is recorded in Jeremiah 52:31-34.

Jeremiah 13:17. Today's key verse is taken from an oracle calling for repentance found in Jeremiah 13:15-17. This verse is a lament that Jeremiah anticipates making over the captivity of the people of Judah.

INTERPRETING THE SCRIPTURE

Prophecy Becomes History

King Jehoiakim (who reigned 609-598 B.C.E.) had entered into a treaty with the powerful Babylon, thereby making Judah a vassal from 604–602 B.C.E. But when the Egyptians beat back Babylonian troops, Jehoiakim mounted a badly timed rebellion that resulted in the plundering of goods from the temple, deportation of leading citizens, and apparently his own death. Jehoiachin ascended the throne and ruled for just three months before he was deported with the first group of exiles to Babylon in 598/97 B.C.E. King Nebuchadnezzar made Mattaniah (Jehoiachin's uncle) the king of Judah and changed his name to Zedekiah. Although Zedekiah reigned for eleven years (597–587/86 B.C.E.), the historian concentrates on the final days of this evil king's reign. In those days, the words of the prophets—words that seemed so unbelievable when they were uttered—came true. Judah's downward spiral toward destruction was almost complete.

When the Egyptian king Psammetichus II began moving into Palestine in 592 B.C.E., King Zedekiah was caught in a political maelstrom. Zedekiah wavered between maintaining Judah as a Babylonian vassal and forging a new political relationship with Egypt. He decided to link Judah's fate with Egypt, a move that had devastating consequences for his people. In January, 587 B.C.E., Babylon responded with a siege lasting eighteen months. As the Deuteronomic historian describes the battle scene in 2 Kings 25:1, we can see Ezekiel's prophetic etching of the siegeworks on a mud brick. Ezekiel's loaf of bread, baked from a variety of ingredients because food was so scarce, comes immediately to mind as the historian notes the lack of food in Jerusalem (2 Kings 25:3).

The Babylonian troops could not be repulsed. Instead, they breached the wall of Jerusalem in July of 586 B.C.E. King Zedekiah and his soldiers fled, heading toward an area between the Sea of Galilee and the Dead Sea. They had managed to escape through a "gate between the two walls" (2 Kings 25:4), the second of which had been built to protect the water supply at the pool of Siloam during a time of siege.

The escape was short-lived, however, for Nebuchadnezzar's forces overtook them on the plains of Jericho. The Judean troops broke rank, scattering in all directions to avoid capture. Zedekiah was quickly apprehended and punished with unimaginable cruelty. His captors took him, along with his sons, to Nebuchadnezzar, who ordered that the sons be killed as their father watched. Then Zedekiah's eyes were put out and he was bound and carted off to Babylon. For all intents and purposes, the line of David had seemed to come to an ignoble end.

Jerusalem Is Destroyed

The people who remained in Jerusalem had been without food for weeks. Their king had been deported. The sons of the king—apparent heirs to David's throne—

had been killed. The people were defeated, but the Babylonians were not finished with them.

In August of 586 B.C.E., Nebuzaradan, one of the Nebuchadnezzar's bodyguards, led the army in a total destruction of Jerusalem. His troops broke the walls that protected the city. They set fire to all the residences, including the king's palace. They desecrated the temple of the Lord by burning it as well. This action seemed scandalous, yet it was not totally unexpected. Centuries ago, God had warned King Solomon (961–928 B.C.E.), the one who had built the temple, that such destruction would occur if the people were ever to forsake God (see 1 Kings 9:6-9). The people had forsaken God, and the punishment was what God had said it would be.

The soothing prophecy of Hananiah (see Jeremiah 28 and Lesson 7) had proved to be false in ways that were beyond belief. Not only had Babylon's grip not been broken, as Hananiah said it would be, but Jerusalem itself lay in ruins. Perhaps the image of Jeremiah wearing a yoke and confronting Hananiah flashed through the minds of survivors in the midst of the chaos of siege and destruction.

The People Are Exiled

As we have already noted, when Nebuchadnezzar first attacked Jerusalem, he and his troops not only plundered the temple and the palace but also had deported thousands of leaders and skilled craftspersons to Babylon (see 2 Kings 24:13-16). Now, approximately eleven years later, the invaders were rounding up those who deserted the king, as well as other citizens of Jerusalem. Anyone who had a skill or was likely to challenge foreign rule was sent into exile in Babylon.

Today's key verse, Jeremiah 13:17, records the prophets lament for the people of God who have been taken captive. This lament reminds us that the events of war and exile came about because the people did not heed the warnings of God. They had refused to turn from their sinful ways. Although the Babylonians (or Chaldeans) had military might and prowess, they only finalized the defeat that the people of Judah had brought upon themselves. As the historian records in 2 Kings 24:2, God is the one who sent invaders into Judah. The people were not being suppressed by a superior military power but punished by God for their infidelity and hardness of heart.

In a very real sense, the liberation of the Exodus has been undone. God had chosen the people and brought them out of slavery. Now, in response to their sinful actions—actions God had repeatedly warned them against—the people were again exiles in a foreign land.

Everything seems to be lost: David's monarchy, Solomon's temple, all the buildings, and the majority of Jerusalem's inhabitants are gone. But perhaps there is a glimmer of hope. The historian records that "some of the poorest people of the land [were left] to be vinedressers and tillers of the soil" (2 Kings 25:12). Food may again be harvested in the land of famine. Some time in the future, the population may be restored and the city rebuilt. Now, however, the people can only mourn the incredible losses they never imagined they would experience.

Crisis in Our Own Lives

Like the people of Judah, we may experience catastrophes, though they will not likely be on the scale of the destruction of an entire city. Yet, in their own way, these disasters are just as life-changing for us. Consider these examples.
- A young adult goes off to war and returns seemingly unharmed, but later has a child who is seriously ill.
- A teenage family member is diagnosed with a rare form of cancer.
- While on vacation, a family's home is ransacked. The family's possessions and peace of mind are taken.

When a crisis occurs, most of us respond by fearing for our safety. Whether a natural disaster, criminal, disease, or some other agent is responsible for the crisis, we become stressed by circumstances that seem beyond our control. We may be unable to think clearly. Even if we want to respond—perhaps retaliate—we feel powerless to do anything. Possibly all we can do is hold tighter to those who are dear to us and to the special possessions that mean so much in our lives. Maybe we seek to protect our valuables by installing a burglar alarm or putting irreplaceable pictures of deceased loved ones in a fireproof file. Whatever we do, our efforts seem inconsequential because we cannot retrieve whatever has already been lost.

We can empathize with at least some of the fears, anguish, and deprivation the Judeans must have experienced. Their entire world collapsed as the city wall succumbed to the battering ram of the Babylonian army. Life would never be the same. When we face crises, we believe that life will never be the same for us either. In fact, we may wonder if we will be able to carry on with life at all. Whether the crisis involves a whole nation or our own family, we find it difficult to comprehend that such a devastating event has happened. Even in the midst of chaos, God is present. We are not alone. In Romans 8:35-39, Paul assures us that nothing—not hardship, distress, persecution, famine, nakedness, peril, or sword—can separate us from the love of Jesus. On the rock of our faith in Jesus we have a foundation that will endure the most trying times. That good news gives us hope in the darkest hours of our lives.

SHARING THE SCRIPTURE

PREPARING TO TEACH

Preparing Our Hearts

As you prepare to teach this week's lesson, remember at least one humanly initiated world crisis (as opposed to a natural disaster) during your lifetime. Think about what happened, who was involved, and reasons why this event was perpetrated. What was your own response? How did this crisis change your outlook?

Also consider a crisis in your own life. You may want to write responses to these questions in your spiritual journal: What caused the crisis? How did you respond to it? Did it change your relationship with another person? How did it affect your relationship with God?

Preparing Our Minds

Read 2 Kings 24–25, as well as the commentary on the verses found in the Under-standing the Scripture portion of the lesson. Pay particular attention to 2 Kings 24:20b–25:12, the focus of our session.

Also read Psalm 74, a plea for help that seems to assume that Jerusalem has already been destroyed.

You may want to review prior lessons to see how what we have studied to date leads up to the siege depicted in 2 Kings. One section, "Prophecy Becomes History," makes reference to particular passages and previous lessons.

Try to imagine yourself within the walled city as the Babylonian army is invading. What might you be thinking about during the eighteen months of this terrible siege? How would you characterize your relationship with God at this time?

Preparing Our Learning Space

Have on hand:
✔ several Bibles for students

✔ newsprint and marker or chalkboard and chalk

✔ paper and pencils

LEADING THE CLASS

(1) Introduction

Begin today's session by asking class members to recall a terrible national experience that occurred in their own lifetime. Information in the first paragraph under Focusing on the Main Question will provide discussion starters or ideas for a lecture. Ask the group to:

• describe the event.

• recall what they were doing when it occurred.

• explain how the event affected them personally.

• comment on how they believe the event changed the mind or heart of the nation.

Note that the people of Judah experienced an unbelievable event—the siege and destruction of Jerusalem—that would forever change their lives. As we study that event today we will ask the following two main questions, which you may want to post on newsprint or a chalkboard: *How did the Babylonians experience the unbelievable event of the destruction of Jerusalem? How do we cope with crises in our own lives?*

(2) Prophecy Becomes History

Select a volunteer to read aloud 2 Kings 24:20b (start at "Zedekiah rebelled") –25:7.

As an option for the class that enjoys hands-on activities, distribute paper and pencils prior to the reading. Have the class members divide the sheet into three sections, labeled: the siege, the king flees, the king's sons are slaughtered. After the reading has concluded, ask each person to select at least one scene from the reading and illustrate it. Stick figures are fine. Some adults may be willing to share their drawings with others. The point of this activity is to get a visual impression of the total destruction, chaos, and death the people of Jerusalem experienced.

Talk with the class about how this scene portrayed in 2 Kings fulfills some of the prophecies we have already studied. This section, "Prophesy Becomes History," found under Interpreting the Scripture, will provide ideas. Additional prophecies may come to mind.

(3) Jerusalem Is Destroyed

Choose a volunteer to read aloud 2 Kings 25:8-10.

Briefly discuss the total destruction of Jerusalem. Use information from Understanding the Scripture and Interpreting the Scripture as needed.

Class members may be able to compare this scene to something they have witnessed or read about in their own lives.

(4) The People Are Exiled

Conclude today's scripture reading with 2 Kings 25:11-12. Note that the poorest people were allowed to remain. Only those persons who had perceived skills or economic value were deported.

Ask if anyone has ever been exiled or held as a prisoner of war. If the individual feels comfortable in discussing this experience, invite him or her to talk about what it feels like to be taken from one's home, separated from loved ones, and forced to readjust to life in a different culture. If you have a church or community member with this kind of firsthand experience who is not a member of the class, you may want to extend a special invitation to this person to come and share the experience.

Suggest that class members read Psalm 74, which is a prayer for help during the time of national disaster. If enough Bibles are not available, you may want to read the psalm aloud. Ask the class to comment on:

- how the people perceive God's relationship to them.
- the nature of their complaint against God. (God did not seem to intervene on their behalf.)
- the motivations the psalmist suggests to encourage God to help the people.

(5) Crisis in Our Own Lives

Help class members to remember and reflect on some crises in their own lives by doing one or more of the following activities.

(1) Distribute paper and pencils. Ask adults to write a letter to a grandchild or other member of another generation about an event that they perceived to be a life-changing crisis. Have them write about what happened, how it affected them, and how they experienced the presence of God in the midst of this difficult situation. Ask the students to consider mailing the letter. If sharing the letter now is not appropriate, perhaps the writer could set it aside for a future time as a testament of faith.

(2) Distribute paper and pencils. Suggest that class members write a diary account of their own perceptions about and reactions to a national crisis. If time permits, invite several persons to read their accounts and have the class respond to them. Be sure to have them comment on how they perceived God to be present in this situation.

(3) Ask the group to list several crises that they perceive will occur in the near future. These crises may be local, national, or international in scale. Ideas may include: landfills loaded to capacity; an increasing number of elderly adults who need assistance; marginal employees who can neither earn a living wage nor qualify for social programs; lack of health care for a larger segment of the population. Then have them work in small teams to identify the problem and make suggestions as how to address it. These suggestions should be based on scriptural principles, such as stewardship of the earth or economic justice for the poor.

HELPING CLASS MEMBERS ACT

Encourage class members to become involved in some type of disaster response or relief work. They may be able to use their talents in an agency such as the Red Cross, a Volunteers in Mission team, or a search and rescue squad. They can offer Christian care to persons who have experienced a major crisis in their lives.

Suggest that students who have lived through an unbelievable event, such as a war or serious fire, arrange to share their story with the church's youth group to help young people empathize with the feelings of helplessness, despair, and physical deprivation that one experiences in such a situation. The class members will need to make arrangements with the youth counselors for such a program.

Challenge class members to learn more about the Holocaust perpetrated by Hitler and his troops. Encourage the students to read authors such as Anne Frank, Dietrich Bonhoeffer, and Elie Wiesel, who endured this terrifying episode of modern history. Their stories provide a personal account, rather than an official history of the war.

PLANNING FOR NEXT SUNDAY

Ask class members to prepare for next Sunday's lesson by reading the entire book of Lamentations. Our lesson, "Longing for Restoration," will focus on chapter 5, verses 1-10 and 19-22. Challenge the students to put themselves in the place of the exiles in Babylon as they read these mournful poems.

LONGING FOR RESTORATION

PREVIEWING THE LESSON

Lesson Scripture: Lamentations 5:1-10, 19-22
Background Scripture: Lamentations
Key Verse: Lamentations 5:21

Focus of the Lesson:
the anguished captives' cries unto God to remember and restore them

Main Question of the Lesson:
Will God ever remember and restore us?

This lesson will enable adult learners to:
(1) hear the lament of the writer, who feels abandoned by God.
(2) recall situations of grief and feelings of abandonment in their own lives.
(3) respond by assisting someone who has experienced loss.

Today's lesson may be outlined as follows:
(1) Introduction
(2) Remember Us, O God
(3) Restore Us, O God
(4) Grieving Our Losses
(5) Seeking Hope in the Midst of Grief

FOCUSING ON THE MAIN QUESTION

Life constantly changes. Some changes, of course, create improvements in our lives. We feel better about ourselves and excited by the promise of the future. Other changes, though, create pain and hardship. A loved one dies. We lose everything we own in a fire. Our company no longer has room for us in its workforce. An unscrupulous financial advisor gambles away our nest egg. At times like these, we must confront unwanted situations that we are powerless to control. When we feel rejected and overcome by grief we repeatedly raise the question: *Will God ever remember and restore us?* This is the same question the writer of Lamentations posed to God, and the question that will guide us as we study today's lesson.

Since all of us have suffered grief or known disappointment, we can identify with the plight of the Judeans now exiled in Babylon. Their world has been turned upside down. Nothing is familiar in this foreign land. Basic necessities, such as food and water, that were readily available in Judah are now either scarce or too expensive to buy or both. Things that the people previously took for granted can no longer be depended upon. The Judeans, who once exercised control over their own lives, now must submit to the king's slaves who are their masters. The exiles are treated more like animals than humans. They are forced to work constantly and do not even have a break for the Sabbath rest that they and their animals enjoyed in Palestine. Like widows and orphans, they are marginalized people who need care. They cry out to God to remember them in their suffering.

Although the exiles feel abandoned, the writer does affirm that God reigns and endures forever. Having recognized God's sovereignty, the people pray that God will restore them. The exiles know that they cannot act on their own behalf, but they want God to reestablish the close, covenantal relationship that they once enjoyed. Like the exiles, we too want to experience hope and restoration when painful circumstances threaten to engulf us. We want to rest securely in the knowledge that no matter how bleak the current situation, God remembers us and enfolds us with loving care that will not let us go.

READING THE SCRIPTURE

NRSV
Lamentations 5:1-10
1 Remember, O LORD, what has
    befallen us;
  look, and see our disgrace!
2Our inheritance has been turned
    over to strangers,
  our homes to aliens.
3We have become orphans,
    fatherless;
  our mothers are like widows.
4We must pay for the water we
    drink;
  the wood we get must be
    bought.
5With a yoke on our necks we
    are hard driven;
  we are weary, we are given no
    rest.
6We have made a pact with
    Egypt and Assyria,
  to get enough bread.
7Our ancestors sinned; they are
    no more,
  and we bear their iniquities.
8Slaves rule over us;

NIV
Lamentations 5:1-10
1 Remember, O LORD, what has happened to
us;
  look, and see our disgrace.
2Our inheritance has been turned over to
    aliens,
  our homes to foreigners.
3We have become orphans and fatherless,
    our mothers like widows.
4We must buy the water we drink;
  our wood can be had only at a price.
5Those who pursue us are at our heels;
  we are weary and find no rest.
6We submitted to Egypt and Assyria
  to get enough bread.
7Our fathers sinned and are no more,
  and we bear their punishment.
8Slaves rule over us,
  and there is none to free us from their
  hands.
9We get our bread at the risk of our lives
  because of the sword in the desert.
10Our skin is hot as an oven,
  feverish from hunger.

there is no one to deliver us
from their hand.
⁹We get our bread at the peril of
our lives,
because of the sword in the
wilderness.
¹⁰Our skin is black as an oven
from the scorching heat
of famine.

NRSV
Lamentations 5:19-22
¹⁹But you, O LORD, reign forever;
your throne endures to all
generations.
²⁰Why have you forgotten us
completely?
Why have you forsaken us
these many days?

Key
Verse

²¹Restore us to yourself, O LORD,
that we may be restored;
renew our days as of old—
²²unless you have utterly rejected
us,
and are angry with us beyond
measure.

NIV
Lamentations 5:19-22
¹⁹You, O LORD, reign forever;
your throne endures from generation to
generation.
²⁰Why do you always forget us?
Why do you forsake us so long?

Ke
Ver

²¹Restore us to yourself, O LORD, that we
may return;
renew our days as of old
²²unless you have utterly rejected us
and are angry with us beyond measure.

UNDERSTANDING THE SCRIPTURE

Lamentations 1:1-22. Chapter 1 is the first of the five poems contained within Lamentations. Each of the poems expresses the writer's grief over the destruction of Jerusalem by King Nebuchadnezzar. Although this entire book has traditionally been ascribed to Jeremiah, modern scholarship calls his authorship into question on the basis of the oldest Hebrew manuscripts and the dissonance between some of the views expressed in this book and other views that can definitely be attributed to the prophet. This first poem, like the ones in chapters 2–4, is written in the form of an acrostic. The first word of each verse corresponds to the successive letters of the Hebrew alphabet. (The New Jerusalem Bible clearly shows the acrostic form by naming each letter of the alphabet.) The

focus of the first poem, a funeral dirge, is on the city of Jerusalem itself. In the first half of the poem, the writer contrasts its former state of glory with the present desolation. Jerusalem is comfortless. In verse 12, Zion itself speaks, urging the reader to enter into the grief and loss of the city. The poet confesses the people's rebellion and acknowledges the appropriateness of God's action.

Lamentations 2:1-22. The second poem, also a funeral dirge, depicts God as a warrior who destroys Zion. The "day of his anger" refers to "the day of the Lord" foretold by the prophets (see, for example, Isaiah 13:6, Ezekiel 7:7-12; Amos 5:18-20). On that day God will pass judgment. Both the temple ("booth" or "tabernacle") and the palace, representing the crucial religious and political facets of life in Judah, were destroyed. The devastation causes the elders to mourn. Food is so scarce that cannibalism is practiced. Jerusalem is ridiculed by enemies who claimed to have "devoured her" (2:16), but in reality, what has happened is the result of action God "ordained long ago" (2:17).

Lamentations 3:1-66. This poem, like the previous two, is written in the form of an acrostic. Here, however, the particular letter of the alphabet begins three consecutive stanzas, for a total of sixty-six verses. The poem is the lament of an individual who has experienced the devastation and has a word to share with the community. God is depicted as a wild animal who has attacked (3:10-11). After detailing his pain, the poet turns in verses 21-23 to a word of hope: God's love and mercy will never end. He asserts that God has ordained all action, including chastisement; therefore, the people should accept it. The lament closes with a request that God pay back the poet's enemies.

Lamentations 4:1-22. Written as a funeral dirge, chapter 4 begins as chapters 1 and 2 do with the word "how." In the Hebrew text, laments begin with a word that means "O how." The poet describes the horrible scenes of the suffering during the final days of Babylon's siege of Jerusalem. The behavior of people and animals is compared, and the people are found wanting. Social standing and class mean nothing now, for everyone is hungry. In fact, the lucky ones are those who have already died. Unlike the pre-invasion days when people believed Jerusalem was invincible, the events of war have shown that the city can be overcome. The poem closes on a hopeful note: The punishment is complete; God will not exile the people again.

Lamentations 5:1-22. This communal lament includes twenty-two verses, but it does not adhere to the acrostic form. The speaker addresses God, calling God to remember what has happened to the people. The inheritance referred to in verse 2 is the land God gave to the people; now that land has passed into other hands. The survivors are described as vulnerable groups (orphans, fatherless, widows) who need special care and protection. Natural resources required for basic necessities must now be bought. So too must bread be purchased. The people are weighed down with the burden of a heavy yoke. Verse 7 expresses a different perspective on sin which, in contrast to Ezekiel 18:2 (see Lesson 9), seems to say that the survivors are suffering for the sins of their ancestors. Yet, in verse 16, the poet depicts the people as taking responsibility for their own sin. Slaves often held positions of authority (5:8). The society is in chaos. The entire situation—marginalization, famine, chaos, the monarchy, and the destruction of Jerusalem—causes the writer to lament. He closes with an affirmation of faith in the sovereign God who reigns forever. The poet calls upon God to remember, restore, and renew the people.

INTERPRETING THE SCRIPTURE

Remember Us, O God

Unimaginable disaster has struck! Not only has the beloved city of Jerusalem been torched, but the people have been carted off to Babylon. Where is God in all of this? Has God forgotten the covenant people? In the agony of their loss, the people cry out for God to remember them. They remind God of the problems that have befallen them. Centuries ago, when they were slaves in Egypt, they had called upon God. In response, God remembered them and raised up Moses to deliver them (see Exodus 2:24 and 3:7). God's people are again praying to be remembered and delivered.

The exiles are a disgraced people. They lament that their inheritance—the land God gave them (see Deuteronomy 26:1)—is now in the hands of strangers. They compare themselves to the most vulnerable members of society, the orphans and widows, who need care and sustenance. The water they drink and the wood they use were freely available in Jerusalem, but here in Babylon they must buy these necessities. Food is so scarce that they risk their lives to obtain it. Life is excruciatingly difficult.

Not only do they have trouble meeting their basic needs, but the exiles are treated more like beasts of burden than as humans. They are abused by their overseers, who themselves are slaves of the Babylonian king. The people are forced to work long hours without the Sabbath rest that was such an important concept in Jewish law and life. They have no time to recreate and rejuvenate themselves. As slaves in a foreign land they have no opportunity to enjoy the God-given gift of Sabbath.

Even as they ask God to remember them, the exiles acknowledge their own sin. At first glance, verse 7 seems to be a lament about the people suffering for the sins of their ancestors, a common idea that was refuted by Ezekiel (see Lesson 9). However, in light of Lamentations 5:16, in which the exiles claim responsibility for the sin that led to their current situation, verse 7 may be understood as the people identifying themselves with their ancestors. They were not suffering because of what their forebears had done but, like their forebears, they too had sinned.

In short, the exiles are living in chaotic, oppressive circumstances. Their surroundings are both unfamiliar and hostile. Without the temple, they cannot worship or offer sacrifices to God. All they can do is lament their situation and call upon God to remember them.

Restore Us, O God

The city of David lies in ruins. God's temple has been reduced to ashes, and David's monarchy apparently no longer exists. The people are in exile. The author fervently asks why God has forgotten the people. We can almost hear the writer asking, "How long, O God, will you continue to abandon us?"

As horrific as this situation is, however, the author of this lamentation can assert that God's reign endures forever. God is still the all-powerful sovereign. Because he can make that affirmation, the writer can also call upon God to restore the people. The people have sinned and cannot restore themselves; only God can lead them back into divine favor. They know that God has rejected them and is angry with them. Yet, the writer has confidence that unless God has utterly rejected the people—a point that the author does not seem to entertain seriously—God will in fact restore them to their former covenantal relationship.

This cry for restoration of the exiles is echoed in other biblical writings, including Psalm 80 (see especially verses 3, 7, 19), Psalm 85 (see especially verse 4), and Jeremiah 31:18. The writers were painfully aware that one's relationship with God can be ruptured by unrepented sin. Only when God steps in and acts can full restoration occur.

Grieving Our Losses

We all have had experiences of grief. The death of someone dear is surely the most traumatic of losses, but it is not the only source of grief. We grieve for friends we have lost track of or for family members who have become estranged. We move to a new location and mourn the loss of our familiar surroundings and neighbors. An accident or illness leaves us with diminished physical abilities, and we feel so frustrated that movements we once took for granted are either impossible or require great concentration. We lose a job and wonder how life can ever be the same for us again. We lament that the "good old days" of a simpler, slower way of life are gone. We grieve for persons whose lives are shattered by violence or natural catastrophe. Grief arises in many situations and assumes a variety of forms in our lives. It is a natural, if unwelcome, part of our existence.

In the midst of our grief we, like the writer of Lamentations, call out to God. On the cross, Jesus quotes the psalmist (22:1) when he cries out, "My God, my God, why have you forsaken me?" (Matthew 27:46). Like Jesus and the author of Lamentations, we want to know that God has not forgotten us. When we feel forsaken, we want reassurance of God's sustaining presence. We long to hear that God knows who we are and cares about our plight. We yearn to be comforted. We want to be certain that God remembers us. We call upon Jesus to make that connection between us and God.

When disaster strikes many questions swirl in our heads, begging for answers. Why did this happen, God? How long is this nightmare going to last? Will things ever be the same again? Some of these questions can only be answered over the course of time. In that agonizingly long period between the tragedy that has precipitated our grief and the final healing or reconciliation, we can only pray and hope. Like the writer of Lamentations, we offer our own impassioned plea for God to remember and restore us.

Seeking Hope in the Midst of Grief

What sustains us in the anguish of trials and grief? We all need hope. We want to know that someone is in charge of our life when it seems to be spinning out of control. We long to believe that beyond the horror of the present situation, we will find reasons to continue living. We need to catch a glimpse of the rainbow while the storm is raging. Even if the tragedy we are experiencing seems senseless, we want the peace of knowing that God is with us.

God uses many different avenues to provide us with hope. We see hope in God's good creation as seemingly dead plants bud and then spring forth in full bloom. We find hope when we read God's Word, for there we see the unmistakable evidence of God's continuing interest in humanity. The record clearly shows that God does care and will intervene for our sakes. The biblical writers not only report what God has done but show us by their example how to cry unto God when we need a loving touch. We also find hope in the life, teachings, and death of Jesus. Through his glorious resurrection, we enter into the hope of eternal life. The community of faith is another source of hope. Church members support us in difficult circumstances, just as we comfort them. Although it has been said that the church is always just one generation away from extinction, it has survived for two thousand years because its members have continued to tell the good news. The success of the past, despite sins and setbacks, gives us hope for the future of the church.

When we experience hope, we begin to believe that there is a future for us. That future may not look like the past. We may in fact be missing someone we love, or a place that is important to us, or something we no longer have the skill to do, but we can go forward, starting over if necessary. Yet, we do not move ahead alone. God is with us, and that knowledge makes all the difference in our lives. As the anonymous author of the familiar poem "Footprints" claims, God has carried us through the places where we see only one set of footprints in the sand. God walks with us in good times and carries us when we are so overwhelmed with grief or overburdened with problems that we cannot move under our own steam. Those footprints do continue to move forward. Like the exiles who one day left Babylon and walked toward Judah, we too can know that God will never fail to be with us on our journey. We may not be able to describe the shape of the future, but we know that our divine tour guide will always be at our side, even as we venture into eternity. That good news gives us hope beyond measure.

SHARING THE SCRIPTURE

PREPARING TO TEACH

Preparing Our Hearts

Think about a time when you felt that God had abandoned you. What caused you to feel that way? What steps did you take to try to "attract God's attention"? How did God respond to your plea?

If you currently are experiencing anguish or grief over a situation in your life, try writing your own lament in your spiritual journal. Your work does not have to follow any special literary form, but it should come from the heart. Tell God your troubles and implore God to remember and restore you.

Preparing Our Minds

Lamentations is a short book, consisting of only five poems. Try to read the entire book several times during the course of the week. Look especially at chapter 5:1-10 and 19-22. Try to put yourself in the place of the exiles as you read and experience the anguish they felt. Think about any experiences you have had that would help you to better understand how the exiles were feeling.

You may also want to read Psalm 80, Psalm 85, and Jeremiah 31:18, all of which speak of restoration.

Preparing Our Learning Space

Have on hand:
- several Bibles for students
- newsprint and marker or chalkboard and chalk
- paper and pencils
- optional hymnal that includes Psalm 85

as a responsive reading (See *The United Methodist Hymnal*, page 806.)

LEADING THE CLASS

(1) Introduction

To open the session, encourage class members to think of a time when they were experiencing such pain or difficulty that they thought God had forgotten or abandoned them. Help them to experience how they felt by directing the class to do one of the following activities.

(1) Ask each person to speak with a partner regarding the painful experience and how they felt about God at the time. What did they do to try to get God's attention, or did they turn aside, believing that God had abandoned them?

(2) Distribute paper and pencils. Ask students to write private letters to God detailing a difficult situation in which they felt that God had forgotten them. Have them tell God how they were feeling about the situation and about their relationship with God. Ask them to cry out to God for help in whatever way seems appropriate within their letter.

(3) Use the following guided imagery as a means to helping individuals remember a painful experience. Remember to pause for about ten seconds when indicated.

Sit back and relax. Take a deep breath. Remember a time when you felt that you were alone, utterly alone. (pause) R

R Picture the place where you experienced this aloneness. Perhaps you were standing next to the casket of a loved one. Maybe you were clutching a pink slip at your office. Possibly you were surveying the scene of your home that had been destroyed by fire or natural disaster. (pause)

Remember how you wanted to respond to this situation. Perhaps you felt like crying or screaming or praying. (pause) Then recall what, if anything, you might have said to God. Maybe you offered thanksgiving that no one was hurt. Or perhaps you asked, "Why me?" Or possibly you told God you were so angry that you would never again worship or come to church. (pause)

Remember how God responded to you. Perhaps you heard a still, small voice within. Possibly someone spoke a word that you knew was from God. Think about whatever happened that let you know that God had remembered you and give thanks. (pause)

Open your eyes whenever you are ready.

Rather than ask class members to discuss their private concerns with the entire group, you may want to read or retell the information in the Focusing on the Main Question portion of the lesson. Be sure to lift up today's main question: *Will God ever remember and restore us?*

(2) Remember Us, O God

You may want to use the Understanding the Scripture portion to provide general information to the class about the book of Lamentations. Then, choose a volunteer to read aloud Lamentations 5:1-10 as expressively as possible.

As the class considers these verses, ask the following questions. Fill in gaps from the "Remember Us, O God" segment of Interpreting the Scripture.

? **(1) What problems do the people, through** the writer of Lamentations, bring before God? ?

(2) On what grounds do you believe that the writer feels confident about bringing these concerns to God?

(3) Restore Us, O God

If possible, ask class members to read aloud Lamentations 5:19-22 in unison. These verses constitute a plea for restoration. Ask:

(1) Why must the writer plead to God for ? **restoration? (The people have sinned and cannot restore themselves. See "Restore Us, O God" under the Interpreting the Scripture portion.)**

(2) What does the writer's willingness to plead say about his understanding of the nature of God?

(3) The writer adds a caveat, an escape clause for God: "unless you have utterly rejected us, and are angry with us beyond measure." Do you think the writer believes that God has utterly rejected the people? Defend your answer.

Help the class to put this plea for restoration in a modern context. Discuss the following questions either with the total group or in small teams:

(1) What reasons would the contemporary ? **church have for longing to be restored? In other words, how have we sinned so as to be in need of restoration?**

(2) In what ways do you see God bringing about restoration?

(3) What changes do we as a church need to make in order for full restoration to occur?

If you have a hymnal available that includes responsive readings from the Psalms, you may wish to read Psalm 85.

(4) Grieving Our Losses

Remind the group that the people of Judah have suffered numerous losses: loved ones were killed; their land was taken from them; their temple was burned; their way of life was shattered. Use newsprint and a marker to record their answers to these questions:

? (1) **What kinds of losses have you or people you know suffered?**
(2) **How did such losses change your life?**

Then discuss how we go about grieving our losses. Ask:

(3) **What are some of the emotions you feel during the crisis of loss?**
(4) **What are some of the ways in which you experience God's presence in the midst of loss or grief?**
(5) **God is always with us, but sometimes we cannot feel God's presence. Have you or someone you know ever turned away from God in a difficult situation because you could not experience God's presence? What happened?**

If the class enjoys hands-on activities, distribute paper and pencils. Ask members to either write their own lament about losses they are grieving or rewrite Lamentations 5 in their own words. Be sure to have them include features of their current life they would miss if they were forced to live elsewhere as an exile.

(5) Seeking Hope in the Midst of Grief

Discuss the following questions with the group. Use information from "Seeking Hope in the Midst of Grief" under Interpreting the Scripture to augment the discussion.

? (1) **Why, as a Christian, are you hopeful? What gives you this hope?**
(2) **What Bible passages do you turn to for hope?**

(3) **What hymns are favorites of yours when you need to hear a word of hope?** ?

Invite several volunteers to share a word of witness about situations in which they found hope in the midst of grief. You may need to set a time limit so as to allow maximum participation. If the class is large, divide it into teams.

HELPING CLASS MEMBERS ACT

Invite each class member to remember someone in the church or community who has recently experienced the death of a loved one or some other serious loss. Suggest that they do something tangible, such as sending a card, preparing a meal, or providing transportation for errands, as a means of demonstrating to the grieving individual that he or she is not alone.

If a large-scale tragedy, such as a deadly hurricane, has recently occurred, encourage class members to do whatever they can to aid the victims. The group may be able to take an offering, collect food or clothing, send a work crew to rebuild, or offer temporary shelter as a means of demonstrating God's love and concern for them.

Suggest that class members recall a time in their own lives when they sustained a serious loss. Have them meditate and perhaps write a spiritual journal entry regarding this time of anguish. Ask them to consider questions such as: What was the significance of this loss to me? How did I cope? How was my life different? How was God present with me?

PLANNING FOR NEXT SUNDAY

Our quarter will end next Sunday with a lesson entitled, "Finding Hope Beyond Despair." To prepare for the lesson, encourage class members to read Ezekiel 37, paying particular attention to verses 1-12 and 14. The familiar story of the valley of the dry bones will enable us to examine the possibility of finding hope in a situation that seems totally hopeless.

FINDING HOPE BEYOND DESPAIR

NOVEMBER 24

PREVIEWING THE LESSON

Lesson Scripture: Ezekiel 37:1-12, 14
Background Scripture: Ezekiel 37
Key Verse: Ezekiel 37:14

Focus of the Lesson:
the hope of God's promise that the captives would return home and renew their relationship with God, as symbolized in Ezekiel's vision by new life in the valley of dry bones

Main Question of the Lesson:
How can the community of faith be infused with new life?

This lesson will enable adult learners to:
(1) study God's prophecy through Ezekiel that the dry bones of the house of Israel will live again.
(2) examine their own need for spiritual renewal, both individually and as a church.
(3) respond by renewing their commitment to God.

Today's lesson may be outlined as follows:
(1) Introduction
(2) The Valley of Dry Bones
(3) These Bones Shall Live Again
(4) Hope for the Future
(5) Revitalizing the Community of Faith

FOCUSING ON THE MAIN QUESTION

"It's too late. There's nothing that can be done now. Even God can't fix this problem." How often we limit the power of God by foreclosing on options! We may profess that God can do anything, but in the secret places of our hearts, we may not truly believe that God can create a new opportunity or bring new life when the door seems so firmly shut. Yet, hope can and does exist in all situations. God is able to do far more than we dare to think or ask.

Ezekiel knew that. That's why when God showed him a vision of a valley of dry bones and asked the prophet if those bones could live again, Ezekiel responded by saying, "O Lord GOD, you know" (Ezekiel 37:3). In other words, Ezekiel did not judge the final outcome by the outward appearance. He trusted God to act in surprising, miraculous ways. In contrast, most of us would have likely said, "You've got to be kidding. Not only are the people dead but the flesh is gone and the skeletons are dismembered. There's no way that life could ever reenter these bones strewn across this field."

Although we would have based our assessment on objective evidence, we would have been totally wrong. Our vision would have been that of death. God, however, looked beyond this hopeless situation and envisioned new life. The prophet Ezekiel, though not completely sure what might happen, was willing to be open to new possibilities because he believed in the power of God to bring about hope and renewal.

Through the power of the spirit that God sent to breathe into the lifeless bones, new life emerged. The separate bones were reunited to form individuals. The individuals were raised up on their feet as the whole community of faith. They were alive, not just as individuals but as the whole people of God. Moreover, God promised the community that they would return to their own homeland—another future that seemed too incredible to contemplate. God graciously gives second chances, even when the entire community of faith turns away from God. As we study today's lesson we will ask: *How can the community of faith be infused with new life?*

READING THE SCRIPTURE

NRSV
Ezekiel 37:1-12, 14

1 The hand of the LORD came upon me, and he brought me out by the spirit of the LORD and set me down in the middle of a valley; it was full of bones. ²He led me all around them; there were very many lying in the valley, and they were very dry. ³He said to me, "Mortal, can these bones live?" I answered, "O Lord GOD, you know." ⁴Then he said to me, "Prophesy to these bones, and say to them: O dry bones, hear the word of the LORD. ⁵Thus says the Lord GOD to these bones: I will cause breath to enter you, and you shall live. ⁶I will lay sinews on you, and will cause flesh to come upon you, and cover you with skin, and put breath in you, and you shall live; and you shall know that I am the LORD."

7 So I prophesied as I had been commanded; and as I prophesied, suddenly there was a noise, a rattling, and the bones came together, bone to its bone. ⁸I looked, and there were sinews on them, and flesh had come upon them, and skin had covered them; but there was no breath in

NIV
Ezekiel 37:1-12, 14

1 The hand of the LORD was upon me, and he brought me out by the Spirit of the LORD and set me in the middle of a valley; it was full of bones. ²He led me back and forth among them, and I saw a great many bones on the floor of the valley, bones that were very dry. ³He asked me, "Son of man, can these bones live?"

I said, "O Sovereign LORD, you alone know."

⁴Then he said to me, "Prophesy to these bones and say to them, 'Dry bones, hear the word of the LORD! ⁵This is what the Sovereign LORD says to these bones: I will make breath enter you, and you will come to life. ⁶I will attach tendons to you and make flesh come upon you and cover you with skin; I will put breath in you, and you will come to life. Then you will know that I am the LORD.' "

⁷So I prophesied as I was commanded. And as I was prophesying, there was a

them. ⁹Then he said to me, "Prophesy to the breath, prophesy, mortal, and say to the breath: Thus says the Lord GOD: Come from the four winds, O breath, and breathe upon these slain, that they may live." ¹⁰I prophesied as he commanded me, and the breath came into them, and they lived, and stood on their feet, a vast multitude.

11 Then he said to me, "Mortal, these bones are the whole house of Israel. They say, 'Our bones are dried up, and our hope is lost; we are cut off completely.' ¹²Therefore prophesy, and say to them, Thus says the Lord GOD: I am going to open your graves, and bring you up from your graves, O my people; and I will bring you back to the land of Israel. . . . ¹⁴I will put my spirit within you, and you shall live, and I will place you on your own soil; then you shall know that I, the LORD, have spoken and will act," says the LORD.

Key Verse

noise, a rattling sound, and the bones came together, bone to bone. ⁸I looked, and tendons and flesh appeared on them and skin covered them, but there was no breath in them.

⁹Then he said to me, "Prophesy to the breath; prophesy, son of man, and say to it, 'This is what the Sovereign LORD says: Come from the four winds, O breath, and breathe into these slain, that they may live.' " ¹⁰So I prophesied as he commanded me, and breath entered them; they came to life and stood up on their feet—a vast army.

¹¹Then he said to me: "Son of man, these bones are the whole house of Israel. They say, 'Our bones are dried up and our hope is gone; we are cut off.' ¹²Therefore prophesy and say to them: 'This is what the Sovereign LORD says: O my people, I am going to open your graves and bring you up from them; I will bring you back to the land of Israel. . . . ¹⁴I will put my Spirit in you and you will live, and I will settle you in your own land. Then you will know that I the LORD have spoken, and I have done it, declares the LORD.' "

Key Verse

UNDERSTANDING THE SCRIPTURE

Ezekiel 37:1-6. The prophet's vision of the valley of dry bones follows God's promise of renewal and repopulation of Israel as detailed in chapter 36. In 37:1, the "hand of the LORD" came upon Ezekiel, an image suggesting spirit possession (see 1:3; 3:22; 8:1) or a trancelike state. The spirit took the prophet (see 3:12, 14) to the middle of a valley or plain (see 3:22; 8:4). In this valley, Ezekiel sees a vision of dry bones, which represent God's people. These scattered, lifeless bones, have no apparent hope of ever reconnecting with one another, much less living again. Addressing the prophet as "mortal," God asks if these bones can live again. Ezekiel does not rule out any possibilities, even in the face

of death, but simply says that God knows. Then God tells him to prophesy to the bones. God's word is that these bones shall be completely revived; sinews and flesh will come upon them. Breath (in Hebrew, *ruah*, which means breath, spirit, or wind) will enter and enliven these bones that apparently had no more hope of life than God's people did of restoration.

Ezekiel 37:7-10. Ezekiel does as God commands, and the bones join together to form skeletons that are then enfleshed. As was the case in the Garden of Eden, the human form is lifeless until breath enters it. In response to the word of prophesy, the bones in fact do live again. However, before they are fully restored to life, these bones move through several phases: from disjointedness (37:1-6); to coming together to form skeletons (37:7); to being covered with flesh and sinews (37:8); to a time when the prophet calls upon the spirit or breath (37:9-10); to the announcement that God "will put my spirit" within the people (37:14). In verse 9, the bones are described as "these slain," indicating that the prophet is standing in the midst of a battlefield.

Ezekiel 37:11-14. In these verses God explains to Ezekiel what has happened. In verse 12, the imagery seems to shift from a battlefield strewn with bones to a cemetery filled with graves. This shift may indicate that verses 12b-13 were later additions to the text. Some early Christians interpreted these two verses in light of their belief in bodily resurrection, a belief that was widespread in first-century Judaism, though repudiated by the Sadducees. However, in Ezekiel's day this image likely would not have been understood as a message about individual resurrection. Instead, the people would have seen the community as a whole being revived. This vision closes with a promise from God that the bones will be reanimated by the breath of God and returned to their own land from the nations to which they have been dispersed. In sum, the vision of the dry bones illustrates the purpose of Ezekiel's prophetic ministry: He is to preach God's word to the people in order to bring new life to them

Ezekiel 37:15-28. This portion of Scripture records an oracle that Ezekiel is to proclaim to the people. The two sticks, Judah and Joseph (or Ephraim), represent the Southern Kingdoms and Northern of the divided monarchy that are both now in ruins. By the symbolic action of writing the name on each one and joining these two sticks to form a whole, the prophet tells the people that God will gather them from the places to which they have been scattered. At the time of Ezekiel's prophecy, the notion of the revitalization and reunification of the former Northern and Southern Kingdoms must have seemed absurd. The people of the North had been defeated, dispersed, and assimilated into other cultures about 150 years prior to Ezekiel's time. Yet, the prophet proclaims that God will recreate a unified nation of these people on their own soil. They will never again be divided. A king from David's line will reign over all of them. Unlike the usual model of kingship, Israel's king will be a servant, not a tyrant who rules by domination. The people will worship and obey God alone. God will reaffirm an everlasting covenant of peace with them. God's sanctuary will be among them. Since the temple was destroyed by the Babylonians, these verses are clearly planting seeds for the rebuilding of that central place of worship. God will bless the people and make them holy. God's action will not only reestablish the relationship between God's people and God but will also send a message to other nations about that relationship. Ezekiel's prophecy embodies four ancient concerns that were embedded in Israel's identity and self-understanding: land, ruler, covenant, and the temple.

INTERPRETING THE SCRIPTURE

The Valley of Dry Bones

In a vision, God shows the prophet Ezekiel a valley of dry, unburied bones that represents the "whole house of Israel" (37:11). God's people have been defeated, slaughtered, dismembered. We cannot imagine how the prophet, who saw this vision in the spirit, must have responded to this scene of dry, sun-bleached bones. Just as the community of faith had been dislocated, these bones were torn from one another and scattered at random, bone upon bone. Nothing in this valley of death would suggest any hope for life. All seems irreparably lost for the community of faith.

From a theological perspective, the people are in the valley not because a stronger military force defeated them, but because they had turned away from God. God allowed this punishment to come upon them. Their casual attitude toward the worship of other gods, their disregard for the covenant and commands of God, and their smug belief that God would never abandon the temple contributed to their downfall. Thus, even before their defeat by the Babylonians, the people were spiritually dead. Their own sinful actions had caused the life to be sapped out of their relationship with God. The community of faith had withered and died.

These Bones Shall Live Again

God had severely punished the people for their apostasy and hardness of heart, but God had not forsaken them. In the midst of this holocaust, God is present. God comes with the prophet not to gloat over their defeat but to proclaim a life-giving word. God asks the prophet if these bones can live. Ezekiel cannot say for certain that such a possibility exists. Yet, he trusts that even in the face of death God can bring about new life. Therefore, the prophet responds by saying to God, "you know" (37:3). Through Ezekiel, God will breathe new life into the dead, just as the breath of God entered and animated Adam in the Garden (Genesis 2:7).

As Ezekiel obeyed God and prophesied that breath might fill the lifeless bones, "a vast multitude" "stood on their feet" (37:10). This miraculous restoration gave the people a second chance for a meaningful relationship with God. As the image shifts from a battlefield to a cemetery in verse 12, we get a glimpse of what some early Christians understood to be a rudimentary doctrine of bodily resurrection of

the individual. Ezekiel probably did not intend to convey that idea. Instead, he was emphasizing the renewal of the entire community of faith.

The bones are reconnected and re-invigorated because God has spoken through the prophet. The word of God has the power to create (Genesis 1) and to restore. Nothing is impossible with God. Even those bones, which were clearly dead, can live again.

Hope for the Future

The prophet Ezekiel is in Babylon along with the other exiles. All hope seemed lost. The only future that the people could envision for themselves was bleak indeed. They were captives whose world had been irreparably shattered. They were a defeated people who would never have expected to return to their homeland, which now lay in ruins. Perhaps worst of all was the knowledge that they had brought their fate upon themselves. Their own disobedience and apostasy were at the root of God's punishment.

We can only imagine how Ezekiel's words would have been received. The people's situation would certainly not have changed. In fact, they would be captives in Babylon for decades before they were freed by King Cyrus of Persia to return home. Yet, there was hope. God had not utterly abandoned them. God was present. Moreover, God had the power to do the impossible: God could breathe new life into the dead community of faith. It would once again rise as a "vast multitude." This "vast army" (37:10, NIV) would then return to the land that God had given them. They would be a unified people once again. When they did return, they would know that God's word had enabled such a return to come about. God speaks and it is so.

Revitalizing the Community of Faith

If God were to show us the state of the modern church in North America, what would it look like? Would it be a vibrant multitude moving forth to witness on God's behalf, or a valley of lifeless bones? Perhaps the most accurate description is somewhere in between. In some portions of the field, a few vital souls exist, but much of the modern church valley, regardless of its denominational label, is filled with dead bones.

What evidence do we have that the church community seems so lifeless? Many people claim not to need the church, or to need it only on high days such as Christmas and Easter. They maintain that their spiritual quest is a personal journey, and in some respects they are, of course, correct. However, neither the house of Israel nor the early church perceived itself as a collection of individuals on their own private spiritual venture. Instead, God was in the midst of a community of faith. The individuals who comprised the church did not necessarily agree at all times, but they were a community. The whole was greater than the sum of its parts. The notion of a relationship with God outside the context of the community would have been strange indeed. The apostle Paul emphasized the unity of the church—one body composed of persons with many gifts—to help us understand that one part of the body could not simply opt out of its relationship. Yet, some church members believe they have an inalienable right to determine if and when they will participate in the life of the community. Without the strength and support that we give each other—just as blood flows from the heart to the various organs and limbs of the body—we can expect to be lifeless bones that are cast about individually with no apparent connection to the other bones.

Even when those bones seem to be knit together, the church may be like the skeletons covered with flesh but lacking the spirit that only God can give. These bodies may look real, just as a church without a dynamic ministry still appears to be a church because it has a congregation and a building. But it cannot go anywhere. It cannot stand as a vast multitude and move forward until the breath of God enlivens it. This type of church community is often struggling to survive. People work to keep the building intact, but very little is happening inside or, more important, outside its walls. There is a fear of growth and the different ideas that new people bring to a congregation. The seven last words of the church—"We've never done it that way before"—are often heard within such congregations.

However, when God puts the divine spirit within these moribund bodies, the church can truly live again. What would such a church do? Or, to phrase it another way, how would we know that this community of faith was truly alive?

The vital church focuses its attention on God. Worship, prayer, and praise are essential. The people seek God's will, whether they are in the middle of a worship service or a board meeting. The congregation acknowledges its identity as the people of God. They spend time educating all of their members (not just the children) so that people can grow to become spiritually mature disciples and stewards who are in fellowship with God and all humanity. The vital congregation reaches out to serve the world by supporting the work of missionaries who preach and teach the word, as well as persons who seek social justice so as to bring about the peace and justice that God wills for all creation. This lively church engages in evangelism—the telling of the good news—so that all persons might come to know and love the Messiah whom God sent into the world for our sakes. Members of the community give of their time, talent, financial resources, and service to enable the church to fulfill its mission. They do not expect the ordained clergy to attend to all the ministry, nor are they sitting on the sidelines criticizing those members who are working on behalf of the church. Instead, they accept their role as baptized ministers who bear responsibility for the church.

In short, Ezekiel's vision of the valley of dry bones can be our vision of the church as well. Even if we feel that our congregation or denomination or the Christian church in general is not the vital force that God intends it to be, we can take heart and affirm that God has the power to change the situation. For that to happen, however, the people of God must recognize God's sovereign will and truly want to live like the people God calls us to be. God can then act in amazing ways to restore, enliven, and unify us so that we may live with hope ourselves and share that hope with others.

SHARING THE SCRIPTURE

PREPARING TO TEACH

Preparing Our Hearts

Think of a time when you felt spiritually dead or somehow cut off from God. What caused you to feel that way? What happened that enabled you to reconnect with God? Do you see any similarities between your own experience and that of the people of Judah who were living as exiles in Babylon? You may want to record your observations in your spiritual journal.

Preparing Our Minds

Our lesson focuses on Ezekiel 37:1-12, 14, but you will want to read all of chapter 37 for background. You may also want to read additional commentary information on this chapter.

Preparing Our Learning Space

Have on hand:
- several Bibles for students
- newsprint and marker or chalkboard and chalk
- optional cassette player and recording of the spiritual "Dem Bones"
- optional paper and pencils

LEADING THE CLASS

(1) Introduction

If you can obtain a cassette of the spiritual "Dem Bones" and a cassette player, have this recording playing as the adults enter the classroom.

Begin the session by asking members if they or someone they know (but do not name) has ever been in difficult circumstances only to find that they suddenly have a second chance. If so, invite them to talk about the situation very briefly and tell how they felt when they moved from despair to hope. If this discussion seems too personal for your group, use community or national situations. For example, some persons may have experienced despair when Pearl Harbor was bombed or when the stock market took a big plunge or a national leader was assassinated.

Move to today's scripture lesson by pointing out how hopeless the situation in Babylon must have seemed to the exiles from Judah. They had no outward reason to hope for a better tomorrow. And yet, just as war has ended, and the stock market has continued to have ups and downs, and new leaders have taken over the reins of government, so, too, the exiles had reason for hope. God was taking the initiative to act on behalf of the people. God was willing to bring them out of the depths of despair and death into the light of a new day.

Conclude the introduction by lifting up today's main question: *How can the community of faith be infused with new life?*

(2) The Valley of Dry Bones

Read aloud Ezekiel 37:1-6. Ask the class members to listen as you read as if God were speaking directly to them. When you have finished, tell class members to pretend that they are Ezekiel and complete the following sentences. You may do this exercise orally or, if you prefer, distribute paper and pencils and encourage the adults to write their answers and then discuss them.

- When I saw this valley of dry bones, all I could think of was . . .
- When God asked me if I thought the bones could live again, I believed that . . .
- When God told me to prophesy to the bones, I . . .

(3) These Bones Shall Live Again

Now read Ezekiel 37:7-10. Tell class members to close their eyes and envision the scene in the valley as you read. As an alternative, all or some of the class members may be willing to act out the story by making simple motions, such as waving their arms or shaking a leg to symbolize the bones coming together. When you read verse 10, the participants are to stand.

Be sure to point out that the bones live not because of any action on their part or curative power on the prophet's part, but only because the word of God has been spoken. Use information under this section of scripture in Understanding the Scripture to help class members see how the bones moved from death to life.

(4) Hope for the Future

Now read aloud Ezekiel 37:11-12, 14.

Ask the class members to put themselves in the place of the exiles. Then ask:

?

(1) **How would you have felt had you heard this word of prophecy?**
(2) **What changes would you be willing to make in your own behavior to enable this prophecy to come true? (Remember that the people's unfaithfulness is what caused the punishment that resulted in exile.)**
(3) **What insight would you gain about God's concerns and plans for you?**

Suggest that group members meditate silently on this thought as it relates to them: As I hear these words of hope to the exiles who lived in despair, I begin to have hope about a specific situation or problem in my own life. I can trust that God will act.

R

(5) Revitalizing the Community of Faith

Now put today's scripture lesson in a modern context. Ask:

?

(1) **If God were to show us the state of the modern church in North America, would it be a vibrant multitude moving forth to witness on God's behalf, or a valley of lifeless bones, or something in between these two extremes?**
(2) **On what evidence do you base your assessment of God's people in today's church?**

Be sure to make clear that people of Judah, as well as the early Christian church, saw themselves as a community of faith, not as a collection of individuals who participated in the life of the church whenever they found it convenient.

Take a sheet of newsprint and divide it in half lengthwise. On the left, write, "evidence that the modern church is a valley of dry bones," and on the right ,"evidence that the modern church is a vibrant multitude." Lead the class in a brainstorming session. As an option for classes that like to work in small groups, divide into teams. Give each team a marker and at least one sheet of newsprint and tell the teams how to label the paper. Instruct each team to choose a recorder. Set a time when the groups will report back to the whole class. As an option for a class that prefers lecture, use information under "Revitalizing the Community of Faith" in the Interpreting the Scripture portion.

Once the class has discerned evidence about the modern church in general, help them to look specifically at their own congregation. Keep the discussion on a fair, objective level so that the pastor or other persons are not blamed for problems. Ask these questions:

(1) **How is our congregation like the vibrant multitude?**

(2) **How are we like the lifeless bones?**

(3) **What changes do we need to make to become a more vital church? (These changes may include adding some new programs or being friendlier to visitors, but they may also include focusing more intently upon God by joining on a regular basis for prayer meetings or covenanting to study together.)**

(4) **What signs of hope do you see for the future of our congregation?**

HELPING CLASS MEMBERS ACT

Challenge class members to consider their own level of spiritual vitality. Encourage them to think about their personal relationship with Jesus. Is Jesus a friend with whom they converse often, or someone they approach only when trouble is at hand? Do the students see themselves as connected to the "vast multitude" of the church, or are they like the individual dead bones? Suggest that as they take stock of their vitality, they make at least one concrete commitment to become more faithful in their relationship with God.

Encourage the class to consider the spiritual vitality of your congregation. Invite them to review the announcements in the church bulletin and newsletter in order to assess what is happening. Ask them to consider what else the church needs to be and do in order to become the spiritually lively place that God calls this congregation to be. Challenge each class member to take one action during the week that will help to strengthen the community of faith. That action may be something like attending a group or participating in a certain missions project. Or it may involve discerning action the church needs to take and letting church leaders know of their concern and suggestions for change.

Invite each class member to seek out at least one person who, for whatever reason, feels hopeless. Encourage the students to do whatever they can to show and announce the life-giving presence of God to give the person in need hope for the future.

PLANNING FOR NEXT SUNDAY

Next Sunday we will begin a new quarter entitled, "New Testament Personalities." In Unit 1 we will be studying key people in Jesus' life and ministry, as well as major figures in the early church. Ask class members to prepare for the first lesson on Elizabeth and Zechariah, the parents of John the Baptist, by reading Luke 1:5-25, 57-80. Class members may also want to consider setting up an Advent wreath in their own homes as a way of preparing for Jesus' birth.

SECOND QUARTER

DECEMBER 1, 1996—FEBRUARY 23, 1997

"New Testament Personalities" is the title of our winter study. This quarter is divided into three units, beginning with "Persons in Jesus' Nativity and Early Life." In the second unit we will meet individuals who are important in Jesus' ministry. The final unit looks at six other persons who play significant roles in the life of the New Testament church.

We begin the first unit on December 1 with two righteous figures, Elizabeth and Zechariah, who experienced God's joy as they were blessed late in life with a son, John. Their story is told in Luke 1:5-13, 24-25, 59-64. Next, we will consider the story of Jesus' mother, Mary, as found in Luke 1:26-42. She willingly surrendered to God's will when the angel Gabriel announced that she would bear God's son. The story of the shepherds, who were the first to receive the message that a Savior had been born, is recounted in Luke 2:8-20. We move to Matthew 2:1-12, 16 to read the story of the magi, their encounter with Herod, and their worship of the baby Jesus. This unit concludes on December 29 with a study of two devout persons, Simeon and Anna, who had believed that God would send the promised Messiah. Their response to him is recorded in Luke 2:22, 25-38.

Unit 2, "Persons in Jesus' Ministry," opens with a lesson from Mark 1:4-11, 14-15, and Luke 7:18-23 in which John bears witness to Jesus and baptizes him. On January 12, we meet the sisters Mary and Martha in Luke 10:38-42 and John 12:1-8. Their story helps us to understand the importance of choosing right priorities. Peter, the disciple who confessed Jesus as the Messiah, is the focus of our attention on January 19. His story is recounted in Matthew 4:18-20 and 16:13-23. The unit closes with a look at Judas Iscariot, the betrayer of Christ, whose actions are detailed in Matthew 26:14-16, 20-25, 47-50 and 27:1-5.

The final unit, "Persons in the New Testament Church," starts on February 2 with a lesson from Acts 4:32, 36-37; 9:26-27, and 11:22-30. Here we meet Barnabas, who was well known for the encouragement he gave to the early church. Our next lesson spotlights Stephen, the first Christian martyr, whose story is told in Acts 6:8-15 and 7:54-60. A husband and wife team, Aquila and Priscilla, who were strong supporters of Paul and ministers in their own right, are introduced to us in Acts 18:1-4, 18-19, 24-26, and Romans 16:3-5a. Our quarter ends on February 23 with selected passages from Acts, 1 Corinthians, Philippians, and 2 Timothy that show Timothy as a faithful companion of Paul and diligent worker in the early church.

As you prepare to teach this quarter, we would recommend that you use *The Devotional Companion to The International Lessons 1996–97* (available from Cokesbury) as a guide for class worship. In keeping with our emphasis on God's Word as the light for our way, you may also want to use the refrain from the song "Thy Word Is a Lamp" (*The United Methodist Hymnal,* page 601) as a regular part of your weekly devotions.

During the lessons for Advent, we suggest that you set up an Advent wreath in your worship area. You may want to make this wreath yourself, or borrow one from the church, or purchase a wreath for the class. Lighting the candles each week can be an important part of class members' preparation for the celebration of the birth of Jesus.

MEET OUR WRITER

DR. MARION L. SOARDS

Dr. Marion L. Soards, an ordained minister in the Presbyterian Church (U.S.A.), is Professor of New Testament Studies at Louisville Presbyterian Theological Seminary. He has been a Fellow of the National Conference of Christians and Jews, the National Endowment for the Humanities (twice), The Association of Theological Schools in the United States and Canada, The Catholic Biblical Association of America, and the Alexander von Humboldt-*Stiftung* (Germany). He is active in a number of scholarly societies and associations, including the Society of Biblical Literature, the Catholic Biblical Association of America, and the international society for New Testament studies, *Studiorum Novi Testamenti Societas*. Soards has published over forty articles in leading theological dictionaries and professional journals worldwide and is the author of eighteen books. Soards served for two years as Editorial Director of *The New Interpreter's Bible* project for The United Methodist Publishing House, Abingdon Press division; and he is on the editorial board for that set of commentaries. Dr. Soards is an associate editor for the *Journal of Biblical Literature*. He is a frequent lecturer at conferences and schools for pastors throughout the United States and a much sought after guest preacher.

EXPERIENCE GOD'S JOY

PREVIEWING THE LESSON

Lesson Scripture: Luke 1:5-13, 24-25, 59-64
Background Scripture: Luke 1:5-25, 57-80
Key Verse: Luke 1:6

Focus of the Lesson:
the joy that Elizabeth and Zechariah experienced as a result of their righteousness before God and the birth of a son in their old age

Main Questions of the Lesson:
In what ways did Elizabeth and Zechariah experience God's joy?
In what ways have we experienced God's gift of joy despite real disappointments?

This lesson will enable adult learners to:
(1) recognize that God gives joy to the righteous.
(2) experience the joy that Zechariah and Elizabeth felt concerning their son.
(3) share the good news of God's joy with others.

Today's lesson may be outlined as follows:
(1) Introduction
(2) Elizabeth and Zechariah Experience God's Joy
(3) Experiencing God's Joy in Our Own Lives

FOCUSING ON THE MAIN QUESTION

The announcement of the birth of John the Baptist by an angel and the account of the naming of the baby John tell us of the grace of God operating in the lives of the pious elderly couple, Zechariah and Elizabeth. Old and childless, the couple's deepest unspoken prayer was for a child. In the verses of this lesson Luke tells of God's grace and of the surprising ways that humans experience the powerful presence of God in their lives.

The sad experience of childlessness, when a child is truly desired, is but one illustration of the profound disappointments that persons experience in the course of their lives. What makes childlessness so poignant an example of many of our disappointments is that it epitomizes the inability of persons of faith to celebrate God's good gift of life by participating in God's creation of life through bringing children into the world.

While all people do not know the pain of an unfulfilled longing for a child, we all

---

face the awful grief of losing family members and others whom we love. Yet, even as we experience the disappointments of unrealized desires and sorrowful losses, through faith we believe in God, who raises the dead and brings joy in the midst of frustration and sadness. One example of this is a young couple who were devastated by the stillbirth of their child and the subsequent news that it would be impossible for them to have children in the future. After a period of grief, they poured their energies into working with young people in their local church. One involvement led to another, and eventually they began working with a group of parents who were concerned with the complexities of raising foster children. As time went by the couple themselves adopted three young children. The sadness of their earlier loss seemed more than offset by the joy and challenge of raising three little ones in the context of their family and in the life of their church.

As we study the story of Zechariah and Elizabeth and consider similar situations, we may ask today's main questions: *In what ways did Elizabeth and Zechariah experience God's joy? In what ways have we experienced God's gift of joy despite real disappointments?*

READING THE SCRIPTURE

NRSV
Luke 1:5-13

5 In the days of King Herod of Judea, there was a priest named Zechariah, who belonged to the priestly order of Abijah. His wife was a descendant of Aaron, and her name was Elizabeth. 6Both of them were righteous before God, living blamelessly according to all the commandments and regulations of the Lord. 7But they had no children, because Elizabeth was barren, and both were getting on in years.

8 Once when he was serving as priest before God and his section was on duty, 9he was chosen by lot, according to the custom of the priesthood, to enter the sanctuary of the Lord and offer incense. 10Now at the time of the incense offering, the whole assembly of the people was praying outside. 11Then there appeared to him an angel of the Lord, standing at the right side of the altar of incense. 12When Zechariah saw him, he was terrified; and fear overwhelmed him. 13But the angel said to him, "Do not be afraid, Zechariah, for your prayer has been heard. Your wife Elizabeth will bear you a son, and you will name him John.

NIV
Luke 1:5-13

5In the time of Herod king of Judea there was a priest named Zechariah, who belonged to the priestly division of Abijah; his wife Elizabeth was also a descendant of Aaron. 6Both of them were upright in the sight of God, observing all the Lord's commandments and regulations blamelessly. 7But they had no children, because Elizabeth was barren; and they were both well along in years.

8Once when Zechariah's division was on duty and he was serving as priest before God, 9he was chosen by lot, according to the custom of the priesthood, to go into the temple of the Lord and burn incense. 10And when the time for the burning of incense came, all the assembled worshipers were praying outside.

11Then an angel of the Lord appeared to him, standing at the right side of the altar of incense. 12When Zechariah saw him, he was startled and was gripped with fear. 13 But the angel said to him: "Do not be afraid, Zechariah; your prayer has been heard. Your wife Elizabeth will bear you a son, and you are to give him the name John.

Key
Verse

NRSV
Luke 1:24-25

24 After those days his wife Elizabeth conceived, and for five months she remained in seclusion. She said, 25"This is what the Lord has done for me when he looked favorably on me and took away the disgrace I have endured among my people."

NRSV
Luke 1:59-64

59 On the eighth day they came to circumcise the child, and they were going to name him Zechariah after his father. 60But his mother said, "No; he is to be called John." 61They said to her, "None of your relatives has this name." 62Then they began motioning to his father to find out what name he wanted to give him. 63He asked for a writing tablet and wrote, "His name is John." And all of them were amazed. 64Immediately his mouth was opened and his tongue freed, and he began to speak, praising God.

NIV
Luke 1:24-25

24After this his wife Elizabeth became pregnant and for five months remained in seclusion. 25"The Lord has done this for me," she said. "In these days he has shown his favor and taken away my disgrace among the people."

NIV
Luke 1:59-64

59On the eighth day they came to circumcise the child, and they were going to name him after his father Zechariah, 60but his mother spoke up and said, "No! He is to be called John."

61They said to her, "There is no one among your relatives who has that name."

62Then they made signs to his father, to find out what he would like to name the child. 63He asked for a writing tablet, and to everyone's astonishment he wrote, "His name is John." 64Immediately his mouth was opened and his tongue was loosed, and he began to speak, praising God.

UNDERSTANDING THE SCRIPTURE

The first two chapters of the Gospel according to Luke are often referred to as the "Infancy Narratives," the "Birth Account," or the "Birth-and-Childhood Stories" of Jesus. The material, however, is not primarily biographical; the focus of the narrative is broader than simply the birth of Jesus, and the story is thoroughly theological—although the Gospel articulates theology by telling the story of selected incidents that took place around the time of Jesus' birth. The verses for this week's lesson fall into two distinct parts: First, verses 5-25 recount the angelic promise of the birth of John the Baptist; second, verses 57-80 tell of events at the birth and naming of John. The major characters in the story are Zechariah and Elizabeth, the parents of John, though we should never forget the commanding presence of the angel Gabriel who tells and foretells the will and work of God in the world.

Luke 1:5-7. The political context and the religious atmosphere of the events are registered immediately in these lines through the mention of Herod the Great and the priestly lines of the families of Zechariah and Elizabeth. The ancient blend of politics and religion characterized the world into which John was born (as was Jesus) and the world in which he lived and died (as did Jesus). Above all, we are told that Zechariah and Elizabeth were "blameless" in their practices of ritual piety; yet, they were old and childless. In the ancient world, childlessness was thought of not only as a tragedy but also as a great social shame. It was even understood to be a sign of God's displeasure, although Luke makes it clear that this elderly couple was scrupulously pious. Tensions fill the air as the story begins.

Luke 1:8-13. There were twenty-four classes or lines of priests among the Jews. Twice each year for one week, one group was responsible for the maintenance of the temple observances. Nevertheless, because of the great number of priests, actual temple service was a rare privilege; and an even rarer assignment, perhaps coming not even once in a lifetime, was the opportunity to offer the incense to the Lord. At this special moment, as Zechariah was performing his sacred duties, he meets the angel Gabriel. Zechariah was in awe, and as Gabriel speaks, we learn that Zechariah himself had been praying to God—obviously for a child.

Luke 1:14-20. The news that his prayer was answered, however, proved too much for Zechariah to accept. Yet, Zechariah's hope was taken seriously by the Lord, for Gabriel foretold not only the birth of John, but also his special purpose and greatness before God. Zechariah's doubts were taken with equal seriousness, for he was rendered speechless until the time of John's birth and naming. God's will and work clearly defy the natural boundaries of existence in this world.

Luke 1:21-23. The report of the people's reaction to Zechariah's delay in the temple and his inability to speak upon coming out are strong confirmations of the reality of God's presence and work in the course of human life.

Luke 1:24-25. The story suddenly shifts to focus on Elizabeth's pregnancy. God's promise is fulfilled. We read that Elizabeth withdrew from the normal routines of living. The report of her activity is not a note about her psychological state, as the report of her words in verse 25 makes clear. Elizabeth's withdrawal focuses the full light of the account on the power and work of God, who blesses humanity despite our seemingly hopeless situations in life.

The lesson skips to a later moment in the story. The next verses we read bring us to the naming of John.

Luke 1:57-58. At the time of John's birth friends and family assemble to celebrate the joyful moment. The reaction of these people emphasizes that the mercy of the Lord is the cause for the celebration. God's goodness brings joy.

Luke 1:59-64. Jewish boys were routinely circumcised on the eighth day after their birth. Frequently boys were named for their fathers or other male relatives as a sign of respect and as a way of keeping the family's heritage alive. The assembly tried to name the baby for his father, and Elizabeth's determination to name the boy John caused a stir. Zechariah confirmed the name, and as he faithfully brought to realization God's will, his speech returned.

Luke 1:65-66. The crowd was already surprised by the naming, but now the miracle of Zechariah's speaking strikes fear—the fear of the Lord—in the hearts of the people, as all see plainly that God has great plans and purposes for the baby called John.

Luke 1:67-75. Zechariah was "filled with the Holy Spirit" and he prophesied. At first, he blessed God as he looked to the present signs of God's salvation that were breaking forth into the world. The words of praise celebrate God's liberating grace that means freedom to serve God as we live day by day.

Luke 1:76-79. In turn, Zechariah focuses on John, foretelling his greatness as a prophet who prepares the way of the Lord. The Lord's way supersedes John's greatness, for it is the path of salvation that means knowing God's forgiveness of sins as we experience God's mercy guiding us as we live according to God's will.

Luke 1:80. The story ends with a statement similar to 1 Samuel 2:26. John's early life anticipates the way of life to which he will later call others—a life in the power and presence of God.

INTERPRETING THE SCRIPTURE

Lifelong Piety

Throughout the Scripture we read about the grace of God at work in the lives of pious couples who experience the disappointment of childlessness. Abraham and Sarah lived into old age before they were blessed by God with the birth of Isaac. Hannah and Elkanah lived faithful year after year, and still Hannah was deeply distressed until God granted her and her husband their son, Samuel. In Luke's story we read of a devout couple, Zechariah and Elizabeth, who wanted children but were old and childless before the birth of John. God's grace ultimately brought joy to the lives of these godly people, granting them the realization of their deepest desires despite the seeming hopelessness of their situations.

Our lesson informs us that Zechariah and Elizabeth were old and "righteous before God." The deep irony in the story is that despite the couple's piety, their heartfelt longing for a child had gone unfulfilled. Yet, note that although the desire for a child had gone without realization, Zechariah and Elizabeth had remained faithful to God.

How often do we create conditions for our own faith that either motivate or sour our piety? Too often, positive experiences produce momentary bursts of gratitude and devotion, while unfulfilled hopes and expectations leave us unable to relate to God with enthusiasm. Answered prayers suggest God cares, whereas when our prayers go unanswered we may take it to mean that God doesn't care or is unable to do anything about our concerns. A sheer theology of experience would have told Zechariah and Elizabeth that (a)there was something wrong with their piety, so they were without a basis for hope, or (b) God was indifferent to their plight or unwilling or unable to do anything for them or both.

But Zechariah and Elizabeth lived in relation to God in a way that went beyond casting God as the Great Wish-Fulfiller. They had the blessings of faithfulness and service, even though their hope for a child had gone unfulfilled. Without the joy of a child in their home, the old couple had nevertheless known the joy of a right relation to God! Zechariah and Elizabeth are models for us as we seek to know God, despite the disappointments of life.

Humility and the Experience of Grace

The actions and words of both Zechariah and Elizabeth show them to be humble before God. When Gabriel appears in the temple, Zechariah displays fear (of the Lord?); he does not puff up with pride at his good fortune. When Elizabeth becomes pregnant, she withdraws in humble joy; she does not put herself on parade to make a show of her blessedness. When Zechariah speaks to Gabriel, he finds the news from God almost too good to be true. He had prayed, but could God now answer his prayer in his and Elizabeth's old age? Zechariah does not assume that his piety had earned him a just reward. In turn, when Elizabeth declares her joy that God has removed her shame, she understands God's goodness as God's own willful act, not as a payment for her life of faithfulness. The couple's humility before God allowed them to see God's grace for what it was, love poured forth freely, amazingly, blessing them beyond reason. As we look at Zechariah and Elizabeth in their experience of grace, we may find our own eyes opened anew to the marvelous compassion of God's grace at work in our lives and in the world around us. Genuine piety fosters humility before God. Such humility is not a passive disposition toward life and its conditions; rather, it is a reverence for God that motivates truly righteous living.

Doubts Are Natural

Although in faith we embrace the conviction that God does have plans and purposes, we are often like Zechariah in that we still experience doubts despite our belief. We may not stand face-to-face with an angel, but we often perceive the will of God for our lives as we face various situations; yet, we still have doubts. We see the deep needs of ourselves and others, both physical and spiritual, and we know that God cares for us and would have us care for one another, to share with those around us the gospel of God's grace given in Jesus Christ. Nevertheless, we wonder whether our efforts will really make a difference, so we hesitate rather than act with confidence. Also like Zechariah we find the truth of our convictions as we faithfully carry out the will and work of God. Zechariah's doubts brought the loss of his speech, but his naming John in accordance with the words of the angel liberated his tongue to sing God's praises with a new courage and clarity that made him the very prophet of God's grace. The reality of our faith manifests itself in our obedience to God's revealed will.

Gratitude to God for Grace

Luke presents Elizabeth and Zechariah as models of gratitude. Elizabeth's statement in verse 25 recognizes God's goodness, declaring that God takes initiative in relation to the difficulties of human life and that God's grace brings liberation from oppression. Elizabeth celebrates God's liberating acts, experiencing in her own physical self the gift of God's goodness. Later, Zechariah uses the gift of his returned speech to bless God and to declare the meaning of God's work. We read that Zechariah was filled with the Holy Spirit (as Elizabeth had been when Mary visited her; see verses 41-45) and that his eyes were opened to the spiritual reality of God's work in the world. Zechariah also speaks of God's liberating love that comes to God's people in order to redeem, save, and deliver them from oppression so that they might freely serve God. The language of Zechariah's prophetic speech is the poetry of theological reflection, and while it is possible to hear this seemingly holy talk and let it do little more than soothe the soul, we should see that our liberating God is the one who keeps promises and directs lives according to God's own purposes for peace. Zechariah celebrates God's faithfulness and that means liberation that frees us for service in order to accomplish God's will. God's aims are real, and our divinely wrought freedom comes for the purpose of God's peace. Here, as in all the Scripture, peace is far more than the absence of strife among persons—although that condition would be one characteristic of God's peace. Indeed, peace is the wholeness of life that God intends for the world and, that God is at work pursuing, even by bringing us humans into the achievement of God's will.

Salvation

The verses of our lesson make clear that salvation can be comprehended and described. First, salvation means the forgiveness of sins. Our misdeeds are pardoned and we are freed from bondage to the forces of evil so that we might have a right, energizing relationship with God. Second, by the mercy of God we are enlightened in our experience of salvation. We are not simply given good information in the place of bad; rather, we know the reality of God's work so that we live with certainty despite the many ambiguities of life. Third, the transformed quality of life and the liberating experience of God's peace come as the Spirit lives and works among us. God's presence and power grasp our lives and give us direction that we may be faithful to the one who in all things is faithful and merciful to us. The benefits of God's salvation come to us as we focus on God, not merely on the good things that God has done and is doing for us, and, in turn, as we live with an awareness of and gratitude for God as our loving Lord.

SHARING THE SCRIPTURE

PREPARING TO TEACH

Preparing Our Hearts

During this season of Advent, consider the ways in which you experience God's joy. Give thanks for the relationship you have with God that enables you to know the joy of God's presence in your life. If you keep a spiritual journal, write about an experience that has brought you joy.

Preparing Our Minds

As you read the background scripture and focus especially on the verses of the lesson scripture, imagine yourself in the place of Zechariah and Elizabeth. Consider how you would feel about being childless and how the angel Gabriel's news transforms your life.

As you read the Understanding the Scripture and Interpreting the Scripture portions, be alert for ways in which God's joy comes unexpectedly into the lives of those whom God loves. Note, as our key verse states, that the son of promise came because Elizabeth and Zechariah were righteous before God.

A word of caution as you make your preparations: Ancient peoples understood childlessness to be a sign of God's displeasure with the woman, who in the Bible is described as barren. Modern medicine has helped us to understand that either the male or the female may have medical conditions that preclude childbearing, but we are not to understand such situations as a sign of judgment from God. Moreover, some modern couples consciously choose not to have children. Therefore, as you deal with this lesson, be sensitive to students in the class who, for whatever reason, do not have children.

This quarter's lessons focus on individuals and groups of people who play an important role in the New Testament. Note that each week we will look at that character's experience with God. Then we will consider how his or her experience may relate to—and be a model for—our own experience. Since it is difficult to limit class interaction about persons to brief passages of scripture, we will read the scripture lesson in its entirety at the beginning, rather than dividing it into smaller segments.

Preparing Our Learning Space

If your class meets in a room of its own, consider setting up an Advent wreath that you can light as a reminder of Jesus' coming. If possible, set the wreath on a blue or purple cloth. Plan to use the wreath during your worship time. Refer to the *Devotional Companion* for suggestions on worship.

If possible, you may want to set up a cassette recorder and play Advent music, such as "O Come, O Come, Emmanuel," to set the mood of anticipation.

You may want to write the questions for the quiet meditation or journal exercise under "Experiencing God's Joy in Our Own Lives" on newsprint or a chalkboard prior to class.

Be sure to have on hand:
- several Bibles for students
- newsprint and marker or chalkboard and chalk

✔ optional paper and pencils
✔ optional Advent wreath and matches; *Devotional Companion*
✔ optional cassette recorder and music

LEADING THE CLASS

(1) Introduction

Introduce the main questions by inviting class members to answer the following questions. You may wish to discuss the answers with the total group, or ask each person to share his or her comments with a partner.

[?] **(1) In what circumstances have you experienced real disappointment?**
(2) How did God bring joy to you?

If the class prefers not to enter into discussion, read or retell the example of the couple who lost a child and later found joy in working with other children, as found under Focusing on the Main Question.

Note that today's lesson will focus on the joy that Elizabeth and Zechariah experienced as a result of their righteousness before God and the birth of a son in their old age. Read or write today's main questions: *In what ways did Elizabeth and Zechariah experience God's joy? In what ways have we experienced God's gift of joy despite real disappointments?*

(2) Elizabeth and Zechariah Experience God's Joy

Choose volunteers to read the parts of the narrator, angel, and Elizabeth. Have them read Luke 1:5-13, 24-25, and 59-64.

Then ask half of the class to consider the story from Zechariah's perspective. Ask the other half to consider it from Elizabeth's perspective. Give each team newsprint and a marker to record their thoughts. Post the questions below on newsprint or a chalkboard where everyone can see them. Have the teams answer the questions from the perspective of their assigned character. Then have the teams share their answers for a total class discussion. Fill in gaps as needed from the Understanding the Scripture and Interpreting the Scripture portions of the lesson. As an alternative, work together rather than in two teams.

• How would other persons have judged Zechariah and Elizabeth's relationship with God if all that was known about this couple was that they were childless? (See Luke 1:5-7 in the Understanding the Scripture portion.)
• Despite their disappointment about being childless when they truly desired children, how did Elizabeth and Zechariah relate to God?
• How did Zechariah respond to the angel's announcement?
• How did Elizabeth respond when she realized she was pregnant?
• What does the couple's willingness to name their son in a non-customary way (that is, by not selecting a family name) say about their relationship to God?

Close this segment by asking:
(1) What lessons can we learn from Zechariah and Elizabeth regarding how we as Christians can experience and celebrate God's joy, even in the midst of disappointment? [?]

(3) Experiencing God's Joy in Our Own Lives

Read or retell the section entitled "Life-long Piety" under Interpreting the Scripture. Ask the class:
(1) In what ways does our relationship with God depend upon a theology of experience? In other words, do we find excitement in that relationship when God seems to be doing what we want, but feel distant when God seems to be unwilling or unable to answer our prayers? Or do we, like Zechariah and Elizabeth, relate faithfully to God no matter what God is—or apparently is not—doing in our lives? Give an example to support your position. [?]

Make the point that Zechariah and

Elizabeth do not assume that the gift of their son was a reward for their piety. Instead, "the couple's humility before God allowed them to see God's grace for what it was, love poured forth freely, amazingly, blessing them beyond reason" (see "Humility and the Experience of Grace" under Interpreting the Scripture). Then ask the class to meditate on the following ideas that you have written on newsprint or a chalkboard. You may want to provide paper and pencils for students who prefer to write their thoughts as a spiritual journal exercise. Provide a few minutes of silence. If time permits, a few volunteers may be willing to share their own story.

• Recall an incident in which you thought God was rewarding you for "good behavior." What had you done?
• How had God responded?
• What was your reaction to God's response?
• As you look back on that incident now, what evidence do you see that the event was the result of God's grace, rather than a reward for your behavior?
• How might the insight about a prior event affect your relationship with God in the future?

Reread Luke 1:25 and this sentence from Interpreting the Scripture under "Gratitude to God for Grace": "Elizabeth's statement in verse 25 recognizes God's goodness, declaring that God takes initiative in relation to the difficulties of human life and that God's grace brings liberation from oppression." Suggest that students discuss with a partner or team how they experience and express gratitude for God's grace.

Close this portion of the lesson by inviting class members who feel comfortable in doing so to utter a sentence prayer of thanksgiving for God's grace. The prayer may be as simple as: Gracious God, I give you thanks for . . .

HELPING CLASS MEMBERS ACT

Challenge class members to think of a time when they were disappointed, perhaps believing that God had not answered their prayers. Then have them recall how such a prayer seemed to be answered unexpectedly. Invite students to write about their experience in their spiritual journal, giving thanks to God for the joy they experienced.

Suggest that each class member identify at least one person he or she knows who is in an unexpected or unfamiliar situation. Perhaps that person recently lost a spouse, or was diagnosed with a serious illness, or experienced a life crisis. Ask the class member to talk with the person and offer words of hope.

Invite class members to tell a family member or friend something that God has done to make them joyful. This event need not be as life-changing as the angel's announcement to Zechariah, but it should be something that brought joy and perhaps drew the class member closer to God.

PLANNING FOR NEXT SUNDAY

Direct the class members to read Luke 1:26-56, paying particular attention to verses 26-42. Ask them to consider how Mary surrenders to God's will. Also ask each person to recall a time when he or she surrendered to God's will. What were the circumstances? How did this surrender bring about transformation?

SURRENDER TO GOD'S WILL

PREVIEWING THE LESSON

Lesson Scripture: Luke 1:26-42
Background Scripture: Luke 1:26-56
Key Verse: Luke 1:38

Focus of the Lesson:
Mary's obedient surrender to God's will as announced to her by the angel

Main Question of the Lesson:
What does it mean to surrender to God's will?

This lesson will enable adult learners to:
(1) become familiar with Mary's joyful acceptance of God's will for her life.
(2) adopt an attitude of joyful surrender in their own lives.
(3) respond by discerning an action or attitude God expects and then following through on it.

Today's lesson may be outlined as follows:
(1) Introduction
(2) Mary Surrenders to God's Will
(3) Surrendering to God's Will in Our Own Lives

FOCUSING ON THE MAIN QUESTION

The story of Gabriel's visit to Mary registers an awkward truth: Finding favor with God can be puzzling, even disturbing, because throughout history God's personal call on human lives has always been a call to faithful service. As Luke puts it in this passage, Mary was "much perplexed by [Gabriel's] words" that called her "favored one" and told her "the Lord is with you." Moreover, as the angel offered an explanation, seemingly as a word of comfort, the heaven-sent message became all the more incomprehensible: Mary, a virgin, was to have a child, and not just any child, but the Son of the Most High. No wonder Mary was perplexed!

Nevertheless, she listened; and although the message of the angel was far from ordinary, Mary trusted in God's will and work She responded, "Here am I, the servant of the Lord; let it be with me according to your word." Although she could not have fully understood the mysterious science of divinely initiated virginal conception, Mary moved on faith to embrace the unknown, the incomprehensible, because of her clear unswerving confidence in God.

God's grace poured out on humanity *always* means God's purposeful choice that brings a commission to service as an intricate part of divine favor. We all may wonder at God's choice and call in our lives; yet, Mary shows us that we can accept God's will without fear. The appropriate response to God's "yes" to us is our own faithful, trusting "yes" to God's will.

Mary's experience is certainly unique, but all humans who are confronted by God's grace are challenged to surrender to God's will in some way. Consider the story of a young businesswoman in New York City. She had risen to the top of her profession, heading a major corporation at an unusually young age. She was a regular churchgoer, and her involvement in the life of a local congregation brought an unexpected development to her life. Through a series of conversations with her pastor, the young woman heard a clear call (as if beckoned by an angel) to resign her corporate position and devote her highly cultivated administrative skills to directing the operations of a small, hard-pressed Christian charity organization. She did not anticipate this call from God, and at first she could not believe it was true. But when she recognized God's will, the young woman devoted herself to God's work with enthusiasm. As we study today's lesson, we may ask with Mary and this corporate executive: *What does it mean to surrender to God's will?*

READING THE SCRIPTURE

NRSV
Luke 1:26-42

26 In the sixth month the angel Gabriel was sent by God to a town in Galilee called Nazareth, 27to a virgin engaged to a man whose name was Joseph, of the house of David. The virgin's name was Mary. 28And he came to her and said, "Greetings, favored one! The Lord is with you." 29But she was much perplexed by his words and pondered what sort of greeting this might be. 30The angel said to her, "Do not be afraid, Mary, for you have found favor with God. 31And now, you will conceive in your womb and bear a son, and you will name him Jesus. 32He will be great, and will be called the Son of the Most High, and the Lord God will give to him the throne of his ancestor David. 33He will reign over the house of Jacob forever, and of his kingdom there will be no end." 34Mary said to the angel, "How can this be, since I am a virgin?" 35The angel said to her, "The Holy Spirit will come upon you, and the power of the Most High will overshadow you; therefore the child to be born will be holy; he will be called Son of God. 36And now, your relative Elizabeth in her old age has also con-

NIV
Luke 1:26-42

26In the sixth month, God sent the angel Gabriel to Nazareth, a town in Galilee, 27to a virgin pledged to be married to a man named Joseph, a descendant of David. The virgin's name was Mary. 28The angel went to her and said, "Greetings, you who are highly favored! The Lord is with you."

29Mary was greatly troubled at his words and wondered what kind of greeting this might be. 30But the angel said to her, "Do not be afraid, Mary, you have found favor with God. 31You will be with child and give birth to a son, and you are to give him the name Jesus. 32He will be great and will be called the Son of the Most High. The Lord God will give him the throne of his father David, 33and he will reign over the house of Jacob forever; his kingdom will never end."

34"How will this be," Mary asked the angel, "since I am a virgin?"

35The angel answered, "The Holy Spirit will come upon you, and the power of the Most High will overshadow you. So the holy one to be born will be called the Son of God. 36Even Elizabeth your relative is going

---

ceived a son; and this is the sixth month for her who was said to be barren. [37]For nothing will be impossible with God." [38]Then Mary said, "Here am I, the servant of the Lord; let it be with me according to your word." Then the angel departed from her.

39 In those days Mary set out and went with haste to a Judean town in the hill country, [40]where she entered the house of Zechariah and greeted Elizabeth. [41]When Elizabeth heard Mary's greeting, the child leaped in her womb. And Elizabeth was filled with the Holy Spirit [42]and exclaimed with a loud cry, "Blessed are you among women, and blessed is the fruit of your womb."

to have a child in her old age, and she who was said to be barren is in her sixth month. [37]For nothing is impossible with God."

[38]"I am the Lord's servant," Mary answered. "May it be to me as you have said." Then the angel left her.

[39]At that time Mary got ready and hurried to a town in the hill country of Judea, [40]where she entered Zechariah's home and greeted Elizabeth. [41]When Elizabeth heard Mary's greeting, the baby leaped in her womb, and Elizabeth was filled with the Holy Spirit. [42] In a loud voice she exclaimed: "Blessed are you among women, and blessed is the child you will bear!"

Key Verse

UNDERSTANDING THE SCRIPTURE

The story of Gabriel's visit to Mary follows a fivefold literary pattern established in the Old Testament for the annunciation of salvific figures (i.e., those who offer salvation): the appearance of the angel, a fearful reaction by the one visited, the angel's delivery of a message, the registering of an objection by the recipient of the visitation, and the offering of a divinely determined sign as a confirmation of the truth of the message. Remarkably, in the account of the annunciation of Jesus' birth we find both these standard elements and other elements that are not in keeping with the Old Testament pattern of annunciation. The extra elements are the virginal conception, the statement of the child's future accomplishments, and the portrait of Mary in verses 34 and 38. These "special" elements are noteworthy for developing a study lesson from this passage.

Luke 1:26-27. The reference to the sixth month in verse 26 relates to the term of Elizabeth's pregnancy and ties the account of Gabriel's visit to Mary to the preceding story about John the Baptist. God's active role in the events recounted here is clear from the note that God sent Gabriel to Nazareth. The description of Mary as being

a virgin (*parthenos* in Greek) forms an allusion to Isaiah 7:14, a powerful prophetic declaration about the birth of a child called Immanuel who is the embodiment of God's promise to protect Jerusalem in a time of grave danger. Thus, while we see the connection to King David in the description of Joseph ("of the house of David"), we can already understand that God's promise to David is being fulfilled as God moves and works among the people.

Luke 1:28-30. Gabriel's initial greeting is strange, and it perplexes Mary. Remarkably, Luke tells us that Gabriel's words, not his appearance, are the cause of Mary's bafflement. As Gabriel continues to speak, the sense of Mary's being favored by God comes clear. Quite literally, in verse 30, Gabriel says, "Fear not, Mary, for you have found *grace* with God!" We are to see that Mary's encounter with the angel and her forthcoming pregnancy are profound experiences of the grace of God.

Luke 1:31-33. The angelic prophecy of the conception, name, identity, and divinely appointed destiny of Jesus recognizes both his greatness and God's special achievements through him. Everything about Jesus is exceptional—from his conception to his eternal reign over an endless kingdom—because of God's own extraordinary involvement with him. God's will and God's work bring forth and establish Jesus as the supernatural Son of the Most High. Jesus' privileged status results from God's own actions, so that in him and through him humanity experiences God's presence and power.

Luke 1:34-35. The exchange between Mary and Gabriel in these verses supplies Luke's readers with vital information. Mary's surprise and lack of comprehension are grounded in plain reality: she is not yet married and living with a husband. Gabriel's answer, however, extends far beyond mundane reality as he speaks of the Holy Spirit, God's power of creativity, and Jesus' divine Sonship. The human and the holy are drawn together as God works in this special way to bring forth Jesus into the course of human history as the embodiment of divine holiness.

Luke 1:36-37. Gabriel offers a sure sign to Mary of the truth of the prophecy of Jesus' conception and sonship: The aged and barren Elizabeth had conceived a child as an indication of the power of God's grace. The story and the bold statement in verse 37 recall elements of the story of Sarah's conception of Isaac in Genesis 18:14. The sovereignty of God is seen in the effectiveness of God's creative power that reaches beyond the limitations of normal human experience.

Luke 1:38. Mary's next words show that she had not been in doubt despite her lack of understanding. Mary submits to God's will, willfully surrendering herself to God that she may participate faithfully in God's work among humanity. Mary recognizes that she belongs to the Lord, that God is a trustworthy sovereign, and that the acceptance of God's will is the appropriate human engagement with God's work among us.

Luke 1:39-41. Mary's confidence in the message of Gabriel moved her to go to the home of Elizabeth and Zechariah. There the truth of Gabriel's words found striking confirmation, for not only was Elizabeth pregnant, but the child in her womb leaped in obvious and joyous recognition of the child that Mary herself was carrying. Lest we ever forget the divine cast of the occurrence in this dramatic story, we read that Elizabeth was filled with the Holy Spirit—a reminder of the presence and power of God at work in the events of which we are told.

Luke 1:42-45. Elizabeth's Spirit-inspired words of praise recognize both the blessing of God's grace that Mary experienced and the divine identity of the child that Mary would bear. Elizabeth regards Mary's presence and the presence of her unborn child as a divine visitation, as a special blessing of unmerited grace. Indeed, in the closing line of Elizabeth's thanksgiving praise we see the recognition that Mary's trust in God was the vehicle of her experience of the grace of God in her life.

Luke 1:46-56. These verses include Mary's well-known song, the Magnificat. Her soul wells up in praise of God as she declares God's gracious goodness that provides the bounty of divine blessing on God's chosen and faithful servants through the ages.

INTERPRETING THE SCRIPTURE

The Miracle of Virginal Conception

The story of Gabriel's annunciation to Mary of her forthcoming virginal conception of the Son of the Most High needs to be approached in a variety of ways. Clearly this is a "miraculous" birth that assumes the unique involvement of God. As God moves to bring forth the promised heir of David, God does so in a way that goes far beyond all possible human expectation. The son of Mary who is the son of David is, above all, the divine Son, who was begotten by the Holy Spirit. At the heart of this story is the Christian conviction and claim that at a particular time and place, in a manner that supersedes the normal course of historical human events, God acted in history in relation to humankind, begetting the beloved Son who comes in fulfillment of God's promises and for the salvation of humanity.

Trusting Despite a Lack of Understanding

Mary is a model of "faith seeking understanding." Perplexed by the words of Gabriel, she nevertheless hears the bizarre, seemingly impossible message about her having a son, and she embraces God's will with modesty and enthusiasm. What seems impossible to Mary is real because, as Gabriel says, "nothing is impossible with God" (1:37, NIV). Thus, never thinking merely of herself, Mary recognizes that the path of blessing runs in the direction of living according to God's will. As readers of this story we still wonder how a virgin can conceive and bear a child. But, imagine being Mary! For us this is a wonderful (if puzzling) story about the amazing creative power of God, but for Mary the events were a direct experience of God's creativity! What is story for us is reality for Mary!

Mary did not completely comprehend the mystery of God's ways, but she demonstrated the bold faith that makes the reality of God's grace present in our lives. Mary's lack of understanding did not prevent her from welcoming and experiencing the power of God's grace. Yet, Mary's faith was not a reckless leap into the dark, for her surrender to God's will came as she accepted the revelation of God's purposes for her life. Gabriel's words to Mary did not attempt to explain away the depths of the mystery of God, but the message did declare the purposes of God in bringing Jesus into the world. Moreover, Gabriel's message underscored the reality of God's gracious power by referring to Elizabeth's remarkable conception of a child in her and Zechariah's old age. As we ponder Mary's actions and reactions in this story we see that the challenge of faith is to trust, to embrace God's revealed purposes even if we lack complete comprehension.

The One to Be Born

Although we focus on Mary and her surrender to God's will in this story, we should never lose sight of the one of whose conception the angel speaks. Mary's surrender brings her to accept intimate involvement with Jesus, her Spirit-conceived son and God's Spirit-filled Son. Indeed, the child whose birth is announced by Gabriel is one whose future accomplishments go far beyond all possible human expectations. Israel may have looked forward to the promised reestablishment of the line of David, even eternally, but there is no basis for the expectation that the child born to occupy the throne of David would reign forever or be the Son of God in anything other than a figurative sense. The eternal reign and the profound holiness of the child are realities beyond all human hopes! Thus, the character and accomplishments of Jesus Christ are the fulfillment of God's promises, demonstrating the extravagant nature of God's grace. Mary's faith in God is exemplary, and her son, Jesus, is now the object of the faith to which we are called by God's grace.

Mary's Place in God's Plan

In this story, Mary becomes far more than a person in history or another character in another story. Her enthusiastic acceptance of God's will (despite the clear scandal that it would have suggested to first-century readers) is in sharp contrast to the cynical laughter of Sarah in the Old Testament. Mary's response is closer to the reaction of Hannah, the mother of Samuel, when she learns that she will bear a child (see 1 Samuel 1:18). The identification of Mary with Hannah prepares the reader for Mary's subsequent recitation of the Magnificat (1:46-55) with its close and pronounced parallels to Hannah's canticle in 1 Samuel 2:1-10. In Luke's story Mary becomes a symbolic representative of the "poor" and faithful remnant of Israel, whose piety and devotion caused them to be completely dependent on God for their well-being and, in turn, always fully accepting of God's will for their lives. Mary serves as a model of true faith, accepting God's will despite her lack of comprehension and even her understandable reservations in relation to the angelic message of God's saving work. Mary's genuine modesty is evident in her surprised reaction to Gabriel's greeting. As the story unfolds we see that her trust in God was not based in a full comprehension of God's ways, but rather in her sheer confidence in God. Above all, the blessing Mary received was not one that this world can appreciate—it was quite scandalous and potentially disgraceful, even dangerous. Nevertheless, in her acceptance of God's will Mary embodies the Christ-like disposition of absolute trust in God ("not my will but yours be done," see Luke 22:42b).

The Heart of the Story

Taken together the various elements of this story form a message about the surprising, unforeseeable, even incomprehensible nature of God's grace. Yet, the message declares that grace is real, despite its strangeness. Grace takes flesh. Grace exists in history, though it comes from beyond history's confines. Indeed, divine grace touches human existence beyond all expectations, perhaps primarily because grace itself becomes human for the genuine humanization of a hoping, but otherwise hopeless, humanity. Through divine initiative God's Spirit raises up the son of David who achieves more than human efforts could even raise up as hope. Mary is more than a mere model for faithful submission to the will of God. She actually incarnates the manner in which we all are called to relate to God, and as she lives faithfully Mary actualizes obedience. No longer do we hope or wish that faithfulness were possible, for in Mary's acceptance of God's will we see that obedience to God's will is real!

The language of "surrender" can give the mistaken impression either of *giving up* or of *defeat*, but nothing could be farther from the sense of this story. Mary's surrender is the joyful comfort of faith. Mary accepted God's will for her life as the gift of pure grace. Through the miracle of divine grace God gave her a son, who is God's own Son. The scandal of virginal conception (to the world, Mary appeared to have a child out of wedlock) did not stop Mary from embracing God's will, and so as we see her in this story Mary reminds us of the sovereignty of God. As Gabriel comes to Mary and speaks, she hears the angelic words that both assure her of God's initiative in her pregnancy and call her to active participation in God's work. Through Mary's surrender to God we see the will and the work of God made real in the context of our world. Mary's trust in God is a clear indication that God is indeed Lord of life.

SHARING THE SCRIPTURE

PREPARING TO TEACH

Preparing Our Hearts

Today's lesson examines Mary's joyful acceptance of God's will for her life as a gracious gift. She surrenders herself to God. As you prepare for this week's lesson, think about times in your own life when God has called you to do something. How did you respond? Can you honestly say that a positive response to God's will was one of joyful acceptance, or did you feel as if you were simply "giving up"? Meditate each day on your understanding of surrender.

Preparing Our Minds

Read the scripture and lesson for this week. The story of the Annunciation—Gabriel's coming unto Mary—has been depicted in art through the centuries. Perhaps you can locate a picture in an art museum or library book. If so, note how the artist has depicted the scene. What evidence do you see that the artist has captured the scene in his or her own time and place? How would you or someone in your own community represent this amazing biblical event in art? What colors, textures, and symbols would you use? If possible, bring the art book, poster, or whatever you could locate to class with you on Sunday.

Mary's Magnificat (Luke 1:46-55) is often compared to Hannah's canticle (1 Samuel 2:1-10). You may want to read both of these passages in order to compare and contrast them.

Preparing Our Learning Space

If you used the Advent wreath last week, you will want to set that up again and light the candles, preferably during your regular class worship time.

If you have located one or more artistic representations of the Annunciation, post the picture or set the book where class members can see it.

Have on hand:

✔ several Bibles for students
✔ newsprint and marker or chalkboard and chalk
✔ optional Advent wreath and matches
✔ optional pictures of the Annunciation

LEADING THE CLASS

(1) Introduction

Begin by asking the class the following question. If the group is large, divide into teams of four or five.

(1) Have you ever had an unexpected event occur that seemed to change the direction of your life? Describe the event and tell how it affected your life.

To spark discussion you may want to tell the story, found at the end of the Focusing on the Main Question portion, of the young woman executive who felt called by God to leave a corporate job and use her skills for a nonprofit Christian organization. Other examples may include a sickly child who became a good athlete or an unemployed person who founded a successful business or a victim of war who became a staunch advocate of peace.

If your class prefers a lecture format, read or retell the Focusing on the Main Question portion.

Lead into today's lesson by pointing out that Mary found her life unexpectedly changed by the angel Gabriel's announcement that she will bear a son named Jesus. Although she was certainly aware of the censure and public ridicule she would likely face as a pregnant, unmarried woman, Mary willingly and joyfully surrendered to God's will. Her story prompts us to ask today's main question: *What does it mean to surrender to God's will?*

(2) Mary Surrenders to God's Will

Focus on the scripture lesson by having the class read aloud the story of the Annunciation and Mary's visit to Elizabeth found in Luke 1:26-42. This passage lends itself to dramatic reading, so you may want to choose volunteers to read the parts of a narrator, Gabriel, Mary, and Elizabeth.

If you obtained an artistic representation of the Annunciation, show it to the class and ask the following questions. If you obtained more than one picture, divide the class into as many teams as you have art for and have them discuss the questions. If you choose the second option, allow time for each team to show its art and briefly share their responses with the class.

- How does this picture accurately depict Luke's account of the Annunciation?
- How might you have painted it differently?
- What kind of mood or attitude do you sense in Mary?
- Had you been Mary, how would you have looked in this picture?

Direct the class's attention to the scripture. Ask them to identify the events of verses 26-38. Record their answers on newsprint or a chalkboard. Then point out that these events follow the following five-fold pattern used in the Old Testament to announce persons who will bring salvation.

- An angel appears.
- The one who is being visited reacts with fear.
- The angel delivers a message.
- The hearer objects.
- A divinely determined sign confirms the truth of the message.

As noted in the introduction to the Understanding the Scripture portion, Luke's story includes other elements not found in similar Old Testament stories: the one who conceives is a virgin; the child's future accomplishments are noted; and the specific information on Mary found in verses 34 and 38. Be sure that the class identifies these elements as well.

Use the section entitled "The Heart of the Story" under Interpreting the Scripture to help the class understand both God's grace and Mary's faithful obedience. You may want to ask class members to give their definition of "surrender" before pointing out that Mary's surrender is a joyful acceptance of God's gracious will for her life.

(3) Surrendering to God's Will in Our Own Lives

Call the class's attention to the key verse from Luke 1:38: "Here am I, the servant of the Lord; let it be with me according to your word." Do this guided imagery as a means of opening the class to God's will in their lives and enabling them to respond. Read the exercise aloud, pausing for ten seconds or so where indicated. Remind the class that they are to make all responses silently.

Sit in a relaxed position, close your eyes, and breathe deeply. Picture yourself in a favorite place. Survey the scene and take in the landscape or the furniture or other distinguishing features. Smell the fragrances that you associate with this place. (pause)

Now envision yourself in this scene doing whatever you normally do in this place. Notice how you are dressed, your posture, the expression on your face, what your hands are doing. Feel the contentment of this place and your activity there. (pause)

Without warning, an angel comes to you and stands before you in shining white. Tell the angel how you are feeling at this moment. (pause)

Hear the angel ease your fears. Then the angel gives to you a message from God. Listen to it. (pause)

Respond to the angel by raising concerns and objections or asking questions. (pause)

Hear the angel's response. (pause)

The moment has come when you must respond to God. (pause)

After you have given your response, note for a few moments how you feel. Do you sense a peace and wholeness that likely indicate you are following God's will, or are you somehow upset or angry? Try to identify and resolve your emotions. (pause)

Open your eyes when you are ready.

Conclude this activity by asking:

(1) In what ways could you identify with Mary's surprise visitor and his announcement?

In teams or as a whole class, consider one or more of the following giants of the faith (or others that you know) as he or she was confronted by God and called to make a decision. You may want to ask these questions about each person you discuss:

(2) Where did this person seem to be headed in life?

(3) How did God's call threaten to change this person's life?

(4) How did the person respond?

(5) What difference did that person's decision make to the community of faith and/or to you personally?

- Paul was traveling toward Damascus to round up suspected Christians when he was blinded on the road by the living Christ.
- Moses was tending his father-in-law's flock of sheep when a voice called to him from the burning bush and then explained that he had been chosen to lead God's people out of slavery and into the land of covenant.
- Hosea the prophet heard the word of God saying that he was to marry and bear children by an unfaithful woman as a sign of Israel's harlotry with the gods of other nations.
- Joan of Arc heard the voice of the archangel Michael and told Charles, whose right to the throne was disputed, to attack Orleans so that he could be crowned. She herself led a force that liberated Orleans in 1429.

HELPING CLASS MEMBERS ACT

Suggest that class members talk with a young person who is confused about the future. Perhaps that teen or young adult has lost a boyfriend/girlfriend, or finds that the required courses for a potential career are not what he or she expected. Encourage the adults to be good listeners by first hearing the concern and then trying to respond with reassuring words about God's will in our lives.

Invite adults to identify a stressful situation in their own lives right now. Challenge them to pray about that situation each day in a way that does not tell God what they want to see happen, but opens them to being receptive to God's will. Encourage them to set aside preconceived notions of how this situation will resolve itself to allow the power of the Holy Spirit to move in a transforming way.

Ask class members to recall a period in their lives when they felt that God was calling them to do something that they, for whatever reason, did not do. For example, some second-career clergy have said that they knew at an earlier age that God wanted them to be ordained, but they chose to follow another path. Suggest that class members pray about any of these missed opportunities in their own lives to see if surrender to God's will is still possible. Since a major life change will likely occur gradually, they may want to keep a spiritual journal to discern new directions.

PLANNING FOR NEXT SUNDAY

Next week we will examine the story of the shepherds in the field as they hear the glorious message of Jesus' birth from the angel. Ask the class to prepare for this lesson by reading Luke 2:1-20, focusing particularly on verses 8-20. Suggest that they consider how they receive God's message in their own lives.

RECEIVE GOD'S MESSAGE

PREVIEWING THE LESSON

Lesson Scripture: Luke 2:8-20
Background Scripture: Luke 2:1-20
Key Verse: Luke 2:20

Focus of the Lesson:
the shepherd's reception of the good news of the birth of the Savior

Main Question of the Lesson:
As we receive God's message of grace, what do we believe God calls us to do?

This lesson will enable adult learners to:
(1) examine the message the shepherds heard from the angel and their response to it.
(2) consider what the good news of Jesus' birth means today.
(3) respond by sharing that news with others.

Today's lesson may be outlined as follows:
(1) Introduction
(2) The Shepherds Receive God's Message
(3) We Hear and Respond to God's Grace

FOCUSING ON THE MAIN QUESTION

Luke's birth narrative of Jesus is one of the best-known and most-loved stories in the Gospels. No Christmas season seems complete without a reading of these verses with their moving description of the humble circumstances into which Jesus was born, the awe-inspiring chorus of angels, and the timid, faithful, and grateful shepherds. These lowly shepherds working the night shift have an experience for which many high and mighty people would gladly pay a great price. The way Luke recounts the shepherds' behavior reveals their humanity. At first, the shepherds

fear, and who wouldn't under the circumstances! Then, as they hear the good news of the birth of the Savior Jesus, their fear gives way to curiosity. The shepherds seem to forget their shepherding as they hurry off to investigate the news from the angels. Next, with their curiosity satisfied, the shepherds act on the information that they have confirmed for themselves; they tell about what they have heard and seen. Finally, Luke tells us that the shepherds went back to their business, but now fear has given way to joy and thanksgiving toward God. The grateful shepherds were the first persons to hear and the first persons to tell the good news of God's salvation made real in Jesus Christ.

The shepherds' fear should most likely be understood as an appropriate, humble reverence. Yet, notice that fear did not paralyze the shepherds. Instead they received the good news and then acted on it. Moreover, the shepherds did not think the gospel a message to be kept to themselves; rather, with exuberant hearts they shared the good news with others as they praised and gave God the glory for the great thing that God did that momentous night in Bethlehem. The gospel is more than something we hear or read about. It is God's good news that takes hold of us and redirects our lives as God works through Jesus Christ to save our world. And so, throughout Christian history, the shepherds, the disciples, Paul, Priscilla and Aquila, Augustine, Luther, Calvin, Knox, Wesley, Mother Teresa, Bishop Tutu, and countless others have heard the gospel and become so caught up in the rush of grace that they were compelled to share the good news with the world around them. *As we receive God's message of grace, what do we believe God calls us to do?*

READING THE SCRIPTURE

NRSV
Luke 2:8-20

8 In that region there were shepherds living in the fields, keeping watch over their flock by night. [9]Then an angel of the Lord stood before them, and the glory of the Lord shone around them, and they were terrified. [10]But the angel said to them, "Do not be afraid; for see—I am bringing you good news of great joy for all the people: [11]to you is born this day in the city of David a Savior, who is the Messiah, the Lord. [12]This will be a sign for you: you will find a child wrapped in bands of cloth and lying in a manger." [13]And suddenly there was with the angel a multitude of the heavenly host, praising God and saying,

[14]"Glory to God in the highest heaven,
and on earth peace among
those whom he favors!"

15 When the angels had left them and gone into heaven, the shepherds said to one another, "Let us go now to Bethlehem and see this thing that has taken place, which the Lord has made known to us." [16]So they went with haste and found Mary and Joseph, and the child lying in the manger. [17]When they saw this, they made known what had been told them about

NIV
Luke 2:8-20

[8]And there were shepherds living out in the fields nearby, keeping watch over their flocks at night. [9]An angel of the Lord appeared to them, and the glory of the Lord shone around them, and they were terrified. [10]But the angel said to them, "Do not be afraid. I bring you good news of great joy that will be for all the people. [11]Today in the town of David a Savior has been born to you; he is Christ the Lord. [12]This will be a sign to you: You will find a baby wrapped in cloths and lying in a manger."

[13]Suddenly a great company of the heavenly host appeared with the angel, praising God and saying,

[14]"Glory to God in the highest,
    and on earth peace to men on whom his favor rests."

[15]When the angels had left them and gone into heaven, the shepherds said to one another, "Let's go to Bethlehem and see this thing that has happened, which the Lord has told us about." [16]So they hurried off and found Mary and Joseph, and the baby, who was lying in the manger. [17]When they had seen him,

this child; [18]and all who heard it were amazed at what the shepherds told them. [19]But Mary treasured all these words and pondered them in her heart. [20]The shepherds returned, glorifying and praising God for all they had heard and seen, as it had been told them.

Key Verse

they spread the word concerning what had been told them about this child, [18]and all who heard it were amazed at what the shepherds said to them. [19]But Mary treasured up all these things and pondered them in her heart. [20]The shepherds returned, glorifying and praising God for all the things they had heard and seen, which were just as they had been told.

Ke Ver

UNDERSTANDING THE SCRIPTURE

The verses from Luke 2 are a crucial part of Luke's story of the events surrounding Jesus' birth in Luke 1–2. This section of the story is dramatic and assumes some familiarity with the Jewish environment in which the events take place. In telling of the census and Jesus' birth, the shepherds and the angels, and the visit of the shepherds to the holy family, Luke makes many important points.

Luke 2:1-3. The historical note at the beginning of this account locates the events in the context of world history. At the time of Jesus' birth the world had achieved a temporary peace under the leadership of the emperor, Caesar Augustus. But the mention of a census immediately points to the fragile nature of that peace. The Jews of Palestine deeply despised and resented such head-counting for the purposes of taxation, and a few years after the birth of Jesus there was actually a rebellion among the Jews in reaction to a census. Thus, the birth of Jesus takes place in a time of peace but in a world that was politically volatile. Nevertheless, we see Jesus' family complying with the terms of the census, not engaging in revolutionary behavior.

Luke 2:4-5. The references to David and Bethlehem emphasize the Jewish world into which Jesus was born. One immediately recalls Israel's former glories in the time of David, and for astute readers the mention of Bethlehem, called the city of

David, would evoke memories of God's promise to David that his heir would reign one day in peaceful glory. Moreover, the references to David and Bethlehem form a fitting frame for the subsequent picture of the shepherds who ply the trade of David himself in his own city.

Luke 2:6-7. With David's name Luke raised certain expectations concerning God's promises, and so we read of the birth of Jesus. The account emphasizes the humble circumstances of Jesus' birth. The inn was full, so there was no room for Mary and Joseph in the normal lodging facilities, even though Mary was about to give birth to a child. The world was peaceful but far from perfect. Luke accentuates the genuine humility of Jesus' family. They were not people of great means or of remarkable social status, and their lack of standing meant that Jesus was born in a stable and laid in a manger. Jesus did not arrive in circles of power and privilege; rather, he was born into meager surroundings that were decorated with only his parents' love. As Luke recounts the manner in which Jesus' parents wrapped him, he tells us of their careful handling of the child in the style of that day.

Luke 2:8. Shepherds keeping the night watch outside Bethlehem were those to whom the angels brought the revelation of God's saving work. Scholars frequently discuss the identity of the shepherds, suggesting that they were likely employees of the temple who were assigned to guard sheep that were designated for sacrifice. The exact identity of the shepherds is uncertain, however, and not crucial for Luke's story. Through the recollection of the shepherds Luke again emphasizes the humility of the situation. The angels did not appear to the rulers of this world; rather, they came to shepherds as Jesus was born in a stable and laid in a feeding trough.

Luke 2:9-14. When the angel appeared the shepherds were afraid, that is, they were awestruck by the heavenly revelation. Yet, the angel immediately comforted the shepherds and explained to them what God had done for the salvation of humanity. God had brought forth the promised Messiah out of the line of David, and his coming meant great joy and salvation for all the people. This Lord, however, was far from the mighty king that many expected. The Lord that came that night in Bethlehem was a baby, born poor and helpless into a world with no room for him and his family. Nevertheless, as the angel told of what God had done a vast host of angels sang God's praise. God had accomplished in Christ the Lord what this unwelcoming world could never do for itself: God brought a divine peace to earth that meant joy and salvation for humanity.

Luke 2:15-20. As the angels receded into heaven, the shepherds determined to see for themselves the sign of which the angel had spoken: a baby wrapped in bands of cloth and lying in a manger. The activities reported in these verses show the dynamic character of faith. The shepherds went to see for themselves, they told others of what they had heard and seen, and they gave God the glory as they offered praise for what they had experienced. Mary, however, models another form of faith as she treasures the words and ponders them in her heart.

INTERPRETING THE SCRIPTURE

The Shepherds' Story

The story of the shepherds at the birth of Jesus provides a remarkably detailed portrait of faith in action. From the fearful beginnings of the encounter with God's messenger of grace to the reverent activity of joyful worship, we follow the unfolding dynamics of faith in the lives of the shepherds as they received the good news of the birth of the Savior. The way that the shepherds receive the good news of God's work in Jesus Christ shows that they heard the gospel as more than striking information; rather, the reception of the gospel meant the transformation of their lives. These shepherds actually become the second evangelists (the angels were the first) as they spread the good news to others around them.

Unexpected Grace

As the shepherds guarded their sheep during the night, they probably were not expecting a visit from an angel, let alone a concert by a chorus of the heavenly host. Nevertheless, as the shepherds were watching the flock, the angels came. As God had once surprised Israel by selecting a shepherd boy, David, to become a great king, here again God's ways are surprising as the angel tells shepherds of the Savior, the Christ, the Lord who was a newborn baby lying in a feed box in a stable. The shepherds were surely surprised by the appearance of the angels, and we should not allow our familiarity with this lovely story to cause us to miss the surprising, even startling way in which God's salvation and peace arrived among humanity.

God's ways of working are clearly unexpected, although this story tells us of a God who is faithful to keep God's promises to God's people.

Fear

The story tells us that the shepherds were terrified at the appearance of the angel. The reaction is understandable, for the angel arrived with the shining glory of the Lord. In a field outside Bethlehem the shepherds were confronted by the heavenly radiance of God Almighty. Yet, because the angel bore good news, the first words were words of comfort. Fear that paralyzes persons into pure passivity is not the goal of God's grace, so the angel called the shepherds forth in faith out of fear to hear the good news of God's promises finding fulfillment in Jesus Christ. God's grace aims at bringing joy into the lives of all people. An encounter with the Divine may begin with the reasonable reaction of fear, but because the news of God's grace at work is good we are called to experience joy as God's own self, God's will, and God's work are revealed to us.

Listening

As they moved from fear to joy, the shepherds listened. The good news of God's active grace came as a message of revelation. No one would ever have guessed the shape of the salvation that God achieved in Jesus. Who could imagine that the Savior, the Christ, the Lord would be born? Such a powerful figure would surely stride forth into the midst of human life and history with magnificent boldness. But, no, that was not God's way. The angel tells of the work of God in the person of a newborn child, delivered into meager circumstances, the unforeseen sign of God's surprising grace. In the infant Jesus who grew up to live in demonstration of God's will and work, we see the clearest evidence that God's ways are different from the methods of this world. Through the power of the Roman army, Caesar Augustus had forged a hard-won peace in this world; but as we know from history that peace was short-lived. Power that merely intimidates all opposition into inactivity brings a peace that simply awaits an end, for as earthly strength fades repressed hostility rises up to even old scores. God's power, which saves and brings real peace, intervenes in the person of Jesus Christ, the suffering Savior who reigns as a loving Lord.

The shepherds heard the angel, and as they listened they learned of God's surprising work in Jesus. God's self-revelation presents us with a fresh understanding of God's will and calls us to reevaluate the way we live in the world. The message that the shepherds heard spoke of God's concern for "all the people (2:10)." Thus, we see that God works in Jesus Christ because of God's concern for all humanity. God's universal purposes for the salvation of humanity in Jesus Christ is a central theme of the gospel. The apparent modesty of the newborn Jesus contrasts sharply with the magnitude of grace established in the Lordship of Christ. The glory of God reveals itself in the form of a baby in whom is embodied the presence of God's all-powerful saving grace.

Exploration

If the joy of God's salvation takes form in our listening, we should also recognize that hearing the news of God's grace calls us to action. The shepherds acted on the message of the angels. They went to see the baby of whom the angel spoke. The message grasped their hearts and minds with a vigor that caused them to step away from their duties of shepherding and go to look at this newborn Savior, Messiah, and Lord. The shepherds were not content merely to hear about grace; they sought out the sign of God's grace and experienced the work of God for themselves. The shepherds' faith was based on more than hearsay; they heard and believed, so they acted. No matter how true the message, had the shepherds only listened they would have missed the blessing of seeing God's grace for themselves. The angel's message moved the shepherds to direct involvement with God's grace made present in the baby Jesus. There is a clear element of adventure in the experience of faith. God's grace calls us to run the risk of new experiences. The gospel calls us not merely to experience the news about Jesus Christ, but to experience direct involvement with Jesus himself.

Proclamation

Having seen the sign of grace of which they had been told, the shepherds told the good news to others. The good news was too good to keep to themselves. The shepherds declared what they had heard, and having witnessed the reality of God's grace in the Christ child they could and did add their own word of confirmation to the message of the angel. The shepherds began the adventure of faith as they received a word of divine revelation, and they continued in the way of faith as they claimed and proclaimed the reality of God's work in Jesus Christ. When we receive the good news of God's saving work in Jesus Christ we are compelled to share that good news with people around us. As the grace of God grasps and saves humanity, that same grace directs us into ministry. God entrusts us with the message of the gospel, the good news of God's saving grace, and God commissions us through the experience of grace to share the good news in word and deed with the rest of the world. When we hear the gospel and believe, when we experience the peaceful power of saving grace, then we are called to tell what we have heard and seen to others.

The shepherds were not powerful priests or learned scholars, but they were God's agents of the gospel. These modest people remind us all that God's grace is not dependent upon the structures and systems of the world for its effectiveness. In the shepherds we see that all who hear, believe, and experience the gospel are capable of sharing the good news with others.

Worship

As the story ends, we see still another outcome of the experience of God's saving grace. The shepherds worshiped. Luke tells us that they glorified and praised God for all they had heard and seen. The language of the passage clearly reflects the practices of worship. God's grace brings forth the reverent response of worship as a natural part of our lives. As we know the reality of God's goodness through the saving work of Jesus Christ, we experience the transformation of our lives. Life itself becomes oriented toward God in true thankfulness. The peace of God inspires and liberates our inmost selves to live in a new relationship to God. Grace grants gratitude. Peace produces praise. We glorify God for salvation that gives us a right relation to God and brings peace as the experience of God's favor. The experience of faith ultimately expresses itself in worship, for it is impossible to contain the gratitude for grace that grows through our relationship to God in and through Jesus Christ.

SHARING THE SCRIPTURE

PREPARING TO TEACH

Preparing Our Hearts

Christmas will soon be upon us. You will likely be hurrying to finish the shopping, mailing, baking, cleaning, wrapping, decorating, and whatever else you do during Advent. In the midst of your hectic schedule, stop and imagine yourself as one of the shepherds. You are tending your sheep in the quiet of the night when a host of angels appears to you with news from God. Let the simplicity of the shepherds' lives and the immediacy of their response guide you so that you can keep your priorities focused on the One whose birth we are about to celebrate.

Preparing Our Minds

Be sure to read Luke 2:1-20, which tells the story of the shepherds. Also read the entire lesson, noting key words chosen for the headings: "the shepherds' story," "unexpected grace," "fear," "listening," "exploration," "proclamation," "worship." Consider how these words and their explanations enable you to see a pattern of faith resulting in action. This information will be used for a class activity.

If you have time, you may want to read Matthew's account of Jesus' birth, as found in Matthew 1:18–2:23. Note that this writer makes no mention of the shepherds. This information may be helpful if some class members try to meld together the details of Matthew and Luke.

Preparing Our Learning Space

If you have been using the Advent wreath, set it up again this week. Be prepared to light the third candle. You may again want to use the *Devotional Companion* as an aid to worship.

In several activities, you will note that information or questions are to be written on newsprint or a chalkboard. You may want to do some of this writing prior to class.

Have on hand:
- several Bibles for students
- newsprint and marker or chalkboard and chalk
- optional Advent wreath and matches; *Devotional Companion*
- optional paper and pencils
- optional hymnals

LEADING THE CLASS

(1) Introduction

Open today's session by inviting each person to tell the best news he or she ever received. If the class is large, you may want to divide into pairs or teams for this activity. Set a time limit and encourage each person to relate the news in two or three sentences.

After all class members have had a chance to convey their news, ask this question:

(1) **What would be the best news that the world could hear?** Explain your answer by stating why you think it is such good news.

If the class prefers a lecture format, read or retell the Focusing on the Main Question portion of the lesson.

Relate the introduction to today's scripture by pointing out that the shepherds received incomparable news one night as they were going about their usual business of overseeing their flocks. They felt compelled to go forth and tell that news to others. Our main question today is: *As we receive God's message of grace, what do we believe God calls us to do?*

(2) The Shepherds Receive God's Message

If all of the class members can see copies of the same version of the Bible, you may want to choose one person to read aloud Luke 2:8-20 and ask the class to join in by reading verse 14 in unison. In addition, a few members who feel comfortable in doing so may pantomime the actions of the shepherds as they draw back in fear, listen, respond by going toward Bethlehem, and glorify God.

Note that this story is familiar to us from carols as well as the Bible itself. If possible, distribute hymnals and have the students locate hymns that tell the story of the angels appearing to the shepherds. One example, "While Shepherds Watched Their Flocks," is number 236 of *The United Methodist Hymnal*. Other hymns may include a verse or two that refer to the story in Luke 2. If you cannot secure a quantity of hymnals, borrow one and read the selected hymn aloud. Either as a class or in teams, discuss how the hymn captures the mood and details of the scripture. Compare and contrast the biblical story with the hymn writer's version of it. Consider how the hymn writer has used imagination to fill in gaps.

Write the words that head the sections under Interpreting the Scripture ("the shepherds' "story," "unexpected grace," "fear," "listening," "exploration," "proclamation," "worship") on newsprint or a chalkboard. Discuss how the reception of God's message creates a pattern in which faith brings about action (see Interpreting the Scripture). You may sum up the progression this way: Shepherds who are going about their daily tasks are unexpectedly the recipients of God's unmerited grace. Their first response to this grace is fear. Then they open themselves to listen to the angel's message. Acting in response to the message, the shepherds set off to Bethlehem. They proclaim to Mary and Joseph, and later to others, what the angel has revealed to them because they could

not keep such good news to themselves. Their faith eventuates in worship as they praise and glorify God. Wrap up the discussion by pointing out that when we receive the message of God's gracious love in Jesus Christ, we are motivated to take action and tell others.

(3) We Hear and Respond to God's Grace

Reread today's key verse from Luke 2:20: "The shepherds returned, glorifying and praising God for all they had heard and seen, as it had been told them." Post newsprint or use a chalkboard on which you record responses to this question for brainstorming:

(1) **What are some examples of messages from God that you have heard or seen enacted or in some other way experienced?**

When everyone has had an opportunity to give at least one answer, ask:

(2) **What action did you take in response to God's message?**

(3) **If you could make any change in your response, what would it be?**

(4) **Do you think most Christians respond with the zeal of the shepherds to God's good news? If not, what inhibits our response?**

Point out that in verse 11, the angel refers to Jesus as "Savior" and "Messiah, the Lord." Give class members a few moments to reflect silently on the news that a Savior has come into the world for them. Ask them to consider the following points, which you may want to write on newsprint or a chalkboard. If some students prefer to write their answers, distribute paper and pencils.

(1) **How do I define the word "Messiah"?**

(2) **What difference does it make in my own life to believe that Jesus is the Messiah?**

(3) **By what words or actions do I proclaim this good news to others?**

Note that the shepherds neither heard the news as isolated individuals nor responded to it by suggesting that each go his own way. Instead, they heard the news in community and responded together. Ask the class to consider ways in which they could respond by joining together as a group. Make a list of their ideas on newsprint or a chalkboard. Here are some suggestions if you need discussion starters:

- Work together on a Habitat for Humanity home as a sign of God's grace in action
- Agree to provide substitutes for a Sunday school class for teens or children as needed
- Spearhead a ministry of caring, perhaps by involving the church in Stephen's Ministry
- Plan to send several class members on a Volunteers in Mission team or other type of hands-on missions project

HELPING CLASS MEMBERS ACT

Suggest that, just as the angels proclaimed the good news of the Savior's birth to the shepherds, each class member select at least one person who needs to hear of God's gracious love and speak a word of witness to that person in a winsome, friendly, humble way.

If someone in the church or community has a new baby, perhaps class members could arrange to help provide food, transportation, or baby-sitting service for the new parents. Class members may also choose to create gifts, such as bibs, blankets, or toys, that could be given to each child born within the congregation. A tradition of giving a gift to a newborn could become a class trademark that would be a long-lasting witness of love.

If the weather permits, encourage class members to take a walk through their own communities. If they go during the day, they will likely notice God's creation. If they walk at night, perhaps Christmas decorations will remind them of the coming of the Christ child. Suggest that as they walk in their familiar surroundings, they invite God to give them new insights about the Messiah and their relationship to him.

PLANNING FOR NEXT SUNDAY

Next Sunday's lesson, entitled "Respond to God's Son," is based on Matthew 2. Ask the class to read the entire chapter, paying particular attention to verses 1-12 and 16. Suggest that they consider why the magi, who had no relationship with Judaism, would want to find and worship the babe in Bethlehem.

RESPOND TO GOD'S SON

PREVIEWING THE LESSON

Lesson Scripture: Matthew 2:1-12, 16
Background Scripture: Matthew 2
Key Verse: Matthew 2:11

Focus of the Lesson:
two contrasting responses to the baby Jesus—the homage paid to him by the wise men and the violent response by Herod

Main Question of the Lesson:
How do we seek and relate to Jesus today?

This lesson will enable adult learners to:
(1) examine the responses of the magi and Herod to the news of Jesus' birth.
(2) consider how they respond to Jesus in their own lives.
(3) respond by making a commitment to Jesus.

Today's lesson may be outlined as follows:
(1) Introduction
(2) The Magi Respond to the News of Jesus' Birth
(3) Herod Responds to the News of Jesus' Birth
(4) Our Response to God's Son

FOCUSING ON THE MAIN QUESTION

The sharply contrasting reactions of the wise men, on one hand, and Herod and "all Jerusalem with him," on the other, register at the birth of Jesus the varying reactions of humanity to Jesus Christ down through history. The wise men employed the best of their knowledge, the best of their resources, indeed the days of their lives to seek out and pay rightful homage to the recently born king of the Jews. Herod and his company, however, react in fear and follow up with deception and outright hostility to the advent of

Jesus. Both responses direct the attention of Matthew's readers to the Christ child, either through legitimate adoration of his majesty or through calculated opposition to one worthy of being feared.

In a swirl of biblical language and images, the story emphasizes the significance of the birth of Jesus Christ. As we focus on the magi we are reminded that in and through Jesus God worked to bring the Gentiles into the divine plan of salvation. Moreover, as the wise men focus on the star of Bethlehem they turn their gaze away from the stars of heaven as a system of knowledge (astrology and magic) and come face-to-face with the true and promised light of the world, Jesus Christ. The wise men model to us the wisdom of following God's guidance, even if that means facing difficulties and uncertainties. As they bring their treasures to Jesus, we see the appropriateness of generosity as a sign of our own genuine gratitude for God's grace. Herod, however, reminds us of the kind of opposition to God's will seen at least since time of the hard-hearted Pharaoh. Clutching to worldly power, Herod shows the magnitude of his malice as he had "all the children in and around Bethlehem who were two years old or under" killed to protect his standing as "king of the Jews."

The act of worship rather than the physical gifts per se is the focus of the account, as is clear from the repeated references to paying homage (the Greek word *proskynein* literally means "to worship"), so that the attitude rather than the act of the wise men constitutes the reality of faith. The story calls us to identify with the wise men. Their tenacity in seeking Jesus and their piety in paying him homage demonstrate the right ways of relating to Jesus. Their attitude calls us to ask: *How do we seek and relate to Jesus today?*

READING THE SCRIPTURE

NRSV

Matthew 2:1-12, 16

1 In the time of King Herod, after Jesus was born in Bethlehem of Judea, wise men from the East came to Jerusalem, ²asking, "Where is the child who has been born king of the Jews? For we observed his star at its rising, and have come to pay him homage." ³When King Herod heard this, he was frightened, and all Jerusalem with him; ⁴and calling together all the chief priests and scribes of the people, he inquired of them where the Messiah was to be born. ⁵They told him, "In Bethlehem of Judea; for so it has been written by the prophet:

⁶'And you, Bethlehem, in the
    land of Judah,
  are by no means least among
    the rulers of Judah;
for from you shall come a ruler
  who is to shepherd my
    people Israel.' "

7 Then Herod secretly called for the wise men and learned from them the exact time when the star had appeared. ⁸Then he sent them to Bethlehem, saying, "Go and search diligently for the child; and when

NIV

Matthew 2:1-12, 16

1 After Jesus was born in Bethlehem in Judea, during the time of King Herod, Magi from the east came to Jerusalem ²and asked, "Where is the one who has been born king of the Jews? We saw his star in the east and have come to worship him."

³When King Herod heard this he was disturbed, and all Jerusalem with him. ⁴When he had called together all the people's chief priests and teachers of the law, he asked them where the Christ was to be born. ⁵"In Bethlehem in Judea," they replied, "for this is what the prophet has written:

⁶" 'But you, Bethlehem, in the land of Judah,
  are by no means least among the rulers of
    Judah;
for out of you will come a ruler
  who will be the shepherd of my people
    Israel.' "

⁷Then Herod called the Magi secretly and found out from them the exact time the star had appeared. ⁸He sent them to Bethlehem and said, "Go and make a careful search for the child. As soon as you find him, report to me, so that I too may go and worship him."

you have found him, bring me word so that I may also go and pay him homage." ⁹When they had heard the king, they set out; and there, ahead of them, went the star that they had seen at its rising, until it stopped over the place where the child was. ¹⁰When they saw that the star had stopped, they were overwhelmed with joy. ¹¹On entering the house, they saw the child with Mary his mother; and they knelt down and paid him homage. Then, opening their treasure chests, they offered him gifts of gold, frankincense, and myrrh. ¹²And having been warned in a dream not to return to Herod, they left for their own country by another road.

⁹After they had heard the king, they went on their way, and the star they had seen in the east went ahead of them until it stopped over the place where the child was. ¹⁰When they saw the star, they were overjoyed. ¹¹On coming to the house, they saw the child with his mother Mary, and they bowed down and worshiped him. Then they opened their treasures and presented him with gifts of gold and of incense and of myrrh. ¹²And having been warned in a dream not to go back to Herod, they returned to their country by another route.

Key Verse

Key Verse

Matthew 2:16

16 When Herod saw that he had been tricked by the wise men, he was infuriated, and he sent and killed all the children in and around Bethlehem who were two years old or under, according to the time that he had learned from the wise men.

Matthew 2:16

¹⁶When Herod realized that he had been outwitted by the Magi, he was furious, and he gave orders to kill all the boys in Bethlehem and its vicinity who were two years old and under, in accordance with the time he had learned from the Magi.

UNDERSTANDING THE SCRIPTURE

The verses of the lesson come from three of five scenes that make up Matthew 2: (1) verses 1-6, (2) verses 7-12, (3) verses 13-15, (4) verses 16-18, and (5) verses 19-23. Together, the parts of this chapter tell of the reactions among humanity to the birth of the Christ child and of God's providential care for the beloved son.

Matthew 2:1-6. The opening scene is filled with details. We meet wise men, who are often called magi because the Greek word usually translated "wise men" is *magoi*. From this term we can tell that the wise men were astrologers, highly regarded ancient "scientists" who were, nevertheless, sometimes associated with sorcerers. Yet, as we see in this story there is no negative cast to these magi. Christian tradition holds that there were three wise men, because in the story we read that there were three gifts:

gold, frankincense, and myrrh. Later pious imagination even provided names for the three magi who were elevated to the rank of kings: Caspar, Melchior, and Balthasar. The purported remains of the three kings are enshrined in the world-famous cathedral in Cologne, Germany.

The mention of the star in this story has given rise to much speculative interpretation. The magi speak of "his star," relating it to the Christ child who was born "king of the Jews." Interpreters have suggested that the magi operated with either the idea that each person has a star that appeared at birth and vanished at death or that they assumed, as many ancients did, that a new star heralded the birth of all truly great persons. Moreover, readers of Matthew have suggested that the star was a new star, a supernova, a comet, or the timely conjunction of planets. All these ideas are interesting and equally unprovable. We can see from the description in verse 9 of the star moving and guiding the magi that Matthew had something extraordinary in mind and that the star in the heavens was a sign for all the people on earth to know of the birth of Jesus.

Herod was neither Jewish nor born a king. He had been appointed king by the Romans in reward for his efficient management of the Jewish population on the Romans' behalf. From ancient historical sources we know he even had his own family members executed in efforts to protect his place on the throne. What is peculiar in these verses is the note that "all Jerusalem" shared Herod's reservations about the birth of Jesus. The population hated Herod, so we might expect them to rejoice at the news of a born king of the Jews. Indeed, Matthew may mean to foreshadow the rejection of Jesus by the people that occurs toward the end of the Gospel (Matthew 21–27). Here, Herod's interaction with the chief priests and the scribes of the people registers two points. Negatively, we can contrast the indifference of these leaders to Jesus' birth with the eagerness of the magi. More important, however, we see the positive point that Jesus' birth accords with scripture and so complies with and fulfills God's purposes.

Matthew 2:7-12. Herod's secret exchange with the magi shows that he operated with stealth in seeking Jesus. Yet, the magi went forth in good faith, following the miraculous star as God guided them to the child. The story emphasizes the joy of the magi, which they express by worshiping the child and giving him costly gifts in recognition of his status as divinely acclaimed king of the Jews. God's active role in the events remains clear as the magi were warned in a dream to avoid Herod.

Matthew 2:13-15. God continues to intervene as Joseph is directed to take the child out of Herod's grasp by moving the family to Egypt. Oddly, Matthew, unlike Luke, seems to assume that the holy family actually resided in Bethlehem until they moved to Egypt. Matthew's chief concern becomes clear as he tells us that this relocation was also a fulfillment of scriptural prophecy. In this event, Jesus relived the story of Israel, which was saved and brought out of Egypt by the power and direction of God.

Matthew 2:16-18. Herod's infamous slaughter of the innocents was an act of desperation. The threat the child Jesus faced was great and real. Matthew again tells the reader that the events fulfilled scripture, but here the distinctive wording of the lines lets us know that God did not will, but foresaw, Herod's wickedness.

Matthew 2:19-23. The final section of Matthew 2 brings another dream, another evasive move by Joseph, and another declaration of the fulfillment of scripture. God's active care for Jesus is clear, as is God's saving will being brought to realization in Jesus' life.

INTERPRETING THE SCRIPTURE

Perceiving God at Work

The magi in this story are Gentiles, and even though we see that they are noble pagans, their involvement with astrology was not the substance of good religion according to Jewish religious sensibilities. Yet, we can see that the magi practiced their ancient science in service to the best of pagan religious concerns. Although the magi *could* have gone astray through astrology to become entangled in magic and the black arts, through their science they focused on divine reality, which they knew was greater than themselves and their acquired knowledge. In the star they recognized the hand of God at work in the context of human history. The simple knowledge that God was at work did not satisfy the magi, so they sought to encounter and acknowledge what God was doing. As the magi perceived God they did not swell up with pride over their superior knowledge. Instead, they knew they could only acknowledge the work of God with gratitude. Like the magi, we too are called to acknowledge the gracious work of God in Jesus Christ with joyful worship.

Diligent Searching

When the magi saw the star they devoted their lives to pursuing God's revelation. Remarkably, from the story we can see that these wise men may have traveled as long as two years as they sought to locate the newborn king of the Jews. Moreover, when the magi had done what they could to locate this king, they continued their search by turning to others who were in a better position to direct them to their desired destination. Their natural assumption was that the One born king of the Jews would be in the circles of the court of the one who was then called the king of the Jews; so the magi called upon Herod. Yet, Herod knew less than they, and when he consulted his own experts they were informed but indifferent. The religious authorities knew where to look for the Christ child, but hearing news of signs of his birth they did nothing, nor did Herod in that moment. The magi alone went out to continue their search for the One whose birth was signaled in the heavens. Called forth in faith, we avail ourselves of all possible resources as we move ever onward, guided by God to where God would lead us.

Fear from Self-Interest

Herod is a model of self-interest. None of the joy of the magi characterized Herod when he heard of the birth of God's long-awaited king. The news of the Christ child only frightened Herod, who apparently thought of God's Christ as nothing more than a threat to himself. Herod, like his father before him, was a truly self-made individual. Like many self-made persons, Herod appears to have had a tendency to worship himself rather than to devote himself to God. When having and holding power become the main concerns of our lives, we are unable to recognize and celebrate the gracious workings of God in our lives. Herod's concern was not with the will of God, but with doing whatever was necessary to keep his earthly throne—even if that meant having the divinely appointed Christ of God killed. The raw lust for power dehumanizes those who fall prey to its grasp. Even God becomes a threat to those who are absolutely intent upon establishing their own position in this world. Although Herod is certainly no model for Christians, he teaches us a crucial lesson about the potential danger of wielding worldly power.

Scripture and Knowledge

From the Scriptures and from persons entrusted with their interpretation, the magi received vital information about God's will and work. The magi responded to the teaching of the Scriptures by acting on what they had learned. Encountering the teachings of the Bible produced definite action by the wise men. Today we continue to turn to the Scriptures to learn of God and of God's will for our lives. In and through our own encounter with the Scriptures we come to know and appreciate what God has done and is doing through Jesus Christ. The texts of our Bible mediate to us a personal knowledge of God and Christ that has the power to mold our lives. The Scriptures not only inform, but even more, they form and direct our living. The Bible is not a book of rules, but God will come to rule in our lives as we devote ourselves to the study of scripture. The magi sought God's will, and the Scriptures brought God's word to bear upon their lives.

Self-Interest in Action: Deception

Herod provides a second negative lesson as he deals deceptively with the wise men. Herod's real concern to protect his power is masked with a sweet-sounding lie about his desire to join the magi in their worshiping of the newborn king. Self-interest drives humanity to dishonesty; it isolates us from one another as we position ourselves behind the cover of our lies. Again, Herod is no model, but his own failed humanity admonishes us to be forthright in our dealings with other persons.

Following God's Lead

In this story, the real models of the appropriate way to respond to God's work in Jesus Christ are the magi. These wise men first followed God's heavenly sign that led them out of their own land and to Jerusalem. Then, in the context of Herod's court, the magi received further insight from the Scriptures that directed them to Bethlehem. Here, the story is remarkable. When the wise men traveled to Jerusalem they were merely responding to the rising of the star. Then, in Jerusalem, they learned from biblical prophecy that the child they sought was in Bethlehem. Only when the magi had this striking combination of a heavenly sign and the reading of scripture do we find that the star itself moved and directed the wise men. The actions of God and the Word of God are the crucial combination that clarifies God's will. The magi model faith because they fully follow God's lead. As disciples of Christ we are called, above all else, to follow the lead of our Lord as revealed through his actions and words.

As the story continues we find that the magi continued to do God's will, even if it meant disobeying or ignoring the wishes of a king. Through the miracle of a dream, God warned the wise men not to return to Herod. They obeyed God and returned to their own country. Although they were somewhat indebted to Herod for the information about Bethlehem, nevertheless, when God revealed the divine will the magi shunted a mere social obligation in obedience to God's word.

Finding the Christ Child

When the magi arrived at Bethlehem they recognized and entered the house where the child Jesus was. Upon seeing the child they worshiped him and offered him lavish gifts. The act of worship directs the reader's attention to the dignity of the child. Here, at the outset of the Gospel, Gentiles are the first to come and worship Jesus as the king of the Jews. This act anticipates the future when God's saving grace will be poured out on all humanity, uniting persons of different backgrounds and origins in a new community of faith gathered around God's Christ. The response of faith is best seen in worship.

Moreover, the gifts of the magi entice the imagination today as they have through centuries of interpretation. The traditional pattern of interpretation holds that gold is for a king, incense for a god, and myrrh for a human. These seemingly sensible suggestions are no more certain than more fanciful interpretations of the three gifts as symbolizing "faith, hope, and love" or "faith, reason, and works" or "mercy, prayer, and purity" or "wisdom, prayer, and mortification of the flesh." What the story does tell us is that the magi presented their treasures in gratitude for the grace they encountered in seeing God's chosen king. As we turn toward Jesus Christ in worship, our reverence is to be characterized by generosity that declares our gratitude for grace.

Self-Interest in Action: Brutality

Herod's actions in Matthew 2:16 provide one final negative lesson for our consideration. Moving from fear through deception, Herod lashed out with unreasonable fury when he found his evil plans had been thwarted. He did not simply seek to destroy the one child he feared was a threat to his throne; instead, he ordered the massacre of every child in the vicinity of Bethlehem who was roughly the age of Jesus. Self-interest is blind to its own penchant for violence and has no regard for others. Indeed, all others are expendable in the cause of saving one's self. When we respond to God's work and will from a perspective of pure self-interest, we fail to experience God's liberating grace that makes us truly human. Herod's brutal behavior reveals the real character of putting self before all others, including God.

SHARING THE SCRIPTURE

PREPARING TO TEACH

Preparing Our Hearts

You may need to make a special effort to schedule some quiet time away from the last minute preparations and hubbub of celebrations. As you meditate on this week's lesson from Matthew, think about the magi and their diligent search to find the Christ child. Also consider the fear and threat that Herod experiences as he learns of the baby's birth. Honestly assess your own response to Jesus. How diligently do you seek him? What are you willing to do or give in order to worship him? Talk with God about your response.

Preparing Our Minds

Read Matthew 2 and all of the lesson material. Find a picture of the magi, perhaps on a Christmas card that you have received. Check the Bible story against the artistic depiction. As noted in the entry for Matthew 2:1-6 in the Understanding the Scripture portion, tradition—not the scripture itself—provides the details for the way in which we perceive the magi.

Preparing Our Learning Space

If you have been using an Advent wreath, be prepared to light it again this week. Again, use the *Devotional Companion* for worship.

Have on hand:
- several Bibles for students
- newsprint and marker or chalkboard and chalk
- optional Advent wreath and matches; *Devotional Companion*
- optional paper and pencils
- optional list of the names and addresses of homebound members (see "Helping Class Members Act")

LEADING THE CLASS

(1) Introduction

Open the lesson by asking class members this question:

(1) Have you ever attended a movie, concert, or play with someone else and found that the two of you had entirely different reactions to the same event? If so, why do you think your responses were so different?

Listen to several answers and try to sum up reasons for the variations in their responses. If possible, write these reasons on newsprint or a chalkboard.

Move to the heart of the lesson by noting that just as we have different reactions to cultural events, so too people have different responses to God's Messiah. Some persons go to extraordinary lengths to seek and worship him, whereas others consistently ignore him or fight against him. In today's lesson we will note how the wise men (magi) and Herod exemplify these two responses. We will also discover how we ourselves respond to Jesus. Read or write today's main question: *How do we seek and relate to Jesus today?*

(2) The Magi Respond to the News of Jesus' Birth

Select a volunteer to read aloud Matthew 2:1-12 and verse 16, omitting verse 6. Choose another volunteer to read verse 6 so that the words of the prophet Micah (5:2) will stand out.

Ask class members:

? (1) What does Matthew's account tell us about the wise men?
(2) What other ideas do we have about them? Where did we get those ideas?

Use information from throughout the lesson to fill in gaps about these figures. See especially Matthew 2:1-6 in the Understanding the Scripture portion. Then ask:

? (3) What words or phrases would you use to describe their attitude and behavior concerning Jesus?

List the responses on the left side of newsprint or a chalkboard. Retain this list, because we will use it later in the session to contrast the magi's attitude with that of Herod.

Read or retell the Interpreting the Scripture section entitled "Following God's Lead." Emphasize the importance of the combination of the action of God (the sign of the star) and the word of God in clearly showing the will of God. The magi had seen the star, but they had to learn about the scripture (verse 6, which Herod had heard from the Jewish leaders) in order to find out where Jesus was.

Point out that the magi not only found the place where the Christ child was but they also brought gifts to worship him. Discuss possible meanings for the gifts of gold, frankincense, and myrrh as in the "Finding the Christ Child" segment of the Interpreting the Scripture portion. Provide a few moments for the students to reflect on the kinds of gifts they bring to worship Christ. Such gifts may include their time, talent, dedication, and praise.

If the class enjoys imaginative activities, distribute paper and pencils. Tell them to pretend that they are the magi. They have been following the star and searching for the Christ child possibly for two years. At last they found the child and came before him with their gifts. Have each class member write a diary entry for the day after their visit. Tell them to include their perceptions about the child, his parents, the surroundings, and how they felt about seeing this king and making their offering to him. If time permits, you may want to have a few volunteers read their entries.

(3) Herod Responds to the News of Jesus' Birth

Ask the class to look at the scripture and note any attitudes or behaviors indicated for Herod. Record their answers on the right side of the newsprint or chalkboard used earlier. Invite the students to comment on the differences they perceive between the response of the magi and the response of Herod.

Point out that Herod is a model of self-interest. Use information in the sections entitled "Fear from Self-Interest," "Self-Interest in Action: Deception," and "Self-Interest in Action: Brutality" under the Interpreting the Scripture portion to explore how Herod uses the information he receives to respond to the Christ child. Then ask:

**(1) Think back over the last two thou- ?
sand years. What other examples can you recall of leaders killing, persecuting, or acting brutally toward a group of people because of their religion? (Examples include: Holocaust of**

?   **World War II, witch trials at Salem in 1692, and Spanish Inquisition.)**

(2) Why do you suppose some persons in power respond so negatively?

(4) Our Response to God's Son

Note that Herod's response of fear is shared by "all Jerusalem" (verse 3). In other words, the very people to whom the Messiah was coming were afraid when they heard that the king of the Jews had been born. Ask:

?   **(1) Put yourself in the position of the Jewish people in Jerusalem. Why do you think you would be afraid if you had heard that the Messiah had been born?**

(2) How would you characterize the reactions of modern persons to the Christmas news that "God is with us"?

(3) What do you think motivates these different reactions?

Again direct the class's attention to the newsprint on which you have listed attitudes and behaviors of both Herod and the magi. Ask the following questions, which you may want to write on another sheet of newsprint or a chalkboard. If class members do not know one another well, you may want to have them reflect on their answers silently. If they are comfortable with one another and willing to keep whatever they hear confidential (a point you will want to emphasize!), ask them to discuss the questions with a partner.

• As you look at both these lists, which attitudes and behaviors would you say best describe you?

• Which attitudes and behaviors would you like to adopt?

• Which attitudes and behaviors would you like to set aside?

You may wish to close this segment with a brief word of prayer, asking God to help the students embody the kinds of attitudes and behaviors that will draw them closer to the Christ they seek to follow.

HELPING CLASS MEMBERS ACT

If class members do not believe that their lives exemplify the level of discipleship that God calls them to, challenge them to take one step to deepen that relationship.

Suggest that students remember homebound members with a card, phone call, or gift. You may want to obtain a list of the names and addresses of these persons from the church office prior to class. Encourage the group to give their gift of time or talent in the same spirit of love that the magi offered their presents to the baby Jesus.

Like Herod, some persons today see Jesus as a threat to their power or lifestyle. Suggest that class members make a special effort this week to talk with someone they know who turns aside from the Messiah because they do not want to reorder their lives or refocus their priorities. Students may want to invite such persons to worship and class next Sunday, or invite them to attend a special Christmas service where they can hear the good news.

PLANNING FOR NEXT SUNDAY

Our lesson for next week, "Believe God's Promises," encompasses Luke 2:21-40, focusing on verses 22 and 25-38. Ask the class members to read this scripture and consider how Simeon and Anna are role models for faithful persons who expect God to perform that which God has promised to do.

BELIEVE GOD'S PROMISES

PREVIEWING THE LESSON

Lesson Scripture: Luke 2:22, 25-38
Background Scripture: Luke 2:21-40
Key Verses: Luke 2:26, 38

Focus of the Lesson:
the unwavering faith of two devout persons, Anna and Simeon, who had believed
God's promise that a Messiah would be sent to Jerusalem

Main Question of the Lesson:
How would your own song of faith express your belief in God's promises?

This lesson will enable adult learners to:
(1) explore the witness of Anna and Simeon as they express their belief in God's
    promises.
(2) examine their confidence in and gratitude for God's presence and action
    through Jesus.
(3) respond by stating their own belief in God's promises.

Today's lesson may be outlined as follows:
(1) Introduction
(2) Simeon and Anna Believed God's Promises
(3) We Keep Expectations and Faith Alive

FOCUSING ON THE MAIN QUESTION

The verses of today's lesson inform us of the timing and performance of two vital Jewish religious rituals: the circumcision and naming of the baby Jesus and the purification rituals that were performed following childbirth. Through Simeon and Anna our eyes and minds come to rest on Jesus. As God's salvation, Jesus enters the world in the context of devotion to doing God's will. Yet, these verses tell us that God's bringing forth Jesus was not a smooth operation, for as God's salvation Jesus produced a division among Israel that exposed humans' real relationship to God. Though this division is real and painful, ultimately God's work in Jesus establishes the universal boundaries of salvation that affect all humanity. As this story unfolds we encounter a striking variety of persons (Jesus' parents, Jesus, Simeon, Anna, unnamed folks looking for the redemption of Israel) and topics (the law, the temple, the Holy Spirit, Old Testament story, prophecy, and vital piety). Yet, the reader should see that Jesus is the focus of Luke's story despite the complex contents of these verses. Simeon and Anna guide our gaze and give expression to the faith we are called to have.

Believing God's promises means that we perceive and state our confidence and gratitude to God for what God has done, is doing, and will do in Jesus Christ. And so through history, Christians have composed songs of praise (as Simeon does here), perhaps none more eloquently than Charles Wesley in myriad and magnificent songs such as, "O For a Thousand Tongues to Sing." Today that song-writing tradition continues, as a look in any of the recent hymnals of the mainline denominations will reveal. Many people are still writing songs of praise, such as Fred Anderson, Jane Parker Huber, Alice Parker, and Tom Troeger, to name a few. While most of us Christians may not be songwriters, we can gain encouragement, inspiration, and even direction from the insightful lyrics of these faithful servants of God who continue to pen songs that focus and express our faith. What songs of faith declare your beliefs? How? Why? *How would your own song of faith express your belief in God's promises?*

READING THE SCRIPTURE

NRSV
Luke 2:22

22 When the time came for their purification according to the law of Moses, they brought him up to Jerusalem to present him to the Lord. . . .

NRSV
Luke 2:25-38

25 Now there was a man in Jerusalem whose name was Simeon; this man was righteous and devout, looking forward to the consolation of Israel, and the Holy Spirit rested on him. 26It had been revealed to him by the Holy Spirit that he would not see death before he had seen the Lord's Messiah. 27Guided by the Spirit, Simeon came into the temple; and when the parents brought in the child Jesus, to do for him what was customary under the law, 28Simeon took him in his arms and praised God, saying,
29"Master, now you are dismissing
    your servant in peace,
    according to your word;
30for my eyes have seen your
    salvation,
31which you have prepared in

NIV
Luke 2:22

22When the time of their purification according to the Law of Moses had been completed, Joseph and Mary took him to Jerusalem to present him to the Lord. . . .

NIV
Luke 2:25-38

25Now there was a man in Jerusalem called Simeon, who was righteous and devout. He was waiting for the consolation of Israel, and the Holy Spirit was upon him. 26It had been revealed to him by the Holy Spirit that he would not die before he had seen the Lord's Christ. 27Moved by the Spirit, he went into the temple courts. When the parents brought in the child Jesus to do for him what the custom of the Law required, 28Simeon took him in his arms and praised God, saying:
29"Sovereign Lord, as you have promised,
    you now dismiss your servant in peace.
30For my eyes have seen your salvation,
31 which you have prepared in the sight of
    all people,
32a light for revelation to the Gentiles
    and for glory to your people Israel."

Key
Verse

Key
Verse

the presence of all
peoples,
³²a light for revelation to the
Gentiles
and for glory to your people
Israel."

33 And the child's father and mother were amazed at what was being said about him. ³⁴Then Simeon blessed them and said to his mother Mary, "This child is destined for the falling and the rising of many in Israel, and to be a sign that will be opposed ³⁵so that the inner thoughts of many will be revealed—and a sword will pierce your own soul too."

36 There was also a prophet, Anna the daughter of Phanuel, of the tribe of Asher. She was of a great age, having lived with her husband seven years after her marriage, ³⁷then as a widow to the age of eighty-four. She never left the temple but worshiped there with fasting and prayer night and day. ³⁸At that moment she came, and began to praise God and to speak about the child to all who were looking for the redemption of Jerusalem.

Key Verse

³³The child's father and mother marveled at what was said about him. ³⁴Then Simeon blessed them and said to Mary, his mother: "This child is destined to cause the falling and rising of many in Israel, and to be a sign that will be spoken against, ³⁵so that the thoughts of many hearts will be revealed. And a sword will pierce your own soul too."

³⁶There was also a prophetess, Anna, the daughter of Phanuel, of the tribe of Asher. She was very old; she had lived with her husband seven years after her marriage, ³⁷and then was a widow until she was eighty-four. She never left the temple but worshiped night and day, fasting and praying. ³⁸Coming up to them at that very moment, she gave thanks to God and spoke about the child to all who were looking forward to the redemption of Jerusalem.

Ke Ver

UNDERSTANDING THE SCRIPTURE

Luke's account of the birth of Jesus is told in such a way that incidents related to the annunciation, birth, circumcision, and naming of John the Baptist precede and alternate with the same kinds of events in the life of Jesus. In Luke 1:5-25 the birth of John is foretold, and in Luke 1:26-38 the forthcoming birth of Jesus is announced. Luke 1:57-66 tells of the birth, circumcision, and naming of John, and Luke 2:1-21 (especially 2:1-7, 21) narrates the birth, circumcision, and naming of Jesus. Luke 2:22-40 forms an imprecise parallel to the prophetic utterance of Zechariah in Luke 1:63b-80. Zechariah's oracle after the naming of John (1:63b-79) foretells the career of the Baptist, and then 1:80 reports that "the

child grew and became strong in spirit, and he was in the wilderness until the day he appeared publicly to Israel." When Jesus' parents bring their baby son to the temple they are met by Simeon and Anna, and Simeon utters prophetic words over Jesus that foretell of his ministry; and then verse 2:40 states, "The child grew and became strong, filled with wisdom; and the favor of God was upon him."

For both structure and content Luke 1–2 draw inspiration from the story of Samuel in 1 Samuel 1–2, so that Samuel, his parents, and the other characters in the Old Testament account become models for John and Jesus, Zechariah and Elizabeth, and Simeon and Anna. The construction of the general birth account invites comparison of John the Baptist and Jesus. Careful study of the stories finds that Luke used this narrative structuring to demonstrate the superiority of Jesus to John the Baptist. But Luke's argument is more positive than negative, since he labored to elevate Jesus rather than to disparage John.

Luke 2:21-24. Jesus was born into a family that lived in a pious relation to God's law. The best of Israel's traditional piety frames, forms, and directs the life of Jesus' family. Luke's story does not reveal a precise knowledge of the legal requirements of Judaism concerning circumcision, naming, purification, and dedication, but it does make clear that Jesus was born and raised in a family that was devoted to observance of the law. Three times in these verses (2:22, 23, 24) and twice in other portions of the presentation account (2:27, 39), the story makes it clear that the law was the norm for Jesus' family's life.

The offering of "a pair of turtledoves or two young pigeons" indicates the economic status of Jesus' family. The law called for giving a lamb, but it permitted the less costly offering for those who could not afford the lamb. Thus, one sees that Jesus' family was not devoted to the law because they were affluent. Instead, Jesus' family belonged to the class of Israel's pious poor; that is, they were persons whose limited means fostered a radical dependence upon God, since they were without possessions in which to invest their trust.

Luke 2:25-38. Simeon and Anna dominate the next verses, although they themselves fully focus on the Christ child. These two aged persons are models of piety. They see as prophets see; that is, they see the will and the work of God in the world. Upon seeing the baby Jesus, both Simeon and Anna recognize the child as the promised Messiah.

Luke 2:39-40. Having "done everything required by the Law of the Lord" (NIV), the family returned to Galilee. Luke relocates the family geographically in 2:39, which is necessary for the story; but his deeper concerns come through in the statement in 2:40, "The child grew and became strong, filled with wisdom; and the favor of God was upon him." This remark testifies both to the humanity of Jesus and to the divine grace that was upon him as he was "filled with wisdom." The mention of God's favor may have been Luke's way of indicating that Jesus was obedient to God's will in the course of his growing up. In Acts 7:46, Luke recorded Stephen speaking of David as one "who found favor with God." The course of Stephen's speech is a selective contrasting of obedient and disobedient responses to God's will throughout Israel's history. If, then, obedience is the occasion of God's favor, Luke's Gospel may be indicating that, from childhood, Jesus was consistently obedient to God's will.

INTERPRETING THE SCRIPTURE

Simeon and the Holy Spirit

At the heart of these verses we see in three rapidly repeated references to the Holy Spirit (2:25, 26, 27) a major motif of this presentation scene. Simeon's coming to the temple at the time that Jesus' family presented him there was not by mere chance. Although Simeon's life was permeated with the presence of the Spirit (2:25), and although he enjoyed the privilege of the insight of inspiration (2:26), he lived a life that was, nevertheless, Spirit-directed (2:27). Simeon was possessed by the Spirit; he did not possess the Spirit. Simeon shows us that we do not rest on the cushion of grace; rather, we walk under the canopy of grace in the path set forth for us.

Simeon and Hope

Simeon personifies the expectations of Israel's piety that had been created by God's promises to Israel. As Simeon had lived in hope with the assurance that the Lord would fulfill the promise of salvation, so the faithful among Israel lived, hoping, trusting, ever ready to obey the direction of the Holy Spirit. Luke's description of Simeon as "righteous and devout, looking forward to the consolation of Israel" echoes the language of the second and third portions of the book of Isaiah, where Israel is consoled through God's restoration of the nation after a time of humiliation. Simeon, who had lived looking for the consolation of Israel, now sees God's promised solace in the infant Jesus. The language of Isaiah employed in the description ultimately provides a clue for interpretating the whole scene.

Simeon and the Nature of Prophecy

As Simeon holds the infant Jesus in his arms, he speaks prophetic words that form two distinct units. First, in 2:29-32 we read the lines of the well-known Nunc Dimittis. This oracle has the form of a prayer of petition. Simeon's words acknowledge that in looking upon the baby Jesus he knew, through the inspiration of the Holy Spirit, that he was beholding God's promised salvation. Simeon's recognition was not only that God had brought to fulfillment the promise to Israel but also that his own God-given lot, one day to behold God's salvation, was completed. Simeon was not so much the possessor of privileged information as he was the recipient of a commission. Simeon fulfilled his appointed role by recognizing God's salvation, Jesus, and by uttering prophetic words that revealed the nature of God's

salvation. The Nunc Dimittis declares the universal character of God's provision of salvation: God "prepared [salvation] in the presence of all peoples, a light for revelation to the Gentiles and for glory to [God's] people Israel" (2:31-32).

Salvation

As a whole, the Nunc Dimittis presents a rich combination of the language and thought of the latter portion of Isaiah (see, for example, portions of Isaiah 40; 42; 46; 49; 52; and 66). But in this text the words and ideas from Isaiah are reconfigured in relation to the infant Jesus; they are not related directly to Israel. Yet, although Jesus, not Israel, is referred to as "salvation" and "a light for revelation to the Gentiles," there are three points of striking continuity between Isaiah's prophetic oracles and Simeon's prophetic utterance in the Nunc Dimittis: (1) God is the actor in the bringing of salvation. Salvation is God's work, not the result of human actions. (2) God's salvation is universal in scope so that it includes Gentiles and Jews alike. The promise of salvation came from God to Israel, but the accomplishment of salvation affects all humans regardless of their religious or ethnic background. (3) God's delivery of salvation in Jesus brings glory to Israel, not as the privileged possessors of God's favor, but as God's chosen servant people through whom God has worked to bring forth the salvation achieved in Jesus.

Simeon's Puzzling Words

The second of Simeon's Spirit-inspired pronouncements (Luke 2:34-35) is more specific than the theologically grand and universalistic Nunc Dimittis, but the passage is nevertheless puzzling and has produced a remarkably diverse history of interpretation. Questions abound: Does the reference to "the falling and the rising of many in Israel" mean that some will fall while others will rise, or does it indicate that first all will fall and then all will rise? What does it mean that Jesus is destined "to be a sign that will be opposed"? What does the parenthetical statement to Mary ("and a sword will pierce your own soul too") mean? The answers to these and other questions come through interpreting this brief text in relation to the whole of Luke's work in Luke and Acts and against the background of Isaiah, which was a key to the interpretation of Simeon's earlier declaration.

A major theme throughout Luke and Acts is that Jesus produces a division among humans as they react favorably or unfavorably to him, both in the course of his earthly ministry and in the course of the disciples' proclamation of the meaning of God's work in Jesus' life, death, resurrection, and exaltation. The reference to "the falling and the rising of many in Israel" in Simeon's oracle is an early sounding of a theme that characterizes Luke's general narrative. In the Gospel, Jesus himself says that he causes division among humans, even in the close-knit structure of family relationships (Luke 12:51-53); and in Acts throughout the evangelistic speeches by the disciples one finds the contrasting of unbelief with belief and guilt for the rejection of Jesus with salvation through belief and repentance. As Peter declares through the inspiration of the Spirit in Acts 4:11-12, "This Jesus is 'the stone that was rejected by you, the builders; it has become the cornerstone.' There is salvation in no one else, for there is no other name under heaven given among mortals by which we must be saved." Luke's story shows that God has acted in Jesus in a final and decisive manner that requires humans to be set for or against God's salvation; neutrality is not an option as God's work confronts humanity. God's saving activity in Jesus exposes the position of humans with regard to God. The remark that "the inner thoughts of many will be revealed" in the last line of Simeon's pronouncement indicates that judgment is inherent in the reac-

tion of humans to Jesus. "Inner thoughts," or better, "innermost thoughts," always refers to a negative human disposition in the New Testament; therefore, Jesus is God's instrument for exposing human resistance to God's work. Consistent with this line of interpretation is the designation of Jesus as a "sign that will be opposed." The idea of a child being a sign takes up the mind of Isaiah once more, wherein the child Immanuel is a sign given as an indication of God's judgment to the house of David (Isaiah 7). And indeed, the theme of Simeon's second oracle is divine judgment that divides.

Interpreters have struggled to make sense of Simeon's puzzling statement to Mary. Suggestions range from the subtle to the ridiculous. Yet, read in the context of Luke and Acts, the text surely means that even Mary, the obedient handmaiden of the Lord, does not escape the dividing judgment brought in God's saving work in Jesus. Mary finds her place in the early church not by virtue of giving birth to Jesus, but as do all others, by coming to believe in God's salvation achieved in him.

Anna and the Reaction of True Faith

Along with Simeon the prophetess Anna appears in the temple alongside Jesus' family. Anna personifies the faith and piety of Israel in the same way that Simeon does. The text does not narrate an encounter between Anna and Joseph, Mary, and Jesus, nor does Luke offer a record of Anna's words. But her reaction to the presentation of Jesus scores two crucial points: (1) Anna gives thanks to God. This is the first and appropriate response of those recognizing the significance of Jesus as the one in whom God accomplishes the promise of salvation. Giving thanks to God is a vital element in the experience of salvation, as is immediately apparent from a reading of Luke. Note throughout Luke's writings that faith without thanksgiving is incomplete faith.

For example, in the story of the healing of the ten lepers in Luke 17:11-19, it is the Samaritan alone who returns to give thanks; and it is to the Samaritan alone that Jesus says, "Get up and go on your way; your faith has made you well." (2) Anna spoke of Jesus as the one to whom all "wcrc looking for the redemption of Jerusalem." This report emphasizes once more that Jesus is the fulfillment of God's promise of salvation. But of equal or greater importance here is the pattern of Anna's action. She recognized Jesus as the one in whom God accomplished redemption, and so she was compelled to testify to God's work. The good news of God's redeeming grace in Jesus Christ is not a private possession to be received and hoarded; rather, the good news must be shared, as Anna demonstrated.

SHARING THE SCRIPTURE

PREPARING TO TEACH

Preparing Our Hearts

Think about the promises of God that are especially meaningful to you. Which of these promises do you believe have been fulfilled? Which ones do you expect to see fulfilled in your lifetime? Which ones do you believe will be fulfilled even if you are not alive to see the outcome? You may want to spend time seeking out these promises in the Scriptures and meditating upon them.

Preparing Our Minds

Read the background scripture, Luke 2:21-40, paying particular attention to verses 2:22, 25-38. The focus of the lesson is not on the temple rituals themselves, but on Anna and Simeon as persons who believed God's promises. However, for your own understanding, you may want to review information concerning the rituals in Exodus 13:2, 12 and Leviticus 12:2-8.

Note Luke 2:31-32, for it shows Jesus as one who is expected to bring about salvation for all persons, including Gentiles. You may wish to read Isaiah 42:6 and 49:6, portions of the first and second servant song, respectively, in order to see that this promise to all peoples or nations was made through the prophet. Simeon's words speak of a promise of God that is now being fulfilled.

Preparing Our Learning Space

Have on hand:
- several Bibles for students
- newsprint and marker or chalkboard and chalk
- optional paper and pencils

LEADING THE CLASS

(1) Introduction

Again this week you may have out-of-town guests visiting the class. Be sure to introduce them at the beginning of class.

Open the session by asking class members to think about traditions their families observe, particularly with respect to Christmas. Invite them to share this information with a partner or small team. Some may discuss certain foods the family eats or rituals the family follows. Others may speak of gift-giving traditions or a special decoration that has been handed down. Allow a few moments for this sharing. Then call the group together and ask:

(1) **Why do you suppose we continue to follow these traditions? Why, for example, do we put an ancient star that needs some sprucing up on the tree?**

(2) **Why do you think members of the older generations work to preserve traditions?**

Guide the discussion toward today's lesson by noting that Mary and Joseph followed the rituals of their Jewish faith by taking Jesus to the temple on the eighth day to be circumcised and named. Mary participated in a ritual of purification following childbirth. Two devout persons at the temple, Simeon and Anna, had awaited the fulfillment of God's promised redemption of Israel. Both of these elderly persons knew that the child brought by Mary and Joseph was the one who would fulfill that promise. The belief that God's promise had been fulfilled prompted both of them to praise God. As we consider their reaction to the Christ child, we are called to ask today's main question: *How would your own song of faith express your belief in God's promises?*

(2) Simeon and Anna Believed God's Promises

Read aloud Luke 2:22 to set the stage for Anna and Simeon's praise to God for Jesus, whom they perceived to be the fulfillment of God's promise. You may want to make brief mention about these rituals, but do not get bogged down. Note that Luke's account clearly shows that Mary and Joseph devoutly observed the law.

If the class enjoys dramatic reading, choose a volunteer to read Luke 2:25-28, 33-34*a*, a second person to read Simeon's words in Luke 2:29-32, 34*b*-35, and a third person to read the description of Anna, Luke 2:36-38. Scripture does come alive for many people when they can hear different voices.

Ask the following questions about Simeon and Anna. You may want to divide the class in half and assign each one a character. Either give each team newsprint and a marker to record their answers, or, if the entire class works together, record the answers yourself using two sheets of newsprint.

[?] (1) **How would you describe the spiritual life of Simeon (Anna)?**

(2) **What did Simeon (Anna) believe that God had promised?**

(3) **How did Simeon (Anna) respond to Jesus?** [?]

If the class worked in teams, provide time for them to share their answers. Add ideas appropriate from the Interpreting the Scripture portion.

(3) We Keep Expectations and Faith Alive

Mention that neither Anna nor Simeon was surprised by Jesus' coming. They believed that God had promised a Messiah to Israel and that Jesus was the Promised One. Ask class members to cite their favorite Bible promises. You may want to have them just call out a promise, possibly paraphrasing it in their own words. Or you may prefer to have them look up the promise and read it from their Bibles, an option that will work well if your students are very familiar with the Bible. Then talk for a few moments about why the expectations or hopes embodied in these promises are so important to them.

Note that Simeon and Anna both dedicated themselves to work in the temple. Luke wrote that Anna fasted and prayed day and night and had not left the temple since she was widowed early in life. Such devotion is reserved for causes to which we are passionately committed. Ask class members to think silently for a few moments about these questions, which you may want to read twice, first together so the class can see where you are going and then separated by pauses so they have time to meditate.

Have you ever felt deeply committed to a cause or ideal? If so what was it? Why did you embrace this cause? [R]

Can you honestly say that your commitment to Jesus is the foremost priority in your life? If so, what evidence can you think of to support your claim? If not, what is keeping you from making Jesus the first priority in your life?

What changes would you ask God to help you make in your life in order to be more devoted to Jesus? [R]

Ask the group to consider ways in which

your congregation keeps the traditions and promises of our faith alive for future generations. Ask them to determine whether each of the following statements is true, partly true, or false. Have them be prepared to give evidence to support their position.

As a congregation, we provide opportunities for our children and teenagers to be active participants in our worship services.

R We have certain traditions that help make us who we are as a congregation.

Certain individuals (either living or now with the Lord) have committed themselves to the work of Christ through this church in such meaningful ways that they have touched my life. (Note: Encourage class members to share the names of others and what they have done. You may find that the people who are named will have no idea that the "little things" they have done have been so meaningful to others.)

When strangers visit our congregation, they encounter the presence of Jesus in a variety of ways. (Class members may make note of the friendliness of the congregation, the support that the parishioners extend to one another, the type of preaching, the variety of programs and groups, and so on.)

Use Simeon's prayer of petition in Luke 2:29-32 as words of dismissal. This portion of scripture is commonly called the Nunc Dimittis. The first verse of these words of praise in Latin reads: "Lord, now let your servant depart in peace." You may want to use the information under "Salvation" in the Interpreting the Scripture portion to help the group better understand this passage. If class members can see the same translation of the Bible, invite them to read this passage together in unison.

HELPING CLASS MEMBERS ACT

Encourage the group to think about how other church members perceive them. Ask them each to consider the role they play in keeping expectations and faith alive and strong within the congregation. Challenge them to take some action this week that will pass traditions of the church on to a succeeding generation. Such action may be as simple as reading a Bible story to a child or explaining why the church observes a certain religious tradition.

Ask class members to select a favorite hymn or Psalm or other word of praise that expresses their belief in God's faithfulness. Suggest that they sing, recite, read, or mentally repeat the words each day this week.

Challenge each member to write a spiritual journal entry this week in which they state something that they hope God will do in their lifetimes. The concern may be a personal one (such as seeing a family member enter into a faithful relationship with God) or a more universal one (such as bringing peace among groups where there has been conflict or war).

PLANNING FOR NEXT SUNDAY

Next week we will begin a new unit entitled, "Persons in Jesus' Ministry." The first lesson will look at the witness of John the Baptist. Ask students to prepare for this lesson by reading Mark 1:1-15 and Luke 7:18-30, paying particular attention to Mark 1:4-11, 14-15 and Luke 7:18-23.

WITNESS ABOUT CHRIST

PREVIEWING THE LESSON

Lesson Scripture: Mark 1:4-11, 14-15; Luke 7:18-23
Background Scripture: Mark 1:1-15; Luke 7:18-30
Key Verse: Mark 1:8

Focus of the Lesson:
the powerful witness of John the baptizer who called persons to change their ways and to be prepared for Jesus and the baptism of the Holy Spirit that he would bestow

Main Question of the Lesson:
In what concrete ways can we live as faithful followers and witnesses of Christ today?

This lesson will enable adult learners to:
(1) experience John the Baptist as an important figure in Jesus' ministry.
(2) examine their own willingness to listen to the witness of someone who is different from them.
(3) respond by witnessing to others.

Today's lesson may be outlined as follows:
(1) Introduction
(2) John the Baptist's Work and Witness
(3) Being Faithful Witnesses and Leaders in Our Own Day

FOCUSING ON THE MAIN QUESTION

Taken together, the materials from the Gospels of Mark and Luke tell the larger story of John the Baptist, especially in his relationship to Jesus. After the striking opening of Mark's Gospel we find a report of the appearance and the ministry of John (Mark 1:2-8). Then, Mark brings Jesus onto the scene and tells of his baptism (Mark 1:9-11), his temptation in the wilderness (1:12-13), and the beginning of his ministry (Mark 1:14-15). Our lesson from Luke's Gospel begins with John's disciples visiting John in prison and telling him about the activities of Jesus (Luke 7:18). John then sent two disciples to inquire of Jesus whether he was the one whom John had awaited and proclaimed to be coming (Luke 7:19-20). Jesus, who had just done mighty acts of healing and exorcism, told John's disciples to report what they had seen and heard to John, adding, "And blessed is anyone who takes no offense at me" (Luke 7:21-23). After the departure of John's messengers Jesus turned to the crowds and spoke about John and his work as a prophet and of John's crucial role as the one who went before Jesus to prepare his way and the way of the coming kingdom of God (Luke 7:24-30).

Jesus' words acknowledge John's greatness and importance. We learn from Jesus' assessment of John that John had played a critical role in God's plan of salvation. He epitomized the kind of radical obedience that God had desired from people throughout history. Jesus also said that with his own ministry a new day had dawned in God's relations with humanity, so that as his own work brought the kingdom, John's labors had brought the conclusion to a former day that had to pass in order for God's future to come among the people of the earth. We may not be called to be a John the Baptist, but as faithful followers of Jesus Christ who devote ourselves to doing God's work, we can be like John as we obey God's will, as we give faithful testimony to God's purposes, as we remain ever open to God's future, and as we keep our focus in faith on Jesus Christ. *In what concrete ways can we live as faithful followers and witnesses of Christ today?*

READING THE SCRIPTURE

NRSV
Mark 1:4-11

⁴John the baptizer appeared in the wilderness, proclaiming a baptism of repentance for the forgiveness of sins. ⁵And people from the whole Judean countryside and all the people of Jerusalem were going out to him, and were baptized by him in the river Jordan, confessing their sins. ⁶Now John was clothed with camel's hair, with a leather belt around his waist, and he ate locusts and wild honey. ⁷He proclaimed, "The one who is more powerful than I is coming after me; I am not worthy to stoop down and untie the thong of his sandals. ⁸I have baptized you with water; but he will baptize you with the Holy Spirit."

Key Verse

9 In those days Jesus came from Nazareth of Galilee and was baptized by John in the Jordan. ¹⁰And just as he was coming up out of the water, he saw the heavens torn apart and the Spirit descending like a dove on him. ¹¹And a voice came from heaven, "You are my Son, the Beloved; with you I am well pleased."

NIV
Mark 1:4-11

⁴And so John came, baptizing in the desert region and preaching a baptism of repentance for the forgiveness of sins. ⁵The whole Judean countryside and all the people of Jerusalem went out to him. Confessing their sins, they were baptized by him in the Jordan River. ⁶John wore clothing made of camel's hair, with a leather belt around his waist, and he ate locusts and wild honey. ⁷And this was his message: "After me will come one more powerful than I, the thongs of whose sandals I am not worthy to stoop down and untie. ⁸I baptize you with water, but he will baptize you with the Holy Spirit."

Key Verse

⁹At that time Jesus came from Nazareth in Galilee and was baptized by John in the Jordan. ¹⁰As Jesus was coming up out of the water, he saw heaven being torn open and the Spirit descending on him like a dove. ¹¹And a voice came from heaven: "You are my Son, whom I love; with you I am well pleased."

NRSV
Mark 1:14-15

14 Now after John was arrested, Jesus came to Galilee, proclaiming the good news of God, [15]and saying, "The time is fulfilled, and the kingdom of God has come near; repent, and believe in the good news."

NIV
Mark 1:14-15

[14]After John was put in prison, Jesus went into Galilee, proclaiming the good news of God. [15]"The time has come," he said. "The kingdom of God is near. Repent and believe the good news!"

NRSV
Luke 7:18-23

18 The disciples of John reported all these things to him. So John summoned two of his disciples [19]and sent them to the Lord to ask, "Are you the one who is to come, or are we to wait for another?" [20]When the men had come to him, they said, "John the Baptist has sent us to you to ask, 'Are you the one who is to come, or are we to wait for another?' " [21]Jesus had just then cured many people of diseases, plagues, and evil spirits, and had given sight to many who were blind. [22]And he answered them, "Go and tell John what you have seen and heard: the blind receive their sight, the lame walk, the lepers are cleansed, the deaf hear, the dead are raised, the poor have good news brought to them. [23]And blessed is anyone who takes no offense at me."

NIV
Luke 7:18-23

[18]John's disciples told him about all these things. Calling two of them, [19]he sent them to the Lord to ask, "Are you the one who was to come, or should we expect someone else?"

[20]When the men came to Jesus, they said, "John the Baptist sent us to you to ask, 'Are you the one who was to come, or should we expect someone else?' "

[21]At that very time Jesus cured many who had diseases, sicknesses and evil spirits, and gave sight to many who were blind. [22]So he replied to the messengers, "Go back and report to John what you have seen and heard: The blind receive sight, the lame walk, those who have leprosy are cured, the deaf hear, the dead are raised, and the good news is preached to the poor. [23]Blessed is the man who does not fall away on account of me."

UNDERSTANDING THE SCRIPTURE

Mark 1:1-8. These opening verses are quite complex. Verse 1 is a title for Mark's account concerning Jesus. Verses 2-3 refer to prophecy and specifically quote Isaiah 40:3 to declare the early Christian conviction that John the Baptist was the forerunner of Jesus. Having explained the significance of John's activity, the lines continue by telling of the character of John's ministry in verse 4, of the popular response to John's work in verse 5, and then of John's striking appearance in verse 6. The concluding verses (Mark 1:7-8) report the content of John's preaching and prompt us to

ask, "What is the meaning of the gospel?" In the verses that follow and throughout the Gospel, Mark offers an answer in the story of Jesus' ministry and passion. We find that the gospel is the fulfillment of God's promises; it is God's own reaching out through faithful witnesses—first, John, and finally, Jesus. Specifically, the gospel is the good news of the coming of God's Son, Jesus Christ, who is ever the focus of the gospel.

John's attire and diet seem appropriate for his ministry in the wilderness, where he acts in fulfillment of the prophecy of

Isaiah. John's clothing, however, reflects Elijah's style of dress in 2 Kings 1:8. Thus, John creates the basis of a comparison between himself and Elijah, who was expected to come again at the end time just before the advent of God. More striking still is the report of John's preaching. The scripture tells us that he is working to "prepare the way of the Lord," and in John's own words we learn this Lord is one who is mightier than John and one whose surpassing power brings baptism with the Holy Spirit. The message looks toward and announces that God is about to do a new and wonderful work among humanity.

Mark 1:9-11. The brief story of Jesus' baptism recalls a puzzling moment. Jesus arrives from Galilee, we learn that the news concerning John had gone near and far. Jesus' baptism by John is a positive response and affirmation of John's preaching. Yet, we recall that John had been "proclaiming a baptism of repentance for the forgiveness of sins." John's message is clear: He calls humanity to repent and experience divine forgiveness *because* there is a Mighty One coming to baptize with the Holy Spirit. John declares God's will, and among those who respond to the call is Jesus himself. At the moment when Jesus is baptized, a heavenly voice confirms his identity as God's Son, the Beloved, with whom God is well pleased.

Mark 1:12-13. These verses recall an interlude between the time of the ministry of John the Baptist and the beginning of Jesus' own public ministry. From the powerful beginning of baptism when Jesus was anointed with the Holy Spirit, we see him move to do ministry only after he faced and withstood temptation in the wilderness, which was thought to be the domain of Satan and the demons.

Mark 1:14-15. With precision, Mark recalls the launching of Jesus' ministry and summarizes Jesus' words and deeds. Here, we see that Jesus' preaching and actions reiterate and advance the eschatological (that is, concerning the end times) tone and content of John's preaching. The time toward which John looked was present; the one for whom John looked had arrived; the kingdom of God had drawn near. Thus, Jesus repeated John's call to repentance with a special, new urgency.

Luke 7:18-20. When Jesus came preaching John's disciples took note. Luke 3:19 records the arrest of John, so we understand that John's disciples visited their master in prison. The reports about Jesus peaked John's curiosity so that he sent messengers to ask Jesus about his identity and aims. Having heard about what Jesus was doing, John found no neat fit between Jesus' actions in ministry and the popular messianic expectations of the day. Yet, John recognized enough of God's power in Jesus' work to make him think that Jesus might be the long-awaited Messiah.

Luke 7:21-23. Jesus did not answer John's questions with a simple "Yes" or "No." Instead, he portrayed his work with the language of faith, drawing on lines from Isaiah (29:18-19; 35:5-6; 61:1) in reply to the faithful John. In Jesus' answer we learn that there is blessing for those who see in Jesus the fulfillment of God's promises, even if his actions cause them to redefine their own assumptions about the Messiah.

Luke 7:24-30. Finally, Jesus' closing words about John the Baptist provide a more complete understanding of John's person and work. Jesus offers a theological re-reading of John as he interprets the Baptist in relation to scripture. John was a great prophet, indeed the greatest. Yet, Jesus also states clearly that he and his hearers stood in a new and altered time and place. The time and the presence of the kingdom of God are greater than anything the world before the kingdom had ever known.

INTERPRETING THE SCRIPTURE

A Faithful Witness in the Biblical Tradition

John the Baptist was a faithful witness, commissioned by God to prepare the way for God's Son. We see from our lesson that John was faithful through faith. He did not know God's full plan, but he had a clear sense of God's will for his life. Even if his role in the accomplishment of God's will was limited, John was completely devoted to doing his part at any cost. Many words characterize John: "bold," "faithful," "devoted," "courageous," "unswerving," "curious." But the words that best summarize this great prophet come from Jesus: "More than a prophet. . . . I tell you, among those born of women no one is greater than John" (Luke 7:26, 28).

John took his calling to be a prophet with utter seriousness. He not only dressed the part, but he also sounded the way a prophet was supposed to sound. An early Christian writing from the late first or early second century entitled *The Didache* discusses true and false prophets. At one point the document reads, "Not everyone who speaks in the spirit is a prophet, except he have the behavior of the Lord. From his behavior, then, the false prophet and the true prophet shall be known. . . . Every prophet who teaches the truth, if he do not what he teaches, is a false prophet" (*Didache* 11.8, 10). John's words and deeds were in harmony with one another.

John actually lived the biblical tradition. In his appearance he relived the dress of Elijah. In his ministry he lived out the message of Isaiah, preparing the way of the Lord as he made straight the path of the Lord in the wilderness. In calling people to repentance for the forgiveness of sins, he articulated a prominent prophetic theme found in Isaiah, Jeremiah, Hosea, Joel, and Zechariah, among others. In John the Baptist we see a faithful life that was actually formed from scripture. John's vision, his person, and all his work are the results of his being so thoroughly steeped in scripture that he physically lived the texts of the Bible. However, John was no mere parrot, simply repeating something he read or heard. In John the Baptist there was a fresh synthesis of the truth of God that had engaged Israel through the centuries. The biblical tradition with its focus on God found new life and fresh expression in John's life and work.

Calling for the Recognition of God's Ways

The call to repentance is a radical message that we sometimes misunderstand and trivialize. The word "repent" means "to change one's mind" or "to become reoriented." Repentance is turning away from false priorities to the way of life that God desires. Moreover, the call to repentance is not an end in itself. As John called people to turn away from the way they had been living (obviously in his estimation not a fashion in keeping with the will of God), he called them to experience forgiveness of their sins. From sin to forgiveness was the pattern of repentance that John preached. People were called from sinful involvements to a new experience of the grace of God that meant forgiveness and, thereby, a fresh relationship with the God who simultaneously judged them sinful and offered them forgiveness.

John the Baptist is often cast in popular culture (such as books and art) as a kind of wild-eyed, fire-and-brimstone preacher who railed against his contemporaries. This image is unfortunate and inaccurate. John does appear ascetic in his dress, his diet, and his taking to the wilderness as a place of ministry; but notice that he was neither so weird nor so isolated as to prevent drawing a large following—even Jesus came from Galilee, which was some distance from where John was preaching and baptizing. John was not cut off from society, although he removed himself from the towns and cities as places of ministry. John's distancing himself from normal society was a physical act that pronounced judgment on the course of normal affairs, but he was not disinterested in the reality of life; rather, he sought to offer a theological critique of the world in which he lived that called it to change as an offer of divine hope. He looked forward to what God would do in the future, and he called others to join him in living for God.

Looking Toward God's Future

The word "eschatology" means "teaching about the end" or "teaching about the last things." John the Baptist came preaching about God's future. In doing so he was an "eschatological prophet." John looked for the coming of God's Messiah, for he knew from the Scripture and the teaching of segments of Judaism in his time that God would send forth a Messiah to judge the world on God's behalf, to set the world straight, to make the world the place that God intended it to be.

As John looked forward to what God would do—to what God was about to do—he spoke about the Holy Spirit. In the New Testament, the talk about the Holy Spirit is not done at the refined level of later Christian doctrine, which works carefully with the notion of the Holy Spirit as a member of the Holy Trinity, One God in Three Persons. Rather, in the New Testament, mention of the Holy Spirit is perhaps best thought of as wholehearted reference to the *presence* and *power* of God. When John speaks of the Mighty One coming, he is an eschatological prophet; and when he speaks of the baptism with the Holy Spirit, he reveals that he thinks the future and any hope that we may have for the future are to be related to the presence and the power of God at work in the world in bold, new ways.

Jesus and John

Without stretching the truth one can say that John was something of a model for Jesus in his outlook and in his preaching. Of course, there are crucial differences between these two figures: John was an ascetic and did his ministry under rigorous conditions in the wilds of Palestine. Jesus worked in villages, towns, and cities among all classes of people and enjoyed a rich social life. John spoke of the future. Jesus spoke of the nearness and even of the presence of the kingdom of God in his own ministry as well as in the future. Yet, like John, Jesus recognized the necessity of repentance—the need for humanity to turn away from self-absorption and to embrace God's presence and will.

Jesus came to be baptized by John. The awkwardness of Jesus' submitting to a baptism of repentance for the forgiveness of sins has long bothered, even embarrassed, the church. But, read Mark and there is no embarrassment for Jesus, for at his baptism he hears God's own voice confirming the extraordinary relationship he had with God. Jesus is God's Son and he hears that truth as he rises from the waters in which John baptized him.

Thus, it should not surprise us that the first words from Jesus echo the preaching of the Baptist. We should not miss seeing in the records of Jesus' teaching in the Gospels that his one and only call to repentance came at the beginning of his ministry as he returned from being baptized and being tempted in the wilderness. Thereafter, Jesus proclaimed the kingdom's presence and the importance of embracing its presence. The language of repentance fades into the background, although the idea of a radical turning away from whatever is distracting us from the kingdom is always present in Jesus' teaching as an assumption.

Ever Faithful

John never flagged in his commitment. He lived in rugged circumstances in order to issue a faithful call to making the path of God's future into the present heard. John faced hostility, as we know from his imprisonment and execution by Herod; nevertheless, he preached the message that God had given to him—even at the cost of his life. Moreover, when Jesus arrived on the scene, John was completely open to what God was doing. John was not skeptical of this possible Messiah, he asked him directly whether he was the one he expected. John was not bitter about being surpassed by someone who followed on his coattails. He knew his role in God's plan and he performed it with dedi-cation and clarity. John did not sit in judgment of Jesus; rather, he recognized in him a Savior he might not have anticipated, but one that God may have sent forth just the same.

According to Jesus, those of us who are privileged to live in the time of the kingdom of God that came in the ministry of Jesus Christ have an advantage over John the Baptist. Even so, anyone alive in the world after the life, death, and resurrection of Jesus will do well to live so faithfully as John did. In John we have a fine model of faith.

SHARING THE SCRIPTURE

PREPARING TO TEACH

Preparing Our Hearts

John the Baptist is well known for his unusual habits and clothing, reminiscent of the prophet Elijah. His distinctive appearance caused him to stand out even in his own day. Yet, he was a witness sent by God, a witness who apparently drew large crowds. Think about how you respond to the witness of persons who do not look or act as you expect them to. Ask God to help you uncover reasons for your reluctance to listen impartially to such persons. Likewise, try to listen and learn this week from someone whose theology is quite different from yours. You may not agree with that person, but you will find an opportunity to sharpen your own understanding as you consider why you believe what you believe.

Preparing Our Minds

Read the assigned scripture from Mark and Luke. Also read the lesson carefully. Note especially how John does not lift up himself but points to Jesus, the one who is greater than he. How would you describe John's personality, given that he takes no credit for himself?

Ponder these questions as you prepare this week's lesson: How can John be a model of faith for you? What aspects of his work and ministry help to give focus to your own ministry as a teacher and church leader?

Preparing Our Learning Space

Several activities suggest that you write information on newsprint or a chalkboard so that everyone can see and remember it. You may want to write the questions and/or sentence stems prior to class and post them. If so, cover the board or fold and tape the newsprint in half until you are ready to use it.

Be sure to have on hand:
- several Bibles for students
- newsprint and marker or chalkboard and chalk
- paper and pencils
- picture (possibly from a magazine) of someone whose appearance is different from your own community's norm.

LEADING THE CLASS

(1) Introduction

If you located a picture of someone whose appearance is different from your own community's norm, hold it up or pass it around. If not, describe someone who would appear different. Ask:

[?] **(1) Suppose I invited this person to lead our class next week. What do you think this person would say to us about Jesus?**

(2) Would you be in class to hear this speaker? Why or why not?

(3) God does in fact use persons who do not meet our preconceived notions to be highly effective witnesses, as we shall see in today's lesson. How might that knowledge affect our openness to different persons, especially those whose words of witness call us to bold action?

Guide the discussion toward the scripture lesson by pointing out that John, the one Jesus had sought out to baptize him, would have been seen as "different" when compared to most of the people to whom he witnessed. Yet, God uses a wide variety of people to call others to repentance. John was a faithful witness whose story prompts us to ask: *In what concrete ways can we live as faithful followers and witnesses of Christ today?*

(2) John the Baptist's Work and Witness

Ask the class members to close their eyes and envision the scene as you read Mark 1:4-11 and 14-15. Discuss with them the sounds, sights, smells, textures, or tastes they could experience in their imaginations as you read the story.
Then ask:

[?] **(1) What is the focus of John's ministry? (See "Calling for the Recognition of God's Ways" under Interpreting the Scripture for ideas.)**

(2) How do John and his message reflect the biblical tradition? (See "A Faithful Witness in the Biblical Tradition" [?] **under Interpreting the Scripture.)**

(3) How does John's witness point toward the future that God wills? (See "Looking Toward God's Future" under Interpreting the Scripture.)

(4) How would you describe the relationship between Jesus and John? (See "Jesus and John" under Interpreting the Scripture.)

If the class prefers a lecture format, use ideas from the cited portions of the lesson to develop a lecture prior to the session.

Now read Luke 7:18-23. Note that John was in prison in Machaerus when he sent his two disciples to Jesus. Ask:

(1) Suppose you had been one of the peo [?] **ple sent by John to Jesus. In response to John's question, Jesus says to you, "Go and tell what you have seen and heard." What would you have thought about Jesus' actions?**

(2) What would you have told John about Jesus' actions?

(3) What would be your message to Christians today?

(3) Being Faithful Witnesses and Leaders in Our Own Day

This activity will help to bring John's story into our own time. If possible, divide the class into teams. Give each team a sheet of newsprint and a marker or paper and a pencil. Ask each team to designate a spokesperson to report to the whole class. Tell the teams to consider these questions. You may want to write the questions on newsprint or a chalkboard.

(1) What characteristics do you believe [?] **John possessed that made him an effective leader and witness?**

(2) Which of his characteristics would be important for today's church leaders to have?

(3) If John were to come into the average church in the United States today, what positive responses would he receive? What kinds of problems or

opposition would you expect him to face?

(4) **What changes would need to be made in the modern church in order to hear a leader who has a radical message that challenges people?**

Point out to the group Mark's report that "people from the whole Judean countryside and all the people of Jerusalem" (1:5) went to hear John's message on repentance. Not only did they hear, but they responded by asking to be baptized. The word from God resulted in action on the part of the people. Distribute paper and pencils and invite the students to complete the following sentence stems that you have written on newsprint or a chalkboard. Some students may choose to meditate rather than write responses. Tell the group that their answers are between them and God and will not be discussed.

- John's words remind me that I am called to repent of . . .
- John's humility before Jesus can serve as a model for my own faith by . . .
- Jesus invited John to baptize him. When I think about what my own baptism means to me, I . . .
- John continued to witness, even though his activity led to imprisonment and death. When I consider that level of commitment to faithful discipleship, I . . .

When John sent two disciples to see if Jesus was the awaited Messiah, the Baptist was seeking reassurance. He wanted to know that he had been on the right track, that his work had meaning. As a modern witness for Jesus, what might you say to reassure the persons in the following scenario that they are on the right track with God?

CASE 1: For about six months, Naomi and her husband, Fred, had been driving to the next state at least three weekends a month to see her ailing mother. A few weeks after her mother died, Naomi's husband suffered a stroke. She had arranged for a caregiver to come in during the week while she worked, but on the weekends Naomi cared for Fred herself. Several church members had begun to question her commitment to God because she was so seldom in church. What would you say to Naomi?

HELPING CLASS MEMBERS ACT

The baptism of a baby is a joyous occasion not only for the child's family but for the church as well. Suggest that class members contact families with a word of congratulations, as well as encouragement to the parents to remain (or become) active in the life of the church. Some class members may take on added responsibilities, such as volunteering to baby-sit, so that new parents have some time alone.

Ask class members to consider the ways in which they are witnesses for God. What kind of message does their behavior, attitude, and speech convey to other persons about God's love in Jesus Christ? Suggest that they examine their own lives to see how they may draw persons toward Jesus or push them away from him. Encourage them to make some kind of positive witness this week.

Invite class members to follow John's example of lifting up Christ and his abilities by complimenting at least one person each day on something that they do well.

PLANNING FOR NEXT SUNDAY

Next Sunday's lesson is based on the familiar personalities of Mary and Martha. "Choose Right Priorities" looks at Luke 10:38-42 and John 12:1-8, which the group should read prior to the session. Ask the class to consider their own priorities in life and how this story may challenge the way in which they order their lives.

CHOOSE RIGHT PRIORITIES

PREVIEWING THE LESSON

Lesson Scripture: Luke 10:38-42; John 12:1-8
Background Scripture: Luke 10:38-42; John 12:1-8
Key Verses: Luke 10:41-42

Focus of the Lesson:
Mary's priorities regarding Jesus and his teaching, though criticized by others including Martha, were rightly ordered and therefore commended by him

Main Question of the Lesson:
What do our priorities reveal about our relationship with Jesus?

This lesson will enable adult learners to:
(1) study the priorities of Mary and Martha.
(2) examine their own priorities.
(3) respond by reordering their priorities if necessary.

Today's lesson may be outlined as follows:
(1) Introduction
(2) Mary's Choice: Discipleship
(3) Mary's Choice: Loving Extravagance
(4) Our Own Priorities

FOCUSING ON THE MAIN QUESTION

The two sets of verses for the lesson bring us glimpses of two moments in the life of Mary and Martha (and one incident including their brother, Lazarus) in "a certain village" or "Bethany." We can identify with different characters in these stories in different ways, and shifting our point of view from one position to another may prove to be a helpful way to think about the stories in our lesson.

We should notice that in both Luke's Gospel and John's Gospel we have come to crucial turning points in the story of Jesus. In Luke 9:51, Jesus "set his face to go to Jerusalem," that is, Jesus determined to visit Jerusalem for the final time in his earthly life. In John 12:1, Jesus draws near to Jerusalem only six days before the time of his final Passover in the holy city. The time in both accounts is charged as Luke and John recall dramatic incidents involving Martha and Mary.

In very different ways these stories deliver the same vital message: In our relationship to Jesus Christ it is necessary to act boldly, deliberately, and decisively, recognizing who Jesus is and how God is working in and through him. When we recognize the importance of full and vital devotion to Jesus Christ, we may be moved to actions that will set us in poor stead with those around us. In Luke, Mary seems insensitive to her sister, and in the context of her own social world she would appear to be doing something that was inappropriate for a woman as she acted as a disciple listening to the teaching of a master. In John, Mary seems reckless, wasteful, foolish, and scandalous as she uses extremely expensive ointment to perform an act that was—bluntly evaluated—overtly sensuous and inappropriate public behavior. Decent first-century Mediterranean women did not let down their hair, and decent single adults did not make contact in the manner recounted in this story.

These stories challenge us as we strive to follow Jesus. What have we ever done because of our intense devotion to Jesus Christ that has caused others to wonder about the appropriateness of our behavior? A successful businessman heard his pastor deliver a series of sermons about the wrongs of racism, and the man was moved to resign his membership in a racially exclusive club. Earlier the man had paid over twenty-five thousand dollars to be initiated into that association. Many of his friends, including a number of the members of his church, thought his actions were extreme or fanatical, certainly unnecessary. But his faith prompted him to do what he did. As we study today's lesson, we will ask: *What do our priorities reveal about our relationship with Jesus?*

READING THE SCRIPTURE

NRSV
Luke 10:38-42

38 Now as they went on their way, he entered a certain village, where a woman named Martha welcomed him into her home. ³⁹She had a sister named Mary, who sat at the Lord's feet and listened to what he was saying. ⁴⁰But Martha was distracted by her many tasks; so she came to him and asked, "Lord, do you not care that my sister has left me to do all the work by myself? Tell her then to help me." ⁴¹But the Lord answered her, "Martha, Martha, you are worried and distracted by many things; ⁴²there is need of only one thing. Mary has chosen the better part, which will not be taken away from her."

NIV
Luke 10:38-42

³⁸As Jesus and his disciples were on their way, he came to a village where a woman named Martha opened her home to him. ³⁹She had a sister called Mary, who sat at the Lord's feet listening to what he said. ⁴⁰But Martha was distracted by all the preparations that had to be made. She came to him and asked, "Lord, don't you care that my sister has left me to do the work by myself? Tell her to help me!"

⁴¹"Martha, Martha," the Lord answered, "you are worried and upset about many things, ⁴²but only one thing is needed. Mary has chosen what is better, and it will not be taken away from her."

Key Verses

NRSV
John 12:1-8

1 Six days before the Passover Jesus came to Bethany, the home of Lazarus, whom he had raised from the dead. ²There

NIV
John 12:1-8

1 Six days before the Passover, Jesus arrived at Bethany, where Lazarus lived, whom Jesus had raised from the dead.

they gave a dinner for him. Martha served, and Lazarus was one of those at the table with him. ³Mary took a pound of costly perfume made of pure nard, anointed Jesus' feet, and wiped them with her hair. The house was filled with the fragrance of the perfume. ⁴But Judas Iscariot, one of his disciples (the one who was about to betray him), said, ⁵"Why was this perfume not sold for three hundred denarii and the money given to the poor?" ⁶(He said this not because he cared about the poor, but because he was a thief; he kept the common purse and used to steal what was put into it.) ⁷Jesus said, "Leave her alone. She bought it so that she might keep it for the day of my burial. ⁸You always have the poor with you, but you do not always have me."

²Here a dinner was given in Jesus' honor. Martha served, while Lazarus was among those reclining at the table with him. ³Then Mary took about a pint of pure nard, an expensive perfume; she poured it on Jesus' feet and wiped his feet with her hair. And the house was filled with the fragrance of the perfume.

⁴But one of his disciples, Judas Iscariot, who was later to betray him, objected, ⁵"Why wasn't this perfume sold and the money given to the poor? It was worth a year's wages." ⁶He did not say this because he cared about the poor but because he was a thief; as keeper of the money bag, he used to help himself to what was put into it.

⁷"Leave her alone," Jesus replied. "It was intended that she should save this perfume for the day of my burial. ⁸You will always have the poor among you, but you will not always have me."

UNDERSTANDING THE SCRIPTURE

Luke 10:38-42. This story in Luke's account of the ministry of Jesus is our first encounter in the Gospel with the sisters Martha and Mary. Although there is no mention here of their having a brother named Lazarus, there is little doubt that the Martha and Mary of this story are the same characters that we meet in the Gospel according to John along with their brother, Lazarus. Remarkably, however, we find in Luke that the house in which the events take place belongs to Martha, whereas in John the house belongs to Lazarus. Whether we should think of one or two houses is impossible to determine.

Interpreters debate the focus or central concern of this story. Does the account create a contrast between two kinds of service, one physical and one spiritual, wherein the latter is "better" than the former? Or, does the story contrast active service and passive listening? Is there a certain inconsistency in the story itself that implies a bias toward the heavenly and against the earthly? Readers of Luke's Gospel will know immediately that Luke does not present Jesus as a spiritual leader with a mild disdain for this world. We should not read too much into the account; we should, read the story carefully.

Martha is concerned in this story with *hospitality*, an obligation that was actually sacred in the ancient world. Strangers and travelers were often at the mercy of people they encountered in their travels, and hospitality was a social necessity. The idea that God was a host, especially to Israel, gave the activity of hosting special theological status in the life of Israel and the early church.

The failure to provide hospitality was a social evil that amounted religiously to sin; and the failure to provide adequate hospitality caused social shame. Families in antiquity lived and died by the notions of honor and shame in a way similar to the modern notions of success and failure. If one member of a family was shamed, the whole family suffered severe social stigma. Thus, when Martha attends to the duties of hospitality, she could expect Mary to be concerned with what she was doing. The family's place in polite society was on the line in relation to the adequacy of the hospitality they provided.

Yet, Mary acts in this story in a peculiar way. She does not take up the role of concerned hostess, intent upon providing hospitality. Rather, she acts in the unusual (in that day *abnormal*) manner of a disciple. Women rarely, if ever, took on this role in society, so that in what she left undone and in what she did Mary acted peculiarly in the eyes of her contemporaries.

John 12:1-8. There are very similar stories to this one in the other three Gospels. This account is unique in several of its features. First, the mention of Lazarus brings a new character and a new tone to the events. One should not miss that in the preceding chapter of John, Jesus had raised Lazarus from the dead. His performing of this life-restoring miracle had angered his enemies who, John tells the reader, determined to kill him to eliminate a political threat to the nation of Israel. Moreover, immediately after the verses of this story, in John 12:9-11, John says the chief priests decided to put Lazarus to death along with Jesus since it was on account of his having been raised from the dead that many of the Jews had come to believe in Jesus. Second, also remarkable here is the note that Martha served while Lazarus was at table with Jesus and while Mary performed the anointing. Martha does here exactly what she did in Luke.

Mary's pound of nard ointment would have been about twelve ounces of exotic perfumed substance from the Orient, probably out of the Himalayas. The rarity of the item and the expense of transportation, along with its being a luxury item, caused it to be costly. The sum mentioned in the story, three hundred denarii, amounted to approximately a year's wages for a laborer. The denarius was the sum typically paid for a day's work. Moreover, Jesus' words about the appropriateness of the action—a shocking deed, at best—relates the anointing to his forthcoming death. Seeming extravagance finds meaning in relation to the even greater extravagance of God's so loving the world that God gave Jesus!

John exposes Judas's hypocrisy as he tells of the protest about the waste of the perfume. On the surface, giving alms to the poor was a sign of piety and devotion to God, who was concerned for the lowly. John interprets Judas's insincerity, attributing it to greed and to John's certain knowledge of Judas's having betrayed Jesus.

Jesus' own pronouncement forms a kind of proverb. He does not mean to trivialize a genuine concern for the poor; rather, the statement identifies the crucial significance of the moment as he looks toward the last days of his earthly life, to his Passion, crucifixion, and resurrection.

INTERPRETING THE SCRIPTURE

Preface

As we follow the scheme of the lesson we shall think our way through two incidents that are different in time and occurrences, but that are remarkably similar in concern. Mary had a way of doing things that made others ask questions about what was appropriate or inappropriate behavior. Once her actions forced a distinction between "good" and "best"; another time her actions caused Jesus to speak of the difference between both "right and wrong" and "better and best."

Jesus Visits Martha and Mary

Luke tells the story vividly in the style of good storytelling. Initially, we locate Jesus and his followers in a village on the way to Jerusalem, and then we follow them into Martha's house. Martha clearly defines the space; it is her house, so that all others, including Mary, seem to be guests. Mary is defined in relation to her sister, although she acts independently by sitting at Jesus' feet to hear his teaching. Thus, Mary assumes the posture and plays the role of a model disciple. By contrast, as the story continues, Martha is distracted from Jesus' teaching by the activities of hospitality. She protests, calling indirectly for Jesus to rebuke Mary and to charge her to assist her sister in providing hospitality. Jesus refuses and instead gently, but clearly, rebukes Martha as he praises Mary's choice of devotion to his teaching.

Showing Concern for Things That Matter

The verses of our lesson from Luke tell a story that shows that persons concerned with embodying God's love and will have nothing better to do than to hear the words of Jesus Christ. The story directs disciples to hear the teaching of Jesus above all else, for all else is secondary and must follow in the wake of listening to Jesus' words. What Martha does is good, but it is less than the best. All her service is lovely—although her call for Jesus to rebuke Mary suggests that a touch of legalism motivates her elaborate performance of hospitality. Moreover, all Martha's efforts pale by comparison with the seemingly passive act of listening to Jesus' teaching—the role that her sister, Mary, elects.

Jesus' answer to Martha contrasts "many things" (good things) with "one thing" that is better because it is deemed "necessary." A clue for deeper understanding of Jesus' statement comes when we note at verse 41 that Luke refers to Jesus as "the Lord." That is who Jesus is! Thus, Mary attends to the one necessary action for true disciples: she hears the word of the Lord. Jesus calls us to an active life of discipleship. Yet, we are not set off for service that merely amounts to doing many good things. Rather, we are called to hear the word of our Lord, for only then are we equipped to understand his will and to undertake the multifaceted service to which he directs us. Indirectly, the story of Martha and Mary contrasts industrious service *to* the Lord with educated service *for* the Lord. From the entire context of Luke's Gospel we should see that simply listening is never an end in itself, but plenty of good work does not replace hearing and, then, doing the word of the Lord.

In studying these verses we should realize that most of us probably find it easier to identify with Martha than with Mary. An engaging question for reflection is, "How would you have felt about things if you had been Martha?" Moreover, we live in a world that is recently and painfully aware that cultures socialize humans to take on certain roles as they grow up. Martha was doing what women were supposed to do, providing hospitality; and she was doing a major task by taking in Jesus and his disciples. We should recall that Luke reported that at least seventy disciples were with Jesus on the road to Jerusalem (10:1). Martha takes on the preparations for a multitude while Mary takes a seat. How would we feel in Martha's place? Mary could have listened another time. Or, could she? We should also recall that Jesus has set his face toward Jerusalem (9:51), so that he moves ever closer to his Passion. In Luke's story-time the moment is crucial. Jesus' call to discipleship places demands on the lives of those around him. Jesus' call to discipleship may even redefine traditional social roles, as was the case with Mary. Those who encounter Jesus are called to recognize the difference between what is good and what is necessarily better, and they are expected to act appropriately. Thus, while we can and should sympathize with Martha, we stand with her before Jesus and we hear his words. Will we listen? Now, with whom will we identify—with Martha or Mary?

Mary Anoints Jesus' Feet

This story locates Jesus in Bethany at a banquet in the company of Lazarus, Martha, and Mary. We learn of Mary's anointing Jesus' feet with costly ointment. We see that Judas objects, and this development gives the author of the Gospel according to John an opportunity to comment on Judas's hypocritical dishonesty. As always in John, however, Jesus has the final word. His complex statement is confrontational, prophetic, and revealing. Jesus' words both conclude and dominate the account. Thus, while Mary's action is the point with which we can identify as we seek to relate through generosity to our Lord, the focus is taken off both Mary's extravagance and Judas's deceitful character by the very striking words of Jesus.

Asking Questions of the Text

John's story is both similar and dissimilar to the stories in Matthew 26:6-13; Mark 14:3-9; and Luke 7:36-50. Read in conjunction with the other accounts of the anointing of Jesus, this story raises far more questions than anyone can answer. For example, when was Jesus anointed? Where did this take place? Was he anointed on the head or the feet? Who did the anointing? How did she do it? Who objected? Why? What did Jesus say? There are still other possible questions, and no one has full or sufficient answers; so, people usually know a homogenized version of this story taken from the different

accounts; and, perhaps most tragically, they twist the harmonized account to whatever end they wish. Thus, one former president loosely quoted Jesus' words about the poor to defend cutting relief programs to those in poverty.

The only real remedy to the impossible interpretive situation and the steady abuse of the account(s) of this event is to take the story as directly as possible in the terms that each particular evangelist presents it. Thus, we must let John be John, we must not ask him to be Mark or Luke—or, Mark and Luke. If we approach John's account in this manner, we must take seriously the mood of the narrative, the development of the story, and move with the text to where it takes us!

Mary Celebrates Jesus' Presence

The story begins by placing Jesus in an atmosphere that recalls and celebrates his many wondrous deeds. Mary's extravagant action celebrates the life and work of Jesus, a life that manifested the power and will of God. In turn, the story focuses on the responses of different humans to Jesus' ministry. What Jesus did produced gratitude and joy, even celebration. We should ask ourselves how the gospel affects our lives today so that we are moved in sheer gratitude to celebrate the goodness of God's work in Jesus Christ.

Yet, lest the mood of festivity run wild, the story brings in the sour, self-centered resentment of Judas who was less than enthused about Jesus' ministry and the joyous reaction of others to it. Simply ignoring this part of the story, however, may impart an artificial sweetness to the rest of the account and, thus, to our thinking! Indeed, the next portion of the story that refers to the death of Jesus will make little sense without some recognition of the real hostility that he encountered in the course of his life and work. A frank recognition that the whole world is not singing Jesus' praises helps us understand the full impact of the gospel.

Jesus Blesses Generosity

The words of Jesus expose the hypocrisy of Judas's objection and point to the cross and resurrection, that is, to Jesus' costly glory achieved in the context of God's saving work in relation to humankind. The difficult reference to the poor surely means that if we are truly grateful to God for the joy of salvation we know in Christ, then, now that our Lord has died and been raised, we have—in relation to the poor—a clear opportunity to express our gratitude. Thus, the story ends with Jesus' call to take seriously the real needs of others! Perhaps when we wrestle with this story in its details we will even be led to react as Mary did, that is, with extravagance.

SHARING THE SCRIPTURE

PREPARING TO TEACH

Preparing Our Hearts

Today's lesson looks at two stories about Mary and Martha that help us to focus on choosing priorities. In the Sermon on the Mount, Jesus calls us to get our priorities in order by seeking first the kingdom of God (see Matthew 6:33). Take a look at your calendar and think over the events of the last week or month. Honestly assess whether your time has been spent on priorities that would win Jesus' approval. Remember that the first priority may not necessarily involve your presence at church. Visiting a lonely neighbor may be, from Jesus' perspective, a far higher priority than serving a church dinner. What changes do you think God is calling you to make in the way that you order your priorities?

Preparing Our Minds

Read the accounts from Luke 10:38-42 and John 12:1-8, along with today's lesson. Try to envision yourself as Mary and then as Martha. As you consider Luke's story, imagine the feelings you might have if you were Martha. Listen carefully to Jesus' words to Martha in Luke and to Judas in John. How do these words help you to understand the priorities to which Jesus calls us?

Note the comments under "Asking Questions of the Text" in the Interpreting the Scripture portion. Although we will not be discussing the accounts of the anointing of Jesus found in the other Gospels, you may want to read these to help class members who want to harmonize the stories to focus on John's account.

Preparing Our Learning Space

Before class begins, write this information on a sheet of newsprint or a chalkboard. Keep the newsprint or chalkboard covered until you come to the "Our Own Priorities" part of the lesson.

Look at this list and rank each item according to the priority that you give it in a normal week. Your highest priority would be number 1 and lowest number 8.
- Work/career or whatever you consider to be your work
- Parents or extended family who do not live in your home
- Children and other family members living in your home
- Housework/yard maintenance
- Church activities during the week
- Personal devotional time for Bible study, prayer, and other spiritual disciplines
- Recreation or socializing with friends
- Attendance at Sunday school and worship

Have on hand:
- several Bibles for students
- newsprint and marker or chalk and chalkboard
- paper and pencils

LEADING THE CLASS

(1) Introduction

Begin today's session by reading or retelling the incident of the businessman who dropped his exclusive club membership, as found in the Focusing on the Main Question portion of the lesson. Then ask class members to share personal incidents of an action they took because of their faith. Have them consider how other persons perceived their behavior. After several examples have been shared, note that Mary, the sister of Martha and Lazarus, took action because of her relationship with Jesus. To Martha, Mary's action seemed inappropriate. Later action by Mary seemed wasteful and extravagant. Yet, Jesus commended her. She had her priorities in order.

Note today's main question as we begin our study of the stories of Mary and Martha as recorded in Luke and John. *What do our priorities reveal about our relationship with Jesus?*

(2) Mary's Choice: Discipleship

Choose a volunteer to read aloud Luke 10:38-42. Use information from the Understanding the Scripture portion for this passage to help class members understand how Martha was acting appropriately by providing hospitality. In contrast, Mary's disciple-like behavior was definitely unusual for a woman of her time.

Refer to the "Showing Concern for Things That Matter" section under Interpreting the Scripture. Point out that what Martha was doing was both good and necessary. Her work was important. However, in response to her protest about Mary's failure to do her share of the work, Jesus commended Mary for the choice she had made. Ask these questions to the class. Or, if you choose, divide the class into two groups, asking one to pretend to be Martha and the other, Mary.

[R] Suppose you had been Martha. You are fulfilling your expected role by inviting guests (perhaps seventy or more who [R] were traveling with Jesus) into your home. Instead of fulfilling her proper role, your sister is sitting around listening to Jesus.

(1) **How would you have felt?** [?]
(2) **What would you have said to Jesus about Mary's behavior?**
(3) **What reaction would you have had to Jesus' words? Would they have caused you to reorder your priorities? Why or why not?**

Suppose you had been Mary. You know [R] you can cook or clean anytime, but you seldom have the chance to hear Jesus. You know that your actions defy social custom, but you decide that Jesus' message is too important to miss.

(1) **How would you feel about Martha's** [?] **protest?**
(2) **What would Jesus' words have helped you to understand about your own priorities?**
(3) **How would you describe your relationship with Jesus?**

(3) Mary's Choice: Loving Extravagance

Choose a volunteer to read aloud John 12:1-8. Consider selecting someone to read Judas's words (verse 5) and Jesus' words (verses 7-8) to give the group the feel for the dialogue.

Refer to this passage of scripture as discussed in the Understanding the Scripture segment. Also refer to "Mary Anoints Jesus' Feet," "Mary Celebrates Jesus' Presence," and "Jesus Blesses Generosity" in the Interpreting the Scripture portion. Use this information to help you fill in gaps of the class's answers to these questions:

(1) **How would Mary's actions have been** [?] **understood by those who were present?**
(2) **What does Judas's concern reveal about his character?**
(3) **What do Jesus' words reveal about his response to Mary and her actions?**
(4) **Had you been present, would you have thought that Judas had unjustly criticized Mary, or would you too**

?

have thought she was being extravagant ? Defend your answer.

(4) Our Own Priorities

Post the sheet with the activities listed under "Preparing Our Learning Space" that you wrote before class. Distribute paper and pencils and provide a few moments for class members to rate their own priorities. By a show of hands, find out what the first and second priority was for the group. Then talk about why we order our lives the way we do. What motivates our commitments? Although church-related activities may rate high, point out that there is no "correct" order here. Remember that the person home caring for a sick relative is acting in a way consistent with Christian discipleship. Some students may express a need to give more attention to their spiritual lives. If so, ask the group for suggestions as to how they go about finding more time for God in their busy lives.

In Jesus' commendation of Mary, we find that personal relationships—the care and attention we give to one another—are more important than agreeing with certain doctrines. Mary showed her belief in Jesus by the way that she listened to him (in Luke) and anointed him with expensive nard (in John). Suggest that class members work with a partner or small team to discuss these questions:

?

(1) What kinds of things do you do to show other persons that you care for them?

(2) How have you experienced God's love through other people?

(3) In what ways do you show your devotion to Jesus?

Provide a few moments for the class to center on these thoughts:

Martha was focused on her task. She did R what was expected of her by providing food and hospitality. In contrast, Mary ignored the task and focused her attention on Jesus. Consider how you are like Martha and like Mary, as well as how you are unlike each of these women. Are there times when you need to learn to let go, to set the task aside, so that you can give your undivided attention to the Savior?

HELPING CLASS MEMBERS ACT

Some people are so bogged down that they cannot get away from a family member who needs care or some other serious situation that demands their attention. Suggest that each class member seek out at least one person this week who would like to attend church or do something else for the Lord but cannot escape pressing responsibilities and volunteer to do something that will allow the caregiver the freedom to concentrate on God.

Encourage class members to surprise someone this week with a meaningful gift to express gratitude. Though it need not be as costly as nard, the gift should be carefully selected or possibly handmade.

Suggest that the students plan to extend hospitality to someone who needs to be remembered. As in Martha's day, the hospitality may include a home-cooked meal, but it may involve lunch at a restaurant or tickets to a show or some other activity that person finds enjoyable.

PLANNING FOR NEXT SUNDAY

Ask the class to read Matthew 4:18-20 and 16:13-23 in preparation for next Sunday's lesson on Peter. This disciple was called to confess Christ, and so he did. Suggest that as class members study their lesson, they consider ways in which they confess (or deny) Jesus.

CONFESS CHRIST

PREVIEWING THE LESSON

Lesson Scripture: Matthew 4:18-20; 16:13-23
Background Scripture: Matthew 4:18-20; 16:13-23
Key Verse: Matthew 16:16

Focus of the Lesson:
Peter, who had answered Jesus' call to follow, confessed his faith in Jesus as the Messiah and Son of God

Main Question of the Lesson:
How do we show and how do we fail to show that we believe what we confess, that Jesus is the Messiah, the Son of the living God?

This lesson will enable adult learners to:
(1) explore the nature of Peter's faith.
(2) examine their own confession of faith.
(3) respond by acting on the strength of their convictions.

Today's lesson may be outlined as follows:
(1) Introduction
(2) Peter's Faith
(3) Confessing Our Own Faith

FOCUSING ON THE MAIN QUESTION

The two sets of verses from Matthew's Gospel tell of three striking incidents in the ministry of Jesus that involved Simon Peter in a significant way. While our lesson emphasizes the confession by Peter at Caesarea Philippi that Jesus was "the Messiah, the Son of the living God," as we study the verses for this week, we first see Peter at the time of his call to discipleship; then as he makes his confession at Caesarea Philippi; and finally as he and Jesus engage in a sharp exchange when Peter tries to tell Jesus how to do God's will.

Peter, like all of us, responded to Jesus in various ways. At the time of his call Peter shows spontaneity, confidence, decisiveness, and courage in simply walking away from his usual manner of everyday life in order to answer Jesus' call to follow him as a disciple. Called to follow, Peter (along with his brother Andrew) did exactly that. As we find this incident reported in scripture, we do not know why Jesus called the sons of Jonah or why Peter and Andrew acted so immediately in answering the call. In turn, as he followed Jesus during the early days of Jesus' ministry, Peter saw the marvelous deeds that Jesus did and he heard the moving teaching about the kingdom of heaven. Having been a disciple, Peter gained insight into who Jesus was, so that when Jesus asked the disciples who they believed him to be, Peter could confess with incisive clarity that Jesus was both the Messiah and the Son of God. Nevertheless, even though Peter trusted Jesus and had some understanding of who he was, when Jesus spoke to his disciples about his forthcoming suffering, death, and resurrection, it was Peter who took Jesus aside and tried to straighten him out about how to be who he was!

Peter is much like the rest of us who call ourselves disciples of Jesus Christ. Sometimes we do what Jesus calls us to do, unhesitatingly with full confidence in our Lord. Yet, at other times we seem to think (although we would not say it) that we know better than Jesus what God wants done in the world. We are called to confess Jesus Christ as Lord, and in that confession is the truth that disciples are to follow, not to try to lead, their master. In what kinds of ways do we (each and all) succeed and fail as disciples? *How do we show and how do we fail to show that we believe what we confess, that Jesus is the Messiah, the Son of the living God?*

READING THE SCRIPTURE

NRSV
Matthew 4:18-20

18 As he walked by the Sea of Galilee, he saw two brothers, Simon, who is called Peter, and Andrew his brother, casting a net into the sea—for they were fishermen. [19]And he said to them, "Follow me, and I will make you fish for people." [20]Immediately they left their nets and followed him.

NIV
Matthew 4:18-20

[18]As Jesus was walking beside the Sea of Galilee, he saw two brothers, Simon called Peter and his brother Andrew. They were casting a net into the lake, for they were fishermen. [19]"Come, follow me," Jesus said, "and I will make you fishers of men." [20]At once they left their nets and followed him.

NRSV
Matthew 16:13-23

13 Now when Jesus came into the district of Caesarea Philippi, he asked his disciples, "Who do people say that the Son of Man is?" [14]And they said, "Some say John the Baptist, but others Elijah, and still others Jeremiah or one of the prophets." [15]He said to them, "But who do you say that I am?" [16]Simon Peter answered, "You are the Messiah, the Son of the living God." [17]And Jesus answered him, "Blessed are you, Simon son of Jonah! For flesh and blood has not revealed this to you, but my Father in heaven. [18]And I tell you, you are Peter, and on this rock I will build my church,

NIV
Matthew 16:13-23

[13]When Jesus came to the region of Caesarea Philippi, he asked his disciples, "Who do people say the Son of Man is?"

[14]They replied, "Some say John the Baptist; others say Elijah; and still others, Jeremiah or one of the prophets."

[15]"But what about you?" he asked. "Who do you say I am?"

[16]Simon Peter answered, "You are the Christ, the Son of the living God."

[17]Jesus replied, "Blessed are you, Simon son of Jonah, for this was not revealed to you by man, but by my Father in heaven. [18]And I tell you that you are Peter, and on

Key
Verse

K
Ve

and the gates of Hades will not prevail against it. ¹⁹I will give you the keys of the kingdom of heaven, and whatever you bind on earth will be bound in heaven, and whatever you loose on earth will be loosed in heaven." ²⁰Then he sternly ordered the disciples not to tell anyone that he was the Messiah.

21 From that time on, Jesus began to show his disciples that he must go to Jerusalem and undergo great suffering at the hands of the elders and chief priests and scribes, and be killed, and on the third day be raised. ²²And Peter took him aside and began to rebuke him, saying, "God forbid it, Lord! This must never happen to you." ²³But he turned and said to Peter, "Get behind me, Satan! You are a stumbling block to me; for you are setting your mind not on divine things but on human things."

this rock I will build my church, and the gates of Hades will not overcome it. ¹⁹I will give you the keys of the kingdom of heaven; whatever you bind on earth will be bound in heaven, and whatever you loose on earth will be loosed in heaven." ²⁰Then he warned his disciples not to tell anyone that he was the Christ.

²¹From that time on Jesus began to explain to his disciples that he must go to Jerusalem and suffer many things at the hands of the elders, chief priests and teachers of the law, and that he must be killed and on the third day be raised to life.

²²Peter took him aside and began to rebuke him. "Never, Lord!" he said. "This shall never happen to you!"

²³Jesus turned and said to Peter, "Get behind me, Satan! You are a stumbling block to me; you do not have in mind the things of God, but the things of men."

UNDERSTANDING THE SCRIPTURE

Matthew 4:18-20. These verses are the initial half of the story of Jesus' calling his first disciples in Matthew 4:18-22. The activity of fishing, the trade of Simon and Andrew, becomes the basis of the metaphor with which Jesus calls and directs the brothers into discipleship. We learn here only that Simon was called Peter, although in the verses of this week's lesson that follow (see Matthew 16:18) we learn that Jesus gave Simon the nickname Peter, that means "rock" and that refers to the solid faith upon which Jesus aimed to build the congregation of those who came to follow him as Lord. In the Greek text the call to discipleship is distinctive, for Jesus says (literally), "Come! after me." The words "after me" are *opisó mou* in Greek, and strikingly, in the later verses of our lesson—at Matthew 16:23 when Jesus says, "Get behind me, Satan!"—the words "behind me" are *opisó mou* in Greek.

Finally, we should not fail to notice that in the very first words with which Jesus called people to be his disciples, there are at least two crucial assumptions: (1) Jesus expected disciples *to follow*, that is, his disciples were to take their lead from him, from his work, from his words, and from his ways; (2) Jesus understood the call to discipleship to be a call toward a ministry of outreach and inclusion. Peter and Andrew (and all the others) were called to become disciples in order to follow Jesus as he led them to bring others into the new reality that he came to proclaim and to establish.

Matthew 16:13-14. Caesarea Philippi was a city north of Galilee. Jesus and his disciples were in the vicinity of this community, which had originally been named Paneas for the pagan god Pan, but renamed Caesarea Philippi in honor of Caesar Tiberius by Herod Philip. This location is perhaps as far north as Jesus ever traveled. There, Jesus asked his disciple about popular perceptions of who he was and, by implication, what he was about in his work. The collection of answers—John the Baptist, Elijah, Jeremiah, one of the prophets—shows that the people who encountered Jesus during the course of his ministry perceived his words and deeds to be those of a prophet.

The reports suggest that people understood Jesus' person and work to signify God's long-awaited, promised, final action in the world. The return of a prophet from the dead, particularly of Elijah, was thought to be the penultimate act of God in judging and redeeming the world.

Matthew 16:15-16. Jesus, however, forced the issue with his disciples directly, "But who do you say that I am?" First, Jesus asked for a report; then, he asked for an opinion. Simon Peter spoke for himself and probably for the group of the disciples. This Jesus who healed the sick, exorcised demons, and spoke with clarity and authority was perhaps a prophet, but he was more than a prophet. Peter recognized in Jesus the one that Israel had long expected and awaited from God. Israel hoped for the Messiah, but in popular expectation this figure was something like a Jewish Caesar—a military leader like King David who would liberate and elevate Israel to a position of international dominance.

The terms "Messiah" and "Son of [the living] God" are used here as if they were synonyms, although they are not. Yet, remarkably, among the writings preserved from the caves near the Dead Sea known as the Dead Sea Scrolls, one of the most recently published texts seems to refer to the Messiah as being God's Son. Thus, Peter recognized in Jesus one who came from God to do God's work on earth that meant the establishment of God's reign among humanity.

Matthew 16:17-18. The use of the phrase "son of Jonah" is a pointed recognition of Simon's human origins. The blessing pronounced by Jesus on Peter illustrates the biblical conviction that what humans know about God comes as the result of God's revelation, not of humans' "figuring out" God. This observation does not disparage valid human reason or intellect, but puts it in its place in the scheme of relations between God and humanity. God comes to us as creator, and we recognize and reflect upon God's presence and actions. Thus, Jesus says Simon was blessed, for he had received the gracious gift of God's opening his eyes to who Jesus was and that God was at work in the world in Jesus' ministry. Moreover, Jesus' words tell us that faith such as Simon's, though imperfect, is the foundation of what God through Christ is establishing in the world.

Matthew 16:19-20. The words about binding and loosing, spoken to Simon Peter here, have a rich history of interpretation. The Roman Catholic Church has at times related these lines to the authority of Peter that is thought to be inherited by the Pope. Various Protestant interpreters, however, have taken the lines in relation to the responsibility of all believers to maintain a clear faith in Christ and to exercise divinely commissioned oversight of the life of the church in full confidence that the presence and the power of the risen Lord inform believers as they seek to do God's will faithfully.

Matthew 16:21-23. Jesus predicted his Passion, and his understanding of God led him to speak about his resurrection. His words, however, could not be heard by Simon Peter. Thus, Peter tried to tell Jesus how to be the Messiah. Jesus would have none of it, and in his reply he put Peter in his place—quite literally. Jesus told Peter to get back into the role of following, for in taking the lead he opposed God and set himself in service to Satan.

INTERPRETING THE SCRIPTURE

Faith Without Flinching

Simon and Andrew answered Jesus on the spot. When Christ comes calling he demands our full attention and a decision. Thus, we do not have the luxury of pondering the gospel. We hear the good news of God's gracious reconciliation of the world in Jesus Christ and we either believe or we do not. Behind this fact is another: God's Spirit working in our lives, our hearts, our minds, either has sufficiently prepared us for the reception of the gospel or has not. Simon and Andrew walked away from job, family, and friends—in other words, they left all forms of earthly security in order to answer the call of Jesus to be his disciples. They seem imprudent. They seem unattached and, therefore, reckless; but remember the rest of the story. Simon had his ups and downs, but Christian tradition has it that after the resurrection of Jesus he traveled far and wide (with his wife) preaching the gospel and that he ultimately died in Rome as a faithful witness to the presence and power of God in Jesus Christ. We can easily say that Peter was impetuous in abandoning his nets and family responsibilities to wander around Palestine with Jesus—until we see the traditional end of the story. Peter died in faithful service to the gospel, his wife being his companion, and he was more embroiled with responsibilities in relation to the life of many early Christian congregations than any fisher could imagine.

The Nature of Faith

The way Matthew tells of the well-known confession of Peter at Caesarea Philippi gives us information about several features of valid faith. In the first place, faith is *informed*. Jesus assumed that his disciples knew what others were saying about him. Jesus' followers were not cut off from society and uninformed about the ideas of others concerning who Jesus was and what he was doing. In the second place, faith is *involved*. The disciples were not allowed merely to repeat the thinking of others. They had to confess who Jesus was for themselves. It is necessary to struggle with the heart of our faith for ourselves and to form a clear belief that is our own. In the third place, faith is *independent*. It may be necessary for us to come to a conclusion about God's will that is different from the typical thinking of others, even those who have long pondered the matter. Jesus Christ calls us to a new way of thinking—to a manner of thought that is focused, concrete, and given to vital proclamation: JESUS IS LORD! In the fourth place, faith is *inspired*. What we know about Jesus—his life and work, along with his will for our own lives—does not simply come from our own reflection; it comes from the presence, power, and persistence of God in our lives. These four qualities of our faith are the bases of Jesus' declaration to Peter, "Blessed are you, Simon son of Jonah!" As we live in faith, we can count on hearing the Lord's blessing for our own lives.

The Dynamics of Faith

Matthew arranges the story of Peter's confession so that we see that faith is not merely static; faith is not simply something that brings us a divine blessing. Having affirmed the authenticity of Simon's faith, Jesus continued to speak so that he commented on the responsibilities inherent in vital faith. Jesus gave the faith-filled Peter the charge to do the work of God on earth and, at the same time, the authority for the doing of that work. Peter was not made a little god; yet, his pregnant faith is charged with God's own power for the accomplishment of God's will.

There are at least two dimensions of the work to which Peter was commissioned. First, he was to give himself to the service of the church. The charge of Christ to ministry was a call to Peter to bear the weight of the church, to provide—through the God-given strength of faith—the support the church needs to be established in the world. Second, Peter was directed beyond the confines of the church to be Christ's worker "on earth." Such work established God's ways among humans. We may call such ministry "social action" or "community service" or "basic gospel work," but we should not miss seeing that Jesus' words assume that Christians have concerns that extend beyond the boundaries of the community of faith.

Faith and Obstacles

In Jesus' own words to Simon Peter we see a warning about the difficulties we are to expect as we minister in the name of Jesus Christ. As Jesus says, "the gates of Hades" will rail against those who live in service through faith. Yet, Jesus' words to the disciples also contain an assurance that his disciples will be sustained in their faithful efforts—"the gates of Hades will *not* prevail" (emphasis added). Thus, the charge to ministry, the gift of authority for ministry that is given to every believer in Christ, is not a call to privilege, position, power, and pleasure; rather, the call of Christ to do his work is a directive to ministry wherein disciples (we) can count on opposition, but it is a call wherein we are guaranteed divine support. Faith that is inspired by God, who inspires and directs us to service, empowers us to serve the same God who is with us in ministry regardless of the difficulties we may face.

The True Role of Discipleship

It should not surprise anyone who reads this story that the nature of ministry, the nature of discipleship to which Jesus calls us, is difficult to understand. When Jesus spoke about his death to the disciples, we should not be surprised to see Simon Peter, the Rock of the Church, trying to set his master straight. After all, Jesus had just told Peter that he had been blessed with the divinely revealed truth that Jesus was the Messiah, the Son of the living God; and in affirmation of Peter's faith Jesus had promised him the authority to do the hard work of ministry. This knowledgeable and empowered disciple heard his master—the Messiah, the Son of the living God—talking about his Passion, and Jesus' words completely threw Peter for a loop. Peter acted logically when he rebuked Jesus. Whatever he said, Peter's words were strong, for the verb translated "to rebuke" is the same word used throughout the Gospel in reference to Jesus' rebuking demons. Yet, it is Jesus, not Peter, who has the final say in this exchange. Jesus' words as they are recorded in Matthew are sharp: "Get behind me, Satan! You are a stumbling block to me; for you are setting your mind not on divine things but on human things (16:23)."

What Jesus Meant

Four items in this sharp exchange demand attention. First, Jesus calls Peter "Satan." As Satan had tempted Jesus in the wilderness, now Peter tempts Jesus by attempting to turn him away from the hard road ahead. Second, Jesus orders Peter, "Get behind me." This is not a dismissal, "Get lost!" but a call (as we noted above in the use of the vocabulary, see Matthew 4:19) to Peter to assume his proper place as a disciple. The same words formed the original call of Peter and Andrew to discipleship. Third, Jesus tells Peter he is a stumbling block, because Peter's call to Jesus to move away from the cross sets before Jesus the scandalous possibility of not suffering for humanity (see Matthew 20:28). Strikingly, the possibility of disobedience to God's will seems real for Jesus, but he rejects this terrible temptation. Fourth, having called Peter "Satan," having called him back into line, and having refused the scandalous option of disobedience, Jesus tells Peter that his mind is set on human, not divine, things. Jesus lived obediently and he served selflessly; but, in contrast, Peter seems to think only of the easy road and the good times. Peter, who recognized Jesus, still did not comprehend the call to discipleship as a call to service; rather, he interpreted it as a call to privilege and power. Jesus labeled such thinking as human and not divine. How shall we understand the call to discipleship? What will be our confession?

SHARING THE SCRIPTURE

PREPARING TO TEACH

Preparing Our Hearts

What, indeed, is your confession? What do you believe about who Jesus is, what he was sent to do, and his relationship with God? Ponder these questions as you prepare to lead the class. Think further about whether your own brand of discipleship is one that follows Jesus by serving others, or if you expect your confession in Jesus to bring you special privilege and power. Record your thoughts in your spiritual journal.

Preparing Our Minds

Carefully read Matthew 4:18-20 and 16:13-23 this week. Also become familiar with the lesson. Note especially the key verse, Matthew 16:16. Imagine how each of your class members might respond to Jesus' question. Be prepared to offer assurance of God's love to those who are searching for a relationship with Jesus.

If time permits, read the Nicene Creed and other creeds, both historic and modern, to gain a better understanding of what the people of God have believed about who Jesus was and what God sent him to accomplish.

Preparing Our Learning Space

Try to have available a hymnal or other worship aid that contains the Apostles' Creed written in question and answer form, such as that found on page 41 of *The United Methodist Hymnal*. If you cannot obtain sufficient copies, write the creed on newsprint so you can post it during the session.

Have on hand:
- several Bibles for students
- newsprint and marker or chalkboard and chalk
- paper and pencils
- copies of the Apostles' Creed

LEADING THE CLASS

(1) Introduction

Begin by telling the class that the Apostles' Creed was originally a series of questions and answers used to help early Christian converts learn what the church believed about the Father, Son, and Holy Spirit. Either distribute copies of the hymnal with the creed or post the newsprint on which you wrote the creed. If you do not have access to a copy of the creed in question and answer form, ask these questions and have the group respond with the appropriate segments:

(1) **Do you believe in God the Father?** (response: I believe in God . . . earth.)
(2) **Do you believe in Jesus Christ?** (response: I believe in Jesus . . . dead.)
(3) **Do you believe in the Holy Spirit?**

?

(response: I believe in the Holy Spirit . . . everlasting.)

Then ask the students to work in small groups and focus on the portion of the creed concerning Jesus. Have them address these questions, which you may want to write on newsprint or a chalkboard:

?

(1) **How does this creed reflect what you believe about Jesus?**

(2) **Which statements about Jesus, if any, are troublesome to you? Why?**

When you bring the class back together, note that today we will be studying an early confession of faith made by Peter. In this session we will ask: *How do we show and how do we fail to show that we believe what we confess, that Jesus is the Messiah, the Son of the living God?*

(2) Peter's Faith

Choose a volunteer to read aloud Matthew 4:18-20. Then give class members these instructions: Put yourself in Peter's place and tell a partner what happened to you when Jesus called. Try to explain why you followed this man Jesus. Describe how you expected your life to change once you said yes to Jesus' invitation to follow him.

If the class prefers a lecture format, use ideas from "Faith Without Flinching" in the Interpreting the Scripture portion and verses 18-20 in the Understanding the Scripture segment to help the group grasp Peter's response to Jesus' call.

Now move the class ahead to a later point in Jesus' ministry to his question to Peter. Read aloud Matthew 16:13-23. To help the group understand the dialogue better, have one person read the narrator's part; another person, the disciples' response; a third person, Peter's words; and someone else to read Jesus' response.

Point out (as noted in "The Dynamics of Faith" portion) that once Peter confesses his faith Jesus speaks to him about the responsibilities of faith. Jesus expects his

disciple to serve and gives him the authority to do so. If class members are good Bible students, ask them to give examples of how Peter's confession of faith resulted in service. Do not spend a great deal of time on this activity. You are using it to show how Peter's confession and Jesus' response shaped Peter's future ministry.

Mention that Peter could have been on the wrong track with Jesus. He had failed to understand the importance of Jesus' suffering for humanity. Use information from "The True Role of Discipleship" and "What Jesus Meant" under Interpreting the Scripture to help the class comprehend Peter's early misunderstanding—despite his confession of faith—of who Jesus was and what he was called to do.

(3) Confessing Our Own Faith

Note under "The Nature of Faith" in the Interpreting the Scripture section that Peter's faith is *informed, involved, independent, and inspired.* We will look at each of these descriptions in turn. State that Jesus assumed that his disciples knew what others were saying about him. In other words, he believed they were informed. Then ask:

(1) **What do you think society as a whole believes about Jesus?**

?

(2) **What do you perceive most church members believe about Jesus?**

(3) **On what do you base your opinions? In other words, where do you look for information?**

Read this quote from the lesson concerning involvement: "They (the disciples) had to confess who Jesus was for themselves." Distribute paper and pencils. Remind the class of your earlier discussion on the Apostles' Creed. Challenge them to write their own confession of faith that would answer Jesus' question: "Who do you say that I am?" If time permits, some members may be willing to share what they have written.

Now read this quote: "In the third place, faith is *independent.*" This means that we may ponder questions just as others have and arrive at different conclusions. The class may want to debate the following statement:

R The historic creeds and Bible stories about Jesus set boundaries around what we can believe about his Lordship; therefore, no new understandings of Jesus' work are possible for us today.

Finally, read this quote concerning the fourth facet of faith: it is *inspired*. "What we know about Jesus—his life and work, along with his will for our own lives—does not simply come from our own reflection; it comes from the presence, power, and persistence of God in our lives." Invite class members to meditate on this thought. Have paper and pencils handy in case some students would like to jot down their thoughts.

• I know that God is present and persistent in my life because . . .

Encourage class members to participate in a brainstorming session in which they answer this question. You may want to record their responses.

? **(1) In what concrete ways can we put our confession of faith into action-oriented discipleship? In other words, how can we demonstrate our faith?**

Conclude the discussion by noting that confessing faith in Jesus and acting upon that confession may lead to suffering. Some early Christians were persecuted, even killed, for their beliefs. Throughout its history the church has lost faithful members who were martyred because they clung to their beliefs or who renounced their confession of faith because of the high price. Even in our supposedly enlightened world, people still suffer religious persecution.

HELPING CLASS MEMBERS ACT

Suggest that each class member interview someone who changed careers, perhaps to become a clergyperson, missionary, or other worker devoted to Christian service. Have the student explore with that person the signs of his or her calling, why he or she chose to say yes, and how life has changed because of this leap of faith.

Encourage members to talk with persons from other Christian traditions about their understanding of who Jesus is and what discipleship involves. Caution students that their purpose is not to sway someone else to their own way of believing in Jesus but to make a witness to that individual and to carefully examine the other person's viewpoint so as to possibly broaden their own spiritual horizon.

Remind the group that a confession of Christ leads to action for Christ. Challenge each person to do at least one Christ-like action each day, especially on behalf of the poor, sick, or lonely, to whom our Lord ministered.

PLANNING FOR NEXT SUNDAY

Our session for next Sunday will focus on one of the best-known and least liked personalities of the Bible, Judas Iscariot. Ask students to prepare for class by reading Matthew 26:14-16, 20-25, 47-50; and 27:1-5. Tell them to consider how they have, at times, failed to be true to Christ.

BE TRUE TO CHRIST

PREVIEWING THE LESSON

Lesson Scripture: Matthew 26:14-16, 20-25, 47-50; 27:1-5
Background Scripture: Matthew 26:14-16, 20-25, 47-50; 27:1-5
Key Verse: Matthew 26:25

Focus of the Lesson:
Judas Iscariot's irrevocable failure to remain true to Christ ultimately led to his downfall

Main Question of the Lesson:
What can we learn from the story of Judas that will help us to be better, more faithful disciples of Jesus Christ?

This lesson will enable adult learners to:
(1) discern Judas's failure to be faithful to Jesus.
(2) consider examples of their own faithlessness.
(3) respond by affirming their loyalty to Jesus.

Today's lesson may be outlined as follows:
(1) Introduction
(2) Judas's Failed Discipleship
(3) Examining Our Own Faithfulness

FOCUSING ON THE MAIN QUESTION

At the outset one should recognize that this is not a happy or pleasant lesson. Squarely facing that fact may make it possible for the materials to help persons of faith. The verses of this week's lesson are parts of the larger account of the Passion of Jesus in Matthew's Gospel. In part the verses have parallels in the other Gospels of the New Testament, but elements of the story that Matthew tells concerning Judas Iscariot are unique. In fact, Matthew's presentation of Judas allows us to follow Judas's motives and actions more carefully than we are able to do in the other Gospels. Matthew alone tells us that Judas asked the chief priests, "What will you give me if I betray him to you?" Thus, we see clearly that Judas was motivated by greed. Matthew alone stipulates that the money Judas received from the chief priests amounted to "thirty pieces of silver." Matthew alone records that Judas repented and attempted to return the money to the chief priests and elders after

Jesus was condemned, and when the leaders refused to take back the "blood money" Judas threw down the pieces of silver in the temple. Thus, we see the guilt of the leaders in the condemnation of the innocent Jesus. Moreover, Matthew heightens the evilness of Judas's actions when he alone records the direct conversation about the betrayal between Jesus and Judas at the Last Supper. Matthew alone has Jesus confront Judas at the time of the arrest by asking, "Friend, do what you are here to do." Finally, Matthew alone tells us that Judas hanged himself.

Matthew's focus on Judas intensifies the matters of faithfulness or failure in discipleship. Judas provides a negative example of how we are to relate to the Lord. Called to be a follower, Judas stepped out on his own and worked a deal for his own gain that ultimately led to the death of Jesus and his own suicide. The traitorous nature of Judas's betrayal drove him to despair and to abandon all hope for life. What seemed to be a path to profit and self-enhancement was the road to self-destruction. As Judas put himself before Jesus, he created conditions that finally caused him to abandon life itself. In lesser ways most Christians fail to live up to our calling in Christ. *What can we learn from the story of Judas that will help us to be better, more faithful disciples of Jesus Christ?*

READING THE SCRIPTURE

NRSV
Matthew 26:14-16

14 Then one of the twelve, who was called Judas Iscariot, went to the chief priests [15]and said, "What will you give me if I betray him to you?" They paid him thirty pieces of silver. [16]And from that moment he began to look for an opportunity to betray him.

NRSV
Matthew 26:20-25

20 When it was evening, he took his place with the twelve; [21]and while they were eating, he said, "Truly I tell you, one of you will betray me." [22]And they became greatly distressed and began to say to him one after another, "Surely not I, Lord?" [23]He answered, "The one who has dipped his hand into the bowl with me will betray me. [24]The Son of Man goes as it is written of him, but woe to that one by whom the Son of Man is betrayed! It would have been better for that one not to have been born."

NIV
Matthew 26:14-16

[14]Then one of the Twelve—the one called Judas Iscariot—went to the chief priests [15]and asked, "What are you willing to give me if I hand him over to you?" So they counted out for him thirty silver coins. [16]From then on Judas watched for an opportunity to hand him over.

NIV
Matthew 26:20-25

[20]When evening came, Jesus was reclining at the table with the Twelve. [21]And while they were eating, he said, "I tell you the truth, one of you will betray me."

[22]They were very sad and began to say to him one after the other, "Surely not I, Lord?"

[23]Jesus replied, "The one who has dipped his hand into the bowl with me will betray me. [24]The Son of Man will go just as it is written about him. But woe to that man who betrays the Son of Man! It would be better for him if he had not been born."

Key Verse

[25]Judas, who betrayed him, said, "Surely not I, Rabbi?" He replied, "You have said so."

[25]Then Judas, the one who would betray him, said, "Surely not I, Rabbi?"
Jesus answered, "Yes, it is you."

K Ve

NRSV

Matthew 26:47-50

47 While he was still speaking, Judas, one of the twelve, arrived; with him was a large crowd with swords and clubs, from the chief priests and the elders of the people. [48]Now the betrayer had given them a sign, saying, "The one I will kiss is the man; arrest him." [49]At once he came up to Jesus and said, "Greetings, Rabbi!" and kissed him. [50]Jesus said to him, "Friend, do what you are here to do." Then they came and laid hands on Jesus and arrested him.

NIV

Matthew 26:47-50

[47]While he was still speaking, Judas, one of the Twelve, arrived. With him was a large crowd armed with swords and clubs, sent from the chief priests and the elders of the people. [48]Now the betrayer had arranged a signal with them: "The one I kiss is the man; arrest him." [49]Going at once to Jesus, Judas said, "Greetings, Rabbi!" and kissed him.

[50]Jesus replied, "Friend, do what you came for."

Then the men stepped forward, seized Jesus and arrested him.

NRSV

Matthew 27:1-5

1 When morning came, all the chief priests and the elders of the people conferred together against Jesus in order to bring about his death. [2]They bound him, led him away, and handed him over to Pilate the governor.

3 When Judas, his betrayer, saw that Jesus was condemned, he repented and brought back the thirty pieces of silver to the chief priests and the elders. [4]He said, "I have sinned by betraying innocent blood." But they said, "What is that to us? See to it yourself." [5]Throwing down the pieces of silver in the temple, he departed; and he went and hanged himself.

NIV

Matthew 27:1-5

1 Early in the morning, all the chief priests and the elders of the people came to the decision to put Jesus to death. [2]They bound him, led him away and handed him over to Pilate, the governor.

[3]When Judas, who had betrayed him, saw that Jesus was condemned, he was seized with remorse and returned the thirty silver coins to the chief priests and the elders. [4]"I have sinned," he said, "for I have betrayed innocent blood."

"What is that to us?" they replied. "That's your responsibility."

[5]So Judas threw the money into the temple and left. Then he went away and hanged himself.

UNDERSTANDING THE SCRIPTURE

This ugly story is rich with details that create emphasis and provide interpretative insights by making connections between the events reported and elements of the Old Testament. Careful consideration of key items will assist us in grasping the depths of the account.

Matthew 26:14-16. Matthew refers to Judas as "one of the twelve." The reader of Matthew's Gospel knows well who Judas was. Matthew 10:1-4 tells of Jesus' summoning his "twelve disciples" and commissioning them for ministry. Among the group Matthew named "Judas Iscariot, the one who betrayed him." By repeating here and again at Matthew 26:47 that Judas was "one of the twelve," Matthew emphasizes the awful truth that one of those who was closest to Jesus was the one who betrayed him. Moreover, here and earlier in the Gospel Matthew gives us the designation "Iscariot" for Judas. Scholars have suggested a variety of meanings for this term, but in fact we do not know what "Iscariot" means. At times New Testament writers use *Iskariótes*, and at other times they use *Iskarióth*. It is probably the case that the authors of the Gospels themselves did not know the meaning of this designation, but they preserved it because it came to them from the earliest traditions of the church.

The reference to thirty pieces of silver is intriguing. First, the amount is the sum that Exodus 21:32 sets as the value of an injured slave. Second, thirty pieces of silver is mentioned explicitly in Zechariah 11:12-13 as the amount paid to the prophet for his services as a shepherd; a payment judged inadequate and rejected in contempt of the leaders of Israel as a sign of God's judgment. Zechariah threw the thirty pieces of silver into the treasury of the temple to declare God's displeasure, and Matthew surely means to allude to God's judgment with the remembrance of Judas's payment and his throwing the money down in the temple.

Matthew 26:20-25. Judas pretended to be a faithful disciple despite his determination to help destroy Jesus. He not only came to the table as Jesus and the other disciples ate the Passover meal, according to Matthew he seems even to have partaken of the elements of the Lord's Supper. Judas's deceitfulness was without bounds, for he had made a deal and he took steps to ensure its success.

Yet, as we read the account, we see that Jesus was aware of the plot against him. From the story we cannot determine how Jesus knew he would be betrayed. Jesus said that as the Son of Man he went to his death "as it [was] written of him." Yet,

even this clear statement is puzzling, for we cannot determine what scripture Jesus meant to indicate by this saying. We can, however, see that Jesus related his forthcoming suffering and death to the will and the work of God. Nevertheless, he pronounced a "woe" on his betrayer. In biblical times the woe-formula was a standard means of pronouncing a divine curse on someone or something; the "woe" indicated God's judgment.

Judas responded to Jesus' words with more insincerity. Pretending alarm at the prospect of his being the one who would betray Jesus, Judas attempted to divert Jesus' suspicion. Jesus' brief reply to Judas's question is difficult to interpret, although literally he said, "You yourself say." Perhaps we should paraphrase it, "You tell me."

Matthew 26:47-50. At the arrest of Jesus Matthew once again emphasizes Judas's treachery by referring to him as "one of the twelve." Here, he leads an armed body out against Jesus, implying that Jesus was a dangerous figure who had to be dealt with by force. Yet, the manner of the betrayal, giving Jesus a kiss, reveals Judas's cunning. In antiquity a kiss was a sign of love and devotion. Judas chose this intimate sign to indicate the one the Jewish leaders apparently believed to be a dangerous force in the national life of Israel. Jesus, however, confronted Judas. "Friend" as an address sounds friendly, but the context in which this designation occurs is not amiable; moreover, a careful study of the word in Matthew's Gospel reveals that "friend" serves to designate an enemy rather than an ally.

Matthew 27:1-5. Apparently Judas was shocked to his senses by the outcome of the arrest. In the past century interpreters have repeatedly suggested that Judas really believed in Jesus but he was impatient with Jesus' timing and tried to force Jesus' hand in bringing the kingdom of God. The New Testament will not bear the weight of this interpretation, for Judas is clearly thought by the authors of the Gospels to operate out of greed. Judas is remembered as a purely reprehensible character. Yet, even Judas was appalled that the innocent Jesus was condemned and executed. Perhaps, at best, Judas thought Jesus was so innocent that he could betray him for profit and be assured that no harm would come to Jesus. This interpretation too is speculation. Judas betrayed Jesus and, then, he killed himself. We simply do not know why.

Judas's attempt to return the money he was paid for betraying Jesus focuses our attention on the deliberate malice and guilt of the Jewish authorities. "Innocent blood" was shed; that is, the death of Jesus polluted the leaders. Both Numbers and Deuteronomy take up this theme. That Judas threw down the blood money in the temple was a clear sign that the temple itself, with its established leadership, was guilty of the death of Jesus.

INTERPRETING THE SCRIPTURE

Intimacy: No Guarantee of Fidelity

Judas Iscariot was not only a follower of Jesus, he was one of the Twelve, one of Jesus' specially chosen disciples who were closest to him. Judas had opportunities to be with Jesus, to watch him work, to listen to his teaching, and to talk with him. Such close contact with Jesus was not generally available to the crowds that followed him. Thus, it is hard to comprehend how one so close to Jesus could have betrayed him unto condemnation and death. The New Testament explains that Judas conspired with the Jewish authorities who were hostile toward Jesus for the sake of gaining money. Luke (22:3) and John (13:27) both contend that Judas operated under the influence of Satan. While that assertion is easy to believe, we should not ignore that whether Judas betrayed Jesus out of simple greed or because of satanic sway or both, his having been close to Jesus did not guarantee that he was beyond treachery and the danger of the lure of evil.

No matter where we think we are in our relationship to Christ, we should remember Judas and devote ourselves with enthusiasm to following our Lord. Being close to Jesus is not the same as being obedient to him. Familiarity does not ensure that we will be faithful followers. Disciples are those called to follow and to obey their masters, so we must always ask whether we are faithfully doing the will and the work of our Lord or going our own way in his name.

Putting Money Before the Lord

Judas's life is evidence of the power of wealth to corrupt humanity. In Matthew's Gospel, Jesus plainly taught his disciples to store up treasure in heaven, not on earth, for as he said, "where your treasure is, there your heart will be also" (6:21). Moreover, Jesus said, "No one can serve two masters. . . . You cannot serve God and wealth" (6:24). As Judas cut his deal with the chief priests, he put money before the Lord because he was serving himself above all else. Judas's concern with money led him to betray the one treasure that is worth all of life, the grace of God in Jesus Christ.

Judas sold his Lord for a slave's wages, an amount that had been an outright insult to the prophet Zechariah. We see that Judas had the wrong priorities, so he put a cheap price on the value of discipleship to Jesus. The act of betrayal was itself dishonorable, but the paltry payment Judas took for his work highlights the sinister nature of the deed. Judas had asked, "What will you give me if I betray him to you?" And, when the insulting offer was made, Judas judged the payment good enough. Because money was more important to Judas than his relationship to Jesus Christ, he found even the pitiful sum of thirty pieces of silver (about 120 days' wages) sufficient for his dirty work. Judas shows us that a singular concern with money will bring a human to the lowest levels of life.

Trying to Play Games with Christ

At the Last Supper when Jesus spoke about this betrayal, surprisingly each of the disciples displays uncertainty about the possibility of his being the betrayer. Judas, however, who knew what he had contracted to do, pretended to be as surprised as the others at the notion that he might betray Jesus. Here is Judas at his worst, for in feigning innocence Judas compounded the evil of betrayal with the evil of dishonesty. Confronted with the terrible truth of his betrayal, Judas acted in a dastardly way to attempt to remove any suspicion Jesus might have had. "Surely not I, Rabbi?" he said, joining the others who had protested, "Surely not I, Lord?" Judas sought to divert Jesus' attention rather than to face his own predicament and to repent of the evil he planned to do. Thinking of himself and the money he anticipated, Judas played at being innocent in order to ensure the success of his plans. The sharpness of this exchange between Jesus and Judas is captured with beauty by J. S. Bach in his Passion oratorio, "St. Matthew Passion," wherein Jesus foretells his betrayal with clear sorrow that is exceeded only by the overdone, artificial remorse of Judas, who seems cut to the quick by the very notion that he could do anything so terrible. The soloist charged with singing Judas's part typically sobs the words of protest.

It is not pleasant to ask about our own behavior in this awful vein, but in sad but real ways most followers of Christ try to play games with the Lord. We hear Christ's words about concern for the poor, and we pretend we are taking them seriously. We know that God is no respecter of persons, yet we tolerate life in a world that is deeply racist, sexist, and ageist—not doing anything inappropriate ourselves, but also not doing anything about the problems. When the teachings of Christ challenge our commitments, we find ways to pay lip service to Jesus that allow us to feel good about not living as he has taught us. We are not Judas. There was only one Judas Iscariot, but we all have a little bit of Judas in our souls. Unlike Judas, we should not miss the chance Christ provides us to repent as he confronts us with our self-serving plans. That we all squirm at these thoughts is some confirmation of their truth.

Divine Confrontation

When Judas led the armed party to Gethsemane, Jesus spoke directly, "Friend, do what you are here to do." Jesus did not play games with Judas; he confronted him. We may be prone to try to persuade ourselves (and others?) that we are busily attending to what God would have us to do with our lives, but as this story recognizes, Jesus knows us and sees to the heart of our actions. Judas tried to mask his betrayal by greeting Jesus and giving him a kiss. On the surface it seemed that Judas was respectful of Jesus. But Jesus saw the ugly nature of Judas's actions and would have nothing to do with the sham that Judas attempted to stage.

We do not fool God. We may fool ourselves into thinking that we can present ourselves to God so as to win a reception, but as this story informs us, we cannot deceive our Lord. In relation to our Lord Jesus Christ our actions remain transparent. This is the bad news, and this is the good news. Our Lord knows us for who we are, and in relationship to him we cannot—and we need not try to—be anything other than who we are. In a wonderful sense, because Jesus Christ sees us and knows what we are doing, we are free: free from the need to pretend that we are anything other than what we are; free for an honest relationship to Christ that calls us to be his full-fledged disciples. Because God is God and we are God's creatures, we are at our best when we face who we are and relate accordingly to God.

The Point of No Return

Judas went too far. He made a plan and he acted on it. Later we see that he reconsidered his actions, but it was too late. The plot Judas had set in motion was going to hatch and there was nothing he could do about it. Repentance came too late for Judas. Throwing the money in the temple did not set Jesus free. Our actions produce consequences, even though we may have a change of heart. When Jesus confronted Judas at the Last Supper, perhaps there was a chance for him to change. Before he led the crowd out to Gethsemane, perhaps Judas could have altered the course of his actions. But Judas did not think about the evil nature of his betrayal until after he saw that he had sold out "innocent blood." Then, however, it was too late. It is a small point, but a vital one—we should think before we act, not after. This moral observation is not the gospel, but it is also not opposed to the truth of the grace of God. Judas's reprehensible behavior is a sad testimony to what we humans can do with the freedom God gives us; but if we have eyes to see, we can learn from Judas what not to do with our lives.

SHARING THE SCRIPTURE

PREPARING TO TEACH

Preparing Our Hearts

At first glance, today's lesson may seem far removed from our own brand of discipleship. As teachers and students of the Word, surely we know who God is and what is expected of us. We apparently bear no similarity to Judas at all. Or do we? Judas was one of Jesus' closest associates. Moreover, he was entrusted with the group's finances. If someone so closely connected to and trusted by Jesus as Judas was could betray him, is it not possible that we too could betray our Lord? Of course, Jesus will never again be handed over to be crucified. But we can betray him in lesser ways every day as we fail to live up to the highest expectations of discipleship. Observe your own behavior this week. Note those times when you failed Jesus because of something you did or neglected to do. Seek repentance.

Preparing Our Minds

Read the lesson as well as Matthew 26:14-16, 20-25, 47-50; 27:1-5. Check the scripture references made within the lesson. Note the points Matthew makes regarding Judas that are not included in the other Gospels as described in the Focusing on the Main Question portion.

Preparing Our Learning Space

If possible, obtain Bach's "St. Matthew Passion" and a cassette or CD player.
Have on hand:
- several Bibles for students
- newsprint and marker or chalkboard and chalk
- paper and pencils
- optional cassette or CD player and J.S. Bach's "St. Matthew Passion" cued to the solo by Judas

LEADING THE CLASS

(1) Introduction

Invite the students to think of a time they felt betrayed by a friend. Possibly the betrayer repeated confidential information, or lied, or turned away when help was needed. A few persons may be willing to recount the incident briefly without mentioning names. If class members feel uncomfortable sharing their own stories, they may be willing to approach this topic in a more generic way by talking about the kinds of betrayal people experience, such as marital infidelity gossip.

Now brainstorm answers to these questions. If possible, record responses on newsprint or a chalkboard.

[?] (1) **How do you feel when someone betrays you?**

(2) **How might the betrayer be affected by his or her actions?**

(3) **What difference does a betrayal make in the relationship between two people?**

Move toward today's scripture by announcing that we will be studying the ultimate act of betrayal—Judas's "selling" of Jesus for thirty pieces of silver. As we discuss Matthew's account of this act, we will keep this main question before us: *What can we learn from the story of Judas that will help us to be better, more faithful disciples of Jesus Christ?*

(2) Judas's Failed Discipleship

Read the story of Judas's betrayal as found in Matthew 26:14-16, 20-25, 47-50; 27:1-5. If you have access to a tape or CD of Bach's "St. Matthew Passion," you may want to play the portion related to today's scripture as a means of conveying the emotion of the event to the class.

Use the Focusing on the Main Question portion to help the students understand the uniqueness of Matthew's presentation of Judas's betrayal. These details describe what Judas did and why, at least as Matthew perceived his motivation.

Use the information under "Putting Money Before the Lord" in the Interpreting the Scripture section and the reference to Matthew 26:14-16 in the Understanding the Scripture section to discuss Matthew's understanding of Judas's motivation to betray Jesus. Then ask:

(1) **Based on Matthew's account, what would you say is Judas's motive for betraying Jesus?** [?]

(Discuss Judas's greed, but point out that thirty pieces of silver was the value set on an injured slave according to Exodus 21:32. Also note that this amount was so small that God had rejected it as payment for the prophet Zechariah's services as a shepherd according to Zechariah 11:12-13. Apparently, Judas placed such a low value on Jesus that he was willing to betray him for a minimal amount.)

(2) **Is this motive one that any other disciple—including ourselves—might be swayed by? Why or why not?** [?]

Note that although Judas had sold out for a paltry sum, he acted at the Supper as if he could not believe that someone would betray Jesus. As the "Trying to Play Games with Christ" section under Interpreting the Scripture notes, "Judas sought to divert Jesus' attention rather than to face his own predicament and to repent of the evil he planned to do. Thinking of himself and the money he anticipated, Judas played at being innocent in order to ensure the success of his plans." Suggest that class members try to envision the scene in the Upper Room as Jesus announced his knowledge of a plot to betray him. Provide a few moments for the students to close their eyes and see themselves at the table, taste the food, and hear Jesus' words. Ask:

(1) **What would you have been feeling and thinking had you been one of the eleven disciples?** [?]

(2) **What would you have been feeling and thinking had you been Judas?**

[?] **(3) What affect do you think Jesus' failure to identify his betrayer had on the eleven disciples?**

(4) What affect do you think Jesus' failure to identify his betrayer had on Judas?

Move the discussion to the scene in Gethsemane (Matthew 27:1-5). Note Jesus' comment to Judas: "Friend, do what you are here to do." As mentioned under "Divine Confrontation" in the Interpreting the Scripture segment, "We do not fool God." Ask:

[?] **(5) How did Jesus' apparently straightforward statement actually confront Judas?**

(Note that "friend" is used in Matthew "to designate an enemy rather than an ally.")

(3) Examining Our Own Faithfulness

Read aloud the paragraph under "Intimacy: No Guarantee of Fidelity" in the Interpreting the Scripture section that begins, "No matter where."

If possible, divide the class into teams and have them debate this statement which you may want to write on newsprint or a chalkboard:

• Had we been among the original twelve disciples, any one of us could have been Judas.

If you have worked in teams, summarize this activity by encouraging each team to share their ideas with the class.

Distribute paper and pencils to each student. Suggest that they write an imaginary dialogue between themselves and Jesus about the ways in which they have been unfaithful to him in their own lives. This exercise may seem fanciful, but the Holy Spirit speaks to us and through us to reveal the Word and will of God if we will but open ourselves and listen. The dialogue may begin with these words from Matthew 26:21, 22, which students may copy from their Bibles:

• Jesus: "Truly I tell you, one of you will betray me."
• You: "Surely not I, Lord?"

Continue the dialogue. This information is not to be discussed with others, so close the activity with a moment of prayer in which you offer thanks for the Spirit's gift of insight and ask for guidance in living more faithfully.

HELPING CLASS MEMBERS ACT

Challenge class members to be aware of ways in which they betray Jesus. An outburst of temper, or unethical behavior are two ways. Suggest that students offer a prayer of repentance as soon as they realize they have acted in ways that betray Jesus.

Matthew reports that Judas's betrayal of Jesus was motivated by greed. Ask students to consider how their concerns about money prompt them to put financial gain ahead of the needs of people. Encourage them to review their financial records this week to determine where their priorities really are.

Suggest that class members recall an action or word that they spoke or wrote that caused a serious strain or complete break in a relationship. Encourage the students to think about what happened and, if possible, to plan a strategy so that a similar problem will not occur again.

PLANNING FOR NEXT SUNDAY

Next Sunday we will begin the final unit of this quarter. "Persons in the New Testament Church" opens with a look at Barnabas. Ask class members to read the references to him found in Acts 4:32-37; 9:23-31; and 11:19-30. Suggest that they look for ways in which Barnabas encouraged members of the early church.

BE A COMMITTED ENCOURAGER

PREVIEWING THE LESSON

Lesson Scripture: Acts 4:32, 36-37; 9:26-27; 11:22-30
Background Scripture: Acts 4:32-37; 9:23-31; 11:19-30
Key Verses: Acts 11:23-24

Focus of the Lesson:
through his words and deeds, Barnabas encouraged others to come to Christ and to remain steadfast and faithful to him

Main Question of the Lesson:
How is Barnabas a role model for us today?

This lesson will enable adult learners to:
(1) examine the ways in which Barnabas encouraged and supported members of the early church.
(2) recognize the important role "encouragers" play in the life of the church.
(3) respond by offering encouragement to others.

Today's lesson may be outlined as follows:
(1) Introduction
(2) Barnabas Encourages Others
(3) Encouragers in the Modern Church

FOCUSING ON THE MAIN QUESTION

This week we focus on a somewhat familiar figure from the life of the early church, Barnabas. As the materials from Acts tell us, this man was actually named Joseph and he came from Cyprus. Barnabas seems to have been an even more significant personality in early Christianity than the references to him in Acts might imply. Paul mentions Barnabas in his letter to the churches in Galatia, recalling his involvement in a controversy over table fellowship between Jewish and Gentile Christians in Antioch. Outside the New Testament in later legendary writings of Christian authors, one finds claims that Barnabas was one of the Seventy sent out by Jesus in Luke 10:1, that he preached in Rome before the death of Jesus and converted Clement of Rome to Christianity, and that he died as a martyr in Cyprus as he conducted a highly successful mission there. Barnabas is said to have been the author of an extra-biblical writing entitled the *Epistle of Barnabas*, and he is credited with having written a Gospel that is now lost. At times it has even been suggested that Barnabas was the author of Hebrews.

The early Christian fascination with Barnabas is largely the result of his presence and activities as they are reported in Acts. We find that he was a model of generosity in the life of the earliest Jerusalem church, that he mediated between the apostle Paul and the Jerusalem church after Paul's call on the road to Damascus, that he brought Paul into the life and mission of the church in Antioch, and that he worked with Paul—perhaps initially as the senior partner—in vital missionary work throughout the eastern Mediterranean.

Barnabas's capacities for generosity and encouragement are an inspiration for us today. Indeed, in almost every congregation there is someone like Barnabas, someone gifted with selfless devotion to the well-being of the Christian community and to the mission of the church in the world. When you think about Barnabas, who comes to mind from your own experience in the church? What was it that was so inspiring about the behavior of such persons? What are some things that all Christians could do to be more like Barnabas? What difference would more Barnabas-like living make in the life of your own congregation? *In short, how is Barnabas a role model for us today?*

READING THE SCRIPTURE

NRSV
Acts 4:32

32 Now the whole group of those who believed were of one heart and soul, and no one claimed private ownership of any possessions, but everything they owned was held in common.

NRSV
Acts 4:36-37

36There was a Levite, a native of Cyprus, Joseph, to whom the apostles gave the name Barnabas (which means "son of encouragement"). 37He sold a field that belonged to him, then brought the money, and laid it at the apostles' feet.

NRSV
Acts 9:26-27

26 When he had come to Jerusalem, he attempted to join the disciples; and they were all afraid of him, for they did not believe that he was a disciple. 27But Barnabas took him, brought him to the apostles, and described for them how on the road he had seen the Lord, who had spo-

NIV
Acts 4:32

32All the believers were one in heart and mind. No one claimed that any of his possessions was his own, but they shared everything they had.

NIV
Acts 4:36-37

36Joseph, a Levite from Cyprus, whom the apostles called Barnabas (which means Son of Encouragement), 37sold a field he owned and brought the money and put it at the apostles' feet.

NIV
Acts 9:26-27

26When he came to Jerusalem, he tried to join the disciples, but they were all afraid of him, not believing that he really was a disciple. 27But Barnabas took him and brought him to the apostles. He told them how Saul on his journey had seen the Lord and that the Lord had spoken to him, and

ken to him, and how in Damascus he had spoken boldly in the name of Jesus.

how in Damascus he had preached fearlessly in the name of Jesus.

NRSV
Acts 11:22-30

22 News of this came to the ears of the church in Jerusalem, and they sent Barnabas to Antioch. 23When he came and saw the grace of God, he rejoiced, and he exhorted them all to remain faithful to the Lord with steadfast devotion; 24for he was a good man, full of the Holy Spirit and of faith. And a great many people were brought to the Lord. 25Then Barnabas went to Tarsus to look for Saul, 26and when he had found him, he brought him to Antioch. So it was that for an entire year they met with the church and taught a great many people, and it was in Antioch that the disciples were first called "Christians."

27 At that time prophets came down from Jerusalem to Antioch. 28One of them named Agabus stood up and predicted by the Spirit that there would be a severe famine over all the world; and this took place during the reign of Claudius. 29The disciples determined that according to their ability, each would send relief to the believers living in Judea; 30this they did, sending it to the elders by Barnabas and Saul.

NIV
Acts 11:22-30

22News of this reached the ears of the church at Jerusalem, and they sent Barnabas to Antioch. 23When he arrived and saw the evidence of the grace of God, he was glad and encouraged them all to remain true to the Lord with all their hearts. 24He was a good man, full of the Holy Spirit and faith, and a great number of people were brought to the Lord.

25Then Barnabas went to Tarsus to look for Saul, 26and when he found him, he brought him to Antioch. So for a whole year Barnabas and Saul met with the church and taught great numbers of people. The disciples were called Christians first at Antioch.

27During this time some prophets came down from Jerusalem to Antioch. 28One of them, named Agabus, stood up and through the Spirit predicted that a severe famine would spread over the entire Roman world. (This happened during the reign of Claudius.) 29The disciples, each according to his ability, decided to provide help for the brothers living in Judea. 30This they did, sending their gift to the elders by Barnabas and Saul.

Key Verses

UNDERSTANDING THE SCRIPTURE

Acts 4:32-35. From time to time throughout the narrative of Acts, the author, Luke, makes summary statements about the growth and the life of the church. These verses are the second of three such summaries that mention the devotion of the Jerusalem church to the apostles and the practice of the members of that congregation of holding their possessions in common. (See Acts 2:42-47; 4:32-37; 5:12-16.)

The frame in which Luke wants the reader of Acts to view the life of the Jerusalem church is that of *unity*. The notice that "the whole group of those who believed were of one heart and soul" uses the language of Greek culture to describe perfect friendship. Thus, Luke emphasizes the harmony of the congregation. In turn, his report that "there was not a needy person among them suggests an ideal fellowship that would have fulfilled Moses' promise to Israel in Deuteronomy 15:4 that there would be no need when the Lord God blessed the people.

The beauty of congregational harmony, the meeting of physical needs, and divine blessing are not simply ends within themselves, as is clear from Luke's deliberate placement of the information in Acts 4:33 within this section. We find that harmony, provision, and blessing were the atmosphere in which the church conducted a vital mission to the world by testifying to Christ's resurrection.

Acts 4:36-37. The information about Barnabas follows the report about the Jerusalem church. Barnabas incarnates the spirit Luke understands to have existed in the earliest days of the church—although the story of Ananias and Sapphira in Acts 5 shows that everything wasn't perfect. Nevertheless, we should see that Joseph of Cyprus's gracious submission to the inspired leadership of the church and his generosity won him the nickname "Barnabas" in recognition that he inspired others as well as providing for their needs.

Acts 9:23-25. The lesson moves to Acts 9, where we focus on Barnabas in relation to Paul. These verses report that after Paul's conversion his preaching in Damascus aroused the ire of certain Damascus Jews as he confounded them with his powerful proofs that Jesus was the Messiah. The hostility forced Paul to flee by slipping away at night. (Paul tells his version of this story in 2 Corinthians 11:30-33.)

Acts 9:26-27. The story told here is Luke's version of events that Paul reports in Galatians 1:18-24, and readers of both accounts will notice that the two versions of the events are distinct. Paul stresses his independence from the original disciples because he wishes to underscore the formative nature of his miraculous encounter with the risen Lord Jesus Christ for his mission and message. Luke has a different motive for writing, however. He labors to show that, despite Paul's conversion from being a persecutor of the church to becoming a key figure in early Christianity, Paul was in continuity with the basic work that began with the apostles in Jerusalem.

We should notice the important role Barnabas plays in this story. Barnabas is the agent of divine continuity. God's work expanded to include Paul, and the early church recognized and approved of what happened because Barnabas brought Paul and the members of the Jerusalem church together. Barnabas's testimony united vital portions of the early church.

Acts 9:28-30. Paul again ran afoul of segments of the Jewish population that had not embraced the gospel of Jesus Christ. Luke says that Paul collided with the "Hellenists," that is, with the Greek-speaking Jews of Jerusalem. This development should be no surprise, since Paul himself was a Hellenistic Jew, as was his key supporter, Barnabas.

Acts 9:31. This verse is another summary of the life of the church, although now the focus expands to larger regions of Palestine. Luke understands the growth theologically. He does not give a mechanical, psychological, or sociological reason for the health and expansion of the church. He sees that the developments were the results of the work of the Holy Spirit.

Acts 11:19-21. Luke tells of a new moment as the church grew beyond Palestine. Jewish Christians from Cyprus and Cyrene fled persecution in Jerusalem and, as some of them came to Antioch, they preached the gospel in an outright fashion to Gentiles who believed.

Acts 11:22-24. When the Jewish Christians in Jerusalem heard of the success among the Gentiles in Antioch, they sent Barnabas to investigate the problem. Barnabas was a natural choice for the job, for he was from Cyprus—a Hellenistic Jewish Christian—and, as he had proven with his willingness to welcome Paul into the life of the church, he was gifted at recognizing the grace of God at work in surprising ways. As Luke puts it, he was "a good man, full of the Holy Spirit and of faith."

Acts 11:25-26. Barnabas not only acknowledged the validity of the work in Antioch, he also sought to enhance the effectiveness of the mission by seeking out Paul and bringing him into the efforts. Barnabas could discern the movement of the Holy Spirit and had the wisdom to recognize fresh ways to contribute to the work that the Spirit was directing.

Acts 11:27-30. The last word in our lesson about Barnabas shows him at work in yet another way. When the church in Antioch learned of the perils of famine that threatened the church in Judea, Barnabas and Paul were chosen to deliver the relief funds to those afflicted. Clearly, Barnabas was considered trustworthy by many Christians in a variety of settings.

INTERPRETING THE SCRIPTURE

Son of Encouragement

Joseph of Cyprus was an extraordinary person—he was generous, really generous, more concerned with the well-being of others than with preserving physical security for himself. Thus, he took what he had and sold it in order to supply the liquidated assets for the benefit of other members of the community of faith of which he was a part. In general, early Christians thought of themselves differently from the way in which we moderns think of ourselves. First-century Christians were less individualistic than twentieth-century persons tend to be, so they saw themselves as more than redeemed individuals—they were part of God's long-awaited and promised redemption of creation. For early Christians, "we/us/our" was more important than "I/me/mine," for God through Christ was at work saving the world, not merely this or that individual. Even in this context, Joseph of Cyprus stood out among the members of the congregation. He was a Levite, a member of the priestly clan; and he was a non-Palestinian Jew. Nevertheless, as a member of the corporate Body of Christ he understood that he was one of God's people, not just a blessed individual; so he took what he had and made it available to all those with whom he shared faith in Jesus Christ. Joseph of Cyprus felt called to share with people who also recognized the reality of what God was at work doing in Jesus Christ. The success of God's own work depended on such care of the fragile early Christian community.

In turn, Joseph of Cyprus was willing to recognize others whom God had chosen to lead the life of the early church. Commentators say he was "submissive," and that word leaves a bad taste in our mouths. We worry about being submissive, for to persons in the twentieth century it implies a poor self-image, a lack of confidence, and the experience of oppression. However, such implications do not apply in a reading of Acts. Joseph of Cyprus was submissive to the presence and the work of the Holy Spirit in the apostles in Jerusalem; that is, he was obedient to God's power at work in the apostles, not to the apostles themselves. When reading Acts we should never lose sight of the constant presence and power of God in the events of the story being told.

Joseph's capacity to recognize and obey the Spirit was his chief characteristic, so the apostles named him "Barnabas," meaning (Luke says) "son of encouragement." The ability to see and obey God in the context of the complex operations of Christian community inspired others to do likewise. Barnabas was indeed a crucial figure in the life of the early church. We should all pray to be as able and willing to contribute to God's work in the life of the church as Barnabas was—here and throughout his ministry.

Embracing God's New Work

When Paul arrived on the scene, newly converted from being a vicious persecutor of the early church to acting as one of the gospel's most effective proclaimers, the majority of the members of the church were afraid of him, perhaps uncertain of the sincerity of his motives (was he a spy?). Yet, Barnabas observed Paul and with confidence welcomed him as a collaborator in Christ. We should not miss the singularity of Barnabas's ability to see God at work in Paul. Almost all others were skeptical, even afraid; yet, Barnabas showed the insight and the courage to acknowledge that God was at work in Paul. Openness to God's new workings, mettle to admit the unexpected, and wisdom to recognize God's will—all these traits characterize Barnabas.

Full of the Holy Spirit

Yet, lest we should think that Barnabas was a superman, Luke explains that Barnabas evinced his extraordinary capacities because he was "full of the Holy Spirit." His remarkable capacities were not the results of his superior character alone—others in the early church were surely noble. But Barnabas had been deeply affected by the presence and the power of the Holy Spirit, and living under the Spirit's influence he did not live only for himself; he lived for others as well.

Let us be honest: We do not think in such "spiritual" terms as Luke tells this story. We say we believe in the Holy Spirit; our confessions tell us that we do. But, what do we believe? The doctrine of the Trinity is a mystery to most Christians; and as a study of scripture shows, the doctrine is present in the Bible only in "kit form." Yet, The New Testament would have us know that while God is sovereign and transcendent, God is also present and active in the world in the person of the Spirit. We fallible humans can be more than who we are because of the divine presence of God's Spirit in our lives.

One example of the Holy Spirit at work in modern-day life concerns a splendid lay leader. Under her influence hundreds of persons came to faith in Christ, and hundreds of others heard and answered a call to devote their lives to full-time Christian ministry. When asked how she was so effective, she astonished people with her answer. She confided that by nature she was shy. If left to her own choices she would have been a pious recluse, but that was not what God wanted her to be. The woman believed that she was called to involvement with others so that their lives could be transformed and invigorated for Christ's service. She had worked her whole life in obedience to and by the power of the Spirit, so that whatever she appeared to have done, she believed the Spirit had accomplished through her obedience. Thus, just as the Holy Spirit empowered Barnabas for faithful service in the early church, the Spirit empowers us today when we are obedient to God's call on our lives.

Recognizing God's Work and Contributing to It

Barnabas did more than recognize God's workings and open up to new developments; he also helped others to see God at work in new, if startling ways. As we follow Barnabas through Acts we see that he was perceptive, open, and *innovative*. Barnabas saw what God was doing, recognized it, encouraged the work on the part of the persons involved, and envisioned new ways to advance the work. Luke, of course, would want us to understand that whatever innovations Barnabas introduced were brought into the work of the early church by the Spirit. Consequently, when Barnabas saw the success of the mission to the Gentiles in Antioch, he affirmed the work and sought out Paul to advance the mission.

Such foresight should inspire us to ask ourselves, What is God doing in the world? What is God's will for my life? Is

God doing a new work that calls for recognition? How, according to God's will, may I contribute to what the Spirit is doing? These questions are enough to take us through all of life; and if we are listening, to the end that God desires.

Providing for the Needs of Others

The lesson began with Barnabas's selling land to provide for others. Now, even with no apparent resources we see that Barnabas (along with Paul and the other early Christians) found ways to care for others. Barnabas was entrusted with the delivery of a charitable contribution to persons in need in Judea. As we look at Barnabas, we see that our ability to help others is not limited to our own physical resources. We may well help others as they assemble the goods that address the needs of still others.

Thus, a man saw the need of the poor of his community. He was not wealthy, but he did not despair. Instead, he organized a city-wide, half-year-long drive to meet the needs of the poor at Christmas. His project began modestly, but it grew over the years and finally became a year-round ministry to supply clothing, medicine, food, and toys to persons in need.

Barnabas had discernment; he had courage; he had fidelity; he had imagination; and he had flexibility. Oh, that we all were like Barnabas—sons and daughters of encouragement!

SHARING THE WORD

PREPARING TO TEACH

Preparing Our Hearts

Barnabas acted like a magnet in the early church—he drew people in, and on the strength of his own example and Christlike life he kept them involved. The Holy Spirit provided the force that powered Barnabas's work. As you study this week's lesson, think about the effect you have on your own class and congregation. How do you act as a role model and encourage others to draw closer to Christ? Be alert for opportunities to invite others into a relationship with Christ and into the life of the church.

Preparing Our Minds

Read the portions of Acts for today's study: Acts 4:32-37; 9:23-31; 11:19-30. Also read the material in the lesson.

If time permits, you may want to check the references to Barnabas that appear in Paul's letters: 1 Corinthians 9:6, Galatians 2:1, 9, 13, and Colossians 4:10. You may also want to read about Barnabas in a Bible dictionary.

Think about people you have known who have acted as "encouragers" in this congregation or others. What qualities made them so helpful to the church?

Preparing Our Learning Space

Have on hand:
- ✔ several Bibles for students
- ✔ newsprint and marker or chalkboard and chalk
- ✔ paper and pencils

LEADING THE CLASS

(1) Introduction

Tell students to think back to when they joined this congregation. Ask them to recall:
- why they chose this church.
- who helped them to become involved in the life of the church.
- how they have invited others in and helped them to feel at home.

R

Note that students who have been life-long members of this congregation will want to concentrate on the last point.

Provide a brief time to discuss these points, either with the entire class or in pairs or teams.

Move to today's Bible lesson by introducing Barnabas. Some students may be able to share information about him if you ask an open-ended question such as:

⟨?⟩ (1) What do you know about Barnabas?

The Focusing on the Main Question portion will help you to fill in gaps. If you prefer, read or retell that section of the lesson. Be sure to highlight today's main question: *How is Barnabas a role model for us today?*

(2) Barnabas Encourages Others

To help the class get a comprehensive picture of who Barnabas was and what he did, select three volunteers to read the passages for today's lessons: Acts 4:32 and 36-37; Acts 9:26-27; and Acts 11:22-30. Note that we will look at each of these passages in turn.

Focus first on Acts 4:32 and 36-37. Invite the class to respond to the following questions. You may want to use information under "Son of Encouragement" in the Interpreting the Scripture section to supplement their answers.

⟨?⟩ (1) **What do you suppose motivated Barnabas to sell his field?**
(2) **How do you think his action encouraged other members of the early church?**
(3) **What could modern church members learn from Barnabas's action?**

Turn the group's attention to Acts 9:26-27, which concerns Barnabas's relationship to Paul. If you have students who may not be familiar with Paul's transforming experience with Christ on the road to Damascus, and the subsequent suspicion with which this persecutor of the church was eyed, you may want to review Paul's story.

Suggest that the students put themselves in Paul's place. Act as an interviewer of Paul as you ask these questions to the group. If the class is large, you may want to divide into teams. If so, try to write the questions on newsprint or a chalkboard.

(1) **Everyone else views you, Paul, with** ⟨?⟩ **suspicion and distrust, yet Barnabas seems to welcome you as a co-laborer. Why? What do you see in his character that enables him to be so open to you?**
(2) **Paul, in what ways do you see the power of the Holy Spirit at work in Barnabas?**
(3) **Barnabas vouched for the authenticity of your conversion, Paul. What do you think his willingness to speak for you may have—or could have—cost him?**

Now consider Barnabas's work in Antioch, as recorded in Acts 11:22-30. You may want to read the first paragraph under "Recognizing God's Work and Contributing to It" in the Interpreting the Scripture segment. Note that Barnabas was a "team player." He did not try to do all of the work himself. Instead, when he saw that he could not harvest all the ripe fields of potential converts, he sought.

Close this part of the lesson by asking students to brainstorm answers to these questions. Write their responses on newsprint or a chalkboard. We will refer to this activity later in the session.

(1) **What words or phrases would you use** ⟨?⟩ **to describe Barnabas's personality?**
(2) **How would you describe his contributions to the early church?**
(3) **Which of his attributes and actions would be helpful in today's church?**

(3) Encouragers in the Modern Church

With the aforementioned description of Barnabas in mind, turn to two examples of contemporary encouragers. First, read or retell the story of the lay leader found in the last paragraphs under "Embracing God's New Work" in the Interpreting the Scripture section. Then, retell the first and second paragraphs under "Providing for the Needs of Others," which describe the man who cared for others.

[?] **(1) In what ways do these two modern Christians follow in the footsteps of Barnabas?**

(2) What other examples can you give to show how people seek to encourage others?

(3) Would you agree with the following statement? Our congregation does enough to encourage children, youth, and adults to come into a relationship with Christ and to live out that relationship as a member of the church. If you agree, cite examples to show effectiveness in this area. If you disagree, point out ways in which we could be better at fostering encouragement for others.

Provide time for class members to meditate on the following questions. You may want to write them on newsprint or a chalkboard. Distribute paper and pencils for students who prefer to write their responses.

• Which aspects of Barnabas's character and work excite you?

• Which of these characteristics do you have or could you develop?

• How do you encourage others in their Christian faith?

• What could you do to be more like Barnabas?

• If you (and others) were more like Barnabas, what difference would that make to your congregation?

Note that not one of us is exactly like Barnabas, but we do likely share some of his characteristics. Call the group's attention to the list of descriptive words and phrases they brainstormed earlier in the session. If class members know one another well, ask one person to mention the name of another class member and cite one "encouraging" trait that he or she has. In order to include as many people as possible in this affirmation exercise, ask the class not to refer to anyone more than once. You may need to make adjustments for very large groups (perhaps by working in teams of five), but try to affirm each person's ability to act as an encourager.

HELPING CLASS MEMBERS ACT

Challenge each member to offer support this week to someone who has a spiritual, physical, material, or emotional need.

Suggest that each person find a way to either encourage an unchurched member to attend church or to listen to the concerns of an inactive member. The class member may want to contact the pastor about this individual so that he or she can arrange for a call.

Remind the group that Barnabas worked not only within the church but also as a missionary beyond it. Suggest that the group take a special offering (perhaps next week) to support the work of a missionary. The class may want to consider some sacrificial, long-term support, such as covenant missionary support in The United Methodist Church.

PLANNING FOR NEXT SUNDAY

The next personality we will study is Stephen, whose story is told by Luke in Acts. Tell the class members to read Acts 6:8-15, 7:54-60, and if possible, the entire background scripture from Acts 6:1–8:3. Ask them to consider how Stephen is a faithful witness to Christ.

BE A FAITHFUL WITNESS

PREVIEWING THE LESSON

Lesson Scripture: Acts 6:8-15; 7:54-60
Background Scripture: Acts 6:1–8:3
Key Verse: Acts 6:8

Focus of the Lesson:
Stephen's faithful witness for Christ, even in the face of a martyr's death

Main Question of the Lesson:
What can we do to grow more like Stephen as we live and work for Jesus Christ?

This lesson will enable adult learners to:
(1) encounter Stephen, a faithful witness who gave his life for the gospel.
(2) discern the faithfulness of their own witness.
(3) respond by witnessing to others, especially in the face of opposition.

Today's lesson may be outlined as follows:
(1) Introduction
(2) Stephen: A Faithful Witness
(3) Discerning Our Own Commitment to Faithful Witness

FOCUSING ON THE MAIN QUESTION

At what price would you bear a faithful witness to God's work in and through Jesus Christ? As we read the story of Stephen in the early chapters of Acts we cannot help but ask ourselves that question. Stephen appears in the pages of Luke's account of the life of the early church as a model of devotion. Over and over Luke offers words of praise that clearly recognize the godly character of this man, paying special attention to the power and blessings of the Holy Spirit in his work and life. As we watch Stephen through the course of this story, we see *the*

embodiment of Christ-likeness: Like his Lord, Stephen was empowered by the Holy Spirit and devoted himself to doing God's will. Like his Lord, his efforts met with strong opposition. Like his Lord, Stephen was called in before the authorities. Like his Lord, he confronted false witnesses. Like his Lord, he stood steadfast in the face of opposition. Like his Lord, he was rejected and killed. And, like his Lord, Stephen died trusting God fully and calling for the forgiveness of those who murdered him. As we ponder his person and his work, Stephen becomes both an inspiration and a challenge for our own faithful living.

The Oxford Dictionary of Saints refers to Stephen as a "protomartyr of the Christian church," meaning that he stands at the head of a long list of individuals who have given their lives in faithful service to Christ through the centuries. The church in the West has celebrated the feast of Saint Stephen on December 26 at least since the fourth century, thereby, placing the date of his martyrdom—his birth into heaven as it were—immediately after the celebration of the birth of Jesus Christ.

That Stephen was the first to follow Christ faithfully unto death gives him a special place in the memory of the church. Today, several major Protestant denominations sponsor a program of "Stephen Ministry" that recognizes and promotes a vigorous combination of ministering to the physical needs of persons with faithful proclamation of the gospel. Since Stephen stands close to Christ in person and work, we may ask ourselves: *What can we do to grow more like Stephen as we live and work for Jesus Christ?*

READING THE SCRIPTURE

NRSV

Acts 6:8-15

8 Stephen, full of grace and power, did great wonders and signs among the people. ⁹Then some of those who belonged to the synagogue of the Freedmen (as it was called), Cyrenians, Alexandrians, and others of those from Cilicia and Asia, stood up and argued with Stephen. ¹⁰But they could not withstand the wisdom and the Spirit with which he spoke. ¹¹Then they secretly instigated some men to say, "We have heard him speak blasphemous words against Moses and God." ¹²They stirred up the people as well as the elders and the scribes; then they suddenly confronted him, seized him, and brought him before the council. ¹³They set up false witnesses who said, "This man never stops saying things against this holy place and the law; ¹⁴for we have heard him say that this Jesus of Nazareth will destroy this place and will change the customs that Moses handed on to us." ¹⁵And all who sat in the council looked intently at him, and they saw that his face was like the face of an angel.

NIV

Acts 6:8-15

⁸Now Stephen, a man full of God's grace and power, did great wonders and miraculous signs among the people. ⁹Opposition arose, however, from members of the Synagogue of the Freedmen (as it was called)—Jews of Cyrene and Alexandria as well as the provinces of Cilicia and Asia. These men began to argue with Stephen, ¹⁰but they could not stand up against his wisdom or the Spirit by whom he spoke.

¹¹Then they secretly persuaded some men to say, "We have heard Stephen speak words of blasphemy against Moses and against God."

¹²So they stirred up the people and the elders and the teachers of the law. They seized Stephen and brought him before the Sanhedrin. ¹³They produced false witnesses, who testified, "This fellow never stops speaking against this holy place and against the law. ¹⁴For we have heard him say that this Jesus of Nazareth will destroy this place and change the customs Moses handed down to us."

¹⁵All who were sitting in the Sanhedrin looked intently at Stephen, and they saw that his face was like the face of an angel.

Key Verse

Key Verse

NRSV
Acts 7:54-60

54 When they heard these things, they became enraged and ground their teeth at Stephen. ⁵⁵But filled with the Holy Spirit, he gazed into heaven and saw the glory of God and Jesus standing at the right hand of God. ⁵⁶"Look," he said, "I see the heavens opened and the Son of Man standing at the right hand of God!" ⁵⁷But they covered their ears, and with a loud shout all rushed together against him. ⁵⁸Then they dragged him out of the city and began to stone him; and the witnesses laid their coats at the feet of a young man named Saul. ⁵⁹While they were stoning Stephen, he prayed, "Lord Jesus, receive my spirit." ⁶⁰Then he knelt down and cried out in a loud voice, "Lord, do not hold this sin against them." When he had said this, he died.

NIV
Acts 7:54-60

⁵⁴When they heard this, they were furious and gnashed their teeth at him. ⁵⁵But Stephen, full of the Holy Spirit, looked up to heaven and saw the glory of God, and Jesus standing at the right hand of God. ⁵⁶"Look," he said, "I see heaven open and the Son of Man standing at the right hand of God."

⁵⁷At this they covered their ears and, yelling at the top of their voices, they all rushed at him, ⁵⁸dragged him out of the city and began to stone him. Meanwhile, the witnesses laid their clothes at the feet of a young man named Saul.

⁵⁹While they were stoning him, Stephen prayed, "Lord Jesus, receive my spirit." ⁶⁰Then he fell on his knees and cried out, "Lord, do not hold this sin against them." When he had said this, he fell asleep.

UNDERSTANDING THE SCRIPTURE

Acts 6:1-6. Luke tells the reader of Acts that as the church grew, a problem arose between the Hellenists and the Hebrews, that is, between the native Greek-speaking Jewish Christians and their Aramaic-speaking fellow believers. The Twelve called together the full number of the disciples and addressed the situation. The Twelve themselves were unwilling to abandon the ministry of prayer and preaching that they were doing in order to take on the supervision of an equitable distribution of the charitable provisions that were being given to those in need. Thus, they called for the assembly to select others, the Seven, who would be given responsibility for this part of the church's life. The Twelve plainly named the qualifications for the Seven: They had to be "of good standing, full of the Spirit and of wisdom," and open to being appointed to the task.

Luke reports that the suggestion of the Twelve pleased the whole group, so they chose and brought the Seven to the apostles, who blessed them for their work. Luke wants the reader to see that the work of the Seven is an outgrowth of the work of the Twelve, that prayer and preaching result in ministering to physical needs—although every person is not charged with the responsibility for every task. Nevertheless, those committed to praying and preaching recognize and bless the necessary work of charity.

Acts 6:7. This verse is a summary concerning the life of the church. The mention of the priests shows that the growth was dramatic, and that there was a warm reception of the gospel among those devoted to God's work in Israel.

Acts 6:8-10. Special notice is given to the work of Stephen, a clearly charismatic figure who did much more than "wait on tables." Indeed, in his role of responsibility Stephen did mighty works in word and deed. Luke tells the reader that Stephen was "full of grace and power," so that we understand his activities to be the outpouring of God's provisions on the people.

Nevertheless, what Stephen said and did brought him into conflict with other Hellenistic Jews who were not Christians. The controversy was obviously sharp, but Stephen appears to have been so "full of grace and power" that Luke reports his opponents "could not withstand the wisdom and the Spirit with which he spoke." The Twelve had wanted to appoint persons filled with Spirit and wisdom, and Stephen turns out to be exactly that in every way. His work was the manifestation of God's will at work through the Spirit in his life. Stephen is impressive, but we should not miss seeing that it is the Spirit in him that made him so effective, powerful, and even offensive.

Acts 6:11-14. False charges concerning the temple were brought against Stephen in context of the council of scribes and elders. While Luke has much less detail in his Gospel concerning the interrogation of Jesus by the Jewish authorities than do the other Gospel writers, one cannot help but see the clear parallels between Jesus and Stephen at this point.

Acts 6:15. Luke continues to emphasize the dramatic manner in which Stephen was Spirit-filled. In the face of accusations, Stephen's visage appeared even to his enemies "like the face of an angel." Of course, we are to understand Stephen's striking countenance as divine testimony to his innocence; yet, as the story continues, we should recall that Stephen's speech and his steadfastness are the outworking of the presence of the Spirit.

Acts 7:1. The high priest demanded a reply from Stephen concerning the charges. Readers of the speech that follows have long since noticed that Stephen does not so much deny the charges against him

as he does level his own charges against his enemies!

Acts 7:2-50. Stephen's speech is the longest and most puzzling address in Acts. In the lengthy initial portions of the address Stephen tells a story, his version of the history of Israel. First, he focuses on God and Abraham (7:2-8); then, he tells of the time of Abraham and the ancestors of Israel, including especially the story of Joseph (7:9-16); then, Stephen speaks of the time of God's promise, that is, an account of the exodus and the wilderness wanderings (7:17-43); finally, the story shifts to focus on the transition from the tabernacle to the temple (7:44-50).

Acts 7:51-53. In these verses Stephen turns on his audience and levels charges against them (7:51) and gives evidence to back up the indictment (7:52-53). Whereas we have seen that Stephen is full of the Spirit and the agent of the Spirit's work, his accusations charge his opponents of "forever opposing the Holy Spirit" and murdering "the Righteous One," that is, Jesus Christ.

Acts 7:54. Luke notes the anger of the crowd and uses idiomatic language to heighten the portrait of their fury.

Acts 7:55-56. Again, Luke reports that Stephen was "filled with the Holy Spirit." Now, in the power of the Spirit he has a vision into the heavens where he sees the risen Jesus in a position of special power alongside God.

Acts 7:57-60. As Stephen faithfully declares his vision, his enemies act with utter malice to kill him. Yet, even as he dies, the Spirit-filled Stephen is completely faithful, even at peace, praying for the forgiveness of those who were in the process of murdering him.

Acts 8:1-3. These final verses recall the severe persecution that came on the church in the wake of the incident with Stephen. Luke records the burial of Stephen and how he was mourned. With Stephen dead, now others faced the hostility he had so faithfully suffered.

INTERPRETING THE SCRIPTURE

On Being Full of Grace and Power

When Stephen was filled with the Holy Spirit, he was charged with divine power for the doing of ministry. Vital religious experience is not purely private, nor is it simply inwardly focused. Stephen shows us that when the Spirit comes into the lives of faithful believers, they act for the good of the gospel mission.

Stephen and the other six members of the Seven were appointed and blessed to do a specific ministry in the life of the early church. The Twelve had prayed for them and had laid hands on them as a sign of blessing. One of the requirements that the Twelve had stipulated for those who were to be among the Seven was that they were to be full of the Spirit. As we ponder this account we see that the Spirit directed Stephen, and in various ways the others, to do far more than the necessary work of waiting on tables. Stephen proved to be a charismatic figure who preached and did mighty works that commanded attention for the gospel.

Under the influence of God's Holy Spirit, faithful believers may do more than anyone would ever have expected. Thus, one man who went through the training to be a "Stephen Minister" in his church anticipated giving about a half day per week to doing visitation. With the passage of time, however, he was directing the work of a Meals-on-Wheels program, teaching a Sunday school class for mentally challenged children, assisting in worship as a liturgist, and finally serving as a lay minister for two rural congregations. He took on one challenge after another, moving into areas neither he nor others anticipated, all because of the Spirit's leadership in his life.

The Security of the Spirit

Stephen was a formidable figure in the exchanges between Hellenistic Jewish Christians and other Hellenistic Jews who did not believe the gospel of Jesus Christ. In the debates between these groups, Stephen manifested the power of the Spirit as he faithfully and forcefully declared the gospel in the power of the Spirit. Wise words were granted to Stephen as he faced people opposed to the message he proclaimed. Stephen was never simply left to his human resources, for as he was faithful to the gospel so the Spirit was faithful to Stephen—or better, as the Spirit was faithful to Stephen, he was faithful to the gospel.

In Luke's Gospel, Jesus had taught his disciples that they would have "an opportunity to testify" (Luke 21:13); and he told them, "So make up your minds not to prepare your defense in advance; for I will give you words and a wisdom that none of your opponents will be able to withstand or contradict" (Luke 21:14-15). As we see Stephen encountering the Hellenistic Jews in Jerusalem, we watch the fulfillment of Jesus' promises as the Spirit secured his faithful witness. The presence and the power of the Spirit are the greatest security for which any of us might hope, and the Scriptures tell us that all we need to do to experience the faithfulness of the Spirit is to be faithful ourselves and step out in word and deed doing the mission to which we are called. The Spirit is present and powerful, but unless we act we will never know the Spirit's presence.

Steadfastness in the Face of Violent Opposition

Stephen faced much more than a tough debate. When his opponents could not withstand the wisdom of his arguments, they formed a strategy to guarantee their success. Yet, even under arrest and charged with blasphemy, Stephen stood firm in the power of the Spirit. As Christ had faced the hostile council, so Stephen emulated his Lord in the same situation. The Spirit empowered Stephen to incarnate the ways of Jesus Christ, so that he did not hang his head in the face of condemnation; rather, he stood transformed by the Spirit to face malicious lies with divine power.

Here, Stephen is an admirable figure; but we must ask ourselves at what distance we stand admiring Stephen as he is under fire. Seldom do we ourselves face situations of real danger because of bearing a faithful witness to Jesus Christ. We will not likely find ourselves in peril for taking fruit baskets to homebound persons at Christmastime, although that is an important and valid form of ministry. What kinds of situations do exist, however, right in our own communities that would bring us into danger if we were to bear a faithful witness for Christ? What forms of injustice, what kinds of oppression exist in our midst and demand from us, as faithful witnesses, a firm word from Christ? Who is speaking for Christ in these situations? Christ has no lips but our lips, no hands but our hands.

Faithful Witness Brings Vision and Trust

Stephen stood under fire and looked into the heavens. As he faced the hazard of certain death, Stephen looked to the source of his faithfulness and he saw his Lord. This vision of the risen Christ was the securing confirmation of all that Stephen had said and done. Having borne testimony to the gospel of Jesus Christ, Stephen was granted a vision that called him forward in faith despite the terrible moment in which he stood.

Turning to Jesus and seeing him with clarity empowered Stephen to trust his Lord with the sacrifice of his life. The reality of Christ gave Stephen spiritual power to continue to embody the ways of his Lord, so that even as he was murdered he prayed for his killers, asking that they be forgiven for their wickedness.

An elderly Christian woman had given her life to being a faithful servant of Jesus Christ. She had cared for people in poverty, fought against wars, marched for social justice, and steadily testified to the transforming grace of God in Jesus Christ. At times she had faced and suffered physical violence, but she had always been faithful despite the terrible situations she had faced. Toward the end of her life she was asked how and why she had done such things. Her reply was another testimony to the gospel. She said, "As a young woman I went with a church group to visit a community of people who were afflicted with Hansen's disease—sometimes called leprosy. As I met those people, as we talked, when I looked into their eyes all I could see were the eyes of Jesus Christ, gazing at me with God's love and calling out to me for help."

The Power to Call for Forgiveness

Perhaps the hardest thing in the world to do is to forgive, to ask God for the forgiveness of persons who have really wronged us, to pray for people who may have done us actual harm. Yet, Stephen petitioned God on behalf of his killers. As Jesus died saying, "Father, forgive them," so the Spirit empowered Stephen to do likewise. Having seen the risen Christ, Stephen died as his Lord had died rather than calling for revenge. Stephen's faith issued in faithfulness as he gave the ultimate testimony by dying like Jesus Christ.

A newspaper ran a remarkable story about a family of Korean Christians who had arrived at the sentencing of a man who had killed a member of their family out of racial hatred. After the judge passed the sentence, the head of the family asked to speak and, talking directly to the convicted killer, he said, "We forgive you, and we pray that you may know God's forgiveness, too."

In a variety of ways the story of Stephen teaches us about Christian faith in action. Called to table service, Stephen took on the work, and in the power of the Spirit he did even more than he was asked to do. Facing opposition, he bore faithful witness. Falsely accused, he boldly spoke the truth. Rejected and attacked, he lived and died like his Lord. As the church's first martyr, Stephen provides us with both testimony and an example of what it means to be a faithful witness to Jesus Christ.

SHARING THE SCRIPTURE

PREPARING TO TEACH

Preparing Our Hearts

As noted in our lesson, "we will not likely find ourselves in peril for taking fruit baskets to homebound persons at Christmastime." The good that we do is necessary to spread the gospel and nurture others, but we seldom find ourselves caught in life and death dramas as Stephen did. Suppose you were confronted with a situation that could only be resolved if you were willing to renounce Christ or suffer the consequences of your faithfulness. Reflect on how you think you would respond. Recall that although Stephen was the first Christian martyr, he was surely not the last. Many have given up jobs, homes, family relationships, and even their lives for the sake of the gospel. What, honestly, are you willing to sacrifice?

Preparing Our Minds

Today's background scripture is lengthy but important for our understanding of who Stephen was and what he did. Be sure to allow sufficient time to study it, along with the Understanding the Scripture section. Read the entire lesson.

If time permits, you may want to do additional research on Stephen by consulting a Bible dictionary. Read Acts 11:19 and Acts 22:20, which also mention Stephen.

Preparing Our Learning Space

If possible, find and display pictures histroical or contemporary of persons who gave their lives because of their faithful witness.

Have on hand:
- ✔ several Bibles for students
- ✔ newsprint and marker or chalkboard and chalk
- ✔ paper and pencils
- ✔ optional pictures of Christian martyrs

LEADING THE CLASS

(1) Introduction

Begin the session by reading this quip: "If you were tried on the charge of being a Christian, would there be enough evidence to convict you?" Ask the class to respond to this question by brainstorming a list of "evidence" that would indicate that a person was indeed "guilty" of being a Christian. Record the answers on newsprint. Then ask:

(1) **Do most Christians you know exhibit these traits?**　 ?

(2) **Which traits do you often see?**

(3) **Which traits seem to be lacking in the lives of many modern Christians?**

Guide the discussion to today's lesson on Stephen by asking the class to note which of the characteristics they brainstormed to describe Stephen. Emphasize that Stephen embodied Christ-likeness. Refer to the first paragraph under Focusing on the Main Question to illustrate the ways in which Stephen was like Jesus. Conclude this part of the lesson by lifting up today's main question: *What can we do to grow more like Stephen as we live and work for Jesus Christ?*

(2) Stephen: A Faithful Witness

Set the stage for the discussion of the end of Stephen's life by sharing whatever you feel the group needs to know of the background scripture from the Understanding the Scripture portion. Do not get bogged down in details, but demonstrate that Stephen's work and witness prior to his martyrdom are examples of faithful Christian witness.

Choose a volunteer to read aloud the scripture lesson, Acts 6:8-15; 7:54-60, in its entirety. Or, to add more drama to the reading, choose a student to read the part of the narrator, others to read the words of the false witnesses (6:11, 13), and another to read Stephen's words (7:56, 59b, 60b).

Point out that in Acts 6:8-15, we see tremendous opposition to Stephen. Yet, as noted in "Steadfastness in the Face of Violent Opposition" in the Interpreting the Scripture section, "Stephen stood firm in the power of the Spirit." Opposition did not defeat him; it opened a window of opportunity for transformation.

Note that opposition mounts in Acts 7:54-60, as Stephen is ultimately stoned to death by his accusers. Ask:

?

(1) What resources does Stephen have in the face of such opposition? (See "The Security of the Spirit" and "Steadfastness in the Face of Violent Opposition.")

(2) In the midst of life-threatening opposition, Stephen had a vision of the risen Christ. Why do you think he saw this vision. In other words, what purpose did it serve? (See "Faithful Witness Brings Vision and Trust.")

(3) In his last moments, Stephen prays that his executioners would be forgiven. This is "the ultimate testimony" that he could give to Christ. What effect would Stephen's prayer of forgiveness have had on you if you had been standing in the crowd with a handful of stones?

(3) Discerning Our Own Commitment to Faithful Witness

Relate the story of Stephen to the class members' lives by doing the following guided imagery exercise. Any church leaders who have dared to take risks will have encountered a milder version of the criticism Stephen experienced. Remember to wait at least ten seconds for each pause before continuing. Read the following:

Sit comfortably and relax. Allow God's Spirit to speak to you as we do this guided imagery exercise. Picture yourself in front of your own church. Note the sounds, sights, and smells. (pause)   R

As you are standing there, the church door flies open, almost yanked off its hinges. Several church leaders and the pastor approach and surround you. They are obviously angry with you, though you are not sure why. Soon the din dies down a bit and one person—to your amazement—is shouting a criticism of what you thought was a very faithful action. Perhaps you tried to encourage the church to engage in a ministry to the hungry or homeless, or suggested that the church increase its support of missions. Whatever you did, some people are obviously upset. Listen as this person criticizes something you did or said. (pause)

Recall how you feel when someone hurls stinging criticism at you. (pause)

Now listen to what Jesus has to say about the action for which you were being criticized. (pause)

Think about the experience. Would you do it again, even though you know it will result in criticism from some people but praise from Christ? Listen to your own feelings (pause).

Now offer forgiveness to your critics. (pause)

• Give thanks to God for opportunities to act in Christlike ways, regardless of the consequences. (pause)

• Open your eyes when you are ready.

Now look at three examples in our les-

R son of persons whose behavior was similar to that of Stephen. You may want to read the cited paragraphs aloud, or retell them, or write them on newsprint. Have the class work together to answer the questions that follow. If you choose to work in teams, provide time for them to share with the whole class.

EXAMPLE 1: the man who trained to be a Stephen Minister (See paragraph three under "On Being Full of Grace and Power.")

EXAMPLE 2: the woman who had a lifelong history of engagement in the quest for social justice (See paragraph three under "Faithful Witness Brings Trust and Vision.")

EXAMPLE 3: the Korean family who forgave the murderer of their family member (See paragraph two under "The Power to Call for Forgiveness.")

For each of the persons cited above, answer these questions:

? (1) **How does this person's behavior seem unusual compared to what most people would do?**

(2) **What do you think you would have done in a similar situation?**

(3) **How does this person's behavior reflect the model of Stephen, who in turn reflects the example of Jesus?**

(4) **What affect do you think this person's behavior may have had on those who witnessed it?**

To conclude this activity, invite class members to share examples of persons they know, either personally or by reputation, who have followed Stephen's example of faithful witness. If you have found pictures of Christian martyrs, this would be an appropriate time to show them.

Help the students to consider their own faithful witness in the face of opposition by discussing these questions:

• What situations in our own community would endanger us physically or socially if we were to bear faithful witness to Christ? (Example: A homeless shelter is needed, but certain citizens insist that it cannot be put in the community.)

• What injustices exist in our community that must be addressed by speaking a faithful word? (Example: A petition is circulating to deny new immigrants housing in the community.)

• How can we, as individuals and as a church class, speak out for Christ in order to overcome injustice in our own community? (Examples: letter-writing campaigns to elected officials and newspapers; education on the issue within the church to enlist support.)

HELPING CLASS MEMBERS ACT

If the class identified a local issue that needs to be addressed, challenge them to develop a strategy that will enable them to bear a faithful witness.

Remind the students that Stephen faced a group of religious people who disagreed with him so strongly that they stoned him to death. Tell them to be alert this week for ideas and opinions voiced within the Christian community that would normally "turn them off." Suggest that they try to empathize with the speaker and understand the ideas, even if they cannot agree.

Invite each person to consider making a commitment to action on Christ's behalf. This witness may be through a well-organized program such as Stephen Ministry, but it can also be done informally.

PLANNING FOR NEXT SUNDAY

Acts 18:1-4, 18-19, 24-26 and Romans 16:3-5a are the scripture readings for next week's lesson. They focus on a dynamic husband and wife team, Priscilla and Aquila, who offer support and companionship to Paul.

BE A SUPPORTIVE COMPANION

PREVIEWING THE LESSON

Lesson Scripture: Acts 18:1-4, 18-19, 24-26; Romans 16:3-5*a*
Background Scripture: Acts 18:1-4, 18-19, 24-26; Romans 16:3-5*a*
Key Verses: Romans 16:3-4

Focus of the Lesson:
the supportive companionship of Priscilla and Aquila that contributed significantly to Paul's ministry

Main Question of the Lesson:
How can we be supportive companions in ministry with others?

This lesson will enable adult learners to:
(1) study the lives and ministry of Priscilla and Aquila.
(2) explore their own willingness to be in ministry.
(3) respond by opening themselves to the possibility of ministry.

Today's lesson may be outlined as follows:
(1) Introduction
(2) Priscilla and Aquila: Supportive Companions
(3) Extending Our Own Hands in Ministry

FOCUSING ON THE MAIN QUESTION

Priscilla and Aquila were an important part of the early Christian missionary activity. They are somewhat distinguished in the mix of prominent persons in the early church by being a married couple, both of whom seem vitally involved in the church's mission. The amount of information about this couple in the New Testament is limited, although beyond the verses of our lesson we find mention of Priscilla and Aquila at 1 Corinthians 16:19 and 2 Timothy 4:19.

From their names we can tell that they were most likely freeborn persons, not for-mer slaves; and from the tendency in the New Testament more often than not to list Priscilla before Aquila, we suspect that she may have come from a higher social class than he did. Moreover, the name Luke uses for the woman in Acts, Priscilla, is a diminutive or a nickname implying famil-iarity or fondness; whereas her more for-mal given name, Prisca, is the one Paul uses in his correspondences.

Paul met this couple in Corinth when he first went there to establish a base of min-istry in the Roman province of Achaia, of which Corinth was the capital. Priscilla and Aquila were Jews, but they were already Christians when Paul met them. They shared not only a Jewish background and Christian faith with Paul, but also their trade-occupation. With much in common, the couple and the apostle formed a firm bond. Paul came to live with them and work with them; and subsequently they joined Paul as he moved doing missions in various settings.

Priscilla and Aquila were important persons in the travels and work of Paul. While we know their names and some information about them, Priscilla and Aquila clearly played a much larger and more important role in the overall ministry of the apostle than one might suppose. We will never know the details of their involvement in the team of ministers with whom Paul associated, but the few data we know with certainty give us important images of ways in which we might go about Christ's work. Priscilla and Aquila remind us of the importance of faithful, unassuming involvement in gospel ministry. Their work prompts us to ask: *How can we be supportive companions in ministry with others?*

READING THE SCRIPTURE

NRSV
Acts 18:1-4

1 After this Paul left Athens and went to Corinth. ²There he found a Jew named Aquila, a native of Pontus, who had recently come from Italy with his wife Priscilla, because Claudius had ordered all Jews to leave Rome. Paul went to see them, ³and, because he was of the same trade, he stayed with them, and they worked together—by trade they were tentmakers. ⁴Every sabbath he would argue in the synagogue and would try to convince Jews and Greeks.

NIV
Acts 18:1-4

1 After this, Paul left Athens and went to Corinth. ²There he met a Jew named Aquila, a native of Pontus, who had recently come from Italy with his wife Priscilla, because Claudius had ordered all the Jews to leave Rome. Paul went to see them, ³and because he was a tentmaker as they were, he stayed and worked with them. ⁴Every Sabbath he reasoned in the synagogue, trying to persuade Jews and Greeks.

NRSV
Acts 18:18-19

18 After staying there for a considerable time, Paul said farewell to the believers and sailed for Syria, accompanied by Priscilla and Aquila. At Cenchreae he had his hair cut, for he was under a vow. ¹⁹ When they reached Ephesus, he left them there, but first he himself went into the synagogue and had a discussion with the Jews.

NIV
Acts 18:18-19

¹⁸Paul stayed on in Corinth for some time. Then he left the brothers and sailed for Syria, accompanied by Priscilla and Aquila. Before he sailed, he had his hair cut off at Cenchrea because of a vow he had taken. ¹⁹They arrived at Ephesus, where Paul left Priscilla and Aquila. He himself went into the synagogue and reasoned with the Jews.

NRSV
Acts 18:24-26

24 Now there came to Ephesus a Jew named Apollos, a native of Alexandria. He

NIV
Acts 18:24-26

²⁴Meanwhile a Jew named Apollos, a native of Alexandria, came to Ephesus. He

was an eloquent man, well-versed in the scriptures. [25]He had been instructed in the Way of the Lord; and he spoke with burning enthusiasm and taught accurately the things concerning Jesus, though he knew only the baptism of John. [26]He began to speak boldly in the synagogue; but when Priscilla and Aquila heard him, they took him aside and explained the Way of God to him more accurately.

NRSV
Romans 16:3-5a

3 Greet Prisca and Aquila, who work with me in Christ Jesus, [4]and who risked their necks for my life, to whom not only I give thanks, but also all the churches of the Gentiles. [5]Greet also the church in their house.

was a learned man, with a thorough knowledge of the Scriptures. [25]He had been instructed in the way of the Lord, and he spoke with great fervor and taught about Jesus accurately, though he knew only the baptism of John. [26]He began to speak boldly in the synagogue. When Priscilla and Aquila heard him, they invited him to their home and explained to him the way of God more adequately.

NIV
Romans 16:3-5a

[3]Greet Priscilla and Aquila, my fellow workers in Christ Jesus. [4]They risked their lives for me. Not only I but all the churches of the Gentiles are grateful to them.
[5]Greet also the church that meets at their house.

UNDERSTANDING THE SCRIPTURE

Acts 18:1-4. From the information in Acts and from a note in the Roman historian Suetonius's *Claudius* (25.4), we can infer that Priscilla and Aquila were Roman Jews who had become Christians while still participating in the life of a synagogue in Rome. They had apparently helped in the dissemination of the gospel, activity that had produced controversy and even rioting among the Roman Jews. Thus, in the year 49 C.E., under the administration of Claudius, the apparent troublemakers had been expelled from the capital. The ban was such that Priscilla and Aquila could have maintained ownership of any property they held in Rome, and they would have been free to return to the city after the death of the emperor.

Fortunately, this couple, like Paul, had an essentially portable profession: they were "tentmakers." This occupation was either weaving canvas or repairing leather, or perhaps both. With a set of tools and the frame of a loom one could practice

tent-making almost anywhere, and indeed some tentmakers lived on the road because they followed the Roman armies in order to make and repair tents and various leather goods that the soldiers used.

As we meet this couple we find them living in the Jewish quarter of Corinth and already affiliated with a synagogue. We should notice that Acts 18:4 recognizes that both Jews and Greeks were active in the synagogue community. This situation was not unusual outside Palestine. Around the first century, Judaism itself was a missionary religion that sought to make converts of Gentiles, many of whom were attracted to the life of the synagogue because of monotheism, the high moral standards of Jews, and the vitality of the synagogue community. Yet, because of the physical pain and social stigma of circumcision, many Greeks never fully converted to become Jews. Paul and his associates often had success in preaching to these Gentiles in the synagogues.

Acts 18:18-19. Priscilla and Aquila left Corinth with Paul. This change is understandable in part because of their mobile trade, but we should not let that social reality obscure the deep commitment to ministry that this move reveals. As they left Corinth they went to Cenchreae, which was the actual port town of Corinth on the Saronic Gulf of the Aegean Sea. In Romans 16:1, Paul writes of a woman named Phoebe, who was a deacon in the church at Cenchreae, so that we know there were more congregations of Christians than one in and around Corinth during this time.

Paul cut his hair because he was under a vow. This remembrance refers to an element of the "nazirite" vow, described in Numbers 6:1-21. This vow was a self-imposed means of special devotion to God. The cutting of one's hair signaled the completion of the period of the vow. Since Paul had been living with Priscilla and Aquila, they would have been at least indirect participants in the conditions to which Paul had devoted himself.

Finally, we see that the group went to Ephesus. Paul left the couple there as he continued to travel.

Acts 18:24-26. In Ephesus, Priscilla and Aquila met Apollos. We find that he was articulate, eloquent, and well-versed in the teaching of scripture. Yet, Apollos has only "book-knowledge" of the reality of or "the Way of God." Having experienced the baptism of John, Apollos was in need of information of "the things concerning Jesus." Priscilla and Aquila gave Apollos the instruction he needed to complete his education and to empower him for even more effective ministry.

Romans 16:3-5a. In Paul's letter to the Romans we find that Priscilla and Aquila eventually returned to their home. At the earliest this could have happened in 54 C.E., when Claudius died. Paul's brief remarks also provide us with other striking pieces of information. Paul confirms that both Prisca (Paul's way of referring to her) and Aquila had worked with him in the gospel ministry of Christ Jesus. The degree of their commitment is evident from Paul's saying that they "risked their necks for [his] life." He probably has in mind something(s) they did during the stay in Ephesus, where Paul encountered serious danger that was apparently life-threatening (see 1 Corinthians 15:32 and 2 Corinthians 1:8-9). As Paul expresses his clear gratitude, we see that he was not alone in his appreciation of the efforts of this couple; for he says that "all the churches of the Gentiles" are thankful for the work of Prisca and Aquila. While we may never know exactly what they did, Paul's expressions and phrases suggest significant activities. He even refers to a church that met in their house.

INTERPRETING THE SCRIPTURE

Preface

Priscilla and Aquila were Jewish Christians whose lives had been dramatically affected by their faith in Jesus Christ. As we read the passages in our lesson concerning this first-century Christian couple, we learn what their faith directed them to do with their lives. Priscilla and Aquila help us to think about certain characteristics of living that are appropriate for Christians. In reflecting on the traits that Priscilla and Aquila demonstrated we should never forget that these early Christians lived as they did because of the presence and the power of the risen Lord in their lives, so that we are considering spiritual characteristics, not merely human niceties.

Priscilla and Aquila Were Bold and Enduring

Priscilla and Aquila took their faith so seriously that they were banned from Rome because of their involvement with the gospel of Jesus Christ. This couple's commitment to Christ was costly; they were literally thrown out of their home because of their Christian faith and actions. Controversy and tumult did not keep Priscilla and Aquila from doing what they were called to do for the gospel. Moreover, having experience being expelled from Rome, Priscilla and Aquila again were active for the gospel mission in Corinth. The unpleasant experience of banishment did not deter this couple from rendering faithful service to their calling. Having paid the price of discipleship in Rome, Priscilla and Aquila stood ready to face the cost of following Christ in Corinth.

How many Christians today would willingly suffer such losses and go through such inconvenience, only to live in such a way that the same thing was likely to happen again? We have heard of missionaries in faraway places who have suffered, even died, as they lived out their calling to Christian ministry; but are we prepared to pay such prices for service ourselves?

Priscilla and Aquila Were Open and Accepting

When Paul came to Corinth, Priscilla and Aquila took him in—both to work with them and to live with them. This couple's openness facilitated the work of Paul in Corinth, in Ephesus, and elsewhere. Although they were not converted to Christianity by Paul, Priscilla and Aquila did not view their relationship to Paul competitively; rather, they acted cooperatively and, thereby, compounded the effectiveness of the early Christian mission. Moreover, as we follow their story in Acts, we see that when Apollos arrived in Ephesus, Priscilla and Aquila dealt graciously with him. Apollos was eloquent, but he was not fully informed. Priscilla and Aquila could have easily perceived him to be dangerous, but instead they embraced what he was doing and provided him with fuller information that gave even more substance to his proclamation. Rather than react to Apollos as if he were an ill-informed threat, the couple saw him as an opportunity to extend the ministry of the early church.

If missionaries arrived in our community would we be committed enough to the gospel mission to help them secure a living and find a place to live? Would we become involved in the work they came to do? Or, would we be skeptical or afraid of such persons and their activities? Priscilla and Aquila show us what it means to embrace the Christian mission as fully as possible.

Priscilla and Aquila Were Flexible

Not only could this couple open their home to Paul, but when he moved on to work in other places they went with him. Having been thrown out of their home in Rome, Priscilla and Aquila came to Corinth, where they welcomed Paul, and then they moved their home to Ephesus, where Paul again used their house as a base of operations for ministry. Later (we do not know exactly when or how) the couple moved back to Rome. New Testament scholars suggest that this move may have been strategically motivated, that is, the couple may have moved on ahead of Paul to establish still another base for the mission that Paul wanted to launch in Spain. The freedom of the gospel freed Priscilla and Aquila to live an adaptable lifestyle devoted to work, Christ's.

The missionaries who are sent out today by most, if not all, churches are required to live as flexibly as Priscilla and Aquila did. They usually serve terms in the situations and settings to which they are sent. Home is where they are more than what they have. Moreover, the standard policy of ministry in The United Methodist Church is *itineracy*, that is, United Methodist ministers are obliged to serve where they are appointed by their bishops. Similar accountability is the norm for ordained ministers in other denominations. While the conditions of ministry for contemporary pastors, priests, and missionaries are not exactly the same as those faced by Priscilla and Aquila, similar flexibility is required for ongoing service. What if all Christians were *required* to be so adaptable? Are there other ways in which all Christians can be flexible without actually having to undergo a physical relocation?

Priscilla and Aquila Were Dedicated and Generous

In both Corinth and Ephesus they opened their home to Paul, and in Rome their home became a house church. All along the way, at every turn of events, we see Priscilla and Aquila giving freely of their resources to the work of the early church. The power of Christ in their lives produced a seemingly boundless generosity and a remarkable willingness to share what they had with others.

Jesus Christ calls his disciples to a new way of relating to the world. As followers of Christ we are to look at all of life as Jesus himself said God views the world—in grace and goodness with a will to serve. God has called all Christians through Jesus Christ in order to accomplish God's will through us. As we read and ponder their story, we see that Priscilla and Aquila recognized that in Jesus Christ the will of God took flesh in order to call them (and us!) to devotion to the gospel. Thus, a little girl named Agnes Bejaxhui from southeastern Europe heard in the gospel the call of Jesus Christ. As she gave full ear to Christ's call, she knew herself to be sent to those in this world who suffer the greatest disabilities in the midst of the worst forms of poverty. In her devotion, at eighteen years of age, Agnes Bejaxhui became a missionary nun who is known to us today as Mother Teresa. It is said that she never doubted for a second that she had done that right thing; that it was the will of God; that it was God's choice. Such remarkable and selfless dedication—seen so clearly in Priscilla and Aquila—can come only from the confidence gained by doing God's will. As we discern God's will and as we devote ourselves to living according to the call of Christ, we will find ourselves living beyond the level of mere human possibilities.

Priscilla and Aquila Were Courageous

In Rome, the couple had risked their security in devotion to the gospel. In Corinth, they risked the danger of involvement with Paul and his controversial work. Later, they took on the real risks of travel in the ancient world as they moved with Paul to Ephesus. There they apparently risked their own lives to assist Paul as he faced peril. Finally, back in Rome where their troubles started, Priscilla and Aquila risked the dangers of hosting a church in their house. The courage of Christ himself to face difficulties, including the reality of death, empowered and motivated this couple to serve others for Christ at all costs.

How can we know and practice the courage of Christ so that we can be as faithful in service as Priscilla and Aquila were? We find the beginning of an answer to this question when we face squarely that the gospel is more than something we have–it is the power of God that takes hold of us and shapes our lives as it works to change the world. Thus, a young woman in Puerto Rico was left on the streets at twelve years of age. She was there in poverty until her teenage brother died from an overdose and a concerned Christian family took her into their home. They told her the gospel, fed her, clothed her, housed her, and saw to her education. Today, having been transformed by the gospel at work in the world, she works among poor Hispanics in Washington, D.C., sharing with them the gospel as she ministers to their real physical needs.

The gospel forms lives like those of Priscilla and Aquila.

SHARING THE SCRIPTURE

PREPARING TO TEACH

Preparing Our Hearts

Priscilla and Aquila were accepting people who courageously took the risks necessary to further the spread of the gospel. They "kept their bags packed," so to speak, ready to move wherever God would call them to go. As you think about these faithful companions of Paul, consider how you not only minister yourself but also support the ministry of others. Ponder the following questions. You may want to respond to them by writing in your spiritual journal. In what ways do I support the ordained clergy of my own church? How do I help the laypersons identify and use their talents in service to Christ? Why would others say that I am supportive of their efforts in ministry? In what ways could I be a more effective supporter?

Preparing Our Minds

Carefully read the lesson and study Acts 18:1-4, 18-19, 24-26; Romans 16:3-5a.

If time permits, you may want to do some research on tent-making or leather-working if you would like to have more information about the trade that Paul had in common with Priscilla and Aquila.

Preparing Our Learning Space

If possible, secure and post a map showing Rome, Corinth, Ephesus, and Alexandria (home of Apollos). Be prepared to point out these places.

Have on hand:
- ✔ several Bibles for students
- ✔ newsprint and marker or chalkboard and chalk
- ✔ paper and pencils
- ✔ map, if possible

LEADING THE CLASS

(1) Introduction

Begin by reminding the group that often in our lives we "need somebody to lean on." That "somebody" may be a friend, family member, co-worker, neighbor, or church member who helped us in a time of transition and adjustment, such as the birth of a child or a serious illness.

Ask class members to share with a partner a time when they needed support or help. Have them discuss with one another this question:

(1) What behaviors or attitudes enabled the person who helped you to be supportive?

Invite the students to call out some of the traits they have identified. List these on newsprint or a chalkboard.

Move to the scripture lesson by noting that Priscilla and Aquila were a married couple who were Christian ministers in their own right and very supportive of the apostle Paul as well. Identify the following traits that enabled them to be supportive over the long haul: boldness, ability to endure, openness and acceptance of others, flexibility, and courage. Close this introduction with the main question: *How can we be supportive companions in ministry with others?*

(2) Priscilla and Aquila: Supportive Companions

To help the class get an overview of the lives and work of Priscilla and Aquila, choose four volunteers to read aloud the scripture passages from Acts 18:1-4, 18-19, 24-26 and Romans 16:3-5*a*. If you have a map available, point out the cities mentioned in the reading.

After the reading, focus first on Acts 18:1-4. Use information from the Understanding the Scripture portion to explain why Priscilla and Aquila had been expelled from Rome. Also provide information on the trade of tent-making. Then ask:

[?] (1) **How would you describe the kind of faith that enabled Priscilla and Aquila to be expelled from one city only to go to another and continue doing what they had been doing?**

(2) **What would prevent you from being willing to suffer a similar loss of home for the sake of Christ?**

Turn now to Acts 18:18-19 and 24-26. Point out that Apollos was apparently enthusiastic about his preaching, but he lacked complete information about Jesus and his work. Priscilla and Aquila could have ignored or criticized Apollos, but they chose to be mentors by instructing him. Ask:

[?] (3) **What does the willingness of Priscilla and Aquila to help Apollos say about their own concerns for the gospel?**

Now look at Romans 16:3-5*a*. Note, as stated in the Understanding the Scripture portion, that we do not know exactly when Priscilla and Aquila returned to Rome, but it certainly was not before 54 C.E. Paul's letter gives several important pieces of information: Priscilla and Aquila had returned to Rome; they had put themselves in physical jeopardy for Paul; Paul and the Gentile churches owed Priscilla and Aquila a debt of gratitude; and a church met in their home.

If the class enjoys hands-on activities, distribute paper and pencils. Ask them to pretend that they are either Paul or a church member who has been helped by Priscilla and Aquila. Have them write a thank-you note expressing appreciation for the support they have received from this faithful Christian couple.

Extending Our Own Hands in Ministry

Read the following fictional article to the class and ask the questions below.

Missionaries Jane and Michael Adams recently fled their host country after the government was overthrown by a military junta. The new leaders are hostile to Christianity, so the Adamses have sought asylum in the United States. They hope to be able to return to their post. All of their belongings were left as they hastily escaped. They are in need of food, clothing, jobs, and a home for an indefinite period. Anyone who can help is asked to call Pastor Drew Goodson at 555-0000.

(1) **What could our church do to help Jane and Michael?** [?]

(2) **How do you honestly think most church members would respond to this appeal?**

(3) **How could you use the example of Priscilla and Aquila to convince skeptical church members of the need to be supportive?**

Begin the next activity by pointing out that Priscilla and Aquila had to move and relocate their business. While employment-related moves are common in our day, few people seem willing to move for the sake of the gospel. Ask:

(1) **How would the church be different if all Christians were expected to "live an adaptable lifestyle devoted to Christ's work"? (See "Priscilla and Aquila Were Flexible.")** [?]

(2) **What problems or risks might accompany such flexibility?**

(3) **What would be the rewards for the individual church member who was adaptable?**

(4) **What would be the rewards for the church at large?**

Read or retell the portion "Priscilla and Aquila Were Dedicated and Generous" under Interpreting the Scripture. Note especially the example of Mother Teresa. Provide a few moments for class members to reflect silently on the following questions, which you may want to write on newsprint. As an option, distribute paper and pencils to students who prefer to write their thoughts.

? (1) **The selfless dedication of Priscilla and Aquila or Mother Teresa "can only come from the confidence gained by doing God's will." How am I fulfilling God's will?**

(2) **If I am not selflessly supporting the work of the gospel, what changes do I need to make in my life?**

Point out that the gospel "is the power of God that takes hold of us and shapes our lives as it works to change the world." Note an example of this statement that is found in the last paragraph under "Priscilla and Aquila Were Courageous." You may want to compare this young woman's experience with that of Apollos, who was also transformed by the power of the gospel as he experienced it in its fullness from Priscilla and Aquila.

Distribute slips of paper and pencils to students. Ask them to write the first name of someone whose support and witness helped them to be transformed by the power of the gospel. They are not to sign their own name. Give them a few moments to decide who this influential companion in their faith journey is. Then collect the papers. Offer a prayer of thanksgiving for these supportive companions, reading each name aloud as you pray.

HELPING CLASS MEMBERS ACT

Ask students to think of someone who needs support in living out his or her Christian faith. Perhaps poor choices or difficult circumstances have caused this individual to step away from God, or maybe he or she, like Apollos, did not have a good grasp of the faith to start. Have the class members take at least one step this week to help this person who needs a companion in the faith.

Suggest that the students call or write a thank-you note to someone (perhaps the person named in the closing exercise) who has helped them to grow in their faith.

Encourage class members to discern at least one way in which they can support others in ministry this week. This support may be as simple as a word of appreciation for a helpful sermon, but it may require greater commitment, such as the pledging of a sacrificial gift to support a missionary.

PLANNING FOR NEXT SUNDAY

Next Sunday's lesson will conclude our study of New Testament personalities by looking at Paul's companion, Timothy. Ask class members to read the references to this faithful worker found in Acts 16:1-5; 1 Corinthians 4:14-17; Philippians 2:19-24; and 2 Timothy 1:3-7 and 3:14-15.

You may want to begin looking ahead to the material in 1 and 2 Thessalonians and Revelation to prepare for the spring quarter entitled "Hope for the Future."

BE A FAITHFUL WORKER

PREVIEWING THE LESSON

Lesson Scripture: Acts 16:1-5; 1 Corinthians 4:14-17; Philippians 2:19-22; 2 Timothy 1:4-7

Background Scripture: Acts 16:1-5; 1 Corinthians 4:14-17; Philippians 2:19-24; 2 Timothy 1:3-7; 3:14-15

Key Verse: 1 Corinthians 4:17

Focus of the Lesson:
the faithful ministry and high reputation of Timothy that made him an invaluable asset to Paul and his ministry

Main Question of the Lesson:
What inspiration and direction for our own faithful living can we gain from Timothy?

This lesson will enable adult learners to:
(1) recognize the traits that enabled Timothy to be a faithful, effective worker.
(2) imagine how the church would function if each member were like Timothy.
(3) respond by making a commitment to increase their own work for Christ.

Today's lesson may be outlined as follows:
(1) Introduction
(2) Timothy's Faithfulness
(3) Our Own Faithful Work for Christ

FOCUSING ON THE MAIN QUESTION

Timothy was one of Paul's most valued, trusted fellow workers. His importance to the overall mission that Paul led can be easily underestimated, but careful attention to the range of reference to Timothy in Acts and the Pauline letters of the New Testament finds that Timothy worked prominently in a number of ways to advance the mission Paul coordinated. Timothy's involvement with Paul extended over a lengthy period of time, probably from 48 or 49 C.E. until Paul's death in the early 60s. The narrative of Acts recalls Timothy's work at various times and places, although often one cannot be certain whether the Acts account assumes Timothy was present with Paul. Nevertheless, a glance through Paul's letters finds Timothy present and active. First, in 1 and 2 Thessalonians, 2 Corinthians, Philippians, and Colossians, one sees that Timothy is named as the co-author or co-sender of the letter with Paul. Second, Timothy is presented as Paul's co-worker in Romans, 1 and 2 Corinthians, Philippians, Colossians, 1 and 2 Thessalonians, 1 and 2 Timothy, and Philemon. Third, the Pauline letters refer to Timothy variously as Paul's "co-worker" (Romans, 1 Thessalonians); "beloved and faithful child in the Lord" (1 Corinthians); "loyal child in the faith" (1 Timothy); "child" (1 Timothy); "beloved child" (2 Timothy); and "brother" (2 Corinthians, Colossians, 1 Thessalonians, Philemon). Fourth, one finds that Paul regularly sent Timothy in his place when he was unable to attend to the critical needs of congregations in faraway places (see 1 Corinthians, Philippians, and 1 Thessalonians).

In Acts 16 one learns that Timothy was from Derbe-Lystra, that his mother was Jewish and his father was Greek, and that before he became Paul's partner on the mission field that Paul circumcised him to avoid hindering the mission among the Jews of Lystra and Iconium. How Timothy became a Christian is unclear from Acts, but Paul's references to him as his "child in the Lord" may mean that Timothy was converted during the so-called first missionary journey of Paul and Barnabas through Asia Minor. Timothy joined Paul as a co-worker during the second missionary journey. However Timothy came to work with Paul, his personal integrity and commitment to ministry made him a highly esteemed personality in the life of the early church. His solid reputation, faithfulness, selflessness, and concern for others made Timothy a paragon of Christian life; thus, Paul could hold him up as a model to the Philippians and speak of him in glowing terms to other congregations. In turn, we can look to Timothy's life as we know it from the New Testament and ask: *What inspiration and direction for our own faithful living can we gain from Timothy?*

FEBRUARY 23

READING THE SCRIPTURE

NRSV
Acts 16:1-5

1 Paul went on also to Derbe and to Lystra, where there was a disciple named Timothy, the son of a Jewish woman who was a believer; but his father was a Greek. [2]He was well spoken of by the believers in Lystra and Iconium. [3]Paul wanted Timothy to accompany him; and he took him and had him circumcised because of the Jews who were in those places, for they all knew that his father was a Greek. [4]As they went from town to town, they delivered to them for observance the decisions that had been reached by the apostles and elders who were in Jerusalem. [5]So the churches were strengthened in the faith and increased in numbers daily.

NIV
Acts 16:1-5

1 He came to Derbe and then to Lystra, where a disciple named Timothy lived, whose mother was a Jewess and a believer, but whose father was a Greek. [2]The brothers at Lystra and Iconium spoke well of him. [3]Paul wanted to take him along on the journey, so he circumcised him because of the Jews who lived in that area, for they all knew that his father was a Greek. [4]As they traveled from town to town, they delivered the decisions reached by the apostles and elders in Jerusalem for the people to obey. [5]So the churches were strengthened in the faith and grew daily in numbers.

NRSV

1 Corinthians 4:14-17

14 I am not writing this to make you ashamed, but to admonish you as my beloved children. [15]For though you might have ten thousand guardians in Christ, you do not have many fathers. Indeed, in Christ Jesus I became your father through the gospel. [16]I appeal to you, then, be imitators of me. [17]For this reason I sent you Timothy, who is my beloved and faithful child in the Lord, to remind you of my ways in Christ Jesus, as I teach them everywhere in every church.

NIV

1 Corinthians 4:14-17

[14]I am not writing this to shame you, but to warn you, as my dear children. [15]Even though you have ten thousand guardians in Christ, you do not have many fathers, for in Christ Jesus I became your father through the gospel. [16]Therefore I urge you to imitate me. [17]For this reason I am sending to you Timothy, my son whom I love, who is faithful in the Lord. He will remind you of my way of life in Christ Jesus, which agrees with what I teach everywhere in every church.

NRSV

Philippians 2:19-22

19 I hope in the Lord Jesus to send Timothy to you soon, so that I may be cheered by news of you. [20]I have no one like him who will be genuinely concerned for your welfare. [21]All of them are seeking their own interests, not those of Jesus Christ. [22]But Timothy's worth you know, how like a son with a father he has served with me in the work of the gospel.

NIV

Philippians 2:19-22

[19]I hope in the Lord Jesus to send Timothy to you soon, that I also may be cheered when I receive news about you. [20]I have no one else like him, who takes a genuine interest in your welfare. [21]For everyone looks out for his own interests, not those of Jesus Christ. [22]But you know that Timothy has proved himself, because as a son with his father he has served with me in the work of the gospel.

NRSV

2 Timothy 1:4-7

[4]Recalling your tears, I long to see you so that I may be filled with joy. [5]I am reminded of your sincere faith, a faith that lived first in your grandmother Lois and your mother Eunice and now, I am sure, lives in you. [6]For this reason I remind you to rekindle the gift of God that is within you through the laying on of my hands; [7]for God did not give us a spirit of cowardice, but rather a spirit of power and of love and of self-discipline.

NIV

2 Timothy 1:4-7

[4]Recalling your tears, I long to see you, so that I may be filled with joy. [5]I have been reminded of your sincere faith, which first lived in your grandmother Lois and in your mother Eunice and, I am persuaded, now lives in you also. [6]For this reason I remind you to fan into flame the gift of God, which is in you through the laying on of my hands. [7]For God did not give us a spirit of timidity, but a spirit of power, of love and of self-discipline.

UNDERSTANDING THE SCRIPTURE

Acts 16:1-5. In Acts 15 one learns that Paul and Barnabas, who had worked as colleagues in missions, parted ways and that Paul took on Silas as his new partner. Early in their work together they came to a section of south-central Asia Minor where the cities of Derbe and Lystra were situated. There, they met Timothy. This brief account relates that Timothy was already a Christian, that his mother, who was Jewish, was also a believer, that his father was a Greek whose religious status is unclear, and that Timothy had not been circumcised. This last item suggests that Timothy's upbringing in Judaism had not been painstaking.

Of central importance in this account, however, is the report about Timothy's good reputation. The word about Timothy among Christians in the area was so positive that Paul added him to his cohort. Timothy's efforts alongside Paul and Silas were focused on proclaiming the news of the decision of the Jerusalem Conference or Apostolic Council of which we read in Acts 15. The results of this work edified the church in the region and promoted growth in the number of believers. Clearly, Timothy's solid standing enhanced and eased the work of Paul and Silas.

1 Corinthians 4:14-17. In 1 Corinthians, Paul faced a complex situation where members of the church were forming factions and proudly engaging in activities that should have shamed the congregation. Paul recalls having established the church in Corinth, so he speaks to the believers there using the metaphor of fatherhood in Christ Jesus to address them. As children often learn by copying the actions of their parents, Paul calls for the Corinthians to imitate him. The reason Paul can suggest such behavior becomes clear later in the letter at 1 Corinthians 11:1, when Paul says the Corinthians should imitate him because he himself imitates Christ. Thus, he offers himself, in imitation of Christ, as a concrete model of Christian life.

As Paul raises the matter of the Corinthians' imitating him as their father in Christ, he moves to speak of Timothy, whom he calls his "beloved and faithful child in the Lord." In metaphorical terms, Paul's words indicate that Timothy and the Corinthians are siblings. Timothy, however, is cast as a kind of older, wiser brother; for Paul is confident that he can

send Timothy to the church in Corinth to encourage, direct, and inform the Corinthians of Paul's "ways in Christ Jesus."

Philippians 2:19-24. In Philippians, Paul wrote to the members of the church in Philippi as they experienced the hardship of opposition by persons who were not part of the congregation (Philippians 1:28-30). The church was also suffering the effects of a quarrel between two prominent women leaders, Euodia and Syntyche (Philippians 4:2-3); and Paul sought to bring about a reconciliation in the life of the church.

Because of the difficulties the church was experiencing, the members needed Paul's encouragement and direction. Paul wrote to offer the Philippians both reassurance and instruction. Paul tells the Philippians he hopes to send Timothy to stand in his place in Philippi and, in turn, Timothy will bring the apostle news of the situation. Paul states explicitly that he had "no one like [Timothy]," meaning, as he explains, that Timothy would be "genuinely concerned for [the Philippians'] welfare." Paul suggests there are two kinds of people, those who seek "their own interests" and those who seek the interests "of Jesus Christ." Timothy was concerned for others rather than for himself because he was devoted to the interests of Christ. Moreover, Paul reminds the Philippians that they were aware of Timothy's character and of his faithfulness to Paul. He presents Timothy as a model figure to the believers in Philippi.

2 Timothy 1:3-7. As we read 2 Timothy we find a picture of Paul in prison in Rome (2 Timothy 1:16-17; 2:9). Timothy seems to be in Ephesus as he clearly was in 1 Timothy. Paul had been through one hearing that went well despite difficult circumstances (2 Timothy 4:16-18), but at the time that we see Paul writing to Timothy the apostle seems to foresee his death (2 Timothy 4:6-8). We learn that the letter was written to Timothy to offer him personal advice and to issue a series of warnings about problems in the life of the church. Paul calls for Timothy to come to him and to bring certain items to the apostle (2 Timothy 4:9-13).

The reason given for Paul's longing to see Timothy is so that he will be filled with joy. This joy is the result of Timothy's "sincere faith," which we learn is a family tradition including Timothy's grandmother Lois and his mother Eunice. Paul recalls blessing Timothy, so that his younger colleague is courageous, powerful, and self-disciplined.

2 Timothy 3:14-15. Later in the second letter to Timothy, Paul issues a call to "orthodoxy" as he admonishes Timothy to continue to think and to live as he has learned and believed. The apostle recalls Timothy's pious upbringing with solid scripture study, and he reminds Timothy of the value of "sacred writings" to instruct for salvation through faith in Christ Jesus. Timothy's life is the result of and a testimony to true piety.

INTERPRETING THE SCRIPTURE

Preface

For many reasons Timothy was a highly regarded, successful, and ever-faithful minister of the gospel of Jesus Christ. The snippets of information that we have examined in this lesson offer profound insights into the life of this important early Christian worker—into his spiritual formation, integrity, activities, disposition, and effectiveness. Timothy appears to be a person of sterling Christian character who embodies the reality of ideal Christian life. Through pondering Timothy we gain insight into the value of crucial dimensions of faithful living.

The Foundation of Faithfulness

As the lines of 2 Timothy recall Timothy's spiritual formation, we learn that he was raised on the nourishment of scripture. Being steeped in the sacred writings of the Bible gave Timothy an outlook on life that resulted in a distinctive lifestyle. The basic perspective of true piety that shaped him came through Timothy's attention to the Scriptures. The recognition of the value of scripture study for the formation of faithful Christian life is as old as Christianity itself; yet, frankly, modern Christians tend to be biblically illiterate and indifferent even when encouraged to study scripture. The church needs desperately to recognize that we encounter, we hear, and we learn God's Word for us in the world today as we attend to Bible study. God's self-revelation is mediated to us through the testimony of scripture, so that if we are to know God and to live in a vital relation to God, we must give our best attention to Bible study.

The Produce of a Life of Faith

As Timothy lived out the vision of God and of human existence that he learned from scripture, his life was characterized by traits that testify to the value of healthy piety. First, Timothy had a good reputation. In the first century and in the late twentieth century a good reputation is a valuable asset. One cannot buy a good reputation. The facts of a person's life are the foundation of being positively regarded by others. People who do bad things certainly do not have good reputations, although they may achieve a certain notoriety and even the glamour of fame; and persons who do nothing are seldom, if ever, highly regarded. Good reputations are typically the results of positive contributions or achievements, and Timothy was well spoken of by the Christians throughout the region in which he lived. We do not know what Timothy did to deserve his positive standing, but as we examine what he did after joining Paul's missionary band we see traits that would have won him high regard from others at any point in his life.

Active Service

As Timothy worked with Paul he often stood in for the apostle. Being a substitute for his apparently more renowned colleague was not a duty that Timothy resisted. As we look at the story in Acts and at Paul's letters, we see that such "filling in" was a regular part of what Timothy did as he worked for Christ. Moreover, Timothy himself made a contribution as he was called on to substitute or to do legwork for Paul. Timothy is presented, particularly in Paul's letters, as having positive relations with the congregations with which he was sent to work. Timothy worked with Paul and other missionary associates so that the various churches they founded and attended to were steadily strengthened. When Timothy found difficult circumstances he also found ways to work so that the churches were edified. In fact, as we read of the work of Timothy, Paul, and the others, we find that the churches to which they were related tended to grow because of the predominantly healthy character of these congregations that existed because of the work of the apostles.

What did Timothy do to strengthen and to build the churches? According to Paul, Timothy encouraged the members. He found ways to lead Christians through problems to new patterns of living that enabled the members to endure hardships and controversies and to profit from confronting the difficulties. One modern-day example of the church confronting such difficulties is a small integrated congregation in a racially mixed neighborhood that experienced regular hostility from persons of the various racial groups in the area.

The non-Christians wanted their own groups to dominate the neighborhood, so the harmony of the church as a rainbow community was an unwelcome presence in the community. A deacon in the church, however, constantly called for the other members of the church to stand courageously and steadfast in the reconciling name of Jesus Christ. Over time the church attracted more and more persons from the neighborhood who wanted to live in a new, peaceful day, rather than in the patterns of old hostilities. Today, after years of struggling to stay in existence, that same church is a thriving endeavor devoted to promoting the peace of Christ beyond the neighborhood in which it is situated—passing the peace of Christ into the city and world around it.

Paul also says that Timothy provided *direction* and *information* to the churches with which he worked. Recall that Timothy was steeped in scripture, so that the materials he would have provided would have been more than just practical advice. With a biblically inspired and Christ-formed vision of life, Timothy would have led other Christians to develop a similar outlook and to devote themselves to living with a constant concern for God's will.

Selflessness

Above all, when we read Acts and the warm references to Timothy in Paul's letters, we see that Timothy put others before himself. This observation does not mean simply that Timothy was a classic "do-gooder." Rather, Timothy embodied a Christlike mentality and style of living. In Philippians Paul admonished the church to have the mind of Christ. As Christ had put God's purposes ahead of all else, as he had devoted himself to obeying God's will even at the cost of his own life, so Paul taught the Philippians that they should live. In illustrating such a lifestyle, Paul held up Timothy as a living example of one who had devoted himself to living according to the mind of Christ. Timothy was caught up in the reality of Christ to the point that he did not spend his time and energy attending to his own interests; instead, because he was primarily concerned with the interests of Christ, Timothy was more concerned with others than with himself. Devotion to Christ produced a life in Christ that made for Christlike living. Thus, Timothy lived to serve others. When Paul needed Timothy to go on the road and to see to a troublesome situation in distant congregations, Timothy went. He willingly represented the apostle in sometimes perilous circumstances, and as we can easily discern he did this repeatedly. Moreover, on the scene in distressed congregations, Timothy put the interests of the members of the congregation before his personal welfare. The churches with which Timothy labored benefited from his selfless devotion to Christ and others.

Joy

We learn that Timothy's faithfulness produced joy—for others. In 2 Timothy we see the apostle Paul deeply longing to see Timothy so that he might experience the joy of Timothy's faithful presence. One hopes and believes that Timothy's faithfulness gave him deep personal joy, but the New Testament memory of Timothy is so focused on his unselfish devotion to Christ and his fellow Christians, that we never hear of his own moods, emotions, and experiences. Timothy was the source of joy, all because of his true piety that focused his life through a serious encounter with scripture on the truth of the liberating gospel of Jesus Christ. The joy of God's salvation reached out through the life of Timothy and effected profound results in the world. The world would be a better place if there were more Timothys among the Christians!

SHARING THE SCRIPTURE

PREPARING TO TEACH

Preparing Our Hearts

Spend some time this week thinking about people you perceive to be faithful workers for Christ. What strikes you about their behavior and attitudes? How have they influenced you personally? What difference has their presence made in the church at large? Give thanks for these dedicated individuals. Also reflect on your own faithfulness as a worker for Christ. Who do you influence? How? What might others say about the affect you have had on their lives? Pray that by God's grace you will remain faithful to the task of showing others who Jesus is.

Preparing Our Minds

Read all of the scripture references for this week's study of Timothy. Read the lesson carefully, paying particular attention to the attributes of Timothy that enable him to be such a faithful worker. These traits include his willingness to serve actively, his selflessness, and his joy.

If time permits, you may want to check these other references to Timothy that are not included in our lesson: Acts 17:14-15; 18:5; 19:22; 20:4; Romans 16:21; 1 Corinthians 16:10; 2 Corinthians 1:1, 19; Philippians 1:1; Colossians 1:1; 1 Thessalonians 1:1; 3:2, 6.

Preparing Our Learning Space

Have on hand:
- several Bibles for students
- newsprint and marker or chalkboard and chalk
- paper and pencils

LEADING THE CLASS

(1) Introduction

Begin by encouraging students to brainstorm answers to this question. Write their responses on newsprint or a chalkboard.

[?] (1) **If you could create the ideal church worker, what attributes would you want this person to possess?**

Now divide into teams or pairs and distribute paper and pencils. Ask each group to write a help wanted ad for the kind of faithful worker they would like to have in their own church. Select a few volunteers to read the descriptions.

Move the discussion to the scripture lesson by pointing out that the church did not have too many ideal workers. Timothy, however, was an exceptional laborer who was well respected for the work he carried out as an associate of Paul. He can be a model worker for us as well. As we study today's lesson we will ask: *What inspiration and direction for our own faithful living can we gain from Timothy?*

(2) Timothy's Faithfulness

Choose four volunteers to read aloud the selected scripture passages regarding Timothy from Acts 16:1-5; 1 Corinthians 4:14-17; Philippians 2:19-22; and 2 Timothy 1:4-7. Then ask the following questions. Use Understanding the Scripture portion to fill in details as needed.

[?] (1) **What do you know about Timothy's family?**

(2) **What influence do you think his family may have had on his beliefs and his willingness to be a worker for the church?**

(3) **How does Paul perceive his relationship with Timothy?**

(4) **What kinds of tasks has Timothy done on behalf of Paul and the church?**

Now turn the group's attention to Timothy's character, perhaps by reminding them of the list they generated at the beginning of the session. Ask the following questions, using information from the Interpreting the Scripture portion to expand answers as needed.

(1) **Which attributes that we thought** [?] **were important does Timothy seem to possess?**

(2) **What other attributes of a faithful worker does Timothy seem to have that we have not mentioned?**

(Be sure to include the ideas that Timothy actively served, was willing to do whatever was necessary, knew how to encourage churches, knew how to give the churches direction, was selfless, and was filled with joy.)

Consider taking the list that the class has created and assigning the four scripture sections to four different teams. Distribute paper and pencils so they can record their answers. Also make sure each group has at least one Bible. Instruct the teams to check their assigned scripture for evidence (either stated or implied) that Timothy possessed the attributes you have discussed. Provide time for the teams to report back to the whole class.

Point out that Timothy had to make adjustments in his life in order to provide the kind of faithful service upon which his reputation was built.

(3) Our Own Faithful Work for Christ

Distribute paper and pencils to each student if you have not already done so. Ask them to write their own name in the center of the paper. Then *above* their name, ask them to write the names of at least three persons who really influenced who they are and what they do. Tell the group to draw arrows from those names pointing to their own name. Now have them think of at least three persons who they think they have influenced. Have them write the names of these persons *below* their own and draw arrows from their name pointing downward to each of these names. Suggest that everyone reflect silently on the kind of influence others have had on them, as well as the kind of influence they have had on others. Ask them to meditate on this question:

R

What comments might Jesus have about the faithfulness of my work and the influence I have on others?

Remind the group that Timothy was known for his ability to encourage and strengthen churches. Read or retell the example of the deacon in the racially mixed community found in the second paragraph under "Active Service" in the Interpreting the Scripture portion. Ask the group to think of other examples of ways people encourage and strengthen the church.

Note that people often refer to teenagers and young adults as "the church of the future." In contrast, Paul saw in Timothy "the church of the present." Timothy's youth was no barrier to service. Paul relied upon Timothy as a partner in ministry. Divide the class in half, if possible. Ask one group to think of all the ways your congregation encourages youth to be in vital ministry (for example, including youth as leaders in worship, engaging youth in service projects, encouraging youth to visit homebound members). Ask the other half to think of ways the congregation discourages young people, perhaps pushing them away from the church (for example, making certain rooms off limits, expecting teens to always clean up after dinners, failing to offer Sunday school classes for youth). Give the groups newsprint and markers. Set a time limit after which the groups are to report back to the whole class. If it seems clear that the church is perceived to be discouraging younger members, ask:

(1) What can we do as a class to be mentors or advocates for our young people, just as Paul was to Timothy? ?

Close this section of the lesson by looking again at the main question and asking class members to offer their own responses, either aloud or silently. *What inspiration and direction for our own faithful living can we gain from Timothy?*

HELPING CLASS MEMBERS ACT

Challenge class members to seek out a teenager or young adult this week. Have the members talk with the younger persons about why they do or do not attend church, how people in the church make them feel, and how they see themselves as being related or unrelated to Christ. Note that this activity will help more mature adults act as mentors, just as Paul did.

Have the students consider at least one way they can encourage a group or person in the church. Perhaps the finance chairperson is discouraged because funding is low. Maybe the missions committee invited an outstanding speaker to describe her ministry but few people came to hear her. Class members may want to offer encouragement by means of a phone call, card, visit, or personal comment.

Suggest that class members examine their own commitment to Christ, especially as expressed in their willingness to work for the church. Note that no one can (or should be expected) to do everything, but everyone can do something. Encourage students to consider prayerfully whether God may be calling them to rearrange their priorities so as to take on new responsibilities or gracefully bow out of others.

PLANNING FOR NEXT SUNDAY

Next Sunday we will begin a new unit entitled "Hope for the Future." The first five sessions will look at selected passages from 1 and 2 Thessalonians. To prepare for the first lesson, "Tell the Good News!" ask class members to read 1 Thessalonians 2:1-13. Suggest that they consider what it must be like to proclaim the gospel in the face of strong opposition.

THIRD QUARTER

MARCH 2, 1997—MAY 25, 1997

Our study for the Spring Quarter is divided into three units, beginning with "Stand Fast in the Lord," a five-session study on Paul's first and second epistles to the Thessalonians. Here the apostle gives directions on how to live as Christians, especially in the face of persecution. The second unit "Letters to Churches" explores the words of commendation and judgment that the risen Christ commanded John to write to the seven churches in Asia Minor. The last four lessons, "A Message of Hope," offer encouragement to God's people for a time when the forces of evil will unsuccessfully attempt to overcome them.

The quarter begins on March 2 with a lesson from 1 Thessalonians 2:1-13 that calls upon believers to stand fast and proclaim the gospel. This lesson is followed by one on 1 Thessalonians 3:12–4:12 in which church members are told to live loving, holy lives. Standing fast also entails praying for others, as Paul calls the people to do in 2 Thessalonians 1. In the lesson for March 23 on 2 Thessalonians 3:1-16, the brothers and sisters are exhorted to do what is right. This unit closes on Easter with a lesson on resurrection hope taken from Matthew 28:1-10 and 1 Thessalonians 4:13-18.

Unit 2, "Letters to Churches," starts on April 6 with an examination of John's call to write the visions he was given on Patmos, as recorded in Revelation 1:4-15. Next, we will look at the letters reported in Revelation 2:8-17 in which believers in the churches at Smyrna and Pergamum are called to be faithful. On April 20, we will study the warning to the church at Thyatira, found in Revelation 2:18-29, that they are not to tolerate a false prophet but to hold fast to sound teaching. This unit ends with a study of the letters to Philadelphia and Laodicea, found in Revelation 3:7-10, 15-21. The church at Philadelphia was commended, but the Laodiceans were admonished because of their lukewarm commitment to Christ.

The final unit opens with a look at Revelation 5:1-10 in which the Lamb is identified as being worthy to open the sealed scroll. Times will be difficult, but the Lamb will provide help and deliverance according to the lesson from Revelation 7:1-3, 9-10, 13-17 on May 11. Unquestionably, the Christ who died on Calvary is victorious, for he is the "King of kings and Lord of lords" referred to in Revelation 19:11-16 and 20:11-15. This quarter concludes with a vision of a new heaven and earth as recorded in Revelation 21:1-7, 22-27.

Again this quarter, we would recommend that you use *The Devotional Companion to The International Lessons 1996–97* (available from Cokesbury, ISBN 0-687-01998-2) to assist you or another class member responsible for leading worship. In keeping with our emphasis on God's Word as the light for our way, you may want to continue to use the refrain from the song "Thy Word Is a Lamp" (*The United Methodist Hymnal*, page 601) as a regular part of your weekly devotions.

Since this quarter's lessons include geographical references, we would again recommend that you have on hand a copy of *Bible Teacher Kit* (available from Cokesbury, ISBN 0-687-77786-0). This teaching resource will provide you with maps, a glossary, and articles that you will find very helpful. Specific suggestions for use are made under the Sharing the Scripture portion in various lessons.

MEET OUR WRITERS

CATHERINE AND JUSTO GONZÁLEZ

Catherine Gunsalus González and Justo L. González have collaborated in writing on several occasions over the past twenty years. Most of the time, however, Justo is a full-time writer, largely in the field of church history, and Catherine is a full-time teacher as Professor of Church History at Columbia Theological Seminary. Justo occasionally teaches and Catherine occasionally writes. Both are ordained ministers; Justo in The United Methodist Church and Catherine in the Presbyterian Church (USA). They live in Decatur, Georgia, which is about halfway between their original homes in Havana and New York.

TELL THE GOOD NEWS!

PREVIEWING THE LESSON

Lesson Scripture: 1 Thessalonians 2:1-13
Background Scripture: 1 Thessalonians 2:1-13
Key Verse: 1 Thessalonians 2:2

Focus of the Lesson:
Paul's willingness to boldly proclaim the gospel to his children in the faith, despite strong opposition, in order to please God

Main Question of the Lesson:
How can Paul's way of sharing the gospel message, both through bold proclamation and by living a life in keeping with the news he proclaims, be a model for us?

This lesson will enable adult learners to:
(1) explore Paul's motivation and attitude in proclaiming the good news.
(2) recognize the importance of one's "walk" (life) reflecting one's "talk" (the gospel message).
(3) respond by sharing both ourselves and the good news with others.

Today's lesson may be outlined as follows:
(1) Introduction
(2) Paul's Message for Us Today
(3) The Unflattered Church
(4) Incarnate Love
(5) We Are the Message

FOCUSING ON THE MAIN QUESTION

It is possible to do a very good deed for a wrong reason. The apostle Paul knew this. Proclaiming the gospel is in itself the best of actions. It is a means of conveying God's offer of salvation to human beings who desperately need to know it. Yet even this action can be undertaken for sinful motives—for financial gain or for personal prestige. Evidently some people were preaching for the wrong reasons, and Paul wished to make clear that he was not among their number.

At the same time, it is quite possible to do the right thing and be accused of wrongdoing. Paul also knew this. Indeed, he had undergone many sufferings in his work to proclaim the gospel to others. He had often been misunderstood by other Christians as well as by the wider society that was not a part of the church.

Proclaiming the gospel can be done out of selfish, sinful motives. That is a constant temptation. It can also be done purely and still be misunderstood and the proclaimer falsely accused of sinful motivation. This is a constant danger.

The problem is not only Paul's; it is ours as well. We may hesitate to speak to our neighbors and friends of what God has done for us in Jesus Christ because they may think us strange. Or we may say the proper words so that others will think we really do belong in the Christian community. Or we may speak easily and constantly of the gospel but only so others will recognize how superior we are. How can we judge ourselves and discern what

our real reasons are for proclaiming the gospel?

Paul deals with all of these questions in terms of his own life. In doing so, he helps us see the necessary connection between the proclaimer and the message; between the speaker and the word. This is the basic question of integrity, that what we say and who we are match. Paul tested himself by the measure of the gospel. He knew that his sufferings had not been in vain. He knew also that his motives had been pure. His writings therefore give us the measure we need to test our own lives. Today's scripture lesson challenges us to ask: *How can Paul's way of sharing the gospel message, both through bold proclamation and by living a life in keeping with the news he proclaims, be a model for us?*

READING THE SCRIPTURE

NRSV

1 Thessalonians 2:1-13

1 You yourselves know, brothers and sisters, that our coming to you was not in vain, [2]but though we had already suffered and been shamefully mistreated at Philippi, as you know, we had courage in our God to declare to you the gospel of God in spite of great opposition. [3]For our appeal does not spring from deceit or impure motives or trickery, [4]but just as we have been approved by God to be entrusted with the message of the gospel, even so we speak, not to please mortals, but to please God who tests our hearts. [5]As you know and as God is our witness, we never came with words of flattery or with a pretext for greed; [6]nor did we seek praise from mortals, whether from you or from others, [7]though we might have made demands as apostles of Christ. But we were gentle among you, like a nurse tenderly caring for her own children. [8]So

NIV

1 Thessalonians 2:1-13

1 You know, brothers, that our visit to you was not a failure. [2]We had previously suffered and been insulted in Philippi, as you know, but with the help of our God we dared to tell you his gospel in spite of strong opposition. [3]For the appeal we make does not spring from error or impure motives, nor are we trying to trick you. [4]On the contrary, we speak as men approved by God to be entrusted with the gospel. We are not trying to please men but God, who tests our hearts. [5]You know we never used flattery, nor did we put on a mask to cover up greed—God is our witness. [6]We were not looking for praise from men, not from you or anyone else.

As apostles of Christ we could have been a burden to you, [7]but we were gentle among you, like a mother caring for her little children. [8]We loved you so much that we were delighted to share with you not

Key Verse

Ke Ver

deeply do we care for you that we are determined to share with you not only the gospel of God but also our own selves, because you have become very dear to us.

9 You remember our labor and toil, brothers and sisters; we worked night and day, so that we might not burden any of you while we proclaimed to you the gospel of God. [10]You are witnesses, and God also, how pure, upright, and blameless our conduct was toward you believers. [11]As you know, we dealt with each one of you like a father with his children, [12]urging and encouraging you and pleading that you lead a life worthy of God, who calls you into his own kingdom and glory.

13 We also constantly give thanks to God for this, that when you received the word of God that you heard from us, you accepted it not as a human word but as what it really is, God's word, which is also at work in you believers.

only the gospel of God but our lives as well, because you had become so dear to us. [9]Surely you remember, brothers, our toil and hardship; we worked night and day in order not to be a burden to anyone while we preached the gospel of God to you.

[10]You are witnesses, and so is God, of how holy, righteous and blameless we were among you who believed. [11]For you know that we dealt with each of you as a father deals with his own children, [12]encouraging, comforting and urging you to live lives worthy of God, who calls you into his kingdom and glory.

[13]And we also thank God continually because, when you received the word of God, which you heard from us, you accepted it not as the word of men, but as it actually is, the word of God, which is at work in you who believe.

UNDERSTANDING THE SCRIPTURE

1 Thessalonians 2:1-2. In many respects we are coming into the middle of an ongoing story in these verses. Not only is there an earlier chapter in this letter, but also Paul's opening words here refer to the fact that he and the Thessalonians had been through a great deal together. We can only guess at some of the mutual understandings that lie behind the apostle's words. He speaks of the faith that the congregation in Thessalonica had developed based on his preaching. They know the difficulties he encountered in his preaching, even before he came to their city, difficulties that led to humiliation and suffering. They know that even in Thessalonica there had been dangers. He had persisted in spite of these difficulties and had proclaimed the gospel to them. They had believed the good news. The new believers had also been persecuted. (See Acts 17:1-9.) Paul

and the church there had a long history together.

1 Thessalonians 2:3-7a. Perhaps other preachers had waged charges that Paul acted only for personal gain, or that his popularity was based on his currying favor with the people. Perhaps Paul simply knows that these are the temptations that face all who proclaim the gospel. The list of temptations is striking: deceit, trickery, flattery, greed, and human praise.

Evidently Paul had had harsh words for the Thessalonians on many occasions, so flattery was certainly not his motive for preaching. Greed could not have been his motive either, since he had not received from his preaching even what an apostle should have been expected to receive. Perhaps Paul had plied his trade as a tentmaker so that he could be self-supporting, or had support from other friends and churches, as we know he did in other places. (See 2 Corinthians 11:7-8).

1 Thessalonians 2:7b-10. These verses point to the heart of Paul's test for integrity regarding proclamation. Paul and his companions—Silvanus and Timothy who join in this letter—had shared more than the gospel. They had shared themselves as well. They loved the people. The image is of a nurse caring for her children. Indeed, the Thessalonians were newborn in the faith. Again, Paul had not even expected them to support him. He calls upon their common history, asking them to remember what had happened. Paul had worked very hard, harder than anyone should have expected. His actions were motivated by love and not by any base motives. All of this is summarized in verse 10: the people of Thessalonica are witnesses of the integrity of his behavior when he was among them.

1 Thessalonians 2:11-13. The imagery changes from a nurse caring for her charges to a father raising his children. It is an interesting balance of gender-specific images. Like a father, Paul has urged, encouraged, and pleaded with them. He was not a heavy-handed disciplinarian. Paul's goal was to have this new, small congregation develop into people who

were really prepared to enter the kingdom of God. This is the calling of all Christians. Clearly, to believe the gospel is not simply an intellectual exercise. Belief is to lead to transformation, to conversion, to new birth, to becoming new creatures, living not on the basis of the values of this fallen world, but on the basis of the values of God's reign and glory.

Paul concludes this section with very important words. When he had proclaimed the gospel to the Thessalonians, they could have readily dismissed the message. But God had used Paul's proclamation so that the Thessalonians had received it as God's word to them. It is God's word that has had such a transforming effect in these new believers. Even if a witness's motives are pure, even if the words are persuasive, it takes more than human words to transform human beings. Only God's word can do that. Yet God's word comes to us in the words of human beings. This points both to the greatness of the task of proclaiming the gospel and to the humility we need to have, realizing that our words alone can do nothing. Paul gives thanks that his human words became for the Thessalonians the word of God. And that has made all the difference in their lives.

INTERPRETING THE SCRIPTURE

Paul's Message for Us Today

Paul's first letter to the Thessalonians contains a message not only to those early Christians but to us as well. Often we assume that many of the problems we face as the church in the late twentieth century are radically different than those faced by churches in the New Testament. Yet there are constants. To be given authority in the community of faith—either by office or by clear commitment of life—is to face temp-

tations. Holiness comes from being aware of such temptations and saying no to them.

Paul knew that there were temptations to use such authority for selfish purposes, for greed, or for personal glory. We need only to read the headlines of the past few years to know that there are such temptations. Ministers have misused their authority. They have sought to gain financial and social prestige through preaching the gospel. We hear of Christian leaders who have abused their authority within the congregation in sexual misbehavior. Fraud in various forms has been a very public charge against ministers of the gospel in many Christian communities in our own day. Ministers have faced the same charges since the earliest years of the church, though that does not excuse the present realities or deny that they may be more common today.

The Unflattered Church

Paul reminds the Thessalonians that he had not yielded to such temptations. They knew he had not flattered them—although we do not know exactly what stories lay behind these words. We may not know what he refers to, but his first readers surely did. Perhaps Paul's financial independence of the church in Thessalonica helped him avoid flattery. It is very difficult to avoid the temptation of flattery when it is so easy for the unflattered to withhold contributions and make life difficult for a pastor. So the temptation to flatter is based also on the desire of the congregation to be flattered. Paul's ability to be faithful to the gospel may have been supported by a congregation that also was faithful and willing to hear unpleasant truths.

Incarnate Love

Paul had avoided the misuse of the authority God had given to him. In spite of the fact that he knows the church in Thessalonica can never accuse him of flattery, he says that he was very gentle with them—"like a nurse tenderly caring for her own children." His authority was used lovingly. It was a gentle and clear, but not self-serving authority. In verse 8 he writes: "So deeply do we care for you that we are determined to share with you not only the gospel of God but our own selves, because you have become very dear to us." Paul's task was to impart the gospel, but because

he had grown to love the people, he gave them not only the gospel, but himself. Nor was this his act alone, for he writes in the plura, "we."

If the gospel we are entrusted with is indeed a gospel of God's great love for us, can it ever be truly communicated if there is no love for those to whom it is given? Probably not very well. Paul's letters are filled with the love he has for the churches. But here there is more said. It is not only that Paul and his co-workers loved the Thessalonians, but this love caused them also to give themselves—or as the NRSV says, "share" themselves as well as the gospel. There was something mutual in the relationship with the church there.

In verse 13, Paul writes, "We also constantly give thanks to God for this, that when you received the word of God that you heard from us, you accepted it not as a human word but as what it really is, God's word. " How amazing that the more Paul and his companions are embodied within their communication of the gospel, the more clearly their words are not their own but God's.

This paradox seems so astonishing: when we share ourselves as well as the gospel, the words the hearers receive are not simply our words but the Word of God. Perhaps it ought not be surprising. After all, the heart of our faith is that the God whom we worship is able to become one of us, without ceasing to be God. In fact, it is the Word of God that became human. And that Word still seeks a human form in its communication to others. The more fully human–in a redeemed humanity, a loving, gracious humanity–the more fully the word is able to be the Word of God to others. Paul is quite right. As Paul and his companions interacted with the Thessalonians they wre not simply sharing their "old" selves, but rather relating to the people as those who were being transformed by the gospel they preached. They loved them, cared about them, dealt with them in terms of the gospel, both when they needed correction and when they needed support. Where this is the action of those who seek to communicate the gospel, there will be little danger of exploiting the gospel for selfish purposes.

We Are the Message

The communication of the gospel hinges upon our giving ourselves. We are part and parcel of the message we proclaim. We cannot withhold ourselves from others on the grounds that we are proclaiming the gospel and not ourselves. A gospel of incarnation is falsified by such thinking. Nor can we impart our "old" selves, untouched by the gospel, as though we were the ones who mattered and not the gospel. The line of demarcation is delicate. Our staying out of the wrong headlines depends on the gospel's work on the self that we give. To put it another way, the gospel is the church's message about the transformation of human beings made possible by Jesus' life, death, and resurrection. Untransformed people or churches that proclaim this message have a difficult time being heard accurately. People may hear them, and even decide to join them, but for all the wrong reasons. The church may be a significant social group in the community and therefore helpful for reasons that have nothing to do with transformation. Joining a church for non-spiritual reasons may be far less common now than it was several decades ago. As the society becomes more secular the church becomes less significant for unrelated to faith reasons. But there are other temptations.

We may be part of the church for what it can do for us in emotional or psychologi-cal ways that still fall short of what we mean by the new creation. In a society often described as "therapeutic," we expect to join groups for what they will do for us. We do not expect them to make demands upon us. If there are demands, we may well decide the organization is not worth it, and withdraw. But the church cannot properly be understood in such categories. Of necessity it will make demands on us. It will tell us the gospel is what it is, and not what we want it to be. It will refuse to flatter us. In fact, it may well tell us we are sinful or that we are mistaken about what we need. But the church also tells us the truth about what a loving and redemptive God has done for us. The church calls us to radical transformation, to a new life. This is not a demand; it is a gracious offer.

A transformed community of faith is a loving community. For the Roman society that surrounded the early church the astonishing thing about the church was how Christians loved each other and how they loved their neighbors—even their enemies. Christians could travel to other cities and think of the church they found there as their own family. That love may well have been the secret of their success as communicators of the gospel to others.

In our individualistic culture, we may find it difficult to think of redemption as having to do with the whole community of faith—not just the local congregation—transformed into a loving society that is a foretaste of the coming reign of God. That is what Paul reminds these ancient Christians to consider. In doing so, he also reminds us and calls us to tell the good news.

SHARING THE SCRIPTURE

PREPARING TO TEACH

Preparing Our Hearts

Like Paul, you have been entrusted with the joy of sharing the good news with your class. Perhaps your proclamation does not require the level of courage that Paul had to muster. But you still need to make a bold witness, especially to students who may be skeptical, or complacent, or unwilling to consider their Christian faith anything more than a Sunday morning exercise. Despite your timidity or feelings of anxiety, you move ahead and trust that God will empower you. As you prepare this week's lesson, think about the obstacles you have courageously overcome to be in the position of teacher. Perhaps you had never imagined yourself in this role. Pray each day that God will lift you up so that in what you say and what you do you will be an inspiring role model for your class members.

Preparing Our Minds

Read 1 Thessalonians 2:1-13, along with the lesson. We will be studying excerpts from both 1 and 2 Thessalonians in this five-week unit entitled "Stand Fast in the Lord." If time permits, you may want to read both of these short letters in their entirety this week to get a feel for Paul's concerns and his relationship with the Christians at Thessalonica.

You may also want to read Acts 16:19-40 to learn how Paul was treated at Philippi. He makes reference to an incident for which he was jailed in that city in 1 Thessalonians 2:2. Paul founded the church in Thessalonica after the incident at Philippi.

Preparing Our Learning Space

Have on hand:
- several Bibles for students
- newsprint and marker or chalkboard and chalk
- paper and pencils

LEADING THE CLASS

(1) Introduction

Begin by reading the following case study to the class:

When the secretary of First Church was fired by the staff-parish committee, the secretary told her side of the story to everyone who would listen. Unfortunately, she omitted some details that would have cast the situation in a different light. Soon, church gossips began to accuse the committee of unfairness and even suggest that they fired the secretary so that the chairperson's daughter could get the job. Determined not to enter into the fray and to keep employee-employer information confidential, the members of the staff-parish committee held their peace and continued to act with love toward everyone. Several months later, a few members learned information from outside sources that prompted them to conclude that the secretary had been fairly treated.

Now ask the class:
(1) **Had you been a part of First Church, what kind of witness would you say the staff-parish committee made in the face of opposition and hostility?**
(2) **How would you have felt had you been part of the committee?**
(3) **How would you, as a committee member, have later explained why you neither yielded to pressure nor expressed hostility and anger toward those who had unjustly accused you of unfairness?**

Bring the discussion to today's scripture lesson by pointing out that Paul too faced opposition, and he continued to act with love and proclaim the good news. When people questioned his motives, Paul responded that he preached as he did in order to please God. Furthermore, his life befit the gospel message in such a way that, as we would say, his walk matched his talk. As we study today's lesson we will ask: *How can Paul's way of sharing the gospel message, both through bold proclamation and by living a life in keeping with the news he proclaims, be a model for us?*

If the class prefers a lecture format, read or retell the Focusing on the Main Question portion, being sure to include the main question.

(2) Paul's Message for Us Today

Read 1 Thessalonians 2:1-2. To show the intense level of opposition toward Paul, you may want to recount briefly the story of his difficulties in Philippi as told by Luke in Acts 16:19-40. Paul had cast out a spirit of divination from a slave whose owners made a great deal of money from her fortune-telling. When she lost this spirit, the owners dragged Paul and Silas into the marketplace and accused them of violating Roman customs. They were thrown in jail but during the night an earthquake struck, loosing their chains and flinging open the doors. Paul witnessed to the distraught jailer and won him to Christ.

Ask the class:

[?] (1) **What hardships have you endured for the sake of the gospel?**
(2) **If tested as Paul was, do you think you would be willing to stand firm against opposition? Why or why not?**
(3) **Do you think Christians who live in a society where freedom of religion is legally guaranteed take their faith too much for granted because they do not**

have to stand fast in the face of opposition? Explain your answer. [?]

(3) The Unflattered Church

Ask a volunteer to read aloud 2 Thessalonians 2:3-7a (end with "Christ"). Note that Paul claims he spoke to please God and, therefore, did not use flattering words to please the church members. Nor did he seek their praise or try to persuade them to give him money. Point out, as stated in verse 7 (and more directly in verse 9), that Paul worked, likely as a tentmaker, to support himself so that he was not dependent upon the church for a salary, though as an apostle he could have requested funding. Ask the class to debate one or both of these statements:

The current practice of churches [R] employing clergy full-time heightens the temptation for a pastor to flatter the church in order to retain the job and earn salary increases.

Church members can reduce a pastor's temptation to tell them what they want to hear—rather than preaching the gospel in its fullness—by continuing to support the church with their prayers, presence, gifts, and service no matter how challenging the message may be.

(4) Incarnate Love

Select a volunteer to read aloud 1 Thessalonians 2:7b-13. Point out that in verse 7 Paul uses a feminine image, that of a nurse tending a child, to describe his relationship with the Thessalonians. Also note that in verse 11 Paul says he was "like a father with his children." Ask the whole class both of these questions. Or, have half answer one question and half the other. You may want to record (or have them record) their answers on newsprint.
(1) **What descriptive words or phrases** [?] **come to your mind when you think of a nurse caring for a child?**

? (2) **What descriptive words or phrases come to your mind when you think of a father with his children?**

If you worked in teams, have them share their ideas with the whole class.

Conclude this part of the lesson by asking:

? (1) **How do these images convey the love of Christ, which is embodied in the one who witnesses to others?**

(5) We Are the Message

Distribute paper and pencils. Ask the students, either working alone or with a partner, to

• reread verse 8.
• rewrite the verse in their own words.
• explain the meaning of the verse, possibly by giving examples of how they understand the idea of sharing themselves.

Invite volunteers to report on what they have discerned from this verse.

Provide a few moments of silence so that class members may reflect on the ways in which they share not only the words of the gospel but also themselves with others. Have them think about the way in which God uses such a witness to transform lives.

HELPING CLASS MEMBERS ACT

Challenge class members to make a special effort this week to share God's love with someone who often opposes them. Such sharing may take the form of a soft word or kind action in response to the other person's anger or criticism. It may involve speaking up for one's enemy among a group of peers. Or, this sharing may be offered in response to a need that the opposer has expressed.

Encourage students to find a way to give generously of themselves this week. Point out that this kind of generosity has nothing to do with money. Instead, the class members may want to phone or visit a lonely person, mow the lawn for a neighbor who cannot do so, play a game with a child, or take someone on an outing. Whatever action is undertaken should be done freely and without the expectation of any return.

Ask class members to do some soul-searching this week. Have them block out some time when they can be alone, perhaps taking a pad or spiritual journal with them. Invite them to think about how their own lives do or do not reflect the gospel message that they proclaim. Challenge them to ask God to show them areas of their lives that need to be changed.

PLANNING FOR NEXT SUNDAY

Next Sunday's lesson, "Live in Love and Holiness!" is based on 1 Thessalonians 3:6–4:12. Ask the class to read these verses, paying particular attention to the key verses, 3:12-13. Encourage students to think about what it means to them to love one another and to live in holiness.

LIVE IN LOVE AND HOLINESS!

PREVIEWING THE LESSON

Lesson Scripture: 1 Thessalonians 3:12–4:12
Background Scripture: 1 Thessalonians 3:6–4:12
Key Verses: 1 Thessalonians 3:12-13

Focus of the Lesson:
Paul's encouragement to the Thessalonians to love other persons and to live holy lives marked by highly moral and ethical behavior

Main Question of the Lesson:
How are we to live as persons who are transformed by God's love and holiness?

This lesson will enable adult learners to:
(1) understand the relationship between experiencing God's love and living a holy life.
(2) enter into Paul's concerns about immoral and unethical behavior that will result in God's judgment.
(3) respond by acting generously.

Today's lesson may be outlined as follows:
(1) Introduction
(2) The Wider Church
(3) God's Love in Us
(4) Love in Action
(5) The Holy Life

FOCUSING ON THE MAIN QUESTION

Real holiness, which includes unselfish love even for those who are our enemies, is not a human possibility. At least, it is not a possibility for old, sinful selves. But for Paul, such love and holiness are the hallmarks of the transformation God creates in us through Christ. Therefore, if the Thessalonians show growth in such love, if their lives are increasingly marked by holiness, if a moral quality shines through them, then the work of God in them is clear. However, if there are no such qualities, or growth toward such qualities, then as far as Paul is concerned, one can question as to whether they really know God or not.

Paul has no such doubts about the Thessalonians, however. He praises them for their love and for the witness their holy love gives to their unbelieving neighbors.

A faithful witness requires both a concern and lack of concern about what others think of us. On the one hand, if we always try to please others, doing what everyone else is doing so that we will not be considered different, we can readily be led into all sorts of unethical and immoral behavior. The way of the world is not a shining example. Even adults who consider themselves quite mature really live by the motto that we may hear from our children when they wish to do something questionable: "But everyone else is doing it." On the other hand, our lives ought not to be lived on the basis of doing what everyone else is doing, but on what God expects of us. This passage from Thessalonians makes that quite clear. Yet, as we fulfill God's expectations we ought also to be concerned about the witness we are giving as to the meaning of the gospel.

The nature of the holiness to which we are called is stated in Paul's letter. It is love that includes self-control in regard to our sexuality so that no one else is wronged; it includes honest labor and peaceful living. These are some of the basic components of a holy community that honor God and bear witness to others. Paul is clear that such living is not possible outside the work of the Holy Spirit in us. The Gentiles who are outside the community of faith do not live such lives. Paul's letter to the church at Thessalonica calls us to ask ourselves: *How are we to live as persons who are transformed by God's love and holiness?*

READING THE SCRIPTURE

NRSV
1 Thessalonians 3:12–4:12

NIV
1 Thessalonians 3:12–4:12

ey
rses

Key
Verse

¹²And may the Lord make you increase and abound in love for one another and for all, just as we abound in love for you. ¹³And may he so strengthen your hearts in holiness that you may be blameless before our God and Father at the coming of our Lord Jesus with all his saints.

4:1 Finally, brothers and sisters, we ask and urge you in the Lord Jesus that, as you learned from us how you ought to live and to please God (as, in fact, you are doing), you should do so more and more. ²For you know what instructions we gave you through the Lord Jesus. ³For this is the will of God, your sanctification: that you abstain from fornication; ⁴that each one of you know how to control your own body in holiness and honor, ⁵not with lustful passion, like the Gentiles who do not know God; ⁶that no

¹²May the Lord make your love increase and overflow for each other and for everyone else, just as ours does for you. ¹³May he strengthen your hearts so that you will be blameless and holy in the presence of our God and Father when our Lord Jesus comes with all his holy ones.

4:1 Finally, brothers, we instructed you how to live in order to please God, as in fact you are living. Now we ask you and urge you in the Lord Jesus to do this more and more. ²For you know what instructions we gave you by the authority of the Lord Jesus.

³It is God's will that you should be sanctified: that you should avoid sexual immorality; ⁴that each of you should learn to control his own body in a way that is holy and honorable, ⁵not in passionate lust like the heathen, who do not know God;

one wrong or exploit a brother or sister in this matter, because the Lord is an avenger in all these things, just as we have already told you beforehand and solemnly warned you. [7]For God did not call us to impurity but in holiness. [8]Therefore whoever rejects this rejects not human authority but God, who also gives his Holy Spirit to you.

9 Now concerning love of the brothers and sisters, you do not need to have anyone write to you, for you yourselves have been taught by God to love one another; [10]and indeed you do love all the brothers and sisters throughout Macedonia. But we urge you, beloved, to do so more and more, [11]to aspire to live quietly, to mind your own affairs, and to work with your hands, as we directed you, [12]so that you may behave properly toward outsiders and be dependent on no one.

[6]and that in this matter no one should wrong his brother or take advantage of him. The Lord will punish men for all such sins, as we have already told you and warned you. [7]For God did not call us to be impure, but to live a holy life. [8]Therefore, he who rejects this instruction does not reject man but God, who gives you his Holy Spirit.

[9]Now about brotherly love we do not need to write to you, for you yourselves have been taught by God to love each other. [10]And in fact, you do love all the brothers throughout Macedonia. Yet we urge you, brothers, to do so more and more.

[11]Make it your ambition to lead a quiet life, to mind your own business and to work with your hands, just as we told you, [12]so that your daily life may win the respect of outsiders and so that you will not be dependent on anybody.

UNDERSTANDING THE SCRIPTURE

1 Thessalonians 3:6-11. One of the major characteristics of the early church that we often overlook is the constant travel that permitted Christians to visit congregations not their own. Timothy had just returned from Thessalonica and had told Paul about the congregation that Paul had been instrumental in founding. Timothy has reported that their faith remains strong, and they long to see Paul. Paul also wants to see them, not only from simple human friendship, but so their faith may be strengthened even further. Their faith has strengthened Paul during his imprisonments and persecutions. Clearly they have been praying for Paul and Paul for them since they were last together. But there is the great desire of Christians not only to hold one another in prayer and love, but also to meet together and worship together.

1 Thessalonians 3:12-13. Love holds the church together across all the miles. As

that love grows, the church itself is strengthened and grows. Such love is the work of God in the church, and not simply a human action. Holiness—of which love is a part and a sign—is also the gift of God. The church is not a gathering, an organization, or a club of like-minded people: it is the creation of God in Jesus Christ. Love is its bond. Holiness of life is its character. Both are the work of God.

This holiness and love have a time line, a goal: when Jesus Christ returns and judgment occurs, the lack of holiness will be revealed. Christians have usually either ignored the whole issue of the return of Christ, or they have tried to discover exactly when it is to be. Neither is helpful. History does have a goal. It will not simply go on forever. Our own personal time line is briefer than that of history, but all history and all individuals in it will face judgment. The demand for holiness is real.

1 Thessalonians 4:1-8. Paul wishes to be quite clear about the character of the holiness to which Christians are called. It is not a matter of how we feel, but of how we act. Holiness should be visible to the world around us. The character of holiness is not simply the opinion of Paul. Paul reminds the Thessalonians of the teaching he gave them earlier. He taught them the will of God as it had been given in Jesus Christ. It is not Paul's authority or that of any other human being, but God's authority that is being challenged by unholy actions. It is the Holy Spirit in us that makes possible the holiness that those outside the community of faith cannot attain.

In this section, Paul is particularly concerned about sexual holiness. Immorality was rampant in the society around the church. Paul makes two important points. First, love does not exploit others or wrong them. Sexual promiscuity does both. It is therefore not compatible with love. Second, the gift of the Holy Spirit implies the power to overcome unholy desires, so that control of what one does with one's body becomes possible. Both the excuses, "but it was an expression of our love at the time" when such love is fleeting, and "I couldn't help myself," deny the power of the Holy Spirit.

1 Thessalonians 4:9-12. Paul again makes clear that he does not doubt the love of the Thessalonians for one another and for the church at large. But there is always room for growth. Their love for one another is their major witness to the world around them.

Paul points to some ways in which their love for one another can be manifest. He mentions three specific ways: live quietly, mind your own affairs, and work with your hands. These may seem rather mundane, but they go to the heart of what he is trying to say. First, live quietly. That obviously does not mean that Christians should shut themselves off from everyone, but rather warns them against creating discord or disharmony, not only in the church but also in the wider neighborhood. Second, mind your own affairs. That is one of the ways to live quietly. Christians are not called upon to reprove their neighbors, but to witness to the love of God for the world. Third, work with your hands. At the time this letter was written, there was an opinion in the Roman world that those who worked with their hands were less honorable than those who did not. Manual labor was beneath the dignity of a lady or gentleman. For Paul, such a view is false. Christians are to do the sort of work that is needful for daily life—producing the food, building the houses, caring for children and the weak, cooking, and cleaning. Christians are not superior to such labor, nor should they be dependent on others when they could take care of themselves.

INTERPRETING THE SCRIPTURE

The Wider Church

Many of us have had the experience of being in a strange city or even another country, aware of not belonging, and then joining in Christian worship with people we do not know at all, and feeling at home. The music may be different, the language may not even be completely understandable. But the love of God, the new life in Christ that this group shares is what makes us and them part of the same family. The church—the Body of Christ—is much bigger than our familiar congregation. Our own faith is strengthened when we have such experiences. Perhaps we hear about Christians in other parts of the world who are suffering, and we feel the need to pray for them, so that their faith is strengthened in the midst of their difficulties when they know they are part of a wider community of faith.

God's Love in Us

The love of which Paul speaks here is very closely related to holiness. He prays that love will abound and the Thessalonians will be strengthened in holiness. In a way, love and holiness are two sides of a coin. Love is an internal feeling; holiness has to do with our actions. Loving actions are holy; holy actions show forth the love that is within us. God's love is a gift, but it also demands to be lived out, not hidden. The living out of this love is holiness.

God's love comes to us in order to be shared, for God's concern is for more than us. We are instruments of God's love in the world, channels that God wishes to use to communicate that love to others. This is the great task of the saints—the holy ones. The seriousness of this mission is made clear by the word of judgment. Now is the time for our mission, our love toward others, our holy lives to witness to others. It is preparation for the end of history, for the kingdom of God. When Christ returns, the time for preparation will have ended. The fulfillment will have come. The saints—the holy ones—will be with Christ when he comes again. We are called to be part of that number.

Love in Action

Much of what passes for love at the human level often leads to unholiness, especially in sexual matters. The love Christians are called to is not simply the expansion of human love, but rather God's own love in us, which is the gift of the Holy Spirit. Human love and God's love may be difficult to distinguish. Often, we think that Christian love is expanding the circle of love that we have within our families, so we treat even strangers as though they were brothers and sisters. But we ought not to romanticize family relationships. Even the love within families needs to be transformed by the Holy Spirit. Possessive, demanding love occurs in the most intimate of relationships, and that is not the gift of the Holy Spirit. Christians are called to holiness in all of their relationships, which means loving others in the way that God loves us, both within our families and within the wider world. A truly Christian family is indeed a good model to be extended to others, and an important nursery for Christian growth in love and holiness.

God is very serious about holiness in our relationships. Paul writes in 4:6 that "the Lord is an avenger in all these things." That is, God will be on the side of the person who suffers from our unholy, unloving actions. We cannot call ourselves Christians and then suppose that God is always on our side rather than on the side of those outside the church. Our unholiness may prevent us from carrying out the mission toward them that God has given us. God has called us because God also loves them and wishes us to be the messengers, the bearers of that love to them.

Paul stresses the authority of these expectations of holiness. He reminds the Thessalonians that what he taught them came through Jesus Christ. Their holiness is clearly the will of God. To reject the notion of holiness is to reject the clear word of God to us and the action of the Holy Spirit in us.

It is helpful to realize that the name "Holy Spirit" does not simply mean that the Spirit is holy because it is the Spirit of God. It is the Holy Spirit because it causes *us* to be holy. We speak of the gift of the Holy Spirit, meaning the dwelling of the Spirit with us or the action of the Spirit in us, causing us, allowing us to be holy in a way that is beyond human ability.

The Holy Life

Growth in holiness and love is a lifelong task. Paul has no complaints about the

Christians at Thessalonica. This letter is not like some of his others, especially to the troubled church at Corinth, where he points out all the unholy things they are doing. The Thessalonian Christians are well on their way to holy lives. There is ample evidence of the work of the Holy Spirit in their actions toward Paul and other Christians well beyond their own small community. Even within the congregation, in their daily life together, they are loving. But all Christians can use a word of encouragement, urging them on to greater and greater holiness. If we ever think we have arrived, that we are sufficiently holy, that our love for others is extensive enough, we will be in great danger of losing what we have attained.

Perhaps Paul knew the particular dangers that faced the Thessalonian Christians. Perhaps the negative attitude toward manual work was strong there, and had even come into the congregation. Perhaps some people felt so holy that they could set themselves up as judges of the rest of the world, and therefore look down upon those outside the church, condemning the unholiness of others rather than bearing witness by their lives to the love of the God who seeks out the lost. Perhaps that is what is meant by minding your own affairs. Perhaps some used their Christian faith as a pretext for disruption, provoking divisions in families and neighborhoods. The words here are very similar to what Paul wrote to the Romans: "Do not repay anyone evil for evil, but take thought for what is noble in the sight of all. If it is possible, so far as it depends on you, live peaceably with all" (Romans 12:17-18). Clearly, this does not mean denying Christ in order to keep the peace, but a confession of faith, a witness to

Christ, should be done peaceably. Christians can control their own actions. If their witness leads to their persecution by others, so be it. Then Christian love shall have to encompass enemies. That is holiness of the highest order. But persecution is not something Christians seek out by stirring up antagonism or by judging the lives of others. Therefore, Paul urges Christians to live quietly and mind their own affairs.

Paul ties his expectation that Christians should work with their hands to the notions that they should not be dependent and should act properly toward outsiders. The early Christians were noted for their charity and generosity toward the poor. It would have been a scandal for the community of faith for a Christian to have been dependent on those outside the church. Such dependency would have indicated a breakdown in the fabric of the church. At the same time, Christians were not to presume upon the generosity of their brothers and sisters in the church. They were to do their share, to provide for themselves so as not to be a burden on others, as well as being generous to those who were truly needy. Becoming a Christian was not an excuse for laziness. In the letter to the Ephesians we find an even stronger statement: "Thieves must give up stealing; rather let them labor and work honestly with their own hands, so as to have something to share with the needy" (Ephesians 4:28). In this verse there is a contrast between the former life where there was a dishonest taking from others and the new life in Christ where there is honest work and a giving to others. Generosity is at the heart of the nature of the church because it is an expression of love and it is the character of holiness.

SHARING THE SCRIPTURE

PREPARING TO TEACH

Preparing Our Hearts

What does it mean to you to live in love and holiness? How do you show the love that God has for you to others? What moral and ethical teachings guide your behavior so that it is holy unto the Lord? Read 1 Thessalonians 3:12-13, our key verses, changing the pronouns to make them a more personal prayer that reads:

> And may the Lord make me increase and abound in love for one another and for all. . . . And may God so strengthen my heart in holiness that I may be blameless before my God and Father at the coming of my Lord Jesus with all his saints.

Pray this prayer each day this week, trusting that God will indeed strengthen you for holy living and loving.

Preparing Our Minds

Carefully read the lesson, along with the scripture found in 1 Thessalonians 3:6–4:12. Note that the Understanding the Scripture section gives background concerning the expectations people would have had regarding work and other behaviors.

If you have access to a map, locate Thessalonica, which was the capital of the Roman province of Macedonia. This city was an important point along both land and sea routes. You may want to consult a Bible dictionary for more information about the city itself.

Preparing Our Learning Space

If possible, post a map of Thessalonica or duplicate copies of the map of Paul's Second Journey found on page 151 of *Bible Teacher Kit* (Abingdon, 1994).

Have on hand:
- ✔ several Bibles for students
- ✔ newsprint and marker or chalkboard and chalk
- ✔ paper and pencils
- ✔ map(s)

LEADING THE CLASS

(1) Introduction

Begin the session by asking this question:

(1) Suppose a bishop (or other church official) sent someone to visit our congregation. What kind of report would this envoy take back to our denominational leaders about who we are and what we do here?

Allow some time for the class to respond. Then read today's key verses, 1 Thessalonians 3:12-13, noting that Paul's words suppose that love and holiness are already present within the congregation at Thessalonica. Finally, ask:

(2) What evidence of love and holiness is present within our congregation?

(3) In what areas could we as a church body show improvement in the way we express love and live holy lives?

Lead into today's lesson by pointing out that, while he was in Athens, Paul did in fact send Timothy to encourage the church at Thessalonica as it faced persecution. Timothy's good report (3:6) prompted Paul to write. Note that in today's session we will focus on living in love and holiness. The main question that will guide us is: *How are we to live as persons who are transformed by God's love and holiness?*

If the class will not engage in discussion, use the Focusing on the Main Question section to introduce the lesson.

(2) The Wider Church

If time permits, you may want to use the background verses from 1 Thessalonians 3:6-11, discussed under this heading in the Interpreting the Scripture portion, to remind the class that we are to extend God's love to all persons, regardless of their geographic location. The bonds of love connect churches no matter where they are located. This understanding was especially clear in the fledgling church because the early leaders did so much traveling. In fact, according to 1 Thessalonians 3:1-2, Paul had sent Timothy from Athens to the church at Thessalonica. Paul writes this letter (possibly from Corinth) after Timothy returns with news of the faith and love of the Thessalonians (3:6).

If you have a classroom map, or copies of map handouts, point out the location of Thessalonica. If your map includes Athens, identify that as well so that students can see where Timothy traveled.

(3) God's Love in Us

Read the following excerpt from "God's Love in Us" under Interpreting the Scripture: "In a way, love and holiness are two sides of a coin. Love is an internal feeling; holiness has to do with our actions. Loving actions are holy; holy actions show forth the love that is within us. God's love is a gift, but it also demands to be lived out, not hidden. The living out of this love is holiness."

Distribute paper and pencils. Have class members draw a circle to represent a coin. Tell them to write the word "Love" in the center on one side and "Holiness" in the center on the other. Then have them write words or phrases that somehow describe or explain each word. Provide a few moments for students to share their ideas with the class or with partners.

Close this part of the lesson by asking the class to read in unison the key verses, 1 Thessalonians 3:12-13.

(4) Love in Action

Choose a volunteer to read 1 Thessalonians 4:1-8. Note that much of this passage deals with unholiness in sexual relationships. Paul speaks out against illicit unions and exploitation. Unfortunately, such unholy behavior is seen as the norm in much of our society. Discuss these questions with the class:

(1) In what ways does our society send signals about what it considers appropriate sexual behavior? ⁇

(2) What behaviors that our society condones would Paul speak out against if he were alive today?

(3) What should be the church's role in setting standards for sexual behavior for its members?

(4) Does the church have the right to impose its teachings on society at large when many citizens do not make any claims to being Christian? Explain your answer.

Note that God will judge relationships in regard to their holiness. Furthermore, God will be on the side of the one who suffers from unholy, unloving actions (4:6). Ask:

(1) If God were to send a plane with a sign trailing behind it to announce God's judgment of our nation's sexual behavior, what would the sign say? ⁇

As verse 8 indicates, Paul is not speaking on his own authority but on the authority given to him by God through the Holy Spirit. In other words, Paul's ideas are not his own opinion but have come from God. Ask:

(2) Many people claim to speak for God, but certainly all do not. What evidence would you have for agreeing that Paul is speaking on God's authority? ⁇

(5) The Holy Life

Choose someone to read aloud 1 Thessalonians 4:9-12. Use information from these verses in the Understanding the Scripture portion, as well as in "The Holy Life" discussion in the Interpreting the Scripture section to help class members understand what Paul is saying here. Especially note the negative attitude toward manual labor.

Now concentrate on Paul's direction to the church to be generous. Read this excerpt from the Interpreting the Scripture portion: "It would have been a scandal for the community of faith for a Christian to have been dependent on those outside the church. Such dependency would have indicated a breakdown in the fabric of the church. At the same time, Christians were not to presume upon the generosity of their brothers and sisters in the church. They were to do their share, to provide for themselves so as not to be a burden on others, as well as being generous to those who were truly needy." Then ask these questions:

(1) In recent years, the downsizing of companies has resulted in the loss of jobs for many workers. What has your church done (or could it do) to provide for those who are unemployed or underemployed while they seek a permanent job?

(2) How would these actions demonstrate God's love and holiness?

Conclude this segment by noting that Paul commends the church in Thessalonica, but he is calling its members—and us—to do more and more to live in God's love and holiness.

HELPING CLASS MEMBERS ACT

Encourage class members to reflect on how their own lives show forth both God's love and God's holiness. Suggest that they try to identify areas of their lives in which they need the Holy Spirit to make them holy. Have them pray about the changes they want to make in their lives, with God's help, so as to be more loving and holy people.

Remind the group that Paul has much to say in this lesson about the need for church members to be generous. Challenge the class members to think about real, long-range generosity toward the church. Some members may begin to consider changing their last will so that the church receives a percentage of their estate. Others may think about setting up a major gift that will be received by the church after the donor's death.

Note that Paul has a high opinion of manual labor. His opinion would not have been shared with the "ladies and gentlemen" of either his day or our own. Suggest that each person do something for someone else this week that requires manual labor. Possibilities range from weeding a garden, to changing the oil, to creating a handicraft. This work should be done for someone who cannot do the task. A handcrafted item could be given as a gift or sold at a church event to raise money for a missions project.

PLANNING FOR NEXT SUNDAY

We will continue our study of Paul's letters to the church at Thessalonica by reading 2 Thessalonians 1. Our lesson for next week, "Pray for One Another!" concerns Paul's fervent prayer that the church would be worthy of its calling in Christ and able to continue to stand fast in the face of persecution.

PRAY FOR ONE ANOTHER!

PREVIEWING THE LESSON

Lesson Scripture: 2 Thessalonians 1
Background Scripture: 2 Thessalonians 1
Key Verse: 2 Thessalonians 1:11

Focus of the Lesson:
Paul's supportive, intercessory prayer for the Thessalonian Christians

Main Question of the Lesson:
How do prayers for one another support us—individually and collectively—as members of the community of faith?

This lesson will enable adult learners to:
(1) explore the use of intercessory prayer as a means of spiritual support in the early church.
(2) examine the need and privilege of supporting others through intercessory prayer.
(3) respond by offering prayers of intercession for others.

Today's lesson may be outlined as follows:
(1) Introduction
(2) Church to Church
(3) Faith in Difficult Times
(4) The Reality of God's Judgment
(5) The Need for Prayer

FOCUSING ON THE MAIN QUESTION

Christians readily understand the purpose of some forms of prayer. We pray to give God praise. We pray to thank God for what we have received—food and shelter; health and well-being. We also pray that God will provide that which we do not have. We offer prayers of confession and ask for forgiveness.

Why, though, should we pray for oth-ers? If we fail to pray for others, does that mean that God will not do what is good for them? Is God impressed by numbers? Similarly, why should we hope that others will pray for us? Surely all things are in the hand of God. Does God withhold good things because no one else has prayed to God for us? Will the prayer of another be more helpful than our own prayer? What is intercessory prayer, and why is it important in the Christian life?

Often we look at the life of prayer very mechanically. What does it accomplish? Is it a means to an end, a way of having God do something God would not do otherwise? But we know that is not an appropriate way to think about it. Experientially, we know that prayer is communion with God, a sharing of our hearts with God and an openness to God's communication with us. It is not a mechanical process. Numbers are not impressive to God. Fifty people praying for something does not necessarily have greater impact than one person praying, just as repeating the same prayer over and over is of no more significance than one heartfelt prayer. So we ask the question again: Why is there value or significance in intercessory prayer?

When we ask such questions, we may be looking at prayer in a very narrow way. Paul is not raising these questions that we so often ask. In fact, much of the way he deals with prayer is based on a very different perspective. It has to do more with the nature of the church and who we are as Christians and members of the community of faith than it has to do with any mechanical process. Prayer undergirds and supports us, especially in the kinds of difficult circumstances the Thessalonians faced. When we pose the question of intercessory prayer in this context, it looks quite different. We ask: *How do prayers for one another support us—individually and collectively—as members of the community of faith?*

READING THE SCRIPTURE

NRSV

2 Thessalonians 1:1-12

1 Paul, Silvanus, and Timothy,

To the church of the Thessalonians in God our Father and the Lord Jesus Christ:

2 Grace to you and peace from God our Father and the Lord Jesus Christ.

3 We must always give thanks to God for you, brothers and sisters, as is right, because your faith is growing abundantly, and the love of everyone of you for one another is increasing. 4Therefore we ourselves boast of you among the churches of God for your steadfastness and faith during all your persecutions and the afflictions that you are enduring.

5 This is evidence of the righteous judgment of God, and is intended to make you worthy of the kingdom of God, for which you are also suffering. 6For it is indeed just of God to repay with affliction those who afflict you, 7and to give relief to the afflicted as well as to us, when the Lord Jesus is revealed from heaven with his

NIV

2 Thessalonians 1:1-12

1 Paul, Silas and Timothy,

To the church of the Thessalonians in God our Father and the Lord Jesus Christ:

2Grace and peace to you from God the Father and the Lord Jesus Christ.

3We ought always to thank God for you, brothers, and rightly so, because your faith is growing more and more, and the love every one of you has for each other is increasing. 4Therefore, among God's churches we boast about your perseverance and faith in all the persecutions and trials you are enduring.

5All this is evidence that God's judgment is right, and as a result you will be counted worthy of the kingdom of God, for which you are suffering. 6God is just: He will pay back trouble to those who trouble you 7and give relief to you who are troubled, and to us as well. This will happen when the Lord Jesus is revealed from heaven in blazing fire with his powerful mighty angels [8]in flaming fire, inflicting vengeance on those who do not know God and on those who do not obey the gospel of our Lord Jesus. [9]These will suffer the punishment of eternal destruction, separated from the presence of the Lord and from the glory of his might, [10]when he comes to be glorified by his saints and to be marveled at on that day among all who have believed, because our testimony to you was believed. [11]To this end we always pray for you, asking that our God will make you worthy of his call and will fulfill by his power every good resolve and work of faith, [12]so that the name of our Lord Jesus may be glorified in you, and you in him, according to the grace of our God and the Lord Jesus Christ.

Key Verse

angels. [8]He will punish those who do not know God and do not obey the gospel of our Lord Jesus. [9]They will be punished with everlasting destruction and shut out from the presence of the Lord and from the majesty of his power [10]on the day he comes to be glorified in his holy people and to be marveled at among all those who have believed. This includes you, because you believed our testimony to you.

[11]With this in mind, we constantly pray for you, that our God may count you worthy of his calling, and that by his power he may fulfill every good purpose of yours and every act prompted by your faith. [12]We pray this so that the name of our Lord Jesus may be glorified in you, and you in him, according to the grace of our God and the Lord Jesus Christ.

Key Verse

UNDERSTANDING THE SCRIPTURE

2 Thessalonians 1:1-3. Paul is not writing this letter alone. It is a letter from two others as well: Timothy and Silvanus. That is to say, it is a letter from one group of Christians to another group. It is from three Christian leaders who have had a connection with the church in Thessalonica. Silvanus is also called Silas, and under that name is associated with Paul in the account we find in Acts. Silas is the name as it is used in Jewish circles; Silvanus is the Latin form in the wider Roman Empire. Silvanus and Timothy were with Paul in many of his journeys and knew many of the churches well. So it is not a private letter from Paul to one person in Thessalonica, but rather a small group of Christians writing to a congregation.

The writers begin the letter with a benediction, a blessing, which is in itself a prayer for grace and peace. Then they insist that they pray always with great thanksgiving for the faith and love of the church in Thessalonica. This congregation is noted for the love its members have for one another. Their faith is growing deeper all the time. Since the three who write the letter were instrumental in the founding of the church, the reader is not surprised that they give great thanks to God that their labor has borne fruit.

2 Thessalonians 1:4-5. It was not easy for the Thessalonians to have faith and love. Their circumstances could have destroyed both. They are being persecuted for their faith, and are suffering considerably. The letter points out that their suffering is a part of God's judgment, and in going through it they are being made worthy of the kingdom of God. It is for the sake of the kingdom they are suffering, and their steadfastness and love for one another are signs that the persecution has not overcome them. The three who write the letter—Paul, Silvanus, and Timothy—know about persecution and suffering for the sake of Christ. They are well aware that such persecution could lead to a loss of faith. The love within the community could turn to suspicion and fear. But this has not happened. The letter writers thank God for the faithfulness of the Thessalonians, and they boast about it to other churches, so that the Thessalonians may provide an example for other congregations.

2 Thessalonians 1:6-10. The writers then point to the justice of God that will repay the persecutors and comfort the afflicted. They assure the Thessalonians that such judgment will occur in the future. All of this will happen when Jesus returns, at the end of history. Judgment is real. For this reason, the mission of the church is real also. The church in Thessalonica will be blessed at the end because it has believed and obeyed the gospel that Paul and the others preached to them. Were they to fall by the wayside now in the midst of persecution, then they would have joined those who do not obey the gospel. Judgment is real and faith has ultimate significance, even though it is often not easy to keep the faith.

2 Thessalonians 1:11-12. Precisely because they know it is difficult to remain steadfast in faith, Paul and his companions pray for the church in Thessalonica. Because of the persecution, they face the temptation of turning from faith, of ceasing to love the others in the congregation. The prayer is that they will remain faithful, that they will be worthy of the kingdom, which is what their suffering can enable them to become. The prayer is that they will not merely survive, but they will do all the good works that faith can do under such circumstances. God has called them for this purpose. Their faith in the midst of suffering will be a witness to the gospel. In their suffering Jesus will be glorified in them and they also will be glorified by Jesus. This is no easy task. In fact, such faithfulness is not a human possibility. But Jesus will be with them. The grace of God will sustain them. As we will see in next week's lesson, in this letter Paul and his companions not only pray for the Thessalonian Christians; they also request prayers for themselves from the Thessalonians (3:1). Mutual prayer support is essential because no Christians are sufficiently strong in themselves. All need the prayer and support of other Christians.

INTERPRETING THE SCRIPTURE

Church to Church

Intercessory prayer may take the form of one person interceding for another. Or an entire congregation may pray for that one person in need. But in this letter we have the instance of a group of Christians praying for a whole congregation. On occasion we pray for congregations that are in trouble, such as those that have been affected by a flood or hurricane. But since most of us pray only for congregations in our own community, how often do we pray for those churches facing persecution in other countries? There are ways of linking ourselves or our congregations to others around the world. If we intentionally pray for congregations in other parts of the globe that face a variety of difficulties, we expand our own sense of the church. If we travel to other countries and make contact with Christians there, we can cultivate a sense of what they need to have others pray for on their behalf. If we do that, we may then have new eyes to see what our congregation needs to pray for itself. We might then also ask for the prayers of other churches to help us to be more faithful. The church is one, all over the earth and across denominational lines. Congregations need the support and prayers of other Christians in order to remain steadfast in their faith.

Faith in Difficult Times

The Thessalonians probably needed to hear Paul's word of commendation. Paul and his friends point out that they boast about the Thessalonian church. They use them as an example to others. If we are trying very hard to do what is right, to be loving and forgiving in the midst of suffering, such a word of praise can make all the difference in the world. We may think that no one knows of our suffering; that what we do makes no difference to anyone else; that we might just as well give up and do whatever is required to end the suffering. But then along comes a word of praise and appreciation. Someone tells us what we are doing is really known to others and makes a difference to them. Other Christians care. They recognize that we are doing what is right, even when our persecutors are telling us we are really stupid for believing what we do and acting as we are. The words of praise are of great significance. In the same way, to hear that other Christians are praying for us, that other congregations are praying for our church, strengthens our faith and our commitment.

The suffering of the Thessalonian church is put in a wider context. What is happening to them is for a purpose. It is helping to perfect their faith. It is strengthening their love. It is proving what they really believe. It is making them ready for the kingdom and worthy of it. Without such judgment they would not be made perfect. So their suffering is not only a witness to others; it is also a help to them.

The Reality of God's Judgment

From the earliest days of the church, Christians have had some difficulty reconciling God's love and God's justice. If God is loving, how can there be judgment and condemnation? Early in the church's life, some Christians tried to solve the problem by saying God loved and forgave some people and judged and condemned others. Others tried to say God loved and did not judge, even going so far as to say that the God of the Old Testament judged, whereas the God of the New Testament loved. The church maintained that these solutions did not work and rejected them as heresies. God loves but also judges. God is holy and demands righteousness. God is loving and forgiving, but love and forgiveness cannot be understood in a way that denies the reality of God's judgment. In the passage we are studying, God judges both the Christians and the people who deny God. The Thessalonian Christians are suffering because of God's righteous judgment. They are being made worthy by their suffering. Often, the Scriptures depict suffering as a purifying fire that burns away all that is unholy. This is the case when in faith we willingly submit to the judgment of God. The passage speaks also of the eternal condemnation of those who are causing the suffering because of their own denial of God. We may not be comfortable with such words, but we must remember that the fate of others is in the hands of God. We are to love our enemies and pray for those who persecute us. We dare not pronounce damnation on anyone. That is God's province, not ours.

The Need for Prayer

If we face no external persecution, if we are not imprisoned or beaten on account of our Christian faith, we may assume that it is very easy for us to remain faithful. Therefore, we may feel that we do not need the prayers of others. But that is not the case. When things seem very easy, when there appears to be no conflict at all between what the society around us expects and what the Christian life demands, we face great temptation. The ease we feel may be a sign that we have lost sight of the real demands of the Christian life. We may have watered them down so that there is no difference at all between a generally decent citizen and a Christian. The Thessalonians knew that they were in danger because they were being persecuted. They knew they needed the grace of God in order to persevere. They knew they needed the prayers of other Christians in order to remain constant. In our comfort, we may not be so aware. We may not feel we need others to pray for us because everything seems all right.

If Paul and his friends always prayed for others but never expected others to pray for them, then their understanding of the church and their role in it would have been quite different than it was. They knew that they needed prayers as much as they needed to pray for others. The same is true for us. If we know we need to pray for other churches but never see that we too need the prayers of other congregations so that we remain faithful, something is lacking in our understanding of our place in the whole church.

What has been said about churches is also true of individuals. Christians who see no need for the prayers of others are not aware of the temptations they face. They think they are strong and able enough to take care of everything. But no one is like that. All of us face difficult choices, temptations to be unfaithful to Christ. All of us need the support of other Christians. To deny that we need the prayers of others is rather like saying we do not need the grace of God. John Calvin, one of the sixteenth-century reformers, wrote that we are often tempted to pray only for the things we cannot take care of ourselves. If we have enough food, we do not pray for that. If we are healthy, we do not pray for that. If life is going well, we have little to pray for. Calvin said that such a prayer life overlooks the fact that all that we have comes from God. If we ask God for our daily bread, even when there is sufficient food in the cupboard, we are acknowledging that even what we have has come from God and is not really under our control. If we pray for health when we are healthy, we acknowledge that that too is a gift of God and not under our control. Prayers are not limited to what we cannot manage ourselves, for we are mistaken about our power to manage. If we have faith, we ought still to pray for faith. And others can pray for us, even when there is no emergency in our lives. Granted, we greatly appreciate the support of others, expressed in prayer, when we face danger and are fearful. But we need to be conscious of the mutual support of Christians for one another all of the time. That is partly what is meant by the priesthood of all believers.

In this letter, Paul and his companions are dealing with the prayers Christians make for one another. In other places in the Scriptures the scope of intercessory prayer is expanded beyond this. The intercessory prayers of Christians are not limited to other Christians. Prayers need to be offered for people who do not or cannot pray. If they do not know God, we can pray for them. We can pray for people ravaged by war, for children who suffer, for the homeless and the poor. We can pray for those who govern, even for tyrants and leaders who commit great evil. We can pray that God will change them, or bring their evil to naught. People who know God can bring the whole world to God in prayer. This is what it means to be God's priestly people.

SHARING THE SCRIPTURE

PREPARING TO TEACH

Preparing Our Hearts

We can study, discuss, and analyze prayer but, most important, we need to spend time praying. We need to be in the kind of relationship with God that impels us to want to communicate, just as we want to keep in touch with our friends and loved ones. Since this week's lesson focuses specifically on intercessory prayer, offer a prayer for others each day. Here are some suggestions to widen what may be your usual circle of concern: pray for all of the Sunday school classes that study the International Lesson Series, for the citizens of a war-torn country, for all the patients in your local hospital, for persons who are homeless, for persons who live alone. In addition, lift up specific persons you know or know of who need to feel God's presence in their lives.

Preparing Our Minds

Read 2 Thessalonians 1. Also note 3:1, the verse in which Paul requests prayers from the church at Thessalonica. Carefully study the lesson. You will soon be aware that chapter 1 is chock full of ideas. Remember, however, that our lesson focuses on intercessory prayer. In the case of the Thessalonians, such intercession is made to help the church stand fast in times of persecution and suffering.

Preparing Our Learning Space

If possible, secure a copy of your denominational prayer or missions calendar. Check with your pastor about such a publication if you are not familiar with it.

Have on hand:
- ✔ several Bibles for students
- ✔ newsprint and marker or chalkboard and chalk
- ✔ paper and pencils
- ✔ optional copy of denominational prayer or missions calendar

LEADING THE CLASS

(1) Introduction

Even if you have already had a prayer as part of your opening worship, plan to introduce today's lesson with an intercessory prayer. To do this, you will need to gather the names of persons or groups for whom the class would like to pray. If students are comfortable speaking names aloud, invite them to do so. You may want to record these names on newsprint. If students prefer not to offer prayer concerns aloud, distribute slips of paper and pencils. Ask each person to write the name of one group or person who needs prayer today. The reason for the prayer (such as surgery or death in the family) may or may not be included, depending upon your congregation's custom.

Once you have gathered the names, you may want to offer the prayer yourself, saying the name of each person or group listed on the newsprint or slips of paper. The prayer need not be lengthy or elaborate, but it should truly speak to God on behalf of others. As an option, if you have a small class where people know each other well, you may want to have them join hands in a circle. Shuffle the slips of paper and redistribute them to each person. Go around the circle with each member offering just a sentence prayer for the person or group whose name is before them.

After the prayer time, spend a few moments asking these questions:
(1) Why do we pray for one another? ?
(Scripture such as James 5:14-15 tells us to pray for others.)

(2) How useful do you think these prayers we have offered will be?

(Scriptures such as Matthew 7:7 and James 5:16 assure us that they will be quite effective.)

(3) What examples can you cite of intercessory prayers being answered?

Close this portion by stating that our lesson today focuses on the need that Christians have to pray for others, especially those who are facing difficult circumstances. The main question for our session is this: *How do prayers for one another support us—individually and collectively—as members of the community of faith?*

(2) Church to Church

Have a volunteer read aloud 2 Thessalonians 1:1-3. Then read or retell the information in "Church to Church" as it appears in the Interpreting the Scripture section. Ask the class as a whole, or in teams, to brainstorm answers to these questions:

(1) If we were to write a letter to a church experiencing difficult times, where would it be? (Try to include a broad geographic area, though class members may not know the name of a specific church in a certain region.)

(2) What kinds of difficulty might this church be experiencing? (Some broad ideas include: effects of natural disaster or war, conflict within the congregation, major problems within the neighborhood.)

If the class enjoys hands-on activities, have them draft a letter to a church expressing their concern and prayer support. The recipient may be an imaginary one but, if possible, plan to polish and send this letter to a congregation experiencing the kind of difficulty the letter addresses. For example, you may be able to obtain from your pastor the name and address of a church that has been devastated by a natural disaster to let the members of that congregation know of your class's support.

(3) Faith in Difficult Times

Now read 2 Thessalonians 1:4-5. Note that Paul is telling the Thessalonians that he brags about them to other congregations. This church has stood firm in the face of opposition and persecution. Ask the class:

(1) If someone were to brag about your congregation, holding you up as a model for other congregations, what points would they make about you?

(4) The Reality of God's Judgment

Read 2 Thessalonians 1:6-10, in which Paul speaks of the reality of God's coming judgment. Point out that the early church expected Jesus to return immediately, to be "revealed from heaven with his mighty angels in flaming fire, inflicting vengeance on those who do not know God and on those who do not obey the gospel of our Lord Jesus" (1:7-8). You may also want to read or retell this section under Interpreting the Scripture because it will likely speak to uncertainties your group has about the relationship between God's judgment and God's love. Provide time for the students to voice their own questions about the reality of God's judgment.

Then ask the following question. You may want to write the answers on newsprint or a chalkboard.

(1) What effect does the notion of impending judgment have on your willingness to be an intercessor in prayer?

(5) The Need for Prayer

Ask students who have the same translation of the Bible to read in unison 2 Thessalonians 1:11-12. Point out that verse 11 is our key verse. Ask the class:

(1) Had you been a member of the church at Thessalonica, how would

[?] **you have felt knowing that Paul and his companions "always pray for you"?**

Point out, as we will read in next week's lesson, that prayer was reciprocal. Paul not only prayed for the Thessalonians but asked (in 3:1) that they pray for him as well.

Create a prayer calendar that may guide class members as they intercede for others. If your denomination has a prayer calendar or missions guide that you have access to, use this resource to create a plan for intercessory prayer. Include persons around the world, as well as those at home. You may set up the calendar on a daily, weekly, or monthly basis, depending upon the time you have for this activity. Here's an example of the kind of plan the class could use to guide their intercessory prayer time in the coming week. Monday: missionaries John and Judy Smith in Northern Ireland; Tuesday: homeless teens in Brazil and the Christians who care for them; Wednesday: the Jones family as they teach and minister in Appalachia; and so on. You may also want to include specific groups within your congregation in order to lift them up in prayer in an intentional way. Distribute paper and pencils so that class members may copy whatever you have agreed upon in order to use the list this week. (See "Helping Class Members Act.")

HELPING CLASS MEMBERS ACT

Ask class members to join you in a covenant to pray for other persons this week. Perhaps together you will have identified specific individuals or groups that you plan to uphold in prayer. While you may have difficulty working out a prayer time that fits everyone's schedule, the effect of the intercession would be enhanced among the students if certain times (for example, 7:00 A.M. and 10:00 P.M.) could be set aside each day when all class members will offer their intercessory prayer.

Note that in his letter, Paul specifically tells the congregation at Thessalonica that he is praying for them. Suggest that students consider writing a note to someone for whom they have been praying to let that person know that thoughts and prayers are with them.

Challenge class members to spend some time this week reflecting on what they truly believe about the judgment of God. Have them ask questions such as: Do I expect God to judge other persons? Do I expect God to judge me? Am I prepared for judgment? If not, what changes do I need to make, with God's help, so I can be ready? Suggest that students write their thoughts in a spiritual journal.

PLANNING FOR NEXT SUNDAY

We will continue our study of 2 Thessalonians next week by reading chapter 3, especially verses 1-16. Ask class members to think about what it means to "do right." Our key verse, 3:13, will help us focus on the need to continue doing what is right.

Do What Is Right!

PREVIEWING THE LESSON

Lesson Scripture: 2 Thessalonians 3:1-16
Background Scripture: 2 Thessalonians 3
Key Verse: 2 Thessalonians 3:13

Focus of the Lesson:
Paul's counsel to the Thessalonians to do what is right

Main Question of the Lesson:
What does "doing right" mean to those who follow Christ?

This lesson will enable adult learners to:
(1) encounter the active, engaged life that Paul models for the Thessalonians.
(2) affirm their own efforts to do right and oppose evil.
(3) respond by taking concrete steps to do what is right.

Today's lesson may be outlined as follows:
(1) Introduction
(2) We Are Not Called to an Easy Way
(3) Tough Love for Idle Christians
(4) The Purpose of Tough Love
(5) Paul's Personal Comments

FOCUSING ON THE MAIN QUESTION

On the surface, it sounds like a simple request: Do what is right! That should be an easy task, for surely doing the right thing comes naturally to us as Christians, right? Besides, we know that doing what is wrong can get us into trouble and make our lives more difficult than necessary. Therefore, to a mature person it makes much more sense to do the right thing in the first place.

Paul, however, is much more realistic about the matter. Doing the right thing is often difficult. The world frequently rewards doing wrong rather than doing right. Sometimes even our closest family and friends may think we are making both our lives and theirs unnecessarily difficult if we do what is really right. Evil is in the world and it battles with good. To do the right thing means to oppose evil. Doing right is not a simple matter of following the path any mature person would take.

We may assume that such contradictions between society's expectations and the Christian vocation to do what is right are no longer a reality since the society has been so influenced by the gospel. But in some ways, that assumption has made it more difficult to determine exactly what is right in any given situation. If most of our friends and family—who also have been influenced by the gospel and perhaps are active church members—think that it is quite possible to follow the expectations of the surrounding society as a good Christian, then we may doubt our own judgment when we disagree.

In today's lesson, Paul deals with some Christians who assume that, because the end of this age is to come soon, they do not need to do much of anything. Others can support them; others can do the work that needs to be done in spreading the gospel. For these people, it is quite enough to believe the right things and let others go on with the daily tasks. We may think we are immune to such mistakes, but we have our own excuses for letting others do the work that needs to be done, and we presume on the goodwill of other Christians for that we should do for ourselves.

Doing what is right is not an easy task, especially over the long haul. It is helpful to have Paul's encouragement as we ask: *What does "doing right" mean to those who follow Christ?*

READING THE SCRIPTURE

NRSV
2 Thessalonians 3:1-16

1 Finally, brothers and sisters, pray for us, so that the word of the Lord may spread rapidly and be glorified everywhere, just as it is among you, ²and that we may be rescued from wicked and evil people; for not all have faith. ³But the Lord is faithful; he will strengthen you and guard you from the evil one. ⁴And we have confidence in the Lord concerning you, that you are doing and will go on doing the things that we command. ⁵May the Lord direct your hearts to the love of God and to the steadfastness of Christ.

6 Now we command you, beloved, in the name of our Lord Jesus Christ, to keep away from believers who are living in idleness and not according to the tradition that they received from us. ⁷For you yourselves know how you ought to imitate us; we were not idle when we were with you, ⁸and we did not eat anyone's bread without paying for it; but with toil and labor we worked night and day, so that we might not burden any of you. ⁹This was

NIV
2 Thessalonians 3:1-16

1 Finally, brothers, pray for us that the message of the Lord may spread rapidly and be honored, just as it was with you. ²And pray that we may be delivered from wicked and evil men, for not everyone has faith. ³But the Lord is faithful, and he will strengthen and protect you from the evil one. ⁴We have confidence in the Lord that you are doing and will continue to do the things we command. ⁵May the Lord direct your hearts into God's love and Christ's perseverance.

⁶In the name of the Lord Jesus Christ, we command you, brothers, to keep away from every brother who is idle and does not live according to the teaching you received from us. ⁷For you yourselves know how you ought to follow our example. We were not idle when we were with you, ⁸nor did we eat anyone's food without paying for it. On the contrary, we worked night and day, laboring and toiling so that we would not be a burden to any of you. ⁹We did this, not because we

not because we do not have that right, but in order to give you an example to imitate. [10]For even when we were with you, we gave you this command: Anyone unwilling to work should not eat. [11]For we hear that some of you are living in idleness, mere busybodies, not doing any work. [12]Now such persons we command and exhort in the Lord Jesus Christ to do their work quietly and to earn their own living. [13]Brothers and sisters, do not be weary in doing what is right.

14 Take note of those who do not obey what we say in this letter; have nothing to do with them, so that they may be ashamed. [15]Do not regard them as enemies, but warn them as believers.

16 Now may the Lord of peace himself give you peace at all times in all ways. The Lord be with all of you.

Key
Verse

do not have the right to such help, but in order to make ourselves a model for you to follow. [10]For even when we were with you, we gave you this rule: "If a man will not work, he shall not eat."

[11]We hear that some among you are idle. They are not busy; they are busybodies. [12]Such people we command and urge in the Lord Jesus Christ to settle down and earn the bread they eat. [13]And as for you, brothers, never tire of doing what is right.

[14]If anyone does not obey our instruction in this letter, take special note of him. Do not associate with him, in order that he may feel ashamed. [15]Yet do not regard him as an enemy, but warn him as a brother.

[16]Now may the Lord of peace himself give you peace at all times and in every way. The Lord be with all of you.

Ke
Ver

UNDERSTANDING THE SCRIPTURE

2 Thessalonians 3:1-5. Paul emphasizes again the theme of last week's lesson, that Christians should pray for one another. Here he asks the Thessalonian Christians to pray for him because his work of spreading the gospel is not an easy task. Wicked people seek to undermine what he is doing. Evil in the world opposes him. It is not within human power to resist such evil, and therefore God's help is needed. The prayers of others for him can strengthen him. Paul begins this section with his own need in the work that he is doing. If Paul, who is known to the Thessalonians as a leader in the church, a man of great faith, needs the prayers of other Christians, how much more do they need God's help? They cannot trust their own strength.

Paul begins with a request for himself, but he quickly turns to the Thessalonian Christians and their need for steadfastness. Perhaps they had been lulled into a false sense of security that the Christian

life was a fairly simple matter, once one had been converted. Paul stresses the need for steadfastness, for continuing effort and intention to lead the life of holiness to which they have been called by the gospel. God's power is needed in order to continue in their love for Christ and in the ways of God.

2 Thessalonians 3:6-13. Paul comes to the heart of the matter. He has heard that some of the Christians in Thessalonica have been presuming on other Christians. They have ceased to work. They have assumed that the Christian community would take care of them, though they contribute nothing to others. Paul reminds them that he has earned his own living when he was with them. We know from Acts 18:1-3 that he was a tentmaker. Evidently, he continued that trade while he spread the gospel and organized a church in their midst. He was not idle.

Paul's words are rather harsh: Christians should avoid those who refuse to work. The faithful should give the idlers a dose of "tough love"; they must earn their own bread. Paul also makes the curious statement that, though he did not "eat anyone's bread" while he was with them, he did have a right to do so. What he is referring to here is a very important debate in the early church as to whether or not those who were given the responsibility of spreading the gospel, that is, those who were missionaries, evangelists, or preachers, should have to support themselves or should be supported by the church. (The same issue is found in 1 Timothy 5:17-18 and in Luke 10:7.) Paul clearly felt that the church should support such ministers and therefore it would have been quite proper for him not to have worked while he was establishing the church in their town. He did not do this, however, but instead worked for his own keep outside the church. Perhaps he already suspected some of the people there would misunderstand his position or use it as an excuse for their own expectation of being supported by the congregation.

Paul clearly is responding to reports that he has heard about the church in Thessalonica. Not only are some of the members idle and relying on the support of the rest of the congregation, but they are using the leisure they have created for themselves in evil ways. In short, the destructive work of being busybodies has replaced constructive work for the church or the society. Faithful Christians are to rebuke such people and remind them of the commands and the example they have received from Paul. They are to work and earn their own living.

The early church was concerned about the kinds of work people did. By the second century, there were lists of occupa-tions that Christians could not hold. These jobs generally would have involved them in idolatry or other evil. In spite of certain limitations, work in the world was considered honorable. Christians were not to withdraw from the society, though that may have been an easier option. Here Paul urges them to work "quietly," which probably implies that they are not to attack others who do not share their faith. The faithful are to go about their business as witnesses in the midst of the non-Christian society. They are to persevere in the midst of the world, and not grow weary. The idle ones have refused this path and, therefore, are to be encouraged and even forced to go back into the world.

2 Thessalonians 3:14-16. Paul concludes with a further exhortation to avoid such idle people. These individuals remain fellow Christians, but they need the harsh lesson of non-support in order to bring them back to the right way. In the concluding benediction Paul prays for peace for the church, even in the midst of the conflict that is sure to follow if they do as he has asked them to do.

2 Thessalonians 3:17-18. Paul adds what amounts to a "P.S." to his letter. He often dictated letters to someone who transcribed them for him, the way someone today would dictate a letter to a secretary. Then, as a friendly gesture, he wrote his own greeting at the end, signing it. Verse 16 is the sort of benediction with which he usually closed his letters. Having added a brief note, he now adds another benediction in verse 18. Benedictions were very important. The letters were intended to be read to the gathered congregation, and the blessing was clearly received as Paul's blessing of the congregation, not as a social formality.

INTERPRETING THE SCRIPTURE

We Are Not Called to an Easy Way

Paul did not make the assumption that some Christians today make, that being a Christian will make us quite acceptable to the world around us. We forget the difficulty. Paul reminds us that evil is a reality and that we will meet opposition if we are truly righteous. If we assume the Christian life will be easy, then we see no need to ask for God's help or seek the support of the community of faith. We may also be surprised by evil and unprepared to deal with it. If we are quite able to trust in our own strength and we find little difficulty in our path, perhaps we have diluted the meaning of righteousness and substituted something that is easier than the faithful life to which God calls us.

Tough Love for Idle Christians

It may seem rather "unchristian" to tell some persons that you will not help them, even if you have the resources to do so. However, we should not take these verses out of context and say that there should be no help for the unemployed. Paul is discussing a very specific situation here. Christians who could be employed have given up their jobs and now expect others in the community to support them. Perhaps the love within the community had been so strong these people assumed they did not need to do anything for themselves. Paul is not saying to cease loving these idle Christians. Rather, the character of the congregation's love needs to change in order to bring these idlers back to the true way.

There are several reasons for Paul's command. First, these idlers are not doing their part in the community. Others are supporting them, but they are not supporting anyone. Second, they seem to have withdrawn from the evil world as though they had no part in it anymore. Paul clearly wishes to change this opinion. The church has a mission to the world and therefore Christians must be in the world. If the persons who cease working for their support in the world are actually carrying out the mission of the church full-time, then the congregation should support them. But if they are merely sitting back and doing nothing useful, then the church needs to take action so that they will change their ways. We should not take the words in verse 10 to mean that children must labor, or that the church should ignore the elderly and the sick, or that we should shun those who wish to be employed but who cannot find work. A third reason for such tough love is that idleness usually leads to destructive behavior. Paul says the idlers have become busybodies. Idleness also hampers the witness of the church as a community in the world when Christians neglect their responsibilities to one another.

Paul recognizes that laboring for one's bread in the midst of an unbelieving world is not an easy matter. Nor is applying the kind of rigorous and restorative love that he has urged. In both cases, Christians are not to give up. They are to follow the right way, even when it is difficult. They are not to grow weary, but instead remain steadfast in the way to which they have been called.

The Purpose of Tough Love

Verses 14-16 are critical to the understanding of Paul's message. There is a purpose to cutting the idlers off from the bounty of the community. Such action is not taken because they are enemies. Rather, they are Christians who have gone astray. They are still part of the church and should be considered that. But they need to feel ashamed of the way they have acted and mend their ways. Within the context of the church, where the word of forgiveness is offered, such shame should lead to repentance, to amendment of life, and to reconciliation.

Our society finds it difficult to imagine that making people ashamed of themselves in any respect could be good. Granted, if someone is made to feel ashamed of something over which he or she has no control, or without the context of love and redemption, that would indeed be negative. But here the context is different. What is desired is that the persons be ashamed of a specific behavior that they can change. They are called to change because such behavior is against the will of God and injurious to the community of faith. Those who seek to bring about such a sense of shame are those who love the ones that have gone astray and who want, above all, to make them part of the community again. The faithful Christians are ready and willing to forgive. Indeed, in a sense they have already forgiven. What is needed is for the idlers to recognize that what they were doing is not to be done.

The love of God for us, and therefore our love for one another, is not a soft and sentimental emotion, glossing over anything that happens. God loves us even though we are sinners, but God does not want us to continue as sinners. Judgment is a part of God's love. The love of the Christian community has the same character. It cannot be reduced to an easygoing acceptance of any and all behavior. In the same way that parents can accept and love a child even when they cannot accept all of the child's behavior, so the community of faith sometimes needs to use discipline in regard to a member. Love is the key. Those who misbehave in the community, as in the family, must be loved. They are not enemies. But they also need to be brought to understand that their behavior is unacceptable. Being ashamed is the sign of their understanding.

The benediction of verse 16 is related to this discussion. One might assume that such tough love would lead to the disruption of the community. The continued idleness of those who could contribute also would eventually disrupt the community. Paul prays that the whole community will know the peace that God can give. It is a peace that seeks the restoration of the wayward and the preservation and strengthening of the love of the community.

Paul's Personal Comments

Paul's words have been rather harsh. But he loves the church in Thessalonica, and he does not wish to end on a biting note. The personal comment, the handwritten note, serves to soften somewhat the hard things he has said before. Paul invokes a blessing for the church, reminding them that all we do is in the power of the grace that is given us in Jesus Christ. Furthermore, by referring to Jesus as the Lord, Paul also makes clear that we all are servants of this Lord, and the commands that he has given are not his, but Christ's.

The church is not a human organization we join because we like the people who are part of it. Rather, it is the people of God, the disciples of Jesus Christ, who acknowledge his lordship and who seek to follow him in their lives. Love is at the heart of the church, but it is a love in the service of discipleship. It is a reflection of God's love for humanity, which seeks to bring us to the goal God has for us, namely, holiness in the lives of the whole community. We live holy lives when we do what is right. In contrast, society has different goals that are incompatible with God's goal of holiness. Therefore, we require perseverance and steadfastness to maintain the course toward God's goal. We are not to be weary in doing what is right. We have the assurance that, because God works with us and through us, such steadfastness is possible.

SHARING THE SCRIPTURE

PREPARING TO TEACH

Preparing Our Hearts

This week's lesson calls us to do what is right. Specifically, Paul called the Christians of Thessalonica to continue to engage in work in the world as they await Christ's return. They were not to divorce themselves from productive work and sit idly by expecting other members of the church family to take care of them. As you prepare to teach this week's lesson, think about ways in which you attempt to work and witness in the world. Do you, like Paul, set an example that others can follow? Or, have you "written off" the world? Pray that God will enable you to be both a good witness and a worker who does what is right in whatever tasks you undertake.

Preparing Our Minds

Read 2 Thessalonians in its entirety, along with the lesson. Be sure that you understand the context of Paul's words about idleness to the church at Thessalonica. Prepare to help the class draw the clear distinction between Paul's insistence that those who are able to work should do so rather than depend upon the community of faith as it awaits the return of Christ, and the notion that Christians should not help those in need (which Paul is not suggesting).

Preparing Our Learning Space

Have on hand:
- several Bibles for students
- newsprint and marker or chalkboard and chalk

LEADING THE CLASS

(1) Introduction

Begin the session by having the students make a list of the temptations that are prevalent in our society. The list will likely include serious sins such as adultery and murder, but be certain that it includes behaviors, such as cheating on income tax returns, that even Christians often rationalize away by saying, "everybody else is doing it." In other words, some Christians will engage in certain behaviors without feeling that these are wrong.

After a few moments, focus on several of the behaviors that prompt mixed reactions from class members as to whether a particular behavior is right or wrong. For example, some may say that it is okay to take stationery supplies (such as notebooks and pens) from their employer because the company knows that everyone does it. Certain employees consider these supplies a fringe benefit. Others will argue that such behavior is theft. The point of the discussion is to demonstrate that Christians may have differing opinions on right and wrong because we have accepted society's attitude toward certain behaviors as the Christian way. Yet, many socially accepted behaviors—even in our so-called Christian society—often do not measure up to biblical standards of right. In our example, taking supplies is theft according to the Ten Commandments, no matter how many co-workers claim otherwise.

Conclude this portion of the lesson by suggesting that Paul encountered Christians who failed to see the sinfulness of their behavior. Paul writes to the church at Thessalonica telling them, as our key verse states, to "not be weary in doing what is right." As we study today's lesson, this main question will guide us: *What does "doing right" mean to those who follow Christ?*

If the class prefers a lecture, use ideas from the Focusing on the Main Question portion to lead into today's lesson.

(2) We Are Not Called to an Easy Way

Ask a student to read aloud 2 Thessalonians 3:1-5. Note that, as we mentioned last week, Paul asks the church to pray for him and his companions. You may also want to read or retell this portion of the lesson as found under Interpreting the Scripture. Then ask:

?

(1) **Why do you think we find it so easy to follow the ways our society dictates, and so difficult to follow the Way of Jesus?**

(2) **Can you give some specific examples of situations in which you would find it easier to follow the way of the crowd, rather than hold steadfast to the way of Christ?**

(3) **How do you feel when you do right, even if you do so as a minority of one?**

(3) Tough Love for Idle Christians

Now ask someone to read aloud 2 Thessalonians 3:6-13. Take great care as you work with these verses. Help the class to recognize that Paul was speaking about persons who were capable of working but had chosen not to. He is not expecting children, the sick, the unemployed person who cannot find work, or the retiree to find work in order to eat. Such a stance would, of course, be counter to the example that we have in Jesus.

If some students are unfamiliar with "tough love," explain that this term refers to taking a stance that may appear harsh but is intended to help someone we love who is on the wrong path. Often, a parent is called to take a tough love approach with a teenager or young adult whose behavior is destructive or dependent. Such an approach, though generally painful for all involved at the time, may ultimately lead to greater maturity, independence, and responsibility on the part of the one who has strayed.

Note in this section under the Interpreting the Scripture portion the reasons given for Paul's insistence that those who had chosen not to work be treated with what we would call tough love. You may want to write these reasons on newsprint or a chalkboard.

- Others are supporting the idlers, but the idlers are not supporting anyone.
- The idlers seemed to withdraw from the evil world as if they had no part in it.
- Idleness usually leads to destructive behavior.

Ask the class, either as a whole or in teams, to consider assumptions that underlie these reasons and discuss their merit. Here are some ideas to spark discussion:

(1) **Paul assumes that all persons who are able should work to support themselves. Do you agree or disagree? Why?**   ?

(2) **Paul assumes that it is wrong for Christians to withdraw from the world, even though the world is evil. Do you agree or disagree? Why?**

(3) **Paul assumes that persons who do not have productive work to do will get into mischief. Do you agree or disagree? Why?**

(4) The Purpose of Tough Love

Have a volunteer read aloud 2 Thessalonians 3:14-15. Encourage class members to restate these two verses in their own words. Be sure that group members understand that Paul's motivation for encouraging a tough love approach is to help Christians who have gone astray to feel ashamed and repent of their sin. His ultimate goal is not the condemnation of an enemy, but the restoration of a loved one.

Point out that a situation similar to that which Paul refers to may exist in homes where grown children have returned to live. Read this case study aloud.

When Jimmy Anderson and his wife Arlene divorced, he moved back into his parents' home. Soon he was a carefree bachelor, expecting his parents to take care of all the household chores, including his laundry. He paid so little attention to his work that he lost his job and depended upon his parents for support. Jimmy was disrupting his parents' lives, begging them for money, and getting in with the wrong crowd.   R

After reading the study, have the students answer these questions, perhaps working in pairs or teams.

[?] (1) **What might Paul suggest that Jimmy Anderson's parents do?**

(2) **Would you agree that tough love is needed in such a situation? Why or why not?**

(3) **What might be the result of the tough love approach?**

(5) Paul's Personal Comments

Read 2 Thessalonians 3:16 and 18 as a benediction for today's lesson.

Allow a few moments for class members to meditate on what difference God's peace would make in their own lives, especially if they are facing difficult circumstances at this time.

HELPING CLASS MEMBERS ACT

Paul's discussion regarding idlers focuses on persons who had chosen not to work. Many people in our society, however, are unemployed through no fault or slothfulness on their part. Encourage class members to contact someone they know who is unemployed and offer some concrete support. Perhaps a listening session over lunch, or a ride to a job interview, or financial assistance graciously given could provide a real boost to one who is in need.

Challenge students to examine their own hearts this week to see if they have grown weary of doing right. Point out that our society does offer many tempting shortcuts, but that God calls us to a higher standard of morals and ethics. Suggest that those who feel that they are not "doing right" should take at least one step to correct their course of action.

Note that Paul closes his letter with a blessing of God's peace. Invite class members to share God's peace with others this week by offering a word of encouragement or a listening ear to those who are experiencing turmoil.

PLANNING FOR NEXT SUNDAY

Our Easter lesson next week will look at both the story of the Resurrection, found in Matthew 28:1-10, and Paul's assurance to the believers in the church at Thessalonica that Jesus had indeed died and been resurrected. Such news, whether we experience it for ourselves at the empty tomb or proclaim it to others, gives those who believe reason to hope. Ask class members to read the account from Matthew, as well as 1 Thessalonians 4:13-18.

WE HAVE HOPE!

PREVIEWING THE LESSON

Lesson Scripture: Matthew 28:1-10; 1 Thessalonians 4:13-18
Background Scripture: Matthew 28:1-10; 1 Thessalonians 4:13-18
Key Verse: 1 Thessalonians 4:14

Focus of the Lesson:
the assurance of Jesus' resurrection gives hope to believers that they will also be resurrected

Main Question of the Lesson:
How does the resurrection of Jesus give us hope?

This lesson will enable adult learners to:
(1) rediscover the hope that Jesus' resurrection offers to all believers.
(2) experience hope in their own lives.
(3) respond by encouraging others to have hope.

Today's lesson may be outlined as follows:
(1) Introduction
(2) The Easter Story
(3) The Church Beyond Death
(4) The Ultimate Future

FOCUSING ON THE MAIN QUESTION

We have looked at various aspects of the Christian vocation. We are called to proclaim the good news, to be holy in our lives, to be concerned for one another in prayer. We have also seen that living out this vocation is not an easy matter because the world opposes the lives we are called to live. Yet, God's loving judgment calls us to persevere in the way of righteousness. Why would anyone follow such a way? Why bother with the discipline, the perseverance that such living requires?

The answer is as simple as it is profound: We have been given hope! This hope is not something that has appeared in our lives for no reason, with no cause. This hope is based on something that has happened centuries ago: the resurrection of Jesus on that first Easter. His resurrection signaled the beginning of a new age, the fulfillment of the promises of God that God's creation would reach the goal God had for it. Human sin and disobedience, no matter how great, would not prevail against God's intentions for the world. Sin and disobedience could be seen at their height in the cross, but in the Resurrection it is clear that they shall not have the last word. Therefore we have hope. In spite of all the opposition, all the difficulties, the way of Christ is the way that brings God's future. All else is false hope, bound to bring disillusionment, bound to pass away.

Therefore, for those who know that Christ has indeed been raised from the dead, there is real hope. Whatever difficulties lie in the path of discipleship are minor in comparison to the goal to which this path leads. It is the pearl of great price (Matthew 13:45). It is the only thing that is not "rubbish" in Paul's eyes (Philippians 3:8). Christ is the goal, and following Christ is the way. This is the meaning of the Resurrection. It does not deny the reality of the cross. Instead, the Resurrection makes clear that the cross is not the last word, but rather the strange, though essential, means to the final goal.

What has happened to Jesus will also happen to his followers, to those who are "in Christ." We, too, see the cross ahead of us. But we know that as Christ was raised from the dead, so too shall we be raised. The cross is a reality for us, but it also is not the last word for us. In today's lesson we shall consider this question: *How does the resurrection of Jesus give us hope?*

READING THE SCRIPTURE

NRSV
Matthew 28:1-10

1 After the sabbath, as the first day of the week was dawning, Mary Magdalene and the other Mary went to see the tomb. 2And suddenly there was a great earthquake; for an angel of the Lord, descending from heaven, came and rolled back the stone and sat on it. 3His appearance was like lightning, and his clothing white as snow. 4For fear of him the guards shook and became like dead men. 5But the angel said to the women, "Do not be afraid; I know that you are looking for Jesus who was crucified. 6He is not here; for he has been raised, as he said. Come, see the place where he lay. 7Then go quickly and tell his disciples, 'He has been raised from the dead, and indeed he is going ahead of you to Galilee; there you will see him.' This is my message for you." 8So they left the tomb quickly with fear and great joy, and ran to tell his disciples. 9Suddenly Jesus met them and said, "Greetings!" And they came to him, took hold of his feet, and worshiped him. 10Then Jesus said

NIV
Matthew 28:1-10

1 After the Sabbath, at dawn on the first day of the week, Mary Magdalene and the other Mary went to look at the tomb.

2There was a violent earthquake, for an angel of the Lord came down from heaven and, going to the tomb, rolled back the stone and sat on it. 3His appearance was like lightning, and his clothes were white as snow. 4The guards were so afraid of him that they shook and became like dead men.

5The angel said to the women, "Do not be afraid, for I know that you are looking for Jesus, who was crucified. 6He is not here; he has risen, just as he said. Come and see the place where he lay. 7Then go quickly and tell his disciples: 'He has risen from the dead and is going ahead of you into Galilee. There you will see him.' Now I have told you."

8So the women hurried away from the tomb, afraid yet filled with joy, and ran to tell his disciples. 9Suddenly Jesus met them. "Greetings," he said. They came to him, clasped his feet and worshiped him.

to them, "Do not be afraid; go and tell my brothers to go to Galilee; there they will see me."

NRSV

1 Thessalonians 4:13-18

13 But we do not want you to be uninformed, brothers and sisters, about those who have died, so that you may not grieve as others do who have no hope. ¹⁴For since we believe that Jesus died and rose again, even so, through Jesus, God will bring with him those who have died. ¹⁵For this we declare to you by the word of the Lord, that we who are alive, who are left until the coming of the Lord, will by no means precede those who have died. ¹⁶For the Lord himself, with a cry of command, with the archangel's call and with the sound of God's trumpet, will descend from heaven, and the dead in Christ will rise first. ¹⁷Then we who are alive, who are left, will be caught up in the clouds together with them to meet the Lord in the air; and so we will be with the Lord forever. ¹⁸Therefore encourage one another with these words.

¹⁰Then Jesus said to them, "Do not be afraid. Go and tell my brothers to go to Galilee; there they will see me."

NIV

1 Thessalonians 4:13-18

¹³Brothers, we do not want you to be ignorant about those who fall asleep, or to grieve like the rest of men, who have no hope. ¹⁴We believe that Jesus died and rose again and so we believe that God will bring with Jesus those who have fallen asleep in him. ¹⁵According to the Lord's own word, we tell you that we who are still alive, who are left till the coming of the Lord, will certainly not precede those who have fallen asleep. ¹⁶For the Lord himself will come down from heaven, with a loud command, with the voice of the archangel and with the trumpet call of God, and the dead in Christ will rise first. ¹⁷After that, we who are still alive and are left will be caught up together with them in the clouds to meet the Lord in the air. And so we will be with the Lord forever. ¹⁸Therefore encourage each other with these words.

Key
Verse

Key
Verse

UNDERSTANDING THE SCRIPTURE

Matthew 28:1-10. The account in Matthew 28 shows the situation of the women who went to the tomb. They had expected to find the dead, to continue their mourning. But instead they hear word of Jesus' resurrection. No wonder they are filled with both fear and joy. What a strange combination of emotions! They hardly dared believe such astonishing news, but when they beheld Jesus, they could not deny it. Of course they were joyful! But their joy included the awareness that everything had changed. A new world was beginning for them, yet the old world was still all around them. This is what hope means for Christians. It

brings both joy and fear, awareness of astonishing new possibilities and awareness that the old world is still all around us, denying the reality of that newness, opposing our living according to that newness.

The one who first greeted the women was an angel, announcing the Resurrection. They did not see Jesus, but they were given a commission, a task of proclamation, to tell the disciples to go to Galilee and Jesus would meet them there. In spite of their fears, the women began to obey the command. At this point, did they really believe that Jesus had been resurrected? Clearly they believed something had happened, that the One who had given them their task of proclamation was no mere mortal. But then, as they were obedient, the risen Christ met them. Now their joy must be full, for they cannot doubt that he is indeed alive. In the conclusion of the chapter, beyond the portion we have studied today, the pattern is repeated. The Eleven went to Galilee as they were commanded, and there they, too, encountered Christ. For both the women and the Eleven, there is a connection between obedience and the certainty of faith. It is not only that we believe and, therefore, are obedient; it is also that we are obedient, and in that obedience, we encounter the risen Christ. To demand intellectual certainty and proof of the Resurrection before we are obedient is the reverse of the way the risen Christ was revealed to his followers on that first Easter. Such a demand is rather like requiring proof that we can swim before we enter the water for the first time.

1 Thessalonians 4:13-14. The church in Thessalonica was one of the earliest congregations in the Christian movement. Surely the time was at hand when Jesus would return and gather together all the faithful. Since that had not yet happened, many questions arose, especially concerning those who had already died. Were they to be separated from the living ones forever? Was their death a punishment that would keep them from the resurrection? Would those who died before the return of Christ be gathered together with those still alive? Is the love that holds the community of faith together strong enough to survive death? Are those who have died still a part of the community? Will they live again? Is the promise of the end of death only true for those alive at the return of Christ?

These questions may seem very strange to us, for we live so long after the time of the first disciples that we know there have already been many generations between the Resurrection and the return of Christ. But it was different for the first generation of the church. Their questions were very real and profound. Paul's answers to them tell us a great deal about our own understanding of death and new life. Paul's response to these questions points to the nature of the Christian hope rooted in the Resurrection. Because Jesus died and rose again, his followers will also be raised with him. Because Christ conquered death the community of faith, the body of Christ, is stronger than death. Therefore we are not separated forever from those who have gone before and are with Christ.

1 Thessalonians 4:15-18. Paul paints a poetic picture of what such a hope means in terms of the final future. Those who died before the return of Christ and those who remain alive at his coming will be reunited in Christ. There is no difference based on the time of death. The resurrection of Christ means that the power of death has been overcome for all those who are in Christ. The "forever" we have with Christ is unaffected by the timing of our death—even if we are part of the final generation that does not experience death in the way that mortals do.

For Paul, and for the earliest Christians, the final return of Christ is not something pertaining only to the future. It has great implications for the present. On the basis of this hope for the future, Christians are to encourage one another even now. Hope that is only a vague promise for the future and has no affect upon how Christians live their lives in the present is not really hope. At most, it is optimism. For Paul, to believe that those who die in Christ will be gathered together and be with him forever—that death has been conquered once and for all—is to have encouragement every day, here, in this world. Encouragement means being able to take courage and to face whatever happens, knowing that the future is secure. It is the power to remain faithful, to continue loving, in a world where evil, hatred, and death still seem very much in charge.

INTERPRETING THE SCRIPTURE

The Easter Story

It is of utmost importance that we realize that Christian hope is based on what God has done for us in the midst of human history. Our hope is based on something that occured before us, without us, and yet for us. The Easter story is an account of events that happened. Though there are several versions, each dealing with the events in a somewhat different fashion, the story itself comes through clearly. Jesus of Nazareth, who was crucified under Pontius Pilate, died, was buried, and was raised from the dead on the third day. He appeared to those who had known him and followed him. His being alive was contrary to all their expectations. His resurrection altered their lives forever. In fact, the awareness that he lived transformed them and transformed the world for them. Everything was new.

The disciples were made new because of the resurrection of Jesus. Even centuries after the events narrated in the Easter story, those who come to know it and believe it are also transformed and made new. The truth of the Resurrection comes to them through the proclamation of the gospel and the power of the Holy Spirit. Before there is new life, before there is hope, before there is faith, there is the fact of the resurrection of Jesus who was crucified.

The Easter story stresses the specific day: it was the first day of the week, the day after the Sabbath. This had much greater significance for the first disciples than we might expect. In the Jewish calendar, the week culminated in the Sabbath, the seventh day. Then a new week began on the first day. Jews looked forward to the great culmination of all of history and sometimes referred to it as the eighth day, that is, the dawning of a day that would not be the beginning of a new week but the end of time itself, the eternal Sabbath, the dawning of the kingdom. The early church saw Easter as the eighth day, the first day of a new age, not the first day of another new week like all the other weeks they had known. Creation began on the first day, and new creation also begins on the first day, a day to end all days.

Though we celebrate Easter Sunday with joy, the women who arrived at the tomb and beheld the angel were afraid. Who would not be in such a circumstance? Surely they were afraid even before they reached the tomb. The One they had followed had been executed by the Roman Empire as a criminal, as a danger to the state. Perhaps they too might be in danger if they presented any problems to the government. At the sight of the angel even the guards are shaking.The angel greets the women with the words, "Do not be afraid" (Matthew 28:5). In the assurance of the angel, in the encounter with the risen Christ, their fear is replaced by the joy that comes from the realization that the new age has really begun. The old, with its fears, has passed away.

The Church Beyond Death

The fears of the Thessalonians are real, too. At first they did not expect believers to die. They reasoned that Christ had conquered death, so those who believed in him would not die. Similar questions were raised elsewhere in the early church. Paul had written to the Corinthians stating that some of them had died because they had received Communion without discerning the body of Christ (1 Corinthians 11:29-30). Given the variety and confusion of opinions on this issue of whether or not believers would die, the Thessalonians had good reason to be concerned.

Although the issue would become clearer after several generations had passed, Paul's words are still of value to us. He tells the Thessalonians that the resurrection of Jesus is the assurance that death is not final for those who are in Christ. His resurrection is the forerunner of our own. Even if we die, we shall be raised. Therefore, as Paul says, we do not grieve as others do.

This view of resurrection does not mean that grieving over the death of a loved one is unchristian or the sign of a lack of faith. Some Christians feel that any sign of mourning is a denial of faith, but that is not what these words mean. Of course there is great pain when a loved one is no longer with us, no longer a part of our daily lives. Of course we grieve and go through the stages of human mourning. But we do not grieve as others do, as those who do not have the sure hope of reunion in Christ. God has won the victory through Christ, and God will bring together all who are in Christ. That promise of the future is sure, even though the pain of the present is also real for those who mourn.

The Ultimate Future

Paul paints a picture of the final future. In some respects it is like other images found in the Bible, with angels and trumpets. In 1 Corinthians 15:51-55, Paul writes of a similar vision of the last trumpet, when all shall be changed and death shall be conquered. The major issue here is that all who have died in Christ will be raised up, and then those still alive will be joined to them. The bottom line is that "we will be with the Lord forever" (1 Thessalonians 4:17).

This chapter from 1 Thessalonians concludes with the admonition to encourage each other with these words about the Resurrection and the hope that it gives to Christians. In a sense, Christians are to proclaim the gospel to each other constantly. We never outgrow our need to hear it. The gospel is to be proclaimed not only to those outside the church, but also to those within. It is to be proclaimed not only by those called to ordained ministry or evangelism, but by every Christian. This is what it means to encourage one another by these words.

Paul writes to the Thessalonians in order to respond to some very specific questions that they have. He affirms that believers who have died before the return of Christ will not be denied the glorious future that is promised. In the chapter that follows, he points to the understanding with which we are more familiar—that we do not need to know when Christ will return. It is not for us to know. Whenever it is, he will come "like a thief in the night" (1 Thessalonians 5:2). We are to be ready at all times, being good stewards while the Master is away, to use the imagery that is more typical of the parables in the Gospels. It is easy to get bogged down in secondary questions. That is what the Thessalonians were doing, so Paul kept pulling them back to the essentials. For Christians, the essential message is that in the resurrection of Christ, death and all else that could separate us from God have been conquered. Therefore, we have real hope.

SHARING THE SCRIPTURE

PREPARING TO TEACH

Preparing Our Hearts

Today's lesson reminds us of the hope that is ours by virtue of our faith in the resurrected Christ. As you prepare to teach this Easter lesson, examine your own heart. Do you truly believe that Jesus was raised from the dead? Do you expect to be raised to new life with God? These are real issues in our own day, for significant numbers of Christians have doubts about the resurrection story and their own eternal future as well. Like the Thessalonians, we do ask questions, though our concerns may be different from those of the people of Thessalonica. If you do not have the assurance that Jesus was resurrected and that you, too, will one day share in that eternal life, pray that God will give you this hope. Also pray for class members who have voiced doubts about these matters.

Preparing Our Minds

Focus on the two scripture readings for today: Matthew 28:1-10 and 1 Thessalonians 4:13-18. Since the Matthew passage will likely be familiar, try reading it from a translation of the Bible that you do not normally use. Fresh words can often shed new light on a well-known story.

Carefully read today's lesson. As you select activities for today's session, be mindful of any time constraints that an extended Easter worship service may place on your class time.

Preparing Our Learning Space

From a magazine or your own photo collection, select one or more pictures of an infant.

Have on hand:
- ✔ several Bibles for students
- ✔ newsprint and marker or chalkboard and chalk
- ✔ paper and pencils
- ✔ optional pictures of infants

LEADING THE CLASS

(1) Introduction

Hold up the picture of the infant you have brought and ask the questions below. Or, if no picture is available, begin by asking one or two people to describe the excitement surrounding the birth of a child or grandchild. Then ask the following questions.

(1) **For most people, the birth of a child is good news. When a child is born the people who love the child have great hope for it. Why does this new, helpless life cause us to hope?**

(2) **What hopes and dreams do you have for the children in your own life?**

Move the discussion to today's scripture lesson by pointing out that the Easter story of Jesus' resurrection gives us great hope. His resurrection gives us hope that we, too, will experience new life with God after life on this earth has ended. Thus, even in the face of the death of our mortal bodies, we can be hopeful about the future. Introduce today's main question: *How does the resurrection of Jesus give us hope?*

If the class prefers a lecture format, use the Focusing on the Main Question portion to introduce today's lesson.

(2) The Easter Story

Before you read Matthew's account of the first Easter morning, you may want to point out that the Gospel accounts do differ in their details, though all tell the same basic story. The points of the story are enumerated in the first paragraph of "The Easter Story" section under Interpreting the Scripture.

Then have one or more volunteers read aloud Matthew 28:1-10. If the class enjoys dramatic reading, this scripture will come alive if you have one person read the narrator's part, another the words of the angel, and a third the words of Jesus.

Ask class members to imagine themselves in the sandals of Mary Magdalene and the other Mary. Then ask:

(1) **How was the situation you encountered at the tomb different from the one you expected to find?**

(2) **After the initial fear and shock that the situation caused, how did you feel?**

(3) **What could you begin to hope for now that you had seen the risen Lord?**

Conclude this portion of the lesson by reading the following paragraph and asking class members to comment on it in whatever way they find appropriate.

The Christians' hope is not an emotion we conjure up for ourselves. Nor is it optimism based on human possibilities and dreams. Christian hope is based on what God has done in raising Christ Jesus from the dead. The Resurrection only makes sense when it is seen in the context of the cross. On Good Friday, it appears that the enemies of God, of good, of the redemption of the world, have won a great victory. Then comes Easter, and all is reversed. What seemed like victory on Friday is now seen as defeat. What appeared to be defeat on Friday is now bursting forth in victory.

(3) The Church Beyond Death

Now ask a volunteer to read aloud 1 Thessalonians 4:13-14. Use information in the first paragraph of this section under Interpreting the Scripture to help students understand that the Thessalonians were both puzzled and troubled about the fate of believers who died before Christ returned.

Point out Paul's comment regarding grief: "so that you may not grieve as others do who have no hope" (4:13). Ask class members for their interpretation of this passage. Do they think that Paul is saying that Christians are not to grieve at all when a loved one dies, or that our grief is somehow different from the grief experienced by those who do not know Christ? The third paragraph of this section in the Interpreting the Scripture portion may help clarify uncertainty among class members as to Paul's meaning in verse 13.

Note that in verse 14, Paul categorically states that Jesus died and rose from the dead and that God will bring with Jesus those who have died believing in him. If your class members feel free to share, open the floor for doubts about eternal life. Studies show that in our scientific age, many persons have difficulty accepting the reality of Jesus' resurrection. Consequently, they do not expect to enter into eternal life themselves. If you choose to do this activity, be sure that those who question or doubt are not belittled for their views. Instead, let this be a time when God's grace may flow and strengthen those who have doubts. Affirm for the class that mature Christian faith does not come by simply agreeing to what you think others would say, but by wrestling with questions of faith and determining answers for yourself, with the help of God.

(4) The Ultimate Future

Choose a volunteer to read aloud 1 Thessalonians 4:15-18. You may also want to read 1 Corinthians 15:51-55. Here Paul uses imagery similar to that in Thessalonians to describe what will happen in the last days. As an option, distribute paper and pencils. After the reading, ask students to do a simple drawing of how they envision Paul's description. Some adults may be willing to share their graphic interpretation with the class.

Ask class members to reread silently

these words to the Thessalonians in verses 15-18. Note in verse 15 that Paul's message is "the word of the Lord," not his own opinion. Ask the group:

(1) What do the events about which Paul speaks say to you about the nature of God?

(2) What do these events say to you about God's concern for humanity?

Invite class members to close their eyes and use their senses to imagine the following scene with you. If you have a class member who has lost a loved one recently, you may want to omit this activity.

Imagine that you suddenly hear Christ calling out a loud command. What is he saying? (pause)

Listen as well to the call of the archangel. Hear God's trumpet playing loudly enough to be heard around the globe. Notice how others react to this blast. (pause)

See the Messiah descend from heaven. What does he look like? How do you and others near you react to such a vision? (pause)

Now envision persons who are dead rising from their graves to meet the Lord in the air. Is the scene one of confusion and panic, or of peace? (pause)

Finally, feel yourself being gathered into the clouds to meet with the Lord. How do you feel? Are you at peace, or terror stricken? (pause)

Imagine yourself with the God in heaven forever. What does heaven look like to you? What do you do there? Who do you see that you know? (pause)

Now direct the group to spend a few moments in silent prayer, asking God to undergird their hope in such a future.

HELPING CLASS MEMBERS ACT

Suggest that class members who know of someone in mourning make a special effort to contact that person this week. Have the students offer whatever help they can to this person. Often, just a willingness to listen and remember the life of a departed loved one is a great source of comfort. If an appropriate opportunity arises, the class members may want to remind the one who is grieving of the hope we have for eternal life as a result of the resurrection of Jesus.

Direct students to seek out an individual who is struggling with a question or problem. Suggest that they offer encouragement to this person, as well as any concrete action that may ease the other's burden.

Challenge students to read and respond to today's key verse, 1 Thessalonians 4:14. Suggest that they write in a spiritual journal what they believe Jesus' death and resurrection mean to their own lives.

PLANNING FOR NEXT SUNDAY

Next week we will begin the second unit of this quarter. Our attention will shift from Paul's letters to the Thessalonians to the book of Revelation. Unit 2, which deals with the letters to the seven churches, will begin with an examination of John's vision of the glorified Christ who commanded him to write. To prepare for this lesson, ask students to read Revelation 1:4-15.

AVAILABLE FOR SERVICE

PREVIEWING THE LESSON

Lesson Scripture: Revelation 1:4-15
Background Scripture: Revelation 1
Key Verse: Revelation 1:11

Focus of the Lesson:
John's willingness to serve God by responding to a vision to write letters to the seven churches of Asia Minor

Main Question of the Lesson:
Are we, like John, available for service?

This lesson will enable adult learners to:
(1) become aware of Christ's call to John to write down the revelation he has been given.
(2) consider their own willingness to be open to God's service.
(3) respond by committing themselves to serve God in some way.

Today's lesson may be outlined as follows:
(1) Introduction
(2) A Reminder of Who We Are
(3) A Message to Friends
(4) A Message from the End

FOCUSING ON THE MAIN QUESTION

In the Easter season we stress the joy and power of the risen Christ. A new age, a new creation has begun. Yet all around us we see signs of the old age, the familiar world in which evil gets ahead, goodness often is pushed out of the way, the gospel is ignored or persecuted, and life goes on as though nothing at all had happened on that first Easter. Why hasn't everything changed? Doubt and despair can set in and make our faith seem unrealistic or futile.

John, the writer of the Revelation to John, was in a similar situation around the end of the first century, more than a generation after that first Easter. There had been time enough for the gospel to be proclaimed to a wide area surrounding the Mediterranean Sea. Most of the converts now were Gentiles, not Jews. Though the church was still a very small fraction of the population of the Roman Empire, it was becoming known to many people, especially in the cities. That growth and awareness also meant that misunderstanding, mistrust, and disapproval were increasing. Christians faced persecution, particularly in areas of the church's greatest growth, in the Roman province of Asia, the area that is now the west coast of Turkey.

Tradition tells us that John was in exile because of this persecution. He was on the small island of Patmos, close to the coast of Turkey, but separated from the rest of the church by captivity and the Aegean Sea. Evidently, he had been a very important part of church life in that area of the province of Asia. But now, what could he do in this helpless condition? He knew that life was going to be difficult for Christians in Asia. Likely, the persecutions would continue and even increase. But here he was, cut off from their fellowship and their worship, unable to help them at all.

In this unlikely setting, a word comes to him. He is to be given a vision. But the vision is not for him alone. It is a vision for the churches from whom he is now separated. He is commanded to write what he sees and what he is told and to send that writing to the churches he has left behind. Even in his current difficult situation, God can use him. He can be helpful to the church even when he is separated from it.

There is no situation in which the call of God cannot come to us. What matters is that we are ready and willing to respond. If John had only felt sorry for himself, or helpless and useless, he could have ignored this call, or perhaps not even heard it. But he was available for God's purposes. As we study today's lesson, we will ask: *Are we, like John, available for service?*

READING THE SCRIPTURE

NRSV
Revelation 1:4-15

4 John to the seven churches that are in Asia:

Grace to you and peace from him who is and who was and who is to come, and from the seven spirits who are before his throne, 5and from Jesus Christ, the faithful witness, the firstborn of the dead, and the ruler of the kings of the earth.

To him who loves us and freed us from our sins by his blood, 6and made us to be a kingdom, priests serving his God and Father, to him be glory and dominion forever and ever. Amen.

7Look! He is coming with the
        clouds;
    every eye will see him,
  even those who pierced him;
      and on his account all the
            tribes of the earth will
            wail.
So it is to be. Amen.

NIV
Revelation 1:4-15

4John,

To the seven churches in the province of Asia:

Grace and peace to you from him who is, and who was, and who is to come, and from the seven spirits before his throne, 5and from Jesus Christ, who is the faithful witness, the firstborn from the dead, and the ruler of the kings of the earth.

To him who loves us and has freed us from our sins by his blood, 6and has made us to be a kingdom and priests to serve his God and Father—to him be glory and power for ever and ever! Amen.

7Look, he is coming with the clouds,
    and every eye will see him,
  even those who pierced him;
      and all the peoples of the earth will mourn
            because of him.
                    So shall it be! Amen.

8 "I am the Alpha and the Omega," says the Lord God, who is and who was and who is to come, the Almighty.

9 I, John, your brother who share with you in Jesus the persecution and the kingdom and the patient endurance, was on the island called Patmos because of the word of God and the testimony of Jesus. ¹⁰I was in the spirit on the Lord's day, and I heard behind me a loud voice like a trumpet ¹¹saying, "Write in a book what you see and send it to the seven churches, to Ephesus, to Smyrna, to Pergamum, to Thyatira, to Sardis, to Philadelphia, and to Laodicea."

12 Then I turned to see whose voice it was that spoke to me, and on turning I saw seven golden lampstands, ¹³and in the midst of the lampstands I saw one like the Son of Man, clothed with a long robe and with a golden sash across his chest. ¹⁴His head and his hair were white as white wool, white as snow; his eyes were like a flame of fire, ¹⁵his feet were like burnished bronze, refined as in a furnace, and his voice was like the sound of many waters.

Key
Verse

⁸"I am the Alpha and the Omega," says the Lord God, "who is, and who was, and who is to come, the Almighty."

⁹I, John, your brother and companion in the suffering and kingdom and patient endurance that are ours in Jesus, was on the island of Patmos because of the word of God and the testimony of Jesus. ¹⁰On the Lord's Day I was in the Spirit, and I heard behind me a loud voice like a trumpet, ¹¹which said: "Write on a scroll what you see and send it to the seven churches: to Ephesus, Smyrna, Pergamum, Thyatira, Sardis, Philadelphia and Laodicea."

¹²I turned around to see the voice that was speaking to me. And when I turned I saw seven golden lampstands, ¹³and among the lampstands was someone "like a son of man," dressed in a robe reaching down to his feet and with a golden sash around his chest. ¹⁴His head and hair were white like wool, as white as snow, and his eyes were like blazing fire. ¹⁵His feet were like bronze glowing in a furnace, and his voice was like the sound of rushing waters.

Key
Verse

UNDERSTANDING THE SCRIPTURE

Revelation 1:1-3. In the midst of persecution, the end of history seemed near. For those who were about to be martyred, the end of their personal history was indeed near. What was God's word to those Christians who would have to face the coming strife? John has received a vision, a revelation from God not only in words but in vivid, dreamlike images that he will have to describe when he writes what he has been shown. Verse 3 commands that the words of this vision be read aloud. The blessing is for those who read them aloud, and for those who hear them. In both cases, the real blessing is for those who keep the words, who take them to heart and live by them.

Why the stress on reading aloud? The

expectation is that these words will be read in the congregations. Partly this is the case because manuscripts were expensive, and literacy could not be assumed. But beyond these mechanical reasons, the message John has received is for the church, for the community of faith, not merely for individuals.

Members of the early church were not part of a highly individualistic culture as we are. They assumed that in baptism they had moved from being part of one kingdom—of darkness—to a new kingdom of light. They were part of a whole new society. The scripture came to them as part of this new society. It was a word to the whole community rather than to them as individuals. This is much clearer in Greek than in English because Greek grammar distinguishes between a singular and a plural "you." In all of the New Testament, the plural form is used almost exclusively. As we read the text, we must remember that it is addressed to the whole community.

Revelation 1:4-8. Verse 4 is the formal beginning of the letter from John to the seven churches of Asia. Again, Asia in this case means the province of the Roman Empire of that name, which today is western Turkey. There is a blessing from God, from seven spirits—which the readers may have understood as having a connection with the seven churches to whom John is writing—and from Jesus, who has been raised from the dead. Redemption from sin comes from his death. The first readers would have understood a reference to baptism as the sign of their being made part of a kingdom of priests. All who are part of that kingdom are committed to serving God.

After the salutation, a hymn points to the expected second coming. The letter comes from an authority far greater than this poor church member now in exile on the island of Patmos. It comes from the One who was there at the beginning and will be there at the end. Alpha and omega are the first and last letters of the Greek alphabet, used here much the way we say "from A to Z."

Revelation 1:9-11. John rehearses how he came to write this manuscript. He makes several important points. First, he is one of them, a brother in the faith. His authority is not the basis on which this book is written. Second, he is writing while in exile on Patmos, and his exile is the result of proclaiming the gospel. This could mean that he was on Patmos in order to preach the gospel, but very early

tradition says that he was there in exile as punishment for holding to the gospel. Third, his vision came to him on a Sunday, while he was caught up in worship, under the influence of the Holy Spirit. He was separated from the congregations but he still was worshiping with them. In this context the word comes to him to write down what he is about to see and hear. He is to send his book to the seven churches that are fairly close to each other near the western coast of the province of Asia. He names the churches. A modern map of Turkey labels these cities using their modern Turkish names: Efes (Ephesus—now only the ruins of the ancient city), Izmir (Smyrna—now a large, modern city), Bergama (Pergamum—a new city near the ruins of the ancient one), Akhisar (Thyatira—still a city), Sardes (Sardis—only the ruins of the ancient city), Alasehir (Philadelphia—still a city), and Laodikeia (Laodicea—only the ruins of the old city remain).

Revelation 1:12-15. The vision begins. The One who spoke is clearly both human—the Son of man—and also beyond the human. The description of this One reminds us of the vision of Daniel (see Daniel 7:9-14). John was familiar with the Scriptures of Israel, and would have known that this One is the judge at the end time, the judge of all people and all history. What is different from Daniel is that this One is here identified with Jesus of Nazareth.

Revelation 1:16-20. This daunting vision of Jesus causes John to fall on his face as if he were dead, but the Son of man calms his fears, assuring him that he has conquered death. John is ordered to write what he has seen, what is, and what will happen in the future.

INTERPRETING THE SCRIPTURE

A Reminder of Who We Are

John and the whole early church understood that Christian faith was based on common assumptions. Faith was not an individual matter, varying from person to person, but the faith of the entire church, confessed in forms similar to the Apostles' Creed. Precisely because John is writing to the church as a whole, he begins by reminding them of who they are as the church. These few verses are really a rehearsal of the total gospel. Jesus Christ, whose death freed us from sin, has been raised from the dead. He has made us a priestly kingdom to serve God. That is who we are. It is clear from the rest of this long letter that not all of the Christians were really acting as though all of this were true. But John is calling them, and us, back to the basics, back to the sense of who we are as the church, who we are called to be in our baptism. He speaks of the Second Coming, of the time of judgment that lies ahead. Whether we live out our calling or whether we ignore it makes a difference. God the creator is also the redeemer. God was in the beginning and God will be at the end. God is the one we are to serve, and no other.

A Message to Friends

Though his words would be valid in many ways for Christians of every age, John is writing specifically to seven churches that he knew. Later on he will have specific messages to each of the congregations. He writes not as a stranger, but as a friend, well acquainted with the situation in which these congregations find themselves. He speaks of himself as their brother. Ancient writers believed John was from Ephesus and was a part of the church there. The other six churches are less than a hundred miles from Ephesus, several

much closer than that. There was constant communication among churches, both by letters and by visitations. Many of the early Christians were tradespeople who moved from city to city. At this time the Roman Empire was at its height, and the roads were fairly good and safe.

A Message from the End

The Revelation to John is an excellent example of what is called apocalyptic literature. That is, it speaks of the end of history in a dramatic fashion and looks at the present difficulties as a sign that the end is near. Judgment is at hand. Persecution is expected. Those who stand fast in their faith will be exonerated. Those who turn aside will be condemned. The troubles of the present are a testing. Apocalyptic literature usually comes, therefore, in times of persecution. It has a cosmic character. Nature as well as human beings are involved. The world as a whole, not just human life, is about to end. Judaism and Christianity are faiths based upon God's actions in history. History is not going around in circles, in some endless cycle we must seek to escape. Rather, human history is in God's hands. It has a beginning, given by God who is the creator of all things. And it has a goal. History is going somewhere. This history will have an end, and a new age of God's creating will then be fully present. Both Judaism and Christianity have produced apocalyptic writings. Since Christianity is based upon Judaism and uses Judaism's Scriptures as its own, it is not surprising that in the Revelation to John there are overtones and parallels to the portions of such literature found in the Old Testament. Parts of the book of Daniel are echoed in Revelation 1:12-15.

Christians of our day usually do one of two things with the apocalyptic portions of the Scriptures. Either we say the end is not near and, therefore, such passages can be dismissed, or we take them very seriously and try to discover which prophecies have been fulfilled and where we are in the historical scheme the passage presents. Neither way is particularly helpful. These writings are not intended to be a neat outline of scheduled events in the distant future. They are visions, and as such have much in common with poetry and dreams. They have a profound meaning, but they cannot be dissected like scientific or logical prose. Because we live in a highly scientific age, we tend either to dismiss non-scientific forms as untrue or unimportant, or to take this strange form of literature as scientific data about the future. We therefore overlook the significance of what the literature is saying in its own form. The early church did not have the same scientific mind-set. It therefore could deal more readily with poetry and visions and understand that both were proper means for conveying serious theological truth in ways that spoke to the heart and to the whole person.

When we say that John received a revelation, we must be clear that we do not mean that John received new doctrines, new information that was not part of the church's faith before. He says nothing that contradicts or even goes beyond the summary of faith that we find in the Apostles' Creed. Even though that particular form of the statement of faith was developed a little after John's time, all its elements are already to be found in the New Testament literature that is earlier than John's Revelation. John stresses the meaning of the Cross and the Resurrection. He points particularly to the coming again of Jesus, as judge of the living and the dead. He picks up on the apocalyptic visions of Israel, which were already part of the Christian tradition. Why then is his vision important if it tells us nothing new?

In a sense John does tell us something new and important. He makes very clear that living as Christians in the world can be dangerous. He knows very well that the old world of sin still is strong, and to live as part of the new creation is not going to be easy. He calls on Christians to be faithful in difficult situations. He reminds us that judgment is a reality and, therefore, compromising with evil on the grounds that it is the only way to get along in this world is not a proper response for Christians. Great commonality exists between John's vision and the rest of the New Testament, although John's revelation is written in different circumstances than were the earlier parts of the New Testament, such as the letters of Paul. The Revelation to John deals with a different social situation and is written in a different form of literature. But the message is the common one.

Christians are not to settle down and be comfortable in the old world. We are to remember who we are. We are to be open to the call of God even though the reality of the new situation brought about by the death and resurrection of Jesus frequently seems very distant from the world in which we live. We are to be ready to respond to God, listening for God's call, even as John was. We are to be ready to be useful to the church and to understand ourselves as part of that whole community, the one society that is now worldwide, the "holy, catholic church" of the creed. There are no circumstances in which God may not find us useful, so we cannot assume that if we are too busy, if our lives are too complex, or if we face too many personal problems, then God cannot use us. Nor can we assume that God speaks to us or lets us understand the word of God only for our own benefit. God uses us for the sake of others, even as God used John in his difficult situation for the sake of the wider church. Faith lets us be open to such a call and available for service.

SHARING THE SCRIPTURE

PREPARING TO TEACH

Preparing Our Hearts

In the midst of exile on the island of Patmos, John was called to write a vision that was to be sent and read aloud to congregations in Asia. In his difficult circumstances, John may have thought that God had no particular use for him. After all, what can an exile do on a rocky island? John did not allow the hardship of his situation to prevent him from making himself open and available for service to God. As you prepare your lesson this week, think about what God might be calling you to do. Are there opportunities for service in addition to (or perhaps instead of) the ones in which you are currently engaged? If God were to give you a vision of service for the Kingdom, what might that vision be? Prayerfully ask God to direct your steps this week as you seek to serve in the name of the Risen One.

Preparing Our Minds

With today's lesson, we begin a two-unit study of the Revelation to John. Before you read Revelation 1, note paragraph two under "A Message from the End" in the Interpreting the Scripture portion. Recognize that we will be taking the words of this book seriously, but will not be attempting to outline the future.

If you have the *Bible Teacher Kit* (Abingdon), you may want to read the article by Keith N. Schoville on pages 71–74, entitled "Apocalyptic Literature: Mystery with Meaning," for additional information on apocalyptic literature.

Carefully read the entire lesson. If you plan to use a map, be sure you can locate the seven cities to which John is commanded to write.

Decide in advance how you will introduce information regarding the seven churches. See the activity under "A Message to Friends."

Preparing Our Learning Space

Paul is writing to specific churches that are named in Revelation 1:11. If possible, post a map to show where these churches are located. The map entitled Paul's Journey, found the *Bible Teacher Kit*, is helpful to you.

If you have access to hymnals with the Charles Wesley hymn, "Lo, He Comes with Clouds Descending," consider using this hymn either in your worship time or as an activity described below. It is found on page 718 of *The United Methodist Hymnal*.

Bring to class a Bible atlas and/or Bible dictionary this week that includes information about the seven churches to which John wrote. If you do not own such references, arrange to borrow them from a church or public library, or from the pastor. Multiple references would be especially helpful.

Have on hand:
- several Bibles for students
- newsprint and marker or chalkboard and chalk
- paper and pencils
- map
- optional hymnals
- Bible atlas and dictionary

LEADING THE CLASS

(1) Introduction

Begin today's session by asking:
(1) How do people usually go about landing a job?
(2) Have you ever had someone offer you a job "out of the blue"? If so, tell us about your experience.

Move to the scripture by pointing out that John was an exile on the island of Patmos. He was not seeking a job. In fact, he probably felt helpless and unable to offer anything. However, God sent an angel to call him to the job God had in mind for him. John was to make known to others what God would reveal to him in a vision. Note that just as people who are offered jobs may choose to turn them down, John could have said no. He did not turn God down but instead made himself available for service in the Kingdom. As we study our lesson from Revelation 1 today, we will ask: *Are we, like John, available for service?*

(2) A Reminder of Who We Are

You may want to introduce the Revelation to John by reading or retelling the first paragraph under the Interpreting the Scripture portion entitled, "A Message from the End." We will discuss more specific information from this segment later in the session.

Read Revelation 1:4-8 with great expression. Note, as discussed in the Understanding the Scripture portion, that verse 7 was originally used as a hymn in the early church. If you have access to a hymnal that includes the Charles Wesley hymn, "Lo, He Comes with Clouds Descending," read this hymn based on verse 7 to the class, or have them look at it. If possible in your setting, sing this hymn. Discuss what Revelation 1:7 means and how this hymn does—or does not—faithfully reflect the meaning and intent of the Bible verse.

Direct the class's attention to verse 6, where John reminds us who we are. Jesus has "made us to be a kingdom, priests serving his God and Father." Ask the students to discuss the following questions. Remind them that since John is writing to the churches, the questions are framed in terms of the whole church, rather than individuals.

(1) What does it mean to your church to be part of the kingdom of God?

(2) How do you see the members of your congregation (not just the ordained clergy) as priests?
(3) In what ways does your congregation serve God?

(3) A Message to Friends

Have a volunteer read aloud Revelation 1:9-11. If you have a map posted, locate the seven churches named in verse 11, which is our key verse. Note in the Understanding the Scripture portion for these verses the modern names and locations of these churches.

Plan ahead how you will handle an introduction to the seven churches. You could do the research on each one yourself and do a short lecture. However, students will learn more if they are empowered to search out the information for themselves. Perhaps a few students could read about an assigned church (see verse 11) during the week and prepare a short report for today. Ideally, you will have several resources available. Divide the class into partners or teams to use whatever you have. Instruct each group to find information about one city to help the class understand what the place was like. Provide time for the students to work. Then have each team report to the total group.

Close this part of the lesson by pointing out that John knew the churches to which he wrote. He was not writing to "occupant," but to people he knew and loved.

(4) A Message from the End

Distribute paper and pencils. Now read Revelation 1:12-15. Read the scripture again, this time asking students to either draw a description of what they are hearing or write key words and phrases that describe what John saw. Ask:

(1) John saw a vision of the glorified Christ in the midst of seven lampstands. He tries to give us a description of what he saw. Would you tend

?

to take his description literally? **Why or why not?**

You may want to refer to paragraph two under "A Message from the End" under the Interpreting the Scripture portion to make clear that these visions would not have been taken literally (in our scientific sense) by John's first hearers. They would, however, have been treated with seriousness and an attempt to understand their mystery.

Review paragraph three and following from the "A Message from the End" portion. Be sure to point out that John's revelation added no new doctrine or information. However, his revelation was important because it alerted Christians to the difficulties of following Christ in a sinful world.

Post these sentence stems on newsprint or a chalkboard so that class members may copy and complete them on paper you distribute:

- If I were to see a vision of the risen Christ I would . . .
- I believe we could (or could not) be living in the end times because . . .
- I believe that God has called me to serve in the Kingdom by . . .
- I have answered that call by saying . . .

Some volunteers may wish to discuss their ideas. Conclude the discussion with a prayer, asking God to keep each person sensitive to God's call and willing to say "I am available, Lord."

HELPING CLASS MEMBERS ACT

Remind the class that John wrote to the churches as one who shared their pain, for he too suffered persecution for his faith. Suggest that class members seek out someone who is experiencing a problem that they too have experienced. For example, a cancer survivor is often able to minister effectively to one who has just been diagnosed with the disease. Similarly, parents whose children have caused heartache may be able to share coping strategies with another parent. Tell the class members to take at least one step this week to assist the person who is suffering.

Encourage class members to think about any personal revelations they have received. These may come in the form of "aha" experiences, or through dreams, visions, or a word from someone else that speaks to their need. Have them think about any revelations and, if they have not already done so, take steps to act upon the word they have received.

Challenge class members to choose one way each day that they will serve God in the coming week.

PLANNING FOR NEXT SUNDAY

Our next lesson, based on Revelation 2:8-17, will focus on the letters to the churches at Smyrna and Pergamum. These churches were called to be faithful, even unto death. Ask class members to read the scripture passage and consider how they would respond if persecuted for their faith in Christ.

CALLED TO BE FAITHFUL

PREVIEWING THE LESSON

Lesson Scripture: Revelation 2:8-17
Background Scripture: Revelation 2:8-17
Key Verse: Revelation 2:10*b*

Focus of the Lesson:
the risen Christ's promise that those who remain faithful to him even unto death
will receive new life

Main Question of the Lesson:
Are we willing to be faithful at all costs?

This lesson will enable adult learners to:
(1) study the letters to the churches at Smyrna and Pergamum.
(2) confront their own willingness to be faithful at all costs.
(3) respond by taking a faithful action in a difficult situation.

Today's lesson may be outlined as follows:
(1) Introduction
(2) The Price of Legitimacy
(3) Fear the True Death
(4) There Is More Than One Temptation
(5) The Secret Life of Christians

FOCUSING ON THE MAIN QUESTION

Churches in various times and places live in very different circumstances. Some are poor, others are rich. Some are respected by the surrounding society, others are persecuted. Each setting brings its own particular opportunities and temptations. We may think that it is far easier to be faithful under some circumstances than under others. The churches we are dealing with in today's lesson are in a difficult setting. Yet the call to be faithful is not suspended until times are easier.

The message to each church makes it clear that Christ knows the particular circumstances they must face. On this basis Christ also outlines the form that faithfulness must take. Christians in any society have some commonalities. They must demonstrate love and forgiveness. They must proclaim the gospel in word and deed. Wherever possible, they must gather together in worship and make evident the meaning of the gospel in corporate as well as individual ways. Beyond these commonalities, however, the Christian life will take different shapes in different circumstances. When there is persecution, faithfulness means not denying Christ. When there is no persecution, faithfulness may mean showing how the demands of the gospel differ from the surrounding culture, or discovering effective ways to proclaim the gospel.

The Christians in Smyrna and Pergamum did face persecution. They could be imprisoned or even killed because they confessed Christ. Faithfulness for them certainly did entail maintaining their confession as Christians. Imagine the difficulty if you were the only Christian in a family and the rest could not understand why you were willing to risk your life for mere words or why you worshiped one particular deity when there were so many to choose from. For a first generation Christian, the pressures from both society at large and the family were great.

When there is a risk of persecution, then the meaning of the Cross and the Resurrection for the Christian become absolutely central. Jesus faced death when he could have avoided it if only he had not been so committed to his calling, to living out his baptism. He was also raised from the dead. Similarly, the Christian is called to live out the meaning of baptism: dying and rising with Christ. Persecution makes the choice of faithfulness very clear. As we study this week's lesson, we will ask: *Are we willing to be faithful at all costs?*

READING THE SCRIPTURE

NRSV
Revelation 2:8-17

8 "And to the angel of the church in Smyrna write: These are the words of the first and the last, who was dead and came to life:

9 "I know your affliction and your poverty, even though you are rich. I know the slander on the part of those who say that they are Jews and are not, but are a synagogue of Satan. 10Do not fear what you are about to suffer. Beware, the devil is about to throw some of you into prison so that you may be tested, and for ten days you will have affliction. **Be faithful until death, and I will give you the crown of life.** 11Let anyone who has an ear listen to what the Spirit is saying to the churches. Whoever conquers will not be harmed by the second death.

12 "And to the angel of the church in Pergamum write: These are the words of him who has the sharp two-edged sword:

13 "I know where you are living, where

NIV
Revelation 2:8-17

8"To the angel of the church in Smyrna write:

These are the words of him who is the First and the Last, who died and came to life again. 9I know your afflictions and your poverty—yet you are rich! I know the slander of those who say they are Jews and are not, but are a synagogue of Satan. 10Do not be afraid of what you are about to suffer. I tell you, the devil will put some of you in prison to test you, and you will suffer persecution for ten days. Be faithful, even to the point of death, and I will give you the crown of life.

11He who has an ear, let him hear what the Spirit says to the churches. He who overcomes will not be hurt at all by the second death.

12"To the angel of the church in Pergamum write: These are the words of him who has the sharp, double-edged sword. 13I know where you live—where Satan has

Key
Verse

Key
Vers

Satan's throne is. Yet you are holding fast to my name, and you did not deny your faith in me even in the days of Antipas my witness, my faithful one, who was killed among you, where Satan lives. [14]But I have a few things against you: you have some there who hold to the teaching of Balaam, who taught Balak to put a stumbling block before the people of Israel, so that they would eat food sacrificed to idols and practice fornication. [15]So you also have some who hold to the teaching of the Nicolaitans. [16]Repent then. If not, I will come to you soon and make war against them with the sword of my mouth. [17]Let anyone who has an ear listen to what the Spirit is saying to the churches. To everyone who conquers I will give some of the hidden manna, and I will give a white stone, and on the white stone is written a new name that no one knows except the one who receives it.

his throne. Yet you remain true to my name. You did not renounce your faith in me, even in the days of Antipas, my faithful witness, who was put to death in your city—where Satan lives.

[14]Nevertheless, I have a few things against you: You have people there who hold to the teaching of Balaam, who taught Balak to entice the Israelites to sin by eating food sacrificed to idols and by committing sexual immorality. [15]Likewise you also have those who hold to the teaching of the Nicolaitans. [16]Repent therefore! Otherwise, I will soon come to you and will fight against them with the sword of my mouth.

[17]He who has an ear, let him hear what the Spirit says to the churches. To him who overcomes, I will give some of the hidden manna. I will also give him a white stone with a new name written on it, known only to him who receives it.

UNDERSTANDING THE SCRIPTURE

Revelation 2:8-10. Christ begins the message to the angel of the church at Smyrna with the reminder of why he is able to speak so authoritatively on the subject of faithfulness unto death. He was killed and resurrected. It is as the Risen One that he speaks to the church. He knows what they are going through.

An important seaport and a commercial center, the city of Smyrna was wealthy. Many of its inhabitants were very affluent. In contrast, the Christians were generally poor; they were not destitute but did not share in the great wealth of the city. The risen Christ tells them they are rich because they are faithful to the gospel, in spite of the fact that they are materially poor. In this, as in the persecution, they are following the pattern of the life of their Lord.

The church in Smyrna was suffering.

There was a sizable Jewish community in Smyrna, and there was conflict between the Jews and the Christians. To understand the conflict, we must take a look at the political situation. At this time—around the end of the first century—the Roman Empire permitted the practice of local religions in conquered areas. But the empire prohibited the establishment of new religions, perhaps because they could be covers for subversive groups that sought to overthrow the power of Rome. An imperial cult that glorified the emperor was practiced throughout the empire as a sign of loyalty. Other religious forms could readily be practiced in addition—as long as they were not new ones. The Christians, therefore, were in an increasingly difficult position. For the first several decades of the church's life, the empire viewed the church as a part of Judaism, with good reason. But by the end of the first century, most of the new converts were Gentiles, not Jews. Differentiation increased between Judaism and Christianity. Was Christianity a new religion, and therefore illegal? Moreover, Jews historically had been exempted from emperor worship in the Roman Empire, since the rulers knew that failure to worship the emperor did not necessarily imply disloyalty on the Jews' part, but rather was the result of their monotheism. Christians wished their religion to be considered legal, and they also wished to have the same exemption from emperor worship as did the Jews. Christians perceived themselves as the true Israel and, therefore, believed these rights belonged to them. Jewish persons resented the implied Christian view that they were disinherited from God's promises. Christianity could no longer be contained within the parties of Judaism and so was labeled a new religion. Imprisonment and even death could follow for the Christians.

Revelation 2:11. In a previous lesson on Thessalonians we saw that some of the earliest Christians did not expect any of their number to die before the return of Christ. Paul dealt with that issue. By the end of the first century, no one held that view. Most of the original Christians had died by this time, and everyone understood that physical death was still a part of human life. The promise of resurrection, however, remained for the household of faith. The "second death" is that which can come after physical death, that which occurs when there is no transition into eternal life.

Revelation 2:12-15. Pergamum was the capital of the whole province of Asia. As such, it was a major area for the imperial cult. In addition, it was home to many religious practices and was filled with famous shrines and altars. The reference to "Satan's throne" may well refer to the seat of imperial government and cult, the political power that carried out the persecu-

tion. Evidently one person, Antipas, had already been killed, but the church remained faithful.

Church members yielded to other temptations, however. Some became lax about practices that made it easier to slide back into idolatry. Eating meat sacrificed to idols is one example, especially since that might imply going to the sacrificial ceremony. "Practicing fornication" in this context probably refers to such possible idolatry rather than to any sexual act. The account of Balaam is found in Numbers 22:1–24:25; 31:8, 16. By the time the Revelation to John was written, Balaam had become shorthand for someone who led others to disobey the law of Israel. The group referred to as the Nicolaitans were evidently the ones accused of leading other Christians to be lax or disobedient, particularly in regard to idolatrous practices.

Revelation 2:16-17. Those who have been weak in their obedience to Christ are not cut off as disciples. Rather, Christ calls them to repentance. If they do not repent, then Christ will make war upon them, but his war will be different than the kind of war the Roman Empire wages. Christ's weapon will be the sword of his mouth. The word of God is powerful. It creates and it destroys. It is more powerful than any empire.

There are several strange references in the latter half of verse 17. Christians who persevere will be rewarded in this life, as well as in the life to come. They will receive hidden manna—bread of heaven given to God's people in the wilderness. They will also receive a white stone, possibly a reference to the stone given to someone on trial when a verdict was reached. Christians in judgment will receive a white stone, which means freedom; a black stone could mean death. The new name they will receive may refer to the new life that faith also gives them. The manna and the name are hidden or secret, which implies that these gifts are not public. The world around the Christians will not know or understand the rewards of faithfulness, but these gifts will indeed be real to Christians.

INTERPRETING THE SCRIPTURE

The Price of Legitimacy

The church in Smyrna had difficulties. It did not have many resources, yet it was located in the heart of a city that prided itself on its wealth. The church faced persecution from the Roman Empire because it was not clearly a legal religious group. The empire might suspect Christians of disloyalty, since they would not worship at the statue of the emperor. Furthermore, Christians withdrew from many of the civil ceremonies because they involved idolatry. Christians called someone other than the emperor "Lord." Their behavior would be akin to an American citizen refusing to pledge allegiance to the flag, or pledging allegiance to some unknown ruler and then refusing to take part in any of the national holidays. Today such behavior might seem strange but not particularly threatening. However, when governments face possible external threats, they then deem loyalty oaths and patriotic displays as very important. That was the case with the Roman Empire. It was strong, but it kept its army ready to fight external enemies and to quell trouble from conquered nationalities within the empire, and it squelched mutinies within the army. Such problems within the empire had happened in recent years.

Many of the Christians were unhappy with this situation. They wanted to worship God as good Christians and also be viewed as good citizens who were loyal to the empire. It was this search for legitimacy that put them into conflict with the large Jewish community in the city. There were good theological reasons for Christians to consider themselves heirs of God's promises to Israel. Whether it would have been possible to make such a claim without thereby disinheriting the Jews is difficult to determine in retrospect. But this attempt to say that Christians are the true Jews and the Jews who are not Christians are false Jews obviously created trouble. Nor was the trouble limited to that immediate time. This tension was the theological beginning of a great deal of misunderstanding and conflict between the two religious communities that continues in some quarters even today.

This attempt to disenfranchise the Jews did not lead to peace for the Christians. As the Christians tried to convince the Roman authorities that they, the Christians, were really the ones who should be exempted from the imperial cult, the Jews reported to the authorities that the Christians were not Jews at all, but a new religion.

The basic question that needs to be asked is whether or not the church should have sought to be legitimate in the eyes of the empire. John of Patmos does not directly address that question, though the tenor of his whole writing is that the empire itself is not legitimate in the eyes of God. In that case, it might have seemed unnecessary or even foolish for the Christians to try and win the favor of the empire. Attempts to escape persecution often fail and involve an unacceptable compromise of the faith. Since the Christians did worship a Lord other than Caesar, conflicting demands would have made loyalty to both an impossibility. The words of Jesus in another context are true here as well: we cannot serve two masters (Matthew 6:24). The attempt to find legitimacy in the Roman Empire may well have involved lessening the loyalty to Christ.

Fear the True Death

In order to avoid persecution, Christians had made attempts to prove their legitimacy in Smyrna. John reminds them that there are things worse than physical death, which is the only kind that the persecutors can inflict. The Christians should fear the second death, the death that is possible after physical death, the death that cuts one off from eternal life, from sharing in the resurrection life of Christ. If Christians try to avoid the first death, inflicted by the empire, and do so by means that imply faithlessness to Christ, then they will be subject to the second death that only God can inflict. John seems to be concerned that some of the Christians in Smyrna may be fearing the wrong thing, and so he calls them back to obedience. Christians must be faithful unto death.

There Is More Than One Temptation

The situation in Pergamum was different than the one in Smyrna. The community in Pergamum seemed prepared to face persecution. One of its members, Antipas, had already been killed. John was not afraid that the community of faith in Pergamum would deny Christ, if called upon to do so by the government officials. That was the major idolatry against which they appeared to be able to stand strong. But there were other idolatries to tempt them, such as eating meat sacrificed to idols. For us, that may seem a strange issue. Why not go to a regular meat market to buy meat, rather than to a temple where the meat had been sacrificed to idols? In a city that had so many temples, with so many sacrifices being offered, probably most of the meat markets were attached to such temples. Kosher meat from a Jewish butcher would have been exempt from such sacrifice, but we do not know if there was a sizable Jewish community in Pergamum, or if the relations between Christians and Jews there would have made the purchase of kosher meat by Christians feasible. John is obviously concerned about the constant interaction between Christians and the common idolatrous practices in Pergamum. Many Christians there may have assumed that if they did not deny Christ in some outright fashion, then they could go on with their lives, making little compromises that did not matter very much. John has a different opinion. Furthermore, it appears that an organized group, the Nicolaitans, is urging such compromised behavior. John wants the Nicolaitans out of the congregation.

The Secret Life of Christians

Even the congregation's faithfulness in the big issues will not let them escape from judgment on the daily, smaller ones. Christ calls them to repentance. They have a choice: either they can oppose the society, or they can oppose Christ. If they oppose the society and its practices, they may lose their lives, but they will win the battle. If they compromise with the society, they may keep their lives for a while, but they will find themselves in a war with Christ. That battle they will lose.

If they are faithful in the small as well as the big ways now, they will find support that the world cannot see or understand. They will receive the hidden manna. This may be a reference to the Lord's Supper in which Christians are united with the risen Christ and strengthened by him. They will receive a white stone, a pledge of new life and the freedom from condemnation that it signifies. They will receive a new name, a new beginning even now. With these powerful gifts, Christians can be empowered to make the difficult choices that often put them in opposition to the world around them. They can remain faithful to Christ and risk persecution, knowing that, in the words of Jesus, "those who want to save their life will lose it, and those who lose their life for Jesus' sake will find it" (Matthew 16:25).

SHARING THE SCRIPTURE

PREPARING TO TEACH

Preparing Our Hearts

The letters to the churches at Smyrna and Pergamum that we read this week in Revelation 2:8-17 call us to be faithful in the face of persecution and repent of our willingness to follow false teachers and cling to false gods. As you prepare for this session, think about your own faithfulness. Most of us, as we have noted in prior lessons, are not concerned about persecution. We may, however, fall prey to smooth talkers who convince us—or perhaps just give us permission to do something we want to do anyway—that we do not have to walk the straight and narrow. Not so, says the risen Christ. We are called to "be faithful until death" and promised a "crown of life" if we are true to Christ. In what ways do you see yourself as being faithful to Christ? In what ways have you failed to be faithful?

Preparing Our Minds

Read today's lesson as well as Revelation 2:8-17. Note that the content of today's session is two letters written by John in accordance with the directions of the vision of the risen Christ he has seen. The first letter, found in verses 8-11, is written to the church in Smyrna. The second, addressed to the congregation at Pergamum, appears in verses 12-17. Be sure you understand the different situations in these two churches.

If the group did not do the research activity in class last week about the cities to which the letters were addressed, be prepared to give that information this week. See especially the Understanding the Scripture portion for details concerning these cities.

Be ready to locate Smyrna and Pergamum on a map.

Preparing Our Learning Space

If possible, post or duplicate maps to show the location of Smyrna and Pergamum. The map of Paul's Third Journey, found on page 153 of the *Bible Teacher Kit,* includes these two cities.

Have on hand:
- several Bibles for students
- newsprint and marker or chalkboard and chalk
- paper and pencils
- map

LEADING THE CLASS

(1) Introduction

Open today's class by dividing the students into teams and giving each team paper and pencils. Have each team choose a recorder. If the class is small, you may want to do this activity with the entire group instead of teams. Tell the class that we are beginning a study of the contents of five of the seven letters that John was instructed to write to the churches. Before we look at the letters to Smyrna and Pergamum today, we are going to consider what kind of letter the risen Christ would write to our own congregation. The letters we will read in the Revelation to John have both commendations and criticisms. Ask the teams to consider both what Christ would commend the congregation for and the criticisms that he would level against it. Caution them against using specific names of groups or individuals. To say, for example, that there often seems to be tension here is quite different from saying that Mrs. Smith's vicious gossip keeps members in an uproar. Depending upon the time you have available, either direct the teams to just list the commendations and criticisms or actually write the letter. Be sure to allow time for the teams to share their ideas with the whole class. Collect these papers. We will look at them again in Lesson 9 and possibly revise them then.

As an alternative, use the Focusing on the Main Question portion to introduce the lesson.

Conclude the introduction by indicating that the churches we will study today faced persecution and the temptation to follow idolatrous and immoral practices. State today's main question: *Are we willing to be faithful at all costs?*

(2) The Price of Legitimacy

Read aloud Revelation 2:8-10. Use information from the Understanding the Scripture section to help class members comprehend the church's situation. If the class did not talk about Smyrna last week, or locate it on a map, this would be an appropriate time to do so.

Focus on the explanation in the Interpreting the Scripture section under "The Price of Legitimacy." Be sure that the class knows that Christians were originally considered a party within Judaism, just as the Pharisees or Essenes and other groups were. Note that it was their "search for legitimacy that put them into conflict with the large Jewish community in the city." Also point out that "this tension was the theological beginning for a great deal of misunderstanding and conflict between the two religious communities that continues in some quarters even today."

Point out that the legal situation Christians in Smyrna faced was vastly different from our own. While the United States provides for both freedom of religion and separation of church and state, Christians in John's day had neither of these legal protections. Yet, comments in the letter to the Christians of Smyrna indicate that they indeed are holding fast to their faith despite forewarning about imprisonment for their faith (2:10). In contrast, many

Christians in the United States rarely attend worship, give little or nothing to God through the church, and engage in moral and ethical practices that sharply differ from those espoused by Jesus, especially as proclaimed in the Sermon on the Mount. Invite class members to debate this statement:

When the church suffers persecution at the hands of the state, Christians are more likely to hold fast to their faith. In other words, Christians respond more faithfully when discipleship is costly than when it is cheap.

R

(3) Fear the True Death

Read verse 11, again using information from the Understanding the Scripture portion and Interpreting the Scripture section if necessary to further explain the situation of the church at Smyrna. Then ask:

(1) If you were being persecuted, how would the knowledge that there is a threat greater than physical death make you feel?

?

(2) Do you honestly think that you would be willing to die for your faith? Explain the reason for your answer.

(4) There Is More Than One Temptation

Tell the class that our focus will now shift to the letter to the church in Pergamum. Point out that although Smyrna and Pergamum are geographically close, the situation in these two congregations is somewhat different. Use information from the Understanding the Scripture and Interpreting the Scripture portions to provide background about the situation in Pergamum. Also, locate this city on a map.

Now have a volunteer read aloud Revelation 2:12-15. Note that the church in Pergamum had faced persecution, and at least one member, Antipas, had already died for the faith. Yet, despite the risen Christ's commendation of their faithfulness, verses 14 and 15 list behaviors that are unacceptable to Christ. Use information from the Understanding the Scripture portion to help students comprehend the nature of these problems.

Although eating meat offered to idols is not a temptation for modern Christians, we do face numerous temptations each day. Have the class brainstorm responses to the questions below. Record the answers on newsprint or a chalkboard. You make want to make two columns, one labeled Temptations, and the other Ways to Resist.

[?] **(1) What temptations exist on a daily basis within our society? (column 1)**

(2) What can we say or do to resist this temptation? (column 2)

Conclude this part of the lesson by asking:

[?] **(1) What difference can our faithful witness make to persons who succumb to temptations, often because they do not know their is another way to live?**

(5) The Secret Life of Christians

Choose a volunteer to read aloud Revelation 2:16-17. Use the Understanding the Scripture portion and the second paragraph under "The Secret Life of Christians" in the Interpreting the Scripture section to help the class understand the meaning of these verses.

Then read aloud the first paragraph under the "Secret Life of Christians." Provide some quiet time for students to review their own lives during the last week. What attitudes or actions—especially ones that are accepted by the larger society—does Christ call them to repent of? Some students may prefer to write their thoughts, so distribute paper and pencils to them.

Close this section by reading again the key verse, Revelation 2:10*b*: "Be faithful until death, and I will give you the crown of life."

HELPING CLASS MEMBERS ACT

Suggest that students write a letter to a friend who is having some difficulty. Commend the person for whatever faith and courage that he or she has displayed during this trying time.

Remind the group that the willingness of Christians to act according to norms that differ from society will not set them up for persecution unto death, but may lead to ridicule about one's beliefs and behaviors. Challenge class members to take a stand this week, even on a small matter such as not laughing at an offensive joke, that they know may cause others to taunt them.

Encourage class members to pray for persons around the world who are suffering for their Christian faith. Perhaps the whole class can agree to pray for persons in a specific location.

PLANNING FOR NEXT SUNDAY

To prepare for next Sunday's lesson on the letter to the church at Thyatira, ask class members to read Revelation 2:18-29. This church had tolerated a false prophet and therefore was called to hold to sound teaching. Ask students to be thinking about false teachings they may encounter.

HOLD TO SOUND TEACHING!

PREVIEWING THE LESSON

Lesson Scripture: Revelation 2:18-29
Background Scripture: Revelation 2:18-29
Key Verse: Revelation 2:23

Focus of the Lesson:
the risen Christ's admonition to reject false teachers and hold fast to sound teaching

Main Question of the Lesson:
How do we hold on to sound teaching at all costs?

This lesson will enable adult learners to:
(1) examine the letter to the church at Thyatira.
(2) consider the steadfastness of their own faith.
(3) respond by standing firm against social pressure.

Today's lesson may be outlined as follows:
(1) Introduction
(2) A Word from the True Lord
(3) The Economic Cause of Idolatry
(4) Holding Fast
(5) The Promised Future

FOCUSING ON THE MAIN QUESTION

In comparison to the great cities on or near the coast—Ephesus, Smyrna, and Pergamum—Thyatira was a small town much farther inland. It was on a plain, without the kinds of high places that were useful for defense or for the ancient religious cults. It was important as a cross-roads for trade, and it had its crafts—especially in metal-working and fabrics. Lydia, who was a companion of Paul, was "from the city of Thyatira and a dealer in purple cloth" (Acts 16:14). Christ praises the church for their love, as well as for their growth in the faith and in endurance. The church at Thyatira does not appear to be in danger of persecution. In spite of the generous praise that begins this letter, however, all is not well.

Unlike the larger cities where a person could be somewhat anonymous, a small city like Thyatira was organized around the craft guilds. In order to earn a living by means of the crafts, one really had to belong to a guild. The guilds were not only trade groups, but religious organizations with their own favorite gods and religious feasts that included sacrifices. How could one be a part of the economic life of such a place and never eat meat offered to idols? For some in the church, the economic and social limitations demanded by the church were simply too great. In contrast to the church's expectations, a prophetess announced that God permits such guild activities, and perhaps even greater accommodation to the social customs of the town than the church had declared. John calls this woman "Jezebel," much as he called the leader of the similar group in Pergamum "Balaam." In both cases, these are references to Old Testament persons who were accused of trying to lead the people of Israel into idolatry. John says her prophecies have come from Satan and not from God. By urging others to commit idolatry she has led them into

unfaithfulness to God, which is probably what adultery refers to here. She had been warned before, and had not repented. She and those who follow her will be condemned. But the Christians in Thyatira who remain faithful, difficult as it is under these circumstances, will receive their reward. They will be raised up to great authority when judgment comes, and will be with Christ himself.

The letter to the church at Thyatira is a call to faithfulness, a warning that living by the standards of society is not acceptable. Even at the cost of economic hardship, Christians are not to be drawn into idolatrous practices. They must remain faithful to the teachings they had received from the beginning, the truth held by all the churches, not to this new, false teaching that "Jezebel" has put forth. This letter challenges us to ask: *How do we hold on to sound teaching at all costs?*

APRIL 20

READING THE SCRIPTURE

NRSV
Revelation 2:18-29

18 "And to the angel of the church in Thyatira write: These are the words of the Son of God, who has eyes like a flame of fire, and whose feet are like burnished bronze:

19 "I know your works—your love, faith, service, and patient endurance. I know that your last works are greater than the first. [20]But I have this against you: you tolerate that woman Jezebel, who calls herself a prophet and is teaching and beguiling my servants to practice fornication and to eat food sacrificed to idols. [21]I gave her time to repent, but she refuses to repent of her fornication. [22]Beware, I am throwing her on a bed, and those who commit adultery with her I am throwing into great distress, unless they repent of her doings;

NIV
Revelation 2:18-29

[18]"To the angel of the church in Thyatira write:

These are the words of the Son of God, whose eyes are like blazing fire and whose feet are like burnished bronze. [19]I know your deeds, your love and faith, your service and perseverance, and that you are now doing more than you did at first.

[20]Nevertheless, I have this against you: You tolerate that woman Jezebel, who calls herself a prophetess. By her teaching she misleads my servants into sexual immorality and the eating of food sacrificed to idols. [21]I have given her time to repent of her immorality, but she is unwilling. [22]So I will cast her on a bed of suffering, and I will make those who commit adultery with her suffer intensely,

Key
Verse

²³and I will strike her children dead. And all the churches will know that I am the one who searches minds and hearts, and I will give to each of you as your works deserve. ²⁴But to the rest of you in Thyatira, who do not hold this teaching, who have not learned what some call 'the deep things of Satan,' to you I say, I do not lay on you any other burden; ²⁵only hold fast to what you have until I come. ²⁶To everyone who conquers and continues to do my works to the end,

I will give authority over the
    nations;
²⁷to rule them with an iron rod,
  as when clay pots are
    shattered—
²⁸even as I also received authority from my Father. To the one who conquers I will also give the morning star. ²⁹Let anyone who has an ear listen to what the Spirit is saying to the churches.

unless they repent of her ways. ²³I will strike her children dead. Then all the churches will know that I am he who searches hearts and minds, and I will repay each of you according to your deeds. ²⁴Now I say to the rest of you in Thyatira, to you who do not hold to her teaching and have not learned Satan's so-called deep secrets (I will not impose any other burden on you): ²⁵Only hold on to what you have until I come.

²⁶To him who overcomes and does my will to the end, I will give authority over the nations—

²⁷'He will rule them with an iron scepter;
  he will dash them to pieces like
    pottery'—
just as I have received authority from my Father. ²⁸I will also give him the morning star. ²⁹He who has an ear, let him hear what the Spirit says to the churches.

K
Ve

UNDERSTANDING THE SCRIPTURE

Revelation 2:18-19. The letter begins with the awesome vision of the One who is speaking. He is the Son of God, a phrase used only once in Revelation. His eyes of flame are able to see through everything, even to see what some may wish to keep hidden. The feet of burnished bronze are a very interesting note in a letter to a city known for its metalworking. In spite of the frightening appearance, the first words to this church are words of praise. They are a loving community and live out their love in actions. In this regard they have grown stronger as the years have gone by.

Revelation 2:20-23. Though the church could be praised for its loving actions, it did not measure up because it was tolerating false teaching. One of the members of the congregation—whom John calls Jezebel—was corrupting the beliefs of others. In fact, a sizable portion of the congregation seemed to be following her teachings and rejecting what had been taught to them earlier by the church. The original Jezebel, the daughter of a foreign king, was the wife of Ahab, king of the Northern Kingdom of Israel in the ninth century before Christ. A Baal worshiper, Jezebel brought priests and idols into Israel, and her new husband joined her in worshiping them. Elijah was the prophet God raised up to oppose this idolatry within Israel. (For the whole story of this conflict, see 1 Kings 16:29–22:40.) The use of the name Jezebel in this letter to Thyatira is very appropriate, beyond any difference in gender between the leader of this group and the similar group in Pergamum. Jezebel was brought into the royal family of Israel because it was assumed the marriage between the king of Israel and the daughter of the king of Sidon would be of economic benefit to Israel.

John is making a parallel with that action and the prophetess's desire to weaken the strictures against idolatry so that the Christians could gain economically in Thyatira. She has been leading her followers astray even as Jezebel led the king astray. He was willing to follow because it enhanced the economic position of his country. The king had allowed an outside influence—the non-Israelite Jezebel—rather than God and God's prophet Elijah—to determine what his obedience to God would be. Now some members of the church in Thyatira are allowing the society around it, through this new Jezebel, rather than God and God's prophets in the form of the recognized leadership of the wider church of Christ, to determine what obedience to Christ is.

The false prophetess had been warned before, but had not repented. This letter gives the warning that Christ is about to punish not only her but also all those who have followed her. They have committed adultery and fornication by practicing idolatry. They have feasted on the comfortable couches of the idolatrous banquets. Now they will be thrown on couches of pain and anguish. Such punishment will be a lesson to all the churches that the Lord of the church will not give up that position to anyone else. Christ can see the true motivations of everyone, and Christians will be dealt with on that basis.

Revelation 2:24-25. There are some in the church in Thyatira who have not followed this Jezebel, and have not agreed that these new teachings are acceptable. They are to remain faithful, to keep on the way they are going. The future punishment will not be leveled against the whole congregation but only against those who follow the false way. Perhaps this faithful group was fairly small and not able to expel or limit the unfaithful ones. At least the words of Christ are that the faithful ones do not need to do anything beyond what they are doing. That will be enough. The phrase "the deep things of Satan" probably is John's portrayal of what she claims are the deep things of God. She professes to be a prophetess because she claims to have insight into God's revelation. Clearly, the source of her revelation is not God.

Revelation 2:26-29. The reward of Christ will come to those who continue to do his works and not the works of another leader. The reward is based on the words of Psalm 2:7-9. Revelation 2:18 uses the image "the Son of God" from Psalm 2:7 for Christ. In Revelation 2:28, Christ makes it clear that the title "Son of God" applies to him. He has been given this authority already. Those who follow him and continue in his ways will finally share in this authority with him. Christ will also give "the morning star." As the Revelation to John closes, the whole series of visions to John include these words: "It is I, Jesus, who sent my angel to you with this testimony for the churches. I am the root and the descendant of David, the bright morning star" (22:16). The gift of the morning star is the gift of the risen and reigning Christ himself.

The letter to Thyatira ends with words of warning that have parallels in all seven letters. In this letter to Thyatira the main issue is to whom the Christians at Thyatira are listening. Are they hearing Jezebel or the Spirit?

INTERPRETING THE SCRIPTURE

A Word from the True Lord

The letters to the churches typically begin with a description of the one who is speaking, thereby relating a specific character or work of Christ to the issue to be addressed in that church. In the case of Thyatira, the description of Christ is of one who is indeed the Lord, ready to judge, ready to punish. He is the judge from whom nothing can be hidden.

The letter begins with words of comfort for the faithful in Thyatira. They have done what is very difficult for many churches to do: they have increased in their love and service. So often churches begin with good intentions. They start with great love for each other. Then, as the years go by, love fades. Service becomes difficult. Patience grows limited. However, in Revelation 2:19, Christ says that in the church at Thyatira their most recent days have been better than their first days. Clearly, they are going in the right direction.

The Economic Cause of Idolatry

The tone of the letter changes in verse 20, when Christ states: "I have this against you: you tolerate that woman Jezebel." The prophetess Jezebel wanted to form alliances with the neighbors of Thyatira who could be of economic advantage. She wanted Christians to be able to join fully in all the economic activity—including guilds that had their own gods—without having their Christian faith limit their participation. In her desire to gain economic benefits, the Jezebel of Thyatira was much like the ancient Jezebel of Sidon. Married to the king of Israel, Ahab, Jezebel was motivated by greed to engage in treachery to gain Naboth's vineyard for her husband (see 1 Kings 21). The Jezebel in Thyatira acts with economic motivation similar to that of her namesake in ancient Israel.

Many people in Thyatira are following this prophetess Jezebel in her sinful, though economically profitable, ways. Neither she nor her followers will repent. Christ makes dire prediction for Jezebel and promises to give her followers what they deserve.

Holding Fast

The letter to the church in Thyatira makes very clear that there is an important connection between what we think and what we do. The Thyatiran Jezebel had a different view of who Christ was and, therefore, how Christians were to behave in the world. At least, there was the assumption that Christ and the world as it was could get along together quite well. This is not the message that the church had understood Christ to be giving to his disciples. Settling down happily in the unredeemed world is hardly the message of the cross. Nor is it the joyful response of the Resurrection.

In this letter, Christ calls upon the faithful in Thyatira to hold fast to what they have. What do they have? They have their love for each other and for Christ. They have their patience and their sense of service. But these are outgrowths of the good teachings that they had received and on which they had based their behavior. Now there were these new teachings. The expectation is that these new teachings will lead to behaviors that are other than love, service, and patience.

Two issues are difficult to balance. The teachings of the church always have to be related to the specific situation of a local setting. We can see this happening in the letters to the seven churches. At the same time, the teachings of the church cannot be an accommodation to an unredeemed world. This is a difficult line to draw. The Thyatiran Jezebel may have assumed she was simply relating Christianity to the local culture, though she did so on the basis of a new revelation. The words of Christ make it clear that the line had indeed been crossed. New revelations are not the authority for the church. Only Christ is.

Underlining the belief that Christians ought not to settle down comfortably in the world is the word of how long the Christians are to hold fast to the teachings they had received: until Christ comes again. This world, unredeemed, can never be the happy home of Christians. When Christ returns, this world will change. The Jezebels and Balaams are forgetting that. But the redeemed cannot be content in an unredeemed world. After listing all those in the past who had been faithful, the Epistle to the Hebrews puts it this way:

> All of these died in faith without having received the promises, but from a distance they saw and greeted them. They confessed that they were strangers and foreigners on the earth, for people who speak in this way make it clear that they are seeking a homeland. If they had been thinking of the land that they had left behind, they would have had opportunity to return. But as it is, they desire a better country, that is, a heavenly one. Therefore God is not ashamed to be called their God; indeed, he has prepared a city for them (Hebrews 11:13-16).

The Promised Future

For the faithful, a great future is promised. Whereas now they are at a disadvantage in regard to the world around them, at least in economic and social mat-

ters, in the future they will be given authority over nations. The unfaithful have no such promise. In fact, the unfaithful are probably presumed to be part of the nations that will be judged and, perhaps, shattered.

As noted in the other letters, the task of Christians is to conquer. The only way to conquer is to be faithful to the gospel, even though that seems like losing out in the present. Jezebel made the other choice, opting for conquering in the present. But that has no promise for the future.

Yet, a future is surely promised. Jesus is the morning star, a phrase used for the expected ruler from the house of David. But why the morning star? The morning star is the sign of the dawn of a new day. It fits well into expectations of the beginning of history's culmination. The kingdom of David had its glory days, though it clearly was not perfect. But promised for the future was a new kingdom, of the line of David, where justice and peace would be perfect. This was the kingdom of God. The birth of Jesus, signaled by a star, was the birth of the one who was indeed the morning star, the sign of a new day. His resurrection was assurance that the day had dawned. But still it was only a sign. The full dawn had not yet come. Condemned are those who decide the night is going to last a long time, so they might as well make their home there. However, blessed are those who hold fast to the teachings of Christ, for they will live in the light of the new dawn.

SHARING THE SCRIPTURE

PREPARING TO TEACH

Preparing Our Hearts

If Christ were to search your heart today, as he promises he will do in Revelation 2:23, what would he find there? Is your heart focused on the things of God, willing at all costs to stand up and witness for God? Or is your heart divided, shifting between the demands of Christianity and the expectations of those around you? How do you know when you have "crossed the line," perhaps caving in to pressure of the society around you? How does your faith bring your back to the ways of God? You may want to record your thoughts in your spiritual journal.

Preparing Our Minds

Read Revelation 2:18-29, along with the lesson. Carefully consider how this message, which at first glance may seem totally unrelated to modern life in the United States, can affect the members of your own church. Consider the social and economic pressures that confront your class members.

Be prepared to point out Thyatira on a map. Also, if the group has not yet done so, provide some background information on the city of Thyatira.

Preparing Our Learning Space

Have on hand:
- several Bibles for students
- newsprint and marker or chalkboard and chalk
- paper and pencils
- map showing Thyatira

LEADING THE CLASS

(1) Introduction

Begin the session by reading and discussing this scenario:

[R] Your state is debating the possibility of legalizing casino gambling. As a United Methodist (or member of another church), your denomination opposes gambling on moral and ethical grounds. Yet, you live in a town that would directly benefit from a casino operation. Some politicians are promising that your taxes would even be lowered. A member of your church is spearheading a drive to support a casino. Where do you stand? Why?

Move the discussion to today's scripture by pointing out that, like the casino supporter in this church, a prophetess named Jezebel taught that Christians could both keep their faith and engage in the economic advantages of guilds, even though these organizations often had their own gods and participated in idolatrous feasts. (See paragraph two of Focusing on the Main Question for a fuller description.) Her teachings were followed by some church members and rejected by others who held fast to the teachings of Christ. Despite the economic advantages of Jezebel's way, Christ's disciples could not follow her. Instead, they were to remain steadfast. The letter to the church at Thyatira that we will study from Revelation 2:18-29 prompts us to ask this main question: *How do we hold on to sound teaching at all costs?*

If you prefer, you may want to begin by using the information in the Focusing on the Main Question portion.

(2) A Word from the True Lord

If you did not introduce Thyatira in an earlier session, this would be an appropriate time to give some background and locate the city on a map.

Choose a volunteer to read aloud Revelation 2:18-19. Point out that the Son of God is seen as one who is ready to judge, prepared to punish. The vision is fearsome, but the first words are ones of praise and assurance. The church at Thyatira was commended for its works, love, *service*, *faith*, and *patient endurance*. If possible, divide the class into five teams. Assign each team one of the areas of commendation. Distribute paper and pencils and have the participants list three examples of how your own church would be commended in the category (example: *works, love*) to which their team has been assigned. Provide time for the teams to create their lists and report back to the whole class. If you prefer, have everyone work together instead of in teams. List their ideas on newsprint. This activity can be very affirming to the group, as long as everyone offers only positive commendations.

Be sure to note, as stated in the second paragraph under "A Word from the True Lord" in the Interpreting the Scripture portion, that the church in Thyatira had actually improved in these areas as the years went by.

(3) The Economic Cause of Idolatry

If you did not do so earlier in the session, lift up paragraph two of the Focusing on the Main Question section so that students may understand the interrelationship between the craft guilds and religious practices of the people. Once that background has been clarified, read aloud Revelation 2:20-23. Note the shift in tone of the letter. No longer is Christ commending the people. Instead, he is warning them about their tolerance of the unrepentant Jezebel and her false teachings. You may also need to note that the reference to fornication and adultery are metaphorical, not literal.

Read this sentence from the Interpreting the Scripture portion aloud: "(Jezebel) wanted Christians to be able to join fully in all the economic activity—including guilds that had their own gods—without having their Christian faith limit their participation." Then ask the class:

[?] (1) **How do you as a Christian handle work-related situations that put you in compromised—or potentially compromised—positions in light of your faith?**

(2) **On what kinds of issues do you draw the line between what is acceptable behavior for you as a Christian and behavior that you cannot engage in because of your faith?**

(3) **What does the fact that so many people are willing to divide their lives into "business behavior" and "church behavior" say about the role that we have allowed money and its attendant status and power to play in our lives?**

(4) Holding Fast

Turn the class's attention to Revelation 2:24-25. Note that the risen Christ did not condemn the whole church at Thyatira because some members do not hold Jezebel's teaching. Ask:

(1) **Do you think the persons whom** [?] **Christ commended belonged to the all-important "network" of the guild in Thyatira? Explain your answer.**

(2) **Perhaps the persons in Thyatira did have some option regarding the guilds, though they clearly would have been economically disadvantaged had they not participated fully. What options do we have in dealing with the business world and its ways while still earning a living?**

Provide a few moments of silent time for individuals to consider the questions below. Some may want to write their answers, so provide them with paper and pencils. You may want to write these questions on newsprint or a chalkboard.

(1) **When tension develops between your** [?] **job and your faith, which one do you give priority to? Why?**

(2) **If you feel a tension between your Christian faith and the expected moral and ethical behaviors of your job, what might God be calling you to do at this moment?**

(3) **How might your action affect you and your family?**

(4) **How might such a change strengthen or weaken your relationship with Christ?**

(5) **What steps can you take within the next month to be employed where God wants you to be, if you are not there now?**

(5) The Promised Future

Have a student read aloud Revelation 2:26-29. Point out that there will be a role reversal. Those who have remained firm in their commitment to Christ, the ones who have been economically disadvantaged by their decision to follow Christ, will be given the morning star. Use information in the final paragraph of "The Promised Future" in the Interpreting the Scripture portion to help class members understand the meaning behind "morning star."

Note that Christ speaks on the basis of authority given by the Father. Verses 26-27 are based on Psalm 2:8-9, which you may want to read aloud. The important point in Revelation is that the conquerors—those who have remained steadfast in the midst of moral and ethical sin—will be given authority. These verses speak of the future, but the promise is sure.

Point out that our ability to withstand pressure—to be a conqueror—is enhanced by prior situations in which we remained steadfast in our commitment despite outside pressure to do otherwise. Invite class members to share stories of situations (particularly those that had economic consequences) that challenged their faith and how they handled these challenges. Suggest that they "file" such stories in their memory banks so that they can draw on them for strength in the future.

Close with a prayer, asking God to allow the light of the new dawn to shine in the lives of your students.

HELPING CLASS MEMBERS ACT

Remind the group that Jesus commended the church in Thyatira for their "love, faith, service, and patient endurance" (Revelation 2:19). Encourage class members to identify someone they feel deserves commendation for his or her Christian witness, perhaps in the face of hardship or crisis. Suggest that they offer a word of praise to the persons they identify.

Challenge class members to be alert this week for situations related to their jobs that they may find questionable in light of their commitment to Christ. Suggest that they consider appropriate steps to give a steadfast witness against moral or ethical behaviors that they as Christians cannot support.

Point out that Jezebel influenced some Christians—but certainly not every one of them—negatively. Ask students to consider the relative ease or difficulty with which someone might influence them. If they find that they are easily swayed by other people, challenge them to pray for God's guidance so that they might be led by the one who wants the best for their lives.

PLANNING FOR NEXT SUNDAY

We will conclude our study of the letters to the seven churches next week by looking at the message of the risen Christ to the churches in Philadelphia and Laodicea. To prepare for this lesson, ask class members to read Revelation 3:7-22, paying particular attention to verses 7-10 and 15-21.

GOOD NEWS, BAD NEWS

PREVIEWING THE LESSON

Lesson Scripture: Revelation 3:7-10, 15-21
Background Scripture: Revelation 3:7-22
Key Verses: Revelation 3:8, 15

Focus of the Lesson:
the commendation or admonishment that results from the risen Christ's knowledge of the works of the church

Main Question of the Lesson:
What is God's word for the churches at Philadelphia and Laodicea and for our own church as well?

This lesson will enable adult learners to:
(1) study the risen Christ's words to the congregations of Philadelphia and Laodicea.
(2) consider how God views their own congregation.
(3) respond by acting upon the good news or bad news God is giving to them.

Today's lesson may be outlined as follows:
(1) Introduction
(2) Who Is in Charge of God's House?
(3) Pillars in the Temple
(4) A Different Message
(5) The Problem of Security
(6) There Is Still Time

FOCUSING ON THE MAIN QUESTION

As we have seen in some of the earlier letters to the churches, God's word to a specific church varies according to the situation and needs of that church. In today's lesson we read of two churches, not too far from each other geographically, but facing very different situations. The church in Philadelphia knew it was quite weak. It had conflicts with the Jewish community in the city. In fact, the Christians there might have felt that it was useless to continue such an unequal battle. They need to hear the encouraging word that the Lord is with them, and that is sufficient. Their victory is assured as long as they remain steadfast.

On the other hand, in the church at Laodicea the Christians evidently were not being persecuted. Instead, they seemed to be participating in the prosperity of the city that was based on several industries: a naturally black woolen cloth; a medicinal salve for the eyes; and banking. The church in Laodicea felt quite self-satisfied. It had no conflict with the society around it. The words of Christ to this church are not for encouragement but rather to oppose its self-satisfaction. In fact, each of the items for which the city could take pride, Jesus claims are an illusion for the church. It is not rich, well-clothed, and endowed with the vision of healthy eyes. Rather, it is poor, naked, and blind. Furthermore, its poverty, nakedness, and blindness cannot be cured by anything produced by Laodicea. Only by turning to Christ can they receive the true riches, the white robes, and the healing ointment for their eyes. What the city offers is of no use to them.

Christ accuses the church in Laodicea of being neither cold nor hot, but rather lukewarm and unfit to drink. This assessment refers to the state of their faith. For them, evidently, the gospel has no contrast at all with the surrounding culture. Therefore Christ said he would spit them out.

If Laodicea had read for itself the message to Philadelphia, or Philadelphia the message to Laodicea, neither would have received the word really meant for it. Both could have remained mired in their problems—Laodicea continuing self-satisfied; Philadelphia becoming even more discouraged. It is quite possible to choose to dwell on scriptures that bring us comfort when what we really need is a critical rebuke, or to choose to hear only words of condemnation when what Christ is really saying to us is a word of grace and comfort. Prayerfully, with the guidance of the Holy Spirit, particularly as given through the witness of the whole church, we are able to discern what our situation is in the eyes of God. Only then are we able to hear the word that is meant for us. As we study today's lesson, we ask: *What is God's word for the churches at Philadelphia and Laodicea and for our own church as well?*

READING THE SCRIPTURE

NRSV
Revelation 3:7-10

7 And to the angel of the church in Philadelphia write:
> These are the words of the holy
> one, the true one,
> who has the key of David,
> who opens and no one will
> shut,
> who shuts and no one
> opens:

8 "I know your works. Look, I have set before you an open door, which no one is able to shut. I know that you have but little power, and yet you have kept my word and have not denied my name. 9I will make those of the synagogue of

NIV
Revelation 3:7-10

7"To the angel of the church in Philadelphia write:

These are the words of him who is holy and true, who holds the key of David. What he opens no one can shut, and what he shuts no one can open. 8I know your deeds. See, I have placed before you an open door that no one can shut. I know that you have little strength, yet you have kept my word and have not denied my name. 9I will make those who are of the synagogue of Satan, who claim to be Jews though they are not, but are liars—I will make them come and fall down at your feet and acknowledge that I have loved you. 10Since you have kept my

Satan who say that they are Jews and are not, but are lying—I will make them come and bow down before your feet, and they will learn that I have loved you. ¹⁰Because you have kept my word of patient endurance, I will keep you from the hour of trial that is coming on the whole world to test the inhabitants of the earth.

command to endure patiently, I will also keep you from the hour of trial that is going to come upon the whole world to test those who live on the earth.

NRSV
Revelation 3:15-21

15 "I know your works; you are neither cold nor hot. I wish that you were either cold or hot. ¹⁶So, because you are lukewarm, and neither cold nor hot, I am about to spit you out of my mouth. ¹⁷For you say, 'I am rich, I have prospered, and I need nothing.' You do not realize that you are wretched, pitiable, poor, blind, and naked. ¹⁸Therefore I counsel you to buy from me gold refined by fire so that you may be rich; and white robes to clothe you and to keep the shame of your nakedness from being seen; and salve to anoint your eyes so that you may see. ¹⁹I reprove and discipline those whom I love. Be earnest, therefore, and repent. ²⁰Listen! I am standing at the door, knocking; if you hear my voice and open the door, I will come in to you and eat with you, and you with me. ²¹To the one who conquers I will give a place with me on my throne, just as I myself conquered and sat down with my Father on his throne.

NIV
Revelation 3:15-21

¹⁵I know your deeds, that you are neither cold nor hot. I wish you were either one or the other! ¹⁶So, because you are lukewarm—neither hot nor cold—I am about to spit you out of my mouth. ¹⁷You say, 'I am rich; I have acquired wealth and do not need a thing.' But you do not realize that you are wretched, pitiful, poor, blind and naked. ¹⁸I counsel you to buy from me gold refined in the fire, so you can become rich; and white clothes to wear, so you can cover your shameful nakedness; and salve to put on your eyes, so you can see.

¹⁹Those whom I love I rebuke and discipline. So be earnest, and repent. ²⁰Here I am! I stand at the door and knock. If anyone hears my voice and opens the door, I will come in and eat with him, and he with me.

²¹To him who overcomes, I will give the right to sit with me on my throne, just as I overcame and sat down with my Father on his throne.

Key
Verse

UNDERSTANDING THE SCRIPTURE

Revelation 3:7-10. The One who speaks identifies himself to the church in Philadelphia by applying to himself words from the prophet Isaiah. In their original context they applied to a new public official who would replace a corrupt one in the house of Israel. Speaking for God, the prophet said: "I will place on his shoulder the key of the house of David; he shall open, and no one shall shut; he shall shut, and no one shall open" (Isaiah 22:22). This new officer shall have full authority in the house of David. What would these words mean to the church in Philadelphia? Much of their conflict was with the Jewish community there, as was the case with the church at Smyrna. Both Jews and Christians claimed to be the heirs of the promise to David. The question arises: Who controls the admission to that people? Jesus claims that he himself does. The church in Philadelphia is weak and powerless, but if the door to the people of God is controlled by Jesus, then they need not be afraid. In fact, Jesus promises that the Jews will eventually see that the Christians truly are God's people. Furthermore, in the persecution that soon will envelop the whole world—evidently persecution by the Roman Empire—the church need not rely on its own strength, for Jesus will keep the congregation safe.

Revelation 3:11-13. These words are a further assurance to the Christians that they are indeed the people of God. If they remain faithful, even in the face of the persecution that may lie ahead, then they will be "a pillar in the temple of God." The Temple in Jerusalem lay in ruins. The pagan temples dominated the city of Philadelphia. But the true temple of God would include these Christians in Philadelphia. The Christians would bear three names: the name of God, the name of the new Jerusalem, and the new name of Christ. All of these names relate to the basic question being raised in Philadelphia: Who are truly God's people?

Revelation 3:14. We are now introduced to the church in Laodicea. This city was situated on a hill, near Colossae. Directly across the valley from Laodicea was the famous city of Hierapolis, known for its hot springs. People journeyed there from all over in order to bathe in the healing waters. As we can see from Paul's letter to the Colossians, some Christians in that area denied the goodness of material creation. That letter refers to the church in Laodicea as having some of the same problems as the church in Colossae (see Colossians 2:1-4; 4:13-16). Some of this erroneous teaching about the material world may have crept into the church in Laodicea, which would explain the identification of Christ as "the origin of God's creation" in Revelation 3:14.

Revelation 3:15-18. In contrast to Colossae, which was known for its cool water,

Laodicea had no good water of its own. Its water came from the hot springs across the valley from Hierapolis. The water in the Hierapolis hot springs was famous for its healing powers, but by the time it reached Laodicea it was lukewarm and terrible for drinking. When the risen Christ says that the church in Laodicea is like that water, it is an insult that would be readily understood by people throughout the area.

The image of a church that thinks of itself as beautifully dressed in its famous black wool, its vision clear because of the good medical care available to it, wealthy and therefore in need of nothing, pictured instead as naked, poverty-stricken, and blind is striking indeed. This letter calls the Laodiceans to realize their situation and turn to Christ, who is the only one who can give them what they need.

Revelation 3:19-21. These words about Jesus standing and knocking are some of the most famous words in the entire Revelation to John. Jesus is often portrayed as waiting at the individual human heart until the door is opened for him to enter. Here, however, his words are clearly addressed to the whole church in Laodicea. The early believers could not have heard these words without thinking of the sacrament of the Lord's Supper. For the early church, there was a strong connection between the Lord's Day and the Lord's Table. The Lord's Day was Sunday, in honor of the Resurrection. At the Lord's Table, in some indefinable way, the church met with the risen Lord, even as those first disciples had met him on the road to Emmaus that first Easter night (Luke 24:13-35). For the church, these words would imply that Jesus had not been with them at their celebrations of the Lord's Supper, and would not be present until they felt the need of that which he offered them.

The letter to Laodicea concludes in the same way as the other letters, with a promise that those who remain faithful, who conquer the temptation of unfaithfulness or falling by the wayside because of the difficulties faith presents, will join Christ on his throne. The parallel between the life of Christ and the way the disciple is to follow is made clear. Christ has conquered these same temptations and difficulties. He was faithful to the end. There-

fore, he joined his Father on the throne and promises that those disciples who continue in the way will join him as well.

Revelation 3:22: The church thinks it can see and hear but in reality is blind and deaf to the word of God.

INTERPRETING THE SCRIPTURE

Who Is in Charge of God's House?

The conflict between the Jews and the Christians for the first several generations was caused by conflicting claims to be God's people. Neither community was able to accept the other without denying itself. At the same time, as we saw in the letter to the church in Smyrna (see Revelation 2:8-11), the political situation regarding legitimacy of religious groups in the Roman Empire added to the problem. Who had the authority to determine who was and who was not a part of God's people? The letter to the church at Philadelphia begins with a quotation from Isaiah (22:22) that prophesied the end of one person's administration of the king's household and the beginning of the administration of a new person who will carry out the office more faithfully. In this context the prophesy is now used to refer to the choosing of the Christ to be over the household of God. The person in charge of the household—the chamberlain—was not the king, but was the person directly under the king. In the parallel presented here, Christ is the new chamberlain appointed by God to rule the household of God's people. If he is in charge, then the church need have no fear of the Jews in Philadelphia. Christ's lordship is hidden at the present, and therefore the Jews can say that the Christians have no part in God's people. But the time will come, says Christ, when his lordship will be made visible, along with Christ's love for the

church. The Jews will have to acknowledge these things. The little community of the church need not be afraid in the coming wide persecution, for Christ is Lord, and he will protect them. Protection here does not necessarily mean keeping them from suffering but rather giving them the strength to endure and remain faithful.

Pillars in the Temple

So often we think of the church as a building, though we know the church is really the community of the faithful, regardless of what building they worship in. Here the metaphor is reversed: it is the building central to worship, the temple, that will be made up of people. The church in Philadelphia will be a pillar in God's temple. This resembles the words in 1 Peter, where the Christians are told to let themselves be living stones, built up into a spiritual building, with Christ, the chosen cornerstone, as the foundation (1 Peter 2:4-6). If the Christians of Philadelphia are a pillar in the temple, then they will never have to worry about being told they are not part of God's people. Furthermore, this new temple will be part of the new holy city of Jerusalem. As we will see in the last of these lessons, the new Jerusalem will not have a physical temple. The Christians in Philadelphia are therefore being prepared for such a time by themselves being part of this temple that is not a building.

One's name is a very important part of a person's identity. Early Christians understood that when they were baptized and anointed with oil, they were being sealed or signed with the name of Christ, which means "the anointed one." Now they are told that if they are faithful and come through the tribulation as conquerors, they will be signed by Christ himself with the name of God, the name of the new city of God, and the new name of Christ. All of this means that they will indeed be part of this redeemed people, inheriting the promises of the eternal kingdom. Surely this is good news!

A Different Message

Now the scene shifts to the church in Laodicea. This congregation needs to hear a true and faithful witness, because they evidently are hearing a different message. Christ is not simply a human being who has lived a very good or even perfect life. He is the One through whom all things were created. He came to redeem a creation that had been created through him. We often try to divide the work of the Trinitarian God in such a fashion that the Father is the creator and the Son is the redeemer. But that does not accord with Scripture. We read here that Christ is the one through whom all things were created. We read the same thing in the prologue of the Gospel of John: "He was in the beginning with God. All things came into being through him, and without him not one thing came into being" (John 1:2-3). And in the Pauline letter to the neighboring city of Colossae we read, "He is the image of the invisible God, the firstborn of all creation; for in him all things in heaven and on earth were created" (Colossians 1:15-16). The Trinity is involved in creation as well as in redemption.

The Problem of Security

Some Christians in poor countries, where their churches have almost no budgets, clergy have almost no salary, and there may not even be a building, say to Christians visiting them from well-to-do congregations in the United States, "It must be difficult to be a Christian in your country!" That often strikes the visitors as a very strange comment, since they were thinking how difficult it would be to be a church without all of the accoutrements we are used to! The church in Laodicea was quite sure that it was a very solid church, able to take care of itself. But the word of Christ to that church showed that all the things that they held most dear were nonessentials. What they lacked was absolutely essential—dependence on Christ and not on themselves. A poor church, especially one that has opposition from the wider society, can make no such mistake. Martin Luther knew this. In his famous hymn, "A Mighty Fortress Is Our God," we read these words from the beginnings of verses 2 and 3 as they appear in *The United Methodist Hymnal* number 110:

> Did we in our own strength confide,
> our striving would be losing,
> were not the right man on our side,
> the man of God's own choosing. . . .
>
> And though this world, with devils filled,
> should threaten to undo us,
> we will not fear, for God hath willed
> his truth to triumph through us.

The church in Laodicea had not yet learned this lesson. It trusted in its own strength and was therefore in great danger. When tribulation came, its source of strength would be gone. What is also clear is that the great gifts of the society around it would be no help at all. In fact, they were precisely what kept the church from finding its strength in the gifts only Christ could give.

There Is Still Time

If the church in Laodicea hears the word of Christ and repents, there is still time for it to place its trust in Christ. Then it will be prepared for the difficulties to come. Christ is ready to come into their midst, to be present at their suppers. Christ loves the church, and wants to be with them.

Those who conquer will be with Christ. Yet, in this life they can expect further persecution. During his ministry, Jesus said to his disciples, "Servants are not greater than their master, nor are messengers greater than the one who sent them" (John 13:16). The disciples of Christ are his servants and his messengers. If Christ suffered persecution and yet was faithful, why should servants expect to do less? But the promise is that, even as Christ conquered and is now on the throne of God, so disciples also who conquer, remaining faithful to the end, will also share in Christ's reign in the eternal kingdom.

SHARING THE SCRIPTURE

PREPARING TO TEACH

Preparing Our Hearts

In today's lesson, we will see that the risen Christ has both good news and bad news for the churches. To the church in Philadelphia, where members are feeling weak and inadequate, Christ sends a good word of encouragement. To the church in Laodicea, which is "neither cold nor hot," the risen Christ sends a word of judgment: He will spit them out. Very possibly Christ has both good news and bad news for most of us. We may be doing well in some areas but in need of real growth in others. As you prepare to teach, listen carefully for the word Christ has for you. Which works of yours would bring commendation? Which would bring condemnation? Pray that God may empower you to be a more faithful servant.

Preparing Our Minds

Today read the letters to Philadelphia and Laodicea, found in Revelation 3:7-22. Our lesson focuses on selected verses from these letters, but we have tried to provide you with sufficient background material to understand the situations in these two churches. Read the lesson thoroughly.

If you have not previously introduced the cities of Philadelphia and Laodicea, plan to give a brief background and locate them on a map.

Review the introductory activity in Lesson 7. Pull together ideas from the lists and letters written for that activity, especially the ideas that appear repeatedly. We will use them for the introductory activity this week.

Preparing Our Learning Space

Have available a map showing Philadelphia and Laodicea.

If possible, have a picture of Christ standing at the door and knocking. Your church may have a copy of the familiar "Heart's Door" by Sallman.

Have on hand:
- ✔ several Bibles for students
- ✔ newsprint and marker or chalkboard and chalk
- ✔ paper and pencils
- ✔ map

LEADING THE CLASS

(1) Introduction

If you did the introductory activity in Lesson 7, consider this one as a follow-up to it. Begin by reviewing the main ideas expressed in the lists or letters the class completed in Lesson 7. If possible, write the list or main points of the letters on newsprint. Then ask:

?

(1) **Now that we have had a chance to study the behaviors and attitudes that the risen Christ commends and condemns, what points do we need to add, subtract, or modify?**

(2) **Christ says in Revelation 3:8 and again in verse 15: "I know your works." If Christ were to make this statement to our congregation, would we consider that good news or bad news?**

(3) **If we believe it is bad news, on what grounds is it negative?**

(4) **What changes do we need to make?**

As an alternative, use the Focusing on the Main Question portion to introduce the lesson.

Conclude the introduction by indicating that the churches we will study today confront conflict and temptation. The risen Christ has a word for these churches: He knows their works. That word can be heard as both good news and bad news, depending upon the nature of their works. Read today's main question: *What is God's word for the churches at Philadelphia and Laodicea and for our own church as well?*

(2) Who Is in Charge of God's House?

If you have not previously introduced Philadelphia, this would be an appropriate time to tell the class something about the city and to locate it on a map.

Choose a volunteer to read aloud Revelation 3:7-10. Use the Understanding the Scripture portion for these verses to help the class comprehend the significance of the quote from Isaiah in verse 7.

Also use the information in this section of the Interpreting the Scripture section, noting that the situation the church in Philadelphia faced is similar to the one we discussed in Lesson 7 on Smyrna.

Point out that the people of Philadelphia "have not denied [Jesus'] name" (3:8).

Because of their steadfastness, the risen Christ has a word of good news: They will be kept "from the hour of trial that is coming on the whole world" (3:10). Ask the class members these questions.

(1) **What examples can you give of persons whose faith was sorely tested, perhaps due to a crisis or serious illness, but who remained faithful to Christ?**

?

(2) **How does Christ transform times of greatest weakness into times of greatest spiritual strength?**

(3) Pillars in the Temple

This section, which includes verses 11-13 of Revelation 3, is from our background scripture. If you have time, you may find it helpful to read or retell this information so that students will have a fuller understanding of the letter to Philadelphia. Note especially the importance of the new name that God will give to those who conquer and become pillars in the temple.

(4) A Different Message

Make the transition to the letter to the church at Laodicea by reading Revelation 3:14. Present any material you have, including a map, to help the class understand the situation in Laodicea.

Use the information in the Understanding the Scripture portion for verse 14 to prepare the class for the allusion to hot and cold water that will appear in verse 16.

(5) The Problem of Security

Now read Revelation 3:15-18. Ask:

(1) **In what ways might the church at Laodicea be similar to a typical church in the United States?**

?

After hearing the class's response, be sure to emphasize that the members thought they could take care of themselves. They had said, according to 3:17, "I am rich, I have prospered, and I need nothing." They were unaware of their wretched condition. Then ask:

? **(2) How do such feelings of self-sufficiency affect our fervor for the gospel message?**

(3) Would you agree that most congregations in the United States are "neither cold nor hot"? If so, what do you think needs to happen for the church to exhibit the red-hot zeal that Christ expects of his followers?

(6) There Is Still Time

Have a volunteer read aloud the concluding verses from Revelation 3:19-21. Point out that the risen Christ has proclaimed a word of judgment, but he has not foreclosed on this congregation. There is still time to repent.

If you have a picture of Christ knocking at the door, display it as you do this closing activity. If not, refer to it; most adults have seen this familiar artwork. Reread verse 20, and then ask the class to meditate on these questions. Read each one and allow a few moments for reflection before reading the next one.

R   If this is the door to our church, what kind of response will the risen Christ receive from us? Do we open the door and joyously welcome him, or do we turn him away? (pause)

HELPING CLASS MEMBERS ACT

Challenge class members to examine their own attitudes toward material wealth, especially if prosperity prompts them to feel self-sufficient, as was the case in Laodicea. Ask the students to consider the possibility that God may regard them as spiritually impoverished, despite their riches. Suggest that they pray about the need to reorder their priorities so that they are no longer lukewarm Christians.

Have each class member identify a person who feels weak and overwhelmed, like the members of the church in Philadelphia. Suggest that the students contact that individual this week and offer a word of affirmation and encouragement.

As a way of making the congregation's presence felt more strongly in the community, encourage class members to seek out opportunities to serve groups that do the kind of work that Jesus would approve of, though not necessarily within the context of the church itself. For example, some members may be willing to volunteer as nursing home visitors, or Meals on Wheels drivers, or Big Brothers or Sisters. Urge them to find places to serve.

PLANNING FOR NEXT SUNDAY

Next week we will begin a new unit, also based on the Revelation to John, entitled "A Message of Hope." Ask class members to prepare for the first lesson, "Who Is Worthy?" by reading Revelation 5:1-10. If time permits, encourage them to read the background scripture, found in chapters 4 and 5. This lesson concerns John's vision of the victorious Christ, the Lamb of God, who is worthy to open the seals of the scroll.

WHO IS WORTHY?

PREVIEWING THE LESSON

Lesson Scripture: Revelation 5:1-10
Background Scripture: Revelation 4–5
Key Verse: Revelation 5:9

Focus of the Lesson:
the worthiness of Christ alone to redeem all persons by his blood

Main Question of the Lesson:
Who is worthy to open the scroll and break its seals?

This lesson will enable adult learners to:
(1) recognize the worthiness of Christ to redeem all persons by his blood.
(2) experience first the bitter disappointment and then the joyous gratitude John must have felt.
(3) respond by joining in worship with others.

Today's lesson may be outlined as follows:
(1) Introduction
(2) A Change of Scene
(3) Is It Hopeless?
(4) The Lamb That Was Slain
(5) The One Who Is Worthy
(6) God and the Lamb

FOCUSING ON THE MAIN QUESTION

The first several chapters of the Revelation of John, though they do contain some visionary characteristics, are mainly concerned with the messages to the seven churches. In this sense, they are like many of the prophetic books of the Old Testament. The prophet receives a word from the Lord to deliver to a part or the whole of Israel. As we move into chapter 4, however, the setting and the content of the book changes. No longer is the writing mainly a word to be received, albeit in a visionary setting. Now it is the vision itself that is central. In fact, from the beginning of chapter 4 until the close of the last chapter, the different visions begin with words like: "Then I saw," or "after that I looked," or "I heard." Gone is the command that was constant in the first three chapters: "Write these words."

With this change in character comes a dramatic change in content. No longer is the major issue the life of the churches in Asia Minor. Now the scene is heaven, God's throne, the heavenly host gathered there in praise. What matters is the purposes and plans of God. This is the context within which those small churches in Asia Minor are called to live their lives faithfully. In the same way that it is instructive for us to read the earlier letters to the Asian churches, it will also be important for us to understand the coming sections of this book. We may at first be discouraged because they are so strange, but we will find them powerful portions of scripture when we ponder their meaning.

Even though the scene and tone change here, we need to read the remainder of the book through the eyes of the struggling churches in Asia Minor to whom the book was written. The major point of the whole book of Revelation is this: God is the true ruler of the whole world because God is its creator. No Roman emperor can make such a claim. God has no equal among the rulers of the earth. God's purposes, not those of other rulers, are the ones that will be carried out. This truth is recognized in heaven. The final stage of God's purposes has now begun, and we need to know what is recorded in a scroll sealed with seven seals. The question in heaven—and for us—is this: *Who is worthy to open the scroll and break its seals?* Since Christ has conquered, he is therefore worthy. The opening of the scroll begins the final fulfillment, leading ultimately, as we shall see in later lessons, to the new heaven and the new earth.

READING THE SCRIPTURE

NRSV
Revelation 5:1-10

1 Then I saw in the right hand of the one seated on the throne a scroll written on the inside and on the back, sealed with seven seals; 2and I saw a mighty angel proclaiming with a loud voice, "Who is worthy to open the scroll and break its seals?" 3And no one in heaven or on earth or under the earth was able to open the scroll or to look into it. 4And I began to weep bitterly because no one was found worthy to open the scroll or to look into it. 5Then one of the elders said to me, "Do not weep. See, the Lion of the tribe of Judah, the Root of David, has conquered, so that he can open the scroll and its seven seals."

6 Then I saw between the throne and the four living creatures and among the elders a Lamb standing as if it had been slaughtered, having seven horns and seven eyes, which are the seven spirits of God sent out into all the earth. 7He went and took the

NIV
Revelation 5:1-10

1 Then I saw in the right hand of him who sat on the throne a scroll with writing on both sides and sealed with seven seals. 2And I saw a mighty angel proclaiming in a loud voice, "Who is worthy to break the seals and open the scroll?" 3But no one in heaven or on earth or under the earth could open the scroll or even look inside it. 4I wept and wept because no one was found who was worthy to open the scroll or look inside. 5Then one of the elders said to me, "Do not weep! See, the Lion of the tribe of Judah, the Root of David, has triumphed. He is able to open the scroll and its seven seals."

6Then I saw a Lamb, looking as if it had been slain, standing in the center of the throne, encircled by the four living creatures and the elders. He had seven horns and seven eyes, which are the seven spirits of God sent out into all the earth. 7He came scroll from the right hand of the one who was seated on the throne. [8]When he had taken the scroll, the four living creatures and the twenty-four elders fell before the Lamb, each holding a harp and golden bowls full of incense, which are the prayers of the saints. [9]They sing a new song:

Key
Verse

> "You are worthy to take the
>   scroll
>   and to open its seals,
> for you were slaughtered and by
>   your blood you ransomed
>   for God
> saints from every tribe and
>   language and people and
>   nation;
> [10] you have made them to be a
>   kingdom and priests
>   serving our God,
> and they will reign on earth."

and took the scroll from the right hand of him who sat on the throne. [8]And when he had taken it, the four living creatures and the twenty-four elders fell down before the Lamb. Each one had a harp and they were holding golden bowls full of incense, which are the prayers of the saints. [9]And they sang a new song:

K
Ve

> "You are worthy to take the scroll
>   and to open its seals,
> because you were slain,
>   and with your blood you purchased
>   men for God
>   from every tribe and language
>   and people and nation.
>
> [10]You have made them to be a kingdom and
>   priests to serve our God,
>   and they will reign on the earth."

UNDERSTANDING THE SCRIPTURE

Revelation 4:1-11. The first verse shows that the scene has changed. It also announces that the reason for John's vision is to see "what must take place after this" (4:1). It is a vision of the future, not simply of what is to unfold in the next few days or years, but of the ultimate future that will be when all human history reaches its goal. John tells us that he was at once "in the spirit" (4:2). This phrase probably implies an ecstatic experience. The same phrase was used earlier to introduce the vision that led to the seven letters (1:10).

The imagery for what follows is influenced by other ecstatic visions in the prophetic literature of Israel, especially of Isaiah and Ezekiel (see Isaiah 6:1-4 and Ezekiel 1:1-18). A whole host surrounds the throne of God: twenty-four elders, who may represent the tribes of Israel and the apostles or may be angelic hosts. Four

strange creatures with features of animals and eyes all over them are evidently keeping watch over all things. God is not directly seen, but described in terms of great light and color, thunder and lightening. The heavenly host sing praise to God, using words familiar to us from our own hymns. The final hymn declares God to be worthy of all such praise, for the whole creation came into being through God's will. The purpose of the description in 4:1-11 is to set the stage for what follows.

Revelation 5:1-4. The event for which this stage has been set is the opening of the scroll that is in God's hand. We need to realize that the scroll is not a matter of giving information. The issue is whether or not the final purposes of God for the whole creation can really begin their final journey to fulfillment. That is what is at stake in the question of who is worthy to open the scroll. If no one worthy is found, then God's plans do not go forward. This is not meant to imply a limitation on God's power. What matters is that God wishes to fulfill those purposes with the cooperation and willingness of the creation, most particularly with the cooperation of the creatures given dominion over creation, human beings. When no one comes forward, John begins to weep, for it appears that the glorious purposes of God for creation will not be carried out.

Revelation 5:5-8: The heavenly host know better. One of the elders tells John that he need not weep, for one from God's people has been found worthy. The worthy one is described in terms that had become familiar in Israel for a future messianic king: a lion from the tribe of Judah and the Root of David. Then there is a very strange twist, the kind that readily occurs in dreamlike states: when John turns to look at the lion of Judah, he sees instead a lamb. The lamb is not even a powerful-looking beast, for it bears the marks of having been slaughtered. The lion is famed for its strength and power in overcoming enemies. The lamb is known for its gentleness and docility, and as a sacrificial animal. The fact that weakness has conquered is what Paul means when he speaks of the foolishness of the cross, the weakness of God that is stronger than what we think of as strength (1 Corinthians 1:22-25). Without hesitation, this Lamb takes the scroll, and the heavenly host worship the Lamb in the same way they worshiped the One on the throne.

Revelation 5:9-10. The heavenly host sings a hymn, declaring that the Lamb is indeed worthy to open the scroll. Furthermore, in this hymn they declare the specific reasons why he is worthy. Their song is a summary of the work of Christ: he was killed and by his death he has redeemed people for God's service. These new servants of God come from all over the world, from all languages and nations. Their task is to serve God as priests, constituting a kingdom whose ruler is God. The Lamb has formed them into this priestly kingdom. These servants will exercise rule on earth. What a message for the struggling churches in Asia Minor!

Revelation 5:11-14. The heavenly choir is increased by the presence of many angels. A thunderous chorus rings out, proclaiming the worthiness of the Lamb. Two points in these verses are significant. First, the whole heavenly host worships the Lamb in the same way it worships God. The two are praised and worshiped jointly in verse 13. Second, at the beginning of verse 13 we read that even more voices join in singing this hymn. Now all of the creatures in God's creation—in heaven, on earth, in the sea, under the earth—proclaim the greatness of God and of the Lamb. Both are involved in the creation of all things. The redemption Christ effects is important not only to human beings but also to the whole of creation.

INTERPRETING THE SCRIPTURE

A Change of Scene

Whereas in the earlier visions a heavenly messenger comes down to earth to give words to John for the churches, in this vision John is taken up into heaven, the place of God. Ezekiel and Isaiah and Paul had received such visions, though the latter refused to describe what he had seen (see 2 Corinthians 12:1-4). There are commonalities among the visions of Isaiah, Ezekiel, and this book, but also differences. One must understand them as visions—dreamlike, impressionistic, poetic, conveying their truth by pictures and drama—rather than as blueprints or photographs. Yet the prophet is allowed to glimpse our world and its future from God's perspective.

All these visions are of God, but not one gives a description of God. From all of them it is clear that God is surrounded by great glory, awe-inspiring, cosmic in scope. Those surrounding the throne cannot help but worship. In John's vision, the worship of the heavenly host also includes giving thanks for what God has done. It is not only the power of God that causes such worship; it is the work of God on behalf of creation. In 4:9 we are told that the creatures around the throne give glory and honor and thanks. The worship of heaven provides a pattern for the worship of the people of God on earth. Gratitude is part of true worship.

Is It Hopeless?

John has been taken up into heaven in order to learn about God's plan for the world and how that will come about. From his perspective, it looks as though the vision will be over very quickly. The purposes and plan of God are spelled out in the scroll sealed with seven seals. Even as God merely speaks and the world is created, so the scroll needs only to be read and God's plan and purposes will be revealed. The whole creation is waiting for God's final work for creation to be accomplished. And then there is a pause. An angel asks, "Who is worthy to open the scroll and break its seals?" We might wonder, why God doesn't do it. God is worthy. Why wait for anyone else? To ponder that question is to go to the heart of the gospel, to the mystery of the Incarnation. The heavenly host knows that the question has been answered, so they are able to console John.

The Lamb That Was Slain

There is no question that the Lamb is worthy. But this Lamb is also the Lion of the tribe of Judah, the Root of David, part of the people of God. He has been killed, slaughtered, and yet now he is alive and is proclaimed the One who can begin the final act of God's creation. When he approaches the throne and takes the scroll the elders and the four creatures begin worshiping the Lamb. Each one holds a golden bowl filled with incense. We are told these are the prayers of the saints. In some mysterious way, the prayers of the saints on earth become part of the worship of the Lamb in heaven.

The One Who Is Worthy

We need to pause for a moment to look at the wider theological context within which Revelations 5:9-10 can be understood. From the beginning, God has worked with humanity, training a people as an instrument for God's purposes. But the people are not worthy because they have sinned. So God becomes human, part of this people, suffering what the righteous will suffer in the midst of a sinful people, made even clearer because his righteousness is complete. From an earthly point of view, it looks like God's plans have failed. But from the point of view of heaven, this sacrifice, the slaughter of the Lamb, was really the turning point. This One is worthy. Now the final act can begin. Now redemption has begun in earnest. The Lamb has conquered. The Lamb is worthy.

The cross of Christ would not have been news to John. His faith is based on it, as well as on the Resurrection. We have already seen this in the earlier parts of this book. At this juncture the vision is not pointing to the future. Rather, it is pointing to the past, to the work of Christ. But it is setting that work in a cosmic context. The work of Christ, particularly his death on the cross, is the turning point of all history. It lets God's plans go forward. For the Christians in Asia Minor, this vision gives encouragement that their faithfulness is part of this same turning point.

Their prayers join the heavenly worship. Their victory is sure if they remain steadfast. They are the kingdom, the priests, created by the Lamb of God.

A kingdom in the midst of the Roman Empire—not even a localized kingdom like the conquered people all around the Mediterranean, but a kingdom made up of all nations, tribes, and languages—would sound very subversive to a Roman emperor. Rome thought of itself as a kingdom. To be priests, a whole kingdom of priests, what would that mean? To the early Christians that was part of their baptismal identity. At baptism they were anointed with oil as were the kings and the priests of Israel. A whole nation of priests was a vision in Israel as well as in the early church (see Exodus 19:6; 1 Peter 2:9). To be priests was to be able to stand before God, interceding on behalf of others, even the whole world. A priestly people was carrying out its office particularly in prayer for others. Perhaps the prayers being offered as incense in verse 8 are part of this priestly activity of the saints.

God and the Lamb

This section of John's vision culminates in the increasing voices in the heavenly choir. It is not surprising that so many hymns and anthems used by the church throughout the centuries have come from Revelation. Music seems a frequent part of the vision. We have the four creatures and the twenty-four elders, now joined by many angels and then by all creatures throughout heaven and earth. All the hymns in chapter 5 are to the Lamb, though the final one praises both the Lamb and the One on the throne. A crescendo is building in this chapter, leading up to the content of the scroll, which will unfold in the next several chapters.

With an understanding of the Incarnation, we can see why both the Lamb and the One on the throne can be worshiped equally without any sense that there are now two gods being worshipped. God's plan included the Incarnation, and the Lamb is that incarnation fulfilling the task. The Lamb is still part of the people of God, but unlike the rest of God's people, the Lamb is one who is worthy. The redeemed are part of a new people, made worthy not by themselves, but by the Lamb whose death ransomed them.

In this chapter the stage is set for much of the rest of the vision. We have the four living creatures, closest to the throne of God, and the twenty-four elders who join in worship with the creatures. We have a host of angels who serve the throne. We have the One seated on the throne, the center of the heavenly scene, and the Lamb who is worshiped with the One on the throne and whose death has opened the door for the completion of God's purposes. We have the scroll that contains the purposes that will be enacted as they are announced. The stage is set. The drama begins.

SHARING THE SCRIPTURE

PREPARING TO TEACH

Preparing Our Hearts

We begin the final unit of this quarter with a lesson that describes in apocalyptic imagery the grandeur of the Lamb who is worthy to open the seals of the scroll, the One who is worthy to be worshiped and praised by the multitude in heaven. As you read today's lesson, imagine yourself in John's place. How would you feel if you were privileged to witness the worship of the Lamb? How do you express gratitude to God for the work of the risen Christ, the Lamb of God? What gifts of worship, praise, and yourself do you bring to the throne of grace? Be mindful this week of the opportunities you have to worship God, especially when those moments include other members of the Body of Christ.

Preparing Our Minds

Read Revelation 4–5. Although our session focuses on 5:1-10, the background material is especially helpful in placing the lesson in its context. Chapter 4 sets the stage, while the conclusion of chapter 5 provides us with a thrilling vision of the worship of God and the Lamb.

Be sure to carefully read the other material in the lesson. Be prepared to read or retell portions of it, as suggested.

Preparing Our Learning Space

If you have access to a tape or CD player and a copy of Handel's *Messiah* (perhaps available from your choir director or local library), consider using the selection entitled "Worthy Is the Lamb," as suggested below in the Introduction. This chorus captures the mood and grandeur of the scene in Revelation.

If you do not have or cannot use the *Messiah* in your learning area, see if you can locate a hymn based on Revelation 5. One such hymn, found on page 638 in *The United Methodist Hymnal*, is entitled "This Is the Feast of Victory." Have hymnals handy if you plan to use a selection for the introductory activity.

Have on hand:
- ✔ several Bibles for students
- ✔ newsprint and marker or chalkboard and chalk
- ✔ paper and pencils
- ✔ optional tape or CD player and copy of Handel's *Messiah*
- ✔ optional hymnals

LEADING THE CLASS

(1) Introduction

Open today's session by asking the main question: **Who is worthy to open the scroll and break its seals?**

Begin to answer that question with music. If you have access to Handel's *Messiah* and a tape or CD player, plan to start the session by playing "Worthy Is the Lamb." This chorus will likely be familiar to many class members. As you play this stirring piece, ask the students to close their eyes and envision themselves in the company of the multitude of heaven as they praise the Lamb. Some adults may even want to sing along. After the song has ended, talk with the group for a few moments about how the song may begin to capture for them the awe and gratitude that John may have felt as he witnessed the scene in heaven.

If you cannot use the *Messiah*, use a hymn based on Revelation 5, such as "This Is the Feast of Victory," to begin the class. Perhaps someone could play this song on the piano. Have everyone sing both the first and final antiphon ("This is the feast . . . Alleluia!") in unison. You may want to have the men sing one verse, the women another, or use some other logical division that works for your class. If music is not possible in your setting, read the hymn aloud using logical divisions as suggested. Offer the hymn as an expression of worship.

This would be an appropriate time to lift a prayer of thanksgiving, based on our key verse in Revelation 5:9, for the incomparable offering of the Lamb by whose blood saints from every tribe and language and people and nation have been ransomed.

(2) A Change of Scene

This segment discusses background scripture from Revelation 4:1-11. If at all possible, plan to spend time explaining the scene found here, for it sets the stage for our lesson. Use information from the Understanding the Scripture section and the Interpreting the Scripture portion that is headed "A Change of Scene" to help the class enter into the unfamiliar world of John's heavenly vision.

If time permits, you may want to read this scripture in its entirety.

(3) Is It Hopeless?

Begin this section by asking:

(1) How do you feel when you are all excited about something, set to go as it were, and then you are disappointed because your expectations are not met?

Note that John was in a similar predicament, as we shall see by reading aloud Revelation 5:1-4.

Use information in the Understanding the Scripture segment for 5:1-4 to explain "what is at stake in the question of who is worthy to open the scroll."

(4) The Lamb That Was Slain

Have a volunteer read aloud Revelation 5:5-8. Then read or retell "The Lamb That Was Slain" section under Interpreting the Scripture. Note the imagery of the messianic king, described in 5:5 as "the Lion of the Tribe of Judah, the Root of David." Include the comments in the Understanding the Scripture portion for these verses concerning the contrast between the lion and lamb. Then ask:

(1) What difference might it make in our individual and corporate prayers if we took seriously the image of our prayers being offered up as incense from golden bowls?

(2) In what way do you think your prayers contribute to the worship of the Lamb in heaven?

If time permits, distribute paper and pencils and ask everyone to write a brief prayer—just a sentence or two—concern-

ing something for which they have to be grateful. Collect these and read them aloud as a litany. After each prayer is read, the class responds by saying, "We give you thanks, O God."

(5) The One Who Is Worthy

This section is vital to the understanding of our lesson. Before reading the text from Revelation 5:9-10, review "the wider theological context" of these verses as found under this heading in the Interpreting the Scripture segment. Now read the appropriate verses. Then ask:

(1) Why do you think the Lamb was worthy to open the scroll?

Supplement the class's ideas with information from Understanding the Scripture for verses 5:9-10. Note the summary of the work of Christ mentioned there: "he was killed and by his death he has redeemed people for God's service."

Mention that there has been much discussion in recent years concerning the effect of Jesus' sacrifice on the cross. Ask class members to share their understanding of what Christ's death on the cross did in fact accomplish and what difference his death makes in their own lives.

Be sure to point out that the Lamb's death has universal significance. According to our key verse, 5:9, by the Lamb's blood "saints from every tribe and language and people and nation" were "ransomed for God." Ask the class:

(2) How does the global, international character of the Christian church affect how we perceive others who are of different races or nationalities, or who live in countries whose political or economic systems are different from our own?

(6) God and the Lamb

This section, which focuses on Revelation 5:11-14, is background information for our lesson, but it directly relates to the worthiness of the Lamb. Students would gain a better understanding of the relationship between God and the Lamb if you include this segment. Use information from the Understanding the Scripture portion and from "God and the Lamb" in the Interpreting the Scripture segment. Especially point out that the Lamb and God are both being worshiped by the heavenly multitude.

HELPING CLASS MEMBERS ACT

Encourage class members to spend time this week worshiping God. Ask them to set aside specific time for prayer and praise. Also invite those who do not regularly participate in corporate worship to attend the church service.

Remind the group that just as the heavenly multitude offered praise to the Lamb, people enjoy being commended for a job well done. Ask each member to think of someone who deserves a pat on the back for some recent accomplishment. Suggest that they call, write to, or visit this person to offer some expression of congratulations.

Note that the heavenly scene that John describes is filled with music. Encourage each person to select one or more hymns in the coming week that they can sing with family, in the car, or alone in the shower as a means of praising and worshiping God.

PLANNING FOR NEXT SUNDAY

Ask the class to prepare for next week's lesson, entitled "Provision for the Redeemed," by reading Revelation 7. This session will help us understand how the Lamb provides shelter and comfort for the multitude of the redeemed.

PROVISION FOR THE REDEEMED

PREVIEWING THE LESSON

Lesson Scripture: Revelation 7:1-3, 9-10, 13-17
Background Scripture: Revelation 7
Key Verse: Revelation 7:17

Focus of the Lesson:
the comfort, guidance, and shelter the Lamb will provide to those who have suffered

Main Question of the Lesson:
What provision will God make for the redeemed?

This lesson will enable adult learners to:
(1) study the provisions promised to the redeemed.
(2) recognize the global nature of mission.
(3) respond by giving thanks for God's provisions in their own lives.

Today's lesson may be outlined as follows:
(1) Introduction
(2) Marked for Redemption
(3) The Great Multitude
(4) The Ultimate Shepherd

FOCUSING ON THE MAIN QUESTION

In the last lesson the scroll with the seven seals had been presented. The Lamb had been found worthy to open the seals and thereby begin the final stage of human history. In the passages between that lesson and this one, that is, chapter 6, six of the seven seals were opened. Each time the Lamb opened a seal, terrible things happened on earth: war, famine, disease, earthquakes, meteors. Chapter 7 comes between the opening of the first six seals and the opening of the seventh. It is a dra-matic break, since the first six seals had been opened one after another with no stated pause between.

From the visions he has seen, John is well aware that serious persecution is coming for faithful Christians. The vision of the first six seals makes clear that there will be wholesale destruction on the earth. What will happen to the church in the midst of all of this? Will they be able to withstand it? Will the whole church be destroyed?

As we have seen in earlier lessons, John is very familiar with the Old Testament. A major theme in the Hebrew Scriptures is the righteous remnant that will survive when God destroys the wicked. This is a major theme of apocalyptic literature as well. As we shall see in this lesson, the pause between the opening of the first six and the seventh seal is a time to give John the reassurance that, once again, as so often in the past, God will save a remnant. Not all will be destroyed. The coming terrible times will be a kind of purifying fire, through which the faithful will be tested and their faith made even more sure by the experience.

The time of judgment is not simply punishment for a fallen creation. It is also part of the process of purifying creation so that the world can reach the goals that God has purposed for it. It is not merely an action of the wrath of God; it is also an action of the redeeming will of God. God's will for the world will come to pass. Human sin will not forever frustrate God's good purposes for the creation. Now, sin blots out much of the goodness of nature and of human society. That sin must be destroyed. God's purposes include the provision of all that we need to make life secure and pleasant. But the life of all creation is quite insecure and often there is terrible suffering. The visions given to John speak of the terrifying transition from the present world filled with sin and destruction to the world God ultimately intends. As we consider this unimaginable period we ask: *What provision will God make for the redeemed?*

READING THE SCRIPTURE

(NRSV)
Revelation 7:1-3

1 After this I saw four angels standing at the four corners of the earth, holding back the four winds of the earth so that no wind could blow on earth or sea or against any tree. ²I saw another angel ascending from the rising of the sun, having the seal of the living God, and he called with a loud voice to the four angels who had been given power to damage earth and sea, ³saying, "Do not damage the earth or the sea or the trees, until we have marked the servants of our God with a seal on their foreheads."

(NRSV)
Revelation 7:9-10

9 After this I looked, and there was a great multitude that no one could count, from every nation, from all tribes and peoples and languages, standing before the throne and before the Lamb, robed in white, with palm branches in their hands. ¹⁰They cried out in a loud voice, saying,

(NIV)
Revelation 7:1-3

1 After this I saw four angels standing at the four corners of the earth, holding back the four winds of the earth to prevent any wind from blowing on the land or on the sea or on any tree. ²Then I saw another angel coming up from the east, having the seal of the living God. He called out in a loud voice to the four angels who had been given power to harm the land and the sea: ³"Do not harm the land or the sea or the trees until we put a seal on the foreheads of the servants of our God."

(NIV)
Revelation 7:9-10

⁹After this I looked and there before me was a great multitude that no one could count, from every nation, tribe, people and language, standing before the throne and in front of the Lamb. They were wearing white robes and were holding palm branches in their hands. ¹⁰And they cried out in a loud voice:

"Salvation belongs to our God
    who is seated on the
    throne, and to the Lamb!"

(NRSV)
Revelation 7:13-17

13 Then one of the elders addressed me, saying, "Who are these, robed in white, and where have they come from?" 14I said to him, "Sir, you are the one that knows." Then he said to me, "These are they who have come out of the great ordeal; they have washed their robes and made them white in the blood of the Lamb.
15 For this reason they are before
    the throne of God,
    and worship him day and night
        within his temple,
    and the one who is seated on
        the throne will shelter
        them.
16 They will hunger no more, and
        thirst no more;
    the sun will not strike them,
        nor any scorching heat;
17 for the Lamb at the center of the
        throne will be their
        shepherd,
    and he will guide them to
        springs of the water of
        life,
    and God will wipe away every
        tear from their eyes."

"Salvation belongs to our God,
    who sits on the throne,
    and to the Lamb."

(NIV)
Revelation 7:13-17

13Then one of the elders asked me, "These in white robes—who are they, and where did they come from?"
14I answered, "Sir, you know."

And he said, "These are they who have come out of the great tribulation; they have washed their robes and made them white in the blood of the Lamb. 15Therefore,
    "they are before the throne of God
        and serve him day and night in his
            temple;
    and he who sits on the throne will spread
        his tent over them.
16Never again will they hunger;
    never again will they thirst.
    The sun will not beat upon them,
        nor any scorching heat.
17For the Lamb at the center of the throne
        will be their shepherd;
    he will lead them to springs of living
        water.
    And God will wipe away every tear from
        their eyes."

Key
Verse

Key
Verse

UNDERSTANDING THE SCRIPTURE

Revelation 7:1-3. The words "after this" at the beginning of the chapter are very important. "This" was the opening of the first six seals. The first four seals involved horses with riders appearing, called forth by one of the four creatures around the throne of God. These are often called "The Four Horsemen of the Apocalypse." Each in its own way brings terrible destruction to the earth and its inhabitants: war, famine, disease. The horsemen do not cause destruction directly, but rather permit or encourage human beings to so order their lives that these terrible things occur. The fifth seal speaks of persecution of the church; the sixth of terrible natural disasters. Therefore, when chapter seven opens, great destruction has already begun.

Now there is a respite. The four angels at the corners of the earth are told not to cause destruction yet. The popular picture of the earth for this society was of a square, flat earth, with great winds at each of the corners. Other winds might be pleasant, but these four winds were highly destructive. The angels controlling the winds are told not to let these winds loose on the earth or sea yet. Likewise, the angels who were given charge of destroying much of the earth and sea by means other than wind were also told to wait. Destruction would come soon, but there needed to be time for the servants of God to be marked. They are to be sealed on their foreheads. After that, the final destruction can occur.

What is this mark, this seal on the forehead of the servants of God? We think of other markings mentioned in the Bible. The mark on Cain indicated God would take vengeance on anyone who harmed him (Genesis 4:15). John's vision reflects the passage concerning the Passover of the firstborn during the last plague against the Egyptians, when the Hebrews put the blood of the lamb on their doorposts so that death would not strike their homes (Exodus 12:3-13), as well as Ezekiel 9:4, a vision of that prophet of the coming destruction of Jerusalem. In that vision, Ezekiel sees a man who is commanded: "Go through the city, through Jerusalem, and put a mark on the foreheads of those who sigh and groan over all the abominations that are committed in it." For the early church, the seal on the forehead would have reminded them immediately of making the sign of the cross with oil on the foreheads of those who had just been baptized.

Revelation 7:4-8. The vision continues with the first group of those to be sealed: 144,000, twelve thousand from each of the twelve tribes of Israel. Twelve was considered a perfect number, and therefore twelve times twelve would be perfection itself. This may be a round number rather than a specific figure. It is also not clear that Israel is meant here, since the church often thought of itself as Israel. But with the listing of the tribes, the passage does seem to apply to the original Israel, and

may thereby be a way of tying together the two peoples. The vision may assume that this perfect number from each of the tribes have already become part of the church.

Revelation 7:9-10. A second, or at least a fuller, group of the redeemed appears. They come from every nation, tribe, people, and language. This group is so large that it cannot be numbered. Some have thought that the 144,000 and this countless multitude might be the same group, but they are described in such different ways that it would seem more likely that the first group is the faithful in Israel and the second group are the Gentiles who were part of the church. They are in heaven and are robed in white. In the early church, persons who had just been baptized were clothed in white robes. They are gathered around the throne and the Lamb, praising God and the Lamb for the salvation that they have received from them. As we saw earlier, the same worship is offered both to God and to the Lamb. They cannot be separated in the work of redemption.

Revelation 7:11-12. This great host of the redeemed has joined those who were worshiping at the throne when this whole vision began: the elders and the four creatures. The worship goes on. God is praised for all the characteristics that make it possible for God's good purposes to be achieved.

Revelation 7:13-17. The final section of this chapter begins with John being questioned by one of the elders. He is asked who those are who are clothed in white robes. The dialogue here is rather like that in Ezekiel, in the famous vision of the Valley of Dry Bones. In that vision, the Spirit of God shows him the scene, and then asks a question, to which Ezekiel replies: "O Lord GOD, you know" (Ezekiel 37:2-3). Here, John has been shown this great throng and then is asked who they are. He responds to the elder: "Sir, you are the one that knows." The elder then goes on to tell him that these are the ones who suffered through the great persecution. It is through the blood of the Lamb that they have been washed and their robes made white. Christians from the beginning understood that their redemption was based on the cross of Christ who had made them clean and forgiven their sin. For this reason, part of the meaning of baptism was washing away sin and then being clothed with the white robe of the new life.

The elder then breaks into poetry: the redeemed worship at the throne of God because of what God has done for them. They clearly are not angry at God for all the pain and terror that they have been through. They understand the purposes of God and know that God has loved them and cared for them even in the midst of their suffering. The time of suffering is past, however. Now all of God's purposes will be fulfilled for them. God will be their tent or tabernacle for a shelter, and will give them the food and the drink that they need, as God gave to Israel in the wilderness. The Lamb will be their shepherd, as they continue to be the flock of God. All of their crying and sorrow will be ended.

INTERPRETING THE SCRIPTURE

Marked for Redemption

What good does it do to be marked for redemption if such a mark singles one out for persecution in the immediate future? Such a question must have been on the minds of many Christians who read this book near the time it was written. If the mark referred to here is baptism, and its accompanying anointing with oil in the sign of the cross, the mark made one part of the Christian community. If that community was about to be persecuted, then the mark left one open to such persecution. Or if the coming terrible times were to include natural disasters on an unprecedented scale, one would think a mark that protected one from all this distress would be much more useful. But no such exemption from suffering is promised to the Christians. What is promised for those who are marked with the seal is strength to endure and, at the end, fulfillment of all of God's promises. At least in our society, we live in the kind of time this chapter speaks of: a time of respite, where there is no serious persecution, no great sense that the world is coming to an end. It is in this time that we have been marked as the servants of God, prepared for whatever lies ahead.

The Great Multitude

By the time this book was written, around the end of the first century, the church, though a very insignificant number in the whole Roman Empire, was growing rapidly. Whereas in the earliest times of the church most of the new members were Jews, by now the vast majority of new members were Gentiles. The church was also growing in areas around the whole Mediterranean basin. It increasingly included different languages and nationalities within the Roman Empire. Though at the time the church could not be said to represent every nation and language, since the Roman world did not even know about a great number of them, it was clear that this was the goal and mission of the church: to include every nation, all tribes and peoples and languages. This is part of the missionary impetus within the life of the church. Only in our own day, some twenty centuries after the time of John, can we say with some truth that the church has indeed become part of almost all nations and languages. These diverse persons are the ones in white robes, most likely a reference to their baptism. Although no mention is made here that these faithful ones are marked with the seal, that is to be understood from the context as well as from the baptismal robes they are wearing.

In the hymn that the redeemed sing, we see another instance of the connection of God and the Lamb, both involved in redemption. If in this case the term God is being used for the first person of the Trinity—the Father—and the Lamb for the incarnate second person—the Son—the distinction between person and purpose is blurred. Along with the Holy Spirit, all are intimately involved in all of the divine activity.

The vision continues in Revelation 7:11-12 with a panoramic picture of the heavenly host, which includes all the angels, the twenty-four elders, and the four strange creatures, evidently responding to the hymn just sung by the great multitude in white robes. One would assume that the 144,000 are also a part of the chorus of the redeemed. We can almost imagine an antiphonal choir: the redeemed from humanity on one side and all the heavenly creatures on the other.

The Ultimate Shepherd

The redeemed in white robes are joyful, worshiping God with great fervor. The elder explains to John who they are. They are not ones who avoided persecution; rather, they are those who remained steadfast in the midst of persecution. To make robes white in the blood of the Lamb is a strange phrase if one thinks of it literally. One does not make anything white by dipping it in blood. The symbolic meaning of the white robes in baptism is the new life, the new birth, the new beginning that is free from the domination of sin. Granted, the new life co-exists with the old as long as this earthly life continues, but by faith the new life conquers and grows stronger. Baptism is also the sign of dying and rising with Christ, of joining him in his death, of taking up our cross and following his way. The baptized, therefore, have symbolically died with Christ, and his blood has washed them of their sins. The white robes are the tokens of this. Because they have been through the great tribulation and have remained faithful, it is also clear that they have lived out the meaning of their baptism. They have taken up their cross. They have answered positively with their lives the question Jesus put to the disciples: "Are you able to . . . be baptized with the baptism that I am baptized with?" (Mark 10:38).

The imagery changes from the terrible ordeal through which they have come to the pastoral scene reminiscent of Psalm 23. The Lamb is now their shepherd. He will bring them to bountiful pastures and the springs of the water of life. The valley of the shadow of death is behind them. They will dwell in God's tent forever. The time of sorrow is gone. God wipes away their tears, just as a parent wipes away the tears of a child. This beautiful picture of the time beyond the tribulation picks up on themes that were a part of Israel's understanding of the great future God has promised. Isaiah 49:10 tells of a time when God's people will no longer hunger or thirst, or be harmed by wind or sun; when God will lead them to the springs of water. And Isaiah 25:4-9 includes a song of the redeemed in the final kingdom, where they shall not hunger or thirst. There shall be a great banquet for all peoples, and God will wipe away all tears. Death shall be no more. John understands these visions very well.

The interlude of chapter 7 is over. Next will come the fateful opening of the seventh seal. But at the end, when all of the destruction and judgment are over, the fullness of the glorious future, glimpsed as though in preview in this chapter, will be seen in all its glory.

SHARING THE SCRIPTURE

PREPARING TO TEACH

Preparing Our Hearts

Begin this week's preparation by listing on a sheet of paper all the "things" for which you are grateful. "Things" may include intangible items, such as relationships. Think about how life would be different if these "things" were not available to you. Give thanks for the provisions that God has given for your life's journey.

Preparing Our Minds

As you prepare to lead this week's lesson, be sure to read Revelation 7, giving particular attention to verses 1-3, 9-10, and 13-17. Read the session material carefully.

Study the verses listed in the scripture study under "The Ultimate Shepherd."

Preparing Our Learning Space

You may want to list the scripture references for study under "The Ultimate Shepherd" on newsprint or a chalkboard prior to class.

Have on hand:
- several Bibles for students
- newsprint and marker or chalkboard and chalk
- paper and pencils

LEADING THE CLASS

(1) Introduction

Tell the students that you all are going on a trip to Israel. Each person may take one piece of carry-on luggage packed with the provisions he or she would find most helpful. Distribute paper and pencils and let the class work for several minutes listing the items they would pack. Then, either with the whole class or divided into teams, discuss the contents of their suitcases. Encourage them to tell why they chose particular items. Wrap up this part of the lesson by noting that most of us make adequate provisions for a journey. In today's lesson we will learn about the provisions that God makes for the redeemed, especially those who will suffer persecution at the close of the age. Present today's main question:

What provision will God make for the redeemed?

You may choose to use the information in the Focusing on the Main Question portion either as an alternative to the previous activity, or in addition to it.

(2) Marked for Redemption

Use the information in the Understanding the Scripture segment for Revelation 7:1-3 to set the stage for today's lesson. Be sure you cover the events of chapter 6 (which we did not study), as well as the meaning of the mark that will seal the servants of God. Also explain the square, flat view of the earth that would have been held by the people of John's day so that the idea of angels standing at the four corners of the earth will make sense.

Then have a volunteer read aloud Revelation 7:1-3. Entertain comments or questions regarding this section.

(3) The Great Multitude

Now read Revelation 7:9-10. Use "The Great Multitude" portion of the Interpreting the Scripture section to illuminate this passage for the class.

Pay particular attention to the fact that the great multitude includes persons "from every nation, from all tribes and peoples and languages" (7:9). Ask:

?

(1) **What is our denomination doing to ensure that persons around the world hear the good news of redemption in Jesus Christ?**

(2) **It has been said that a fire that does not burn is no fire at all. Likewise, a congregation that is not in mission is not truly the church of Jesus Christ. What, therefore, is our own congregation doing to make a witness to all nations, just as the Lord calls us to do in the Great Commission (Matthew 28:19-20)?**

(3) **What else could our congregation be doing to be faithful to the task of mission?**

(4) The Ultimate Shepherd

Plan to spend considerable time on this part of the lesson, for it contains our key verse and a discussion of the provision for the redeemed. Begin by selecting students to read the parts of the narrator, the elder, and John in Revelation 7:13-17.

Since many of the verses in this section refer to other biblical passages or ideas, we will do a scripture study to help us understand the allusions. Information about these verses may be found in the Understanding the Scripture portion and the Interpreting the Scripture section, as well. Make sure the class understands the following points:

- We are standing with John before the throne of God as an innumerable multitude is shouting and singing praise.
- John's response (7:14) to the elder's question (7:13) is similar to Ezekiel's response to God's question about whether dry bones can live again (Ezekiel 37:2-3). This vision came at a time when Israel was suffering in exile in Babylon and surely did not expect to be given new life as a people and returned to their homeland.
- The white robes are worn by those who have been baptized; paradoxi-

cally, these robes have been made white by the blood of the Lamb. In other words, their sins have been forgiving by the atoning death of Jesus. Note, as verse 15 makes clear, that the forgiveness brought about by Jesus' atoning death is the "reason they are before the throne of God and worship him day and night."

Now ask the class to look again at verses 16 and 17. Encourage them to associate the words and images in these verses with other biblical passages to get a fuller understanding of the provisions for the redeemed. Here are some associations, though the group may think of others. Ask class members to look up and read these references. If you choose, you may want to write these references on newsprint or a chalkboard for all to see.

- The images in verse 16 are found in Isaiah 49:10, which promises deliverance to the exiles in Babylon, and Psalm 121:6, which speaks of God's protection.
- The idea of hungering and thirsting no more (7:16) is related to Jesus' statement in John 6:35: "I am the bread of life. Whoever comes to me will never be hungry, and whoever believes in me will never be thirsty."
- The idea of the shepherd as the one who dies for the sheep is clearly stated in John 10:11: "I am the good shepherd. The good shepherd lays down his life for the sheep." In Revelation 7:17, the Lamb who was slain has now become the shepherd.
- Additional references to God as the shepherd are found in Psalm 23:1 and Ezekiel 34:23-24, among others.
- The "springs of the water of life" or "springs of living water" may refer to water that flows freely, as opposed to water contained in a cistern, or it may be used as a metaphor for God's salvation. References to "living water" can be found in Jeremiah 17:13; John 4:10-15; John 6:35; John 7:37-38, as well as Isaiah 49:10.

• God's promise to wipe away tears shows us that sorrow will have no place in the new order that is being ushered in. A similar idea is found in Isaiah 25:8: "Then the Lord GOD will wipe away the tears from all faces, and the disgrace of his people he will take away from all the earth, for the LORD has spoken."

After class members have completed this scripture study, tell them to write their own understanding of how God will provide for those who have been redeemed. You may do this by distributing paper and pencils and having each person first work alone and then share ideas with the class. Or, you may divide the class into teams and have each team write its understanding. Or, you may want to work with the entire class to see if a consensus can be reached as to God's provision for us.

Conclude this section with a prayer of praise and thanksgiving for the provision that God makes for those who are redeemed.

HELPING CLASS MEMBERS ACT

Remind class members that the Lamb becomes the shepherd, the one who cares for the sheep. Suggest that they read or recite Psalm 23 each day this week. As they do, invite them to give thanks to the Lamb for the provisions he makes for their lives. Some students may want to rewrite this beloved psalm, updating it to show the ways in which God provides for them.

Note that we learn from Revelation 7 that God does not exempt the redeemed from suffering. In fact, God's mark may cause greater persecution. They are, however, cared for by the Lamb. Suggest that each class member select someone who may be suffering and perform some tangible act this week so that this individual may know that God does indeed care for him or her.

Encourage students to recall a time in their own lives when they suffered, perhaps physically or mentally. Suggest that they look back on this painful period for signs that Christ was present with them, even if they were not fully aware of his presence at that time. They may want to write their thoughts about this period in a spiritual journal. Or, they may be willing to share their experience with someone else who is suffering as a testimony of God's abiding presence in the worst circumstances.

PLANNING FOR NEXT SUNDAY

Ask class members to read the lesson scripture, Revelation 19:11-16 and 20:11-15 in preparation for next Sunday's lesson, entitled "The Victorious Christ." If time permits, they may choose to read the background scripture that includes chapters 19 and 20 in their entirety. Encourage students to think about the risen Christ as the King of kings and Lord of lords.

THE VICTORIOUS CHRIST

PREVIEWING THE LESSON

Lesson Scripture: Revelation 19:11-16; 20:11-15
Background Scripture: Revelation 19–20
Key Verse: Revelation 19:16

Focus of the Lesson:
the triumph of the King of kings and Lord of lords, who rules with righteousness and judgment

Main Question of the Lesson:
How will Christ be victorious over the powers of evil?

This lesson will enable adult learners to:
(1) recognize that the victory over sin and death that was won on the cross is proclaimed in John's vision of the end time.
(2) enter into the victory of Christ and celebration in heaven.
(3) respond by becoming more accountable to God for their actions, attitudes, and words.

Today's lesson may be outlined as follows:
(1) Introduction
(2) The Feast of Rejoicing
(3) The Bloodstained Rider
(4) The Millennium
(5) The Judgment

FOCUSING ON THE MAIN QUESTION

Between the last lesson and this one, in the whole middle section of the Revelation to John, there have been visions of great destruction on the earth, confrontation between the powers of evil and the Lamb. As chapter 19 begins, we now come to the vision of the final battles and the final victory. Throughout the book it has always been certain that God would be victorious, so our question for today is: *How will Christ be victorious over the powers of evil?* In fact, it is clear that the victory has already been won, in the sense that the decisive battle has taken place on the cross. But throughout the book we are given a kind of two-story drama: what is happening on earth, where evil still has great power over human society and

MAY 18

human lives, and in heaven, where the awareness of God's omnipotence, the unwavering belief in God's power over evil, is celebrated. The Lamb is the connection: the one who on earth won a victory already clear in heaven, but unacknowledged by the powers of evil on earth. The faithful are called to live on the basis of their belief that the cross and the Resurrection signal that great victory while living in the midst of a world that does not acknowledge it, and where evil seems the order of the day.

The battles that take place between the Lamb and evil are strange indeed. We are prepared for great conflict, but the Lamb has only to appear and the battle ends. All of the evil powers are captured or destroyed; none of the righteous are harmed. In a sense, the battles are more occasions to make public and effective the victory already won by the Lamb.

There is another characteristic of these passages about the conflict between God and evil. The major players are not individual human beings. The players they are God and the powers of evil, variously described as beasts, Babylon, or the great harlot of Babylon. All are representations or agents of Satan. Human beings and even societies give their loyalty to either God or evil, either the Lamb or Satan, but the conflict is of a more cosmic scale than the humans who are caught up in it. As a part of this conflict contrasting pairs that have been set up in the earlier chapters now come into play as we begin this last section. One pair is the great harlot who is dressed in scarlet and many jewels (17:1-6), in contrast to the bride of the Lamb dressed in white linen (19:7-8). A second pair is the great city of Babylon, certainly representing the Roman Empire with its wealth and idolatry (18:1-24), and the city of the saints that is being inaugurated (20:9). With all of the contrasts that are made, we must remember that John and the other faithful Christians had absolutely no doubt at any time who was going to be victorious. The victory is over the forces of evil that destroy and warp human life and human society by injustice and sin. The end of these forces means that human beings can live the way God intended them to, with righteousness and with justice.

READING THE SCRIPTURE

NRSV
Revelation 19:11-16

11 Then I saw heaven opened, and there was a white horse! Its rider is called Faithful and True, and in righteousness he judges and makes war. [12]His eyes are like a flame of fire, and on his head are many diadems; and he has a name inscribed that no one knows but himself. [13]He is clothed in a robe dipped in blood, and his name is called The Word of God. [14]And the armies of heaven, wearing fine linen, white and pure, were following him on white horses. [15]From his mouth comes a sharp sword with which to strike down the nations,

NIV
Revelation 19:11-16

[11]I saw heaven standing open and there before me was a white horse, whose rider is called Faithful and True. With justice he judges and makes war. [12]His eyes are like blazing fire, and on his head are many crowns. He has a name written on him that no one knows but he himself. [13]He is dressed in a robe dipped in blood, and his name is the Word of God. [14]The armies of heaven were following him, riding on white horses and dressed in fine linen, white and clean. [15]Out of his mouth comes a sharp sword with which to strike down

and he will rule them with a rod of iron; he will tread the wine press of the fury of the wrath of God the Almighty. [16]On his robe and on his thigh he has a name inscribed, "King of kings and Lord of lords."

the nations. "He will rule them with an iron scepter." He treads the winepress of the fury of the wrath of God Almighty. [16]On his robe and on his thigh he has this name written:

KING OF KINGS AND LORD OF LORDS.

Key Verse

Ke Ver

NRSV
Revelation 20:11-15

11 Then I saw a great white throne and the one who sat on it; the earth and the heaven fled from his presence, and no place was found for them. [12]And I saw the dead, great and small, standing before the throne, and books were opened. Also another book was opened, the book of life. And the dead were judged according to their works, as recorded in the books. [13]And the sea gave up the dead that were in it, Death and Hades gave up the dead that were in them, and all were judged according to what they had done. [14]Then Death and Hades were thrown into the lake of fire. This is the second death, the lake of fire; [15]and anyone whose name was not found written in the book of life was thrown into the lake of fire.

NIV
Revelation 20:11-15

[11]Then I saw a great white throne and him who was seated on it. Earth and sky fled from his presence, and there was no place for them. [12]And I saw the dead, great and small, standing before the throne, and books were opened. Another book was opened, which is the book of life. The dead were judged according to what they had done as recorded in the books. [13]The sea gave up the dead that were in it, and death and Hades gave up the dead that were in them, and each person was judged according to what he had done. [14]Then death and Hades were thrown into the lake of fire. The lake of fire is the second death. [15]If anyone's name was not found written in the book of life, he was thrown into the lake of fire.

UNDERSTANDING THE SCRIPTURE

Revelation 19:1-10. As chapter 19 begins, the time of victory is clear. A great Hallelujah chorus breaks out in heaven. They are rejoicing at the fall of the great harlot, Babylon. Babylon was the mighty empire that had conquered ancient Judah in 587 B.C.E., taking many of its leading citizens and skilled workers into captivity. The new Babylon is the Roman Empire, at its height at the time of this vision. It controlled a great part of the inhabited Western world, from the Middle East to Spain and parts of Britain. The wealth of the conquered parts of the empire came to the city of Rome. Already there had been persecutions of some Christians within the

empire, and John's earlier visions make it obvious that he expected much more in the future.

The chorus changes from praise for the destruction that has occurred to the great wedding feast that is about to happen. It is the marriage of the Lamb and his bride, who later will be clearly identified as the church. The imagery of God as the groom and Israel as the bride is a constant theme in the prophets (see Isaiah 54:5-8; 62:4-5; Hosea 2:2-20). The use of this imagery shows both the intimacy and personal relationship between God and God's people and the covenant character of that relationship. In the New Testament the imagery of Christ as the husband and the church as the wife is used not only in Revelation but also in Ephesians 5:25-33.

This section concludes with a dialogue between John and the angel. John tries to worship the angel who has brought such great news, and is told by the angel that only God is to be worshiped. This might have been a strong word to some Christians who worshiped angels as well as God.

Revelation 19:11-16. The one who emerges from heaven on a white horse to engage in the final battle is clearly Christ, the Lamb. Again, the battle is over before it begins. Verse 13 clearly draws on Isaiah 63:1-6, where God says that in vengeance he has trampled down the enemies of the people, and therefore his garments are stained crimson, as though he had been treading grapes in a winepress. Here the rider is called "The Word of God" and "King of kings and Lord of lords." His robe is stained with blood as he comes from heaven, before the battle with the nations begins. Also alluded to here is Psalm 2, that God's anointed will rule the nations with a rod of iron. This is the same passage that was quoted in the letter to Thyatira (Revelation 2:26).

Revelation 19:17-21. An angel announces the end of the battle. The beast that headed the armies of evil and a major servant of his are captured. The angel invites birds of carrion to come and feast on the dead. This is a contrast to the wedding feast to which the righteous have been invited.

Revelation 20:1-10. Though the beast, here clearly identified as Satan, had been captured, now he is thrown into a pit, and the door is locked over him. What follows are verses that have caused great controversy in church circles. Satan is imprisoned only for a thousand years—a millennium—during which time the saints who were martyred in the persecutions rule with Christ over the earth now free from Satan's works. After that thousand years, Satan is let loose briefly and the enemies of God come out for battle again, but fire from heaven destroys them. The leaders of evil, identified here as Satan, the beast and his servant the false prophet, are all cast into the lake of fire forever. The major message is clear: God wins the final victory over all the forces of evil. The terms Gog and Magog come from Ezekiel 38:1–39:20, a battle against the enemies of God. Eventually, such evil will have no place at all in God's world and will be no threat for anyone.

Christians have disagreed about the millennium, the thousand-year reign. Does it come with the return of Christ at the end of history, or does it come in human history before the final end? Could we be living in it now? Augustine believed it was the thousand years between the birth of Jesus and the year 1000. This was believed for centuries in the West and caused great panic around the year 1000. Later times have been suggested, leading to frequent attempts even today to date the return of Christ and the beginning of the thousand years. The major point of the visions, however, is not to fix exact times and sequences of events, but to proclaim the certainty of God's victory, no matter how strong the powers of evil may seem to be in our world.

Revelation 20:11-15: After all the power of evil has been destroyed, then comes the final judgment. For John, there are two resurrections: the first is for the martyrs at the beginning of the thousand-year reign (Revelation 20:4). The second is after the final defeat of Satan, when all the dead shall be raised to face judgment (Revelation 20:5). At that point, death itself shall be defeated. There will be no more Hades—the place for the dead. In fact, from verse 11 we see that even the earth and heaven disappear at this time. The end of all history has indeed arrived. All the dead shall be judged on the basis of their works, but those whose names have not been written in the book of life will be thrown into the lake of fire. This is the second death, from which there is no resurrection.

INTERPRETING THE SCRIPTURE

The Feast of Rejoicing

The defeat of the Roman Empire is cause for great rejoicing. The judgment on the empire was not simply that some Christians were killed. Rather, it was that the ways of the empire were so unrighteous that the saints whose faith called them to support justice and righteousness were seen as enemies of the state and therefore were killed. Idolatry leads to injustice and unrighteousness.

The feast is the wedding banquet. We find in Revelation that, throughout its historical pilgrimage, the church is, in a sense, engaged to Christ. The wedding is to take place at the end, when the bride is fully prepared. The preparation is the wedding dress of white linen to be made up of "righteous deeds of the saints." This has overtones of the parable in Matthew 22:1-14, when the ones invited late to the wedding banquet were expelled and punished because they did not have on the proper wedding garments. There is a constant tension in Revelation between what we might term "salvation by works" and "salvation by grace." That is, the saints are saints because they have done what is just and righteous. At the same time, it is clear that they are righteous because they have been washed in the blood of the Lamb. Both are true. To be redeemed by Christ does not mean that we can make no changes in our behavior, take no risks for the sake of justice and righteousness, and expect to be part of Christ's kingdom.

If Revelation 19:9-10 is intended to discourage the worship of angels, it is a warning about the ease with which we are able to acknowledge the true God and then go on worshiping what we did before. The angel makes very clear that all true prophecy is a proclamation of and witness to the work of Jesus.

The Bloodstained Rider

In Revelation 19:13 we see that the rider is already stained with blood before the current battle. This verse may imply that this rider is stained with blood from the cross, the true final battle, and now appears clad in a bloodstained robe. But it is his own blood. He is now claiming in full view of all the fruits of his victory, which is the destruction of the powers of evil. For John, as for the rest of the New Testament writers, the central moment of history, the point at which the power of evil is ended, is the Cross. The battles at the end are quick—almost notifications to the enemies that the game is over, making them realize and acknowledge what happened on that Good Friday so long ago. This is very important for the faithful to realize, for we live between the time of the Cross and the end. We are not waiting to see if God will win, but rather proclaiming to an unbelieving world that no matter how strong evil seems to be at the moment, its days are numbered because it has already been struck a fatal blow. Christ is Lord and King because of the cross, not because of some battle as yet undecided that lies in the future.

The Millennium

If one studies the history of the church and sees how many guesses have been made as to the identity of the beast, of Gog and Magog, of the false prophet, of the nearness of the beginning or the end of the thousand years, one would come to the conclusion that it is best not to guess. If God wished us to know, the language would have been plain. As it is, authentic visions are not intended to be road maps of the future, but proclamations to the great truths about God on which we can base our lives. We can see from this passage that human history does not simply progress upward. Even the presence of the church in the midst of the world has not meant necessarily a lessening of evil. Hitler and the Holocaust, terrible savagery between nations, horrible crimes against children, abuse of all forms, even in the midst of families–these have not ended and have even been found in the midst of nations and homes influenced by the church. Yet there are also times of great progress. It is not an even, upward march of righteousness. Satan seems bound, only to be loosed again. Yet, Revelation makes clear that God is always in control. The angel of God binds Satan and the angel looses, as God seeks the willing obedience of the human creation.

The Judgment

As the judgment begins, the throne of God appears. Heaven and earth disappear. The judgment is the end of all that was, all of the old. It is clearing the decks for the new that will be seen in the next chapter. Some elements of this judgment scene fit in very well with the image we may have had from our childhood. Yet, other elements are very different. The traditional image includes all the dead being judged on the basis of their lives. It includes the books being opened, so that no one can hide from what they did or did not do during their lifetime. So much is familiar. Familiar also is the image of the book of life, with names being inscribed in it on the basis of faithfulness to Christ. Again we see a tension between being judged on the basis of works and on the basis of what Christ has done for us.

What is not familiar is the resurrection of all at the end of time, rather than facing judgment immediately after death. For the early church, as for Judaism, death is real. There is not something eternal that goes on forever when the body dies. Resurrection means giving new life to those who have died. It is a new act of creation, rather than the natural process of something immortal going on after physical death. This is why the creeds speak of "resurrection of the body" or "resurrection of the dead." Later Christians, only a few centuries after the New Testament, combined the Christian belief in resurrection together with a Greek understanding of an immortal soul that, by its very nature, survives death. This is an unstable combination. John's vision shows—as does the judgment scene in Matthew 25:31-46—a general resurrection all at once, at the end of history. For John, as we have seen, this is a second resurrection after the resurrection of the martyrs with Christ at the beginning of the millennium. This idea of a general resurrection must be held in tension with the belief, strong in the letters of Paul, of the unity of the church, the Body of Christ, even across the boundary of death. We cannot imagine exactly what all of this means. We are indeed joined with those who have died in Christ; yet the dead shall be raised together at the end of history. We do not understand the nature of time that spans the bridge between this world and the next, nor do we understand the connection of time as we experience it here and the eternal that even now impinges upon us. That is a mystery that remains.

SHARING THE SCRIPTURE

PREPARING TO TEACH

Preparing Our Hearts

What does it mean to you to know that Jesus Christ is victorious over the powers of evil and death? How does this knowledge affect your relationship with Christ? How does it affect your ability to take a long-term view of the tragedies, violence, crimes, abuse, and other evil that is heralded in our newspapers and emblazoned on our television screens?

As you prepare to teach this lesson, examine your own heart. Do you, as a member of the church of Christ, perceive yourself to be committed to him alone, as two persons pledge that faithfulness in their wedding vows? Or, are you just casually "dating" Christ, checking out other options and seeking out his company only when his presence seems convenient or useful in your life? Pray that God will strengthen your commitment to the one who is King of kings and Lord of lords.

Preparing Our Minds

In today's lesson, we are again immersed in the visionary world of John. As you read Revelation 19–20, try to imagine yourself as John and among the multitude offering praise to God. Consider how you would feel if you participated in such strange and glorious events.

Read the session and note the suggestions for teaching.

Preparing Our Learning Space

Have on hand:
- ✔ several Bibles for students
- ✔ newsprint and marker or chalkboard and chalk
- ✔ paper and pencils

LEADING THE CLASS

(1) Introduction

Set the stage for today's lesson by reading this imaginary scene. Tell the students to sit quietly with their eyes closed so that they might see, hear, smell, taste, and feel the events of this scene.

As a class, we have decided to go to 〔R〕 (name of a nearby stadium where a team, professional or amateur, plays) to watch a baseball game. We have eaten our fill of hot dogs and popcorn, and it is now the bottom of the ninth. Two batters are out, and two men stand poised for action on first and third. We are two runs behind, but we need this victory if we are to stay in contention for a pennant. The crowd is hushed as the visitors' pitcher delivers the 2-2 pitch. At the mighty crack of the bat, the crowd leaps to its feet. The ball sails into the left field bleachers for a home run. The victory celebration begins as we and all the other fans go wild.

After reading this scenario, ask the class:
(1) **Have you ever experienced a glorious** 〔?〕 **victory when defeat seemed to be so close at hand?**
(2) **How do you celebrate victories in your own life?**

Note that during this session we will be studying Christ's victory over sin and death and the celebration that attends it. We know that Christ will be victorious, so our main question for today is: *How will Christ be victorious over the powers of evil?*

As an alternative, or in addition to this activity, use the Focusing on the Main Question segment to introduce the lesson.

(2) The Feast of Rejoicing

This section, based on Revelation 19:1-10, is actually part of our background scripture. Some students, therefore, may not have read it. You will find it helpful to include this material in the session because it bears directly on the celebration surrounding the victory of Christ and what that means to the church. You may want to present the information here, as found under these verses in the Understanding the Scripture portion, as well as under "The Feast of Rejoicing" in the Interpreting the Scripture segment, in the form of a brief lecture to help set the stage for the rest of the lesson. If so, consider including these points:

• Readers understood this vision to be a celebration of victory over the fall of the Roman Empire, a state that stood against justice and righteousness and persecuted Christians.

• A celebration is at hand, though it is imaged as a wedding feast rather than a victory party. The marriage of the Lamb and bride, identified as the church, is the focus of the festivities.

• This portion of scripture reveals a tension between what we would term "salvation by works" and "salvation by grace." On one hand, "the saints are saints because they have done what is just and righteous." On the other hand, "they are righteous because they have "been washed in the blood of the Lamb." Both God's grace and our response to that grace, as seen in changes in our behavior and attitude, are important.

(3) The Bloodstained Rider

Choose a volunteer to read aloud Revelation 19:11-16. If the class finds visual representations helpful, you may want to distribute paper and pencils. Read the passage again, slowly, and let the students draw what they are hearing. Or, if someone in the class is artistically talented, you may want this student to draw his or her interpretation of this vision on newsprint or a chalkboard.

Pose these questions for discussion:

(1) Note that the rider of the white horse rides into battle with a bloodstained robe. Why?

(See "The Bloodstained Rider" under the Interpreting the Scripture portion for a discussion on this topic.)

(2) The description of the rider clearly shows that he will judge the nations. In other words, they will be held accountable for their actions. What judgments do you think the rider will level against our own nation?

(3) Do you think that knowing a judgment is to come prompts some people to claim a religious faith? Explain your answer.

(4) How does the often one-sided picture of God as loving and merciful lull us into complacency about the other side of God, the side that judges?

(5) What does it mean in your own life to acknowledge that Christ is "King of kings and Lord of lords"?

(4) The Millennium

This portion on the millennium is also based on background scripture, Revelation 20:1-10. We have included it for discussion because, as noted in the Understanding the Scripture portion, Christians throughout church history have disagreed on the timing of this event. Many Christians are familiar with the image of Satan bound for a thousand years, so be prepared to give an overview of these verses and their interpretation if time permits. Present the viewpoints, but do not get bogged down here. Some persons in the class may have strong, and quite different, opinions about this. However, we cannot say for certainty when the millennium will occur; only God knows that. What we can affirm is that God is always in control, no matter how things may appear.

As you talk about these verses, be sure to point out 4-5. They will be important in the next section because verse 4 shows a resurrection of martyrs before Satan's thousand-year reign, while verse 5 shows that other persons will not be resurrected until after the millennium.

(5) The Judgment

Have someone read aloud Revelation 20:11-15.

Divide a sheet of newsprint, or space on a chalkboard, in half. Label the left side, "Familiar Elements," and the right side, "Unfamiliar Elements." Ask class members to recall teachings from these verses that seem familiar to them, perhaps ones they learned in childhood. Also invite them to list elements of this description that seem unfamiliar to them.

Use information from the Understanding the Scripture section for 20:11-15 and "The Judgment" portion under Interpreting the Scripture to get a more comprehensive view of John's understanding of judgment and resurrection.

Conclude today's lesson by providing some quiet moments so that students may reflect on these questions.

R Which of your works do you think God will judge positively so as to praise?

Which of your works do you think God will judge negatively so as to punish?

If you knew that this age would close and judgment would come tomorrow, R what would you do to prepare?

What does Christ's victory over sin and death mean to you personally?

HELPING CLASS MEMBERS ACT

Encourage students to seek out persons they know who are able to celebrate a victory in their own lives. Perhaps they have won an award, overcome a habit such as smoking, or found a new job. Suggest that the class members find a way to celebrate with these victorious ones.

Challenge class members to consider their own accountability before God for their actions, attitudes, and words. Encourage them to take steps if necessary, with God's help, to be able to give a better account of their words and deeds.

Note that Revelation 19 begins with a triumphant song about the end of an idolatrous, unjust, unrighteous government. Point out that Christians can influence their government by running for office, voting, contacting elected officials, and voicing opinions about how tax dollars should be spent. Encourage class members to take some form of action this week to help make their government one that is characterized by righteousness and justice.

PLANNING FOR NEXT SUNDAY

Next week's lesson will conclude our study of Revelation. The session, entitled "A New Heaven and Earth," focuses on Revelation 21:1-7, 22-27. Tell students to read these passages and, if possible, the background scripture from Revelation 21:1–22:5. Ask them to consider their own vision of a new and better world.

You may want to look ahead to the first unit of the fourth quarter, entitled "Guidance for Ministry." This five-session unit is rooted in the Pastoral Epistles to Timothy (1 and 2) and Titus. If time permits, you may want to read all three of these brief letters this week.

A NEW HEAVEN AND EARTH

PREVIEWING THE LESSON

Lesson Scripture: Revelation 21:1-7, 22-27
Background Scripture: Revelation 21:1–22:5
Key Verse: Revelation 21:1

Focus of the Lesson:
the expectation of a new heaven and earth filled with the presence of God, free of evil and sorrow

Main Question of the Lesson:
What are the characteristics of the new heaven and earth?

This lesson will enable adult learners to:
(1) explore John's vision of a new heaven and earth.
(2) begin to experience the closeness that will exist between humanity and God in this just, new world.
(3) respond by taking an action to make their world more like the promised new heaven and earth.

Today's lesson may be outlined as follows:
(1) Introduction
(2) The New Closeness
(3) The City of Light
(4) Face to Face

FOCUSING ON THE MAIN QUESTION

All of the judgment and destruction that John's visions have presented in the bulk of this book are for a redemptive and loving purpose: the creation of a world that fulfills God's intentions, a world in which righteousness is the way of life, where injustice does not occur. Even if everyone became completely righteous, in the biblical view, there are still some results of sin that human beings cannot eliminate: death, sickness, and sorrow would remain because they are brought about by nature itself, not only by human action. This is the result of the curse on the earth and on humanity that was enunciated at the point of the first sin (Genesis 3:15-19). In the final redeemed creation, God will wipe away even these curses.

This final goal of all creation will also differ from all previous reality in that God will relate to humanity in a new and more direct way. Up to this point in human history, God has related to humanity in somewhat indirect ways: through prophets, through the temple, through the Incarnation, through the sacraments. One could always doubt that it was really God who had spoken or acted. Faith was always needed. For the early church, God's indirect ways of dealings with humanity were understood as God's respect for our freedom. If God had appeared to us directly, we would have been so overwhelmed that there would have been no choice, no freedom, no decision-making on our part. But in this new time, this time beyond history where life is eternal and the choices made earlier have been sorted out in the judgment that occurred just before this new time, God will come close to a perfect humanity, to be in fellowship with them.

The image of marriage returns. Whereas earlier there was preparation for the marriage feast, now the bride and groom actually come together. Now their new life together begins. And they will indeed live happily ever after, for the time of sin, sorrow, and death is gone. Unlike some cultures, Judaism and Christianity did not imagine history going around in circles, reaching an end only to start at the beginning again. Once God has redeemed the creation, there will be no new fall. The new relationship to God guarantees this. As we shall see in this lesson, John draws heavily on elements of Old Testament expectation and hope for the future reign of God.

If one views the whole book of Revelation from the perspective of what it tells us about God, what we learn is that God wills a good creation, undisrupted by sin and evil. God will accomplish this. Such a creation was God's intention at the beginning of Genesis, and it is fulfilled in these last chapters of Revelation. The end is not exactly like the beginning, however. The world is different, we are different, our relationship to God is different; but through it all, God remains the same, the Alpha and the Omega.

During today's study, we will ask: *What are the characteristics of the new heaven and earth?*

READING THE SCRIPTURE

NRSV
Revelation 21:1-7

NIV
Revelation 21:1-7

Key Verse

1 Then I saw a new heaven and a new earth; for the first heaven and the first earth had passed away, and the sea was no more. ²And I saw the holy city, the new Jerusalem, coming down out of heaven from God, prepared as a bride adorned for her husband. ³And I heard a loud voice from the throne saying,
"See, the home of God is
     among mortals.
He will dwell with them as
     their God;
they will be his peoples,

1 Then I saw a new heaven and a new earth, for the first heaven and the first earth had passed away, and there was no longer any sea. ²I saw the Holy City, the new Jerusalem, coming down out of heaven from God, prepared as a bride beautifully dressed for her husband. ³And I heard a loud voice from the throne saying, "Now the dwelling of God is with men, and he will live with them. They will be his people, and God himself will be with them and be their God. ⁴He will wipe every tear from their eyes. There will be

and God himself will be with
them;
⁴ he will wipe every tear from
their eyes.
Death will be no more;
mourning and crying and pain
will be no more,
for the first things have passed
away."

5 And the one who was seated on the throne said, "See, I am making all things new." Also he said, "Write this, for these words are trustworthy and true." ⁶Then he said to me, "It is done! I am the Alpha and the Omega, the beginning and the end. To the thirsty I will give water as a gift from the spring of the water of life. ⁷Those who conquer will inherit these things, and I will be their God and they will be my children.

no more death or mourning or crying or pain, for the old order of things has passed away."

⁵He who was seated on the throne said, "I am making everything new!" Then he said, "Write this down, for these words are trustworthy and true."

⁶He said to me: "It is done. I am the Alpha and the Omega, the Beginning and the End. To him who is thirsty I will give to drink without cost from the spring of the water of life. ⁷He who overcomes will inherit all this, and I will be his God and he will be my son.

NRSV
Revelation 21:22-27

22 I saw no temple in the city, for its temple is the Lord God the Almighty and the Lamb. ²³And the city has no need of sun or moon to shine on it, for the glory of God is its light, and its lamp is the Lamb. ²⁴The nations will walk by its light, and the kings of the earth will bring their glory into it. ²⁵Its gates will never be shut by day—and there will be no night there. ²⁶People will bring into it the glory and the honor of the nations. ²⁷But nothing unclean will enter it, nor anyone who practices abomination or falsehood, but only those who are written in the Lamb's book of life.

NIV
Revelation 21:22-27

²²I did not see a temple in the city, because the Lord God Almighty and the Lamb are its temple. ²³The city does not need the sun or the moon to shine on it, for the glory of God gives it light, and the Lamb is its lamp. ²⁴The nations will walk by its light, and the kings of the earth will bring their splendor into it. ²⁵On no day will its gates ever be shut, for there will be no night there. ²⁶The glory and honor of the nations will be brought into it. ²⁷Nothing impure will ever enter it, nor will anyone who does what is shameful or deceitful, but only those whose names are written in the Lamb's book of life.

UNDERSTANDING THE SCRIPTURE

Revelation 21:1-7. The final vision begins with the creation of the new heaven and the new earth. Evidently, even heaven and earth had been so tainted by sin and evil that they could not be the fit habitation of the redeemed. The previous ones had disappeared just as the final judgment began (Revelation 20:11). There are some interesting details here. We are told that the sea disappears. Why was the sea negative? It was negative for John because the sea separated him on the island of Patmos from the churches in the province of Asia. But in the visions he has had, the sea is also the spawning ground of the terrible beasts that represent evil. There had been a long tradition of such imagery in the Old Testament, as seen in Job 3:8 and Isaiah 27:1.

In contrast to the earlier vision of the whore of Babylon (Revelation 17:1-6) we now see the city of God, the new Jerusalem, who is the bride of the Lamb. The time of preparation is ended; the wedding is now to take place. This implies a new union, a new closeness and intimacy within the covenant between God and humanity. God will dwell with humans— God will be in the world of humans, not in a distant heaven. Because of this new closeness there will be no tears or mourning or death. All of the characteristics of the curse on the earth because of sin will be removed. This is the reward of the righteous. It bears great resemblance to the vision of the final future to be found in the prophets (see Isaiah 25:6-9).

Revelation 21:8-21. On the other hand, the wicked will have no place in this new creation. They would corrupt it. In the judgment, they have been given over to the second death (Revelation 20:14-15). John is invited to see the bride of the Lamb, the holy city. Jerusalem is coming down from this new heaven to dwell on the new earth. Clearly, the vision was beyond human capacity to describe, and John paints an extraordinary picture. The whole city shines and sparkles. It is made of jewels that pick up the glory of God that dwells within it. It has walls as all cities did, and it has twelve gates. It is important to note that the gates are named for the twelve tribes of Israel. The twelve foundations are named for the twelve apostles of the Lamb. The two peoples of God are represented here in this city. It is a huge city, over a thousand miles in every direction. It is even twelve hundred miles high! The walls are only two hundred feet high, so most of the city could be seen readily.

Revelation 21:22-27. Israel had been accustomed to a presence of God in the midst of the people. It had been the pillar of cloud and fire in the time in the wilderness. It was the tabernacle that housed the ark of the covenant. Next it was the great Temple in Jerusalem. In Solomon's prayer at the temple dedication (2 Chronicles 6:18-21) we find a description of what Israel believed concerning the temple. Solomon knows that God cannot be contained in a temple created by human beings. God cannot even be contained in the whole earth. But God has promised that God's name will dwell there. Those who go to the temple can be assured that God will hear them. In some way, God's indirect presence is to be found in the temple. Ezekiel has a vision that the presence of God leaves the temple just before it is destroyed (Ezekiel 10:18-19). Jesus proclaims that if the temple is destroyed, he will raise it up again in three days. The interpretation is added that Jesus meant his own body (John 2:19-22). This implies that in the Incarnation, the presence of God is now with the people in Jesus. It is an equally indirect form, for many could see only a human being, and not the presence of God. In this new city, God will be present directly. There will be no temple.

The presence of God is symbolized by great light. If God is directly present with the people, they will need no sun or moon. There will be no night. Night was when cities closed their gates so that no unwelcome people could enter. The walls of the new city are not for security, however, for there is nothing that could threaten the peace and justice of this city. Therefore, the gates are always open. The light shines so brightly that even for nations outside the city the brightness of the city is their sun. Through these open gates all of the nations will come to bring glory and honor. Especially in Isaiah, the promised future included Israel being a light to the nations so that they too could be saved (Isaiah 49:6). Many of the details found in this description of the new Jerusalem are also found in the vision of the future in Isaiah 60. Even the song of Simeon, spoken by the righteous Simeon when Jesus is presented in the temple in the old Jerusalem, includes the belief that in him, God's promised future of salvation for the world through the light coming from Israel had now begun (Luke 2:29-32). No sin shall corrupt this new Jerusalem.

Revelation 22:1-5. Though the final goal of God's creation far surpasses the beginning, there are some commonalities that tie them together. There is a river with the tree of life, now readily available for human consumption. In Genesis, humanity had been expelled from Eden before they could eat of this tree, because they had been disobedient (Genesis 3:22-23). The tree of life provides food and healing for the people. The Lamb and God are constantly intertwined throughout these verses. Themes from the preceding chapter are reiterated: no temple needed, no sun, no night, for God is the light of the city. All of the city will worship God and the Lamb, a continuation of the worship in the old heaven recorded in earlier portions of John's vision.

INTERPRETING THE SCRIPTURE

The New Closeness

In the traditional picture of eternal life that many of us hold, the blessed go to be with God in heaven and life on earth disappears. But that is not the vision that John received and presents to us. For John, there is both a new heaven and a new earth. Why would there need to be a new heaven? Why a new earth? Neither makes sense within the traditional view of eternal life. Yet God intentionally created the earth and its human inhabitants and loved the whole creation. A redeemed earth is part of God's intention, not a disembodied humanity. Heaven has for so long been concerned with the struggle against evil. Heaven's relationship to earth has been on a war footing. Now that peace has come, a new heaven is needed along with a new earth. The whole dynamic has changed. Furthermore, God will dwell with humanity on this new earth. The path from earth to heaven will be open. Heaven and earth are close, not distant.

John's vision is of the end time, the final goal of history. God says that it has been accomplished. For us, it has not happened yet, but it is guaranteed, for God in Christ has finished that which is needed. For the Christians in Asia Minor, the vision of the new heaven and the new earth would strengthen their resolve to be faithful. John's vision would also help them to interpret the terrible events that were to happen, so they would not think God had abandoned them or was unable to save them from their enemies.

The City of Light

In some ways, verses 22-27 of chapter 21 are the climax of the vision. The redemption of the world is no return to the perfection of the beginning of the creation. In the beginning, God created the heavens and the earth, with the sun and the moon to give light by day and by night, creating day and night (Genesis 1:1-5,14-19). Here we are told that at the end there is no more need for a sun and a moon in this new heaven and earth, for there will be no night. God created both the beginning and the end. They are different. Both were perfect, for God's creation was good. But God's final purpose was not completed at the beginning, for God intended history, the development of humanity and its learning to be obedient to God. Sin clearly made this development and learning difficult and confused. But in the midst of this, God was working toward redemption, and this involved the preparation of a people who would be a means for the redemption of the world. Through Israel and the church, God is working toward this final goal.

It is very interesting in this image of the templeless and sunless city, that the light, which is God, flows from the city to the whole world. Not everyone is in the city, though the whole world is redeemed. Nations and kings still freely come in and out of the city. There are gates because there is constant traffic—communication—between the city and the rest of this new earth. The world is functioning as it was intended to, even when the temple and the sun were the source of light. But now it has reached its final stage of development where God is in the midst of the city and, therefore, no temple and no sun are necessary.

Face to Face

Revelation 22:1-5 repeats much of what we have read in the previous section. Added, however, are the direct references to Eden, though here also there are changes, so the old and the new are again related. "The nations" are referred to, which implies that there is more than the holy city on this new earth. Unlike in the old world, all the nations are healed and live together in peace. The servants of God are marked with a seal. A sign on the forehead showing to whom one belongs has been a common theme throughout the Revelation to John. The redeemed have been marked; the servants of the beast have been sealed. In this present world, where God and the powers of evil compete for domination, the individual is never simply a private actor. Our actions put us in the service of one side or the other, and we thus bear the mark of our service. For Christians, baptism is the sign that we belong to God. It is important that our actions show to the world that we indeed belong to God.

The servants of God will see God's face. This is an astonishing statement. For Israel, Moses stood above all other prophets because God spoke to him face-to-face (Exodus 33:11; Numbers 12:7-8). Paul said our vision of God is now like seeing in a dim mirror (1 Corinthians 13:12). In the life to come, however, all the redeemed will see God face-to-face. When Jacob wrestled with the angel, he was astonished that he was still alive, since he had gotten so close to God (Genesis 32:30). Anyone who understands who God is and who we are would be astonished that we could be so close to God and not be destroyed. But in the life to come, there can be this closeness and intimacy between God and humanity, and we will not only remain alive, but indeed, such closeness will give us eternal life.

SHARING THE SCRIPTURE

PREPARING TO TEACH

Preparing Our Hearts

As this fascinating unit on John's vision at Patmos draws to a close, we will consider the new heaven and earth that are promised to us at the close of the age. In those days sorrow and evil will no longer exist. God will be intimately present in the future city, surrounding it and giving light to all. In preparation for leading this session, think about what you hope God's new heaven and earth will be like. What would you hope to find more of there? What would you expect to find missing? What changes would be necessary in your own life to be able to fit into such a place? Prayerfully ask God to help you begin to make those changes now.

Preparing Our Minds

Read Revelation 21:1–22:5, along with the lesson, as you prepare to teach.
If you have *The United Methodist Hymnal* available, read "O Holy City, Seen of John" on page 726. If not, you may be able to find this or another song based on John's vision in Revelation 21 in another hymnal. If you will have someone play the hymn, contact the accompanist early in the week.

Also read "Canticle of Hope" on page 734 of *The United Methodist Hymnal*. This responsive reading is suggested for use as an activity under "Face to Face."

Preparing Our Learning Space

Secure copies of hymnals if you plan to use a hymn and/or responsive reading.

Have on hand:
- ✔ several Bibles for students
- ✔ newsprint and marker or chalkboard and chalk
- ✔ paper and pencils
- ✔ hymnals, if possible

LEADING THE CLASS

(1) Introduction

Begin today's session by telling the class that they have just received a contract to design a city. They are responsible not only for the physical appearance of this new city but also for the moral and ethical values that will guide the lives of its inhabitants. If the class is small, have class members call out their ideas for this new city. Record them on newsprint or a chalkboard. If the class is larger, you may want to divide into teams and give each team pencils and paper on which to write their ideas. Have the teams share their thoughts with the class.

Move to the scripture lesson for today by pointing out that God has already done this work for us. In addition, God has shown John a vision of what this city will look like and be like. Today, as we conclude our study of the Revelation to John, we will ask:

(1) What are the characteristics of the new heaven and earth?

As an alternative way to introduce the lesson, read or retell the Focusing on the Main Question portion.

If possible, sing a hymn based on Revelation 21–22:5, such as "O Holy City, Seen of John," found on page 726 of *The United Methodist Hymnal.* If you cannot sing in your class area, consider reading the hymn in unison.

(2) The New Closeness

Invite students to open their Bibles and follow along as you read Revelation 21:1-7.

Then ask:

? **(1) What does this passage tell you about who God is and what God intends to do?**

(2) What does this passage imply about the kind of relationship God wants to have with humanity?

Discuss the idea of closeness between God and humanity, using the Understanding the Scripture portion to help you. Continue the discussion by asking:

? **(3) If you can picture the kind of world that John is describing, what prevents us from living in such a world now, even though that is what God wills for us?**

(3) The City of Light

Read aloud Revelation 21:22-27. Point out that the new city has no sun, moon, or temple. Do a Bible study to show the importance of these elements in Israel's history. The Understanding the Scripture segment will help you discuss these ideas related to light and God's presence. You may want to ask individuals to locate these passages and read them aloud.

- Genesis 1:1-5, 14-19 tells us that God created night and day and the sun and moon to give light.
- Exodus 13:21-22 states that God was present with the people fleeing Egypt as a pillar of cloud and pillar of fire.
- Exodus 33:10 records that the people would bow down in front of the tent where the pillar of cloud stood.
- 2 Chronicles 6:18-21 discusses Solomon's understanding that the temple cannot contain God, though God is present.
- Ezekiel 10:18-19 records the prophet's vision of God leaving the temple just before its destruction.
- Luke 2:29-32, which is known as the song of Simeon, speaks of Jesus in terms of "a light for revelation."
- John 2:19-22 reports Jesus' proclamation about his own body as the temple.

Summarize this study by reading or retelling "The City of Light" portion under Interpreting the Scripture. Emphasize that neither the sun nor the moon will be needed because God is light. Moreover, the temple will be unnecessary because God is in the midst of the new heaven and earth.

Use this guided imagery exercise to help the class members imagine this new city of God. Be sure to pause so that they may reflect on what your words suggest to them.

Sit back comfortably and relax. (pause)　**R**

Imagine that you have taken a plane ride to the most beautiful, peaceful city you can imagine. Spend some time mentally wandering the streets of this city. Take in the architecture. (pause)

Suddenly you are attracted by a brilliant light. You see no sun and soon realize that God's own self is radiating this dazzling brilliance. Let yourself be bathed in the glow of this light. How does it make you feel? Think how you would describe it to someone else. (pause)

As you are walking, you notice that people—even important-looking people like kings—walk back and forth between heaven and earth. There is no guard or wall or closed gate to keep persons in or shut them out. Instead, there is unlimited freedom to come and go in peace. Think about what it would be like if we need not fear anyone but could go about freely. (pause)

As you begin to talk with the inhabitants of this city, you recognize that no one is suffering. Evil and sorrow have vanished. What hope does that give you for the future? (pause)

Now you must return to the plane and go home. Open your eyes when you are ready.

(4) Face to Face

This section, based on the background scripture from Revelation 22:1-5, reiterates some of the same themes found in the previous chapter. Unlike all prior history, where God was present but not fully revealed, in the new heaven and earth we will be able to see God face-to-face.

Provide a few moments of silence for class members to contemplate:

- what it might feel like to see God face-to-face.
- a word of thanksgiving they would like to say directly to God.
- a question they would like to ask God.

Conclude today's session by reading responsively "Canticle of Hope," found on page 734 of *The United Methodist Hymnal,* or another reading based on Revelation 21–22. If you do not have access to a hymnal, work with the students to write a class litany. Here are some suggested parts for the leader. The group will have to provide responses. You may want to write all of this on newsprint or a chalkboard.

R **Leader:** Rejoice, for the old has passed away and we shall soon live in a new heaven and earth.

People:

Leader: In this city, we will need no sun.

People:

Leader: There will be no temple, for God is with us.

People:

Leader: We will live in joy and peace, for the ways of our God are just.

People:

HELPING CLASS MEMBERS ACT

Mention that the new heaven and earth that John envisions is one of justice and peace. It is a place of shalom—a place where people are whole, healthy, and lovingly related to each other and to God. Challenge class members to do something this week to loosen the grip that evil has on the world and in their lives. For example, they could offer an apology to someone they have wronged, or make an effort to get to know someone of a racial or ethnic group.

Challenge class members to learn more about a conflict or war that is in the headlines. Suggest that they find out why the parties are divided, what the effect of this conflict has on the people and the region in which they live, how this hostility affects the children and their future, and any other pertinent information. Encourage the students to try to create a peace plan that would enable the two sides to live amicably.

Some persons may see the promise of a new heaven and earth as an invitation to start over. Suggest that anyone who has been thinking about changing a career or moving into retirement to think about these shifts in light of the newer, better heaven and earth that are to come. Have students consider reasons why such a change may be beneficial to them. Encourage any who are ready to make a move to give it very prayerful consideration.

PLANNING FOR NEXT SUNDAY

Tell the class that we will begin a new unit next week, "Guidance for Ministry," that will focus our attention on 1 and 2 Timothy and Titus. Our first lesson from this unit, entitled "Practice What You Preach," is based on 1 Timothy 4:6-16.

FOURTH QUARTER

Guidance for Ministry
JUNE 1, 1997—JUNE 29, 1997

A Call to Faithfulness
JULY 6, 1997—AUGUST 31, 1997

Our final quarter for the 1996–97 Sunday school year is divided into two sections. The first, which we will study during the five Sundays in June, focuses on the "Guidance for Ministry" given in the Pastoral Epistles. We will explore the advice given to early servants of the church, Timothy and Titus. The second section, entitled "A Call to Faithfulness," is a nine-week study of The Letter to the Hebrews. Our unit for July, called "The Greatness of Christ," looks at who Jesus is. The last unit, "Be Faithful Followers of Christ" calls the original readers of Hebrews and us as well to be faithful disciples.

On June 1, we begin with a look at 1 Timothy 4:6-16 where Timothy is urged to set an example for others. The following week, in 1 Timothy 6:2b-21 he is also directed to pursue godliness. In the lesson for June 15 from 2 Timothy 2:1-13, the young leader is told to share in suffering as a good soldier of Christ. During the last two lessons we learn that Timothy is also to be faithful and teach that faithfulness to others (2 Timothy 4:1-8), and Titus is to encourage members of the Christian community to be good to one another (Titus 3:1-11).

In July, we will explore the lordship of Jesus Christ. The writer of Hebrews reminds us that Jesus is not simply a messenger from God but God's own Son (Hebrews 1:1-5; 3:1-6) and our Savior (Hebrews 2:5-11, 14-18). Using images of the temple and its practices, the author of Hebrews states that Jesus is both our high priest (Hebrews 4:14–5:10) and the perfect sacrifice (Hebrews 10:1-14).

Once we are aware of who Christ is, we must decide how we will respond to him. Our final unit begins on August 3 with a call for Christians to go on toward mature faith (Hebrews 5:11–6:10). One way to do this is to remain close to God, even as we endure hard times (Hebrews 10:19-25, 32-39). We can also increase in faithfulness as we remember those who were faithful in the past and learn from their example (Hebrews 11:1-2, 6-10, 13-16, 39-40). Growth in faithfulness in a process and, therefore, we must continually renew our commitment to God (Hebrews 12:1-11). Finally, we are to live responsibly, exercising Christlike care and loving concern for others (Hebrews 13:1-16).

As you prepare to teach this quarter, we again suggest that you use *The Devotional Companion to The International Lessons 1996–97* (available from Cokesbury) as a guide for class worship. In keeping with our emphasis on God's Word as the light for our way, you may want to continue to use the refrain from the song "Thy Word Is a Lamp" (*The United Methodist Hymnal,* page 601) as a regular part of your weekly devotions.

If you have not already done so, you will want to order your copy of the 1997–98 edition of *The New International Lesson Annual.* The first unit, "God Leads a People Home," will focus on Judah's history from the fall of Jerusalem in 587 B.C.E. to the end of the Old Testament era. During the winter we will examine passages from the Letters of 1 John, 1 and 2 Peter, and Jude in the course entitled "God's People in a Troubled World." In the spring, we will study Jesus' ministry and teachings as recorded in the Gospel of Mark. During our last quarter, we will delve into the books of Ecclesiastes, Job, and Proverbs in order to gain "Wisdom for Living."

MEET OUR WRITER

DR. CHARLES E. WOLFE

Charles E. Wolfe, a United Methodist minister, has a B.A. from Northern Iowa University, B.D. from Austin Presbyterian Theological Seminary, and D.Min. from Wesley Theological Seminary. He has been a pastor in Texas, New York, and Maryland, and an Army chaplain. Dr. Wolfe has taught Old and New Testament courses at Western Maryland College. At Wesley Theological Seminary he has taught Bible in various programs, including the Course of Study for local pastors, the Lay Resource Institute, and certification for diaconal ministry. For sixteen years he edited *Exegetical Resource*. A resident of Westminster, Maryland, Dr. Wolfe is married and the father of four sons.

PRACTICE WHAT YOU PREACH

PREVIEWING THE LESSON

Lesson Scripture: 1 Timothy 4:6-16
Background Scripture: 1 Timothy 4:6-16
Key Verses: 1 Timothy 4:7*b*-8

Focus of the Lesson:
Paul's counsel to Timothy that Christ's servants must practice godly living to be an example to others

Main Question of the Lesson:
How can we live up to the standards of Christian behavior to which we are called?

This lesson will enable adult learners to:
(1) explore the kind of example that Timothy is exhorted to set.
(2) understand the behaviors and attitudes associated with being a servant who sets an example.
(3) respond by acting in ways that set a good example for others.

Today's lesson may be outlined as follows:
(1) Introduction
(2) Godliness
(3) Training
(4) Example

FOCUSING ON THE MAIN QUESTION

I heard an old joke from a county agent in upstate New York who, with a sly grin, explained the frustration of a younger colleague in his first months on the job. At last the new county agent asked an old farmer, "Why won't you at least try some of these new techniques that I'm trying to teach you?" The old farmer replied, "Well, son, I'm not farming now half as well as I know how to!"

This is the point as we struggle with discipleship, and especially with the relationship between our own conduct and our witness to others. Obviously there is a lot that the old farmer does not know, and he needs to be open to improvement; but he also understands that forays into the unknown must not distract from living up to what he already knows. There are hotly debated topics in Christian ethics that are important: our stance toward capital punishment, organ transplants, abortions, and on and on. We debate, change our minds, and may become confused. But in the midst of the confusions and ambiguities that confront us, we still know enough to embody Christian ideals better than we actually do. That is the point in James Baldwin's play *Blues for Mister Charlie*. I saw it on Broadway in 1964 and can still sense the hushed tenseness of the audience as an angry young black man bursts out that he can be as bad as any white man who ever lived. His pastor cuts through with a powerful, "No . . . . Because you know better!"

That is pretty much our story as well. It would be so easy to let go, to act like everybody else, to sink to the level of the lowest common denominator of acceptable behavior. But we cannot because we know better. And even if we do not have all of the answers, we have enough of them, as our lesson urges us, to be good servants of Jesus Christ (1 Timothy 4:6), to set an example (4:12), and to practice what we preach so that all may see our progress (4:15). Today's scripture prompts us to ask: *How can we live up to the standards of Christian behavior to which we are called?*

JUNE 1

READING THE SCRIPTURE

NRSV

1 Timothy 4:6-16

6 If you put these instructions before the brothers and sisters, you will be a good servant of Christ Jesus, nourished on the words of the faith and of the sound teaching that you have followed. 7Have nothing to do with profane myths and old wives' tales. Train yourself in godliness, 8for, while physical training is of some value, godliness is valuable in every way, holding promise for both the present life and the life to come. 9The saying is sure and worthy of full acceptance. 10For to this end we toil and struggle, because we have our hope set on the living God, who is the Savior of all people, especially of those who believe.

11 These are the things you must insist on and teach. 12Let no one despise your youth, but set the believers an example in speech and conduct, in love, in faith, in purity. 13Until I arrive, give attention to the public reading of scripture, to exhorting, to teaching. 14Do not neglect the gift that is in you, which was given to you through prophecy with the laying on of hands by

NIV

1 Timothy 4:6-16

6If you point these things out to the brothers, you will be a good minister of Christ Jesus, brought up in the truths of the faith and of the good teaching that you have followed. 7Have nothing to do with godless myths and old wives' tales; rather, train yourself to be godly. 8For physical training is of some value, but godliness has value for all things, holding promise for both the present life and the life to come.

9This is a trustworthy saying that deserves full acceptance 10(and for this we labor and strive), that we have put our hope in the living God, who is the Savior of all men, and especially of those who believe.

11Command and teach these things. 12Don't let anyone look down on you because you are young, but set an example for the believers in speech, in life, in love, in faith and in purity. 13Until I come, devote yourself to the public reading of Scripture, to preaching and to teaching. 14Do not neglect your gift, which was given

Key
Verses

Key
Verses

the council of elders. [15]Put these things into practice, devote yourself to them, so that all may see your progress. [16]Pay close attention to yourself and to your teaching; continue in these things, for in doing this you will save both yourself and your hearers.

you through a prophetic message when the body of elders laid their hands on you.

[15]Be diligent in these matters; give yourself wholly to them, so that everyone may see your progress. [16]Watch your life and doctrine closely. Persevere in them, because if you do, you will save both yourself and your hearers.

UNDERSTANDING THE SCRIPTURE

1 Timothy 4:6-9. False teachers, probably from within the congregation itself, have caused trouble in Ephesus. They are teaching a different doctrine from that of the apostle (1:3), one that is intent upon myths and genealogies. They promote speculations that seem to lead nowhere (1:4). In reality, they lead away from the faith (4:1). They are like the old stagecoach line from San Diego to San Antonio that was described as "from no place through nothing to nowhere." Along this dismal route they forbid marriage and demand abstinence from foods (4:1-3). There is no scholarly consensus concerning the details; but their way to purity is dismissed as a myth that is profane (rather than sacred) and as superstition (rather than sound doctrine) to be avoided (4:7). They had probably mixed elements from other religions with Christianity, perhaps the dualism that was to become gnosticism. This would account for the ascetic devaluation of the body. Religious syncretism was in the air. In other words, people were blending the beliefs and practices of other religions together with Christianity.

In contrast, Timothy is to bring to the brothers and sisters religious instruction that flows out of his own life. If the words of the faith have nourished his spirit, as food and water vitalize the body, surely they will nourish the members of the congregation as well (4:6). Sound teaching, in parallelism with the words of the faith, has also fed him, and it can be expected to feed the church as well. Timothy has followed this teaching, in the sense of studying to understand and then being loyal to it no matter what. The Old Testament is a major source of the words and the doctrines (4:13). The hope in the living God as Savior of believers (4:10) is at least part of what is to be taught.

1 Timothy 4:10-12. We Christians are defined as people who believe that God is our Savior (4:10). The salvation is the blessing of the world to come (4:8). This is the end for which we "toil" (NRSV) or "labor" (NKJV) in the present life of discipleship (4:10). It is like the muscle-pulling, nerve-stretching exertion of heavy lifting, or perhaps the exhausting strain of the athlete giving 110 percent effort in the arena. The second verb, "struggle" (NRSV) or "strive" (NIV) or "battling" (NJB), is used of gladiators or soldiers in combat and of athletic competition in general. These two verbs, therefore, reflect the intensity with which we are to live as Christians. NKJV, however, has "suffer reproach" instead of "struggle" for the second verb. The manuscript evidence is not decisive, but most English translations have understood "struggle" as the expected conclusion of the training in verse 8 and have considered persecution as an unexpected intrusion.

1 Timothy 4:13-14. Timothy is to instruct the people (4:13). This instruction consists, among other things, of reading (NKJV). The NRSV clarifies this as "the public reading of scripture." The scripture to be read, of course, is the Old Testament. Public reading, which was a tradition adopted by the early church from the synagogue, was important because many people in attendance would have been unable to read, and the shortage of manuscripts meant that even many of those who could read would not have access to a copy of the Bible. Reading the scripture, however, is not enough. It is to be followed by "exhortation" (NKJV) or "preaching" (NIV), which explains or expounds the text and applies it to everyday life. Exhortation can also be encouragement. The "teaching" (NRSV) or "doctrine" (NKJV) places the specific text within the wider context of the general principles of the Christian faith.

1 Timothy 4:15-16. Yet, as important as the reading, preaching, and teaching are,

they are but half the equation. Equally important is the teacher's own state of grace. And so Timothy is to "pay close attention" to himself (NRSV) or to "take heed" to himself (NKJV) before he speaks to others (4:16). Here the writer is reminding Timothy that we teach in our attitudes and behaviors as well as in words. We cannot cut ethical corners ourselves at the same time that we preach godliness to others. We cannot exhort or encourage others to persevere while we whine about our own problems. We cannot urge others to fix their eye upon the coming world while we are totally consumed by our secular environment. We are, in short, to model the gospel that we preach. This practice will result in our own salvation. And that practice, together with our teaching, tends to the salvation of our listeners.

INTERPRETING THE SCRIPTURE

Godliness

Godliness is a special theme in the Pastoral Epistles (1 and 2 Timothy and Titus). The Greek word for godliness occurs fifteen times in the New Testament. Two-thirds of these instances are in the Pastoral Epistles. Elsewhere it is found only in Acts and in 2 Peter. Six of the ten occurrences, furthermore, are concentrated in two of our lessons, today's and next week's. But the variety in translation shows that no single English word captures its complete meaning. In 1 Timothy 4:7, for example, we find "godliness" (NKJV, NRSV, and NIV), "spirituality" (JB), the "discipline of religion" (NAB), "spiritual exercise" (GNB), and the "practice of religion" (REV). In 4:8 we may add the "benefits of religion" (REB), "godly" (GNB and NIV), and "piety" (NAB).

The basic idea in the word is respect or

reverence for the good, and especially for the divine. This inner attitude is then expressed in outward actions, including worship and the conduct in general that God approves of. In 4 Maccabees 5:20 (found in the Apocrypha) that conduct is specified as obedience to the Law. In 1 Timothy 3:16, the NRSV translates it in very general terms as "our religion." In Acts 3:12 it is the power of personal piety. Godliness is associated with endurance in 2 Peter 1:6, with mutual affection in 2 Peter 1:7, with holiness in 2 Peter 3:11, and with dignity in 1 Timothy 2:2. In 2 Peter 1:3, Christ's power provides what we need for godliness, and in 2 Timothy 3:5, godliness gives us power for living effectively in the here and now. So the word includes the Christian way of life—doctrine, worship, and the nitty-gritty of everyday behavior all wrapped up in one indivisible package.

In 1 Timothy 4:8 godliness is "valuable" (NRSV) or "profitable" (NKJV) in "every way," which is defined in terms of a double promise, for this life and for the life to come. All too often we think of godliness as the prerequisite for the one promise, that of the blessings of heaven. Godliness is then something we have to engage in so that some day we might have our reward. But according to the text this is to short-change ourselves, for godliness is expected to enrich our lives now also. For the godly, accordingly, discipleship is more than a dose of medicine. It is a joy in its own right. This dimension was caught by an elderly man in a church I once served as pastor. He said, "Even if heaven were not to be, it still would have been worth it to be a Christian for the joy it has given me all my life." Anything that can generate such current happiness along with the prospect of so much more to come is certainly valuable or profitable. And that means it is worth any effort.

Training

So Timothy is urged to "train" (NRSV) or to "exercise" himself (NKJV) in godliness (4:7). The "physical training" (NRSV) or the "bodily exercise" (NKJV) has some value (4:8). The Greek word for exercise has entered English as "gymnasium," and the verb in verse 7 means to work out in a gym. Intense practice is required if the body is to be developed and the skills acquired that will enable a person to compete in the games. We are to approach our spiritual development with the same intensity, consistency, and deliberate plan—even more so. For if it is important to run fast or to play the clarinet well, how much more important is it to train for the exercise of discipleship—for so much depends on it, in this life as well as in the life to come.

Through the training theme, the text stresses the interplay between free grace and personal effort. God is our Savior

(4:10) and yet we save ourselves (4:16). We cannot generate the gospel itself. The possibility of salvation is beyond our control. We can only respond when it is offered to us. That response, of course, is faith (4:10). The training is then the lifelong effort to equip ourselves to embody that faith as we labor and struggle through the here and now on our way to the life to come.

Part of the training is learning to use the tools that God has given us, and so Timothy is advised not to neglect his gift (4:14). The word translated as "gift" has entered English as "charisma" and as the phrase "charismatic gifts." Often we restrict the term to the spectacular phenomena associated with the Holy Spirit, such as speaking in unknown tongues and healing. Paul, however, had a wider view of the charismatic. In 1 Corinthians 12:8, for example, the ability to teach is a charismatic gift (NRSV says "the utterance of wisdom"). Timothy's gift, then, need not be tongues. Instead, it is more likely the ability to explain and inspire. In 2 Timothy 1:6-7, the gift is explained in terms of God's having given him the power, love, and self-discipline he needs in order to fulfill his ministry. Prophecies about Timothy, mentioned in 1 Timothy 1:18, may indicate a special revelation that someone had concerning him, but may also be the kind of thing that is often experienced when we sense that an individual is peculiarly suited for a particular ministry and suggest that there is a calling. The laying on of hands is often understood as an ordination; but that is perhaps reading later ceremony back into the text. We are on safer ground to explain it more generally as the public recognition that the congregation has entrusted a specific task to him.

To nurture the gift, and not neglect it, Timothy is to "put these things into practice" (NRSV) or to "meditate" (NKJV) on them (4:15). The Greek verb has the two meanings. NRSV has chosen to follow through the athletic image in the training: be diligent in your workouts, practice until you get it better than right. NKJV, on the other hand, has chosen to follow through the reading, exhorting, and teaching: ponder, reflect, meditate, think about. The immediate reference of "these things" (NKJV) is the activities of 4:13; but the hope of 4:10 (NRSV) should also be included. The second verb in verse 15, translated by NRSV as "devote yourself to them" and by NKJV as "give yourself entirely to them," is actually the imperative "be in them." Timothy is to be in these things so that they become his very nature. He is to immerse himself in them, to sink into them so that they are the very atmosphere within which he moves, as much so as the air he breathes.

Example

There is more to the training for godliness than personal salvation. There is also the salvation of those around us. And so the progress is for a purpose: it is for everyone to see (4:15). The glass house, therefore, is not to be resented as an invasion of privacy. It is to be understood, rather, as a manner for effective evangelism. There will, on occasion, be something that people can hold against us and use as a shield against the gospel. In Timothy's case it is relative youth—he would be older than thirty but not yet a graybeard. In our case it might be upbringing in a non-Christian home, or a lack of formal education, or a host of other reasons. But we are to forge ahead anyway, setting the

example in word and conduct (4:12). In other words, we are to practice what we preach! Both NRSV and NKJV suggest that the example is aimed at believers. The Greek permits a different interpretation, however, which is held by many scholars. The example is "of believers," in the sense of modeling what a believer ought to be like. In this case the example is for other believers, that they might improve themselves, and also for nonbelievers, that they might become believers.

St. Francis of Assisi understood this. One day he went with a monk to the village square to preach. He petted a dog, helped a poor woman across a street, and spoke kindly to the people they passed. When St. Francis headed for home the monk objected, saying that they had come to preach. St. Francis replied that they had preached: "We just went about loving people, and dogs, and life. That was of itself a sermon."

Speech and conduct are to be examples of love. This is not romantic love, of course, or parent-child love, or friendship; but it is the familiar agape, the care for the another's welfare. Speech and conduct are also to be examples of faith. Here it is faithfulness or loyalty or trustworthiness or dependability more than belief itself. Furthermore, speech and conduct are to be examples of purity in thought and deed. NKJV, following manuscripts less favored by NRSV, has a fourth characteristic of the example: it is "in spirit" (4:12), in the sense of spiritual rather than material.

SHARING THE SCRIPTURE

PREPARING TO TEACH

Preparing Our Hearts

Whether you are a Sunday school teacher, elected church official, choir member, usher, or other church worker, you have likely

faced problems in the church. Like all other human organizations, the church has its stumbling blocks and pitfalls. At times, everyone needs encouragement to continue their work, no matter what the obstacles seem to be. As you prepare to teach this week's lesson concerning guidance given to Timothy for ministry, ask yourself this question: What encouragement do I need for the ministry in which I am now engaged? You may wish to speak with your pastor or a trusted friend about concerns you have and possible future directions for your own work within the church.

Preparing Our Minds

In addition to studying today's lesson, read the accompanying scripture, 1 Timothy 4:6-16. If possible, read all of 1 and 2 Timothy and Titus. These three letters, known as the Pastoral Epistles, are the basis for our study over the next five weeks. Although they have historically been attributed to Paul, many modern scholars feel that they were written by a follower of Paul. In the ancient world, followers often signed their teacher's name to documents that reflected the teacher's ideas. This point about authorship may be raised by someone, but it need not bog down the class. Remember that the purpose of this unit is to learn what is expected of a faithful servant of Christ. That advice remains sound regardless of who authored the letters.

Preparing Our Learning Space

To do the scripture study suggested under the heading "Godliness," write on note cards the reference to the passages listed below under that activity.

Have on hand:
- ✔ several Bibles for students
- ✔ newsprint and marker or chalkboard and chalk
- ✔ paper and pencils
- ✔ note cards on which scripture references to godliness have been written

LEADING THE CLASS

(1) Introduction

Begin today's session by asking class members to identify persons who helped them learn their work. Perhaps these individuals were master craftspersons who showed newcomers the tricks of the trade. Maybe they were experienced mothers who showed new moms how to care for their children. They may have been mentors who took a new graduate under their wings to advise, counsel, and show by example how to treat a patient, or teach a class, or close a major sale. After class members have had an opportunity to think of someone, ask these questions:

(1) What methods did the person use to help you learn your job?

(2) As you think back over what you learned, how important would you say the person's example was to you?

(3) What problems arose for you when the person told you to do one thing but then you observed that he or she did something very different?

Link this discussion to today's scripture lesson by pointing out most of us learn more from someone else's example than we do from their words. Timothy was admonished to practice what he preached. Not only would he benefit from such advice, but his example would benefit those to whom he ministered as well. As Christians, we too are called to be faithful servants of Christ by setting an example that others can follow. We may not know exactly what to do in all cases, but we may not even be living up to the standards of behavior to which we know Christians are called. As we study this week's lesson we will ask: *How can we live up to the standards of Christian behavior to which we are called?*

As an alternative introduction, read or retell the Focusing on the Main Question portion of the lesson.

(2) Godliness

Select a volunteer to read aloud today's scripture, 1 Timothy 4:6-16. Use information for 1 Timothy 4:6-9 in the Understanding the Scripture section to contrast the false teachings that have caused problems in Ephesus with the sound teaching that Timothy can offer in both word and deed.

Focus on today's key verses 7*b*-8: "Train yourself in godliness, for, while physical training is of some value, godliness is valuable in every way, holding promise for both the present life and the life to come." If possible, write this passage on newsprint or a chalkboard.

In this segment of the lesson, we will consider the idea of godliness. One way to do this, as seen in the Interpreting the Scripture portion, is to do a word study. Ask students to look up and read the following verses in order to determine what is meant by "godliness." You may want them to work with a partner, or to read their assigned verse to the entire class. As noted, translations from the Greek will vary, but the word "godliness" may be found in the New Revised Standard Version (NRSV) in these verses. You may want to write the reference on note cards in advance to save time in class.

1 Timothy 2:1-2	1 Timothy 4:7-8
1 Timothy 6:3-4*a*	1 Timothy 6:4*b*-5
1 Timothy 6:6	1 Timothy 6:11
2 Timothy 3:2-5	Titus 1:1
2 Peter 1:3	2 Peter 1:5-7
2 Peter 3:11	

In addition, the word "godliness" appears in the New International Version (NIV) in these verses:

Acts 3:12	1 Timothy 3:16

Add information from the Interpreting the Scripture section to the discussion as appropriate. Be sure to include these ideas:
• The basic idea in the word "godliness" is respect or reverence for the good, and especially for the divine.
• The word includes the Christian way of life—doctrine, worship, and the nitty-gritty of everyday behavior all wrapped up in one indivisible package.
• In 1 Timothy 4:8, godliness is described as "valuable" (NRSV) or "profitable" (NKJV) in "every way," which is defined in terms of a double promise, for this life and for the life to come.

(3) Training

Note that godliness does not just happen to us, but we, like Timothy, are urged in 4:7 to train ourselves in godliness. Ask:
(1) **What value do you see in training to do something, whether it be run a marathon, or play a trombone, or paint a picture?**
(2) **What are some ways that you think you could train yourself in godliness?**
Use information in this section under the Interpreting the Scripture portion to help the class understand the nature of the training to which Timothy is called. Emphasize these points:
• At minimum, we are to approach our spiritual development with the same intensity, consistency, and deliberate plan that we approach skill development in other facets of our lives.
• Salvation comes by grace through our Savior, but we respond with faith. Training is the lifelong effort to equip ourselves to embody that faith as we labor and struggle through the here and now on our way to the life to come.
• Part of the training is learning to use the tools—the gifts—God has given us.
• Like Timothy, we are to nurture the gifts and not neglect them. This nurture may take place through training or practice.

(4) Example

Read these sentences from the Interpreting the Scripture portion: "There is more to the training for godliness than personal salvation. There is also the salvation of those around us. And so the progress is for a purpose: it is for everyone to see (4:15). The glass house, therefore, is not to be resented as an invasion of privacy. It is to be understood, rather, as a manner for effective evangelism."

Provide some silent time for students to reflect on these questions. Distribute paper and pencils to those who would like to record their thoughts.

R   As people observe the way I talk and act every day, what kind of example of Christ are they seeing in me?

What changes do I need to make, with God's help, to become a servant who follows more nearly in the Savior's footsteps?

Conclude this silent time with a brief prayer, asking that God will enable each person to go forth to continue training in godliness so that he or she might be an effective example to others.

HELPING CLASS MEMBERS ACT

Encourage class members to think of skills or talents they have that they can share with others. Perhaps they could serve as a teacher or mentor for someone who would like to learn the skill they possess. Help them to see that their knowledge and expertise are valuable to others.

Invite the students to think of someone who needs to see an example of speech and conduct, love, faith, and purity of life (1 Timothy 4:12). Challenge them to take this person under their wing and show by example how a follower of Jesus lives. Assure them that even an exemplary person is not perfect. However, Christlike actions and attitudes can teach someone far more than pious words that are not reflected in one's life.

Suggest that class members find some quiet time this week to reflect on the similarities or differences between what they say and what they do. Have them think about the mixed messages they may be sending to children or neighbors or co-workers when they claim to follow Christ and yet act in ways that run counter to our Lord's own teaching and example. Challenge them to seek God's help in making their "walk" match their "talk."

PLANNING FOR NEXT SUNDAY

Next week's lesson will focus on 1 Timothy 6:2b-21, which students should be asked to read. During this session we will continue our study of "Guidance for Ministry" by exploring godliness as an attribute of the faithful

PURSUE GODLINESS

PREVIEWING THE LESSON

Lesson Scripture: 1 Timothy 6:2*b*-21
Background Scripture: 1 Timothy 6:2*b*-21
Key Verses: 1 Timothy 6:11-12

Focus of the Lesson:
Paul's exhortation to Timothy to pursue godliness

Main Question of the Lesson:
What is the value of godliness, and why should we pursue it?

This lesson will enable adult learners to:
(1) consider why godliness is so valuable that they will want to pursue it.
(2) recognize that an important result of the pursuit of godliness is contentment in their lives.
(3) respond by taking action in keeping with the pursuit of godliness.

Today's lesson may be outlined as follows:
(1) Introduction
(2) Contentment
(3) The Good Fight
(4) Teaching

FOCUSING ON THE MAIN QUESTION

We all want what is best for us. We do not deliberately blight our happiness; for even behavior that appears to be self-defeating turns out, upon close analysis, to be the lesser of evils, even if the perception is unconscious rather than conscious. The suicide, the alcoholic, the drug addict, for example, all intend to escape a greater pain. Always there is a price to pay as we balance one pain against another or one pleasure against another. Our problem, of course, is the difficulty in determining what is actually best for us. We make mistakes and end up marring our happiness. When we want the wrong thing, getting what we want is the worst thing that can happen to us.

So, as we pick our way through the minefield on the way to happiness, we come across the admonition to pursue godliness. But godliness, we cannot help thinking, relates to a very far off happiness; and there is the "meanwhile back at the ranch" problem of happiness—or lack thereof—in the real world close at hand. Godliness is not going to pay the rent, and the rent does have to be paid. And there is a more serious problem than this. Not only does godliness not pay the rent; if we were to take godliness seriously, it could possibly interfere with our efforts to pay the rent. What does the real world have to do with heaven anyway? Or heaven with the real world? So we ask our main question: *What is the value of godliness, and why should we pursue it?*

W. Somerset Maugham struggled with this issue in his play *Sheppey*. Sheppey is a barber who wins the lottery. When he decides to invest the money in "treasures in heaven" by helping the poor with it, his family is aghast. They had better ways to spend the money. Ernie, his son-in-law, tries to straighten Sheppey out: "Why do you suppose they have professors of theology and doctors of divinity? They're there to explain to people that whatever Jesus said he didn't really mean it, but something quite different."

So there we have it. Paul could not be serious about pursuing godliness, right now, in the real world, could he?

READING THE SCRIPTURE

NRSV
1 Timothy 6:2b-21

2b Teach and urge these duties. 3Whoever teaches otherwise and does not agree with the sound words of our Lord Jesus Christ and the teaching that is in accordance with godliness, 4is conceited, understanding nothing, and has a morbid craving for controversy and for disputes about words. From these come envy, dissension, slander, base suspicions, 5and wrangling among those who are depraved in mind and bereft of the truth, imagining that godliness is a means of gain. 6Of course, there is great gain in godliness combined with contentment; 7for we brought nothing into the world, so that we can take nothing out of it; 8but if we have food and clothing, we will be content with these. 9But those who want to be rich fall into temptation and are trapped by many senseless and harmful desires that plunge people into ruin and destruction. 10For the love of money is a root of all kinds of evil, and in their eagerness to be rich some have wandered away from the faith and pierced themselves with many pains.

NIV
1 Timothy 6:2b-21

2b These are the things you are to teach and urge on them.

3If anyone teaches false doctrines and does not agree to the sound instruction of our Lord Jesus Christ and to godly teaching, 4he is conceited and understands nothing. He has an unhealthy interest in controversies and quarrels about words that result in envy, strife, malicious talk, evil suspicions 5and constant friction between men of corrupt mind, who have been robbed of the truth and who think that godliness is a means to financial gain.

6But godliness with contentment is great gain. 7For we brought nothing into the world, and we can take nothing out of it. 8But if we have food and clothing, we will be content with that. 9People who want to get rich fall into temptation and a trap and into many foolish and harmful desires that plunge men into ruin and destruction. 10For the love of money is a root of all kinds of evil. Some people, eager for money, have wandered from the faith and pierced themselves with many griefs.

11 But as for you, man of God, shun all this; pursue righteousness, godliness, faith, love, endurance, gentleness. ¹²Fight the good fight of the faith; take hold of the eternal life, to which you were called and for which you made the good confession in the presence of many witnesses. ¹³In the presence of God, who gives life to all things, and of Christ Jesus, who in his testimony before Pontius Pilate made the good confession, I charge you ¹⁴to keep the commandment without spot or blame until the manifestation of our Lord Jesus Christ, ¹⁵which he will bring about at the right time—he who is the blessed and only Sovereign, the King of kings and Lord of lords. ¹⁶It is he alone who has immortality and dwells in unapproachable light, whom no one has ever seen or can see; to him be honor and eternal dominion. Amen.

17 As for those who in the present age are rich, command them not to be haughty, or to set their hopes on the uncertainty of riches, but rather on God who richly provides us with everything for our enjoyment. ¹⁸They are to do good, to be rich in good works, generous, and ready to share, ¹⁹thus storing up for themselves the treasure of a good foundation for the future, so that they may take hold of the life that really is life.

²⁰Timothy, guard what has been entrusted to you. Avoid the profane chatter and contradictions of what is falsely called knowledge; ²¹by professing it some have missed the mark as regards the faith.

Grace be with you.

¹¹But you, man of God, flee from all this, and pursue righteousness, godliness, faith, love, endurance and gentleness. ¹²Fight the good fight of the faith. Take hold of the eternal life to which you were called when you made your good confession in the presence of many witnesses. ¹³In the sight of God, who gives life to everything, and of Christ Jesus, who while testifying before Pontius Pilate made the good confession, I charge you ¹⁴to keep this command without spot or blame until the appearing of our Lord Jesus Christ, ¹⁵which God will bring about in his own time—God, the blessed and only Ruler, the King of kings and Lord of lords, ¹⁶who alone is immortal and who lives in unapproachable light, whom no one has seen or can see. To him be honor and might forever. Amen.

¹⁷Command those who are rich in this present world not to be arrogant nor to put their hope in wealth, which is so uncertain, but to put their hope in God, who richly provides us with everything for our enjoyment. ¹⁸Command them to do good, to be rich in good deeds, and to be generous and willing to share. ¹⁹In this way they will lay up treasure for themselves as a firm foundation for the coming age, so that they may take hold of the life that is truly life.

²⁰Timothy, guard what has been entrusted to your care. Turn away from godless chatter and the opposing ideas of what is falsely called knowledge, ²¹which some have professed and in so doing have wandered from the faith.

Grace be with you.

UNDERSTANDING THE SCRIPTURE

1 Timothy 6:2b-10. Our teaching is to reflect the "sound" (NRSV) or "wholesome" (NKJV) or healthy words of Christ and thus to square with godliness (6:3). When we are controlled by greed (6:5), rather than godliness, we lose our way. The false teachers are full of themselves rather than full of Christ, and so they are "conceited" (NRSV) or "proud" (NKJV)—puffed up (6:4). Their "morbid craving"

(NRSV) or obsession with (NKJV) contro-versy is destructive; for it leads to "envy" and to "dissension" (NRSV) or to "strife" (NKJV) and to "slander" (NRSV) or "revil-ing" (NKJV) and to "base" (NRSV) or "evil" (NKJV) suspicions. Their minds are so "corrupt" (NKJV) or "depraved" (NRSV) because they no longer have the truth. Thus, they end up thinking that godliness is a way of making money (6:5). But if our contentment is in money rather than in godliness (6:6-9), we risk chasing money so intently that we hardly notice that it has led us away from the faith (6:10).

1 Timothy 6:11-15. Instead, we are to chase after godliness (6:11). If "birds of a feather flock together" we may expect to understand something of godliness by the company it keeps. Righteousness is con-duct and thought that conform to the stan-dard that is expected of us in both direc-tions, toward God and toward others. Faith is dependability or trustworthiness, and love is the unselfish desire for another person's welfare. Patience or endurance is sticking it out to the end. Gentleness, sometimes translated as meekness or for-bearance, does not have the connotation of weakness we sometimes give it. It has more the idea of strength that is brought under control, here by the commitment to Christ. This then leads well into the idea of fighting the good fight of the faith (6:12), actively taking hold of eternal life, making the good confession in public. The confes-sion may be a witness to fellow Christians; but the endurance enables, if need be, the witness to a hostile world (6:13). The good confession involves keeping the com-mandment faithfully (6:14). The com-mandment here may indicate Timothy's ministry more than the specific behaviors enjoined in the Ten Commandments or in the vice and virtue lists. The faithfulness is to continue until the final consummation or Timothy's death, whichever comes first.

1 Timothy 6:16-19. The thought of the "manifestation" (6:14) reminds us that we serve an unimaginable God, "the King of kings and Lord of lords" (6:15), immortal by nature, so holy that none can penetrate that "unapproachable light," invisible (6:16). But the manifestation, the coming to us, is our invitation to approach God after all, and that approach is the pursuit of godliness. That pursuit highlights the dif-ference between this present age (6:17), which is destined to pass away, and the future (6:19), which, as God's home, remains forever. The phrase "until the manifestation" (6:14) indicates that we all, believer and nonbeliever alike, operate in this present age. The critical issue, of course, is the relationship of this present age to the age to come. If we do not see a relationship, or if we do not even think there is an age to come, we will set our hopes on the riches of this world (6:17). And if we have riches it is hard not to be haughty, to think we are more special than those who have less. Such riches, however, provide an uncertain hope at best. We may lose them in the next financial panic, and we will certainly lose them when we die, for we cannot take them with us.

The alternative, the pursuit of godliness, is to set our hope on God, trusting that everything we need has been provided and that we are to enjoy everything that has been provided. And the best way to enjoy what we have is to share (6:18). This makes us rich in good works. And this we can take with us, for it is the treasure for the future (6:19). In this way we "take hold of the life that really is life." The manu-scripts followed by NKJV add "eternal" to define that life.

1 Timothy 6:20-21. The closing admoni-tion is to guard the gospel that has been entrusted to us.

INTERPRETING THE SCRIPTURE

Contentment

The "profit" (NJB; 6:5) that makes the bottom line of the balance sheet a success, the "dividends" (GNB) or the gain (NRSV; 6:6), are more than financial assets. For godliness also has its bottom line. And that bottom line is contentment. When these resources are provided by Christ, we are content or "satisfied" (GNB). We may therefore speak of two ways of calculating net worth, one dealing with money and the other dealing with godliness. They track together part of the way, for we need the tangible essentials that keep body and soul together (6:8). Although, of course, a deeper contentment or Christ-empowered sufficiency permits us to rise above their absence, here the assumption is that we will have what we need. The issue is this: After we have the necessities, then what? If we cannot take our money with us (6:7), can it have much to do with who we are? Does it make sense to be so preoccupied with accumulating what is so external and unimportant to our destiny?

The desire to be rich (6:9) goes beyond the necessities—and even beyond the luxuries that ease the daily struggle to stay afloat—until it elbows the godliness aside in order to take center stage. The desire snowballs, taking on a life of its own, ever pushing the limits of what we are willing to do for it. Temptation beckons and we fall from the standards that are appropriate for Christians. Before we know it we have been snared or trapped like an animal going after the bait. The desire to be rich, the greed, generates a whole host of dependent desires that are foolish and harmful. At last we are swamped by the greed, as a ship that takes on too much water in heavy seas. Once swamped, no longer controlling the desire for material possessions, we are plunged to the depths, to ruin and destruction. The ruin may occur in this life, for the love of money is the root of all kinds or types of evil, as when we overreach and get caught or so narrow our interests that nothing else matters. But 6:10 shows that spiritual destruction is primarily in view. In such single-minded pursuit of money we are apt to take a wrong turn and wander from the faith. At the end, when the enormity of our loss dawns on us, we will understand that we did it to ourselves. We pierce ourselves with many sorrows (GNB; 6:10), with fatal wounds.

The love of money, when we do not have it, is a problem because of the way it takes over our life, driving us to acquire it any way we can. But 6:17 says that actually having the money is also a problem; for it can work against our spiritual health by inducing pride, as if we are better than the brothers and sisters who have no money. And it can compromise our faith if we hope in, or locate our sense of security in, our material possessions. Our hope, our security, is to be located in God alone; and then wealth, beyond the necessities, is a matter of stewardship. The reminder that God gives us what we have eliminates pride, for in the final analysis we do not even earn money. And the reminder that God gives it for a purpose, to be used in good works (6:18), in relieving the wants of others, eliminates pride; for it is not a reward for our personal goodness. And that our enjoyment (6:17) is in using the gift in good works sets in order the relative importance of money, the brothers and sisters, and God. If, then, the value of the riches is in the good works that they enable (6:18), the uncertainty of riches in this earthly life (6:17) yields to the certainty of the true life of the future (6:19). For the good works are the treasures that we can take with us because they are the evidence of discipleship, the by-products of our determined effort to take hold of or make our own the true life in Christ.

The Good Fight

To return to our main question, we ask again: What is the value of godliness, and why should we pursue it? The first reason we should pursue godliness is that contentment in the gospel enables us to use our possessions—and not be used by them—and thus keeps us on track toward God's promised blessings. The second answer is the association of godliness with "patience" (NKJV) or "endurance" (NRSV, NIV), which enables us to take hold of eternal life (6:11-12).

The laying hold is both an avoidance or shunning and an embracing (6:11). On the one hand, it is a flight from the passion for money with its temptations that lead us away from the faith, and a flight from other vices that would interfere with discipleship. On the other hand, it is a self-conscious following of another path, the discipleship that uses money to enable good works. Such a person is righteous, in that he or she behaves the way a Christian is expected to behave: godly or religious, faithful and loving, patient or enduring, and meek or gentle.

Life in Christ is eternal (6:12) and therefore future; but it must also penetrate this life if we are to take hold of it now. The penetration is not complete, however, for the taking hold is a constant struggle, whether the fight is athletic competition or military campaigning. This struggle is separated from the many other struggles of our life in that it is "the good fight of the faith." Thus it is worth it in the ultimate sense, while the rewards or frustrations of the other fights are fleeting. We are encouraged in our struggle by the assurance that God intends eternal life for us, and so we are called into it (6:12). When we answered the call we confessed publicly our commitment to it. And in our continuing struggle to embody that call in our world we imitate our Lord, who made the confession before Pilate (6:13), faithful to the end, no matter what.

The confession involves keeping the commandment in a spotless and unblamable way (6:14). The command is comprehensive, embracing all that we have been told, the doctrines that explain the faith and the conduct that the doctrines envision. We obey these orders in the sight of God. But this scrutiny is not threatening; for the Watcher maintains us in the eternal life (6:13) to which we have been called, so long as we fight to take hold of it.

God maintains us in the true life in Christ, then, so we can persevere until the very end of time. The end of time, of course, is the appearance of Christ (6:14)—unless it is cut short by our death. This ultimate *epiphany* (the Greek word for the appearance or manifestation in verse 14) is more often called a *parousia* (the Greek word for arrival). It is popularly referred to as the Second Coming or the Second Advent. It is certain to occur because God intends it; but it can be neither hurried nor delayed because it is on a divine timetable (6:15). In the meantime we are to work and witness, not sit down and wait.

We can confidently work in the meantime, whether society is indifferent or even hostile, because we serve the ultimate authority. There are earthly kings and lords, but their limited power is not to blind us to *the* King and Lord, the "only Sovereign" (6:15). This One is self-existent and thus immortal (6:16), while all others, from kings to peasants, have their life only on divine sufferance. So to be dazzled by the glitter of the famous and the powerful is to be sidetracked from godliness as surely as by the love of money. Our Immortal, in contrast, dwells in heaven, the "unapproachable light" that is holiness, invisible to the eye of flesh. And so we praise our God, to whom honor and power are—and will be and ought to be—forever.

Teaching

In today's lesson, we have seen that godliness occurs within two contexts. Its pursuit leads to "contentment" (6:5-6) and to "endurance" (6:11). Both have to do with the daily Christian life that at last results in the blessings of heaven. The third context, 6:2b-3, is the effort to assist others to attain that goal, whether it be through evangelism or the nurturing of those who are already Christians. Godliness is the standard that controls what we do and say.

SHARING THE SCRIPTURE

PREPARING TO TEACH

Preparing Our Hearts

"Godliness." There is that word again. Last week we were told to train ourselves in godliness (1 Timothy 4:7). This week we are being directed to pursue godliness (1 Timothy 6:11). Think back over last week's word study on godliness. What does godliness mean to you? How do you pursue godliness in your own life? How does godliness enable you to be content? What behaviors and attitudes detour you from the path of godliness? What harmful desires ensnare you when you are busy pursuing money? Meditate on these questions. You may want to write your thoughts in your spiritual journal.

Preparing Our Minds

Read 1 Timothy 6:2b-21, as well as the lesson. If possible, read the scripture in several different translations. Pay particular attention to our key verses, 1 Timothy 6:11-12.

Preparing Our Learning Space

Have on hand:
- ✔ several Bibles for students
- ✔ newsprint and marker or chalkboard and chalk
- ✔ paper and pencils

LEADING THE CLASS

(1) Introduction

Open today's session by asking class members to brainstorm answers to these questions. Record their responses on newsprint. Be sure to have an answer in column 2 to correspond to each answer in column 1.

(1) **What do people in our society value? (Write answers in column 1.)** ?

(2) **Why do you think people find this of value? (Write answers in column 2.)**

Look back over the list the group has generated and then ask:

(3) **What conflicts do you see between what many people value and what the Bible teaches us to value?** ?

Move to today's scripture lesson by pointing out that while people in our society are often told to value money, status, power, and fame and to pursue these at all costs, 1 Timothy 6 tells us that godliness is of great value and should be pursued. Note our main question for today's lesson: *What is the value of godliness, and why should we pursue it?*

As an alternative, use the Focusing on the Main Question portion to introduce the lesson.

(2) Contentment

Ask two students to read today's lesson from 1 Timothy 6. One should read 2b (beginning with the word "teach") through 10. The other should read verses 11-21.

Look at verses 2b-5. Discuss these questions for a few moments. You may want to set a time limit in advance if you think some persons will engage in a tirade about a pet concern.

(1) **What examples of "controversy" or "disputes about words" do you see in the church today?**

(2) **Where do "the sound words of our Lord Jesus Christ" fit into this argument? Is it possible that both sides are shaping his words to suit their own purposes, rather than reflecting his teachings in a larger context? Explain your answer.**

(3) **What attitudes and behaviors has this debate produced?**

(4) **Are these attitudes and behaviors godly? If not, how would you describe them?**

Now look at verses 6-8. Distribute paper and pencils and ask each person to complete one or more of these statements:

• I am content when . . .

• Contentment is . . .

Have several people share their ideas with the group or a partner. Note any areas of agreement as to what contentment is or what gives rise to it. Also point out that, though not the goal of the pursuit of godliness, contentment is certainly a by-product of that pursuit. When we pursue godliness we set our hope on God, trusting that everything we need has been provided and that we are able to enjoy everything that has been provided.

Note that many persons in our society do not acknowledge God's provisions. Instead, they equate contentment with the getting, spending, and amassing of money. Paul points out in 1 Timothy 6:9-10 that the quest for money has led many people away from the faith. Read or retell the last paragraph under "Contentment" in the Interpreting the Scripture portion to help students understand the teachings concerning money. Then ask:

(1) **If we understand ourselves to be stewards of what God has entrusted to us—not owners of what we have**

amassed for ourselves—how does this understanding enable us to be content with whatever we have?

(2) **How does this contentment assist us in staying on the path of godliness, rather than veering off course to pursue wealth?**

(3) The Good Fight

In 1 Timothy 6:11 Timothy is told to shun all these useless debates and the temptation to accumulate wealth. Instead, he is to pursue characteristics listed in verse 11 and to "fight the good fight of the faith" (6:12). You may want to read or retell "The Good Fight" section in the Interpreting the Scripture portion to help class members understand what the good fight entails and what is at stake in the struggle. Be sure the class comprehends that godliness leads to the endurance necessary to fight the good fight.

Note that fighting the good fight is necessary as we try to live out our faith in a world that is often hostile to the Christian witness. Read the following scenarios aloud and ask class members to finish the stories. If the class is large, you may want to break into groups to do this activity.

SCENARIO 1: You work in a science lab and have become aware that a colleague is falsifying test data to obtain more grant money for experiments. You know that his tests are clearly not working, but his trumped-up results suggest that he is on the path to a major breakthrough in finding a cure for AIDS. Your job is important to you, but you feel the need to fight the good fight of faith in light of your colleague's deceit, so you . . .

SCENARIO 2: An influential church member has been spreading rumors about the pastor. There seems to be a grain of truth in what you have heard, but you think the member is putting her own spin on the situation. You cannot sit by and let the pastor's reputation be ruined just because she does not personally care for him. You

[R] want to see justice here, so you fight the good fight by . . . .

(4) Teaching

As we saw last week, we train for godliness and pursue it not just for our own selves and our salvation but for the sake of others who may follow our example. Paul tells Timothy to teach others "in accordance with godliness" (1 Timothy 6:2b-3). Ask class members to vote, by a show of hands, to determine which of the following situations teach godliness as they understand the term.

A father teaches his college-age daughter that she should live morally, though she knows her father has cheated on her mother.

[R] A single mother on welfare reports income for baby-sitting knowing that her benefits will be cut.

A parent screams at a child in order to get him to share his toys.

A soup kitchen volunteer continues to work even though two supper guests have been verbally abusive.

Wrap up this section by pointing out that we teach others not only by our words but also by our actions. Sometimes, as was the case with the father in our first example and the parent in the third case, we do not even realize that others are aware that our actions and our words are at odds with one another. Other times, we are in difficult situations, such as the single mother and soup kitchen volunteer, but we continue to do the right thing even though that action may cost us something such as money or self-esteem. In the end, however, those who pursue godliness give a faithful witness that teaches others who Jesus is and what godliness is all about.

HELPING CLASS MEMBERS ACT

Challenge class members to evaluate the importance of money and material objects in their own lives. Ask them to imagine that all of their worldly goods are burned. Since the family was away no one was hurt, but everything else is wiped out. Ask the students to list what they have left of value. Suggest that they keep this list where they can easily refer to it during the week and give thanks for the "things" in life—the real "things"—that give value and meaning to their existence.

Suggest that class members read or view a video of Charles Dickens's *A Christmas Carol*. This classic tale clearly shows how the love of money causes Ebenezer Scrooge to set aside all values, including love and concern for others, as he single-mindedly pursues wealth. Scrooge has a conversion experience that turns his whole life around when the Christmas ghosts appear to him. Ask students to reflect on how this tale illustrates the teachings given to Timothy about the dangers of pursuing money and the importance of pursuing godliness.

Encourage students to decide how they can best witness to others what it means to live a godly, faith-filled life.

PLANNING FOR NEXT SUNDAY

Next week's lesson, entitled "The Cost of Commitment," is based on 2 Timothy 2:1-13. Ask them to consider what hardships they have endured, or may be willing to endure, for the sake of the gospel.

THE COST OF COMMITMENT

PREVIEWING THE LESSON

Lesson Scripture: 2 Timothy 2:1-13
Background Scripture: 2 Timothy 2:1-13
Key Verse: 2 Timothy 2:3

Focus of the Lesson:
Paul's message to Timothy that faithful service to Christ includes the willingness to endure suffering as the cost of commitment to him

Main Question of the Lesson:
What price am I willing to pay for the sake of Jesus Christ and the gospel?

This lesson will enable adult learners to:
(1) examine Paul's message about suffering for Christ.
(2) determine what the cost of discipleship might be in their own lives.
(3) respond by considering what they are willing to pay to be faithful to Christ.

Today's lesson may be outlined as follows:
(1) Introduction
(2) Sharing in Suffering
(3) Endurance of Suffering
(4) The Reward for Endurance
(5) Christ's Faithfulness

FOCUSING ON THE MAIN QUESTION

All of us are confronted constantly with the necessity of making choices. Something we want or need is available, but there is a price tag. So the question then is whether we want it enough to pay for it. Not long ago, for example, I decided to buy a new pair of bedroom slippers. I priced good looking slippers in one store in the twenty-five to thirty dollar range—I had sense enough not to go to a store where they would be fifty dollars—but I decided that I did not want to pay even that much. So in another store I found them at fifteen to twenty dollars. They looked pretty good, but I thought the price was still a little high. At last I found them in the third store at five dollars. And these are the ones I bought.

But, you know, I did not get any more than I paid for. I do not kid myself that I got good slippers for five dollars. It is just that that was all I was willing to pay. Perhaps this applies also in the matter of our faith in Christ. We want some kind of faith, so we shop around to see what is available and at what price. How much time am I expected to invest in it? How much of my property is to be devoted to it? *What price am I willing to pay for the sake of Jesus Christ and the gospel? That is our main question.*

At last we make our decision. And then we read all that stuff in today's lesson about sharing in suffering (2:3) and hardship (2:9) and dying (2:11) and enduring

(2:12). This sounds like more faith than we had in mind. We want five-dollar slippers rather than go barefoot. We want a small comfortable faith—so long as it does not cost too much to commit to it. But all those "ifs" before the "died" and the "endure" and the command to share in the suffering tell us that it is all or nothing. There is no five-dollar faith. What a downer. Why should faith be any different from slippers? I thought salvation was a way out of—not into—suffering.

READING THE SCRIPTURE

NRSV
2 Timothy 2:1-13

1 You then, my child, be strong in the grace that is in Christ Jesus; ²and what you have heard from me through many witnesses entrust to faithful people who will be able to teach others as well. ³Share in suffering like a good soldier of Christ Jesus. ⁴No one serving in the army gets entangled in everyday affairs; the soldier's aim is to please the enlisting officer. ⁵And in the case of an athlete, no one is crowned without competing according to the rules. ⁶It is the farmer who does the work who ought to have the first share of the crops. ⁷Think over what I say, for the Lord will give you understanding in all things.

8 Remember Jesus Christ, raised from the dead, a descendant of David—that is my gospel, ⁹for which I suffer hardship, even to the point of being chained like a criminal. But the word of God is not chained. ¹⁰Therefore I endure everything for the sake of the elect, so that they may also obtain the salvation that is in Christ Jesus, with eternal glory. ¹¹The saying is sure:

If we have died with him, we
    will also live with him;

NIV
2 Timothy 2:1-13

1 You then, my son, be strong in the grace that is in Christ Jesus. ²And the things you have heard me say in the presence of many witnesses entrust to reliable men who will also be qualified to teach others. ³Endure hardship with us like a good soldier of Christ Jesus. ⁴No one serving as a soldier gets involved in civilian affairs—he wants to please his commanding officer. ⁵Similarly, if anyone competes as an athlete, he does not receive the victor's crown unless he competes according to the rules. ⁶The hardworking farmer should be the first to receive a share of the crops. ⁷Reflect on what I am saying, for the Lord will give you insight into all this.

⁸Remember Jesus Christ, raised from the dead, descended from David. This is my gospel, ⁹for which I am suffering even to the point of being chained like a criminal. But God's word is not chained. ¹⁰Therefore I endure everything for the sake of the elect, that they too may obtain the salvation that is in Christ Jesus, with eternal glory.

¹¹Here is a trustworthy saying:

If we died with him,
    we will also live with him;

Key
Verse

Key
Verse

¹²if we endure, we will also reign
            with him;
    if we deny him, he will also deny
            us;
¹³if we are faithless, he remains
            faithful—
    for he cannot deny himself.

¹²if we endure,
        we will also reign with him.
    If we disown him,
        he will also disown us;
¹³if we are faithless,
        he will remain faithful,
        for he cannot disown himself.

UNDERSTANDING THE SCRIPTURE

2 Timothy 2:1-2. Timothy is to "be strong in the grace" (2:1). The verb form used in the Greek indicates that the source of the strength is the divine grace and therefore beyond our control. And yet it also commands us to do something ourselves to co-operate with that grace. The grace is God's undeserved gift, but here it also includes the idea of enabling for ministry. The strength may be by means of the grace or it may come as a result of our living in the sphere of grace. To speak of grace, moreover, is to speak of Christ. But we are not to soak up this grace like a sponge. Instead we are to be the conduit through which it flows to others. Timothy is to "entrust" (NRSV) or "commit" (NKJV) to others what he has heard from Paul (2:2). There is a link with 1:14: Timothy has been entrusted with "good treasure" (NRSV) or "good deposit" (NIV) that he is now to entrust to others. Paul's teaching, moreover, has been verified by many other witnesses, and so we have more than his unsupported word.

2 Timothy 2:3-6. The all-consuming nature of ministry or discipleship, which goes so far as to include a share in the suffering (2:3), is illustrated with the soldier (2:3-4), the athlete (2:5), and the farmer (2:6). In all three cases there is a reward. The soldier pleases the officer, just as the Christian aims to please Christ. The athlete gains the crown, which in 4:8 (see Lesson 4) suggests eternal life. The farmer gets a crop, which is a common New Testament image for the joys of heaven. In all three cases there is a single-minded effort on the way to the reward. The soldier is the most likely of the three to have to suffer in the course of his or her duty (2:3). The special lesson from the soldier is to avoid entanglements with the affairs of "this [that is, nonmilitary] life" (NKJV) or "everyday affairs" (NRSV) that would interfere with the mission (2:4). The athlete teaches us to train according to the rules of the games (2:5). The professional athlete rather than the amateur is in mind, and so the point is year-round self-discipline. The farmer's characteristic is labor (2:6).

2 Timothy 2:7-13. Timothy is to "think over" (NRSV) or "consider" (NKJV) the implications of the three illustrations (2:7). And as he turns them over in his mind the Lord will give him the insight to shape his ministry accordingly. The "all things" (NRSV) he is to understand coalesce around the gospel, and the gospel centers on Jesus Christ (2:8). The thinking, therefore, begins with remembering Christ, and insight granted by the Lord brings us back to Christ. The first of the two key points in the gospel is the resurrection of Christ from the dead. This is the key to all else; for it is the guarantee of the promised salvation, the source of our strength. Without it, in fact, there is no Christian faith at all. But it is the living Christ as a present experience that is primary, not a historical fact. For the historical fact acquires its meaning from our being "in Christ" as a living force right now. Descent from David is the other key point in the gospel. Perhaps this intends to stress the Incarnation, and then the two points give us the divine and human natures. In addition, the descent from David stresses that Christ is the Messiah of prophecy, and therefore genuine. Compare the identification of Christ in Revelation 5:4, where the Lamb is the Lion of Judah, the Root of David.

The gospel brings us back to Paul's predicament; Paul's service for the gospel has resulted in the hardship he is now suffering (2:9). The seriousness of the charge is suggested by the word "criminal." In Luke 23:32 this word describes the two who were crucified with Jesus. But even though Paul's own wings are clipped, the word of God is not in chains. Others are preaching, and so the work continues. As Luther's "A Mighty Fortress Is Our God" reminds us "the body they may kill; God's truth abideth still." And so Paul will be all right after all (2:12).

INTERPRETING THE SCRIPTURE

Sharing in Suffering

The believer's relationship with Christ must involve both the death and the Resurrection. If we wish to enjoy the life of the Lord we must first embrace the Cross (2:11). We cannot have the one without the other. In one sense, of course, the death of Christ is so unique that none can share in it. He had to walk the "lonesome valley" alone. In a derived sense, however, the faithful must identify completely with the cross. The basic Christian experience is the death of the old sinful nature and the birth of the new spiritual nature through the faith given by the Holy Spirit. This is symbolized most vividly in baptism, for going under the water is equated with the death and coming out of the water is the appropriation of the life of the Savior. In Romans 6:4, the resurrection of the Lord is paired with newness of life for disciples. In accordance with the general New Testament usage, "new" describes existence within the kingdom of God, beginning now and continuing beyond physical death. Romans 6:8 affirms that we shall live with Christ if we thus die with him. Paul here defines the death as to sin and the life as righteousness. The primary reference is thus to holiness of life or the progressive sanctification by which we realize our faith in the details of our daily activities. Such a death to sin is the basic meaning of our identification with the Cross.

When we move from the death to sin with the resulting new life in Christ to the witness, from sanctification to ministry, we move to the second level of identification with the Cross. Then, as our key verse points out, we "share in suffering." (2:3, NRSV). The verb is a rare triple compound: to suffer + evils + along with some one else. In its other New Testament occurrence, 2 Timothy 1:8, the suffering is "together with" Paul, as here, qualified by "for the gospel." In 2:3, the suffering is qualified with the words "of Christ Jesus." Paul is in chains because of his preaching (2:9) and Timothy may well be next. The sharing, then, is with Christ's own suffering on the cross and with Christ's other soldiers who have paid or are paying such a heavy price for their commitment.

NKJV's "endure hardship," however, follows a group of manuscripts that do not have the "together with" idea. At least for the English reader this takes us down a somewhat different path. On rare occasion we may have to face persecution, to suffer evil along with Christ and the martyrs. But more commonly we are required to make the good confession through other types of pain and suffering. The way in which we take hard knocks—financial reverses, the death of a loved one, our own debilitating and life-threatening illness—tells those around us whether our faith really means anything to us or not. Although our hardship has not been imposed upon us because we are Christians, we place our attitude toward hardship in the service of Christ. And then perhaps it is not too far-fetched to say that we suffer "for the gospel."

Endurance of Suffering

Next week's lesson, "Keep the Faith," will deal with faithful discipleship throughout the entire course of our earthly life. Here, in 2:10 and 2:12, we see that life-long discipleship in terms of endurance. The root idea in the verb is to remain behind when the others have gone—to persevere. This is not a willy-nilly kind of endurance; that is, enduring something because we have no choice in the matter. In the movie *The New Centurions* a police officer is shot in the stomach. While he is in the hospital, a rookie police officer says to his companion, "I don't think I could stand the pain." The wounded cop replies, "What's to stand? If it hurts it hurts!" The endurance in our scripture text has a moral quality beyond "if it hurts it hurts." It is the endurance that bears up patiently under any burden—for the gospel.

The "everything" of 2:10 is all-inclusive. We cannot really predict what the cost of our commitment will be in terms of suffering, and we cannot predict what tragedy around the next corner is about to offer us the special opportunity to make a witness. But the scripture gives us two reasons why it is important that we bear up to the very end. The first is "for the sake of the elect" (2:10). The "elect" is a Pauline term for Christians, including those who have already confessed their faith and those who might yet become Christians. The

point here is that the way in which we bear our troubles has an affect upon others, to strengthen the faith of some and to induce faith in others.

The Reward for Endurance

The other reason for patient endurance is the reward that we shall receive (2:12). There will be no crown if there has been no cross, no throne if there has been no thorn in the flesh. Endurance may become numbingly difficult, and we wear out; but there is revival in the encouragement that comes with the knowledge of the life to come. Because we shared in his death, the Redeemer offers us his own joy. But only if we hold out to the end. The reward for this steadfastness is a share in Christ's heavenly rule as the glorified Messiah blesses his people. Baptism, accordingly, is to be characterized by its staying power.

The reverse is also possible, sad to say, for under the pressure of persecution we might deny the Lord. In this case his resulting denial of us represents condemnation at the Last Judgment. Today it is very seldom that anyone denies Christ under the threat of persecution, at least in my experience; but all too commonly we deny the name of Christ by not valuing it enough to pay much attention to it one way or the other. Compare Esau's willingness to trade his birthright for a bowl of soup. Esau is treated more harshly in the biblical record than is Jacob, for at least Jacob valued the birthright.

Christ's Faithfulness

The chief problem for interpretation in today's lesson is to connect 2:13 with the promises and warnings of 2:11-12. We would expect our faithlessness to be followed by Christ's rejection; but instead we are told that Christ remains faithful. Three major efforts have been made to relate the faithfulness of the Savior to the faithlessness of his people.

(1) The simplest answer refers 2:11-12 to the individual and 2:13 to Christ's general purpose of providing salvation for those who will be faithful to him. The faithlessness of some individuals, resulting in their condemnation, does not make Christ abandon the idea of offering salvation to others.

(2) Christ is faithful to his promises, including both salvation and judgment. To give mercy to the faithless would be to deny his own character as righteous. In this case the faithlessness means apostasy or that there never was any genuine faith at all. It is not, therefore, a temporary lapse into sin. This interpretation stresses the consequences of behavior and the quality of faith itself.

(3) Even when we lapse into sin, Christ remains faithful and this is our hope of forgiveness. In this case the faithfulness is a momentary lapse rather than a permanent apostasy. Furthermore, there is an assumption that there is a genuine faith even behind the sin. Since we cannot depend upon our own strength, we need this hope that the mercy of God will not cast us off but will enable us to return to God again.

It is hard to know how to approach a text when competent scholars are unable to agree. There is enough truth in all of these interpretations that we cannot dismiss any of them easily. We are responsible for the consequences of our actions. As the detective on an old television show used to say, "Don't do the crime if you can't do the time!" But that cannot be the last word, because it so easily slips into counting up gold stars and black marks. We cannot help believing that Christ is a bit more merciful than we would be if the situation were reversed. Faithlessness itself, moreover, wears more than one hat. In some cases it really is apostasy, whether overt or not, and then there is nothing more to be said. To renounce commitment to the only source of salvation is the sin against the Holy Spirit. A faithful Christ has remained in place, but the apostate has left. Scripture knows of no way to return from such a departure. But in other cases there never was a genuine faith and we may still hope for the future. I guess I settle on the temporary lapse into sin and my hope for forgiveness.

SHARING THE SCRIPTURE

PREPARING TO TEACH

Preparing Our Hearts

We like to think that Jesus paid it all at Calvary, and of course in a very real sense he did. Yet, grace is not cheap; discipleship is costly. How much are you willing to pay for your faith? Is your relationship with Jesus Christ so important that you are willing to endure hardship, to suffer if need be, in order to live out your commitment to him? Or are you, like so many of us, willing to give or serve or do only when you find it convenient? Do you draw boundaries around areas of your life that you refuse to offer unto God? As you prepare to teach this week's lesson, give prayerful consideration to what you are willing to endure for the sake of the gospel.

Preparing Our Minds

Read today's lesson, as well as 2 Timothy 2:1-13.

Be prepared to tell the story of Joan of Arc found under the "Introduction."

Preparing Our Learning Space

Have on hand:
- several Bibles for students
- newsprint and marker or chalkboard and chalk
- paper and pencils

LEADING THE CLASS

(1) Introduction

Open today's session by reading or retelling this well-known story:

Born about 1412 near Lorraine, France, Joan of Arc began hearing voices and seeing visions at about the age of thirteen. She was particularly guided by Michael the archangel and two female saints, Catherine of Siena and Margaret. In an attempt to claim the French crown, English troops occupied northern France and were besieging Orleans on behalf of their king, Henry VI. Voices convinced Joan that the dauphin Charles was the rightful heir to the throne and that she should help him be crowned at Rheims. Although Rheims was the seat of French kings, the British troops ruled it. Joan, armed for battle, led an attack on Orleans and freed the city from the British in 1429. Charles was then able to go to Rheims. Although Joan wanted to return home, having completed her mission, Charles convinced her not to go. Consequently, she became involved in petty conflicts and was captured, condemned for heresy, and burned at the stake in 1431. The guilty verdict was later annulled and Joan was canonized as a saint in 1920.

After recounting this story, ask the class these questions:
(1) Why do you think Joan was willing to engage in combat?
(2) Would you be willing to endure suffering if you believed that God, or representatives of God, had spoken to you and told you to act? Why or why not?

(3) What lessons can we learn from Joan about the cost of commitment to God and God's purposes?

Guide the discussion to today's lesson by noting that Paul tells young Timothy to "Share in suffering like a good soldier of Christ Jesus" (key verse, 2 Timothy 2:3). These words remind us that discipleship is not cheap but may cost us a great deal. Joan of Arc is an example of one who literally suffered as a soldier in order to be true to what she understood to be messages from God. Joan paid for her commitment with her life. As we study today's lesson, we will ask: **What price am I willing to pay for the sake of Jesus Christ and the gospel?**

As an alternative, read or retell the Focusing on the Main Question portion of the lesson. Give special attention to the example about the cost of the bedroom slippers versus the willingness to pay the price for them.

(2) Sharing in Suffering

Read today's key verse, 2 Timothy 2:3. Point out that we often share in the sufferings of others. Encourage class members to relate instances when they shared in suffering with others. You may want to record their answers. Here are some ideas: the heart of the world goes out to a community devastated by a natural disaster; relatives share in the suffering of a family member who is ill; a town grieves the loss of a family in a car accident.

Now read aloud today's scripture lesson, 2 Timothy 2:1-13, in its entirety. Ask:
(1) We have some idea of what it means to share in the suffering of others. What does it mean to you to share in the suffering of Jesus?
(2) In what ways do you perceive that people who serve Jesus are like soldiers (verse 3), athletes (verse 5), or farmers (verse 6)?

After hearing the students' responses, fill in gaps from this section of the Interpreting the Scripture portion. Be sure to emphasize the need for Christians to identify with the Cross and the death of our sinful nature as symbolized in baptism.

(3) Endurance of Suffering

Note that in order to truly share in the suffering of Jesus, we must be able to endure. Reread verse 10 aloud. Point out that Paul says he endures "everything." We know from Paul's other letters and the book of Acts that he did endure whatever came his way—persecution, physical abuse, shipwrecks, and prison—because he was faithful to the gospel. Also point out that Paul is not enduring these hardships for self-aggrandizement but "for the sake of the elect."

Many Bible personalities endured hardship for the sake of God's people. Distribute paper and pencils and, if possible, divide the class into teams. Direct the teams to list as many Bible characters as they can think of who endured hardship. Ask each team to report to the total group. Here is a brief list: Hagar who bore Ishmael; Joseph in Egypt; Ruth, for her mother-in-law, Naomi; Rahab, the prostitute who risked her life in Jericho; the prophet Jeremiah; the prophet Hosea; Stephen, the first martyr; Peter; John.

Invite the class to talk for a few minutes about how the Bible's portrayal of persons who suffer for God's people differs sharply from a commonly held belief that the Christian life should shield one from hardship and problems. Wrap up this section by noting that Paul made the point to Timothy, and to us, that faithful discipleship unquestionably involves suffering.

(4) The Reward for Endurance

The suffering, though difficult, is not in vain. Second Timothy 2:12 assures us that if we endure we will also be rewarded because we will reign with Christ. You may want to read or retell "The Reward for Endurance"

as found under the Interpreting the Scripture section.

Then ask students to think silently about the relationship between the Cross and the crown in their own lives. Be sure to pause after reading each of the following questions so that class members can consider their own responses. These questions are not to be answered aloud.

In what ways have I experienced suffering or hardship because of my Christian faith? R

How willing am I to endure hardship in order to help others in need?

If Christ were to rate me on a scale of 1 to 10, with 1 being the least amount of endurance and 10 being the most, what score would I receive?

What kinds of rewards have I expected from God in this life?

What kinds of rewards do I expect in the life to come?

On what do I base my hope for rewards?

(5) Christ's Faithfulness

Choose a student to read aloud 2 Timothy 2:11-13. Ask:

(1) Paul says that "the saying is sure." Do you see any apparent contradictions between verses 11 and 12 and verse 13? ?

Use the information in this section under Interpreting the Scripture to help students understand the three main ways that scholars have tried to interpret these verses. You may want to ask class members to indicate which of the three ways seems the best to them. Perhaps some students will have additional interpretations.

See if a few volunteers would be willing to recount briefly an incident in which Christ was clearly faithful despite their unfaithfulness. Such incidents may be confidential, so remind the class members to treat the information as privileged if it is shared.

In addition to, or instead of, the previous activity you may want to use a New Testament personality to show how Christ remained faithful even when someone else was unfaithful. Peter, for instance, had been one of Jesus' closest associates. He had professed his belief that Jesus was indeed the Messiah (Luke 9:20) and had promised to follow Jesus to prison and death (Luke 22:33). When the test of suffering came after Jesus' arrest, however, Peter denied Jesus three times (Luke 22:54-62), just as Jesus had said he would (Luke 22:34). Yet, Jesus was faithful, despite Peter's faithlessness, for in a post-resurrection meeting with the disciples, Jesus told Peter to feed his sheep (John 21:15-17). Such faithfulness would ultimately lead to Peter's suffering and death (John 21:18-19).

HELPING CLASS MEMBERS ACT

Suggest that some students may want to read about Christians who paid the ultimate price for their commitment. John Foxe's *Book of Martyrs*, written in the sixteenth century, is a classic available in most libraries and bookstores. Another source of information is Acts 6–7, which tells the story of the first martyr, Stephen. Encourage class members to put themselves in the place of those who were willing to die and measure their own level of faith against that of the martyrs.

Invite class members to pray for persons who are persecuted for their faith in our world today. Some specific names or places of persecution may be mentioned.

Challenge students to sit quietly and make a list of what they would be willing to lose or suffer in order to be faithful to the gospel. Ask them to prayerfully consider how much they are willing to pay for authentic discipleship.

PLANNING FOR NEXT SUNDAY

Our lesson for next week focuses on 2 Timothy 4:1-8. Ask class members to read the entire background scripture, 2 Timothy 4:1-18. During this session we will study what it means for Christians to keep the faith.

KEEP THE FAITH

PREVIEWING THE LESSON

Lesson Scripture: 2 Timothy 4:1-8
Background Scripture: 2 Timothy 4:1-18.
Key Verses: 2 Timothy 4:1-2

Focus of the Lesson:
Paul's encouragement to Timothy to preach God's message with faith, courage, and perseverance

Main Question of the Lesson:
How can we keep the faith when times are tough?

This lesson will enable adult learners to:
(1) examine the message to Timothy concerning steadfast endurance in keeping the faith.
(2) evaluate their own faithfulness in running the race for the gospel.
(3) respond by assisting someone else who is trying to endure.

Today's lesson may be outlined as follows:
(1) Introduction
(2) The Departure
(3) Keeping the Faith
(4) The Ministry

FOCUSING ON THE MAIN QUESTION

The famous quote "I have fought the good fight, I have finished the race, I have kept the faith," from today's lesson suggest that it is how we end up rather than how we start that matters. The hare gets far ahead with a burst of speed out of the starting gate. But when it fools around and does not get across the finish line, the fast start is irrelevant. Conversely, the tortoise's slow start is not definitive; for it maintains a steady, albeit slow, pace and never quits until it crosses the finish line. This steadfast endurance is what counts. I have known, as no doubt you have also, all too many "used-to-be" Christians who have slowed down, lost interest, or even quit. They fought the good fight—for a couple of rounds. They ran the race—part of it anyway.

Just before Harry S. Truman left the White House, he told his daughter Margaret: "Your dad will never be reckoned among the great. But you can be sure he did his level best and gave all he had to his country." Truman continued: "There is an epitaph in Boothill Cemetery in Tombstone, Arizona, which reads, 'Here lies Jack Williams; he done his dammedest.' What more can a person do?" And, we might add, what less can a person do?

The epitaph is appropriate, for only after Jack Williams has actually finished his race can his friends make such an assessment. We, on the other hand, are still in the race, and it does not yet appear how it will come out. How fast we run does not seem to be an issue, and so we need not be discouraged by the grey-

hounds who fly by us. And, strange to say, the finish line is movable rather than stationary. No one can ever reach it and then relax, for it is always just ahead. So the race never ends, and that means the only losers are those who quit. The swift have no advantage over the slow, for each is expected to do his or her best—no more, no less. Sometimes the race goes pretty well—"the time is favorable" (2 Timothy 4:2). But sometimes it does not go so well—the time is "unfavorable" (4:2). So as we approach our lesson today we ask: *How can we keep the faith when times are tough?*

READING THE SCRIPTURE

NRSV
2 Timothy 4:1-8

1 In the presence of God and of Christ Jesus, who is to judge the living and the dead, and in view of his appearing and his kingdom, I solemnly urge you: ²proclaim the message; be persistent whether the time is favorable or unfavorable; convince, rebuke, and encourage, with the utmost patience in teaching. ³For the time is coming when people will not put up with sound doctrine, but having itching ears, they will accumulate for themselves teachers to suit their own desires, ⁴and will turn away from listening to the truth and wander away to myths. ⁵As for you, always be sober, endure suffering, do the work of an evangelist, carry out your ministry fully.

6 As for me, I am already being poured out as a libation, and the time of my departure has come. ⁷I have fought the good fight, I have finished the race, I have kept the faith. ⁸From now on there is reserved for me the crown of righteousness, which the Lord, the righteous judge, will give me on that day, and not only to me but also to all who have longed for his appearing.

NIV
2 Timothy 4:1-8

1 In the presence of God and of Christ Jesus, who will judge the living and the dead, and in view of his appearing and his kingdom, I give you this charge: ²Preach the Word; be prepared in season and out of season; correct, rebuke and encourage—with great patience and careful instruction. ³For the time will come when men will not put up with sound doctrine. Instead, to suit their own desires, they will gather around them a great number of teachers to say what their itching ears want to hear. ⁴They will turn their ears away from the truth and turn aside to myths. ⁵But you, keep your head in all situations, endure hardship, do the work of an evangelist, discharge all the duties of your ministry.

⁶For I am already being poured out like a drink offering, and the time has come for my departure. ⁷I have fought the good fight, I have finished the race, I have kept the faith. ⁸Now there is in store for me the crown of righteousness, which the Lord, the righteous Judge, will award to me on that day—and not only to me, but also to all who have longed for his appearing.

Key
Verses

UNDERSTANDING THE SCRIPTURE

2 Timothy 4:1-8. In the presence of Christ, against a backdrop of ultimate accountability at the Last Judgment (4:1), Paul charges Timothy to proclaim the gospel (4:2). This proclaiming or preaching (NIV) is defined by three additional imperatives: to "convince," to "rebuke," and to "encourage" (NRSV) the congregation. It is important that Timothy be patient, never losing his temper; for the time is coming when the people will not listen (4:3). They want something new, like "God is dead!" They will not stand still for "'that old-time religion,'" and so they will wander from the truth to myths (4:4). It is all the more important, therefore, that Timothy be "sober" (NRSV) or "watchful" (NKJV), that he "keep [his] head" (NIV) when others are losing theirs (4:5). The soberness is self-control and alertness to know what is going on. His readiness to "endure suffering" (NRSV) or "afflictions" (NKJV) is about to be tested; for Paul's departure or death is at hand (4:6-8). This means that Timothy will have to take over in the apostle's place.

2 Timothy 4:9-15. Paul knows that the "crown of righteousness" is his (4:8); but he is lonely in his confinement awaiting the Roman sentence and he wants the strength and comfort that Timothy's presence will offer. It would be several months before the letter could get to Ephesus and Timothy could get to Rome. But Timothy is told to do his best (4:9). Demas, who had been with Paul during an earlier imprisonment (Colossians 4:14), has now deserted the apostle. We are not told why he left, but Paul takes it personally, accusing Demas of loving this present world more than he loves the gospel (4:10). It is an open question whether his going to Thessalonica represents apostasy or a desire to get on with his life, deciding that he had already given enough years to full-time missionary activity.

The missionary work must continue, however, and so Crescens (4:10), of whom nothing is known, has gone on a mission to Galatia (in Turkey). Titus (4:10), whose work in Crete is finished, has been sent to Dalmatia (Yugoslavia). Tychicus (4:12), who most likely carried the letter, is on his way to Ephesus to take Timothy's place. Only Luke is left to help the apostle in his hour of trial. But he needs more help, so Timothy is to pick up Mark on the way and bring him to Rome (4:11). The matter of the cloak (4:13) is a touching personal note. This is the winter overcoat, and the aging apostle is beginning to feel the chill. Troas is on the way from Ephesus to Rome, so it is not a problem for Timothy to stop there. All we know about the books and parchments is that Paul wanted them. We do not know why Paul left those things at Troas. And we do not know anything about Alexander the coppersmith (4:14), except that he continues to be dangerous (4:15).

2 Timothy 4:16-18. Upon arrival in Rome under guard, Paul would first have a preliminary hearing or an investigation of his case. The trial itself might be delayed as long as two years after the hearing. It was usual for friends to accompany the accused to this hearing as character witnesses and to offer moral support. Paul would have expected Christians in Rome to step forward in this capacity, but he had to endure the ordeal alone (4:16). He prays, however, that the desertion not be held against those too fearful to step forward and make their witness together with him. But even though the brothers and sisters abandoned him, he was not left alone after all. Christ stood at his side (4:17), invisible to others, but experienced by the apostle. The presence of Christ gave him the strength he needed, so Paul did not defend himself so much as proclaim the gospel with effectiveness to the Gentiles. Since the court at Rome was the center of the world, to preach there is to preach to the entire world. Paul expects that the Lord will rescue him from every evil attack that attempts to undermine his work (4:18).

INTERPRETING THE SCRIPTURE

The Departure

There are three dimensions of faithfulness in today's lesson: the faithfulness of Christ's people to Christ, his faithfulness to them, and their faithfulness to each other within their allegiance to Christ. Even if on this occasion they did not prove faithful to each other, the faithfulness of Christ makes up the lack, and they may do better in the future.

The dominant aspect of faithfulness in today's lesson is the steadfastness that endures all the way to the end. Paul seems to feel that his trial will not go well, and he speaks of his imminent death, calling it a "departure" (4:6). The verb means to untie what has been tied up, whether weighing anchor so a ship can leave port or an army striking its tents preparatory to setting out on a march. As an image for death it is dynamic rather than static. By using this word Paul is saying that death is not the end at all, but it is movement from one sphere to another, from this earthly life to eternal life. It is like a voyage or a march. But the departure from this life involves the shedding of blood, and this suggests the image of his life being poured out as a drink offering. Since wine was poured at an animal sacrifice (Numbers 15:5), the life of the apostle is portrayed as a sacrifice to God. Paul has offered himself in the Lord's work and now he is about to set sail for a better country.

Paul himself can do no more, so his last action is to ask Timothy to take his place in the succession of Christian witnesses. It is like the passing of the baton in a relay race. Each runner runs his or her own laps alone and some are faster than others, but the race is for the team rather than for any individual on the team. What matters is that each person run the entire race and not quit before the end. At Princeton Theological Seminary a wall plaque gives the names of the Princeton graduates who have been martyred over the years on distant mission fields. They too had been poured out as drink offerings to God. But always a new class of graduates pick up the baton and take their places so that the race may continue. Timothy, accordingly, is to proclaim the message so that there is no break in the witness when Paul departs. Each of us, in turn, is part of this great relay race that is the church. We have taken the baton from someone before us, and we are expected to pass it on to another coming after us.

This does not happen if we short-circuit the process, if we do not complete our assigned laps, if our discipleship falters. Note that Paul does not decide when his work is done. The departure comes to him, for it is God who has assigned the number of laps he is to run.

Keeping the Faith

Endurance to the end is compared with combat (4:7). The good fight was discussed in Lesson 2; however, here we stress the past tense. Since Paul had already fought, it is the end. He never quit, but endured faithfully. We can't say this until it is indeed over; for we never know for sure if we'll fail to get our second wind. So we cling to the Spirit which has been poured out upon us (see Lesson 5).

The end of the fight and the idea of endurance lead Paul to think that his life has been more like the long-distance race than the sprint with its short burst of speed (4:7). He has finished the course that has been marked out for him. He may be thinking of the 400 yard race in full armor, which would lead naturally from the combat theme, or of the two or three mile marathon race, which goes well with the endurance theme. In either case, he did not drop out of the race, but now stands at the finish line, exhausted and drained of life energy, but with the satisfaction that he has kept the faith.

There are two possible interpretations of the faith that is to be kept or guarded. First, the faith was the promise that an ancient athlete made to abide by the rules of competition, both in private training and in the actual public competition. In this case, God had laid down the rules of the Christian life and Paul had promised to obey them. Now he says that he has indeed been as obedient as he had promised to be. We, too, have pledged ourselves to obey the rules of the faith as they have been laid down for us by the Scriptures and by the church that we have joined. And we, too, at the finish line, must give account of the way in which we have kept that faith over the long haul.

Second, the faith was a deposit given into another's keeping. It may be a guarantee of our intention to do something at a later time, as when we make a down payment on a purchase, whether to hold a house until closing or to reserve a seat on a trip or whatever. Or perhaps we are leaving town for a time and we entrust something of value to another, such as money to a bank or a dog to a friend. The one who receives the deposit is expected to guard it and return it at the specified time. In this case, God had given Paul the gospel. Paul had kept the faith by being obedient, by transmitting it intact to others, and is now ready to return it to God. He had kept the faith against all temptation to deny it in his various difficulties, including the pending martyrdom. And we, too, at the finish line, must return to God the gospel we had been given for a time to use in ministry (4:5)

The Ministry

Paul is standing at the finish line, the course completed, nothing more to do. The wreath had been prepared before the race and so the judge is able to crown the victor at once. Paul's crown had also been prepared ahead of time, and had been kept secure by God against his finishing the race (4:8). Now God will present to Paul the crown of righteousness. The crown is eternal life. It may be described as "the crown of righteousness" because it is the reward for a faithful and righteous life; or, more probably, it is the gift of perfect righteousness appropriate to the life of the saints in heaven—no more temptation, no more hostility, no more testing, no more difficulty. The analogy with athletic competition breaks down, however, for in athletic competition there is only one crown for a single winner in a race. But the crown of righteousness is for all who complete the course. It is for each individual who has longed for the appearance of Christ at the Second Coming.

The good fight, the race to be run, consists in ministry (4:5). The word means service, like waiting on tables in the mess hall. It expanded to include general service in the cause of the gospel. Here it is defined in terms of evangelism and in 4:2 of proclaiming the message. Both activities, of course, stretch out to include every word or action that testifies to the reality of the gospel in everyday life. Next week we shall see how good works in general are intended to have the same result. To "carry out [this] ministry fully" (NRSV; 4:5) or to "fulfill" it (NKJV) is to do it, to leave nothing undone. In the papyri the verb refers to the discharge of debts and carrying a project through to completion.

Fulfilling the ministry is the result of the readiness (NKJV) or the persistence

(NRSV) of 4:2. Actually, it is a verb that means to place upon, to stand over, and thus to be pressing or earnest. If we take the word in its sense of standing near or standing by, it means that we are to be always prepared, that we are never off duty, that we are to keep at it. If we take it in its sense of pressing, the meaning is the intensity with which we are to embrace the work. In either case—and both have relevance for our discipleship today—we are to persist in the witness "in season *and* out of season" (NKJV; 4:2), whether the time is "favorable or unfavorable" (NRSV). The idea embodied in the word is convenient or opportune, as in Mark 14:11 where Judas looks for a convenient way to betray Jesus. We are, then, to witness whether people listen or not, whether we are in the mood or not. This was illustrated for me at the Rose Bowl. I saw various Christian groups make their witness by trailing behind the official parade, by handing out leaflets at the stadium, and by preaching in the parking lots. It was certainly not a convenient setting, but they did it anyway.

SHARING THE SCRIPTURE

PREPARING TO TEACH

Preparing Our Hearts

In our modern society we often use the term "rat race" to describe the daily round of endless activities that seem to move us nowhere. We are like caged rodents twirling around on a treadmill. Our feet may move faster or slower, but we never really go anywhere. In contrast, Paul writes in 2 Timothy 4:7 about the race he has finished. He was definitely not on a treadmill going nowhere. Instead, as described in the Focusing on the Main Question section, he participated in a relay race. As he ends his life, Paul knows that he has run his appointed laps for the sake of the gospel and so he prepares to hand off the baton to Timothy. As you read the material for this week's lesson, think about the kind of race that you are running. Ask God to show you how you can be a more faithful servant who persistently runs the race, proclaiming the gospel message in both good times and bad. You may want to record ideas in your spiritual journal.

Preparing Our Minds

Read 2 Timothy 4:1-18, especially verses 1-8. Also read all of the material in the lesson.

Try to put yourself in Paul's place. How would you feel if you knew that you would soon be called upon to sacrifice your life for the sake of the gospel? What provisions would you be making so that someone else would be ready to take the baton from you and continue the race? Also put yourself in Timothy's place. What is Paul calling you to do? How will you respond, especially in light of Paul's imprisonment and impending death?

Preparing Our Learning Space

For the ranking activity under "Keeping the Faith," you may want to write each sentence on newsprint or a chalkboard prior to class. If so, cover this work until it is time to use it.

Have on hand:
- several Bibles for students
- newsprint and marker or chalkboard and chalk
- paper and pencils

LEADING THE CLASS

(1) Introduction

Use the Focusing on the Main Question portion to introduce today's lesson, or do the activity below.

Tell the class that today's lesson focuses on faithfulness, particularly the steadfastness that endures to the end. Ask them to give examples of people who have been faithful to the end, especially in the face of difficult circumstances. Here are some examples if you need ideas to spark discussion: a cancer patient who fights valiantly until death; a teacher who perseveres with challenging students; a business owner who fights back from impending bankruptcy; a homeowner who vows to rebuild after everything was lost in a tornado. When several instances have been cited, ask the class:

? (1) **What do you think motivated these persons to hang on despite the odds against them?**

(2) **What would you do under similar circumstances?**

(3) **How might these examples help us to understand faithfulness, in the sense of steadfast endurance?**

Move the discussion to today's scripture lesson by pointing out that Paul recognizes that he has finished his own race in this life. Soon he will be poured out as a sacrifice because of his faithfulness in proclaiming the gospel. He is indeed facing uncertainty and tough times as he writes to Timothy, but his faith never wavers. Paul's situation prompts us to ask our main question for today's lesson: *How can we keep the faith when times are tough?*

(2) The Departure

Choose someone to read 2 Timothy 4:1-8. First, direct class members to put themselves in Timothy's place as they read this letter. Then ask:

? (1) **If you were Timothy, how would feel** knowing that your friend and mentor **?** expected to die soon?

(2) **Since you are aware that your friend's impending death is due to his witness for Christ, what would be your response to his command that you are to "proclaim the message; be persistent whether the time is favorable or unfavorable" (4:2)?**

(3) **What is your reaction to Paul's passing of the baton to you with the command that you are to "do the work of an evangelist" (4:5)?**

(4) **How do you feel about Paul's request that you come to see him in prison?**

Now ask the students to put themselves in Paul's place and answer these questions:

(5) **As you look back over your own life and work, how would you evaluate the race you have run for the sake of the gospel?** **?**

(6) **Now that your departure is imminent, what are your hopes and dreams for the work that Timothy will do?**

(3) Keeping the Faith

Use information from the "Keeping the Faith" section of the Interpreting the Scripture portion to help students gain a better understanding of the faith that Paul is calling Timothy to keep.

Especially note that Paul was called by God to keep the faith in the sense that he was to be obedient in sharing it with others, no matter what difficulties might tempt him to deny it. Just as he told Timothy to do, Paul was persistent in proclaiming the message. Challenge class members to think about their willingness to keep the faith by sharing the good news of Jesus with others. Distribute paper and pencils and have them rank the situations below. Number 1 is the situation in which they think they would have the least difficulty keeping the faith, while number 5 would be the most difficult circumstance for them. Tell the students they must use all five numbers, and no number may be repeated. You may want to read these situations once and then reread them slowly. Or, you may prefer to write them on newsprint or a chalkboard.

- You are visiting a nonbelieving friend who has recently learned that he is terminally ill.
- A co-worker has been laid off and has come to you to tell her story.
- A neighbor's child is seriously injured by a hit-and-run driver who speeds down your street. You really do not know the neighbor well but you want to offer assistance.
- A church member has seemingly had one family crisis after another. She cannot be as active right now as she would like to be, and she feels guilty.
- You go to see your adult son who is in prison on charges of armed robbery.

When the students have finished their individual ranking, talk about how they perceived each situation and why they feel it would or would not be difficult for them to share the good news in each situation.

If time permits, encourage volunteers to share stories about their own experiences of keeping the faith under difficulty circumstances.

(4) The Ministry

You may want to use "The Ministry" section in the Interpreting the Scripture portion to help students understand that the race Paul has run consists of ministry. Ministry takes many forms, such as service, good works, and evangelism. The apostle is able to fulfill his ministry because he has been ready and persistent.

Invite the class to think of images or roles that they associate with ministry. Be sure that they think in inclusive terms, rather than just seeing Christian ministry as the domain of ordained persons. List their ideas on newsprint or a chalkboard. Here are some suggestions to add to the list: teacher, evangelist, prophet, preacher, servant, liberator, counselor, and peace-maker.

Once the list is complete, suggest that each student write a sentence or two about how they perceive themselves to fulfill any of the ministry roles they have identified. Distribute paper and pencils if you have not already done so. When the students have finished, have them share their ideas with a partner or the entire class.

Conclude this part of the lesson by asking class members to review their lists. Have them silently meditate on where they see themselves as fitting into ministry. You may want to close the quiet time by asking God to guide each of you as you steadfastly try to keep the faith and share the message that has been entrusted to you.

HELPING CLASS MEMBERS ACT

Suggest that class members make a special effort to support someone this week who is engaged in an all-out endurance race. Perhaps they can help a terminally ill person, or provide respite for someone who cares full-time for another. The students' willingness to meet the other persons' needs can be a real witness to God's love and care.

Challenge the class members to evaluate themselves as to how faithfully they are running the race. Ask them to consider whether they are just sprinters, in the race with just a short burst of speed and energy, or marathoners who can go the distance. Encourage them to pray that God will give them the stamina needed to finish the race of faith.

Paul's comments about the coming end of his life (2 Timothy 4:6) provide an opportunity for students to consider their own mortality. Suggest that they try to write an obituary for themselves in which they list their accomplishments and indicate how they want to be remembered by others. Class members may want to reflect on the degree to which who they are and what they have done embodies the kind of faithful Christian life they are called to live.

PLANNING FOR NEXT SUNDAY

Ask class members to read Titus 3:1-11 in preparation for next week's session. We will be talking about how those who serve Christ work for the good of others.

BE GOOD TO ONE ANOTHER

PREVIEWING THE LESSON

Lesson Scripture: Titus 3:1-11
Background Scripture: Titus 3:1-11
Key Verse: Titus 3:8

Focus of the Lesson:
Paul's teaching to Titus that believers are to live obediently and harmoniously as members of the Christian community of faith

Main Question of the Lesson:
How can we be good to everyone, including those we think are undeserving?

This lesson will enable adult learners to:
(1) examine the teaching given to Timothy concerning doing good works for everyone.
(2) consider how God's loving-kindness has been poured out upon them.
(3) respond by doing a good work for someone in need.

Today's lesson may be outlined as follows:
(1) Introduction
(2) Good Works
(3) The Divine Kindness
(4) Profitable

FOCUSING ON THE MAIN QUESTION

Several years ago my wife, Helen, and I were in the Dallas airport trying to get back to Baltimore. So many flights had been canceled due to unusually severe weather that our plane was loaded to the gills—not a single empty seat. On edge, nerves frayed, people jostled each other as they hunted for seats and struggled with too much carry-on luggage. I was strapped into my seat and engrossed in my book, almost oblivious to what was going on,

when Helen told me to get up. We were changing our seats. She had noticed a small child crying because the airline had not been able to seat her with her mother. Helen spoke to the flight attendant, and by splitting us up she was able to seat mother and child together.

Helen was ready to perform a "good work" (Titus 3:1), and she did it, and it was "profitable to everyone" (3:8), to the mother and child, to the other passengers, and to the stressed-out flight attendants. But I also was ready to perform a good work, and my willingness to change my seat was required in order to accomplish the task. Degrees of readiness, however, are revealed in the story. Helen identified the need and worked out the solution while I merely agreed after she pointed it out. Perhaps most of the time we act as I did. Someone else spots a need and suggests something that we can do. And on the larger world screen it probably has to be that way. But there is something to be said for the person who looks around to see what needs are to be met rather than becoming too quickly engrossed in a book.

The lesson instructs us to be ready for "every" good work (3:1) and to do it for "everyone" (3:2). But that "everyone" is distressingly comprehensive. Dorothy Day, a Roman Catholic laywoman who spent her life ministering to the down-and-out in New York, spoke of Jesus' comparison of the church to the net cast into the sea and hauled in, filled with fish, which a friend of Day's observed, "include some blowfish and quite a few sharks." This mandate to do good for everyone prompts today's main question: *How can we be good to everyone, including those we think are undeserving?*

READING THE SCRIPTURE

NRSV
Titus 3:1-11

1 Remind them to be subject to rulers and authorities, to be obedient, to be ready for every good work, [2]to speak evil of no one, to avoid quarreling, to be gentle, and to show every courtesy to everyone. [3]For we ourselves were once foolish, disobedient, led astray, slaves to various passions and pleasures, passing our days in malice and envy, despicable, hating one another. [4]But when the goodness and loving kindness of God our Savior appeared, [5]he saved us, not because of any works of righteousness that we had done, but according to his mercy, through the water of rebirth and renewal by the Holy Spirit. [6]This Spirit he poured out on us richly through Jesus Christ our Savior, [7]so that, having been justified by his grace, we might become heirs according to the hope of eternal life. [8]The saying is sure.

I desire that you insist on these things, so that those who have come to believe in God may be careful to devote themselves to good works; these things are excellent and profitable to everyone. [9]But avoid stupid controversies, genealogies, dissen-

NIV
Titus 3:1-11

1 Remind the people to be subject to rulers and authorities, to be obedient, to be ready to do whatever is good, [2]to slander no one, to be peaceable and considerate, and to show true humility toward all men.

[3]At one time we too were foolish, disobedient, deceived and enslaved by all kinds of passions and pleasures. We lived in malice and envy, being hated and hating one another. [4]But when the kindness and love of God our Savior appeared, [5]he saved us, not because of righteous things we had done, but because of his mercy. He saved us through the washing of rebirth and renewal by the Holy Spirit, [6]whom he poured out on us generously through Jesus Christ our Savior, [7]so that, having been justified by his grace, we might become heirs having the hope of eternal life. [8]This is a trustworthy saying. And I want you to stress these things, so that those who have trusted in God may be careful to devote themselves to doing what is good. These things are excellent and profitable for everyone.

[9]But avoid foolish controversies and

Key
Verse

Key
Verse

sions, and quarrels about the law, for they are unprofitable and worthless. [10]After a first and second admonition, have nothing more to do with anyone who causes divisions, [11] since you know that such a person is perverted and sinful, being self-condemned.

genealogies and arguments and quarrels about the law, because these are unprofitable and useless. [10]Warn a divisive person once, and then warn him a second time. After that, have nothing to do with him. [11]You may be sure that such a man is warped and sinful; he is self-condemned.

UNDERSTANDING THE SCRIPTURE

Titus 3:1-2. Titus is to remind the congregation of what they already know: that their behavior toward outsiders is an important part of their discipleship. Christians are to be good citizens, obeying the law and getting along with everyone. We are not to slander anyone and we are not to be dog-in-the-manger quarrelsome. Instead, we are to be gentle and humble (NKJV) or courteous (NRSV) to everyone—even to those who cannot hurt us if we are not!

Titus 3:3-7. We are to treat everyone this way, even those we think are undeserving, because we were not always like we are now. Once we were as the nonbelievers still are: foolish in the sense that we did not understand God, disobedient to God, led astray from the truth by the Devil, slaves to destructive passions, malicious and envious, "hateful" (NKJV) or "despicable" (NRSV) and hating one another (3:3). It was when we were like this that the kindness and consideration of God appeared to us (3:4). Since it simply appeared, we can only respond. We cannot control it by making it come or go and we cannot manipulate it while it is here. The idea is suddenness and unexpectedness. The appearance resulted in our salvation, but was motivated by divine mercy rather than by any goodness of our own (3:5).

The "water" (NRSV) or "washing" (NKJV) is baptism. It is associated with "rebirth" (NRSV) or "regeneration" (NKJV). This unusual word occurs else-

where in the New Testament only in Matthew 19:28. The world will be reborn when the Son of man is upon his throne. There, however, the physical world has passed away and the newly born world is heaven. Here the reborn remain in the old world. The same idea, in different language, is the newness of life experienced by the Christian after baptism (Romans 6:4). And so the rebirth is explained as renewal by the Holy Spirit. Either the new birth is followed by an ever-increasing growth in grace, or the new birth and the renewal take place at the same time and they define each other. God poured out upon us this Holy Spirit through Christ (3:6). Note the Trinitarian language.

The goodness, consideration, mercy, and grace are the characteristics of God the Father. The appearance (3:4), the salvation (3:5), and the justification (3:7) relate to Christ. The words "having been justified" (NRSV) may also be translated as "be put right with God" (GNB). The verb has the flavor of the courtroom. It means to have a right standing before the law. This is normally achieved by obeying the law. When innocence is proven in court, the verb means vindication or acquittal. This cannot be transferred into Christian metaphor, however, because none are innocent. But a king may grant amnesty and they are then safe before the law. This possibility has allowed the use of the term in Christian theology. If the court is the Last Judgment, and if all are guilty, then amnesty can only be granted by God through grace as a gift. The justification is the removal of the guilt so that the individual is right with God. When this happens, based upon the Cross, of course, a person is set free for a new and positive relationship with God. So justification is the beginning of the Christian life in the expectation that it will have final confirmation at the Last Judgment.

The verb translated as "saved" in 3:5 means to rescue someone from danger, whether physical, moral, or religious. Often, especially in the miracle stories in the Gospels, it means to save from sickness. Salvation then came to mean rescue from the greatest danger of all, that of condemnation at the Last Judgment. The rescue must always be future so long as a person lives in the flesh, and yet here the verb is in the past tense. The rescue actually occurred when God's kindness appeared and became part of the believer through the new birth. The past tense, therefore, represents the conviction of faith that salvation for the believer is so certain that it is as if it had already happened.

Titus 3:8-11. The movement is from the divine grace (3:7) to our response in good works (3:8). The focus then shifts from the affect of the Christian behavior upon nonbelievers to the proper conduct within the church (3:9). We are to avoid arguments about arcane doctrines, for that is useless for our spiritual development. We are to have nothing to do with anyone who generates divisions within the church (3:10).

INTERPRETING THE SCRIPTURE

Good Works

The phrase "good works" occurs thirteen times in our three short books. Therefore, it may be taken as a significant theme in the Pastoral Epistles. The word "work" implies that we actually do something; and what we do is qualified by the word "good." Two different Greek words for "good" are used in the phrase, one connoting beautiful, pleasant, and excellent, along with the ideas of useful or profitable and upright or virtuous, which both words share. We cannot detect any real difference, however, for both words are in today's lesson, one in 3:1 and the other in 3:8. So the English translations do not distinguish, consistently rendering the Greek as "good work," the sole exception being NRSV's "noble task" for the office of bishop in 1 Timothy 3:1.

If we "believe in" (Titus 3:8) or have "reverence for"(1 Timothy 2:10) God, then we will perform the good deeds. For we affirm or deny faith according to the character of our actions (Titus 1:16). So we are to be ready to do good to one another (2 Timothy 2:21 and Titus 3:1). Such conduct is not optional; for Christ redeems us for this purpose (Titus 2:14), and we are equipped to do it through our study of the Scriptures (2 Timothy 3:17). Obviously we are not to blow our own horns over it, insisting like Little Jack Horner, "What a good boy am I!" But at the same time the actions are "conspicuous" (1 Timothy 5:25). We are to "model" them (Titus 2:7) so that others can learn from us.

For the most part, the texts simply urge the good works in general terms, although 1 Timothy 6:18 defines them in terms of generosity and readiness to share, and 1 Timothy 5:10 offers several examples: bringing up children, showing hospitality, washing the feet of the saints, and helping the afflicted. The conclusion of 5:10, "doing good in every way," correlates with the "urgent needs" of others of Titus

3:14. Since we cannot know in advance what those needs will be, of necessity the admonition must be open-ended. My list will be different from your list because my situation is different from yours. But that we both will have a list is a given.

The Divine Kindness

So we know that we are to do all kinds of good deeds for everyone all the time. Such a tall order recalls our main question: How can we be good to everyone, including those we think are undeserving? In answer, today's lesson steers us to God's treatment of us when we were the undeserving.

We are Christians today because of the "goodness" (NRSV) of God (3:4). This is the "kindness" of NKJV. The Greek word suggests a quality that penetrates the entire nature, replacing harshness with gentleness. The spirit of the word is "sweetness" or "niceness" in concern to help those in need. In funeral inscriptions there is occasional testimony to such a character in the deceased. Applied to God, the kindness expresses readiness to bless and to forgive. God revealed the kindness in Christ (Ephesians 2:7). The Holy Spirit gives us this kindness as a gift (Galatians 5:22) so that we can display it to others in our own daily life (Colossians 3:12).

The goodness is in tandem with "loving kindness" (NRSV; Titus 3:4) or "love" (NKJV). The Greek word used here is not the normal one for love. Its only other use in the New Testament is in Acts 28:2. The natives on Malta built a fire for Paul and his companions because it was cold and beginning to rain. Their motive was "philanthropy" (as the word came into English), kindly humanitarian treatment of others. The word includes kindness toward equals and graciousness toward subordinates, as well as pity for those who are in trouble. It has the nuance of "consideration," and thus it goes with the gentleness and courtesy we are to show each other (3:1). God's consideration has revealed itself in saving us from the penalty due to our sinfulness. The idea of "Savior" includes our helplessness to save ourselves.

Our salvation is not a reward for any works of righteousness that we have done (3:5). Far from having done any good deeds, we had been committing the sins listed in 3:3. Instead, our salvation is due to the divine mercy that, along with the goodness and consideration, is the third character trait that motivates God's treatment of us. The mercy is activated by Christ and mediated by the Holy Spirit. God, therefore, "poured out" the Holy Spirit on us "through Jesus Christ our Savior" (3:6). The transforming and renewing Holy Spirit was given at Pentecost, and the power continues to work in the lives of Christians. The verb suggests a bowl turned upside down so that all of its contents drain out. Nothing is held back, and the gift is sufficient for all the needs of everyone because it has been done "richly" (NRSV) or "abundantly" (NKJV).

The appearance of the goodness, consideration, and mercy of God in Christ is for a specific purpose: in order that "we might become heirs" (3:7). That purpose is realized through the Holy Spirit. The idea of the inheritance is based upon the concept of the believer's being adopted by God through his or her identification with Christ by faith. We are the heirs now, of course, but it is a potential possession of the inheritance. We may be said to have eternal life now, since it is so certain to become ours, but it is potential so long as the heir is in the flesh. The "might become" and the introduction of the hope point to a future consummation and leave the present free for our good works.

The "grace" of 3:7 has two possibilities in relation to our current conduct. Grace, especially in connection with justification, is the unmerited favor that God extends to us in salvation. Justification is the beginning of the Christian life in the hope and expectation that it will have final confirmation at the Last Judgment. The justification then gives us the potential to achieve righteousness in Christ. The other possibility assumes that the unmerited favor is implied in the justification itself. The grace, then, may be the Holy Spirit, given by God and active in our daily life.

Profitable

We have thus moved from the contemplation of the divine character as the model for our discipleship to the activity of the Holy Spirit to make the imitation possible. The second answer to our main question is that the good works are profitable to us (3:8) aside from any "feel good" by-product and apart from the moral quality of the people who receive our goodnesses, our considerations, our mercies.

All four occurrences of the word in the New Testament are in the Pastoral Epistles. NKJV uniformly translates the Greek word as "profitable" but NRSV also has "valuable" (1 Timothy 4:8) and "useful" (2 Timothy 3:16). In 1 Timothy 4:8 (see Lesson 1), godliness is profitable both for this life and the life to come. In 2 Timothy 3:16, scripture is profitable for training in righteousness. And here good works are profitable for everyone. They are profitable for the doer in that they reflect the discipleship that is on the way to eternal life. And they are profitable for the recipient in two

ways: their urgent needs are met and they are attracted to the faith of one who acts like this.

If the good works are profitable for everyone, ourselves as well as the recipients, and if they are a reflection of our God's nature, then we are to be ready or prepared to do them (3:1; see also 2 Timothy 2:21). Arthur John Gossip has called this readiness "The Galilean Accent." He writes in a book by that title:

> Only when to think in Christ's way has become as instinctive, and spontaneous, and natural, and unconscious as the dialect of one's native place—and who ever notices his own accent, or is so much as aware that it exists? . . . are we fully Christian men and women. . . . all unconsciously, as we move to and fro about our lives a hundred little nothings we ourselves never observe are dropping from our hands that keep betraying accurately whose we are and whom we serve—God or the world, Christ or our self. . . . [those who have] the Galilean accent, the spirit of Christ. . . . have quiet eyes and steady pulses; they face life with cheerfulness and a brave intrepidity. . . . The Galilean spirit means to have a shoulder ready for our neighbour's burdens, a life at the disposal of those in want or need, a mind that has time for others, even for those who seem to have no claim on us, or who on their side have been thoughtless and unjust; for it is not for nothing that when people speak of showing a Christian spirit they mean a forgiving one.

SHARING THE SCRIPTURE

PREPARING TO TEACH

Preparing Our Hearts

What does it mean to do good to one another? Are we truly willing to offer a helping hand to any who need it, or are we selective about who we will assist? We

may choose to share our time, talents, and resources with persons we think are worthy of our love and attention, forgetting for the moment that Jesus reached out to everyone. What about you? Are your heart and hand and purse open to all, including those who you feel are undeserving of your generosity? Try making a list of the persons you have helped in the last week. Likely the list will include family members and perhaps neighbors, church members, and co-workers as well. Does it also include the lonely man you chatted with at the bus stop, or the homeless woman you passed on the street? As you review your list, pray that God will show you ways to expand it. In doing so, remember that you will be doing for others what God has already done for you—reaching out to you when you did not merit favor.

Preparing Our Minds

Read Titus 3:1-11, preferably in several translations. Note that this letter, like those addressed to Timothy, was likely written by a follower of Paul, rather than the apostle himself. Although no specific mention is made of Titus in Acts, which is Luke's record of Paul's work, the letter to the Galatians (2:1) indicates that he was with Paul in Jerusalem. Questions arose about Titus, a Greek, who was not circumcised. Titus is mentioned in another letter that scholars are sure was written by Paul, 2 Corinthians (7:6-7, 13-14 and 8:6, 16-17). The letter to Titus, which concerns the administration of the church in Crete (1:5), highlights the requirements of church leaders, the relationships and treatment of various groups within the church, and the expectations that believers are to live responsibly in this world. The latter section of the letter is the portion from which today's lesson is drawn.

Preparing Our Learning Space

If you choose to use a song for the introductory activity, you will need to select it and secure hymnals for the class.

Have on hand:
- several Bibles for students
- newsprint and marker or chalkboard and chalk
- paper and pencils
- optional hymnals

LEADING THE CLASS

(1) Introduction

Use the Focusing on the Main Question portion to introduce today's lesson, or do the following activity.

Invite class members to sing or say a familiar hymn that speaks of love and care for one another. "Blest Be the Tie That Binds" or "We Are One in the Spirit" (also known by the words of the refrain, "They'll know we are Christians by our love") would be good choices. Then ask:

(1) **How do you think those who are outside the church perceive church members?**

(2) **What kinds of behaviors among Christians do you think give other people their ideas about church members?**

Point out that loving actions by church members have a tendency to pull people toward Christ and his church, while actions that do not reflect the love of God tend to push people away. Lead the class to today's lesson by noting that the portion of the letter to Titus that we will study was written to help church members know how to behave. Their loving actions and good works benefited not only themselves but were "profitable to everyone" (3:8). The author of the letter, who may have been Paul but was more likely one of his followers, recognized that God had been good to us not because we deserved mercy and salvation but because of God's own grace. In light of the loving-kindness poured out upon us, we are to be good to others as well. The question that will guide our study today is this: *How can we be good to everyone, including those we think are undeserving?*

(2) Good Works

Introduce this part of the lesson by reading or retelling the first paragraph under "Good Works" in the Interpreting the

Scripture portion. Tell the group to listen for the words "good work" as a student reads aloud Titus 3:1-11.

Distribute paper and pencils and ask each class member to write a list of good works—large or seemingly insignificant—that they have done in the last three days. Tell them to be honest; the authors of the lists will not be identified. Set a short time limit. Collect the papers and either redistribute them and have students read lists that are not their own, or read some of the lists aloud to the group yourself. Talk about these actions. Affirm the group's willingness to do good deeds.

Then ask the class to brainstorm answers to the following question. Record their responses on newsprint or a chalkboard for reference later in the session.

(3) What other good works could we be doing to show God's mercy and grace to those with whom we come in contact?

As students share ideas, be alert for responses that indicate they do not want to do certain things for people they deem unworthy. Use such comments as an opportunity to gently remind the group that we do not deserve the goodness that God has lavished upon us, but God has acted graciously despite our unworthiness.

(3) The Divine Kindness

Use information in "The Divine Kindness" section of the Interpreting the Scripture portion to help the class more fully understand God's goodness and how we are to reflect the loving-kindness that God has poured out on us.

The following guided imagery activity may help adults relate God's loving actions to their own. Tell the students to sit comfortably in their chairs with their eyes closed. Read these statements, pausing long enough to give the students an opportunity to reflect.

Picture yourself as one of Jesus' followers.

You are standing at some distance as he approaches a woman at a well. You cannot imagine what he is thinking. He is a prominent Jewish teacher talking to a woman. Not just any woman, which in itself was unthinkable, but a despised Samaritan. You see her give him a drink of water. Think for a few moments about this improbable scene and how difficult Jesus' actions are for you to comprehend. (pause)

You have moved closer now and can hear him telling her about all the men in her life. This is truly astounding! He must have known all along that he was talking to a Samaritan woman of very questionable reputation. As you are wondering who she thinks she is to be talking to Jesus, he tells her that he is the Messiah. Surely he cannot be suggesting that salvation is for one such as her. You pause to catch your breath. (pause)

Suddenly the scene changes and you realize that you are the one to whom Jesus is speaking. Jesus offers you the living water of salvation, just as he offered it to the Samaritan woman. Consider how you, like the woman, did not deserve the grace that God was so freely willing to give. (pause)

And now you, like the Samaritan woman who responded by bringing others to Jesus, want to respond to God's kindness to you by doing a good work for someone else. Reflect on who that person may be and what you might do. (pause)

Give thanks for God's grace, knowing that you, like all others, do not merit the loving-kindness that God has so freely and graciously poured out. (pause)

Open your eyes when you are ready.

(4) Profitable

Have the class read the key verse, Titus 3:8, in unison if possible. Remind the group that good works, which were modeled for us by God, are profitable to everyone, including ourselves. You may want to read the second paragraph under "Profitable" in the Interpreting the Scripture section to help the class understand the meaning of "profitable."

Note that in our society many people perform actions that they think will profit them, without regard to how the actions will affect others. In Titus, however, the accent is on doing works that are "profitable to everyone." The spotlight is not on the individual but on the group. Ask the class to consider situations in your own church or community where certain actions would be profitable to many. If the class has difficulty getting started, here is an example they may want to discuss:

R First Church can only be entered by those who can walk up six concrete steps. Some parishioners want to borrow the money needed to make the church accessible. What would you say to those members who opposed the plan because they felt the cost could not be justified?

Sum up the discussion by noting that actions that attempt to include everyone in the church family often make such a witness that people who would not otherwise be a part of the church come in and establish a relationship with Christ.

HELPING CLASS MEMBERS ACT

If you brainstormed ideas earlier in the session for doing good works for others, suggest that each student select one action they could follow through on this week.

Challenge class members to do some special kindness for someone they have considered to be undeserving of their efforts and resources.

Encourage students to take a careful look at the criteria they use to determine how profitable an action is. Do they measure value only in terms of money or their own personal gain, or do they look at the broader picture so as to help others profit from their actions? Suggest that they pray about the matter this week and make changes as God prompts them.

PLANNING FOR NEXT SUNDAY

Ask students to prepare for the next session by reading Hebrews 1, especially verses 1-5, and 3:1-6. Tell them to think about how God's sending Jesus into the world was a new and different way of relating to humanity.

GOD DOES A NEW THING

PREVIEWING THE LESSON

Lesson Scripture: Hebrews 1:1-5; 3:1-6
Background Scripture: Hebrews 1; 3:1-6
Key Verses: Hebrews 3:1-2

Focus of the Lesson:
God's sending of a Son as a new means of speaking to humanity

Main Question of the Lesson:
Who is this Jesus, that his faithfulness to God should be so critical to the ultimate meaning of my life, and what does that make me?

This lesson will enable adult learners to:
(1) explore the greatness of Christ, the Son of God.
(2) consider their understandings of the importance of the Old Testament.
(3) respond by taking action that will show forth their own faithfulness.

Today's lesson may be outlined as follows:
(1) Introduction
(2) The Old Testament
(3) Angels
(4) Moses
(5) Faithfulness

FOCUSING ON THE MAIN QUESTION

Most people assume some sort of power or force beyond a world that we may see, hear, touch, taste, or smell. But for many the effort to relate that "beyond" to the "here and now" results in failure. Samuel Beckett struggled with this problem in a strangely moving play entitled *Act Without Words*. A lone actor is on a bare stage. This is his world. An offstage whistle is heard. Something from the outside has intruded upon his world. He goes to the edge of the stage to investigate and is hurled to the floor. He gets to his feet, wondering what has happened. The whistle sounds from the other side of the stage. Again he goes to investigate and again he is hurled to the floor. The whistle sounds from above and fruit descends; however, the fruit is just beyond his reaching fingers. The whistle sounds again and a box descends. When he stands on the box to reach the fruit the box collapses. He sits down. The whistle sounds again but he does not respond. The whistle had failed to deliver on its promises.

Today's text tells of a different Whistle, one who cares about our hungers and our barked shins, and who chose to do something about it. This God understands our frustration with the vagueness of the offstage whistle and our discouragement over collapsing boxes and receding fruit. And so God sent a Son into our world as a new means of speaking to us, ensuring that there is but one voice and that it is clear. We can understand this Son because he is one of us and, therefore, he under-

stands our sore throats, disappointments, and sorrows.

But we need more than the empathy of one like ourselves. We need one who can take us into a relationship with God that will not disappoint. Therefore we key in on Hebrews 3:1-2; for this Son, the one we know as Jesus, was faithful to the God who appointed him to speak to us. These verses bring us to the main question: *Who is this Jesus, that his faithfulness to God should be so critical to the ultimate meaning of my own life, and what does that make me?*

READING THE SCRIPTURE

NRSV
Hebrews 1:1-5

1 Long ago God spoke to our ancestors in many and various ways by the prophets, ²but in these last days he has spoken to us by a Son, whom he appointed heir of all things, through whom he also created the worlds. ³He is the reflection of God's glory and the exact imprint of God's very being, and he sustains all things by his powerful word. When he had made purification for sins, he sat down at the right hand of the Majesty on high, ⁴having become as much superior to angels as the name he has inherited is more excellent than theirs.

5 For to which of the angels did God ever say,

    "You are my Son;
      today I have begotten you"?
Or again,
    "I will be his Father,
      and he will be my Son"?

NIV
Hebrews 1:1-5

1 In the past God spoke to our forefathers through the prophets at many times and in various ways, ²but in these last days he has spoken to us by his Son, whom he appointed heir of all things, and through whom he made the universe. ³The Son is the radiance of God's glory and the exact representation of his being, sustaining all things by his powerful word. After he had provided purification for sins, he sat down at the right hand of the Majesty in heaven. ⁴So he became as much superior to the angels as the name he has inherited is superior to theirs.

⁵ For to which of the angels did God ever say,

    "You are my Son;
      today I have become your Father"?
Or again,
    "I will be his Father,
      and he will be my Son"?

NRSV
Hebrews 3:1-6

1 Therefore, brothers and sisters, holy partners in a heavenly calling, consider that Jesus, the apostle and high priest of our confession, ²was faithful to the one who appointed him, just as Moses also "was faithful in all God's house." ³Yet Jesus is worthy of more glory than Moses, just as the builder of a house has more honor than the house itself. ⁴(For every house is built by someone, but the builder of all things is God.) ⁵Now Moses was faithful in all God's house as a servant, to testify to the things that would be spoken later. ⁶Christ, however, was faithful over God's house as a Son, and we are his house if we hold firm the confidence and the pride that belong to hope.

NIV
Hebrews 3:1-6

1 Therefore, holy brothers, who share in the heavenly calling, fix your thoughts on Jesus, the apostle and high priest whom we confess. ²He was faithful to the one who appointed him, just as Moses was faithful in all God's house. ³Jesus has been found worthy of greater honor than Moses, just as the builder of a house has greater honor than the house itself. ⁴For every house is built by someone, but God is the builder of everything. ⁵Moses was faithful as a servant in all God's house, testifying to what would be said in the future. ⁶But Christ is faithful as a Son over God's house. And we are his house, if we hold on to our courage and the hope of which we boast.

Key Verses

UNDERSTANDING THE SCRIPTURE

Hebrews 1:1-14. God has not remained silent and hidden, but has spoken many times in the past in order to make sure that men and women would be able to find God (1:1). These past revelations, however, were fragmentary in nature, diverse in geographical location and in method of disclosure. Since these revelations were made in the former times, they were made to the Hebrews of the Old Testament. They are the "forefathers" (NIV) or "ancestors" (NRSV) of all Christians, whether Jewish or Gentile, because they are the roots of our religious tradition. The unity of the revelation is guaranteed by God's being the author of it all, but the variety shows that no revelation is complete or final. Each is preparatory to the final revelation, which is Jesus Christ as the Son of God. The prophets are the organs by which the revelation is made, but the Son is the revelation itself. There is an inner unity of Old and New Testaments, therefore, in the flow of the partial toward the complete, of preparation to the fulfillment.

In these last days, which the New Jerusalem Bible defines as our own time, the Christian era, God has spoken to us in the Son (1:2). The Son is able to make the full revelation of God because he is the "radiance" (NIV) or the "reflection" (NRSV) of the divine glory (1:3). We may think of Christ as radiating the divine glory, as the sun gives forth rays of light (as NIV), or as a reflector that catches the headlights of a car (as NRSV). In either case, Christ translates the glory of God into human life, maintaining oneness with the Source of the glory, and yet reaching out into the world. The Son can reflect the glory because he is the "image" (NKJV) or "representation" (NIV) or "imprint" (NRSV) of God's person or being. The Greek word generally means the reproduction of an original design, such as the mark on a coin that determines its value, or the mark left on wax or metal by a seal to indicate ownership. It may also be an idea in the mind of an artist, which is then expressed in a picture or a statue. In the case of a person, the reproduction is that of a specific and unique character trait. The essence of the Father is printed on the Son so that he is the perfect expression of the Father. It is not the exactness of cloning but is the way in which a child expresses the form and personality of the parent. By revealing himself, therefore, the Son reveals the Father.

The purification for sins, followed by its verification in the return to the "right hand of the Majesty on high," is the heart of the word that God has spoken to us in the Son. Since angels are servants, the Son is obviously superior to them (1:4-14).

Hebrews 3:1-6. Jesus is worthy of greater glory than Moses, just as the builder has greater honor than the house that he or she builds (3:3). The difference is that between Creator and creature; for the builder of all things is God (3:4). And since God created through the Son (1:2), the Son must be superior to Moses.

In addition to the world, the word "house" can also mean the religious community within the larger creation. Moses was faithful in God's house (3:2) as a ser-

vant (3:5); but Christ owns the house and all that is in it (3:6) by inheritance (1:2). The house in which Moses was faithful, of course, was the Israel of the Old Testament; and the house that Christ has inherited is the Christian church. We, then, are that house with all of its implied blessing, because Jesus is the "apostle and high priest" (3:1). An apostle is one who has been sent on a mission with the authority to speak on behalf of the sender, and a priest is one who mediates with deity on behalf of men and women. Since the Sender is God and the Sent is the Son, the combination of terms expresses the twofold movement involved in establishing a relationship with God that will not disappoint. The apostle brings God to us and the high priest brings us to God.

This bonds us together in two directions, with each other and with Christ, as partners in a heavenly calling (3:1). The heavenly calling describes the Christian community as given the privilege of access to God. And the brothers and sisters are holy in that they have been separated out from the secular world.

INTERPRETING THE SCRIPTURE

The Old Testament

There are some exciting stories in the Old Testament—like Abraham and Moses at Mount Sinai and David taking on Goliath. And there are some good passages—like the Twenty-third Psalm—and some wonderful prophecies—Isaiah's peaceable kingdom at Christmas and the Suffering Servant at Easter. But there are so many "begats" in between. So, for the most part, we tend to set aside the Old Testament in order to move more quickly to the New Testament, where we feel more at home. But when we notice the refer-

ences in the margins of our Bibles, we quickly see that the New Testament does not set aside the Old Testament. And that means that we should not either. For although God's sending of a Son is a new means of speaking to us, the Old Testament leads up to it. We say that the child is the father or mother of the man or woman and that we need to know our roots if we are to understand ourselves. In this sense, the Old Testament is the parent of the New Testament and, therefore, we find there our ultimate religious roots.

This is especially true in Hebrews. In 1:5 we encounter two quotations. The first is from Psalm 2:7, which originally referred to the coronation of the king of Israel and reassured the people that God would bless the nation through this new king. The second is from 2 Samuel 7:14, which is part of God's promise to David that, through an endless series of descendants, his throne would be established forever (2 Samuel 7:16). Note that these two verses are used very differently in our passage. Now the Son is Jesus rather than the king of Israel, and the point is Jesus' superiority to the angels rather than divine approval of the king. There is movement, therefore, from the king to the Son of God. This movement, in which New Testament writers use Old Testament texts to explain Christian experience, is called progressive revelation.

It is revelation in that it is genuine. After all, God did speak in many ways to our ancestors in the faith by means of the prophets (1:1). So we have never been willing to discard the Old Testament, and it remains as the front part of our Bible. But it is also progressive, and so we have not been willing to have only the Old Testament. So the New Testament is the back part of our Bible. And, like the horse and carriage, you cannot have the one without the other.

The progress of these two texts, of course, begins with the historical fact of the fall of Israel and Judah to foreign invaders. What do you do with passages about the king when there is no longer a throne for the king to sit on? The first step is to transfer the reference of the texts from the king to the Messiah. Then, when Jesus is identified as the Messiah, the "Son" aspect is used naturally rather than symbolically. Now the "Son" indicates deity, and this makes Jesus superior to the angels, for they are not divine.

Sometimes the quotations in the New Testament do not jibe when we look them up in the Old Testament. There are two possible explanations for this. First, the writer is not quoting from memory, with "almost but not quite" accuracy. Second, he or she is using the Greek Old Testament (the Septuagint) rather than the Hebrew Old Testament. Usually the text is the same; but in Lesson 9 we will see significant differences in the two versions of Psalm 40:6-8 as they appear in the Old Testament and in Hebrews 10:5-7.

Angels

This special status of the Son is defined in Hebrews 1:2-3 by a series of unimaginable activities. God created the world itself through the Son. And since God created through the Son, God also revealed through the Son; and the revelation can be trusted, for it is the Creator who is the Revealer. Creation is a beginning, however, and not an end; for the Son sustains the world, in the sense of maintaining its existence. The idea here is the Son who guides the world to its final destiny rather than the Atlas who bears the dead weight of the world on his shoulders. This guidance is toward the final fulfillment of God's intent in appointing the Son as the heir of all creation. The guidance itself begins with the Son's making purification for our sins and then it is empowered by the Son's sitting on the right hand of the Majesty on high. The act of sitting represents the Son's assumption of authority over all of creation.

When the Son took his seat at the right hand of God he became superior to the angels (1:4). During his earthly life, culminating in the Cross, the Son was inferior to the angels in power and glory. After the Resurrection, however, and the ascension into heaven, he "became" greater; for the angels remain part of creation, but the Son is above creation. The angels recognize this by paying homage to him (1:6).

The lesson scripture, and even more the background scripture, has a surprising emphasis on angels. The most obvious explanation begins with the stunning power and brilliance of angels. If Jesus commands such creatures, we can trust his ability to deliver on the gospel promises. The second explanation assumes that the point is to guard against angel worship. This can lead into a consideration of the ways in which we venerate lesser things at the expense of our commitment to the Son. The third interpretation begins with 2:2, the angels as messengers who delivered the Law to Israel, and considers that the angels lead us to Moses and the Law (3:2-5).

Moses

Moses, according to Numbers 12:7, was entrusted with all of God's house, and therefore the Law itself is called "Mosaic." But Moses was God's earlier means of speaking to humans, for his task was to testify to the things that would be spoken later (3:5). And the life, death, and exultation of Jesus is that word of God that has indeed now been spoken (1:1). So Jesus, the Son, is worthy of more glory than Moses (3:3)—as the final culmination is greater than that which prepares for it and points to it, as the Son and heir is greater than the servant, and as the successor is greater than the predecessor.

Now if we as Christians are Jesus' house (3:6), then Moses does not have the ultimate word for us. But there are many who belong to the house with which Moses was entrusted. We are to hold firm to our "confidence and the pride" (NRSV) that belong to our hope for the future in Christ. The danger of holding fast, however, is the ease with which we slip into its flip side, condemning those not of our house. Anti-Semitism, in particular, too often flows out of our appropriation of the progressive revelation from Moses to Christ. We need to be faithful to the revelation we have received, share it with others, and respect those who are faithful to a different revelation.

When I was an army chaplain in Vietnam, I was sent to interview a Buddhist woman who had requested that we repair the road to the temple in which she worshiped. She said to me, "I prayed to Buddha and you came. I know you think the American army sent you, but I know that Buddha sent you to me." I am a Christian, of course, and not a Buddhist. But I do not have to embrace Buddhism, or dilute my Christian faith in any way, in order to respect such a faith, and in the end leave it to God to evaluate its value.

Faithfulness

Moses and Jesus were both faithful to the various tasks that God set before them (3:2). They are alike in their dependability, even if unlike in the nature of the tasks to which they were appointed. The likeness and unlikeness is an instructive example for us as we struggle to be faithful in the particularity of our varying conditions. We are judged according to what we can do, not according to what we cannot do.

Jesus' faithfulness was displayed above all in his death upon the cross, which made purification for sins (1:3). The Greek word normally means "cleansed." The world was defiled by sin and therefore unable to approach God. The verb was used of worshipers cleansing themselves from ritual defilement and also of the removal of disease in the healing miracles. Christ accomplished this cleansing, scrubbing our sins away, so to speak, by his sacrifice upon the cross and removing the barrier of sin. Now we can enter the divine presence. This cleansing, the removal of our defilement so that we can worship, prepares for the emphasis upon Christ as our High Priest, which is to become increasingly prominent as we continue in Hebrews.

SHARING THE SCRIPTURE

PREPARING TO TEACH

Preparing Our Hearts

Jesus is great because he is God's Son. God had clearly been active throughout the course of human history, but in sending Jesus—"the exact imprint of God's very being"—into the world God was indeed doing a new thing. God's word and will had been revealed through the Law and spokespersons such as angels, Moses, and the prophets. For the first time, however, God sent Jesus—God in the flesh—to dwell among humanity. The writer of Hebrews wants us to know how incomparably great this Jesus is. Is that what you think about Jesus? Is he the Son who reveals the greatness of God, or is he just another messenger from God? As you prepare this week's lesson, prayerfully consider what you believe about Jesus and his relationship to God. Pray that God will in some way reveal to you the greatness and specialness of the One whom we have been taught to call God's Son.

Preparing Our Minds

Read today's lesson, along with Hebrews 1, especially verses 1-5, and 3:1-6. Note that on Sunday we will begin a new unit on the Letter to the Hebrews. Both the date and author of this work are unknown. The writer argues strongly in favor of the finality of salvation through Christ. The author also encourages and warns the readers, who apparently faced persecution, not to turn away from that salvation. While Hebrews reads more like a treatise than a letter, it is classified as an epistle because of its closing verses.

Preparing Our Learning Space

You may want to write the sentences for the final activity on newsprint or a chalkboard prior to class.

Have on hand:
- ✔ several Bibles for students
- ✔ newsprint and marker or chalkboard and chalk
- ✔ paper and pencils

LEADING THE CLASS

(1) Introduction

Start today's lesson by asking if anyone has traced their family's genealogy or read a history of their family. Provide a brief time for a few students who have undertaken this research to answer these questions:
(1) What interesting discoveries did you make about those who had gone before you?
(2) How has knowledge of the ancestry to which you are heir helped to shape your own identity?
Relate this activity to the lesson by pointing out that we begin our study of Hebrews with a look at Jesus, the Son of God. He was the One whom God "appointed heir of all things" (1:2). As God's heir, he is superior to Moses, the prophets, and even the angels. Through the Son, who was faithful to his own calling and identity, God offered us salvation. As we study today's lesson we will ask: *Who is this Jesus, that his faithfulness to God should be so critical to the ultimate meaning of my life, and what does that make me?*
As an alternative activity, read or retell the Focusing on the Main Question portion.

(2) The Old Testament

Move into the scripture by reading Hebrews 1:1-5. Ask:
(1) How do we know how "God spoke to our ancestors" (1:1)?
Note that we know how God spoke and dealt with our ancestors because we have

the record that Jewish persons call the Bible and we Christians call the Old Testament. The Hebrew Scriptures enable us to know the actions between God and the Israelites. You may want to spend a few moments discussing the following points:

- The Old Testament is critically important to our understanding of the New Testament because, like a family's genealogy, it tells us who we are and where we have come from.
- Jesus, the heir of God, was a Jew who practiced the customs of his faith and ministered mostly to other Jews.
- Some Christians try to ignore the Old Testament or read only selected portions such as the Psalms. However, most of the New Testament writers assume a thorough knowledge of the Old, for the New is filled with references to people, places, events, and direct quotations from the earlier testament. It is part of our heritage that we dare not set aside if we are to be biblically grounded, mature Christians.

As an example of the relationship between the Old and New Testaments, point out the two quotations in Hebrews 1:1-5; the first is from Psalm 2:7 and the second comes from 2 Samuel 7:14. Suggest that the class look up these references. See the second paragraph under "The Old Testament" in the Interpreting the Scripture portion for more information. To help students understand why quotations in the New Testament may appear to be different from the way they do in the Old Testament, refer to the last paragraph in that portion.

(3) Angels

Move to the next part of the lesson by asking the class:

[?] **(1) How would you describe an angel?**
(2) What do you believe is the purpose or mission of the angels?

You may mention that there is a modern resurgence of interest in angels. Some people see them as heavenly messengers, or guardians, or guides. Angels have attracted the attention of many persons, including those who are neither Jewish nor Christian. In fact, some people seem to worship angels, though the Bible teaches that they are not to be worshiped. Ask:

(3) What is Christ's relationship with the angels as mentioned in Hebrews 1:3-4? [?]

Use the information in the section entitled "Angels" in the Interpreting the Scripture section to clarify the Son's role in creation and his authority over it, his relationship to angels during his earthly life, and the angels' worship of the Son who is seated at the right hand of God.

(4) Moses

Choose a volunteer to read aloud the second scripture selection, Hebrews 3:1-6. Read or retell the section entitled "Moses" in the Interpreting the Scripture portion to help students think about the relationship between Moses and Christ. Be sure to note the warning against anti-Semitism in the second paragraph.

Divide a sheet of newsprint (or a chalkboard) in half. On the left write "Moses" and on the right, "Jesus." Ask class members to brainstorm as many similarities between these two as possible. For example, Matthew's account of Jesus' birth (though not Luke's) bears great resemblance to the story of Moses' birth. Moses initiated the Passover at God's request, whereas Jesus became the Passover Lamb. Moses led the people out of Egyptian enslavement, while Jesus invites all persons to be saved from slavery to sin and death. Point out the greatness of Moses, but note that the writer of Hebrews reminds us that "Jesus is worthy of more glory than Moses" (3:3).

(5) Faithfulness

Continue the comparison between Jesus and Moses by noting that Jesus and Moses were both faithful to God in fulfilling their respective roles (3:2). Read or retell the second paragraph under "Faithfulness" in the Interpreting the Scripture portion to show that "Jesus' faithfulness was displayed above all in his death upon the cross, which made purification for sins" (1:3).

You may want to refer to the Understanding the Scripture material for Hebrews 3:1-6 to help the class discern the similarities and differences between the house built by Moses and the one built by Jesus.

We have shown the relationship between Moses' faithfulness and that of Jesus. Now encourage class members to consider their own degree of faithfulness to God, for the writer of Hebrews describes us as "holy partners in a heavenly calling" (3:1). Distribute paper and pencils. Write these sentence stems on newsprint or a chalkboard and direct the students to complete them.

• Some of the ways I express my faithfulness to God through Christ include . . .
• I honor Christ in my life by . . .
• Memories are important. I can have confidence for the future because I know that in the past Christ has . . .

You may want to close the session with a prayer asking God to help each person to follow in the footsteps of the Son as they seek to be faithful to God.

HELPING CLASS MEMBERS ACT

Encourage class members to choose a book or part of the Old Testament that is relatively unfamiliar to them. Suggest that they read a chapter or two each day until they have completed their selection. Ask them to be aware of any ways they note that the New Testament is rooted in or dependent upon the portion they have read.

Some students may wish to do research on angels. Books and articles about these heavenly beings are appearing with great frequency. Ask students who are interested in this project to give careful attention to the relationship between Christ and the angels, as well as differentiate between an interest in angels and angel worship.

Remind the class that both Jesus and Moses were faithful to God, who had appointed them to their respective tasks. Challenge the group to be aware this week of ways in which they are faithful—or unfaithful—to the work that God has given them to do. Encourage them to seek ways to be more faithful to God's will and purpose for their lives.

PLANNING FOR NEXT SUNDAY

The second lesson in this unit on "The Greatness of Christ" looks at Jesus as the Pioneer of Salvation. To prepare for class, ask the class to read Hebrews 2, particularly verses 5-11 and 14-18. Suggest that students think about what it means to them to know that Jesus is their Savior.

Jesus, Pioneer of Salvation

PREVIEWING THE LESSON

Lesson Scripture: Hebrews 2:5-11, 14-18
Background Scripture: Hebrews 2
Key Verse: Hebrews 2:9

Focus of the Lesson:
the saving work of Jesus, God's incarnate Son

Main Question of the Lesson:
Is there a Savior who can do for us what we cannot do for ourselves?

This lesson will enable adult learners to:
(1) understand the greatness of Jesus, especially in terms of his willingness to be our Savior.
(2) consider Jesus' suffering and death in light of their own.
(3) respond by recognizing the affect Christ's saving work has had on their own lives.

Today's lesson may be outlined as follows:
(1) Introduction
(2) Son of Man
(3) Pioneer
(4) Tasting Death
(5) The Coming World

FOCUSING ON THE MAIN QUESTION

Today's lesson reminds us of the big, wide, wonderful world that the Creator spread out before us. The stars appeared to be within our grasp as humanity began its journey to Camelot. And so our attention is directed, in Hebrews 2:6-8, to Psalm 8:4-6. It is truly amazing that we should have such great expectations. For, after all, what are we—really, when we think about it—that God should notice or "visit" (KJV) us to do something nice for us? What are we that we are only temporarily lower than the very angels, those magnificent, stunning creatures? What are we that we are to be crowned with honor and glory? What are we that all things have been subjected to our control?

Such a vision would fill us with pride and joy—had we reached our promised Camelot. But something went wrong. Nothing was left outside our control, and yet we do not see, even after all these millennia, everything in subjection to us. And that is the problem. For, like the rebellious knights in Camelot, we, too, sang our "Fie on goodness, fie!" And we slid into a slavery (2:15) to a hostile force (2:14) that frustrates the Creator's intent for our happiness.

We long to be freed from this treadmill that we fear is steadily taking us where we do not want to go. We cannot get off and we cannot change its direction. We try, but our efforts never seem to amount to much more than the proverbial drop in the bucket. We recycle our household trash, but the rising tide of pollution promises to overwhelm us. We work hard and plan for the future, but we lose our job because someone improves the bottom line by downsizing the company. We are haunted by the specters of crime and nuclear bombs and drunk drivers and cancer and childhood traumas that we cannot shake off. Goodness seems out of reach, and we fear that death will make it all meaningless anyway.

Does life have to be the way it is? *Is there a Savior who can do for us what we cannot do for ourselves?*

READING THE SCRIPTURE

NRSV
Hebrews 2:5-11

5 Now God did not subject the coming world, about which we are speaking, to angels. 6 But someone has testified somewhere,

"What are human beings that
you are mindful of them,
or mortals, that you care for them?
7You have made them for a little
while lower than the angels;
you have crowned them with glory and
honor,
8subjecting all things under their feet."

Now in subjecting all things to them, God left nothing outside their control. As it is, we do not yet see everything in subjection to them, 9but we do see Jesus, who for a little while was made lower than the angels, now crowned with glory and honor because of the suffering of death, so that by the grace of God he might taste death for everyone.
10 It was fitting that God, for whom and through whom all things exist, in bringing many children to glory, should make the pioneer of their salvation perfect through

NIV
Hebrews 2:5-11

5 It is not to angels that he has subjected the world to come, about which we are speaking. 6But there is a place where someone has testified:

"What is man that you are mindful of him,
the son of man that you care for him?
7You made him a little lower than the
angels;
you crowned him with glory and honor
8and put everything under his feet."

In putting everything under him, God left nothing that is not subject to him. Yet at present we do not see everything subject to him. 9But we see Jesus, who was made a little lower than the angels, now crowned with glory and honor because he suffered death, so that by the grace of God he might taste death for everyone.
10In bringing many sons to glory, it was fitting that God, for whom and through whom everything exists, should make the

Key
Verse

sufferings. ¹¹For the one who sanctifies and those who are sanctified all have one Father. For this reason Jesus is not ashamed to call them brothers and sisters.

NRSV
Hebrews 2:14-18

14 Since, therefore, the children share flesh and blood, he himself likewise shared the same things, so that through death he might destroy the one who has the power of death, that is, the devil, ¹⁵and free those who all their lives were held in slavery by the fear of death. ¹⁶For it is clear that he did not come to help angels, but the descendants of Abraham. ¹⁷Therefore he had to become like his brothers and sisters in every respect, so that he might be a merciful and faithful high priest in the service of God, to make a sacrifice of atonement for the sins of the people. ¹⁸Because he himself was tested by what he suffered, he is able to help those who are being tested.

author of their salvation perfect through suffering. ¹¹Both the one who makes men holy and those who are made holy are of the same family. So Jesus is not ashamed to call them brothers.

NIV
Hebrews 2:14-18

¹⁴Since the children have flesh and blood, he too shared in their humanity so that by his death he might destroy him who holds the power of death—that is, the devil— ¹⁵and free those who all their lives were held in slavery by their fear of death. ¹⁶For surely it is not angels he helps, but Abraham's descendants. ¹⁷For this reason he had to be made like his brothers in every way, in order that he might become a merciful and faithful high priest in service to God, and that he might make atonement for the sins of the people. ¹⁸Because he himself suffered when he was tempted, he is able to help those who are being tempted.

UNDERSTANDING THE SCRIPTURE

Hebrews 2:1-11. Last week we were told to consider Jesus' faithfulness (Hebrews 3:1-2). Today we are to pay attention to what we heard when God spoke to us by the Son (2:1). We are to keep this gospel in mind lest we drift away from it, like a ship whose anchor fails to hold. The importance of the message correlates with the importance of the One who delivers it; and since the Speaker ranks above the angels, "therefore" we pay a correspondingly "greater" attention to the message. For if the message delivered through the angels (that is, the Mosaic Law) was valid, so that transgressions were punished (2:2), how could we expect to escape punishment if we neglect the greater message (2:3)? This

message was "announced" (NIV) or "declared" (NRSV) by the Lord, our Jesus, who is the Son of God. It was then "confirmed" (NIV) or "attested" (NRSV) to us by the apostles, who heard and believed and handed it down to us. God added God's own testimony, in the miracles that verified Jesus' own ministry and the preaching of the apostles, and in the charismatic gifts of the Holy Spirit, which empower the Christian life.

The word "salvation" occurs twice, in verses 3 and 10. It is, accordingly, the word that God spoke by the Son and it is the glory to which God brings the children by the Pioneer. Salvation is a rescue from some threat. We may be saved from an illness, and then we are healed. The word is often used this way in the healing miracles in the Gospels. But here we are kept from the consequence of sin, which separates us from God and thereby results in death. When the threat is slavery, the salvation is freedom (2:15); and when the danger is testing or temptation (2:18) salvation is the help that strengthens.

When the subject is salvation, all too often we center so directly on the Cross and its suffering that God the Father becomes an angry judge to be satisfied. Here, in contrast, no wedge is driven between Father and Son; for it is the Father who distributes the gifts of the Holy Spirit according to God's will (2:4). What Christ does for us, in fact, is by the grace of God (2:9). And if it is necessary for the Son to become one of us, to be perfected in suffering, in order that we might be brought to glory, then the cross is fitting or becoming to the Father who desires our salvation (2:10). This desire is reinforced in the family image throughout the passage. Instead of creatures before their Creator, we now are children before our Parent. The Son as the sanctifier and we as the sanctified have the same Father (2:11). And so, identifying himself with us, Jesus is not ashamed to call us brothers and sisters.

Hebrews 2:12-13. This is the point in the Old Testament quotations in 2:12-13. Psalm 22:22, quoted in verse 12, is the joyous public proclamation that a prayer has been answered. The psalmist has suffered to the point where life itself hangs in the balance. A cry for deliverance has been answered and, in gratitude, the psalmist offers the testimony of praise to fellow worshipers. Early Christians saw in this psalm, especially in light of the gambling for clothing in verse 18, a prophetic description of the crucifixion. So in our text from Hebrews the psalmist's deliverance has become the Resurrection/Ascension. The testimony is given by the risen Christ. When the Son of God, therefore, calls us brothers and sisters, it is tantamount to the assurance of salvation.

If the Son's identification with us in our human condition involved the suffering that culminates in death, the first quotation in 2:13 shows the spirit in which our Brother mounted the cross. Isaiah 8:17*b* reflects the prophet's trust in God when he is rejected by his fellows. Jesus, then, had to "faith his way" through his ordeal just as we have to do today. But the next quotation, Isaiah 8:18*a*, also in Hebrews 2:13, is a clue that the faith is more than just a pipe dream. Isaiah walked around Jerusalem with his children as a sign that his prophecy would come true. So the children of today, the Christians whom God has given to the Son, are a sign that the ordeal is succeeded by the salvation.

Hebrews 2:14-18. Jesus came to help the descendants of Abraham rather than the angels; and so he had to take on our humanity in order to atone for the sins of the people and mediate with God as our high priest.

INTERPRETING THE SCRIPTURE

Son of Man

Somehow we got off the track that God intended for us, as quoted in Hebrews 2:6-8 from Psalm 8:4-6, and headed for the devil's terminal, marked by slavery to the fear of death. The "slavery" shows that we could never get back on the right track by ourselves. We cannot lift ourselves up by our own bootstraps, no matter how hard we try. If, therefore, we are to change course, it can only be with the help of a Savior. Now the gospel, the good news, is that the Son of God determined to do just that. And so, as KJV has it, he "took on" the seed of Abraham (2:16). The Greek verb often has the idea of taking hold with the intent to help. NRSV, accordingly, simply has "help." The NKJV, with "he does give aid to," agrees.

In order to help us, however, Jesus had to make purification for sins (1:3), as we read last week. The Son of God purifies us from sin by tasting death on our behalf (2:9). But, in order to taste death, he must become one of us; and so the Incarnation is the precondition for the sacrifice on the cross, which provides the help we need. So the Son of God, who created the angels (1:2), was made lower than them "for a little while" (2:9). From Christmas to Easter, therefore, the Son of God was "like his brothers and sisters in every respect" (2:17), sharing our flesh and blood (2:14). The Son of God became the Son of man.

"Son of" is a Hebraic expression that indicates belonging to or characteristic of the next term. A "son of anger," for example, is an angry person—whether male or female. And a "son of man" (KJV; 2:6) is a "human being" or "mortal" (NRSV). Hebrews 2:9—"lower than the angels"—has plainly appropriated the words of the psalm in Hebrews 2:6 to show the Incarnation. The rendering "mortals" for "son of man," however, while correct, obscures the familiar term that the Gospels use of the incarnate Jesus. The Son of man is so vulnerable in his mortality that he has no place to lay his head (Matthew 8:20) and must suffer (Luke 9:22).

But there is more to the Son of man than mortality. He does not remain lower than the angels. Because of and following the suffering and death for all of us, the Son of man has been crowned with honor and glory (2:9). This is the Resurrection/Ascension that verifies and enables as saving the suffering of the Son of man. This status is new and different from that which the Son enjoyed in pre-temporal eternity. Then the Son could create. Now he can re-create or save.

So, even though we do not see everything in subjection to us now, as God intended before it went sour (2:8), we do see Jesus (2:9). And we know that the coming world (2:5) belongs to Jesus, when the will of God prevails as completely on earth as it now does in heaven. Jesus' world is our world. This focuses our discipleship—we act now in the light of then.

Pioneer

Because the Son of God became the Son of man, because he shared our flesh and blood, because he suffered and died for us (2:9), to help us (2:17), and because he was then crowned with honor and glory, he is able to be the agent by which God brings us to glory (2:10). This makes him, as NRSV translates in 2:10, the "pioneer of [our] salvation." The idea is that he goes first, blazing the trail, marking the wilderness, so that we can follow. Because the goal beyond the trackless wilderness is glory, the Son of man is the pioneer of salvation. The word also occurs at Hebrews 12:2 (see Lesson 13), where NRSV also translates as "pioneer," this time of our faith. This pioneer, therefore, is more like the scout who returns to lead the wagon train west than the settler who clears the land on the far edge of civilization.

Of the translations I consulted, however, only NRSV has "pioneer." The primary dictionary definition of the Greek word is "leader" (as NAB, and NJB). This can relate to pioneer, I suppose, in the sense of the scout who guides the wagon train. But the meaning of leader is further defined as ruler or prince. This is why KJV and NKJV have "captain" of our salvation. The Greek word also occurs in Acts 5:31, where NRSV has "leader" and KJV and NKJV have "Prince." So the pioneer is the leader in the sense that he is Lord over our destinies.

The Greek word can also mean the originator or founder of something that continues on. The NIV and NASB, accordingly, have "author" of our salvation. At Acts 3:15, NRSV has adopted this meaning. So in the four occurrences in the New Testament it is assigned three different meanings: pioneer or leader, captain or prince or leader, and author. All of them describe our relationship with Christ in regard to salvation. And, as the various translations reveal, no matter which one we select for a given verse, the others are implied. Some scholars, in fact, using instances of the word in non-biblical literature, would add even two more meanings: champion or defender from enemy attack and the guardian deity or patron saint who looks after us.

So our Jesus is the pioneer, leader, captain, author, champion, guardian of our salvation.

Tasting Death

In order for the Son of man to become the pioneer of salvation God had to make him perfect through suffering (2:10). To perfect is to accomplish, fulfill, complete, or mature. Since the Scriptures tells us that Christ was sinless (4:15), the perfection cannot involve moral or spiritual development. But he did have something to learn from suffering—the obedience (5:8) and the identification with men and women that qualified him to be the high priest (7:28; see Lesson 8). When at the right hand of God, accordingly, he is ready to intercede for those who are tried as he was (2:17-18; 7:25). So the perfection in suffering completes the purpose of the Incarnation, which is to enable our salvation.

The first of the two reasons our passage gives for the necessity of the suffering relates to sin. Our sin is a barrier that bars access to our holy God. An "atonement" (NRSV) or "reconciliation" (KJV) must be made for our sin (2:17) if we are to be sanctified (2:11) and thereby admitted to God's presence, which is the ultimate meaning of salvation. This atonement has to go all the way. It is not enough if I pull a thistle in my backyard. Unless I get the entire root, which in my corner of Maryland can be up to six feet long, it will come right back again. The end of sin's root, so to speak, is death, and so the Pioneer had to taste death for us (2:9). Because of the crowning with honor and glory, this taste of death destroyed the power of death (2:14). And so we can follow our leader through our own taste of death to the glory beyond.

The second of the two reasons for the necessity of the suffering relates to sympathy. Because he suffered while he was lower than the angels, the Son of God is merciful toward us in our sin and weakness, even though now he is crowned with heavenly glory and power. We can turn to this merciful pioneer because he is faithful to God and therefore able to be our Savior, and to us even after we have come to faith and are "tempted" (KJV; 2:18) or "tested" (NRSV) as we struggle to live as Christians.

Mother Teresa picked up on suffering as the middle term between salvation and discipleship. She wrote: "Jesus wanted to help by sharing our life, our loneliness, our agony and death. Only by being one with us has He redeemed us. We are allowed to do the same; all the desolation of the poor people . . . must be redeemed, and we must share it, for only by being one with them can we redeem them, that is by bringing God into their lives and by bringing them to God."

The Coming World

The gospel promise is for the world to come (2:5) rather than for the present world. We still face a physical death, and the problems of life hardly seem changed. The garbage continues to pile up, crime skyrockets out of control, values erode as we watch, and the misery of grinding poverty haunts us. But, in spite of all this, Christians have bet their future on the mercy and faithfulness of our High Priest. And our trust in his help to overcome our

own testing (2:18) energizes our discipleship. The fear of death recedes before the

confidence in the future, and we can tackle
the problems of our "now" world.

SHARING THE SCRIPTURE

PREPARING TO TEACH

Preparing Our Hearts

Our main question for today's lesson asks: Is there a Savior who can do for us what we cannot do for ourselves? We, of course, would expect Christians to respond with a resounding, yes! But far too many people in our "enlightened" age question who Jesus is, for they perceive him to be a good man but not necessarily the Savior whom God sent into the world as a Son. Other modern persons—including some Christians—wonder why they even need a savior. They perceive themselves as law-abiding, wholesome people who are not accurately described by the word "sinful." Perhaps people who hold such opinions are in the class you teach. Maybe you lack clarity about these matters in your own life. As you prepare to teach this lesson on Jesus as the pioneer of our salvation, pray that God will give you the insight needed to convey to others the precious gift that is ours through the work of Christ on the cross.

Preparing Our Minds

The writer of Hebrews presents an in-depth analysis that may require additional study time on your part. Be sure to read the lesson and all of Hebrews 2. Look especially at verses 5-11 and 14-18. Also read Psalm 8, particularly verses 4-8. These verses are quoted in today's lesson.

Preparing Our Learning Space

Have on hand:
- several Bibles for students
- newsprint and marker or chalkboard and chalk
- paper and pencils

LEADING THE CLASS

(1) Introduction

Open today's session by asking if anyone in the class has a story to tell about being saved—perhaps from a fire, drowning, or enemy attack—or saving someone else whose life was in danger. If no one has had such an experience, maybe someone can relate an incident from the news or local history. Then ask the class:
(1) **How did you (or would you) feel as the person who was in need of rescue?**
(2) **When the rescue was complete, how did you feel about the person who had saved you? (Or, if you were the rescuer, how did the one you saved respond to your work?)**
(3) **Having been given a new lease on life, what, if anything, did you resolve to do differently?**
Guide the class to the heart of the lesson by noting that the author of Hebrews refers to Jesus as the pioneer of our salvation. As we study this facet of Jesus' greatness—his ability and willingness to be our Savior—we will ask ourselves this question: *Is there a Savior who can do for us what we cannot do for ourselves?*
As an alternative to the activity above, use the Focusing on the Main Question portion of the lesson.

(2) Son of Man

Choose two volunteers to read aloud today's scripture. One should read Hebrews 2:5-6a, 8b-11, and 14-18, and the other should be the voice that testifies in verses 6b-8a.

Read or retell the information under "Son of Man" in the Interpreting the Scripture portion to help the class understand this term, which is also sometimes translated "mortal." Also make sure they recognize that God's Son became a mortal for the sake of all humanity. Christ tasted death and was resurrected to save us all. The point here is that Jesus shared in our mortal nature and could, therefore, partake in the suffering of death.

(3) Pioneer

Again in the Interpreting the Scripture portion you will find information on the word "pioneer" that will help the class explore the fullest meaning of this term. If possible, ask students who have differing translations to read Hebrews 2:10. Note that the word, which is used to describe Jesus, includes the meanings of pioneer, leader, captain, author, champion, and guardian of our salvation.

If time permits and the class enjoys creative activities, you may work with them as a whole or in small groups to create a litany that uses the variety of meanings noted above to describe Jesus. Distribute paper and pencils to do this.

(4) Tasting Death

Remark that our key verse, Hebrews 2:9, includes the phrase "that by the grace of God [Jesus] might taste death for everyone." In other words, we have a Savior who understands the fear and pain we may experience in the face of death. Ask class members to turn to a partner and discuss these questions:

[?] **(1) What fears do you have as you face the prospect of your own death?**

[?] **(2) What assurance does the fact that Jesus has preceded you in the experience of death give you as you consider this point of transition from this world to the next?**

Note that Jesus' sufferings were intended to make him perfect. As noted in the Interpreting the Scripture portion, "To perfect is to accomplish, fulfill, complete, or mature. Since the scripture tells us that Christ was sinless, the perfection cannot involve moral or spiritual development. But he did have something to learn from suffering—the obedience and the identification with men and women that qualified him to be the high priest (7:28). When at the right hand of God, accordingly, he is ready to intercede for those who are tried as he was (2:17-18; 7:25). So the perfection in suffering completes the purpose of the Incarnation, which is to enable our salvation. Provide a few moments of silence for class members to contemplate these questions:

[R] What does it mean to you to realize that Jesus suffered so that he could bring about your salvation?

How would your own life be different if Jesus had not been willing to taste suffering and death for you?

(5) The Coming World

Have the class look again at verses 5-8a. Ask these questions:

[?] **(1) What does God's willingness to allow all things to be under the subjection or control of humanity say about God's assessment of us?**

(2) How would you personally evaluate the way in which we are taking responsibility for the world? Give examples to support your answer.

Suggest that the class consider the following stories. Have them finish one or more stories in each of two ways: (1) as the story might end if the world were under the control of humans as God had intended in Eden, and (2) as a more likely ending, given the sinful nature of all persons.

STORY 1: A mother and her young son just left a bank, having cashed a check so that they could go shopping. They are approached from behind by a man menacingly waving a handgun and demanding money. Just as the woman tries to respond, the thief . . .

STORY 2: A business owner has completed a job that involved toxic waste. The owner weighs the pros and cons of how to dispose of the waste. The environment is important, he muses, but the cost of properly disposing of these chemicals is astronomical. The owner decides to . . .

Wrap up this section by asking class members to describe what they think the world would be like if everyone took responsibility for controlling the world as God intended.

HELPING CLASS MEMBERS ACT

Some students may wish to do a study of the term "Son of man." If so, encourage them to look up the term in a concordance and read some of its occurrences in order to gain a greater understanding of how the word is used. The NIV uses the term 186 times, whereas the NRSV uses that translation 85 times.

Remind the class that because Jesus has tasted suffering and death he knows what we go through when death is approaching. Suggest that each student visit with someone who is facing a terminal or serious illness and encourage the patient with caring words concerning Christ's saving presence in their lives.

Challenge class members to spend some time alone this week contemplating the things or habits or fears that may enslave them, even though they have been saved by Christ. Suggest that they record their thoughts in a spiritual journal and bring them in prayer before the One who is able to save us from them.

PLANNING FOR NEXT SUNDAY

To prepare for the next session, ask students to read Hebrews 4:14–5:10. Chapter 7 is part of the background scripture and should be read if time permits. The lesson will focus on another aspect of the greatness of Christ: his fulfillment of the role of high priest.

JESUS, THE GREAT HIGH PRIEST

PREVIEWING THE LESSON

Lesson Scripture: Hebrews 4:14–5:10
Background Scripture: Hebrews 4:14–5:10; 7
Key Verse: Hebrews 4:16

Focus of the Lesson:
the priestly work of Jesus, who represented the people before God and offered sacrifice for their sins

Main Question of the Lesson:
Who can put in a good word for us with God, and why would he?

This lesson will enable adult learners to:
(1) understand the role of the high priest.
(2) contemplate how Jesus' sacrificial action enabled him to become the source of our salvation.
(3) respond by putting in a good word for someone.

Today's lesson may be outlined as follows:
(1) Introduction
(2) Holding Fast
(3) High Priest
(4) Source of Salvation
(5) Mercy

FOCUSING ON THE MAIN QUESTION

Many of us, as we go through life, have occasions on which we hope someone will put in a good word for us. We want to apply for a job or admission to a school and need a reference. We like to hear a good word about us by a friend. We long to be offered a word of forgiveness after we have stepped out of line. But in order to do us any good, that word must be spoken by a person of standing who can influence the outcome of our situation. Even if an influential speaker is available, we still wonder if this person would be willing to intercede on our behalf.

That willingness is usually based upon a personal relationship, whether with a family member, friend, teacher, neighbor, or former employer. The touchier our situation, the more we seek out someone who will care what happens to us. Often, especially if we are in pain or struggling to overcome a serious problem, we turn to those who have been there themselves. Alcoholics who desire to quit drinking seek help from recovering alcoholics, and single parents gain strength from other single parents. We do not place our hope in the "business is business" crowd, for the bottom line on the ledger outranks our personal plight. The good-hearted persons who are burned out with "compassion fatigue" and persons who are insensitive to our struggles have nothing to offer. In *The Growing Edge*, Howard Thurman, the black pastor who became dean of the chapel at Boston University, tells of an incident from his boyhood in Florida. One of his after-school jobs was raking leaves. One day the daughter of the household, a little white girl, had fun scattering the leaves as fast as he raked them up. Finally, in exasperation, he threatened to tell her mother what she was doing. Enraged, the child rushed up, took a pin out of her pinafore, and stuck him with it. She was nonplussed when he shouted at her. She said, "But that didn't hurt you, you can't feel!"

We want an advocate who knows that we can feel and cares that we do. The main question is, therefore: *Who can put in a good word for us with God, and why would he?*

READING THE SCRIPTURE

NRSV

Hebrews 4:14–5:10

14 Since, then, we have a great high priest who has passed through the heavens, Jesus, the Son of God, let us hold fast to our confession. [15]For we do not have a high priest who is unable to sympathize with our weaknesses, but we have one who in every respect has been tested as we are, yet without sin. [16]Let us therefore approach the throne of grace with boldness, so that we may receive mercy and find grace to help in time of need.

5:1 Every high priest chosen from among mortals is put in charge of things pertaining to God on their behalf, to offer gifts and sacrifices for sins. [2]He is able to deal gently with the ignorant and wayward, since he himself is subject to weakness; [3]and because of this he must offer sacrifice for his own sins as well as for those of the people. [4]And one does not presume to take this honor, but takes it only when called by God, just as Aaron was.

[5]So also Christ did not glorify himself in

NIV

Hebrews 4:14–5:10

[14]Therefore, since we have a great high priest who has gone through the heavens, Jesus the Son of God, let us hold firmly to the faith we profess. [15]For we do not have a high priest who is unable to sympathize with our weaknesses, but we have one who has been tempted in every way, just as we are—yet was without sin. [16]Let us then approach the throne of grace with confidence, so that we may receive mercy and find grace to help us in our time of need.

5:1 Every high priest is selected from among men and is appointed to represent them in matters related to God, to offer gifts and sacrifices for sins. [2]He is able to deal gently with those who are ignorant and are going astray, since he himself is subject to weakness. [3]This is why he has to offer sacrifices for his own sins, as well as for the sins of the people.

[4]No one takes this honor upon himself; he must be called by God, just as Aaron was. [5]So Christ also did not take upon

Key
Verse

Ke
Ver

becoming a high priest, but was appointed by the one who said to him,

"You are my Son,
    today I have begotten you";
⁶as he says also in another place,
    "You are a priest forever,
    according to the order of
        Melchizedek."

7 In the days of his flesh, Jesus offered up prayers and supplications, with loud cries and tears, to the one who was able to save him from death, and he was heard because of his reverent submission. ⁸Although he was a Son, he learned obedience through what he suffered; ⁹and having been made perfect, he became the source of eternal salvation for all who obey him, ¹⁰having been designated by God a high priest according to the order of Melchizedek.

himself the glory of becoming a high priest. But God said to him,

"You are my Son;
today I have become your Father."
⁶And he says in another place,

    "You are a priest forever,
    in the order of Melchizedek."

⁷During the days of Jesus' life on earth, he offered up prayers and petitions with loud cries and tears to the one who could save him from death, and he was heard because of his reverent submission. ⁸Although he was a son, he learned obedience from what he suffered ⁹and, once made perfect, he became the source of eternal salvation for all who obey him ¹⁰and was designated by God to be high priest in the order of Melchizedek.

UNDERSTANDING THE SCRIPTURE

Hebrews 4:14–5:10. Jesus has been described as the Son of God (see Lesson 6) and as Savior (see Lesson 7). Now the writer of Hebrews moves to the major interpretive category of the book. The saving activity of the Son of God may be understood in terms of Israel's high priest (4:14). The task of the Old Testament high priest was to offer gifts and sacrifices for sins (5:1). This makes him a mediator between the people and God. He is called by God to this office (5:4); and since he is a man, he is subject to human weakness. Therefore he must, as on the Day of Atonement, offer sacrifices for his own sins (Leviticus 16) as well as for the sins of the people (5:3). Because of his own weakness, he deals gently with the ignorant and wayward (5:2).

The theme of superiority to Moses (3:2; see Lesson 6) continues, for Jesus is all that the high priest is—and more. Christ was called by God to be the high priest (5:5).

He sympathizes with us because he was tested as we are (4:15). In next week's lesson we are told that he offers his life as a sacrifice to God. He is more than the high priest because he is the Son (5:5) and without sin (4:15) and the source of all salvation (5:9). Today's text culminates in the assertion that Jesus is a priest forever after the order of Melchizedek (5:6, 10). The background scripture explains the title by reflecting upon Genesis 14:17-20 in the light of Psalm 110:4, and by understanding the psalm in terms of the ascension of Christ.

Hebrews 7:1-10. Hebrews 7:1-2 begins with a reference to the story in Genesis 14:17-20. Abraham, in response to a blessing, gives a tenth of what he has to Melchizedek, the priest of Abraham's God, the Most High. Obviously this makes Melchizedek superior to Abraham (7:7, 4), and therefore superior to the Levitical priesthood. For the Levitical priests, who are descendants of Abraham, collect tithes from the people; but Melchizedek collected tithes from Abraham himself (7:5-6). Levi himself, insofar as he was still in Abraham's loins, paid tribute to Melchizedek (7:9-10). Beyond this, Genesis is silent concerning Melchizedek's parents. This silence is understood to mean that he has no beginning and no end. Therefore he remains a priest forever, in contrast to the Levitical priests, who are mortal (7:3, 8).

Hebrews 7:11-24. By 7:11 we have moved to Psalm 110:4, which associates the royalty of the Son of God with the "forever" nature of the priesthood of Melchizedek. There would have been no new priesthood if the old one had been able to bring people to perfection (7:11). The old priesthood was by law, and a new priesthood based on God's oath (7:20) means that the law is changed (7:12)—abrogated because it was ineffectual (7:18). Melchizedek, since we do not know his parents, could not have become a priest on the basis of the tribe to which he belonged (7:16). The oath, moreover, shows the "foreverness" of this one priest, in contrast to the many priests of the old order (7:21, 23-24).

In contrast to the failure of the old priesthood, our Jesus has indeed been perfected (5:9). He fulfills the Melchizedek prophecy. His coming from the tribe of Judah, which the law does not associate with the priesthood (7:13-14), ties together the royalty of the Son of God (because of David) and the priesthood of the psalm. His perfection introduces a better hope for our approach to God than the law had given us (7:19); for he is the "surety" (KJV) or "guarantee" (NRSV) of a better covenant (7:22). It is as if Christ had pledged himself for us, as if he had gone bail for us. We can depend on the effectiveness of that bail, furthermore, because of God's oath (7:21).

Hebrews 7:25-28. We have left Melchizedek behind by the time we reach 7:25; for now we read of One who died for our sins as a sacrifice that has such ultimate value that it need never be repeated (7:27). The Resurrection and Ascension, of course, are assumed in the statement that "he always lives" (7:25). This means that he is able to save "for all time"—not just during some narrow window of opportunity—all those who approach God through him. That approach will be successful, for he intercedes on our behalf— he puts in a good word for us.

INTERPRETING THE SCRIPTURE

Holding Fast

In Hebrews 3:1 we were told to consider Jesus' faithfulness and in 3:6 to "hold fast" (KJV) or "hold firm" (NRSV) the confidence we have in our hope of salvation. Now in 4:14 we are urged to hold fast to our faith, to tighten our grip on salvation, to hang on through thick and thin. We hang on because of the power involved in Jesus' movement through the heavens. But also we dare to hang on because our High Priest is willing to intercede for us in spite of, or even because of, our weaknesses.

The weaknesses are what undermine our resistance, just as we are more susceptible to catching a cold when we are run down than when we are in good physical condition. Our weaknesses make us more susceptible to temptation by undermining our resistance, and we thus continue to sin. Because Christ is in heaven, it might seem that he would have little patience with our weaknesses since he has none of his own. This thought induces the fear that he might reject us if our holiness does not come up to speed.

We are reassured that because our High

Priest, during the period of his earthly life, was tempted as we are, he sympathizes with us in our failures rather than rejects us (4:15). The Greek verb is stronger than sympathy or compassion in English. It is entering into the suffering of another and making it one's own rather than observing it from without. It is genuinely feeling another's pain, temptation, or failure. The sinlessness, reflecting victory over temptation, might have led to the condemnation of those of us who have succumbed to temptation; but the sympathy has instead moved our Lord to extend the helping hand.

In prayer and worship Christians approach the throne, the seat of divine authority. This access is for all believers because Christ feels for us and because he has passed through the heavens to sit at the right hand of power. We do not come hesitantly or fearfully as if uncertain of our reception, but we come boldly (4:16). Such boldness is based upon an unquestioned right to approach God, and has been given to us by Christ our high priest. We come confidently because we know that we will find a throne of grace rather than of judgment. Mercy and grace, always available to us as a counterpoint to our weakness, broker the divine strength that enables us to rise to the challenge before us. The help comes in time of need. It is not wasted by being given before it is needed, and it is not rendered futile by being given too late. But we do have to make the approach, stay in touch, to request assistance, for not even God can give us help we do not want and will not accept or use.

High Priest

The high priest, because of his function as mediator between God and the people, is a major interpretive category in the book of Hebrews for understanding the work of Christ. He is appointed by God, and yet is himself human, and so he can represent his fellows in the things for which they are responsible to God. Specifically, he is to offer gifts and sacrifices for the sins of the people (5:1). Since the background here is the Day of Atonement, the bloody sacrifice is probably in mind. This then leads us to make a connection with the Crucifixion.

The necessity that the high priest be selected by God to be the representative of sinful humanity indicates God's love for us before we could love God (5:1, 4-5, 10). The high priest represents the people in offering the sacrifice and then mediates the forgiving grace of God to the people. The high priest can mediate because he is fully human and yet has been divinely chosen. The unique idea in the text is that the human weakness of the high priest is the required ingredient that makes his ministry effective (5:2). Because such a person is aware of his or her own feelings before God, there is awareness that others also feel deeply. Because such a person understands human frailty in a loving way, others may find the love of God in him or her. By this reasoning, Christ's incarnation is essential if he is to function as a savior; for a Christ who does not identify with us in weakness and in fear, in sin and in anxiety, cannot be our redeemer. Christ did not have to sin in order to identify with sinful people any more than the high priest had to experience every problem in order to be compassionate; but there has to be an empathetic understanding of the weakness that leads to sin and a willingness to deal with others totally from within their own context rather than looking at them from the outside. Christ knows us in the concrete rather than in the abstract. He can help us because he did not sin, and he chooses to help us because he knows our problems.

Source of Salvation

Christ knows our problems, of course, because in the days of his flesh he too prayed for deliverance (5:7). When we falter, therefore, it is strengthening to know that we reach out to a Savior who understands; for his heart also sank at the prospect that faced him, and he cried out with the intensity of tears. Just as a cancer patient prays to be saved from the ravages of the disease, so the Son prayed to be spared the cruelty of the cross. The prayer was not answered seemingly, however, for the Son must die. So if the prayer was heard, and thus by implication answered, and if there was to be no mitigation of pain, God's answer must lie in another direction. It is the strength to endure what must be in order to become the source of salvation. The clue is in the reason why the prayer is heard. It is because of his "reverent submission" (NRSV) or "fear" (KJV) of the Lord. The Greek word means awe or reverence before deity, and then the humility that is submission. The prayer for deliverance from the cross, therefore, contains within it the implicit "nevertheless, not my will but Yours be done."

Jesus learned obedience (5:8) because he voluntarily accepted the suffering as the will of God. As the Son of God he had the right of access to the Father from all eternity, without doing anything like this to earn it. By his obedience to the Father on the cross in the form of a man, however, he won access to the Father on behalf of sinful humanity. The death on the cross perfected Jesus (5:9) in the sense that the work of salvation was then completed. The Resurrection and Ascension show God's acceptance of that work, and therefore Christ is the source of eternal life. The Son (5:5; the quotation is from Psalm 2:7) has become the high priest (5:6; the quotation is from Psalm 110:4).

As the Son passed through the ordeal of obedience to the Father, so those who would be saved by him must pass through their own ordeal of obedience to the Son (5:9). Continuous, active obedience to Christ is the sign of saving faith.

Mercy

Christ sympathizes with our weakness, then, because of his own experience of testing during the Incarnation (4:15). In 2:17 (see Lesson 7), in fact, the Greek word for "merciful" is connected to the Incarnation. In 8:12 the mercy is connected with the forgiveness of sins and in 4:16 with the help we need to keep going when the road gets bumpy. If we leave out the Old Testament legal quotation in 10:28, these are the only three instances of the actual word "mercy" in Hebrews. It is, therefore, associated with strength and forgiveness as well as with compassion. This range is significant; for even though the feeling tone is important, there is more to mercy than emotion.

Feelings are notoriously undependable. When we come to the throne of grace in time of need we hope for a predictable response. The New Testament, accordingly, defines mercy primarily in terms of the Hebrew word that shows how we are supposed to act when we are in covenant with God. It is, for example, the mercy shown by the Good Samaritan to the wounded man (Luke 10:37). The point is not his feeling compassion, but his fulfilling his covenant obligations to love his neighbor. The mercy is the action rather than the feeling.

Our sin, however, breaks the covenant; and then God has no further obligation to us. But when God chooses to keep the covenant anyway, the obligation shades into grace or mercy. This is the mercy that led to Christ's appointment as our high priest. The compassion, then, is important; but it is the divine will to keep the covenant even when we have broken it that is the mercy we receive in our time of need.

SHARING THE SCRIPTURE

PREPARING TO TEACH

Preparing Our Hearts

Do you recall a favorite teacher writing a recommendation for you that convinced an employer to hire you or a college to admit you? If so, you likely felt thrilled that someone you respected thought highly enough of you to put his or her own reputation on the line by offering a glowing report. Jesus has also put in a good word for us, not one written with ink but with the shedding of his blood on the cross. His sacrificial death is a testament to his profound concern for humanity. As you prepare this week's lesson, meditate on the sacrifice Jesus made on your behalf. Experience awe and wonder that the Son of God was willing to die on your behalf, to act as a priest before God who can put in a good word for you. You may want to record your thoughts in your spiritual journal.

Preparing Our Minds

In addition to the lesson, read the lesson scripture, Hebrews 4:14–5:10, which along with chapter 7 is the background scripture.

In today's lesson we see Jesus' work understood in terms of the work of the high priest of Israel in the order of Melchizedek. To understand more about Melchizedek, be sure you carefully read the Understanding the Scripture portion. Try to do some research on Melchizedek, whose name often appears in Hebrews (5:10; 6:20; 7:1, 10-11, 15, 17). This priest is first mentioned in Genesis 14:17-20. He is again referred to in Psalm 110:4, which is quoted in today's lesson, Hebrews 5:6.

Preparing Our Learning Space

If possible, locate a crucifix (that is a cross with Jesus hanging on it as is commonly used in Roman Catholic churches). While Protestants tend to emphasize the empty cross and its symbolism of the Resurrection, the crucifix will help the class focus on the sacrifice of Christ. If you cannot secure a crucifix, perhaps you can find a picture of Jesus on the cross that you can set on your classroom altar or attach to the wall.

For the final activity under "Mercy," you will need to secure hymnals that include songs related to God's mercy, such as "There's a Wideness in God's Mercy" (*The United Methodist Hymnal*, page 121) or "Great Is Thy Faithfulness" (*UMH*, page 140).

Have on hand:
- several Bibles for students
- newsprint and marker or chalkboard and chalk
- paper and pencils
- hymnals
- optional crucifix or picture of Jesus on the cross

LEADING THE CLASS

(1) Introduction

Begin today's session by distributing paper and pencils. Ask each student to select someone for whom they could write a character reference. This person may even be their spouse or another family member. Students are to write a brief letter detailing the individual's qualities but using a fictitious name to avoid embarrassing anyone. Set a time limit. When you call time, invite several students to read their letters. Then ask:
(1) **If this individual were really applying for a job, loan, or scholarship, would it make any difference who put in a good word for him or her? Why or why not?**
(2) **Why are you willing to put your own reputation on the line by writing a character reference?**

?

(3) How has the willingness of someone else to put in a good word for you enabled you to move toward your own goals?

Guide the discussion toward today's scripture by mentioning that Jesus acted on our behalf as the single perfect sacrifice. Through his work, he was able, if you will, to put in a good word for us with God. As we study today's lesson from Hebrews 10, we will ask: *Who can put in a good word for us with God, and why would he?*

As an alternative activity, use the Focusing on the Main Question portion to begin the lesson.

(2) Holding Fast

Choose someone to read aloud Hebrews 4:14-16. Use the information under "Holding Fast" in the Interpreting the Scripture section to help students understand why we are to hold fast to our faith and how Jesus enables us to do that. Emphasize that because Jesus lived as a human and was tempted as we are, he is able to feel our pain, temptation, or failure.

Ask class members to close their eyes and try to envision this scene as you read it.

R

You are an inexperienced teenage driver. Offering assurances that you will be very careful, you have borrowed your parents' car. As you are backing the car up to pull away from your parking space at the curb, you accidentally give it too much gas. Metal strikes metal and glass shatters. Heartsick, you get out of the car to check on the damage. Fortunately, the car behind you was not damaged, but your car, well actually the car you have borrowed, is going to need some work. You go to tell your parents, assuming that you will be grounded forever. Instead, your parents are very sympathetic. Your dad remembers a similar experience with your grandparents' car. Although you will have to pay for the damage, they forgive you and will allow you to drive again.

Now ask the class:

(1) How many of you can identify with this scene, either because of an incident with a car or another experience where you expected punishment because you were guilty but found sympathy and forgiveness instead?

?

Invite a few students who have raised their hands to briefly tell their own stories, being sure to include these points:

- How they felt about what had happened
- How they felt when they found out that the anger and rejection they had expected were not forthcoming
- How this experience has helped them to respond with empathy and forgiveness when others have fallen short

Relate this activity to the scripture by pointing out that if we know what it is to experience failure and feel the compassion and forgiveness someone offers to us, and if we can offer empathy and forgiveness to those who have experienced some kind of failure, then we can begin to understand Christ's continuing identification with us as sinful humans and his willingness to intercede with a good word on our behalf.

(3) High Priest

Select a reader for Hebrews 5:1-6. Use information in the "High Priest" section of the Interpreting the Scripture portion to help students understand the role of the high priest. Be sure to note the importance of the priest being able to identify with the people. This is an appropriate place to discuss Melchizedek, mentioned in verse 6, as well as read the source of the quote in verse 6, which is Psalm 110:4.

(4) Source of Salvation

Before reading Hebrews 5:7-10 aloud, direct the group's attention to the crucifix or picture of Jesus on the cross if you were able to bring one of these to class. Tell them that after you finish the passage, you will provide a few moments of silence for them to reflect on the suffering that Jesus had to endure in order to become the source of our salvation.

Use information from the Interpreting the Scripture portion under the heading "Source of Salvation" to discuss how Jesus voluntarily accepted the suffering on the cross in order to win access to the Father, not for himself because he had always had that right, but on behalf of sinful humanity.

(5) Mercy

Try to have several students read today's key verse, Hebrews 4:16, from different translations. We want to emphasize "mercy," which is more than just a feeling but is "associated with strength and forgiveness as well as with compassion."

To get a fuller understanding of the mercy we experience because Christ is our high priest, invite the class to sing or say a hymn such as "There's a Wideness in God's Mercy" or "Great Is Thy Faithfulness." You may want to close the session with a hymn, or you may want to add a prayer that gives thanks to God for our high priest, Jesus Christ, who through suffering and death offered us mercy and compassion.

HELPING CLASS MEMBERS ACT

Suggest that class members make a special effort this week to put in a good word for someone. Perhaps they will have an opportunity to serve as a reference for someone, but they will more likely be able to give a pat on the back to someone who has done a good job. Encourage them to spend the few moments needed to compliment a salesperson and let the store manager know how much they appreciated this employee's help.

Prompt students to spend some time this week remembering some sacrifices that another person made for them. Perhaps a wife had worked tirelessly to put her husband through school. Maybe parents chose to forgo all but the basic necessities for themselves so that their children would have a good life. Ask the class to consider how the willingness of the other person to sacrifice on their behalf made them feel. Suggest that they put this human example in an eternal context by contemplating how Jesus' sacrifice on the cross shapes their feelings toward him and, in turn, their actions toward others.

Challenge the group to be aware of opportunities in which they can take an action that shows mercy.

PLANNING FOR NEXT SUNDAY

Next week's lesson will conclude our unit on "The Greatness of Christ." We will be looking at Jesus as the perfect sacrifice. To prepare for the session, ask students to read Hebrews 9:11–10:18. Our study will spotlight 10:1-14.

JESUS, THE PERFECT SACRIFICE

Lesson Scripture: Hebrews 10:1-14
Background Scripture: Hebrews 9:11–10:18
Key Verse: Hebrews 10:14

Focus of the Lesson:
the single, perfect sacrifice of Jesus made on behalf of humanity

Main Question of the Lesson:
Why did Christ have to die, and how does his death on the cross affect my life?

This lesson will enable adult learners to:
(1) consider the sacrificial death of Jesus.
(2) recognize how his death affects their lives.
(3) respond by making a sacrifice for someone else.

Today's lesson may be outlined as follows:
(1) Introduction
(2) Sacrifice
(3) Body
(4) Sitting
(5) Perfection

FOCUSING ON THE MAIN QUESTION

It is a truism that there is no such thing, really, as a free lunch; that, in one way or another, we pay for what we get. So, consciously or unconsciously, we are always assessing the cost against the benefit, whether it is the price tag in a store, the drudgery to attain a skill, or skimping on one thing in order to splurge on something else. For most of us, sacrifice is a constant—giving up in order to get. But, sadly, we sometimes bump up against a cost that we cannot pay. The benefit remains out of reach no matter how much we are willing to sacrifice.

If we are ever to receive such a benefit, it can only be a gift from another's sacrifice. We are thus dependent, at least in this one area. On occasion I will comment to my wife that a particular household task she has assigned me is difficult. Her invariable response is, "If it was easy, I'd do it myself!" The dependency, of course, ratchets up when the benefit we desire is the restoration of a relationship that we have broken. We cannot compel forgiveness no matter what we do—repent, make the sacrifice of a gift in the attempt to turn away anger, or take any other action.

This is also the story of our broken relationship with God. Our sin acts as the barrier that prevents access to the holiness that is God. We may not be as bad as we could be, but we are bad enough to break the connection. So we cannot get through—even if we repent, even if we pray, even if we offer a gift. Our sacrifice does not matter because it does not do what a sacrifice is supposed to do—make us holy.

God chose to break the impasse by appointing Christ to be our high priest (5:5) and making us holy or sanctifying us (10:10). But this holiness comes to us through the offering up of the body of Christ. We wonder: *Why did Christ have to die, and how does his death on the cross affect my life?*

READING THE SCRIPTURE

NRSV
Hebrews 10:1-14

1 Since the law has only a shadow of the good things to come and not the true form of these realities, it can never, by the same sacrifices that are continually offered year after year, make perfect those who approach. [2]Otherwise, would they not have ceased being offered, since the worshipers, cleansed once for all, would no longer have any consciousness of sin? [3]But in these sacrifices there is a reminder of sin year after year. [4]For it is impossible for the blood of bulls and goats to take away sins. [5]Consequently, when Christ came into the world, he said,

"Sacrifices and offerings you
        have not desired,
    but a body you have prepared
        for me;
[6] in burnt offerings and sin
        offerings you have taken no pleasure.
[7] Then I said, 'See, God, I have
        come to do your will, O
            God'
        (in the scroll of the book it is
written of me)."

[8]When he said above, "You have neither desired nor taken pleasure in sacrifices and offerings and burnt offerings and sin offerings" (these are offered according to

NIV
Hebrews 10:1-14

1 The law is only a shadow of the good things that are coming—not the realities themselves. For this reason it can never, by the same sacrifices repeated endlessly year after year, make perfect those who draw near to worship. [2]If it could, would they not have stopped being offered? For the worshipers would have been cleansed once for all, and would no longer have felt guilty for their sins. [3]But those sacrifices are an annual reminder of sins, [4]because it is impossible for the blood of bulls and goats to take away sins.

[5]Therefore, when Christ came into the world, he said:

"Sacrifice and offering you did not desire,
    but a body you prepared for me;
[6]with burnt offerings and sin offerings
    you were not pleased.
[7]Then I said, 'Here I am—it is written about me in the scroll—
    I have come to do your will, O God.'"

[8]First he said, "Sacrifices and offerings, burnt offerings and sin offerings you did not desire, nor were you pleased with them" (although the law required them to be made). [9]Then he said, "Here I am, I have come to do your will." He sets aside

the law), ⁹then he added, "See, I have come to do your will." He abolishes the first in order to establish the second. ¹⁰And it is by God's will that we have been sanctified through the offering of the body of Jesus Christ once for all.

11 And every priest stands day after day at his service, offering again and again the same sacrifices that can never take away sins. ¹²But when Christ had offered for all time a single sacrifice for sins, "he sat down at the right hand of God," ¹³and since then has been waiting "until his enemies would be made a footstool for his feet." ¹⁴For by a single offering he has perfected for all time those who are sanctified.

Key Verse

the first to establish the second. ¹⁰And by that will, we have been made holy through the sacrifice of the body of Jesus Christ once for all.

¹¹Day after day every priest stands and performs his religious duties; again and again he offers the same sacrifices, which can never take away sins. ¹²But when this priest had offered for all time one sacrifice for sins, he sat down at the right hand of God. ¹³Since that time he waits for his enemies to be made his footstool, ¹⁴because by one sacrifice he has made perfect forever those who are being made holy.

Key Verse

UNDERSTANDING THE SCRIPTURE

Hebrews 9:11-28. As 9:18-21 recalls from Exodus 24:3-8, Moses inaugurated the Sinai covenant by sprinkling the people and the implements of worship with the blood of bulls. Since the life is in the blood (Deuteronomy 12:23), this has the effect of bonding God and the covenant people together into the single life that is blessing for the people. If God's people had not sinned after the inauguration of the covenant, of course, that blood would have been enough. But there was sin, and it was not enough. So the law provided for additional blood to sanctify and purify the defiled (9:13, 22), with the daily sacrifice offered by ordinary priests (10:11) and the special annual sacrifice offered by the high priest on the Day of Atonement (9:25). The blood "sanctifies" in the sense of making holy; and since God is holy by definition, sanctification permits our approach to God. And the blood "purifies" (9:13, 14, 22) our sins. The blood of the sacrifice, therefore, enables us to worship. Or at least it would if it worked. For the flesh is purified (9:13), but not the conscience (9:14).

So if blood sanctifies, but the blood of the animal sacrifices does not, we must look for another blood. And that blood, of course, is Christ's. So we have a new high priest who enters a new holy place, one not made with hands, not of this earthly creation (9:11). The sacrifice that he presents to God in this heavenly sanctuary is his own death (9:12). The first covenant (9:15) is a sketch of the "heavenly things" (9:23) and can purify the flesh (9:13) with animal sacrifices. But heavenly things need a better sacrifice (9:23). Since our welfare depends upon our relationship with God, and since that is of the heavenly things, our future hangs upon that better sacrifice. The death of Christ, accordingly, obtains for us the "eternal redemption" (9:12) that we could not obtain for ourselves. It purifies our conscience so that we may effectively worship the living God (9:14). It is a better sacrifice in that it is without blemish and therefore has to be made only once (9:26). It is offered through the eternal Spirit, and thus by God's will, and its acceptance is shown by the admission of our High Priest to heaven (9:24).

The High Priest not only offers a sacrifice on our behalf. He also mediates a new covenant (9:15). The first covenant requires death as a penalty for transgression; and since we have transgressed we are under sentence of death. His death pays that price and we are thereby redeemed from transgressions, with the result that we may receive the promised eternal inheritance. The thought of inheritance leads to a play on words in 9:16-17. The Greek word for "covenant" can also mean "will." Our author cannot resist the pun. The death that mediated the new covenant executed the will by which we are to inherit eternal life. The eternal inheritance does not mean that we do not die a physical death (9:27), but it does mean that we do not stay dead (9:28).

Hebrews 10:1-14. If the animal sacrifices of the first covenant had done the trick, they would not continue to be offered. As it is, however, since the conscience remains guilty, the sacrifices are offered year after year, always in the hope that they will do what they cannot do. Bulls and goats have no relationship with human sin; and so such a sacrifice can be no more than a symbol or "shadow" (10:1), unable to "take away sins" (10:4). The word picture behind the phrase "take away sins" is that of removing a heavy load that has been fastened on a person's back and must be carried. Christ, on the other hand, does have a relationship with human sin through his body (10:5), and so by the offering of this body once for all we are sanctified (10:10) by the removal of our sins (10:12).

Hebrews 10:15-18. The Holy Spirit "testifies to us" (10:15), by inspiring our updated interpretation of the inspired Scriptures of old, that Jeremiah 31:31-34 foresaw the new covenant (10:16-17). What was future expectation is now present reality. Our High Priest mediated, or brought into existence, that new covenant by the death on the cross and the presentation of that sacrifice to God in the heavenly sanctuary. The result is the twin blessings of Jeremiah's prophecy, forgiveness for the past and a new heart for the future.

INTERPRETING THE SCRIPTURE

Sacrifice

The death of Jesus on a Roman cross outside Jerusalem is a historical fact, but its meaning is a matter of interpretation. One model is that of the victim, whether of mob violence or a miscarriage of justice. Another model is that of the martyr who suffers for a cause. But these models do not satisfy the writer of Hebrews. In this unit, accordingly, we have looked at the identity of the one who died in order to understand the death itself. Jesus is Son of God, Savior, and High Priest. Surely such a one cannot be victim or martyr. But high priest is promising; for that involves animal sacrifice, and that involves the shedding of blood. So today's lesson interprets the Cross as the perfect sacrifice.

The background scripture deals with the movement from the ineffectiveness of the animal sacrifices to the effectiveness of Christ's sacrifice. The law, as a "shadow of the good things to come" (10:1), is somewhat like a trial run. It is in the right direction, but it does not quite get the job done. A shadow indicates that a reality exists; but at the same time it can provide only a rough and distorted outline. The law reveals the will of God, but so indistinctly that it would not allow anyone to identify the reality before Christ revealed it. The "image" (KJV), translated variously as "true form" (NRSV) or reality itself (NIV), by contrast, is what casts the shadow and therefore it is substantive. The image is accurate to the ultimate reality, which is God. So there is an implied progression: the law is the shadow, Christ is the image who casts the shadow, and the reality is God. The shadow does not bring the worshiper to God, and no amount of repetition can turn it into an image.

The thread from shadow to image to reality is blood, and that means progression from animal sacrifice to the Cross. Somehow the blood sanctifies us and thereby enables our salvation. That it is a sacrifice means that we could not do it ourselves. We can try to understand it in terms of Christ in heaven praying for us or as mediating a new covenant with the required sacrifice or bearing our guilt. And maybe we can just accept Christ's sacrifice in gratitude as God's will to bless us.

Body

In Lesson 7 we saw that the Incarnation is a precondition for the Cross, if the Son of God is to purify us by tasting death on our behalf (2:9). The lesson gave two reasons for the necessity of Christ's suffering: to atone for sin and to share our humanity in order to sympathize with us in our weakness. Today's lesson has an additional reason: to carry out the divine will to provide salvation for us.

The quotation in Hebrews 10:5-9 is from Psalm 40:6-8. In the original psalm, the psalmist sings a song of thanksgiving because God has rescued him from some great danger. God does not desire that he show his gratitude by offering sacrifices, however, because God has given him ears to hear and he finds his instructions in the law. But we cannot find references to an "ear" in 10:5, nor can we find the word "body" in the psalm. This is because the Greek Old Testament, the Septuagint,

made the change, and the writer of Hebrews has used the Septuagint rather than the Hebrew text. The idea, then, is that obedience to the law while living on earth (that is, in a body) is more pleasing to God than the performance of sacrificial rites. Instead of ears to hear, God gave the whole body for the purpose of obedient service, for discipleship in all of its forms.

The word "ear" would not lead us to the Incarnation, but "body" allows our author to move to the Christmas event as the precondition for the sacrifice that saves. God gave Christ a physical body when he came into the world at the Incarnation, and with this body he was to do the will of God. Since God desires obedience rather than sacrifice, and since Christ was obedient even to death, it follows that the sacrifice of Christ upon the cross has replaced the sacrificial system (10:9b). The sacrifices could give no pleasure to God because they were shadows, but Christ pleases because he is the very image itself.

The psalmist found his duty plainly written in the law (Psalm 40:7-8), and Christ also knew his duty plainly because it was written in the book of God's eternal purpose for men and women. Christ accepted the body from God and consciously used it to accomplish the divine will. Christ's sacrifice, therefore, is by God's will. This guarantees its effectiveness, and so it need be offered only once.

Sitting

The contrast between standing and sitting in 10:11-12 has two implications. Standing suggests that there is still work to be done, the repetition of the sacrifices; and it also indicates subservience in the presence of a superior who sits. Sitting has the two opposite implications. The work is done, so there is no need to stand. The sacrifice for sin has been offered, and it does not have to be repeated, for it is effective forever. So Christ "sat down." The verb is in a tense that indicates that the action is past and complete. He does not have to get up and go back to work again. The sitting, moreover, is not on some back bench in a locker room; but it is at the right hand of God. This side-by-side sitting expresses the close relationship between God and Christ, and the consequent authority that Christ exercises over those who must stand in such a presence.

Sitting down shows that the work has been completed insofar as the work is defined in terms of offering the sacrifice for sins. The sitting, however, does not mean that Christ has nothing more to do. The offering, made once and for all, effective forever, must yet be applied to the work of the individual believer. The sitting, also called the session, therefore embraces the work of intercession, enabling us to come to God through Christ (7:25). We are not to consider the sitting as passive, as if Christ never moves. He gets up from the throne and moves about, so to speak, as an active savior. But he "sat down" in the sense that no enemy can remove him from the position of authority.

The sitting also involves waiting for the final victory over his enemies. The Greek passive in 10:13, "are placed" (usually translated "be made") as a footstool, means that God will do the placing. This reinforces the closeness between God and Christ that is implied in sitting at the right hand—Christ's enemies are God's enemies—and it stresses the inevitability of the ultimate outcome. The enemies are all who resist the divine will as revealed in Christ. This point is encouraging to Christians who are being persecuted.

Perfection

By the single sacrifice on the cross Christ has made perfect those who are sanctified (10:14). In the first phrase we are the

objects and in the second we are the subjects, but in the passive. This is a reminder that something is done for us that we could not have done for ourselves. The "made perfect" (NIV) is in the perfect tense, which in Greek generally describes a past action whose effects continue into the present. The past action, of course, is Jesus' death on the cross. That is what made us perfect. The continuing effect of that past action is the state of grace that is the Christian life. It is, in short, Christ's goodness applied to us rather than our own achievement. "Are sanctified" is a present passive that gives a sense of timelessness. "Sanctified" means "made holy." Since holiness is the characteristic of the divine, to make holy is to make fit for God's presence. Such sanctification, by cleansing our sins and making us fit for God's presence, enables us in our turn to regard our lives as received from the Lord to the end that we may do the Lord's will (10:9).

Perfection and sanctification are brought together here. Both terms relate to the forgiveness of sins and they define each other. The primary thought is Christ's perfection. Each successive Christian then partakes of perfection by being in Christ. Sanctification is usually considered in terms of progressive growth in the Christian life; but here sanctification is used in the way that Paul used justification, that initial cleansing from sin when a person comes to faith.

A positive thrust to the passage should be stressed. The yearning for communion with God is assumed. That yearning is frustrated by sin as the barricade between God and people. Salvation, then, as the removal of sin is not the negative movement from the fear of hell, but is the positive movement toward the joys of communion with God.

SHARING THE SCRIPTURE

PREPARING TO TEACH

Preparing Our Hearts

Sometimes our actions seem so futile. Sisyphus, the legendary king of Corinth, was condemned to roll a heavy rock uphill in Hades only to have it roll back upon him as it neared the top. He did this not once, but over and over again without ever getting the rock to the peak. Perhaps the writer of Hebrews saw the endless round of animal sacrifices from a similar perspective. The priest offered the sacrifices, but they could not perfect anyone. The people were still conscious of their sin. But then Jesus came along and with a single offering of himself perfected the people for all time. As you prepare to teach this week's lesson, search your own heart. Are you trying on your own to "get right with God"? Are you, in essence, going through useless motions that cannot achieve what only Jesus can do? Pray that God will lead you and those you teach to a greater understanding of Jesus' sacrifice and the transforming effect that the Cross has on your life.

Preparing Our Minds

Read today's lesson, along with Hebrews 9:11–10:18. The lesson will focus on Hebrews 10:1-14.

If you plan to do the additional activity under "Sacrifice," familiarize yourself with the information in Leviticus 16.

Preparing Our Learning Space

For the introductory activity, check the hymnals available to you to find hymns that deal with blood or sacrifice. Some that you may want to consider include: "And Can It Be that I Should Gain" (page 363), "It Is Well with My Soul (*UMH*, page 377),

and "Victory in Jesus" (*UMH*, page 370). Have on hand:
- several Bibles for students
- newsprint and marker or chalkboard and chalk
- paper and pencils
- hymnals

LEADING THE CLASS

(1) Introduction

To begin the class, distribute hymnals. Have the class sing or say at least one of the hymns you have selected that deal with the sacrificial blood of Jesus. If copies of the hymnal are not available, recite the hymn yourself. You may want to follow up the singing or recitation with these questions. They may be answered in small teams or by the entire group.
(1) **What does the songwriter seem to believe about Jesus' shedding of blood?**
(2) **What do you believe?**
(3) **What difference does it make in your life to know and believe that Jesus offered himself as the only sacrifice needed on your behalf?**

Move further toward today's lesson by telling the group that they will be continuing their study of Hebrews by studying the writer's perspective on Jesus as the perfect sacrifice. As they study the lesson, ask them to keep in mind this main question: *Why did Christ have to die, and how does his death on the cross affect my life?*

If you prefer, read or retell the Focusing on the Main Question portion as a way to introduce today's lesson.

(2) Sacrifice

Choose someone to read aloud Hebrews 10:1-4. Read or retell the section entitled "Sacrifice" under the Interpreting the

Scripture portion. Note that last week we saw Jesus as the high priest, the one who offers the sacrifice. This week we see him as the sacrifice itself.

As an additional activity, you may want to have class members study the directions for the handling of sacrifices on the Day of Atonement, as found in Leviticus 16. Reference is made to this description in the background scripture from Hebrews (9:13). Note the importance of the blood of the animal in this description (Leviticus 16:14-16). You may do this study by dividing the class into teams and assigning each team certain verses. Or, you may want to consult a commentary and prepare your own lecture or discussion on this. Make the point that even those who followed the law scrupulously still had to repeat the sacrifice on a regular basis. Such sacrifice is the foundation of Jesus' sacrifice but is not comparable to it, for he can atone for us once, for all.

(3) Body

Select a reader for Hebrews 10:5-10. Use the information under "Body" in the Interpreting the Scripture segment. Show students that it was important for Jesus to come in the flesh in order to:
• atone for sin.
• share our humanity so as to sympathize with our weakness.
• carry out the divine will to provide salvation for us.

Note, as stated in that section, that "God gave Christ a physical body when he came into the world at the Incarnation, and with this body he was to do the will of God." No other human is God-enfleshed in the way that Jesus was, but all humanity is created in the image of God. In his first letter to the church at Corinth Paul writes: "Or do you not know that your body is a temple of the Holy Spirit within you, which you have from God, and that you are not your own? For you were bought with a price; therefore glorify God in your body" (1 Corinthians 6:19-20). Distribute paper and pencils and have the students respond to these questions that will not be discussed by the group:

In what ways do I use my body—perhaps especially my hands, feet, ears, and eyes—to do the will of God?

In what ways have I allowed my body to become less than the temple of God?

What changes do I need to make in the way I use and treat my body so as to glorify God with my body?

(4) Sitting

Ask someone to read aloud Hebrews 10:11-13. If students enjoy artistic activities, be sure they have paper and pencils. Then ask them to draw the scene they hear depicted in these verses. Another way to show visually the contrast between the priest and Christ would be to ask one student who can make a quick sketch to do so on newsprint or a chalkboard. A third way to show this contrast would be to have certain members of the group stand as if they are the priests while the others remain seated as Christ sat down. The point here is to show the priest must stand because there is work to be done, the sacrifice needs to be offered repeatedly. Christ, however, is seated at the right hand of God because his sacrificial work has been completed. He does sit in close relationship with God, continuing to do the work of intercession on behalf of humanity.

Use the information from the "Sitting" section of the Interpreting the Scripture segment to help the class more fully understand the implications of Christ's seated position.

(5) Perfection

Select someone to read Hebrews 10:14, or invite the class to read this key verse in unison. Ask students to either rewrite that verse in their own words or explain what it means to them. If the class is large, have them discuss their work with a partner or small team. If the class is small, have volunteers share what they have written with the entire group.

Add information from the "Perfection" portion of the Interpreting the Scripture part of the lesson to fill in gaps as needed. The terms "single offering," "perfected," and "sanctified" are especially important here.

Conclude this part of the lesson by returning to the main question: *Why did Christ have to die, and how does his death on the cross affect my life?* Provide a few moments for students to reflect on the sacrificial offering of Christ that puts us right with God. When it seems appropriate, offer a prayer of thanksgiving for Christ's sacrifice on our behalf and the removal of the barricade of sin that had separated us from God so that we may now enjoy communion with God.

HELPING CLASS MEMBERS ACT

Tell class members to consider some different ways that they have dealt with guilt. Perhaps they have tried to ignore it altogether, or maybe they have become so overwhelmed by it that they cannot live effectively. Suggest that they reread today's scripture lesson this week, particularly the key verse, Hebrews 10:14, and try to accept and experience the healing that comes when we know we have been cleansed from sin.

Remind the class that in being the perfect sacrifice, Jesus was willing to give up his life for them. Challenge them to be alert this week for opportunities to give up something they wanted to do or own in order to offer their time or resources to someone else. Ask them to reflect on why they would be willing to make a sacrifice for another and how that person may have benefited from their action.

Suggest that students examine their spiritual lives for repetitive activities. Have them consider whether they are doing something numerous times because they want to do it (for example, attending worship), or engaging in activities because they somehow feel obligated to do them or perhaps have carried an unexamined habit over from childhood. Encourage them to make changes as they feel God leads them to do so.

PLANNING FOR NEXT SUNDAY

Next week we will begin the final unit of our summer quarter, "Be Faithful Followers of Christ," which is also rooted in Hebrews. The lesson for next week encourages us to grow in faithfulness. To prepare for the session, ask class members to read Hebrews 5:11–6:12.

GROW IN FAITHFULNESS

PREVIEWING THE LESSON

Lesson Scripture: Hebrews 5:11–6:10
Background Scripture: Hebrews 5:11–6:12
Key Verse: Hebrews 6:1

Focus of the Lesson:
the need to grow beyond basic teachings in order to grow in faithfulness and move toward maturity

Main Question of the Lesson:
How can our faithfulness to God continue to grow and keep pace with the demands of everyday life?

This lesson will enable adult learners to:
(1) comprehend the concerns of the writer of Hebrews about the people's lack of spiritual maturity.
(2) hear the call to grow in faith in their own lives.
(3) respond by inviting others to participate in class so that they, too, might grow.

Today's lesson may be outlined as follows:
(1) Introduction
(2) The Transition
(3) The Basics
(4) The Next Step
(5) The Crop

FOCUSING ON THE MAIN QUESTION

Many of us have various unfinished projects around the house: the blank pages following the opening of an old diary, a sweater started years ago, the beginner's piano book, the loose pictures still waiting to go into the new photo album, the closet that never got cleaned out, the unread four-volume set of the world's greatest philosophers. My latest project is a dollhouse that I was asked to complete. Now, as I shingle the roof and it begins to realize the intentions of the person who began it so long ago, it somehow seems sad that I should be having the pleasure that by rights should have been enjoyed by another.

But this often happens. We study something—ballet, the clarinet, karate, another language—but we quit before the joy of competence succeeds the drudgery of endless practice. My seven-year-old granddaughter's self-portrait proudly graces the refrigerator door. It is wonderful—for a seven-year-old. But if she is still at this artistic level when she is thirty, it will be a different story indeed. Her growth in artistic ability, of course, is to be paralleled by her growth in personality and in faith. The developmental stage of the picture on the refrigerator door, however, is more obvious to many of us than the developmental stage of our religious convictions. But here also, unless we progress beyond the basics, we will never realize religion's potential to transform our lives.

Something about the static is unfulfilling. If we are not progressing, we are regressing. That regression, however, is usually at such a comfortable pace that we hardly notice it. Its primary effect is to render the faith irrelevant. We then assume that we have faith, but it never gets in our way. And we hardly notice that it does not help us either. The first compromise perhaps gives us pause. But the second is easier. And at last we persuade ourselves that we have not compromised at all. If we do not go beyond the basics, our faith loses its cutting edge in the face of our society's increasing complexities. So the main question is: *How can our faithfulness to God continue to grow and keep pace with the demands of everyday life?*

READING THE SCRIPTURE

NRSV
Hebrews 5:11–6:10

11 About this we have much to say that is hard to explain, since you have become dull in understanding. ¹²For though by this time you ought to be teachers, you need someone to teach you again the basic elements of the oracles of God. You need milk, not solid food; ¹³for everyone who lives on milk, being still an infant, is unskilled in the word of righteousness. ¹⁴But solid food is for the mature, for those whose faculties have been trained by practice to distinguish good from evil.

Key Verse

6:1 Therefore let us go on toward perfection, leaving behind the basic teaching about Christ, and not laying again the foundation: repentance from dead works and faith toward God, ²instruction about baptisms, laying on of hands, resurrection of the dead, and eternal judgment. ³And we will do this, if God permits. ⁴For it is impossible to restore again to repentance those who have once been enlightened, and have tasted the heavenly gift, and have shared in the Holy Spirit, ⁵and have tasted the goodness of the word of God

NIV
Hebrews 5:11–6:10

¹¹We have much to say about this, but it is hard to explain because you are slow to learn. ¹²In fact, though by this time you ought to be teachers, you need someone to teach you the elementary truths of God's word all over again. You need milk, not solid food! ¹³Anyone who lives on milk, being still an infant, is not acquainted with the teaching about righteousness. ¹⁴But solid food is for the mature, who by constant use have trained themselves to distinguish good from evil.

6:1 Therefore let us leave the elementary teachings about Christ and go on to maturity, not laying again the foundation of repentance from acts that lead to death, and of faith in God, ²instruction about baptisms, the laying on of hands, the resurrection of the dead, and eternal judgment. ³And God permitting, we will do so.

⁴It is impossible for those who have once been enlightened, who have tasted the heavenly gift, who have shared in the Holy Spirit, ⁵who have tasted the goodness of the word of God and the powers of the

and the powers of the age to come, ⁶and then have fallen away, since on their own they are crucifying again the Son of God and are holding him up to contempt. ⁷Ground that drinks up the rain falling on it repeatedly, and that produces a crop useful to those for whom it is cultivated, receives a blessing from God. ⁸But if it produces thorns and thistles, it is worthless and on the verge of being cursed; its end is to be burned over.

9 Even though we speak in this way, beloved, we are confident of better things in your case, things that belong to salvation. ¹⁰For God is not unjust; he will not overlook your work and the love that you showed for his sake in serving the saints, as you still do.

coming age, ⁶if they fall away, to be brought back to repentance, because to their loss they are crucifying the Son of God all over again and subjecting him to public disgrace.

⁷Land that drinks in the rain often falling on it and that produces a crop useful to those for whom it is farmed receives the blessing of God. ⁸But land that produces thorns and thistles is worthless and is in danger of being cursed. In the end it will be burned.

⁹Even though we speak like this, dear friends, we are confident of better things in your case—things that accompany salvation. ¹⁰God is not unjust; he will not forget your work and the love you have shown him as you have helped his people and continue to help them.

UNDERSTANDING THE SCRIPTURE

Hebrews 5:11–6:3. In the preceding verses, the writer mentions Christ as the source of our salvation and the priesthood of Melchizedek. (Review Lesson 8.) There is much more to say about this matter, and it will be expanded upon in Hebrews 7. The concept itself is hard enough to explain even when close attention is paid. It is even harder because the Hebrews, who once were quick to understand, are now "slow to learn" (NIV) or "dull in understanding" (NRSV; 5:11). But it is too important to neglect, and "if God permits" (6:3), the writer will try once again to explain the Melchizedek priesthood. It is not that the people lack intelligence, of course, but that they are careless about obedience to the demands of the gospel. Such sluggishness concerning discipleship is a threat to salvation itself (6:6).

The members of this church had completed their "New Members Class" with such flying colors that they are competent

to teach the basic Christian doctrines to others. They were past the milk stage and were ready to advance to solid food. The foundation had been laid and new construction should begin. They already understand dead works and faith and baptism and laying on of hands and resurrection and judgment. But it looks as if they have regressed to the milk stage again. In contrast, those with mature faith pick their way through the maze that society presents them, unerringly choosing the good over the evil (5:14). If we can never get beyond the foundation, continually retracing ground already covered, we will never make any progress toward the perfection that God expects of us (6:1). We will go on to perfection, that is, if God permits (6:3); for we are all ultimately dependent upon God's will.

Hebrews 6:4-6. It is critical that we get our engines running again, for sluggishness can lead to falling away, and such backsliding is catastrophic. This is not backsliding from superstar saintliness into a sin such as drunkenness. For such sins there is repentance, forgiveness, and a fresh start as we try anew with God's help. This is backsliding from the enlightenment that is our acceptance of the gospel itself. It is the retreat from the taste of, or the personal experience of, the heavenly gift, which is salvation. It is backing away from a personal share in the Holy Spirit, who has provided the taste of, or personal experience of, the goodness of God's word. And so it is losing out on the powers of the coming age, which is where and how the eternal blessing is ultimately activated. "If they fall away" (NIV) or "and then have fallen away" (NRSV; 6:6) is in a Greek verb tense that indicates a single decisive action in the past. It is, therefore, a decisive move into apostasy rather than a continuing struggle against some vice.

The apostate cannot be brought back to repentance because he or she has rejected the only basis upon which repentance is meaningful. This backsliding, in effect, crucifies the Son of God all over again and holds in contempt the source of salvation. This obviously makes salvation impossible. Therefore it is vital that we stop being babies, that we take the next step, that we grow in our faithfulness—lest we start to slide and end up, by default if not by design, as apostates.

Hebrews 6:7-8. The parable is a truism. When conditions for growth are favorable the farmer expects a good crop. A field cannot be rewarded or punished, of course, but the blessing and burning lead into the thought of our accountability before God.

Hebrews 6:9-12. Although the readers need to be warned of potential danger, the writer is satisfied that they will pay attention, with the resulting better things of salvation (6:9). God will give them full credit for the good works they have performed in the past (6:10). In 10:32-34 (see Lesson 11) their past work is identified as boldness in the face of persecution. Their love for God had moved them, for God's sake, to help God's people (NIV) or serve the saints (NRSV). The reference may be to their refusal to melt into the crowd when fellow Christians are under attack. They "continue to help" (NIV) or they "still do" (NRSV). The verb is a present participle, indicating continuing action. The verb translated as "help" has come into English as "diaconate." But the people need to deepen and intensify this service, to show diligence (6:11).

INTERPRETING THE SCRIPTURE

The Transition

The previous unit, "The Greatness of Christ" (Lessons 6–9), emphasizes theological themes as we struggle with Jesus' true identity—God's Son, Savior, High Priest, Sacrifice. This unit, "Be Faithful Followers of Christ" (Lessons 10–14), emphasizes our response to Jesus' true identity—faithfulness, nearness to God, memory, commitment, and responsible living. This transition from theology to response, intended to encourage and exhort, is aimed at peo-ple who are already Christians; and so it is pastoral rather than evangelistic. Therefore, we are to "grow" in faithfulness rather than to come to faith, to "remain" near to God, to "remember" the past as a spur to the present, to "renew" a commitment already made, and to "live" responsibly.

In addition to a transition from theology to response in discipleship, today's lesson also points to a second transition that we must make, from the original audience to our own day. The congregation to which this letter was addressed, like the other New Testament churches, was of necessity small enough to fit into somebody's living room—certainly no more than fifty, and probably closer to twenty or thirty. The writing is specific to that particular group. That specificity makes it vivid and real, of course, rather than abstract; but it also increases our difficulty in relating to it, for our specifics are different from their specifics. But God's intent to bless through the Cross is the same for us as for them; and the requirement to respond in the face of an indifferent or hostile society is the same for us as for them. And so, always careful not to paper over the differences, enough churches in enough places and across enough centuries have found help here to assist their discipleship that it has become part of the canon, part of our Bible. We, too, may expect to find help here.

We listen in on a congregation that has done great things in the past, but has slowed down now and perhaps even drawn back in the face of pending persecution. We hear a friend's concern over the congregation's sagging faith, even the worry that some of the members might give up the faith altogether. And so he or she urges them to respond to God's absolute claim on their lives and grow in faithfulness rather than chug along at best, fall behind at worst. Just as this writer heard the Old Testament speak to the Hebrews, in spite of the different specifics of Abraham and Moses and all the rest, so we may hear Hebrews speak to us.

The Basics

The Hebrews have mastered their catechism. They know the "basic elements" (NRSV) or the "elementary truths" (NIV) of the "oracles of God" (NRSV) or "God's word" (NIV; 5:12). They have, in fact, progressed to the point where they can teach others about Christ—or at least they should have. They have passed beyond their infancy in Christ and so they no longer need milk (5:13)—or at least they should not. The beginning Christian has to be spoon-fed because he or she has not yet learned how to apply the doctrine to a new situation. He or she is as yet "unskilled in the word of righteousness" (NRSV) or is not yet "acquainted with the teaching about righteousness" (NIV). Some scholars assume that the application of doctrine to the situation in question leads to martyrdom. So the regression to the milk stage implies a failure of nerve.

The basics are listed in Hebrews 6:1-2. They are certainly not denigrated, for they are the foundation for all that follows. Repentance is a change of mind, and more than that, the "about face" that orients a person in a new direction. The conversion experience is such an about face. It has a *from* and a *to*. The from is "acts that lead to death" (NIV), conceived as the sins that keep us from God and thus result in judgment; or perhaps "dead works" (NRSV), understood as the animal sacrifices that do not have the power to forgive sins. The *to* is God through faith. The instruction about baptisms may contrast Christian baptism with the Levitical washings. The laying on of hands is associated with the conferral of blessing, with consecration to a special discipleship, and especially with empowerment by the Holy Spirit. The resurrection of the dead and the accountability of judgment round out the six fundamentals as the basic foundation for faith.

The readers do not really need to be taught the fundamentals, for they have not forgotten anything. They could still pass their exam in Theology 101. The writer hopes, however, that calling them "babies" is the slap in the face that will wake them up from their sluggishness before it gets even worse.

The Next Step

Because the foundation really is intact, the writer will not go over the basics again. Instead, he will leave the foundation behind and go on from the milk to the solid food. The solid food is for the mature, the full-grown in contrast to the infants. They are mature in that "by practice" (NRSV) or "constant use" (NIV) they have been trained to distinguish between good and evil (5:14). It is more than being able to tell the difference between good and evil. They already know that. It is, rather, the determination to choose the good and reject the evil, whatever the cost. The solid food, as it appears in the epistle, which builds upon the basics, is the high priesthood after the order of Melchizedek and all that implies.

Therefore, since we are able to distinguish good from evil, let us assume that the foundation still holds and take the next step. Let us go on "toward perfection" (NRSV) or "to maturity" (NIV; 6:1). The Greek word is built on the stem that means "end" in the sense of goal. The perfection, then, is the life that God intends for us to live. The English word "perfect" carries an overload of the saintliness that is unattainable. Due to the translation, we can then dismiss "perfection" as for the special saint but not for us, and so it is irrelevant. Or our inability to measure up can be so discouraging that we quit. "Maturity" does not have quite the same connotation of impossibility, and so it can serve as a more meaningful expression of our end or goal. The going on to perfection can be understood on several levels. As the harvest discussion in 6:7-8 indicates, it is the growth in grace that reveals a fully developed Christian character, and it is the growth in ministry that is helpful to others. It is also growth in understanding more complex doctrines. But above all, it is ever-increasing faithfulness to God, enduring through to the end, the successful appropriation of the promises (6:12).

The Crop

If we grow in faithfulness and move on toward perfection, we are like a field that has been cultivated and planted in the expectation of a harvest that will help the farmer pay the bills. The rain falls repeatedly upon it and it responds with the hoped-for crop. Such a field, in its fertility, receives God's blessing (6:7). The Hebrews have certainly been well watered with the repeated blessings of 6:4-5: enlightenment, the heavenly gift, the Holy Spirit, the word of God, and the power of the coming age. Active discipleship is the crop that is useful to God, who has watered our field, and that triggers the divine blessing.

But suppose that the field next to it, cultivated and watered with the same care, does not produce the cash crop that keeps the farm family going. Instead, it yields a disappointing harvest of thorns and thistles. They have no value. The field is in danger of being cursed. Its end, in fact, is to be "burned over" rather than blessed (6:8). The analogy does not quite work, for burning the field prepares it for another crop rather than punishes it for its failure. But the burning is an image for judgment and so it provides the transition to the case of the readers of the epistle. We have received the same list of blessings (6:4-5); but instead of going on to perfection, we have retreated into apostasy (6:4-6). There is no road back, and our end is judgment rather than blessing. Therefore regression to babyhood is deadly serious business, to be avoided at all costs.

The writer is convinced that the slap in the face will have the desired effect, that the readers will snap out of their dangerous drift. The Hebrews are not apostates, but they cannot stand still any more than we can. We will move in one direction or the other, produce one of the two possible crops. And if past performance is the best predictor for the future, the kindnesses we have done for others herald our continued service. Better things, the things that belong to salvation, are therefore in store for us as God takes account of what we do (6:9-10).

SHARING THE SCRIPTURE

PREPARING TO TEACH

Preparing Our Hearts

Where are you in your own faith journey? Have you continued to grow and change in the time that you have known the Lord? Or are you like the employee who, after thirty years with the company, had no greater knowledge or insight about his work than he did in his first year on the job? The writer of Hebrews knows that his readers should have been far enough along in their faith development that they could have taught others. However, they were not moving toward maturity of faith but were acting as if they needed help with the basics of the faith. As you prepare to teach this week's lesson, think back over your own growth in the faith. If you have kept a spiritual journal, go back and read earlier entries and compare the thoughts and concerns you had then with those you have now.

Preparing Our Minds

Read today's lesson and the background scripture from Hebrews 5:11–6:12.

Today's lesson concerns growing in faithfulness. Mature Christians—the ones who have grown beyond the basics—are those who have both a close, personal relationship with God through Jesus Christ and a desire to serve others. The most important factor in helping adolescents and adults grow toward a mature faith is Christian education, according to the findings of a large study of six major Protestant denominations conducted by Search Institute. Recognize the important role you play as the class leader in helping the students grow. Also affirm their willingness to participate in a class that will allow them to be open to the Holy Spirit's leading of their growth.

Preparing Our Learning Space

For this week's introduction, try to locate some art, music, or poetry created by a child, as well as some created by one or more accomplished adults. For example, you may bring in some "refrigerator art" drawn by a child or grandchild, as well as a picture painted by a famous artist. Or you might bring in a homemade tape recording of a youngster playing a simple piece on the piano, as well as a tape of a renowned performer or orchestra.

Have on hand:
- several Bibles for students
- newsprint and marker or chalkboard and chalk
- paper and pencils
- optional art, music, or poetry by both a child and accomplished adult
- if needed, tape player

LEADING THE CLASS

(1) Introduction

Start the class by holding up the art or reading the poetry or playing the music of a child. Ask the class these questions:
(1) **How old do you think the artist, writer, or musician is?**
(2) **How would you rate this work?**
(3) **By what standards do you judge this creation?**

Now hold up the art or read the poetry or play the music of a professional artist, writer, or musician. Ask:
(4) **How would you rate this work?**
(5) **By what standards do you judge this creation?**
(6) **What is the difference between the standards you use to judge the work of the child and the work of the professional?**

Talk for a few moments about the development that we expect of persons as they mature. Use information from the Focusing on the Main Question portion. Then relate this activity to today's discussion of growing in faithfulness by noting that some adults who should be "accomplished" Christians, are still at the level of faith of the young child. They have not delved deeply into the teachings and practices of their faith, as fine artists or writers or musicians learn their craft. Instead, they have allowed their growth to be stunted, to remain at the level of "refrigerator art" or grade school recitals or adolescent verse. The writer of Hebrews was concerned about the lack of growth in the faith that he observed and challenged the readers about it. Their faith did not begin to keep pace with their lives. As we study today's lesson, we will ask ourselves this question: *How can our faithfulness to God continue to grow and keep pace with the demands of everyday life?*

(2) The Transition

Read or retell "The Transition" from the Interpreting the Scripture portion. This segment will help students relate the previous unit concerning Jesus' identity to the unit that we are beginning today that calls for our response to Jesus. Comments here may also help students see some similarities and differences between their church and the people to whom the writer addressed this letter.

(3) The Basics

Choose one or more students to read aloud Hebrews 5:11–6:10. Then ask the following questions for discussion:

[?] **(1) How would you sum up the writer's concerns in a single sentence?**
(2) What are the basics to which the writer refers? (List the six fundamentals on newsprint or a chalkboard as they are named. See the Interpreting the Scripture portion.)

(3) Do you agree with the writer of [?] **Hebrews that these are, in fact, the fundamentals of the faith? If not, what basic teachings would you add? Which of his would you subtract?**
(4) Think about Christians you know. If the author of Hebrews were to write to you and this group of people, would he perceive you, as a group, to be spiritually immature or closer to maturity? Explain your answer.

(4) The Next Step

Have the class read today's key verse, Hebrews 6:1, in unison. Recall that the Greek word translated as "perfection" does not refer to some unattainable state, but rather to maturity or full development or endurance to the end.

Distribute paper and pencils and read these directions to the class:

Draw a straight line across a sheet of [R] paper. On the left, put the date of your birth or the date when you consciously decided to become a follower of Jesus. About two-thirds of the way across put today's date. Fill in important milestones along your spiritual journey, perhaps including baptism, confirmation, a conversion experience, time of renewal or recommitment, healing, and so on. On the far right side of the line, write the word "perfection" or "maturity."

Now consider what you may need to know or do or experience in order to reach spiritual maturity. Fill in steps you need to take, though not necessarily dates, to move from where you are now toward this important goal.

These questions, which you may want to write on newsprint or a chalkboard, may help students consider their future steps:
• Am I still in need of the basics of the faith, or do I have a firm foundation on which to grow? How do I know?
• What question, concern, or doctrine am

I wrestling with right now?

• What are my next steps toward maturity?

You may want to close this section with a word of prayer asking God to direct our steps toward maturity and completeness in the faith.

(5) The Crop

Direct the group's attention to Hebrews 6:7-8. Also read or retell "The Crop" from the Interpreting the Scripture portion. Note that the field that yielded only thistles and thorns had failed to achieve its potential. The carefully tended seeds did not bring forth the mature grain that can be harvested and used but instead created a nuisance that had to be removed. Ask class members to try to create some analogies that will help them remember the difference between the faithful Christian who has grown to maturity and the one who has failed to mature. Here are some simple examples:

• A mature Christian is like a big, juicy red tomato; an immature one remains stunted, withering on the vine.

• A mature Christian is like a mighty river, flowing strongly and watering the ground along its shores; an immature one meanders like a shallow streambed that only infrequently holds life-giving water.

HELPING CLASS MEMBERS ACT

Encourage class members to invite someone to attend Sunday school with them next week. Ask them to think especially of church members who feel that education is for children and that they need not do anything to grow in faith. Suggest that students be prepared to talk with their potential guests about what Sunday school means to them and how it helps them to grow in their faith.

As a symbol of their growth in faith, suggest that students plant flower seeds in a garden or pot or a small tree in their yard. Tell them to keep an eye on this plant, noting its growth spurts, times of apparent dormancy, and needs, such as for water, sunshine, weeding, and food. Encourage them to think of tending their own spiritual lives so as to grow in faithfulness whenever they tend to this particular plant.

Tell students to review the basic beliefs listed in Hebrews 6:1-2. Challenge them to consider seriously which of these beliefs they have settled in their own minds and which they need to think and pray about further. Students who keep a spiritual journal will want to record their insights.

PLANNING FOR NEXT SUNDAY

Ask the class to prepare for next week's session by reading Hebrews 10:19-39, focusing particularly on 10:19-25 and 32-39. That lesson calls us to remain close to God even as we endure hard times. Invite students to think about some difficult times they have encountered and how their nearness to (or distance from) God affected their ability to cope with the situation.

ENDURING HARD TIMES

PREVIEWING THE LESSON

Lesson Scripture: Hebrews 10:19-25, 32-39
Background Scripture: Hebrews 10:19-39
Key Verse: Hebrews 10:23

Focus of the Lesson:
the encouragement to the readers of Hebrews to hold fast to their faith in God, for God will remain faithful to them even in hard times

Main Question of the Lesson:
What enables us to maintain our faith through hard times?

This lesson will enable adult learners to:
(1) consider boldness, fellowship, and memory as keys to enabling believers to maintain their faith.
(2) recall a difficult time that challenged their faith.
(3) respond by encouraging someone who is struggling.

Today's lesson may be outlined as follows:
(1) Introduction
(2) Boldness
(3) Fellowship
(4) Memory

FOCUSING ON THE MAIN QUESTION

"The Martyrdom of Polycarp," part of a collection of early Christian writings called *The Apostolic Fathers*, tells the story of the martyrdom of Christians in the arena in Smyrna (Izmir in modern-day Turkey) in the late 150s. When Polycarp was led into the arena, Christian observers claim they heard a voice from heaven say, "Be strong, Polycarp, and act like a man." So when he was offered an opportunity to save his life by swearing the oath to Caesar and revil-

ing Christ, the revered old bishop replied with a ringing affirmation of faith: "For eighty-six years I have been [Christ's] servant, and he has done me no wrong. How can I blaspheme my King who saved me?" The Romans determined to burn him at the stake, and he gave thanks to God through his heavenly High Priest as the fire was lit.

On that same day, in order to vary the spectacle for the crowd, other Christians were killed by wild beasts. We are told that some of the Christians in the arena were afraid when they saw the wild beasts and so were in danger of renouncing their faith. Young Germanicus encouraged his fellows by his own patient endurance, for his reply to the proconsul's offer to save his life by renouncing his faith was to grab hold of the wild beast and hang on until it killed him. But Quintus is another story. In that same arena, when he saw the same wild beasts, he turned coward and saved himself by swearing the oath to Caesar. This is tragic, for Quintus had been an

eager and intense disciple. He had offered himself as a martyr and had encouraged others to make the ultimate witness in the arena. He had started out to run a good race, but he had faded in the stretch. And it is how you end up that counts.

The main question for us, coming out of that March afternoon in ancient Smyrna, is suggested by the difference between Germanicus and Polycarp on the one hand and Quintus on the other hand. *What enables us to maintain our faith through hard times?*

READING THE SCRIPTURE

NRSV
Hebrews 10:19-25

19 Therefore, my friends, since we have confidence to enter the sanctuary by the blood of Jesus, 20by the new and living way that he opened for us through the curtain (that is, through his flesh), 21and since we have a great priest over the house of God, 22let us approach with a true heart in full assurance of faith, with our hearts sprinkled clean from an evil conscience and our bodies washed with pure water. 23Let us hold fast to the confession of our hope without wavering, for he who has promised is faithful. 24And let us consider how to provoke one another to love and good deeds, 25not neglecting to meet together, as is the habit of some, but encouraging one another, and all the more as you see the Day approaching.

NIV
Hebrews 10:19-25

19Therefore, brothers, since we have confidence to enter the Most Holy Place by the blood of Jesus, 20by a new and living way opened for us through the curtain, that is, his body, 21and since we have a great priest over the house of God, 22let us draw near to God with a sincere heart in full assurance of faith, having our hearts sprinkled to cleanse us from a guilty conscience and having our bodies washed with pure water. 23Let us hold unswervingly to the hope we profess, for he who promised is faithful. 24And let us consider how we may spur one another on toward love and good deeds. 25Let us not give up meeting together, as some are in the habit of doing, but let us encourage one another—and all the more as you see the Day approaching.

Key
Verse

Key
Verse

NRSV
Hebrews 10:32-39

32 But recall those earlier days when, after you had been enlightened, you endured a hard struggle with sufferings, 33sometimes being publicly exposed to abuse and persecution, and sometimes being partners with those so treated. 34For you had compassion for those who were

NIV
Hebrews 10:32-39

32Remember those earlier days after you had received the light, when you stood your ground in a great contest in the face of suffering. 33Sometimes you were publicly exposed to insult and persecution; at other times you stood side by side with in prison, and you cheerfully accepted the plundering of your possessions, knowing that you yourselves possessed something better and more lasting. [35]Do not, therefore, abandon that confidence of yours; it brings a great reward. [36]For you need endurance, so that when you have done the will of God, you may receive what was promised.

[37] For yet "in a very little while,
    the one who is coming will
        come and will not delay;
[38] but my righteous one will live by
      faith.
    My soul takes no pleasure in
      anyone who shrinks
      back."

[39]But we are not among those who shrink back and so are lost, but among those who have faith and so are saved.

those who were so treated. [34]You sympathized with those in prison and joyfully accepted the confiscation of your property, because you knew that you yourselves had better and lasting possessions.

[35]So do not throw away your confidence; it will be richly rewarded. [36]You need to persevere so that when you have done the will of God, you will receive what he has promised. [37]For in just a very little while,

"He who is coming will come and will not
delay.
  [38] But my righteous one will live by faith.
  And if he shrinks back,
    I will not be pleased with him."

[39]But we are not of those who shrink back and are destroyed, but of those who believe and are saved.

UNDERSTANDING THE SCRIPTURE

Hebrews 10:19-25. Earlier in the chapter (10:1-14), the blood of bulls and goats was contrasted with the blood of Christ. The sacrifice of animals cannot remove the consciousness of sin and so is constantly repeated in a vain effort to reach God. The sacrifice of Christ, however, is able to remove sin and therefore is not repeated. In 10:15-18 the Christian faith has replaced the sacrificial system in fulfillment of the prophecy of the new covenant (Jeremiah 31:31-34). Since in Christ Christians are brought to God (10:19-22), their earthly lives should reflect the heavenly reality, and so this section concludes with three exhortations (10:23-25). We are to hold fast to the faith without wavering, to stir each other up to love and the performance of good works, and not to abandon the congregational worship in which we encourage each other as we wait for the Second Coming of Christ.

Hebrews 10:26-31. There can be no forgiveness if we deliberately continue sinning (present participle) even after we have received the knowledge of the truth of God in Christ (10:26). This can only be apostasy, the renunciation of the faith. It is unforgivable because the sacrifice of Christ has been rejected and there is no other sacrifice that is effective for the forgiveness of sins. The sacrifice of Christ is so effective that it does not have to be repeated, but that also means that it *cannot* be repeated. God has done all that can be done in Christ, and if this is renounced for whatever reason, not even God can do more. And so what remains after apostasy is judgment (10:27). Those who end up being judged are God's "enemies" (NIV) or "adversaries" (NRSV), those who rebel against the divine authority. If the old covenant put apostates to death, how much worse must be the penalty for those who have rejected the new covenant (10:28-29).

In 10:29 the apostate is defined in three graphic ways. Such a person "has trampled the Son of God under foot" (NIV). We do not trample carelessly upon something unless it has no value for us, and so NRSV interprets it as spurning the Son of God. The faith has been thrown out like garbage, and there is little chance of finding it again in the city dump. We do not trample on the Son of God, of course, unless we deny that Christ's death has any value for our lives. This is to treat as unholy (NIV) or to profane (NRSV) the only blood that can provide the blessings of eternal life by sanctifying us. This is to insult (NIV) or outrage (NRSV) the Holy Spirit who brings grace and life to the believer. A person who will mock the only power that can save him or her is beyond repentance. This is the sin against the Holy Spirit (Matthew 12:31).

We would probably rather not talk about judgment, but it cannot be left out of account if we are to talk about reward. Heaven and hell define each other. The point for us is that faith matters, that it is not an "extra" when and if we have time and energy after we have met all the demands that the world places upon us. The unforgivable sin, however, is not the ordinary sin that we all commit, for unless there is forgiveness for sins committed after becoming Christians none of us could hope to be saved. The unforgivable is to conclude that Christ does not matter one way or the other.

Hebrews 10:32-39. The Christians to whom the book was originally addressed were in danger of renouncing their faith under the pressure of persecution, as Quintus. But it does not have to be that way. They can rise to the occasion, like Polycarp. And we can listen in; for even though we are more apt to squander our faith away for no good reason rather than cave in under persecution, the end result is the same. The faith is gone. The Hebrews can become their own examples, remembering when their discipleship was powerful. They need endure but a little while longer in order to gain the promised reward. Hebrews 10:37-38 puts together phrases from Isaiah 26:20 and Habakkuk 2:3-4. Both Old Testament passages deal with the oppressed people of God being required to endure patiently until God brings deliverance. Shrinking back is the fear that prevents active discipleship, the abandonment of the confession of hope; but those who do not grow weary gain their souls (10:39).

INTERPRETING THE SCRIPTURE

Boldness

"Boldness" (KJV) before God (10:19) is the first of three major answers that today's lesson offers to the question: What enables us to maintain our faith through hard times? Rendered as "confidence" by NIV and NRSV, the Greek word means the boldness to speak freely without fear. A natural fear associated with entering the presence of a powerful king because one never knew what he would do (Esther 4:10-11). A sense of awe and fear was associated with entrance into God's presence, for holiness was a dangerous quality. The high priest entered the holy of holies only under carefully controlled conditions. The people worried when Zechariah was slow in reappearing from the holy place (Luke 1:21). But Christians may enter God's presence at any time without restrictions and without fear. We may approach God and speak freely because we know we will be accepted.

Our confidence is based upon the blood of Christ, which opened up for us a new way into the divine presence (10:20). The way had previously been inaccessible, but now Christ has opened it up for traffic. He made the way himself and opened it by first using it himself. Then it may be used by others coming after him. The way is described as "living" because it has the power to take the believer to life eternal, because it leads to fellowship with a living person. The curtain is the barrier of sin, which blocks access to God. The flesh of Christ, the sacrificial death, is what leads through the curtain. This suggests that the resurrected body of Christ takes humanity into heaven.

Christ is now the great high priest over the house of God because he has sovereign authority (10:21). As high priest Christ introduces us to God, and so we may use the new way with boldness or confidence. The approach is to be made with a "true" (NRSV) or "sincere" (NIV) heart (10:22). English has followed Latin in using the heart as a symbol for the emotions; but in Greek the emotions are symbolized by the intestines and lower internal organs, the "bowels" as noted so often in the KJV. The heart symbolizes the mind as a whole, including the emotions and memory and reasoning power, but also the will. A hard heart, for example, is a closed mind rather than callousness. Here it is the mind, and especially the will, that is true or sincere in its approach to God. So faith is tied to the mind more than to the emotions. The assurance of faith, then, is the firm conviction of the will.

This conviction results from the sprinkling of our hearts with the blood of Christ so that we no longer have a guilty conscience. The sprinkling, of course, is the application of the benefit of Christ's death to us; and that application is marked by our baptism, that is, by being washed with pure water. The sprinkling and the washing signify the confession of our hope for the future in Christ (10:23). We must hang on to this hope without wavering (NRSV) or swerving (NIV). We can cling to this

hope because it is the promise of God, and it is guaranteed by the faithfulness of God to his promise. We can, so to speak, take this to the bank. The original promise was to Abraham (Genesis 12:2-3), and now it has been fulfilled in Christ.

Fellowship

If boldness, based upon the new way to God opened up for us by the death of Christ and guaranteed by the divine faithfulness, is the first answer to maintaining our faith through hard times, the second answer in today's lesson revolves around the idea of Christian fellowship.

Enthusiasm begins at fever pitch and then cools off, so effort is required to keep the hope alive. Christians are to be concerned for each other and counter discouragement. Believers are to "provoke" (NRSV) or "spur" (NIV) each other (10:24). The Greek word means stimulate, whether to good or to evil. An incitement to evil may embitter, as the sharp contention that caused Paul and Barnabas to separate (Acts 15:39). The point is that we do stimulate each other, whether deliberately or not. We may spur each other to bitterness by our indifference or sharp criticism. But we can also provoke each other to healing love and growth in grace that is then expressed in the daily Christian life of the other person as well as in our own life.

Gathering together for worship is placed within the context of the hope of eternal life (10:25). To give up on regular attendance is to swerve aside from the hope and be in danger of losing the promise. We are not to forsake (KJV) or neglect (NRSV) or give up (NIV) on such fellowship. The Greek verb means to abandon or to forsake, and probably implies more than simply not going to church on Sunday morning. This is the word from the cross, "Why have you forsaken me?" (Matthew 27:46; Mark 15:34). God, who is faithful to the promise, will never forsake us (Hebrews 13:5); but men and women abandon God or each other, as Demas abandoned Paul in his trouble (2 Timothy 4:10). Some may have forsaken the fellowship because of the fear of persecution. This weakens the ability of the community to hold fast to the confession of its hope and leaves fellow church members in the lurch by setting a dangerous example of apostasy. Others may have given up the meetings because of the pressure of business engagements. This leaves the community in the lurch because it denies the weaker members the benefit of the encouragement of the stronger. It is also spiritually dangerous because in isolation a person is exposed to the danger of losing faith altogether.

Rather than forsaking each other by not attending worship services, we are to be present and encourage each other. The word for "encourage" has come into English as *Paraclete*, John's special word for the Holy Spirit. The basic idea is to strengthen. This may be done by exhortation or instruction, by stiffening the backbone to face martyrdom, and by comforting those in danger of collapse. Christians owe this strengthening to each other in the facing of difficulty and in the growth of grace. This is a primary purpose of gathering for public worship. The nearness of the Day, the Second Coming of Christ, gives greater urgency to the task of strengthening each other.

Memory

The third answer to our main question is memory. The Hebrews are encouraged to endure through their current persecution by being reminded of how well they had endured persecution in the past (10:32). They have a good record and that memory should help them maintain it in the future. They had a hard time, but they survived. They had been made a laughingstock (10:33*a*). As a modern audience can laugh at someone's trouble through the

medium of a clown slipping on a banana peel, so an ancient audience could find the sufferings of Christians entertaining. Christians were humiliated through insults (NIV) or abuse (NRSV). The jeers had stung, but the Christians had borne them patiently. They were also persecuted physically. These are more than insults. No doubt the crowds physically abused them and vandalized their property. Perhaps some Christians had lost their jobs, as well as their friends, after their conversion. No doubt some of them spent an occasional night in jail on some trumped-up charge. Their property was confiscated, but they accepted the loss with joy because they knew they still had a better property than what had been taken from them (10:34*b*). That better property, of course, is their faith in Christ. Not only did they endure their own persecution, but they actively helped other Christians bear up (10:33*b*, 34*a*). They did not turn away or melt into the crowd, but they stepped up to their side, becoming partners with the abused. They are urged not to throw away such boldness now (10:35), when only a little more patient endurance will secure their reward (10:36).

It is possible, however, to remember the past in a destructive way. In the movie *On Golden Pond*, for example, Chelsea, a grown woman, is still bitter over her relationship with her father. At last her exasperated mother tells her that a great many people had unhappy childhoods. Life marches on, and she had better get with it. We can dwell on the pain, whether past or present, and then we are weakened by memory. The Hebrews, as they remembered the past, might have concluded that discipleship is just not worth it. When life gets too hard for us, we also may be tempted to wonder if faith in Christ means anything. Then we are to remember the reward, our share in Christ's resurrection, as the far end of our pain.

SHARING THE SCRIPTURE

PREPARING TO TEACH

Preparing Our Hearts

Very few people escape the challenge of hard times. A layoff results in economic hardship. Substance abuse eats away at the fabric of a family. Serious illness causes life to become unpredictable. The death of a loved one leaves a void that can never be completely filled. Some people manage to weather these storms, keeping their boat on course despite the pounding of the wind and waves. Others, however, jump overboard in a state of despair. How about you? Do you have the kind of faith that enables you to endure hard times? Can your faith be sorely tested and yet remain strong? Or do you rail against God and seek safe harbor somewhere else when the storms of life unleash their fury upon you? As you study this week's lesson, consider what enables you to maintain your faith through hard times. Think about how you might respond if the difficulties you had to endure came about as a direct result of your faith in Christ. Pray that God might give you the strength to remain faithful regardless of the circumstances.

Preparing Our Minds

Read Hebrews 10:19-39 and the lesson as you prepare to teach this week's session.

Become familiar with the examples of Polycarp, Germanicus, and Quintus given in the Focusing on the Main Question portion.

Preparing Our Learning Space

Select a familiar hymn that highlights the assurance of faith in Christ. Two well-known hymns by Fanny Crosby, "I Am Thine, O Lord" (page 419) and "Blessed Assurance" (page 369) would be very appropriate choices.

Have on hand:
- several Bibles for students
- newsprint and marker or chalkboard and chalk
- paper and pencils
- hymnals

LEADING THE CLASS

(1) Introduction

Begin today's session by inviting students to share stories of the triumph of faith in the midst of hard times that (1) they have personally encountered, or (2) people they know have weathered, or (3) they have been made aware of through the media. If they choose the second option, ask them to omit names to protect the person's privacy. Then ask some other students to recount situations in which they or other persons gave up on their faith. Again, no names should be used unless the story is one that was reported in the media. After hearing several of these reports, ask class members:

(1) **What do you suppose motivates some people to hold fast to their faith in difficult circumstances, whereas others just let go?**
(2) **What role do you think the church might play when someone is experiencing a difficult situation?**

Relate these personal stories to today's scripture lesson by pointing out that the writer of Hebrews was keenly aware that people were suffering for their faith. In the midst of their hard times, he called them to remain near to God. As we study this lesson from Hebrews 10, we will ask: *What enables us to maintain our faith through hard times?*

(2) Boldness

Choose someone to read aloud Hebrews 10:19-23. Then ask these questions:

[?] **(1) What gives believers the assurance that they can, in fact, approach God?**

(2) Why are we told to "hold fast to the confession of our hope"?

Note that it is boldness or confidence before God that enables us to maintain our faith through hard times. We can speak freely before God, knowing that God accepts us. Use information under "Boldness" in the Interpreting the Scripture section to explain the concept of boldness further.

This would be an appropriate place to sing or say the hymn you have selected that highlights our assurance of faith in Christ.

(3) Fellowship

Now read Hebrews 10:24-25. Note that we can maintain our faith in the midst of hardship with the help of the community of faith. As explained in the Interpreting the Scripture portion, believers are to provoke or spur one another to perform deeds. We are to encourage one another. To demonstrate how important the church fellowship can be in supporting each other, have the class brainstorm answers to these questions as quickly as possible. Make a list on newsprint or a chalkboard.

[?] **(1) What good deeds have other church members performed that supported you or your family in some way?**

(2) What good deeds performed by others spurred you to do a good deed of your own?

Point out that verse 25 admonishes us not to neglect meeting together. Some persons argue that they can be good Christians without worshiping or otherwise participating in the life of the church. Their reasoning is based on the notion of a private relationship between themselves and God. Yet, the history of Israel and the writings of the early church reveal that God's people have seen themselves not as individuals who had no need of others but as parts of the body, to use Paul's metaphor. Each has its own function and role, but all work together for the good of the whole. You may want to ask students to debate the following statement. Perhaps you will want to divide into groups so that everyone can voice an opinion.

Although we are called to make a personal decision as to our relationship with Jesus Christ, once we make that decision we are expected to live as members in community so as to support, nurture, and edify one another. Acting as a spiritual maverick is neither good for the individual Christian nor the church as a whole. [R]

(4) Memory

Call for a volunteer to read aloud Hebrews 10:32-39. Point out that the writer reminds the Hebrews that they can endure suffering in the present because they have been able to do so before.

To help the class understand the kind of "hard struggle with suffering" that members of the early church endured, tell the stories of Polycarp, Germanicus, and Quintus as found in the Focusing on the Main Question portion. Provide a few moments for the students to reflect silently on how they might have reacted in similar situations.

Talk with the class about how memories of their own past successes in dealing with struggles, as individuals and as a congregation, have enabled them to deal with difficult circumstances. Direct the group to think of specific instances when the church or neighborhood faced a serious problem. Perhaps the church burned or a factory closed, leaving the community in desperate economic straits. Ask:

(1) What was the problem?

(2) How did people pull together to meet [?] **this challenge?**

(3) What was the result?

?

(4) In what ways did we see God at work?

(5) How has the memory of that situation enabled us to face other hard times with greater confidence?

Note that the writer of Hebrews records that persons have responded to persecution and hard times by being compassionate and forgiving toward those who have wronged them. Discuss the following situations. This exercise lends itself well to role-playing if the class enjoys that type of activity.

SCENARIO 1: Your child, an innocent bystander, was accidentally killed as warring gang members were engaged in a shoot-out. One of those involved in the shooting has convinced the jury that he is a changed person, so the jury may choose to impose the minimum sentence. How do you respond as a victim?

SCENARIO 2: A drunk driver plowed into your car at a high rate of speed. You have been left paralyzed because of this person's decision to drink and drive. She comes to see you in the hospital to say she is sorry. How do you respond?

SCENARIO 3: A co-worker who was competing against you for a promotion has been spreading rumors that damage your chances for advancement. Neither of you is chosen, so he wants to reestablish a close working relationship with you. How do you respond?

HELPING CLASS MEMBERS ACT

Remind the class that the writer of Hebrews tells the readers to encourage one another. Suggest that each class member select someone who is experiencing hard times and take some specific action to help that individual or family know that God loves them and is with them in their difficult circumstances.

Note that the writer of Hebrews also tells his audience to remember their previous struggles. Sometimes the memory of overcoming obstacles gives people the hope and the confidence to endure another hardship. Encourage class members to recall such an incident in their own lives that may help them whenever they experience difficult times. In their spiritual journal, they may want to record an account of this event and how their faith helped them go through it.

Mention that the writer of Hebrews reminds the readers that they "cheerfully accepted the plundering of [their] possessions" (10:34). Suggest that class members perform a compassionate action for someone who has wronged them.

PLANNING FOR NEXT SUNDAY

To prepare for next week's lesson, ask class members to read Hebrews 11:1-40. This familiar chapter bears testimony to the role faith has played throughout the history of God's people. Suggest that students recall stories or examples of faith in the lives of memorable persons in their own history. Encourage them to bring to class next week a picture or special memento of a person, place, or event that had significance in their own past.

REMEMBER THE PAST

PREVIEWING THE LESSON

Lesson Scripture: Hebrews 11:1-2, 6-10, 13-16, 39-40
Background Scripture: Hebrews 11:1-40
Key Verse: Hebrews 11:1

Focus of the Lesson:
the remembrance of heroic people throughout Jewish history who remained faithful to their convictions

Main Question of the Lesson:
What does our memory of the past do to our attitudes and behaviors in the present?

This lesson will enable adult learners to:
(1) explore the meaning of faith.
(2) consider Bible personalities whose attitudes and actions demonstrated faith.
(3) respond by determining the role faith plays in their own lives.

Today's lesson may be outlined as follows:
(1) Introduction
(2) Assurance
(3) Conviction
(4) Pilgrimage
(5) Example

FOCUSING ON THE MAIN QUESTION

Sometimes we remember the past through a nostalgic filter, so that we call "the good old days" as being better than they really were. The apple corer, now painted black and placed on a shelf as a decoration, for example, is more attractive than it ever was when grandmother had to use it to core apples. We long for "that old-time religion"—until we try to find guidance for twentieth-century problems in nineteenth-century principles. The nostalgic filter may render the past irrelevant as a shaping force for conduct in the present.

Sometimes we remember the past through a bitter filter, however, and then it does become a shaping force for conduct—but a destructive one. Unless we can change filters, amnesia is preferable to memory. At least that is what Robert E. Lee thought. After the Civil War, the famous Confederate general visited a Kentucky home. His hostess showed him the remains of a giant old tree in front of her house. She complained about the federal artillery fire that had mangled her tree. She expected Lee to join her in hostility toward the North. Instead he said, "Cut it down, my dear Madam, and forget it."

Obviously, it is better to get over the bitterness than to forget the past, for we remember the bad in order to learn from it how to live in the present so we can improve the future. And even if the lesson never becomes clear to us, we are better equipped for present adversity by the thought that we did survive. The Pilgrims had thanksgiving after a successful har-vest; but the settlers who arrived at Berkeley near Jamestown on December 4, 1619, held thanksgiving in advance for blessings they had not yet received. Instead of dwelling upon their difficulties, past and present, they were energized by a vision for the future.

So we can remember the past to find bad examples to avoid and good examples to imitate. The memory can be pleasantly irrelevant for the present; or it can be bitterly paralyzing. But it can also enable us to live more effectively. The main question, therefore, is: *What does our memory of the past do to our attitudes and behaviors in the present?*

READING THE SCRIPTURE

NRSV
Hebrews 11:1-2

Key Verse 1 Now faith is the assurance of things hoped for, the conviction of things not seen. [2]Indeed, by faith our ancestors received approval.

NIV
Hebrews 11:1-2

1 Now faith is being sure of what we hope for and certain of what we do not see. [2]This is what the ancients were commended for.

NRSV
Hebrews 11:6-10

[6]And without faith it is impossible to please God, for whoever would approach him must believe that he exists and that he rewards those who seek him. [7]By faith Noah, warned by God about events as yet unseen, respected the warning and built an ark to save his household; by this he condemned the world and became an heir to the righteousness that is in accordance with faith.

8 By faith Abraham obeyed when he was called to set out for a place that he was to receive as an inheritance; and he set out, not knowing where he was going. [9]By faith he stayed for a time in the land he had been promised, as in a foreign land, living in tents, as did Isaac and Jacob, who were heirs with him of the same promise. [10]For he

NIV
Hebrews 11:6-10

[6]And without faith it is impossible to please God, because anyone who comes to him must believe that he exists and that he rewards those who earnestly seek him.

[7]By faith Noah, when warned about things not yet seen, in holy fear built an ark to save his family. By his faith he condemned the world and became heir of the righteousness that comes by faith.

[8]By faith Abraham, when called to go to a place he would later receive as his inheritance, obeyed and went, even though he did not know where he was going. [9]By faith he made his home in the promised land like a stranger in a foreign country; he lived in tents, as did Isaac and Jacob, who were heirs with him of the same promise. [10]For he was looking forward to

looked forward to the city that has foundations, whose architect and builder is God.

NRSV
Hebrews 11:13-16

13 All of these died in faith without having received the promises, but from a distance they saw and greeted them. They confessed that they were strangers and foreigners on the earth, [14]for people who speak in this way make it clear that they are seeking a homeland. [15]If they had been thinking of the land that they had left behind, they would have had opportunity to return. [16]But as it is, they desire a better country, that is, a heavenly one. Therefore God is not ashamed to be called their God; indeed, he has prepared a city for them.

NRSV
Hebrews 11:39-40

39 Yet all these, though they were commended for their faith, did not receive what was promised, [40]since God had provided something better so that they would not, apart from us, be made perfect.

the city with foundations, whose architect and builder is God.

NIV
Hebrews 11:13-16

[13]All these people were still living by faith when they died. They did not receive the things promised; they only saw them and welcomed them from a distance. And they admitted that they were aliens and strangers on earth. [14]People who say such things show that they are looking for a country of their own. [15]If they had been thinking of the country they had left, they would have had opportunity to return. [16]Instead, they were longing for a better country—a heavenly one. Therefore God is not ashamed to be called their God, for he has prepared a city for them.

NIV
Hebrews 11:39-40

[39]These were all commended for their faith, yet none of them received what had been promised. [40]God had planned something better for us so that only together with us would they be made perfect.

UNDERSTANDING THE SCRIPTURE

Hebrews 11:1-7. Faith sets the goal for human life, making a future hope real, setting the visible against the backdrop of the invisible, providing meaning to the present. By faith our ancestors, who lived our religion before us and who therefore established the pattern for our own relationship with God, received the divine approval. And if Abel still speaks to us, then so do all the others—if only we will remember them in order to hear their word. Enoch was taken directly into heaven because he had pleased God. Such a reward is the direct result of faith, for obviously we do not approach God unless we "believe that he exists and that he rewards those who earnestly seek him"

(11:6). Noah demonstrates that such belief leads to obedience. And if he is an "heir," then we expect to share his righteousness if we imitate his faith.

Hebrews 11:8-22. Abraham shows us that faith is more than intellectual assent that something is true even if it cannot be proven. It is commitment that results in obedience. Abraham trusts the One who promises, and risks everything in response—like the gambler letting it all ride on a single roll of the dice. Once the promise is internalized, everywhere he goes is a foreign land; for he looks for a homeland, a heavenly city built by God for him. He now endures the insecurity of living in a tent, but then his dwelling will have the solidity of foundations that will endure forever. God's faithfulness, moreover, which merits our commitment, is demonstrated in the birth of Isaac. This birth is of special importance to us, for it is the transference of the promise to the next generation, and so, by implication, to us. Abraham's commitment, however, is to be complete. He is to trust God beyond any reasonable level, to the point where he sacrifices the son who is to transfer the promise to the next generation. It turns out all right, of course, and Isaac, Jacob, and Joseph all pass on the faith in the expected blessing. But perhaps it continues only because Abraham did not hold back anything from God.

Hebrews 11:23-31. Moses' parents feared God, in the sense of awe or reverence that engenders obedience, more than the secular might have feared Pharaoh. Their faith is replicated in their son, for Moses gave up the court in order to share the ill-treatment of God's people. The abuse is greater than the wealth of Egypt, for he kept his eye on the reward to come. Since Christ is identified with the reward (11:39-40), and since the abuse is the price to be paid for the reward, Moses' abuse can be said to have been endured for Christ. Moses was able to persevere through all these difficulties because he kept before him, as a real presence, the invisible. This means, in essence, that he always took the long view, the blessing beyond the suffering. The saving power of the blood at Passover cannot help but evoke the final sacrifice of our High Priest. And by faith the people walked into the water, in obedience to God's word, trusting that it would be all right. By faith the people marched around Jericho and did not even feel foolish when they shouted for the walls to tumble down. And Rahab somehow, somewhere, found the faith to cast in with the God of these invaders.

Hebrews 11:32-40. The names in 11:32 are not in chronological order. The random nature of the list thus suggests the endless supply of heroes. At last, beginning with "the prophets," we can consider them only in groups. These heroes of the faith succeeded in many ways, from conquering kingdoms to escaping the edge of the sword, from stopping the mouths of lions to putting foreign armies to flight. But the success of many others was bought at a terrible price, for they were tortured in an effort to break down their faith. They could have had release, in that the torturing would stop if they renounced their allegiance to God (11:35). But they remained faithful to the very end, believing that they would enjoy the resurrection to eternal life, a "better" resurrection than the return to life after a close call. These heroes of the faith, our role models for discipleship, share in the salvation that Christ has wrought for us.

INTERPRETING THE SCRIPTURE

Assurance

"Faith is the assurance of things hoped for" (11:1). The root meaning of the Greek word is "that which has been placed under," whether the foundation of a building or the basis of an argument in logic. The medical writers added another meaning: the sediment that appears on the bottom in liquids. This is a revelation in solid form of what had previously been invisible because it was dissolved in a liquid. In a similar development, the word came to designate a plan that would make something happen or appear, either a strategic plan by which troops would be deployed to achieve a measurable result or the architect's drawing, which would eventually become a pyramid.

Two specific applications of "that which has been placed under" have been selected by various English translations. (1) The foundation may be the steadiness of veteran troops, in contrast with the skittishness of raw recruits, which gives them the expectation of victory. In this sense, faith is the "assurance" (NRSV) or "confidence" (Phillips) of things hoped for. It is what we are "sure of" (NIV and GNB) and so it is a "guarantee" (NJB). The veteran believer has support for daily life from this certainty concerning the future. (2) If, on the other hand, the foundation is the inner essence or substance or ground of being, the intrinsic nature as opposed to its outward form, "the real me," it is the "substance" (KJV) of things hoped for. Certainty is not possible. In Hebrews 1:3, it is the substance or nature of God as revealed in Christ and is variously translated as "the express image of his person" (KJV), "the exact imprint" (NRSV), and "the exact representation" (NIV). But in Hebrews 3:14, the same word is the confidence with which we become Christians. An English translation must choose one of the two major possibilities, but for a Greek reader both ideas, substance and confidence, would be present. Even if one is dominant and the other is recessive, both are there. The faith of the believers of old gave substance to their vision of the future and afforded them the confidence to move toward it.

The things hoped for, the vision of the future, are defined throughout the passage. They are the inheritance (11:8), the promise (11:9, 39), the heavenly city (11:10, 13), the homeland (11:14), the heavenly country (11:16), the blessings for the future (11:20), and a better resurrection (11:35).

Conviction

Faith is not only the substance or confidence in the reality of the blessings we hope for. Faith is the "evidence" (KJV; 11:1) or what "proves the existence" (NJB) of things not seen. This meaning of the word is established by its occurrence in an Egyptian papyrus of 186 B.C.E.: "then if he has confidence in the *proofs* of accusations, he shall enter upon the more serious lawsuit." It is a means of testing the truth. Until it is proved, however, it is the conviction (NRSV) or certainty (NIV) that it will survive any testing. The tension between evidence and confidence is best retained, however, for the evidence is not apparent to all. Some reject it and content themselves with a horizon limited by material existence. Others are enabled to perceive that the physical world cannot explain itself, for it was created by God (11:3). The invisible, accordingly, is more "real" than the visible. Because he understood through faith that ultimate value lay in the unseen world, Abraham was willing to abandon the security of this world and become a homeless wanderer on the say-so of a mysterious Creator (11:8).

Pilgrimage

Faith, then, which deals with hope and the unseen, is oriented toward the future. But it is not "pie in the sky by and by," for the assurance or substance and the conviction or evidence bring that future into the present to shape and energize our lives in the here and now. Therefore, faith involves obedience. Abraham, accordingly, blindly follows the Voice, not even demanding to know the destination, and at last arrives in the land that has been promised to him. Unable to take possession, he is a foreigner (11:9). He is a "stranger" (NIV) or an "alien" (REB), without the rights of citizenship or tribal protection. Yahweh's heir must live in a tent while others have houses and cities. Abraham's faith generates the patience to look past the land of milk and honey to the heavenly city (11:10). This is worth waiting for. Nothing less will do.

While they are alive, the patriarchs and

matriarchs do not actually receive any of the things God has promised them (11:13). They are like travelers who see the towers of the city in the distance, but they must camp at least one more night in the desert before they can get there. Since they consider themselves no more than strangers and aliens in Canaan, they must still be searching for a country of their own (11:14). They no longer feel at home in the land from which they came, for they could have returned at any time. Instead, they desire a better country than Canaan or Mesopotamia or any place in between. Only in heaven with their God will they truly feel at home. This longing for a homeland draws Christians into pilgrimage. (See Philippians 3:20.)

"The Epistle to Diognetus," part of a collection of early Christian literature known as *The Apostolic Fathers*, reflects upon the idea of pilgrimage:

For Christians are not distinguished from the rest of humanity by country, language, or custom. For nowhere do they live in cities of their own, nor do they speak some unusual dialect, nor do they practice an eccentric life-style. . . . But while they live in both Greek and barbarian cities, as each one's lot was cast, and follow the local customs in dress and food and other aspects of life, at the same time they demonstrate the remarkable and admittedly unusual character of their own citizenship. They live in their own countries, but only as aliens; they participate in everything as citizens, and endure everything as foreigners. They are "in the flesh," but they do not live "according to the flesh." They live on earth, but their citizenship is in heaven.

"The Shepherd of Hermas," also part of *The Apostolic Fathers*, understands pilgrimage in terms of discipleship. If we are too much at home here, preparing fields and expensive possessions and buildings and useless rooms, it looks as if we are no longer planning to return to our heavenly city.

Take care, therefore, that you serve God and have him in your heart; work God's works, remembering his commandments and promises that he made. . . . So, instead of fields buy souls that are in distress, as anyone is able, and visit widows and orphans . . . and spend your wealth and all your possessions, which you received from God, on fields and houses of this kind. For this is why the Master made you rich, so that you might perform these ministries for him. It is much better to purchase fields and possessions and houses of this kind, which you will find in your own city when you go home to it.

Example

All of the heroic people throughout Jewish history, who remained faithful to their convictions, were commended by God (11:39). This commendation places them before us as examples to imitate. We recognize our religious roots in them, for they are our ancestors (1:1) in that they believed in God's existence (11:6). It was not an intellectual or abstract proposition for them, however, but the directing influence in their daily activities. They really thought that God rewards those who seek him; and since God's reward is the only ultimate value, their constant seeking can be considered a pilgrimage.

The roll call includes the famous names—Noah, Abraham, Isaac, Jacob, Moses, David—whose successes established and shaped the covenant itself. But it also includes unnamed saints whose suffering was the price the world exacted for their faithfulness. The common thread that unites them all in the divine commendation, however, is their hope in the future blessing, their faith in the unseen city prepared for them, and their single-minded journey through the world to God, allowing nothing to deflect them from their course.

Their endurance is all the more remarkable in that they never received the promise. The promise was not withheld from them because of any defect in their discipleship, of course, or because of divine fickleness or inability to deliver. Instead, God had provided something for them even better than they understood or expected (11:40). That something better is the salvation wrought by Christ, the fulfillment of the covenant, the final form of the blessing. So they were not to be made perfect apart from us; but then we are not perfected apart from them either.

SHARING THE SCRIPTURE

PREPARING TO TEACH

Preparing Our Hearts

Last week's lesson, which included a segment on memory, leads us from Hebrews 10 to this lesson on Hebrews 11. In this chapter the writer presents a brief history of persons who demonstrated their faith in God. As we remember them, we are reminded of the assurance of their faith and their conviction that the ultimate value of their faith lay in the unseen world. These faithful ones perceive themselves to be pilgrims in this world who are on their way to a heavenly home. Moreover, the recollection of their faith can serve as an example for us. As you consider these points, think about Bible personalities who have special meaning for you. With whom do you identify? How has their witness to the faith served to bolster your own discipleship? Choose one or two of these characters and list qualities of theirs that you find helpful for your own spiritual journey.

Preparing Our Minds

Carefully read Hebrews 11:1-40, paying particular attention to verses 1-2, 6-10, 13-16, and 39-40. Also read the lesson in its entirety. If any Bible figures mentioned in today's reading are unfamiliar to you, use a Bible dictionary or concordance to locate information.

As you gather your books and other supplies this week, be sure to include your own photo or memento of a person, place, or event that is important to you.

Preparing Our Learning Space

Have hymnals available if you choose to sing a song concerning faith or assurance, as suggested under "Assurance." Select a hymn prior to class, or give the class their choice of hymns. You may want to write the questions for the activity under "Example" prior to class.

Have on hand:
- ✔ several Bibles for students
- ✔ newsprint and marker or chalkboard and chalk
- ✔ paper and pencils
- ✔ hymnals

LEADING THE CLASS

(1) Introduction

Start today's session by asking students who have brought pictures or mementos to share them. You will want them to tell the group why this photo or souvenir is meaningful. If a number of people have brought pictures, consider having them discuss their treasures in groups so that more people will have a chance to tell their stories. Set a time limit. When the sharing is complete, ask the class:
(1) **What role do memories play in our lives?**
(2) **How do recollections of the past influence our lives in the present?**

Move this discussion of personal memories to today's session by noting that the author of Hebrews presented a roll call of the faithful to help his audience remember how our ancestors in the faith, related to God. As we study this lesson, we will see how their lives can serve as models for our own discipleship. We will ask: *What does our memory of the past do to our attitudes and behaviors in the present?*

As an alternative, read or retell the Focusing on the Main Question segment of the lesson.

(2) Assurance

Read aloud Hebrews 11:1-2. Note that 11:1 is our key verse for today's lesson. If the class enjoys singing, you may want to sing one of the many hymns that focus either on faith or assurance.

Use information in the "Assurance" section of the Interpreting the Scripture portion to explain what is meant by the word "assurance."

Now have one or more students read aloud Hebrews 11:6-10, 13-16, and 39-40. Then, noting that "faith is the assurance of things hoped for," ask:

(1) What did the people in these passages hope for? (See the final paragraph under "Assurance" for answers.)

You can help the class members to express faith and a vision for the future of their congregation by asking:

(2) What vision do you have for our own church?

(3) What memories of the past give you hope that this future might become a reality?

(3) Conviction

Continue the prior discussion on verses 1-2 by highlighting information under "Conviction" in the Interpreting the Scripture section to explain the meaning of conviction.

(4) Pilgrimage

Have the class look again at verses 8-10 concerning Abraham. Ask them to list on newsprint or a chalkboard the actions that Abraham undertook on faith. Information can be found in the "Pilgrimage" section of the Interpreting the Scripture portion.

Then ask them to meditate silently on these questions:

If God had called me to have the faith of Abraham, would I have the level of assurance and conviction needed to do what God had commanded me to do?

What experiences in my past cause me to think that I would, or would not, have such faith?

Call attention to Hebrews 11:13-16. These verses indicate that people of faith have perceived themselves to be foreigners here on earth, for their real home is in heaven. Read aloud the excerpt from "The Epistle to Diognetus" found under "Pilgrimage" in the Interpreting the Scripture portion. Discuss these questions:

(1) Do you agree with the notion that since our citizenship is in heaven our earthly existence is just a station where we have a layover along the way? Or, do you believe that God intended for us to see this earthly life as valuable in and of itself? Give reasons to support your answer.

(2) Do you believe that most Christians see themselves as pilgrims on their journey toward the heavenly city, or are they residents with their feet firmly planted here on earth? Support your answer with actions or attitudes that cause you to think as you do.

Now read the excerpt from "The Shepherd of Hermas," also found in the Interpreting the Scripture portion. Point out that this author "understands pilgrimage in terms of discipleship." Then ask:

(3) If we really saw heaven as our home, what changes might we make in our present life concerning our possessions, work, and use of time?

? **(4) Would such changes enable us to be more faithful disciples? If so, how?**

(5) Example

Direct the class to look over the list of people of faith in Hebrews 11. Have the class call out the names of individuals or groups they see listed here. You may want to write the names on newsprint or a chalkboard. Ask:

? **(1) Why do you think the author of Hebrews provided this list for people whose endurance was being tested?**

(2) How might the knowledge of these pillars of faith be helpful to us in our own faith journeys?

If time permits, you might want to single out several individuals—such as Noah, Abraham, Isaac, Jacob, Moses, and David—and ask this question:

? **(3) What specific traits about this person provide an example for my own life?**

Distribute paper and pencils. Ask the students to write the answers to the questions below. Assure them that their answers will not be read aloud. You may want to post the questions where everyone can see them.

? **(4) Who have been significant examples of Christian disciples in my own life?**

(5) What would God say about the kind of example my life offers to other people?

(6) How can I be a better example of a faithful Christian before people in my own life.

Conclude this quiet time with a prayer that God will enable us both to remember the examples that have been set before us and to be the kind of example to others that will encourage them to live more faithfully unto God.

HELPING CLASS MEMBERS ACT

Suggest that class members spend some quiet time thinking about what faith means to them and how they have drawn strength from their faith in difficult circumstances. They may want to meditate on their faith, or they may prefer to write their thoughts in a spiritual journal.

Encourage adults to think about preserving their own history for a family member of the next generation. Suggest that they write or tape record stories from their own past. Stories related to their faith may be especially meaningful. For example, they may want to tell what Sunday school was like when they were children, or how the family gathered around the piano to sing hymns, or where the church members went for a picnic. This information will enable children or teens to see a connection with the past, while being aware of how things have changed.

Challenge class members to consider how the lessons of their nation's history may help us to avoid mistakes in the present. What can be learned, for example, from prior wars, or economic conditions, or political positions? Suggest that students use the results of their findings to influence elected officials to follow an appropriate course of action.

PLANNING FOR NEXT SUNDAY

Next week's lesson, entitled "Renew Your Commitment," focuses on Hebrews 12:1-11. This lesson reminds us that we are called to persevere in our discipleship, despite struggles and discipline. Ask students to consider their own understanding of discipline as they prepare for this session.

RENEW YOUR COMMITMENT

PREVIEWING THE LESSON

Lesson Scripture: Hebrews 12:1-11
Background Scripture: Hebrews 12:1-11
Key Verse: Hebrews 12:1

Focus of the Lesson:
the call to renew commitment to God and persevere in the faith

Main Question of the Lesson:
How can we keep our faith shined up to the very end?

The lesson will enable adult learners to:
(1) think about their own spiritual ancestors who are cheering them on in the race of faith.
(2) recognize that Jesus is our model of the faithful, totally committed servant of God.
(3) respond by shedding baggage that impedes their ability to run the race.

Today's lesson may be outlined as follows:
(1) Introduction
(2) The Cloud
(3) The Baggage
(4) The Perfecter
(5) The Scriptures

FOCUSING ON THE MAIN QUESTION

The annual ritual of making New Year's resolutions reveals that most of us admit we could make some improvements in our personal lives. The end of the year, with its image of the old man tottering ahead of the Grim Reaper, cuts through the celebration to remind us that this world is passing by at its predetermined pace. But the image of the New Year baby tells us that making resolutions to improve is worthwhile, that renewal is yet possible. And so we make our lists—to lose weight, to spend more quality time with the children, to be more diligent in our discipleship, whatever. But somehow many of us have to make pretty much the same resolutions next year because we did not have the endurance, the staying power, through to the end of the year to make them happen.

We want to improve, otherwise we

---

would not make the resolutions in the first place, but we all are apt to fail in our quest for perfection. The consistency of this failure points to the tendency of a long-term commitment to lose its luster—or at least the danger that it will. We try to counteract that tendency by renewing our important commitments from time to time. Several times during the course of my ministry couples have renewed their wedding vows in public, and once or twice I have offered everyone at the morning worship service the opportunity to renew the marriage commitment. Such a renewal provides an impetus to the relationship

and encourages the rest of us. In the church I now attend, all of us in the pews are asked to recommit to our own baptismal vows each time new members become part of us.

Our lesson speaks to a small congregation that had started on the journey of faith with excitement, resolved to make a difference for Christ. And they did it—at least for a time. We are never told that they quit or that they had failed. But they slowed down. The main question, for them and for us as well, is: *How can we keep our faith shined up to the very end?*

AUGUST 24

READING THE SCRIPTURE

NRSV
Hebrews 12:1-11

Key Verse

1 Therefore, since we are surrounded by so great a cloud of witnesses, let us also lay aside every weight and the sin that clings so closely, and let us run with perseverance the race that is set before us, ² looking to Jesus the pioneer and perfecter of our faith, who for the sake of the joy that was set before him endured the cross, disregarding its shame, and has taken his seat at the right hand of the throne of God.

3 Consider him who endured such hostility against himself from sinners, so that you may not grow weary or lose heart. ⁴In your struggle against sin you have not yet resisted to the point of shedding your blood. ⁵And you have forgotten the exhortation that addresses you as children—

"My child, do not regard lightly
    the discipline of the Lord,
  or lose heart when you are
        punished by him;
⁶ for the Lord disciplines those
    whom he loves,
  and chastises every child
    whom he accepts."

NIV
Hebrews 12:1-11

1 Therefore, since we are surrounded by such a great cloud of witnesses, let us throw off everything that hinders and the sin that so easily entangles, and let us run with perseverance the race marked out for us. ²Let us fix our eyes on Jesus, the author and perfecter of our faith, who for the joy set before him endured the cross, scorning its shame, and sat down at the right hand of the throne of God. ³Consider him who endured such opposition from sinful men, so that you will not grow weary and lose heart.

⁴In your struggle against sin, you have not yet resisted to the point of shedding your blood. ⁵And you have forgotten that word of encouragement that addresses you as sons:
"My son, do not make light of the Lord's
        discipline,
  and do not lose heart when he rebukes you,
⁶because the Lord disciplines those he loves,
    and he punishes everyone he accepts as a
        son."

Key Verse

⁷Endure trials for the sake of discipline. God is treating you as children; for what child is there whom a parent does not discipline? ⁸If you do not have that discipline in which all children share, then you are illegitimate and not his children. ⁹Moreover, we had human parents to discipline us, and we respected them. Should we not be even more willing to be subject to the Father of spirits and live? ¹⁰For they disciplined us for a short time as seemed best to them, but he disciplines us for our good, in order that we may share his holiness. ¹¹Now, discipline always seems painful rather than pleasant at the time, but later it yields the peaceful fruit of righteousness to those who have been trained by it.

⁷Endure hardship as discipline; God is treating you as sons. For what son is not disciplined by his father? ⁸If you are not disciplined (and everyone undergoes discipline), then you are illegitimate children and not true sons. ⁹Moreover, we have all had human fathers who disciplined us and we respected them for it. How much more should we submit to the Father of our spirits and live! ¹⁰Our fathers disciplined us for a little while as they thought best; but God disciplines us for our good, that we may share in his holiness. ¹¹No discipline seems pleasant at the time, but painful. Later on, however, it produces a harvest of righteousness and peace for those who have been trained by it.

UNDERSTANDING THE SCRIPTURE

Hebrews 12:1-4. Last week, we studied the Jewish heroes of the past who were faithful to God no matter what it cost them. Since their God is our God, and since Christ is the fulfillment of their hope, we share the same perfection (11:39-40). "Therefore" (12:1) they are present with us in our struggles to be faithful. Their example encourages us "also" to run the race set before us with the same perseverance. The perseverance, translated as "patience" (KJV), "steadily" (JB), and "with determination" (GNB), appears in 12:7 as the verb rendered "endure" (NRSV, NIV). It is more than gritting-your-teeth endurance, however, and the "hanging in there" has to be more than stubbornness. The inward attitude is just as important as the outward conduct, and so patience in the sense of submission to the divine will is always part of the endurance or the perseverance. It is the virtue exhibited by the martyrs; but since we have not been tested to the point of shedding our blood, for us it is the dependability of our Christian witness over the long haul, whether or not there are difficulties to overcome.

Hebrews 12:5-11. The difficulties, however, sometimes derail the dependability. Suffering can break down faith. It is important, therefore, that we persevere through suffering for the sake of our witness to others as they must absorb their own pain, as well as for the quality of our own continuing relationship with God. In 12:3 we are warned of the danger of losing heart in the face of trouble. That phrase, losing heart, reminds our writer of Proverbs 3:11-12, which is quoted in Hebrews 12:5-6. This leads to an interpretation of suffering as discipline. The point is the relationship between discipline and membership within the family circle. We discipline our children because we care how they turn out. If we are reprimanded, therefore, it is evidence that we belong and that the One who corrects us loves us too much to let us drift off on our own.

So the troubles, far from being a threat to faith, may instead be seen as evidence of God's love for us. They show that we are accepted as God's own children. The text from Proverbs is introduced as an "exhortation" (NRSV) or an "encouragement" (NIV)—the Greek word carries both meanings. In either case, God is speaking to us through the Scriptures and calling us children (12:5). The suffering is intended to guide us to responsible and obedient maturity as the adult children of our heavenly Father, shaped and perfected for the blessings of eternity. God's motive in disciplining us is love. If, then, the purpose of our pain is our ultimate good, we should not take it lightly or lose heart. That would be to misinterpret. The suffering should, on the contrary, lift our spirits because it is evidence that we really are God's children (12:8). When things go too easily we wonder if that means that we are so much of the world that we have slipped out of God's family.

Our human parents must shape our attitudes and behaviors if we are to develop into mature adults. Their discipline is not successful until we respect them. That respect for the human parent correlates with submission to "the Father of spirits"

(12:9). This designation for God stresses the transcendent authority in heaven and hell as well as on earth, reminiscent of the clause in the Lord's Prayer, "your will be done on earth as it is in heaven." The submission to this Father results in life eternal. The parents discipline their children as seems best (NRSV) or as they think best (NIV). This is an important corrective in the use of the parental analogy; for at times parental discipline, or its lack, is destructive to the child. Such children, when they become adults, have problems thinking of God as Father. Perhaps this was in the back of our writer's mind as he stresses that God always acts in our best interests (12:10). And that best interest is defined as sharing God's holiness. Holiness, as the essential nature of deity, represents heaven itself, and so to share in it is to enjoy salvation in its ultimate sense. The sharing is further defined as a "harvest of righteousness and peace" (NIV; 12:11).

INTERPRETING THE SCRIPTURE

The Cloud

The image in 12:1 is the familiar comparison of the Christian life with athletic competition. The basic decision that each contestant must make is whether or not to compete in a given event. The potential competitor may walk over the course before the race, estimate its length and difficulty, and study the rules. The athlete may decide not to compete, but he or she cannot alter the course or its rules. In similar fashion, a person may look over the Christian course and its rules before deciding whether or not to enter the race. This examination of the course would have to include Christ's endurance of the shame of the Cross as well as the joy of the glory (12:2). The decision to enter the race is made at the time of coming to faith. When this occurs, the Christian must know that

he or she cannot change the rules or the course, for it has already been laid out by Another. The task of the Christian, then, is to run the race that is "set before us" (NRSV) or "marked out for us" (NIV). We can quit and we can run it poorly, but we cannot run a different race by different rules and think we have competed in this particular event. That would be like the case of the two farmers who decided to race their horses against each other. One hired a professional jockey, hoping to gain an edge. During the race both horses threw their riders at the same obstacle. The jockey recovered more quickly than the amateur rider, remounted, and went on to win the race. But it was all for nought. He won the race on the wrong horse!

When his or her event is called, the secular runner steps into the stadium and hears the roar of the crowd shouting its approval and encouraging a top effort. These are non-competing spectators and their cheers have a strengthening effect on the athlete. The Christian runner also has a crowd watching and giving encouragement, but it is a different kind of a crowd. These witnesses are former competitors in the event and all have been victorious. Rather than the roar of the spectator crowd, therefore, the picture is that of the nervous young athlete who is approached by the veteran champions in his or her event. They pat the young runner on the back, offer advice on how to run, and say, "We're rooting for you and we know you can do it!" This is the steadying effect that the younger athlete needs as he or she competes for the first time in a major race. This is the ever-present role of the witnesses from the past in relation to the present-day Christian. Their pat on the back revs us up to renew our commitment. They are a "cloud" in that they are one, while at the same time they are many.

The Baggage

The starting time approaches, and the runner strips off "every weight" (NRSV; 12:1), "everything that hinders" (NIV). No extra weight will be on the feet. No pockets will be filled with material not needed in the race itself. No loose clothing will be allowed to flap in the wind. The runner strips down from street clothes to a track suit. The hindrance or the weight that interferes with the Christian race, of course, is sin. This slows the runner down so that the extra effort required endangers the strength needed to complete the entire race. It is hard enough to keep going when we are not carrying any extra baggage. With sin clinging to us, it is like trying to run the marathon with a loaded suitcase in each hand. We get tired and lose heart (12:3) before we have gone very far.

The sin to be laid aside is described as that which "clings so closely" (NRSV; 12:1)

or "so easily entangles" (NIV). Phillips has an expressive paraphrase: "sin which dogs our feet." The rare word is a passive participle with a prefix, which means "readily being surrounded." From this the translators derive the idea of something that clings. The sin is a clinging obstacle like weeds that cling to a swimmer or clothing that is tied and yet billows out to slow us down. It might be mud that clings to our shoes or practice weights that the runner forgot to remove. No more can we afford to carry prejudice or selfishness or any other attitude that does not contribute to our sharing God's holiness.

NRSV has an alternative reading in the margin, based on other ancient manuscripts. Instead of "the sin that clings so closely" we read "the sin that easily distracts." Like the image of stripping away the weights, this reading continues the image of the race by understanding sin as that which distracts us from the business at hand, which is running the race that God has placed before us. The word "elsewhere" is used of the way in which marriage distracts a philosopher from thought or luxurious food distracts a hermit from prayer. In 1 Corinthians 7:35 Paul uses the negative of this word to indicate the necessity of being undisturbed or undivided in our devotion to the Lord.

The Perfecter

In spite of our best efforts, however, we no doubt continue to carry more baggage than we would like. If the race of 12:1 is the marathon, then we can expect to hit the "wall of pain" sooner or later. Unless we can get our second wind, we are in danger of falling behind and at last dropping out altogether. That critical second wind comes from "looking to" (NRSV; 12:2) or "fix[ing] our eyes on" (NIV) Jesus. The idea is that Jesus is at the finish line, and by fixing our attention on him, by not losing our concentration on the promised eternal blessing, we see beyond the wall of pain and are thereby enabled to continue on through it. This seeing is a continual recommitment to the "author" (NIV) or "pioneer" (NRSV) of our faith. (Review the discussion in Lesson 7.) Jesus is the perfecter of our faith in the sense that he completes it. (Review the discussion in Lesson 9.) Jesus was perfected by enduring the Cross and then ascending to the right hand of God the Father Almighty. Note that the joy, which relates to the right hand, comes before the Cross, and that the shame is between the Cross and the right hand. So Jesus sees the joy, but must endure the shame before it can be realized. The shame is mentioned because crucifixion, which the Romans mostly restricted to slaves and foreigners, humiliated the victim in addition to inflicting great pain.

We are to "consider" (12:3) that Jesus "endured such hostility against himself from sinners" (12:3). To "consider" is to allow Jesus to become an example to imitate when we get tired or lose heart as our faith begins to cost us something. Such consideration generates the second wind at the critical moment. Note the NRSV margin. Instead of "hostility against himself from sinners" some manuscripts read, "such hostility from sinners against themselves." This reading stresses the self-destructive nature of sin. We hurt ourselves more than we hurt others in that we halt the process of perfection that would have been our salvation.

The Scriptures

We are encouraged to persevere in the faith by the cloud of witnesses who are looking over our shoulder and by putting wings on our feet as we jettison the baggage that weakens our commitment. We also persevere through intense and persistent consideration of Jesus' own endurance and by pondering the Scriptures. The text in Proverbs provides for us a new interpretation of suffering in terms of discipline. The pain is still there. No one pretends that it is pleasant (12:11). But this new spin on an old problem insists that the pain is not meaningless, that the cosmos is getting even with us for our sin, or that we are in the clutches of the Devil. Instead it is in order to bless, it is the training that prepares us for heaven. Then the pain looks different. And that new insight shines up our faith again.

When James A. Garfield was president of Hiram College a man came to him to request that his son take a shorter course of studies than the other students were taking. "My son can never take all those studies," the father said. Garfield replied, "Oh, yes. He can take a short course; it all depends on what you want to make of him. When God wants to make an oak he takes a hundred years, but he takes only two months to make a squash." Well, God has decided what God wants to make of us; and we have agreed with this vision of our future by enrolling in the course of study that enables it.

SHARING THE SCRIPTURE

PREPARING TO TEACH

Preparing Our Hearts

What kinds of commitments have you made? How have you renewed them? Perhaps you have publicly renewed your wedding vows or reaffirmed your baptismal vows. Maybe you have stood before your congregation and promised to teach Sunday school or serve on a church committee for another year. Possibly you renewed your commitment to a branch of the armed forces by re-enlisting. Sometimes we find it easy to renew a commitment. Other times, however, we have faced a difficult situation and asked, "Why am I doing this to myself? I should let someone else do it." Yet, if we are willing to meet a challenge head-on, we often find that with perseverance we can rise to the occasion. We put our faith in gear and keep on trying. An awareness that others have overcome similar odds may give us the courage to overcome whatever difficulties face us. During the week, reflect on the witness of the saints as a helpful means of keeping your commitment to God firm.

Preparing Our Minds

This week's lesson continues our study of Hebrews by focusing on chapter 12. The chapter links with last week's study by reminding us that we are surrounded by a cloud of witnesses. We run the race of faith in the presence of these witnesses who are our spiritual ancestors and examples. We may experience persecution and discipline from the Lord, but we are to continue forging ahead with perseverance. Be sure to read Hebrews 12:1-11, along with this lesson in preparation for Sunday's class.

Review the discussions in Lessons 7 and 9 on Jesus as the pioneer and perfecter of our faith. Note these references under "The Perfecter" in the Interpreting the Scripture portion.

Preparing Our Learning Space

The well-known hymn, "For All the Saints," is found in many hymnals (for example, *The United Methodist Hymnal*, page 711). If you have books available that include this hymn, plan to use it during the introductory activity.

You may want to set up a graffiti board for students on which they can list the names of persons who have made a difference in their spiritual lives. To do this, affix a large sheet of butcher paper or newsprint to a wall. Provide markers. Label the sheet "Our Great Cloud of Witnesses" and invite students to add names as they arrive.

Have on hand:
- ✔ several Bibles for students
- ✔ newsprint and marker or chalkboard and chalk
- ✔ hymnals
- ✔ optional newsprint or butcher paper and several markers

LEADING THE CLASS

(1) Introduction

As students enter the classroom, encourage them to write the names of persons now deceased who they believe have had made a significant contribution to their spiritual lives. To begin the session, read the names aloud, provided there is enough time to read all of them. Observe a moment of silence in which the group gives thanks for these persons. Then, if possible, sing "For All the Saints," based on Hebrews 12:1, as a tribute to these people who have meant so much to group members.

Point out that these persons must have made a long-term commitment to God, for their lives have touched ours in a deep and meaningful way. They have fought the good fight, persevered to the end, and now, in some manner that we cannot truly understand, they surround us as we run our own race of faith. It is as if they are cheering us on. Today as we study Hebrews 12, we remember these spiritual forebears and ask: *How can we keep our faith shined up to the very end?*

As an alternative, read or retell the Focusing on the Main Question portion.

(2) The Cloud

Choose someone to read aloud today's scripture, Hebrews 12:1-11, in its entirety.

Then invite the class to read in unison today's key verse, Hebrews 12:1. Note that this verse speaks of the Christian life in terms of an athletic competition, a race. Ask these questions:

?

(1) **If you were to run a marathon, what would you do to prepare?**

(2) **What would the judges expect of you?**

(3) **How does the cheering of the crowd on the sidelines affect your own commitment to the race?**

Supplement the group's answers with information from "The Cloud," under the Interpreting the Scripture portion. Be sure to include the anecdote about the jockey who rode the wrong horse to the finish line.

(3) The Baggage

Direct the group's attention to the words in verse 1, "let us also lay aside every weight and the sin that clings so closely." Ask class members to close their eyes and relax as you read this guided imagery exercise. Be sure to pause at the places so marked.

R

Finally, the big day has arrived. You are ready to run your first marathon. You take your position, awaiting the signal you have been anxious to hear. Feel the excitement and enthusiasm of the moment. (pause)

With the report of the pistol, you begin the race. The other racers dart ahead of you. Notice that they are wearing running shoes while you have on heavy hiking boots that slow your steps and tire your feet. Feel the weight of these boots. (pause)

Your arms also feel heavy. Everyone else seems to be running with a cadenced stride, but your steps are awkward and off balance because you are carrying two suitcases, one in each hand. Peer inside of this luggage. What sins or concerns are hindering your steps? How has this baggage weakened your commitment to Christ? (pause)

Ask God to take these boots from your feet and this luggage from your hands so that you might run the good race. Feel these sins and burdens being lifted from you. (pause)

Offer a prayer of thanksgiving and a renewal of your commitment to run life's race as a faithful disciple. (pause)

Open your eyes when you are ready.

(4) The Perfecter

Point out that, as verse 2 states, we are to look at Jesus, the perfecter of our faith. You may want to read or retell this section as found in the Interpreting the Scripture portion. Then ask:

(1) **How can Jesus be an example for us when we are feeling down and our commitment is lagging?** ?

Note that God disciplines those whom God loves. The purpose of this discipline is to perfect us so that we might be able to yield the fruit of righteousness. Ask:

(2) **Does discipline generally cause you to become aware of your shortcomings and sins? If so, do you get discouraged and give up, assuming that God does not love you? Or do you allow chastisement to help you renew your commitment to Christ? If possible, give a concrete example to explain your position.** ?

(5) The Scriptures

So far, we have seen that we are encouraged to renew our commitment by the cloud of witnesses that surrounds us, by throwing off the baggage of sin that weakens our commitment, and by considering Jesus' own endurance as an example of commitment that we can imitate. The Scriptures can also help us renew our commitment. Invite class members to mention favorite scripture passages that may help them to bolster their faith when it is sagging. You may want to list these on newsprint or a chalkboard.

Close by reading the anecdote in the last paragraph of the Interpreting the Scripture portion. Note that if we are only interested in a short-term, "squash-like" faith, we will not have to endure long. However, to grow in faith to the stature of an oak tree, we will have to endure. Our faith will be tested. We will suffer persecution and discipline from God. But, in the end, our faith will be deeply rooted. As the storms of life and seasons of spiritual dryness have caused our faith commitment to wane, we will have countless opportunities to recommit ourselves to the living God and the Christ who showed by his example what a life of faithful commitment is really all about.

HELPING CLASS MEMBERS ACT

Encourage students to think seriously this week about the sin and other heavy baggage that they are carrying around as they attempt to run the race of faith. Invite them to list these concerns. Students who are artistic may want to draw a picture of a suitcase and write their sins or concerns inside. Suggest that they pray about this matter and envision God carrying away this luggage for them so they need not be burdened by it again.

Encourage class members to memorize Hebrews 12:1-2 so that they might be able to call it to mind in difficult situations.

Challenge class members who are parents or grandparents to pay special attention to how they discipline children this week. Are they offering discipline that will enable the child to learn from mistakes and grow? Or are they simply taking out their anger and frustration on the child? Encourage them to pray that they may be more like God as they mete out necessary discipline.

PLANNING FOR NEXT SUNDAY

Next week's lesson, entitled "Live Responsibly," concludes our quarter. In preparation for this lesson, direct students to read Hebrews 13, instructing them to pay special attention to verses 1-16. If you have not already secured a copy of *The New International Lesson Annual, 1997-98* you will want to do so immediately. The first quarter in that series will focus on the history of Judah from the fall in 587 B.C.E. to the end of the Old Testament era.

LIVE RESPONSIBLY

PREVIEWING THE LESSON

Lesson Scripture: Hebrews 13:1-16
Background Scripture: Hebrews 13
Key Verse: Hebrews 13:16

Focus of the Lesson:
the responsibility that Christians are called to exhibit in acts of love and generosity

Main Question of the Lesson:
What is my Christian responsibility in the particular case that confronts me at the moment?

The lesson will enable adult learners to:
(1) explore the characteristics of responsible Christian living.
(2) consider how they embody these characteristics in their own lives.
(3) respond by taking concrete steps to exhibit God's love to others.

Today's lesson may be outlined as follows:
(1) Introduction
(2) Entertaining Angels
(3) That Old-Time Religion
(4) Outside the Camp
(5) The Sacrifice of Praise

FOCUSING ON THE MAIN QUESTION

A sign in front of the Washington Monument in Washington, D.C., points out that George Washington set the precedent for all U.S. presidents coming after him. After all, as our nation's first president, he had no examples to draw from. In like manner, Martha Washington set the precedent for how to be a first lady. She chose to define the office in terms of her responsibility to be a supportive wife. This led to the public expectation that the first lady will be a gracious hostess and that her dress will embody good taste.

Abigail Adams saw a second responsibility, to engage her own mind in the issues of the day. The public embraced this responsibility, and now the first ladies are expected to improve the life of the nation in some way. Each has received the general mandate but has fulfilled it in terms of the specificity of her own life and times. And so the first ladies have worked on everything from urban renewal to drug rehabilitation, from reading to race relations.

They are alike in that they have struggled to discharge an interlocking network of responsibilities—to their husbands, to their children, to the country, and, increasingly, to the world. But, as often noted, "the devil is in the details." And so they are unlike in the precise ways they have fulfilled these responsibilities. No matter the models provided by their predecessors, the challenges facing them are as different as are their skills. Each first lady is required to step out onto new ground.

As Christians, we to struggle to fulfill the interlocking network of responsibilities that we call discipleship. But, like the first ladies, we are unique individuals. We have a general mandate—to show hospitality, to remember those in prison, to be content with what we have, to do good, to share what we have. But our lives are specific rather than general. And so the main question is: *What is my Christian responsibility in the particular case that confronts me at the moment?*

READING THE SCRIPTURE

NRSV
Hebrews 13:1-16

1 Let mutual love continue. ²Do not neglect to show hospitality to strangers, for by doing that some have entertained angels without knowing it. ³Remember those who are in prison, as though you were in prison with them; those who are being tortured, as though you yourselves were being tortured. ⁴Let marriage be held in honor by all, and let the marriage bed be kept undefiled; for God will judge fornicators and adulterers. ⁵Keep your lives free from the love of money, and be content with what you have; for he has said, "I will never leave you or forsake you." ⁶So we can say with confidence,
"The Lord is my helper;
I will not be afraid.
What can anyone do to me?"
⁷Remember your leaders, those who spoke the word of God to you; consider the outcome of their way of life, and imitate their faith. ⁸Jesus Christ is the same yesterday and today and forever. ⁹Do not be carried away by all kinds of strange teachings; for it is well for the heart to be strengthened by grace, not by regulations about food, which have not benefited those who observe them. ¹⁰We have an altar from

NIV
Hebrews 13:1-16

1 Keep on loving each other as brothers. ²Do not forget to entertain strangers, for by so doing some people have entertained angels without knowing it. ³Remember those in prison as if you were their fellow prisoners, and those who are mistreated as if you yourselves were suffering.
⁴Marriage should be honored by all, and the marriage bed kept pure, for God will judge the adulterer and all the sexually immoral. ⁵Keep your lives free from the love of money and be content with what you have, because God has said,
"Never will I leave you;
never will I forsake you."

⁶So we say with confidence,

"The Lord is my helper; I will not be afraid.
What can man do to me?"
⁷Remember your leaders, who spoke the word of God to you. Consider the outcome of their way of life and imitate their faith. ⁸Jesus Christ is the same yesterday and today and forever.
⁹Do not be carried away by all kinds of strange teachings. It is good for our hearts

which those who officiate in the tent have no right to eat. ¹¹For the bodies of those animals whose blood is brought into the sanctuary by the high priest as a sacrifice for sin are burned outside the camp. ¹²Therefore Jesus also suffered outside the city gate in order to sanctify the people by his own blood. ¹³Let us then go to him outside the camp and bear the abuse he endured. ¹⁴For here we have no lasting city, but we are looking for the city that is to come. ¹⁵Through him, then, let us continually offer a sacrifice of praise to God, that is, the fruit of lips that confess his name.

Key Verse
¹⁶Do not neglect to do good and to share what you have, for such sacrifices are pleasing to God.

to be strengthened by grace, not by ceremonial foods, which are of no value to those who eat them. ¹⁰We have an altar from which those who minister at the tabernacle have no right to eat.

¹¹The high priest carries the blood of animals into the Most Holy Place as a sin offering, but the bodies are burned outside the camp. ¹²And so Jesus also suffered outside the city gate to make the people holy through his own blood. ¹³Let us, then, go to him outside the camp, bearing the disgrace he bore. ¹⁴For here we do not have an enduring city, but we are looking for the city that is to come.

¹⁵Through Jesus, therefore, let us continually offer to God a sacrifice of praise—the fruit of lips that confess his name. ¹⁶And do not forget to do good and to share with others, for with such sacrifices God is pleased.

Key Verse

UNDERSTANDING THE SCRIPTURE

Hebrews 13:1-6. We are to serve God within an atmosphere of love for those who are on pilgrimage with us (13:1). This means that we are to extend hospitality to Christians passing through our town even if we do not know them personally (13:2). We are to remember Christians who are imprisoned and tortured for their faith (13:3). To remember them is to do something for them. Faithfulness to strangers, moreover, is to be paralleled by faithfulness within the home (13:4). Fear of not having enough for our own needs, however, inhibits our generosity even when we do feel concern for the unfortunate, and anxiety about our own safety and comfort makes us hesitant to take our place beside those being persecuted for the faith. Such fear is branded as greed (13:5). The antidote is contentment with what we have, which is trust in God's protective providence (13:6).

Hebrews 13:7-9. Those who had established the congregation by their preaching are now gone, but their faith is worthy of imitation (13:7). Strength for the present comes from remembering the outcome of their faith. They sealed their words with their actions to the end. Our imitation leads to their Christ; for even though they are gone, their Christ remains (13:8). Unless we anchor ourselves in this Christ we risk being pulled off course by strange teachings (13:9). We do not know exactly what these strange teachings were and how they relate to food regulations, but they do not strengthen the heart. Only divine grace can do that.

Hebrews 13:10-13. The source of that grace is Christ's sacrifice—"we have an altar" (13:10). Those who serve in the "tent" (NRSV) or "tabernacle" (NKJV), of course, are the Jews who have no right to eat from the Christian altar. Some scholars have suggested that the implied conclusion is, "but we Christians do have that right." The food that we eat from the altar is then the Lord's Supper. But the altar symbolism will lead to the spiritual sacrifices of 13:15-16 instead of to the Lord's Supper, and the tabernacle will lead to the pilgrimage theme of 13:13. So it is best to understand the eating as symbolic. To eat from the altar is to participate in the death of Christ and thereby gain the salvation that it enables.

Verse 13:10 introduces a key point about Jesus' death: that it took place outside the city. Hebrews 13:11 begins with a reference to Leviticus 16:27, that portion of the Day of Atonement ritual specifies that the bodies of the sacrificial animals are to be burned outside the camp but the blood is to be brought into the Holy of Holies by the high priest. Therefore (13:12), since the blood is inside and the bodies are burned outside, Christ was crucified outside the city in order that his blood may work inside, that is, that the people might be sanctified by his blood.

The "outside" of 13:12 and 13 connects Jesus and Jesus' people, for the community must always be with its Savior. The "outside" is expulsion from the sacred space, rejection by the very people who claim the Old Testament promises to which we also turn. For us to go to Jesus outside the camp is to bear the "abuse" (NRSV) or "reproach" (NKJV) that forced him outside the camp. And that is the cross. To go to him is to carry our own crosses (Mark 8:34). Since Jesus is out there, a risen Savior rather than a burned carcass, his blood is also out there. So going forth to him involves also taking his saving blood to the world.

Hebrews 13:14-16. The city is more than Jerusalem, for in 13:14 the contrast is between heaven and earth. We are on the pilgrimage (Hebrews 11:13-16) that is characterized by the "sacrifice of praise" (13:15), which includes good works (13:16).

Hebrews 13:17-25. Our leaders "watch over [our] souls" (13:17) by keeping us pointed in the right direction. The author identifies with these congregational leaders. Obey *them* (13:17) and pray for *us* (13:18). The leaders must one day give account to God for the guidance they have provided. Their conscience is clear because they really want to do the right thing. But all of us, leaders as well as followers, in the final analysis depend upon God, through the indwelling power of Jesus Christ, to give us the strength "to walk the walk" that will take us to the city to come.

INTERPRETING THE SCRIPTURE

Entertaining Angels

The "mutual love" (NRSV) or "brotherly love" (NKJV) in 13:1 is the relatively rare *philadelphia*. In secular Greek it is used only of the affection that natural siblings have for each other. In the New Testament the word implies the new reality of the family of God in Christ. We have been taught by God to love one another (1 Thessalonians 4:9), and therefore the love for the brothers and sisters is to be sincere (1 Peter 1:22), affectionate (Romans 12:10), and part of our very relationship to the Lord (that is, our godliness; 2 Peter 1:7). We are urged to continue or "keep on" (NIV) loving each other because the relationship is constantly threatened by the root of bitterness within and by the world without.

If blood is thicker than water, *philadelphia* implies more than a friendly hello and hearty handshake on Sunday morning. Although elsewhere in the Bible we are told to house the homeless without qualification, here the strangers to be welcomed into our homes are fellow Christians, either passing through on secular business or itinerant missionaries. We recognize them as part of our extended family, kin rather than foreigners. We are spiritually enriched by offering such hospitality, for this entertaining is surely to be included within the spiritual sacrifices that are pleasing to God (13:16). And who knows? We might end up with an angel at our dinner table (13:2).

There is general agreement that the specific reference to angels in 13:2 is to the three strangers who came to Abraham and Sarah (Genesis 18:1-21). Not since Lessons 6 and 7 have we encountered angels in our study of Hebrews. Lest we fixate on wings and glory, however, Hebrews 1:14 stresses the root meaning. An angel is a messenger, and thus a ministering spirit. When the wings are folded back under street clothes, therefore, the angel at our dining room table looks like any other guest. But the ordinary guest also is an angel, sent to us to provide a specific trigger for the *philadelphia* that pleases God. Then, as Howard Thurman so vividly expressed it, our angel spreads "a halo over an ordinary moment or a commonplace event."

Philadelphia implies more than the inconvenience and expense of changing the sheets and cooking for a guest. We are to put ourselves at risk if Christians suffer for the faith (13:3). To visit and assist those in prison is to admit publicly that we share their religious and political views. We are to minister to those who are "mistreated" (NKJV), perhaps by an unruly mob, by stepping to their side in plain view of their persecutors. Their plight is to be of as much concern to us as if we were in prison with them. We remember the mistreated because we also "are in the body" (NKJV). This phrase has been understood in two different ways: (1) If it is physical existence, then we feel their pain as if we also were "being tortured" (NRSV). (2) If it is common membership in the body of Christ (as JB), the idea is that if one member suffers, all suffer (see 1 Corinthians 12:26).

That Old-Time Religion

We keep the *philadelphia* vibrant and effective by remembering "that old-time religion." It was good enough for the leaders who had established our church by the preaching of the word. They are gone now, but their religion is good enough for us. And so we are enjoined to pay attention to the legacy which they have left us (13:7). Lesson 12 concluded with the roll call of the Old Testament heroes of the faith as an inspiring example for us; and Lesson 13 opened with the cloud of witnesses encouraging us in our discipleship. Now we are told to think about them, intentionally, systematically.

To remember, in essence, is to collect the raw data. To consider or "reflect" (NJB) or "think back on" (GNB) is to analyze the data, to probe for meaning. That meaning is to be found in the outcome of their behavior or "conduct" (NKJV). The conduct may be expanded to mean their way of life in general (NRSV) or it may be restricted to the fidelity with which they preached the word of God. In either case the outcome indicates that they have died (GNB). Their faith emerges from the analysis, and this is what we are to "imitate" (NRSV) or "follow" (NKJV).

Remembrance and the analysis are critical prerequisites to the imitation. Third John 11 warns us not to "imitate" (NIV) evil. Calvin Coolidge advises us to know what it is that we propose to imitate. A breakfast guest at the White House once saw President Coolidge pour coffee from his cup into a saucer and add cream and sugar to it. The visitor followed suit and then was stunned to see Coolidge place his saucer on the floor for the cat.

Outside the Camp

The reference to the city in 13:12 and the camp in 13:13 is the same; but the combination of terms adds the wilderness wandering, with exodus and Sinai, to the

Jerusalem image of the holy city. Camp and city, centered on the tabernacle and the temple respectively, may indicate Judaism. The word "outside" then means that the church and synagogue have parted company; for we are to leave the sacred space for the shameful places where carcasses are burned and criminals are executed. That is where Christ is, and if we are to be his we must go to him.

In the *Word Biblical Commentary*, William L. Lane expands on this concept:

[T]he golden calf signified the rejection of God. Consequently, God departed from the formerly sacred enclosure and displayed his presence only at the tent pitched "outside the camp"(Exodus 33:7-10). An attractive proposal is that the play on the phrase "outside the camp" in v 11-13 was designed to call to mind the occasion when God manifested his presence outside the wilderness encampment. The humiliation of Jesus and his death as an outcast show that God has again been rejected by his people. His presence can be enjoyed only "outside the camp," where Jesus was treated with contempt. Anyone who seeks to draw near to God must go "outside the camp" and approach him through Jesus.

The movement may, on the other hand, pick up on the idea of pilgrimage, of passing through this world on the way to heaven. (See Lesson 12.) Camp and city then go beyond Judaism to include the world. To go outside this camp is then to find our meaning in Christ rather than in the world. (See John 15:19 and Romans 12:2.)

The movement has also been understood in terms of mission. In this case the camp/city is the church. We are to go beyond the security of fellowship with like-minded brothers and sisters. Christ is "outside"—where the world hurts—and we are to go forth to him in mission. And when we do, we are sure that he is with us always, even to the end of the earth (Matthew 28:20). This interpretation leads well into the good deeds of 13:16.

All of these interpretations—to move out from Judaism, into pilgrimage, and into mission—make sense. And on different days any one of them might be adopted. But whichever interpretation we choose, the constant is the willingness to go wherever, to do whatever, in order that we might be with Christ.

The Sacrifice of Praise

In Lesson 9 we went from the blood of animals to the blood of Christ, and in 13:13 we bear Christ's abuse, that is, we take up our cross and follow him. Even if this cross-bearing should turn into a literal cross, however, martyrdom is understood in terms of discipleship rather than as sacrifice. For after Christ there can be no more sacrifice. The access to God has already been attained for us "through him" (13:15). The sacrifices of 13:15-16, therefore, which are pleasing to God, are metaphoric rather than literal. These sacrifices, continual rather than occasional, define our ordinary everyday discipleship; and their value comes from Christ.

The first of these sacrifices, the conduct that embodies the attitude with which we go outside the camp, is worship. The worship is praise offered to God (13:15). The phrase "the fruit of lips" comes from Hosea 14:2. NRSV's "confess his name" could be taken as evangelism, as if we confess the name of God to others. The confession in this context, however, is thanksgiving for salvation; and the Greek case construction, represented by the "to" in NKJV, shows that the confession, or thanksgiving, is offered to God rather than to other people.

The second of these sacrifices, so tightly connected that we cannot have the one without the other, is a constant flow of good deeds (13:16). The good deed, at bottom, is the sharing of whatever is appropriate in the specific case before us.

SHARING THE SCRIPTURE

PREPARING TO TEACH

Preparing Our Hearts

We live in an age when no one seems to be responsible for anything. A patron slips on wet pavement and sues the shopkeeper. A driver has an accident and blames the car manufacturer. Criminals refuse to be accountable for their illegal actions. A marriage disintegrates and each partner points an accusing finger at the other. What does it mean to live responsibly? The writer of Hebrews tells us that responsible living includes loving others, showing hospitality to strangers, caring for prisoners, upholding the sanctity of marriage, and being content with what we have. As you prepare to lead this week's session, think about the level of responsibility you are willing to assume. Do you accept positions of leadership, knowing that you will likely be criticized? Are you willing to be accountable when a problem arises? Are you willing to take up your own cross in order to be a responsible disciple of Jesus Christ?

Preparing Our Minds

Read this lesson, along with Hebrews 13. Carefully study verses 1-16.

Give some thought this week to how you, the students in the class, your congregation, and your denomination as a whole all take responsibility for those who need help.

Preparing Our Learning Space

If possible, bring in one or more news articles detailing how persons have helped others in need. The article may, for example, speak of groups helping to rescue survivors after a natural disaster. Or it may talk about how volunteers built a Habitat for Humanity home, or other kind of project.

For the activity under "Outside the Camp," secure information about missions projects from your pastor prior to class, or ask a member of the Missions Committee to be a guest speaker. You may want to secure a videotape and player.

Have on hand:
- several Bibles for students
- newsprint and marker or chalkboard and chalk
- optional paper and pencils
- optional newspaper articles
- missions information, possibly including a videotape and recorder
- optional hymnals

LEADING THE CLASS

(1) Introduction

If you secured news articles describing people helping others, retell two or three of these stories. If not, ask class members to recount how people, particularly church people, have taken responsibility for helping others who needed assistance. Maybe students can recall some events in your own congregation—such as going to a neighboring state to rebuild after a flood or regularly preparing and serving meals at a soup kitchen—in which your own members demonstrated responsible Christian living.

After sharing a few of these memories (or perhaps visions that are on the drawing board), guide the discussion to today's lesson on Hebrews. Note that the writer makes clear that we have many responsibilities because we are called to go with Christ outside the security of our church's walls to minister to a hurting world. As we discuss Hebrews 13, we will ask: **What is my Christian responsibility in the par-**

ticular case that confronts me at the moment?

As an alternative, use the Focusing on the Main Question portion, being certain to include the main question.

(2) Entertaining Angels

Choose someone to read aloud Hebrews 13:1-6. Use the information in the "Entertaining Angels" section of the Interpreting the Scripture portion to help the class understand the meaning of "mutual love," which is translated from the Greek word *philadelphia*.

Note that the writer of Hebrews calls the people to responsible living in both the public and private spheres. Do as many of the following activities related to the author's words as you can in the time you have available.

* Talk about why we are, or are not, willing to extend hospitality to strangers.
* Discuss with the group ways in which they can voice their opposition to torture and other human rights violations around the world. Note that such atrocities may afflict Christians, or be inflicted by them as was the case in Hitler's Germany.
* Invite the class to spend a few moments in silent prayer for persons they know whose marriages are troubled. Mention no names aloud.
* Distribute paper and pencils. Ask students to write some words or phrases that describe what money means to them or the role that money plays in their lives. Are they content with what they have? Do they live within their means? Or are they reckless with money and often in debt? Assure the group their answers will not be shared aloud.

(3) That Old-Time Religion

Select a student to read aloud Hebrews 13:7-9. Use information for these verses in the Understanding the Scripture portion to explain their meaning.

Note that the writer of Hebrews calls us to remember our religious leaders and pay attention to the legacy they have left us. If your congregation belongs to a specific denomination, you may want to ask:

(1) **What are some of the specific teachings and practices that the founder of our denomination (mention the name) set forth?**

(2) **How have these teachings and practices changed since the early years?**

(3) **In what ways have these changes been for the worse?**

(4) **In what ways have they enabled us to be more faithful disciples of Jesus Christ?**

(5) **Do you think it is ever possible to go back to "that old-time religion," or must every era find ways to reform and reshape the church? Give reasons for your answer.**

(4) Outside the Camp

Read aloud Hebrews 13:10-13. Again, information in the Understanding the Scripture portion for these verses will help the class to comprehend the ideas presented here. You may need to review briefly the idea of the wilderness wanderings in the days of Moses if you have some students who are unfamiliar with the Bible. Emphasize that we must be willing to go wherever, to do whatever, in order that we might be with Christ.

Use these verses as an opening to promote missions opportunities within the class. Many adults are willing to sit within the confines of their own sanctuary and contribute to its upkeep. Some are less willing, however, to participate in a missions project. They choose not to give of their time, talent, or finances. You may want to get some information about missions projects from your pastor prior to class, or ask a member of the Missions Committee to be a guest speaker. Do one or more of the following:

* Suggest a way that class members can

become involved in a hands-on, local missions project, such as providing health kits for the homeless.

• View a video of a missions project located in your own country and learn how you can participate through giving needed supplies, money, or your own time.

• Hear a guest speaker (perhaps from the Missions Committee) who can give an overview of what the congregation is doing, what it could be doing, and how class members can be involved.

• Challenge the class to pledge a certain amount of money to support a missionary/evangelist.

Some students may respond with ideas. If so, list them on newsprint or a chalkboard.

(5) The Sacrifice of Praise

Read aloud Hebrews 13:14-16. Use information in "The Sacrifice of Praise" section of Interpreting the Scripture to explain the meaning of these verses.

Since worship is one means that we have to offer praise to God, close today's lesson, which ends the 1996–97 year, with songs and psalms of praise. If you have a musical instrument and a musician capable of playing requests in your class, you may want to let the students make some selections. You will need to distribute hymnals. Another way to give praise to God is to read psalms of praise, either from the Bible or from a hymnal that includes a Psalter. If you use the Psalter, students can read responsively and possibly sing a response. Psalms 146–150 are especially jubilant psalms of praise.

HELPING CLASS MEMBERS ACT

As noted in the lesson, the understanding of *philadelphia* includes the idea of putting oneself at risk if Christians suffer for the faith. Challenge class members to consider going on a missions trip to an area of the world where Christians are at risk and suffering. Volunteer missionaries are often able to assist such persons by building structures, digging wells, or providing other services.

Check to see if any groups (such as choirs or lay witness teams) from other areas will be traveling to your community and in need of shelter. If so, try to enlist class members to house these visitors.

Challenge the class to spearhead the opening of a homeless shelter in your own church or neighborhood. One suburban community, for example, sponsors a shelter that rotates weekly among fifteen churches of all denominations so that the homeless are housed during the winter. The churches sign up for weeks that they will house and feed those who need a place to stay. An additional fifteen churches participate by offering donations.

PLANNING FOR NEXT SUNDAY

Next week we will begin a new Sunday school year. Our unit for September, October, and November is entitled "God Leads a People Home." We will be studying Judah's history from the fall of Jerusalem, which we examined earlier this year, to the end of the Old Testament era. The first unit, "The Opportunity to Return," begins with a message from Isaiah 44:21–45:8. Ask the class to read this background information, focusing especially on 44:24-26 and 45:1, 4-7.